KV-167-467

OXFORD HISTORICAL MONOGRAPHS

Editors

BARBARA HARVEY A. D. MACINTYRE
R. W. SOUTHERN A. F. THOMPSON
H. R. TREVOR-ROPER

THE STRUCTURE OF THE TERROR

The example of Javogues and the Loire

BY

COLIN LUCAS

HATFIELD POLYTECHNIC
P.O. BOX 110, HATFIELD
CONTROL
0198218435
CLASS
944.58044 LUC
ITEM
10 02 73088 5
WALL HALL

OXFORD UNIVERSITY PRESS

1973

Oxford University Press, Ely House, London W. 1
GLASGOW NEW YORK TORONTO MELBOURNE WELLINGTON
CAPE TOWN IBADAN NAIROBI DAR ES SALAAM LUSAKA ADDIS ABABA
DELHI BOMBAY CALCUTTA MADRAS KARACHI LAHORE DACCA
KUALA LUMPUR SINGAPORE HONG KONG TOKYO

© *Oxford University Press 1973*

Printed in Great Britain
at the University Press, Oxford
by Vivian Ridler
Printer to the University

POUR
CHRISTIANE
ET
JEAN-BAPTISTE

PREFACE

THIS book is a study of the department of the Loire and of the mission there of the *Représentant du peuple* Javogues between mid September 1793 and late pluviôse an II. This period corresponds to the 'anarchical' Terror, which was characterized by the absence of governmental control and, in parts of France, by the unrestrained initiatives of local extra-ordinary authorities, by intensive repression, dechristianization, and the proliferation of terrorist weapons.

Javogues and the Loire provide an excellent illustration of this phenomenon. As a result of its implication in the federalist revolt, the Loire presented a particularly suitable terrain for terrorist activity in its extremest forms. Its history during this period is typical of that of other areas of intensive repression—neighbouring Lyon, Marseille and the Midi, Nantes and the Vendée, the frontier regions, etc. Javogues himself typified the violent, insubordinate proconsuls like Chasles, Mallarmé, Taillefer, and Dartigoëyte, who were implementing a particular brand of Terror at this time. The measures which the Committee of Public Safety took against him illustrate not merely the means by which the central government progressively brought the Terror under its control during the late winter and spring of the Year II, but also the limits on the extent to which it was able to exercise effective government in France at this time.

However, this study attempts to move away from the classic mould of monographs on individual *Représentants en mission*. As the title indicates, its purpose is to put the proconsul into a local context. This is, first of all, a geographical and political context. But above all, it is an institutional context, for the proconsul was only one element in a whole structure of institutions which together implemented the Terror. The department of the Loire favours such an approach since all the institutions of the Terror, including a revolutionary tribunal and an *armée révolutionnaire*, were present there. Each institution has been studied separately with a view to demonstrating both its particular contribution to the system of Terror and also its relationship with the other elements in the structure of institutions. This work does not only illustrate the way in which these institutions developed in the autumn of 1793 and how they functioned during the winter of the Year II. It tries to show that, despite ambiguities and duality of function, a coherent and clearly defined structure of revolutionary government emerged in the departments during the 'anarchical' Terror. In this sense, the Committee of Public Safety did not create a structure of Terror, it merely eliminated the elements of disorder from one that already existed.

But, in revolution, the character of institutions is very much dictated by the men in them. It is, of course, important to give some account of the personality and ideas of the *Représentant en mission*, since he was the most powerful man in the department. But it is much more important to provide some assessment of the local terrorists, because it was above all they who gave continuity and reality to the Terror in the departments. This therefore is an attempt to describe the terrorists as a social and political group. Although little work of this kind has been done outside Paris, there is no reason to doubt that the terrorists of the Loire were typical of their colleagues in most of the other departments of France.

I should like to express here my deep sense of gratitude to all those without whose help this book would never have been written. I am indebted above all to Richard Cobb and Albert Soboul, both of whom have so generously given me inspiration and allowed me to explore the treasure-house of their great knowledge of this period, as well as to John Roberts, without whose good-humoured encouragement I would never have written a word. I am also grateful to John Owen, who first introduced me to the pleasures of eighteenth-century history, to Marc Bouloiseau and Albert Goodwin, who advised me on points of detail in this study, and to William Carr, who painstakingly corrected my manuscript. I wish to thank the staffs of the libraries and archives where I worked, especially M. Lacour at Lyon and Mlle Poirier-Coutansais at Saint-Étienne. I can only offer general, nameless thanks to all those people—*secrétaires de mairie*, village schoolmasters, *érudits locaux*, bar acquaintances, and so on—who gave me so many insights into their towns and villages, into the mountains and the plain. Finally, I acknowledge gratefully a grant from the Sheffield University Research Fund, which allowed me to complete my research.

C. R. L.

Manchester
14 January 1971

CONTENTS

LIST OF MAPS

DIAGRAM

ABBREVIATIONS

IN THE TEXT: the terms 'Department', 'District', and 'Municipality' have been used with capitals to indicate administrative bodies, while the terms 'department' and 'district' without capitals indicate the geographical administrative division.

IN THE NOTES: the revolutionary and Gregorian names of months have been abbreviated: brum., frim., niv., etc.; Sept., Oct., etc.

ARCHIVAL REFERENCES are given thus:

A.N.	Archives nationales
A.D.R.	Archives départementales du Rhône
A.D.L.	Archives départementales de la Loire
A.D. P.-de-D.	Archives départementales du Puy-de-Dôme
A.D. S.-et-L.	Archives départementales de la Saône-et-Loire
A.C.	Archives communales
Bibl.	Bibliothèque municipale

THE TITLES OF PERIODICALS are given thus:

La Révolution française	*R.f.*
Annales révolutionnaires	*Ann. rév.*
Annales historiques de la Révolution française	*A.H.R.F.*

OTHER ABBREVIATIONS used are as follows:

armée rév.	*armée révolutionnaire*
Cne-aff.	Commune-affranchie
Comm. mil.	*Commission militaire*
Comm. pop.	*Commission populaire*
Comm. rév.	*Commission révolutionnaire*
Comm. Temp.	*Commission Temporaire*
C.P.S.	Committee of Public Safety
C.G.S.	Committee of General Security
Depart., depart.	Department, department
Dist., dist.	District, district
Mun.	Municipality
reg. dél.	*registre des délibérations*
Repr.	*Représentant du peuple*
rev. com.	revolutionary committee
rev. trib.	revolutionary tribunal
taxe rév.	*taxe révolutionnaire*

REVOLUTIONARY NAMES

THE practice has been adopted of using the name by which a place was known at the time referred to. Thus, Saint-Étienne becomes Commune d'Armes or Armeville after 22 October 1793. Except for localities familiar to the reader through frequent reference, the *vieux style* equivalent is also given when a revolutionary name is used, thus: Rambert-Loire/Saint-Rambert, (Saint) Bonnet-la-Montagne/-le-Château, Fontfort/Saint-Galmier, etc.

Armeville Commune d'Armes Arme-Commune (rare)	Saint-Étienne
Montbrisé	Montbrison
Commune-affranchie Ville-affranchie	Lyon
Bel-Air	Saint-Haon-le-Châtel
Bellevue-les-Vignes	Saint-Cyr-les-Vignes
Bœuf	Saint-Pierre-de-Bœuf
(Saint-) Bonnet-la-Montagne	Saint-Bonnet-le-Château
Chalain-sur-Loire	Chalain-le-Comtal
Chalier (rare)	Charlieu
Chazelles-sur-Commune-affranchie Chazelles-la-Victoire (rare)	Chazelles-sur-Lyon
Clivier	Saint-Paul-de-Vézelin
Conche-sur-Loire (La)	Saint-Laurent-la-Conche
Déome	Saint-Sauveur
Jars-la-Montagne	Saint-Martin-d'Estreaux
Jodard-sur-Loire	Saint-Jodard
Lay	Saint-Symphorien-de-Lay
Marcel-la-Montagne-sous-Urphé	Saint-Marcel-d'Urphé
Marcellin-la-Plaine Donjon-la-Plaine	Saint-Marcellin
Marcilly-le-Pavé	Marcilly-le-Comtal
Montchalier-Laval Montpurifié	Saint-Germain-Laval
Mont-d'Uzore	Saint-Paul-d'Uzore
Montmarat	Saint-Just-en-Chevalet
Mont-Pailloux	Saint-Héand
Raisins (Les)	Saint-Vincent-de-Boisset
Rambert-Loire Commune vignoble (rare)	Saint-Rambert

Roche-libre	Saint-Polgues
Romain-les-Vergers	Saint-Romain-en-Jarez
Semeine-et-Furan	Saint-Genest-Malifaux
Sury-la-Chaux	Sury-le-Comtal
Val-d'Armes (rare)	Valbenoîte
Valdorlay	Saint-Paul-en-Jarez
Vallée-Rousseau Vallée-sous-Mont-Rousseau	Saint-Chamond
(Ville) Fontfort	Saint-Galmier

Many communities bearing the name of a saint were content merely to abandon the appellation 'Saint'; e.g. (Saint-) Jean-Soleymieux, (Saint-) Martin-la-Plaine, etc.

The list printed by Figuères, *Les Noms révolutionnaires des communes de France* (Paris, 1901) is incomplete.

MAP 1. The Loire and its regional location

I

THE DEPARTMENT OF THE LOIRE

On 12 August 1793 the *Représentants en mission* directing operations against the rebellion in Lyon provisionally divided the department of Rhône-et-Loire into two new departments, the Rhône and the Loire.[1] Their decision was ratified by a decree of the Convention on 29 brumaire an II/19 November 1793, which thus established the Loire as the eighty-eighth department of metropolitan France.

Administratively and geographically, this decision made good sense. The original department of Rhône-et-Loire coincided almost exactly with the boundaries of the Ancien Régime *généralité*. These boundaries were clearly marked by physical features: by a line of high mountains in the west and, in the east, by the course of the river Rhône, and then, north of Lyon, by that of the river Saône. But, within these limits, the department comprised two distinct geographical halves: to the west, the valley of the Loire, and to the east, the western slopes of the valleys of the Saône and of the Rhône. Between the two lay the north–south range of the Monts du Beaujolais and the Monts du Lyonnais. The internal administrative divisions of the department of Rhône-et-Loire differed only slightly from those of the *généralité*.[2] The adjustments made to the territory of the districts which replaced the *élections* were for the most part simply intended to identify the administrative geography of the department more closely with this physical character. Thus, for example, the district of Villefranche in the north-east ceded to the district of Roanne in the north-west those parishes of the western slopes of the Monts du Beaujolais which looked

1 A.N., AF II 114 (860) 11; AF II 36, d. 293, p. 36, C.P.S. to Laporte, Gauthier, and Javogues, 6 Sept., approving this.

2 For the administration of the *généralité* of Lyon, see M.-C. Guyonnet, 'Jacques de Flesselles, Intendant de Lyon (1768–1784)', *Albums du Crocodile*, 1956, i. 26–7, 36.

Map 2. Administrative divisions, 1793

towards the Loire. Similarly, the district of Saint-Étienne ceded to the district of Campagne de Lyon some, though not all, of those lands in the south-east corner of the department which faced the valley of the Rhône.[1] Therefore, to each of the distinct physical units there now corresponded almost exactly a coherent administrative unit: one in the west, comprising the three districts of Roanne, Montbrison, and Saint-Étienne and covering the valley of the Loire; the other in the east, comprising the three districts of Villefranche, Lyon, and Campagne de Lyon and covering the western half of the Saône-Rhône valley and its hinterland of mountains. The common frontier of these two administrative units ran along the westernmost crest of the north–south ridges of the central mountains. Therefore, the separation of the one department of the Rhône-et-Loire into the two departments of the Rhône and the Loire merely recognized divisions that already existed. The districts of Villefranche, Lyon, and Campagne de Lyon became the department of the Rhône; those of Roanne, Montbrison, and Saint-Étienne became the department of the Loire and thus resurrected the ancient province of the Forez. The new department of the Loire was surrounded by seven other departments: to the north, the Saône-et-Loire; to the north-west, the Allier; to the west, the Puy-de-Dôme; to the south, the Haute-Loire; to the south-east, the Ardèche and the Isère; to the east, the Rhône.

As a whole, the new department was a geographical cul-de-sac. Only in the north did the Plaine du Roannais, following the river valley, open out into the Charolais in the Saône-et-Loire. The department was bounded in the west by the range of the Monts du Forez and of the Monts de la Madeleine, in the east by the Monts du Lyonnais and the Monts du Beaujolais, and in the south by the Monts du Pilat, which the Loire, flowing from the department of the Haute-Loire, crossed by a series of narrow gorges. To the west and to the south, the mountains reached heights of well over 3,500 feet;

1 G. Cuinet, 'La formation territoriale du département de la Loire et l'ancien Forez', *Bulletin de la Diana*, 1942, pp. 133–65. There was also some adjustment between the districts of Roanne and Montbrison in order to bring the frontier more into line with local geographical features.

to the east, the range was slightly less formidable, rising to about 3,500 feet. Today, the town of Saint-Étienne, beset by the economic difficulties of an obsolescent industrial structure, is still struggling to overcome the disadvantages of its geographical situation.

Moreover, the three districts of the department coincided with three geographical subdivisions. The Plaine du Roannais in the north was clearly separated from the rest of the department by the Seuil de Neulize, a line of hills which stretched across the department between the flanking mountain ranges. The Loire crossed them through another gorge. In the centre, around Montbrison, lay the small and enclosed Plaine du Forez, which had no natural outlet. In the south, the district of Saint-Étienne consisted of the mountain mass of the Pilat, relieved only by the narrow valley of the Gier, which flowed eastwards from near Saint-Étienne through Saint-Chamond and Rive-de-Gier to join the Rhône at Givors.

Another important geographical feature is the contrast between mountain and plain. Nearly two-thirds of the department may be classed as mountain or as hill country difficult of access. Although the district of Roanne was dominated by the Plaine du Roannais, it also contained, in the west, the steep flanks of the Monts de la Madeleine, in the east, the western slopes of the Monts du Beaujolais, and, in the south, the Seuil de Neulize. The district of Montbrison with its central plain was similar in character to that of Roanne. Moreover, an extensive portion of its south-east corner was occupied by the high plateau of the Haut-Forez. The district of Saint-Étienne had its own particular geographical problem. Almost entirely mountainous, one-third of this district lay on the other side of the watershed from Saint-Étienne. Centres such as Bourg-Argental, hidden in the folds of the Pilat, or Saint-Pierre-de-Bœuf, overlooking the Rhône, had even less connection with the rest of the district than Saint-Bonnet-le-Château had with the district of Montbrison or the parishes of the Seuil de Neulize with the district of Roanne. A lot of the department was wild country: during the first seven months of 1793 five wolves, three she-wolves, and twenty-four wolf cubs were destroyed in the district of

Roanne, one of them on 30 July in the town of Roanne itself. Nobody found this remarkable.[1]

Language differences also had a disintegrating effect on the department. The frontier between the *langue d'oïl* and

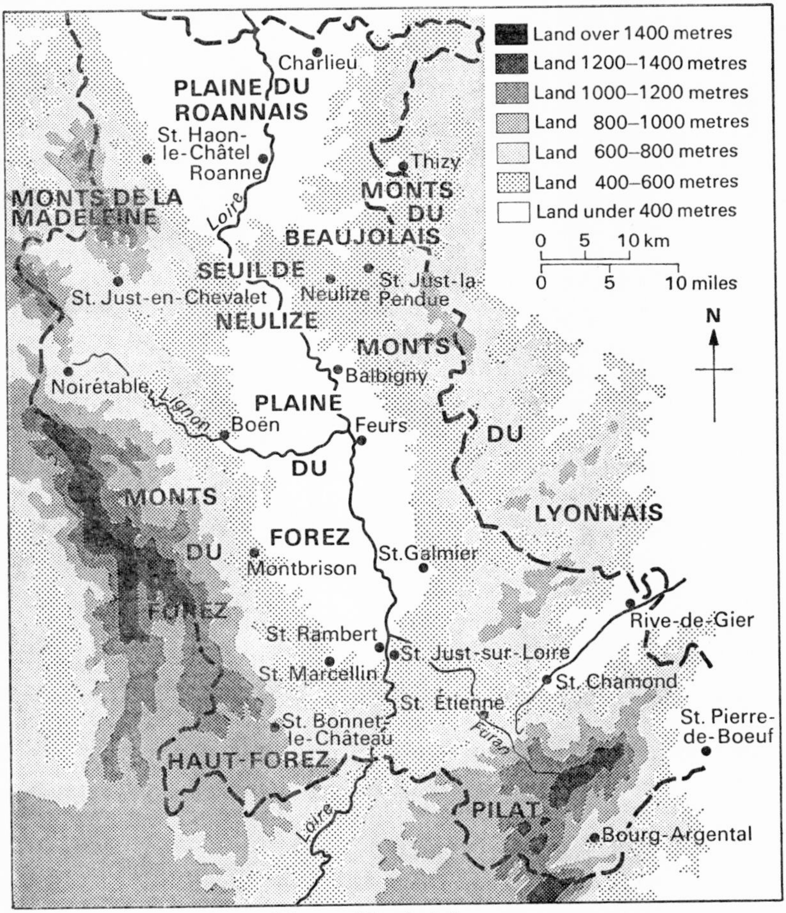

MAP 3. Physical features

the *langue d'oc* ran across this area, with the result that the department was divided into three distinct dialect regions. The inhabitants of the Roannais north of the Seuil de Neulize spoke a patois strongly influenced by French. Most

[1] A.D.L., L 187.

of the department south of this was a twilight zone, where people spoke an intermediate Franco-Provençal dialect. But the dialect spoken in the extreme west and south of the department was specifically Provençal. This area included the high plateau round Noirétable, the higher slopes of the Monts du Forez, the Haut-Forez, and all the district of Saint-Étienne south of the crest of the Pilat. The Puy-de-Dôme, the Haute-Loire, and the Ardèche were linguistically Provençal.[1] These differences of language were a factor of importance. Although all the documents of the period were written in more or less correctly spelt French, patois was the commonest vehicle of speech, as is revealed by the decision of the terrorist administration of Commune d'Armes/Saint-Étienne to speak French at its meetings.[2]

In addition to the geographical differences between them, each of the three districts had its own distinctive economic character. To a certain degree, each was typified by its *chef-lieu*; Saint-Étienne, a populous, industrial city; Montbrison, an aristocratic little town of landowners and lawyers; Roanne, a town of hard-headed merchants, whose interests lay outside rather than inside the department.

The district of Saint-Étienne, almost exclusively mountainous, had no agricultural resources to speak of. An official report of the Year II divided the area into three classes.[3] The smallest of these (the canton of Saint-Romain-en-Jarez) was reasonably fertile, but in fact the villages there concentrated more on the profitable market for fruit at Lyon and Saint-Étienne. The slopes overlooking the Rhône were devoted to growing vines which, at Malleval at least, produced a good-quality wine. In the second class was placed the land that could be sown every other year on the condition that it was well manured. In the third and by far the most extensive class, however, the land could not be tilled; some could be used as pasture in the spring and summer, but most was covered by forests. The report concluded that the grain crop did not generally meet the needs of more than a third of the population. The mountain villages barely

[1] P. Gardette, 'Carte linquistique du Forez', *Bulletin de la Diana*, 1943, pp. 269–81.

[2] A.C. St. Étienne, 1 D 10 (3), fol. 85.

[3] A.D.L., L 156, fol. 109.

supplied their own requirements, leaving the urban centres of Saint-Étienne, Saint-Chamond, and Rive-de-Gier totally unprovided for. Yet this district, with a total population of 118,981, was more populous than either Montbrison (99,413) or Roanne (98,791).[1] It contained by far the largest town of the department Saint-Étienne (13,836), whilst both Saint-Chamond and Rive-de-Gier had about 5,000 inhabitants. The reason for such a concentration of population is that this was one of the most highly industrialized areas of France at the end of the eighteenth century.

The industry of the district of Saint-Étienne may be divided broadly into three categories: coal-mining, metallurgy, and silk.[2] A rich coal-field ran north of the Pilat mountains from Firminy in the west through Saint-Étienne and along the valley of Gier to Rive-de-Gier in the east. About 20 miles long, it was only 5 miles wide at its broadest point west of Saint-Étienne. The main mining centres were Rive-de-Gier, Saint-Chamond, and the villages around Saint-Étienne, such as Roche-la-Molière, Saint-Genest-Lerpt, Saint-Jean-Bonnefonds, and Terre-Noire. A great deal of this coal was exported from the department, shipped either from Rive-de-Gier along the Canal de Givors to the Rhône and Lyon or the south, or else down the Loire from Saint-Just-sur-Loire in the direction of Paris or the west. The remainder supplied various minor industries, such as glass at Rive-de-Gier, and an important metallurgical industry, made possible by the presence of the coal-field and

[1] It is extremely difficult to obtain reliable statistics, and these figures should be treated with caution. The figure for the dist. of Saint-Étienne is given by its administration, 11 vent. an II (A.D.L., L 156, fol. 109); the dist. of Montbrison from a general table of its population dated 5 fruct. an II (A.N., D IVbis 51, d. 70); the dist. of Roanne from a 1792 table by cantons (D IVbis 49, d. 68). The figure for the town of Saint-Étienne is quoted by J. B. Galley, *L'Élection de Saint-Étienne à la fin de l'Ancien Régime*, p. 584, based on a house-to-house survey of 1790, which I have not seen. The figure for Saint-Chamond, ibid. For Rive-de-Gier, (Mun. of Rive-de-Gier) *A l'Assemblée nationale* (1789).

[2] The major source for the industry of the whole depart. is A.D.L., L suppl. 131, 'Brouillon de rapport sur l'industrie de la région stéphanoise' (an VIII), referred to hereafter as *Brouillon*; additional material on the dist. of Saint-Étienne in A.N., F10 236, d. 2, 'Mémoire sur le commerce passé, présent et futur de la ville de Saint-Étienne' (mess. an III), referred to hereafter as *Mémoire*; also in Bibl. Lyon Coste MS. 1267, no. 8, 'Tableau des manufactures à Saint-Étienne-en-Forêt à l'époque de 1789', referred to hereafter as *Tableau*. All figures quoted in the text for the Year VIII are taken from the *Brouillon*.

by the particular qualities of the waters of the river Furan, on which the town of Saint-Étienne stood, 'perpétuellement ensevelie dans la fumée du charbon qui pénètre partout et s'exhale au loin'.[1]

The object for which Saint-Étienne was most famous was the manufacture of firearms, both military and civil. Before the Revolution the production of army muskets was small-scale in character, being in the hands of a monopoly company of three entrepreneurs known as 'La Manufacture royale' which worked on government contracts. The town's reputation in this field rested especially on non-military weapons such as shotguns, pistols, etc. In the closing years of the Ancien Régime the town produced about 45,000–50,000 shotguns and pairs of pistols each year, that is more than any other town in the kingdom. Some of these weapons, finely decorated by *damasquineurs*, were an important article of export, reaching the Sublime Porte and India. But arms were not Saint-Étienne's most important industry: Roland de la Platière calculated that the manufacture of arms occupied one-third of the urban population, whereas 'clincaillerie' occupied two-thirds.[2] Under this term one must count all forms of domestic hardware, cutlery, tools, locks, spurs, etc. In 1789 this industry had as its market the whole of France and the French colonies, Spain and her colonies, Piedmont, the Swiss cantons, and sometimes the Middle East. However, the quality of these articles was often as low as their price, and this had given rise in the trade to the derogatory term 'un ouvrage du Forez'. Even the better articles could not rival the English in this field. The metallurgical industry was not confined to the single town of Saint-Étienne. Saint-Chamond and Firminy were both important centres of nail-casting, whilst Le Chambon specialized in cutlery. Indeed, in all the villages within reach of the coal-field there were forges producing all the various types of hardware.[3] A whole host of industrial hamlets clustered round Saint-Étienne.[4]

[1] J. M. Roland de la Platière, *Lettres écrites de Suisse, d'Italie, de Malte*, vi. 460.

[2] Galley, op. cit., p. 370.

[3] *Tableau.*

[4] A.N., D IVbis 84, d. Loire, 'Adresse de la Commune d'Outrefuran au Conseil des 500', 25 germ. an IV: 'sa population s'élevant (à) 5064 individus . . . le grand nombre d'usines qu'elle a dans son enceinte'.

But the greatest fortunes in the district (for example, the Dugas of Saint-Chamond or the Neyron of Saint-Étienne) came from silk. A calculation of 1789 for Saint-Étienne shows the annual turnover in silk to have been more than triple that in hardware.[1] The two centres of the silk industry were Saint-Chamond and Saint-Étienne, towns which had maintained a fierce rivalry over the last twenty years of the Ancien Régime. The weaving of silk ribbons and of silken lace was carried on in the mountain villages behind these two towns. It provided a livelihood for the population of an area stretching from La Fouillouse, Sorbiers, and Saint-Chamond in the north, down into the department of the Haute-Loire, and westwards into the district of Montbrison as far as Rozier, Saint-Maurice-en-Gourgois, and Chambles. Lists drawn up in 1787 by the parish priests showed that about 28,000–30,000 people were employed in this industry. Nail-casting in the areas within easy reach of the Gier valley and, more generally, silk-weaving were the most remunerative occupations for the inhabitants of these overcrowded and inhospitable mountains. One observer remarked that 'chaque habitant a une forge dans sa maison ou chaumière. C'est à cette industrie [nails] . . . et plus encore à la fabrication des rubans . . . qu'est due la population considérable de ces montagnes, qui n'est en rapport ni avec l'étendue du sol ni avec son infertilité naturelle.'[2] And the Municipality of Saint-Étienne emphasized that this was true of even the more well-to-do *laboureurs*.[3] In the valley, the women would work at the loom, whilst the men were employed either in agriculture, or in the mines, or in metallurgy, and the girls went to market to buy the raw materials and to sell the family produce, whether foodstuffs or silk or hardware.[4]

[1] Bibl. Lyon, Coste MS. 1267, no. 9. For the market of the silk industry, cf. A.D.R., 42 L 185, d. Neyron, letter to Javogues, 14 vent.: 'environ 240,000 livres de débiteurs en Espagne, à Naples, à Paris, à Bordeaux, à Ville-affranchie, à Commune d'Armes . . .'.

[2] *Brouillon.*

[3] *Tableau.*

[4] This reliance on multiple sources of revenue and the fact that children became profitable at an early age encouraged marriage and large families both in the town and in the countryside, and helps to explain the large population of the district. Thus, the silk and metallurgical industries not only sustained a large population, but also encouraged people to breed overlarge families in a desperate attempt to survive on the minimal earnings of several children. Cf. Roland de la Platière, op. cit. vi.

This dispersal of production was characteristic not only of the silk-weaving, but also of the metallurgical industry, which, although not quite so dispersed geographically, was fragmented into numerous small artisan workshops. As was the case in the silk industry, the *négociant* would undertake the heavy work involved in roughly preparing the raw material, which he would then sell to the artisan. The artisan would make up the article and sell it back to the *négociant*. Thus, there were only eleven foundries and twenty-six tilt-hammers preparing the iron and steel, but over 4,000 forges producing hardware. This system maintained a large population of poor workers in the manufacturing towns. The *échevins* of Saint-Étienne noted in 1755 that some workers could earn 3 *livres* a day, but that others, such as the *forgeurs* and *limeurs de boucles*, only earned 10 *sous*; an official report of the early Napoleonic period estimated the average daily earning of the *compagnon* between 1786 and 1790 to have been 14 *sous*.[1] As for Saint-Chamond, in the 1770's the price of labour was so low there that one could get seven gross of tacks for 7½ *sous* and as many plank nails for 14 *sous*.[2] In silk-weaving a hard-working person could get 20 *sous* for his day's work before the Revolution.[3] The fertility of this area as a recruiting-ground for the Ancien Régime army points to the essential poverty of its population.[4]

Moreover, the early years of the Revolution were a time of industrial crisis and of increasing hardship and unrest among the *menu peuple*. In the first place, unrest was caused by the introduction of new methods of production. In the silk industry the introduction of the Zürich loom, capable of weaving thirty ribbons at once but demanding a relatively large capital outlay, led slowly towards a factory system. In 1786, for example, a certain Calmard *cadet* installed 200 looms at his own expense in the canton of Firminy and

451; 'On voit jusqu'à vingt-quatre enfants dans une famille: et l'esprit marital règne beaucoup dans toutes ces contrées'; and p. 462: 'On fait ici des enfants à souhait: Saint-Étienne en est une fourmilière.'

[1] Both cited by Galley, op. cit., pp. 378–9.

[2] Roland de la Platière, op. cit. vi. 450.

[3] A.D.L., L 393, fol. 9.

[4] Roland de la Platière, op. cit. vi. 462: 'Peu de pays fournissent autant de soldats, et par la Milice, et beaucoup plus par les engagements.'

employed people to teach their use.[1] These looms proliferated rapidly during the Revolution, with the result that in the Year VIII there were about 1,200 of them in Saint-Étienne and Saint-Chamond; but their cost, coupled with the stagnation of business, prevented their spreading to the mountain villages which consequently suffered from their competition.[2] A similar situation prevailed in the metallurgical industry. In 1792 or 1793 the populace of Saint-Étienne nearly lynched two artisans from Liège who were introducing labour-saving devices in the treatment of iron.[3] This was merely one of a series of similar riots during the last years of the Ancien Régime and the first of the Revolution.[4] In the second place, the financial instability and the political uncertainty, and then the war, which ruined trade, all combined to paralyse production in most sectors of industry. In the Year VIII, the number of people employed in the silk industry had fallen to one-seventh of the Ancien Régime figure. In nivôse an II, the revolutionary committee of Saint-Genest-Malifaux noted that 'cette montagne avait pour richesse principale et moyen d'existence la fabrication des rubans. Tout était ouvrier . . . Cet avantage a cessé et jusqu'à ce que quelqu'autre le supplée ce pays ne peut être que misérable.'[5] In the same month, the club at Saint-Chamond urgently begged the Committee of Public Safety to permit the export abroad of silk ribbons.[6] As far as *clincaillerie* was concerned, it was not so affected by the closure of foreign markets and should have benefited from the exclusion of better foreign ware; nevertheless, in the Year VIII the annual turnover was reduced by more than a third of the pre-Revolution figure. Only coal-mining and

[1] A.N., W 393, d. 911, certificate delivered to Calmard by Mun. of Firminy, 15 prair. an II.

[2] *Brouillon*.

[3] A.D.R., 42 L 182, d. Journet, petition by Claude Journet to Javogues, n.d. Just before the Revolution Jourjon *père* and *fils* built furnaces near Saint-Étienne imitating those of Germany and England for the manufacture of 'acier de cimentation' (A.D.L. L suppl. 131).

[4] J. B. Galley, *Saint-Étienne et son district pendant la Révolution*, i. 71–2, 74–82, 143–54.

[5] A.D.L., L 393, fol. 9.

[6] Gustave Lefebvre, *Registre des procès-verbaux de la Société républicaine de Saint-Chamond*, p. 114 (4 niv.).

firearms, which had occupied the least number of workers in 1789, were momentarily stimulated by the Revolution.[1]

The district of Montbrison formed on the whole an industrial and commercial no man's land between the district of Saint-Étienne in the south and the district of Roanne in the north. There was some overlap from other areas. The silk industry of Saint-Étienne extended into the east of the Haut-Forez, while further west the lace industry centred on Saint-Bonnet-le-Château and Le Puy employed about 1,200 women in the villages. Unlike the silk industry, the prosperity of the lace industry was unaffected by the Revolution.[2] Saint-Bonnet-le-Château itself maintained a flourishing lock-making business. In the east of the district, Chazelles-sur-Lyon enclosed a feeble branch of the famous hat industry of Lyon: about fifty workshops employed about 500 people doing piece-work for the master hatters of Lyon.[3] At Saint-Galmier about eighty people produced chamois leather. A few villages in the Monts du Lyonnais, centred round Panissières, formed the southern extremity of the rural cloth industry of the Monts du Beaujolais. The only native industry of the district was to be found at Saint-Rambert and its port, Saint-Just-sur-Loire, where some 1,200 boats were built each year in order to take the coal down the Loire. These boats were frail craft, which made only one journey and were broken up on arrival at Paris or at Nantes to be used as scaffolding.[4] Thus there were in effect only three centres where one might expect to find a sizeable urban population of *menu peuple*, Saint-Bonnet-le-Château, Chazelles, and Saint-Rambert, though in this last instance, the itinerant nature of the watermen's job reduced their importance.

[1] Guyonnet, op. cit. iii. 96, gives the figures for the number of miners in the 1770's as 800 at Rive-de-Gier and 600 in the mines round Saint-Étienne; by 1789 the rapid growth of Rive-de-Gier had brought the number there up to 900 ((Rive-de-Gier) *A l'Assemblée nationale*). A.N., AF II* 120, no. 49, 12 niv. an II, states that in the normal year Paris received 1,800 'voies' of coal from Saint-Just-sur-Loire, but that now the figure was 27,000.

[2] Except where stated otherwise, all information about the industry of the dist. comes from the *Brouillon*.

[3] A.D.L., L 431, Mun., club, and rev. com. to Dist. and Depart., 4 pluv. an II.

[4] *Mémoire*. Cf. Restif de la Bretonne's man who bred rabbits in his room used boat planks for partitions (Restif de la Bretonne, *Les Nuits de Paris*, 'L'Homme aux lapins'). These were the boats used for the *noyades* at Nantes (G. Martin, *Carrier et sa mission à Nantes*, p. 277).

This was predominantly an agricultural area.[1] In the centre lay the plain, some 25 miles long by 7 or 10 wide. The earth was light and sandy, but rich in comparison with the rest of the department. A slight surplus over local needs could be grown in cereals, but the largest crop was a fine quality hemp, which supplied both the navy and the nearby mountain cloth industry. Fish thrived in the innumerable malaria-ridden ponds and pools, some of which were dried out every two or three years and sown.[2] The first foothills surrounding the plain were covered with vineyards, producing an indifferent wine for local consumption.[3] The population of the Monts du Forez worked the forests and bred cattle on the rich mountain pastures by a system of transhumance.

The lands of the plain belonged, for the most part, to large landowners living in the urban centres and notably in Montbrison.[4] Their holdings appear to have been usually farmed in big units by *grangers*.[5] There was, therefore, little peasant ownership, and what there was had to be supplemented by some form of tenancy on other land. It is reasonable to assume the existence of a large rural *menu peuple* also,

1 *Mémoire présenté à M. Necker . . . par les citoyens de Mont-Brison et de son département*, 27 Jan. 1789; Abbé Expilly, *Dictionnaire géographique*, iii. 320 ff.; Alléon-Dulac, *Mémoires*, i. 58–65.

2 A.D.L., L 259, fol. 83.

3 Alléon-Dulac, op. cit. ii. 307; 'Les vins de *Saint-Rambert*, et de la plaine du Forez, du côté de Montbrison, sont les pires de tous.'

4 François Tomas, 'Géographie sociale du Forez en 1788', *Bulletin de la Diana*, 1965, pp. 80–117. In Sept. 1788 the Muns drew up 'tableaux des propriétaires et habitants', which categorized the inhabitants according to the amount of tax they paid. Quite a number entered the person's status and occupation. These documents are only a rough guide to the social structure, since they are largely dependent on the whim of the scribe and ignore all non-taxpaying members of the community. As far as the distribution of peasant property as compared with non-peasant property is concerned, the indications of these documents are largely confirmed by A.D.L. Chaleyer MS. 134, 'propriétaires séquestrés dans le district de Boën', n.d. (end pluv. an II?), which gives the following distribution by canton (to be compared with population figures): Boën 86, Feurs 66, Moingt 93, Saint-Jean-Soleymieux 14, Saint-Georges-en-Couzan 7, Saint-Bonnet-le-Château 47, Chazelles 24. Cf. A.D.L. L 329, fol. 20, Dist. of Montbrison to *Commission de commerce et d'approvisionnements*, 15 therm. an II, stating that three-quarters of the plain belonged to rich men, arrested since for federalist crimes.

5 *Grangeage* was a form of *métayage* known as *métayage des quatre grains*, where the division of produce was confined to cereals as was appropriate to the sort of farming in the plain.

needed to work the land, yet excluded from all property. The vineyard communities of the first slopes were completely different in character, possessing a high proportion of peasant owners. Yet, to judge by the tax returns of this area, their holdings were pitifully small in more than a third of the cases. Moreover, an examination of the registers of the *état civil* for the parish of Chandieu for the last four years of the Ancien Régime reveals twice the number of *vignerons* than figure on the tax rolls there, together with an important group of *journaliers* and of *domestiques*.[1] Thus, here also, there was a considerable population of very poor people, probably more numerous than that of the plain. In the hills behind the vineyards the picture was different again. In the Monts du Forez the land was solidly in the hands of a prosperous peasantry. This pattern was slightly modified in the south, where, in the Haut-Forez, the extensive peasant ownership appears to have been less prosperous, whilst non-peasant property increases (perhaps that of the noble canons of Saint-Bonnet-le-Château). This may be one of the reasons for the importance of cottage industry in this area. Similarly, in the Monts du Lyonnais, despite a clear predominance of peasant owners, their holdings were markedly smaller than in the Monts du Forez and there was a much greater proportion of the land in the hands of non-residents, perhaps town-dwellers from Feurs, Chazelles, Saint-Galmier, and even Saint-Étienne.

The fertile plain was the most thinly populated area of the district.[2] The predominantly plain cantons of Moingt, Boën, and Sury had an average population per parish of 496·6, 551·4, and 479·2 respectively. In contrast, the cantons of the Monts du Forez (Saint-Bonnet-le-Château, Saint-Jean-Soleymieux, and Saint-Georges-en-Couzan) had averages of 1,399·5, 1,182, and 1,118·3 respectively. After Montbrison (6,245), the most densely populated commune of the district was Usson, high up in the Haut-Forez with its 3,659 inhabitants; the third was Panissières, in the

[1] Tomas, art. cit., p. 99.

[2] The figures cited come from A.D.L., L suppl. 59, 'État de la population et du taux de la dîme du district de Montbrison' (4 Oct. 1791). The figure for Montbrison is from a house-to-house survey dated 29 pluv. an II (ibid.). See also Tomas, art. cit., fig. 2, 'Densité de la population forézienne en 1801'.

Monts du Lyonnais, with 3,196. The *chef-lieu* of the new department, Feurs, only had 2,600. These figures, however, do not indicate the existence of towns in the mountains, but rather the density of a population scattered through far-flung parishes. With the exception of Feurs, Saint-Bonnet-le-Château, and Chazelles-sur-Lyon, all the townships of the district were situated round the edge of the plain in the first foothills—Boën, Montbrison, Saint-Marcellin, Saint-Rambert, and Saint-Galmier. Apart from Montbrison, they were really little more than townlets with populations of between 1,500 and 2,500. Montbrison was the commercial, administrative, and judicial centre of this little world. Under the Ancien Régime it had been the seat of a *bailliage*, whose jurisdiction had extended over the whole of the ancient province of the Forez. A multitude of courts and administrative bodies (*Sénéchaussée*, *Élection*, *Bureau des aides*, *Hypothèques*, *Gabelles*, *Traites foraines*, *Eaux et Forêts*, *Maréchaussée*, etc.) provided employment for a plethora of men in the legal professions, ranging from judges, *avocats*, and *notaires* to *huissiers*, *commis*, and scribes.[1] It was the winter home of a numerous minor nobility, both *épée* and *robe*, whose lands were scattered over the plain and the adjacent hills. Religious establishments abounded: a noble Chapter, the *Cordeliers*, *Capucins*, *Récollets*, *Visitandines*, *Clarisses*, *Ursulines*, *Pénitents*, not to mention the three parishes, the *Hôtel-Dieu*, the *Charité*, and the College of the Oratorians. Tradesmen and artisans served the needs of this aristocratic, ecclesiastical, and professional society.[2] All those who could afford it owned some land, however little, in the surrounding countryside. The position of such a community—and the other townlets were all very much miniature versions of Montbrison—was essentially parasitic. It drained off the greater part of the countryside's revenues and offered in return only the services of its tradesmen, administrators, and lawyers. In 1771 the *subdélégué* at Saint-Just-en-Chevalet wrote to the *Intendant*: 'C'est elle [la Plaine du Forez] qui nourrit nos montagnes de son superflu et c'est là aussi que nous versons tout l'argent que nous avons.'[3] This money, of course, went into

[1] Expilly, op. cit. iv. 815–16, article on Montbrison.

[2] Alléon-Dulac, op. cit. i. 55.

[3] Quoted in Guyonnet, op. cit. ii. 77.

the pockets of the urban owners of the majority of the land. Thus, the towns of the district of Montbrison differed sharply from those of the district of Saint-Étienne, which distributed work and thus money to the countryside.

The district of Roanne presented a more complex picture than its southern neighbour. Roanne itself, a town of 8,500 inhabitants,[1] owed its prosperity to its position on the river Loire. Indeed, it had been the highest navigable point until the first years of the eighteenth century, when a monopoly company had managed to extend this to Saint-Just-sur-Loire by dredging the river. But between Saint-Just and Roanne navigation remained aleatory: in its upper reaches the water became too shallow in summer, while lower down dangerous rocks littered its bed.[2] At the best of times the boats coming down from Saint-Just with coal and manufactured goods from the Saint-Étienne area could only be partially laden in order to keep their draught slight. Once they were in the deeper waters at Roanne, they could be more heavily loaded, whilst some 300 boats built annually at Roanne provided any surplus space required.[3] Thus Roanne remained the first significant port on the river and, as a result, the town handled a large transit trade in virtually all those goods travelling from the south to the north and west of France that did not make the journey by sea.[4] Merchandise would come up the river Rhône to Lyon, from whence it would be sent overland to Roanne (some thirty miles) to be enshipped on the Loire either in the direction of Paris (via the Canal de Briare) or to the west. Some impression of the importance of Roanne's transit trade may be gained from the destinations of two cargoes of soap from Marseille shipped out of Roanne on 27 pluviôse/15 February and 17 floréal an II/6 May 1794: the departments of the

[1] A.D.L., L suppl. 172. [2] *Mémoire*. [3] *Brouillon*.

[4] Alléon-Dulac, op. cit. i. 68. In 1762 the *Intendant* at Lyon noted that it was most active in time of war when the *négociants* of the Midi were afraid of the English, 'dont la marine a acquis une si grande supériorité depuis le commencement du siècle' (M. Labouré, *Roanne et le Roannais*, p. 469). There seems to have been very little movement from north and west to the south: we find no mention of goods travelling in this direction through Roanne, while the fact that the boats were made for one journey only indicates the absence of return traffic. Even some stronger boats made of oak at Roanne did not come back, but were used on the Seine below Paris (*Brouillon*).

Cher, Loiret, Creuse, Loir-et-Cher, Eure-et-Loire, Eure, Indre-et-Loire, Indre, Vienne, Loire-Inférieure (twice), Deux-Sèvres, Charente (twice), Charente-Inférieure (twice), Mayenne, Ille-et-Vilaine (twice), Manche, Morbihan (twice), Côtes-du-Nord, and Finistère (twice).[1] This intensive commercial activity gave rise to a relatively large population of river workers. But the itinerant nature of their livelihood prevented them from ever becoming an element of any importance in the political life of the town. Moreover, their work was essentially seasonal, full employment depending upon a sufficient depth of water in the river.[2] In the late autumn and early winter, when the Terror was getting under way, this condition was fulfilled.

In the villages of the eastern half of the district, from the right bank of the Loire and up the slopes of the Monts du Beaujolais, the situation was similar to that of the Pilat mountain mass; a large and predominantly mountain population relied heavily upon the textile industry for its survival.[3] In this case, it was an important cotton industry, known under the Ancien Régime as the 'Fabriques du Beaujolais', giving work to about 60,000 people scattered over these mountains in the three departments of the Rhône, the Loire, and the Saône-et-Loire. As in the case of mountains elsewhere in the Loire, this large population did not create urban centres: for example, the parish of Belmont had a population of 2,111, of which only 123 lived within the village.[4] This

1 A.D.L., L 176, fols. 174–5. The floods of 11 Nov. 1790 caused damage amounting to 4,000,000 *livres* in the warehouses along the river bank, excluding damage to the actual buildings (F. Pothier, *Le Pont de Roanne et les inondations de la Loire*, p. 6).

2 e.g. A.D.L., L 176, fol. 136, 28 vent. an II: a number of watermen ask the Dist. to be allowed to charge more for transport to Nevers and Orléans because they can only load to 15 or 16 inches owing to low water.

3 A.D.L., L 416, fol. 1: the club at Régny noted that most of the commune lived uniquely off spinning. In fact, weaving and spinning were widespread throughout the mountain areas: the standard phrase for telling someone to mind his own business appears to have been 'va faire ta toile' (O. Ricau, 'La Révolution vue de Grézolles', *Actes du 88e Congrès national des sociétés savantes*, 1963, p. 238). But in the Beaujolais it assumed the proportions of a major industry. Alléon-Dulac, op. cit. i. 97, hints at a high proportion of children in the population, when he recounts that one priest said that there were 400 children under seven in his parish of less than 600 communicants. This situation corresponded to that existing in the dist. of Saint-Étienne and had the same origins (above, p. 9, n. 4).

4 A.D.L., L suppl. 172.

was a cottage industry functioning in much the same manner as the silk industry in the south of the department. Even the humble spinner worked independently. Each market-day she sold her thread and that spun by her children from the age of seven or eight and purchased the cotton wool or the raw flax and hemp which she would spin before the next market-day.[1] The most important markets were Thizy, Amplepuis, and Tarare (Rhône), Chauffailles (Saône-et-Loire), Saint-Symphorien-de-Lay, and Panissières (Loire). The spun thread was bought by other local people, the *fabricants*. The *fabricant* would have one or two or three looms himself and perhaps also a number of poorer people in his service, to whom he would give piece-work.[2] He would sell his cloth at the same markets as those at which the spinners sold the thread. It would be bought by *négociants*, who would have it bleached and dyed. In the Loire the *négociants* came mostly from Roanne and Charlieu, and, to a lesser extent, from Saint-Symphorien-de-Lay.[3]

On the whole the population of the Monts du Beaujolais was more wretched at this time than that of other comparable areas in the department.[4] The spinners could only expect to earn 9 *sous* for a day's work as compared with the 20 *sous* of the silk-weaver.[5] Labrousse shows that, during the eighteenth century, the price of cloth rose proportionately far less than the price of raw materials and that, therefore, the price of labour in this sphere must have fallen in real terms. He also shows that, whatever the causal relationship may have been, a period of high food prices always corresponded in fact with a falling off in textile production. Thus, in general throughout France at the time of the Revolution, on the one hand the textile worker was getting an increasingly unrealistic return for his labour, and on the other, each food crisis was met by an even more devastating drop in his

[1] *Brouillon*. Alléon-Dulac, op. cit. i. 88, says that children start work at the age of four.

[2] At Cours, one of the largest villages of these mountains, even the curé was a minor *fabricant* possessing a loom (A.N., W 495, d. 505).

[3] In the Rhône they were based on Lyon, Villefranche, and Thizy.

[4] Alléon-Dulac, op. cit. i. 81, writing in the 1760's, recounts that the Inspector of the *Manufactures du Beaujolais* had recently seen at Ranchal 'un père, une mère et sept enfants sans lit, sans feu, sans habits et sans pain'.

[5] *Brouillon*.

purchasing power than was normal for the poorer sections of the population.[1] More particularly, during the early years of the Revolution, the cloth industry of the Beaujolais experienced the same double crisis as the industry of the district of Saint-Étienne. In the first place, machines were being installed, which led to riots such as, for example, those in August 1791 at Thizy, which resulted in the destruction of the machines and the emigration of their owners to Roanne.[2] In the second place, by the time of the Year VIII, the general stagnation had caused a fall in the annual turnover to two-fifths of the figure for 1789. The number of people employed by this industry had fallen over the same period by nearly two-thirds, whilst those who remained had had to cut their already slender profits to such an extent that hand-spun cotton was almost as cheap as that spun on machines.[3]

In that part of the district lying to the west of the Loire, with its well-exposed slopes, vine-growing dominated all other activities. Although not highly regarded today by connoisseurs, the wine of the Roannais was then of sufficient quality for most of it to be exported to Paris, especially that grown round Renaison.[4] The same was true of the wine produced in the area round Saint-Germain-Laval which, although administratively in the district of Roanne, was geographically part of the foothills surrounding the Plaine du Forez. The small arable plain of the Roannais west of the Loire and the vineyards behind it were largely in the hands of non-resident owners, for the most part in those of religious houses (for example, the abbey of La Bénissons-Dieu) and of rich bourgeois from Roanne, together with a few noble families.[5] The arable lands were leased in large units to

1 C.-E. Labrousse, *Esquisse du mouvement des prix et des revenus en France au XVIIIe siècle*, ii. 327–33 and 544–64 *passim*.

2 A.D.R., 38 L 33, for Thizy; M. Dumoulin, *En pays roannais*, p. 188 for Roanne.

3 *Brouillon*.

4 *Mémoire présenté à M. Necker . . . par les citoyens de Mont-Brison*, 27 Jan. 1789; Alléon-Dulac, op. cit. i. 61. F. Pothier, *Roanne pendant la Révolution*, p. 153, estimates that more than 30,000 'pièces' of wine were embarked each year on the Loire at the port of Pouilly-sous-Charlieu.

5 The picture of the distribution of property in the Roannais is obtained by applying to the 'tableaux des propriétaires et habitants' of the 'département' of

grangers, but the vineyards appear to have been leased in medium-sized lots.[1] Thus, although the arable lands of the Plaine du Roannais resembled those of the Plaine du Forez, the vineyards differed radically from those of the Forez, where a multitude of small peasant owners was the rule. The problems facing the village of Saint-Martin-de-Boisy on the death of the mayor and of the second *officier municipal* in the Year II were characteristic of the situation in the Roannais. The remaining *officier* was illiterate, and the *agent national* was a tenant farmer whose landlord had given him notice to quit in brumaire an III and who would then leave the commune because he could not find any other land there. Of the rest of the 195 inhabitants, only four or five owned their holdings; the others rented theirs on a share-cropping basis.[2] This contrast between the Roannais and the Forez was doubtless due to the fact that, since the wine of the Roannais was of good quality, the vineyards attracted investors much more readily than in the Forez.

As far as the surviving peasant owners were concerned, there is no reason to suppose that conditions were any different in this good wine-producing area from those in the neighbouring one of the Beaujolais. There, only the well-to-do could make a good profit because they alone could afford to keep their harvest until the price was right; the small man was obliged to sell immediately to the *commissionnaires*, the sole buyers in the area, with the result that often he had no wine of his own to drink despite spending the whole year in the vineyards.[3] Moreover, the last four years of the Ancien Régime witnessed a complete collapse of wine prices

Roanne the techniques used by Tomas, art. cit., when considering those of the 'département' of Montbrison (above, p. 13, n. 4)—A.D.L. C 69 (1), Renaison, Pouilly-les-Nonains, Mably, Lentigny, Riorges, Noailly-en-Roannais, Ouches, and C 69 (2), Villerest, Saint-Sulpice, Vernay, Saint-Romain-la-Motte, Saint-Martin-de-Boisy, Saint-Maurice, Saint-Haon-le-Vieux, Saint-André-d'Apchon; C 82, Briennon.

[1] 70·5 per cent of the *grangers* paid more than 30 *livres* in taxes; only 15·9 per cent of leasehold *vignerons* paid more than 30 *livres* and 3·9 per cent paid less than 5 *livres*.

[2] A.D.R. 1 L 190, Dist. of Roanne to *Repr.* at Cne-aff., 16 fruct. an II.

[3] A.N., F[20] 129, report by Gonchon to Minister of Interior on agriculture in the Rhône-et-Loire, 1793. See Labouré, op. cit., pp. 440, 459, and 460 for the activities of the *commissionnaires* in the Roannais.

throughout France and consequent misery in vineyard communities. In any case, during the late eighteenth century, the price of wine had become increasingly subject to extremely violent cyclical fluctuations. There was little that the growers could do to protect themselves, for little can be grown simultaneously with the vine or substituted for it in times of crisis.[1]

Information is scarce about landholding in the Monts du Beaujolais in the east of the district. In the far north-east round Belmont, peasant ownership appears to have been strongly entrenched: those properties not in the hands of members of the village belonged to prosperous peasants from neighbouring communities.[2] Further south, towards Saint-Symphorien-de-Lay, a few non-residents had some large properties and peasant holding was mostly restricted to smaller units, but it is probable that these strangers were the cloth merchants from Saint-Symphorien itself.[3] The area centred on Charlieu presents a more complicated picture. Whereas at Saint-Pierre-la-Noaille and Saint-Hilaire there were few signs of infiltration by strangers, Saint-Denis-de-Cabanne and Maizilly suffered considerably from it.[4] Similarly, whereas the majority of peasants at Saint-Hilaire were comfortably prosperous, on the other hand, at Saint-Denis, peasant holdings tended to be small. As in the case of Belmont, the strangers in this area came from nearby Charlieu and from the surrounding villages.[5] Therefore, beyond the immediate neighbourhood of Roanne, the bourgeois of that town do not appear to have owned much land east of the Loire, when compared with their holdings west of that river. This pattern is perhaps a commentary on the boom which the vine experienced during the first half of the eighteenth century.

In the Monts de la Madeleine, to the west, beyond the vineyards, a prosperous and indigenous peasantry held the

[1] Labrousse, op. cit. i. 269–72.

[2] A.D.L., C 82, Belleroche, Belmont, Cuinzier.

[3] A.D.L. C 69 (2), Petit-Saint-Symphorien; C 82, Combre.

[4] A.D.L. C 69 (1), Saint-Pierre-la-Noaille, Saint-Hilaire, Saint-Denis-de-Cabanne, Maizilly, Villers; C 82, Aillant (parcelle de Pouilly), and Chandon.

[5] Ibid. The *tableau* of Maizilly gives the place of origin of all non-resident landowners.

land in the same way as in the highlands of the Monts du Forez.[1] Their hold on the land was weakened somewhat in the south by urban landowners from the small town of Saint-Just-en-Chevalet, but the influence of the latter was only slight and already scarcely noticeable at Saint-Priest-la-Prugne, only six miles away. In the north-west of the district, however, round La Pacaudière where the mountain slopes were gentler, non-peasant properties were extensive, being often in the hands of prosperous citizens from Roanne.[2]

Finally, as far as the villages of the Seuil de Neulize in the south of the district were concerned, the parishes of the southern slopes that looked towards the Plaine du Forez followed much the same pattern as those of the Monts du Lyonnais.[3] Peasant property predominated, but the majority of holdings tended to be fairly small and non-resident land-holders were widespread. This was especially true in the west, which was influenced by the small towns of Saint-Germain-Laval and Boën, but it was also noticeable to the east round Néronde. The same was true of the parishes in the north, where the Seuil de Neulize formed the rim of the Plaine du Roannais and fell into the orbit of the lowland landowners.[4] In the centre, however, round such villages as Saint-Just-la-Pendue, where the hills were more difficult of access, non-resident property largely disappeared, leaving a solid peasantry only slightly less prosperous than that to be found in the Monts du Forez or in the Monts de la Madeleine.[5]

The system of communications emphasized both this disparity between the three districts and also the contrast between mountain and plain.[6] In this long and narrow department, three major roads crossed from east to west, one

[1] A.D.L., C 69 (2), Les Forges (annexe des Noës), Saint-Rirand; Forestier (parcelle de Saint-Just-en-Chevalet), Saint-Priest-la-Prugne; C 82, Arcon.

[2] A.D.L., C 69 (1), Montaiguët; C 69 (2), Vivans, Saint-Martin-d'Estreaux; C 82, Changy, Chenay-le-Châtel, Crozet, Urbize.

[3] A.D.L., C 69 (1), Néronde, Grézolles, Noailly-en-Donzy; Souternon, Violey-Villette; C 82, Amions, Ailleux-en-Bussy.

[4] A.D.L., C 82, Cordelles and Cherier.

[5] A.D.L., C 69 (1), Neulize and Pinay; C 69 (2), Saint-Just-la-Pendue, Saint-Jodard, Saint-Priest, Saint-Thurin; C 82, Bully, Chantois (parcelle de Bully), Crémeaux, Dancé.

[6] Except where otherwise stated, this paragraph is based on engineers' reports contained in A.D.L., L 541. See also Guyonnet, op. cit. ii. 70–1, and F. Imberdis, *Le Réseau routier de l'Auvergne au XVIIIe siècle*, pp. 91, 107, 232, 293–4.

through each district. Yet only one major road linked the three districts together from north to south. One of the two roads from Lyon to Paris crossed the district of Roanne over the Col du Pin Bouchain and through Roanne to Saint-Martin-d'Estreaux in the direction of Moulins, Nevers, and Paris. Through the district of Montbrison there ran the road from Lyon to Clermont-Ferrand through Feurs, Boën, and Noirétable. In the south of the department the road from Lyon to the Languedoc via Le Puy ran along the valley of the Gier and through Saint-Étienne and Firminy. The only road to run through the department from north to south was the road from Paris to the Languedoc, which, leaving the Paris–Lyon road at Roanne, led over the Seuil de Neulize through Saint-Polgues and Saint-Germain-Laval, crossed the Plaine du Forez via Boën and Montbrison, forded the Loire at Saint-Just-sur-Loire, and joined the Lyon–Languedoc road at Saint-Étienne. But to what extent even this road was a useful unifying factor is doubtful. In all probability the amount of traffic along it was small when compared with the other three roads. Whereas public transport services ran regularly on the other roads, no one had considered it worth while in this case.[1] Except for a person travelling from Roanne to Paris or from Saint-Étienne to the south-west, any inhabitant of the department embarking on a long journey was obliged to make his way first to Lyon.[2] Even a stranger to the department, with fortune enough to permit him to travel in his own coach, would be likely to make the slight detour which would allow him to break his journey at Lyon. The plan for a new north–south road linking Roanne to Saint-Étienne along the right bank of the Loire (today's *Route nationale* 82) had been accepted in 1764.[3] But, at the time of the Revolution, only the exit from Saint Étienne had been built over a distance of one and a half miles.[4]

[1] J. B. Galley, *Ancien Régime*, p. 340. Equally significant on this level is the subservient attitude that the Mun. of Saint-Polgues still preserved towards its former *seigneur* in 1793, although its position should have laid it open to the influence of the events of the Revolution (Colin Lucas, 'Le Désarmement du comte de Saint-Polgues', *A.H.R.F.* 1965, pp. 367–8).

[2] L. J. Gras, *Les Routes du Forez et du Jarez*, p. 117.

[3] A.D.L., L 46, 26 vend. an III.

[4] A.N., F10 236, d. 2, *Bureau de commerce* of Saint-Étienne to C.P.S., 15 mess. an III.

A few second-class roads also existed. In the district of Roanne, three ran out from the *chef-lieu*: one along the right bank of the Loire to Marcigny, one to Thizy and thence to Villefranche, and one through Saint-Just-en-Chevalet into the Auvergne. Another led tortuously from Belleville and Beaujeu in the Rhône to Charlieu and thence into the Saône-et-Loire. In the district of Montbrison, an ill-defined road ran from Lyon through Chazelles-sur-Lyon across to Montbrison and thence to Ambert (Puy-de-Dôme). Even more hypothetical was the road that was supposed to run from Chazelles-sur-Lyon through Saint-Galmier and Saint-Marcellin to Saint-Bonnet-le-Château and thence into the Haute-Loire.[1] Finally, in the district of Saint-Étienne, the very ancient road from Saint-Chamond over the Pilat to Pélussin and thence to Annonay (Ardèche) was still rendering signal service, doubtless because it was the only link between the Loire and the Ardèche.[2] However, apart from the roads from Roanne to Marcigny and from Saint-Chamond to Annonay, which were nothing more than exits from the department, even these secondary roads crossed the department from east to west and did no more to link the three districts together than did all but one of the major roads. Moreover, they were of doubtful practicability. Javogues was born at Bellegarde on the Montbrison–Lyon road through Chazelles, and his family still lived there at the time of the Revolution. Nevertheless, in September 1793, when he was pursuing a group of *muscadins* who had chosen this route back to Lyon, he found it necessary to obtain a guide at Bellegarde in order to show him the way on from there.[3]

Within the department, therefore, lines of communication remained largely primeval, especially in the mountains; and two-thirds of the department were mountain or hill country. For example, an inhabitant of Saint-Genest-Malifaux wishing to travel to Saint-Étienne had the choice between several very

[1] A.D.L., L suppl. 591: an engineer's report of frim. an III says that this road is difficult and sinuous between Chazelles and Saint-Galmier, that the section from Saint-Galmier to the Montbrison–Saint-Étienne road is not open, and that the section from there to Saint-Marcellin has hardly been sketched out; the part from Saint-Marcellin to Saint-Bonnet is not even mentioned.

[2] Galley, op. cit., p. 334.

[3] A.D.R., 42 L 173, d. Blanc.

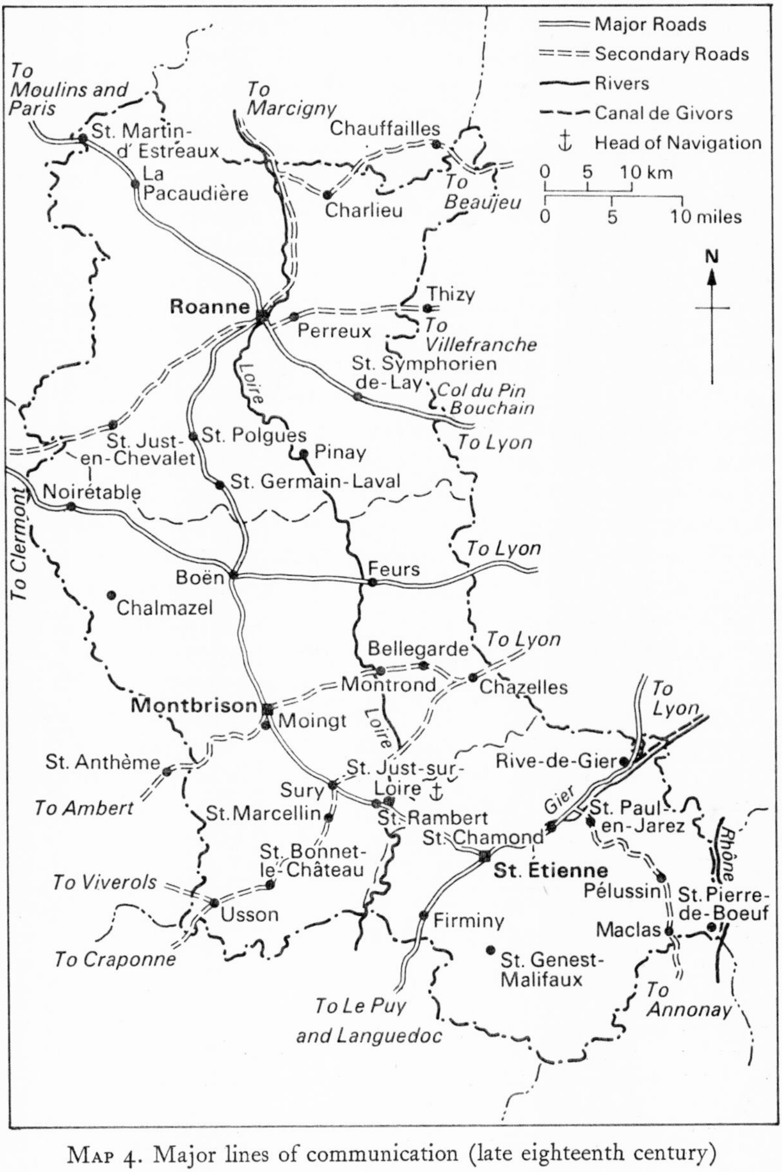

Map 4. Major lines of communication (late eighteenth century)

narrow and equally bad tracks as far as the abrupt descent into the *chef-lieu*. At this point, the bends became so tight that it was impossible to get a cart round them if the load hung over the end, while the gradient was so steep that a pair of oxen could not hold an ordinary load on the way down and could get only an empty cart up. Indeed, the whole enterprise was so strenuous that each year a lot of oxen collapsed.[1] In winter, snow paralysed communications; then travel was dangerous even on the main roads. An engineer's report of 1791 remarked that, during the preceding winter, several people had been injured and their horses killed on the hill just outside Saint-Étienne on the main road to Montbrison.[2] The major lines of communication could easily be blocked by snow as they crossed the mountains on their way out of the department.[3] Few would hazard a journey in the mountains away from the major roads except in a case of emergency. The Municipality of Violay in the Seuil de Neulize informed the administration of the department at the beginning of pluviôse an II that ice had forced a visiting gendarme to lead his horse on foot up to the village.[4] Similarly, one of the leading militants in the district of Saint-Étienne completely missed an appointment with Javogues at Saint-Étienne because the latter's courier who had left on 23 nivôse/12 January at 10 o'clock in the evening, travelling an icy, snowy track through the mountains, did not arrive at [Saint-Pierre-de-] Bœuf until 4 o'clock the following afternoon.[5] Even the hill communes near the major roads were no less isolated than the others in winter. The postmaster of Saint-Martin-d'Estreaux notified the administration of the district of Roanne in nivôse an III that the snow had interrupted all communication along the side roads off the Lyon–Paris road.[6]

[1] A.D.L., L suppl. 549, Saint-Genest and Marlhes to 'département' of Saint-Étienne, 18 Nov. 1787. During the Ancien Régime, the royal subsidy for the *ateliers de charité* had always been used for the upkeep of village communications. The subsidy of 1788 for the *élection* of Saint-Étienne never reached its destination and the whole system disappeared with the Revolution (Galley, *Révolution*, i. 19).

[2] A.D.L., loc. cit., report by Buisson, Oct. 1791.

[3] A.N., D IVbis 84, d. Loire, club at Montbrison to Convention, frim. an III, points out that it was extremely difficult to reach Lyon in winter.

[4] A.D.L., L 18.

[5] A.D.R., 42 L 170, d. Pignon, Pignon to Javogues, 25 niv. an II.

[6] A.D.L., L 227.

The river Loire could constitute another formidable obstacle. In 1793 not a single bridge remained on it. For the previous sixty years people had been clamouring to have the bridge rebuilt at Saint-Just-sur-Loire, where the Paris–Languedoc road crossed the river. At Pinay, only the foundations remained, with the result that the major roads had long ceased to pass that way. One petition acidly remarked that the main road from Lyon to Clermont-Ferrand via Feurs would only become fit for traffic when bridges were built over the Loire and the Lignon; this would cost perhaps 2,000,000 *livres* without any guarantee as to their soundness, given the shifting, sandy beds of these rivers.[1] The only means of crossing was by ford or ferry. During the autumn, winter, and spring months, both were frequently impracticable either because of flood or because of frost. At Roanne, the most important road centre in the department, the wooden bridge collapsed during floods in November 1790, and it was not until 1799 that a temporary substitute was erected.[2] On 25 brumaire an II/15 November 1793, the Municipality of Parigny had no hesitation in sending all the young soldiers of the first requisition back home when 'les gens de l'art' advised that it would be extremely dangerous to use the ferry across to Roanne at that moment.[3] Not only did the capricious nature of the Loire virtually split the department into two halves in times of bad weather, but the numerous small streams running down from the mountains on each side of the valley were also liable to produce the same conditions within each of these halves. In frimaire an II, the *société populaire* at Roanne urgently requested the administration of this district to have a plank thrown across a stream called the Oudan, because, otherwise, the rising water-level was bound to make the road from Roanne to Marcigny impassable.[4]

It was inevitable that the character of the department should have helped to shape the nature of the actions of the

1 A.N., D IVbis 84, d. Loire, 'Délibération de la ville de Saint-Germain-Laval-en-Forez, le 24 janvier 1790', for all the first part of this paragraph.

2 F. Pothier, *Le Pont de Roanne et les inondations de la Loire*, pp. 5–13. Such an incident was not unique: for instance, the stone bridge over the Loire at Tours collapsed under the effect of frost in 1789, although in this case a temporary substitute was erected within six days (de Ferrières, *Correspondance inédite*, p. 27 n. 1).

3 A.D.L., L 373, fol. 106.

4 A.D.L., L 176, 8 frim. an II.

Représentant sent there on mission. Generally speaking, we can see that the department remained on the whole isolated from the rest of France. The effect of this on the population was sufficiently pronounced to move the *Représentant* Méaulle, on mission there in ventôse an II, to write to the Committee of Public Safety describing 'l'intolérance grossière' of the inhabitants of this department for all other Frenchmen.[1] Questions of national importance, such as the federalist crisis, did, of course, impinge upon the department, but they tended to become rapidly absorbed into issues of local significance. The Terror of the Year II was not exempt from this evolution.

More particularly, winter aggravated the general isolation of the department from the outside world. Javogues was at his most active in the Loire during the period between late frimaire and late pluviôse, that is in the depth of winter. It was difficult for outsiders to obtain precise up-to-date information about events in the department during these months. In nivôse, wild rumours circulated at Commune-affranchie/Lyon of troubles in which Javogues was supposed to have been assassinated. Pilot, who, as postmaster, was better placed than most to get at the truth, obviously considered the tales credible enough, since he relayed them to his friend Gravier in Paris, although he did point out how exaggerated it all might be.[2] Similarly, in frimaire the *Journal de Commune-affranchie* remarked that it had done all it could to gain information about the activities of the revolutionary tribunal at Feurs; its letters to the departmental administration had remained unanswered.[3] This newspaper was the semi-official organ of the *Représentants* at Commune-affranchie/Lyon, men who had the important task of supervising and of co-ordinating work in the departments around this city. As such, this statement must be taken to express the ignorance of these *Représentants* about the situation in the Loire at that time. The authorities in Paris had even more difficulty in obtaining reliable information quickly. Such conditions influenced the orientation of Javogues's mission. They explain at least in

[1] A.N., BB[30] 30, d. 5, analysis of a letter dated 6 germ. an II.
[2] *Papiers inédits omis ou supprimés par Courtois*, ii. 203.
[3] *Journal de Lyon ou Moniteur du département de Rhône-et-Loire*, 21 frim.

part why he was able, unchecked during these months, to take measures and make pronouncements that were neither politically advisable nor even, at times, legal.

Nevertheless, although these winter conditions facilitated the general orientation of the mission, conversely they also limited its scope within the department, since the deterioration of internal communications emphasized the fragmented character of the area. Javogues made Feurs the *chef-lieu* of the new department and the revolutionary tribunal was also installed there. Yet, the complaints of the inhabitants of this town show that the river Loire, whether by flood or by frost, frequently interrupted all communication with the western half of the department and more especially with the vital Paris–Languedoc road that linked the three districts together.[1] The administrator Palley was not an isolated example, when he wrote to the administration of the department in late brumaire an II that he was unable to reach Feurs because of the flooding.[2] Another member, sent to Montbrison and to Saint-Étienne on urgent business, wrote back that the flooding of the Loire and the Lignon had considerably retarded his arrival at Montbrison and that he had had to abandon the idea of going any further because he would be unable to get even as far as Saint-Just-sur-Loire, let alone cross the river there and push on to Saint-Étienne.[3] In practice, such conditions seriously impaired the effectiveness of this administration which, by the nature of its functions, might otherwise have served to unite the contrasting elements of the department. The revolutionary tribunal, which was the hub of the machine of repression, evidently laboured under similar handicaps.

More important, the increased isolation of the extensive mountain areas under snow tended to make their population impervious to, when not ignorant of, the directives both of the ordinary administrations and of the extra-ordinary organs of the Terror. And snow lasted a long time in this region: in the Year II it fell as late as 21 floréal/10 May in the canton of

1 Bibl. Lyon, Coste MS. 1255, no. 1, 'La ville de Feurs . . . à Nosseigneurs de l'Assemblée nationale'.

2 A.D.L., L 81, letter of 29 brum.

3 A.D.L., L suppl. 419, no date, no signature.

Saint-Just-en-Chevalet.[1] One writer of the eighteenth century calculated that full winter conditions prevailed in some parts of the Forez for as much as two-thirds of the year, and another remarked that snow frequently lay on the slopes of Mt. Pilat until the feast of St. John Baptist (24 June).[2] Under such conditions, much of the department was affected far less intensely by the Terror than the activities of the *Représentant en mission* and the resolutions of the clubs and revolutionary committees would lead us to suppose. Both the Terror and ordinary administration relied heavily upon *commissaires* in order to reach the rural population. The peasant, naturally inclined to 'immobilism', would only act if he felt at the mercy of constant and unpredictable inspection. Physical difficulties dissuaded the *commissaires* from penetrating frequently to the mountain communes in winter and, on the contrary, did all to reinforce the peasant in a feeling of security born of isolation. For example, the village of Grézolles, lying in the Monts de la Madeleine, but by no means in the remotest part of these mountains, received only two visits from *commissaires* from the revolutionary committee of Saint-Germain-Laval, the *chef-lieu* of the canton. Significantly enough, both of these visits (6 pluviôse/25 January and 21 pluviôse/9 February) took place at the very end of the period of Javogues's mission, that is at a time when the worst of the winter was beginning to be over. The village was not visited by *commissaires* from either the *Représentant* or the regular administrations.[3] The case of Grézolles seems to be typical of the mountain villages of its kind. During the winter of the Year II, religious fanaticism, non-juror priests, and refractory conscripts plagued the hill country of the department. When, in certain areas, drastic action became necessary, it tended to take the form of a minor military campaign, as, for example, the expedition of the *armée révolutionnaire* against Saint-Just-la-Pendue at the end of frimaire.

But, at the best of times, the tenuous nature of communications helped to foster a divorce between the plain and large tracts of the mountains. In 1966 the inhabitants of the Haut-

[1] A.D.L., L 176, fol. 179.

[2] Alléon-Dulac, op. cit. i. 58; Roland de la Platière, op. cit. vi. 459.

[3] Ricau, art. cit., *passim*.

Forez supported their vehement protest against the projected suppression of the train service to Saint-Étienne by claiming that 'nos routes sont parfois impraticables en hiver . . . le train quotidien ou bi-quotidien est, pour nos communes du Haut-Forez, un lien avec la plaine et la ville'.[1] In the eighteenth century only the few roads, even the most doubtful of them, afforded any really permanent measure of contact between the plain and the mountain. But beyond their immediate vicinity the influence of the plain was hardly felt at all. Chantelauze *aîné*, in evidence given in the Year VI about the Thermidorian Reaction, expressly remarked that the proximity of the road from Montbrison to Lyon had prevented him from finding a safe hiding-place at Bellegarde; yet he was subsequently able to remain in comparative security for two months at Chalmazel in the Monts du Forez.[2] Certain changes in place-names during the Revolution indicate that people were conscious of a distinction between mountain and plain, and indeed that the inhabitants of each sought to emphasize their identity as such. Saint-Bonnet-le-Château adopted the name of Saint-Bonnet-la-Montagne, and nearby Saint-Marcellin changed to Marcellin-la-Plaine or Donjon-la-Plaine.[3] In both cases political considerations can be discounted. Saint-Bonnet changed on 21 April 1793 at a time when 'la montagne' was not yet officially synonymous with political purity; Saint-Marcellin adopted its new name in nivôse an II at a time when 'la plaine' was politically anathema. The names, therefore, have an exclusively geographical significance, and one cannot but wonder whether Saint-Marcellin's choice, made after that of Saint-Bonnet, was not dictated by a desire to draw attention to a clearly felt difference between itself and its neighbour. It is certain that the plainsman feared the over-populated mountains, whilst the villagers of the hills saw the plain as a land of milk and honey to supplement their own lean resources. This relationship was to form the back-cloth of much of the history of Montbrison during the Terror. The isolation of the mountain developed yet further the already existent divorce in mentality between town and country: it intensified the

1 *Le Monde*, le 24 août 1966, 'Défense et illustration de l'omnibus rural'.

2 A.N., BB18 690.

3 A.D.L., L 376, fol. 40; L 382, fol. 25.

introspective, xenophobic nature of rural communities and exaggerated the immobilism of political and social outlook characteristic of the peasantry in general. A recent ecclesiastical historian remarks of Sainte-Agathe-en-Donzy, a village of the Monts du Lyonnais, that during the Revolution it became 'une sorte d'îlot fermé, groupement ramassé en lui-même, hermétique aux idées nouvelles, acquis d'avance aux victimes des terroristes'.[1] In the department of the Loire the Terror remained essentially a phenomenon of the plain: more exactly, the Terror was an urban phenomenon which imposed itself upon those rural communities of the surrounding countryside that were easily accessible. Beyond this area terrorist activity resulted either from the pressure of outside agents (e.g. Lapalus in the Beaujolais) or else from the energy of minority groups (e.g. Saint-Bonnet-le-Château) or of individual militants (e.g. Rochat at Saint-Jean-Soleymieux). The peasant population of the mountains, already alienated from the Revolution by industrial slump and religious schism, could not be anything but hostile to the lowlander protagonists of the Terror and to its economic, social, and religious implications.[2] The significance of the winter in this context was that it helped to prevent the coercive measures of the period from overcoming the dichotomy between mountain and plain and dragging the mountain communities willy-nilly in the wake of an urban plain-based Terror. After the recall of Javogues, when the conditions of climate became more favourable again, it was too late, since the main impulse to co-ordinated terrorist activity had been withdrawn.

Since the Terror was urban and lowland in character, it is tempting to relate the varying degrees of its intensity to the economic and social geography of the department. Whilst not denying that the predominance of peasant landowning in the hill country may have been one factor in shaping the attitude

[1] Dom D. Buenner, *Madame de Bavoz, abbesse de Pradines de l'ordre de Saint-Benoît*, p. 155. Something of the atmosphere of the mountain communities of the Forez in the late eighteenth century is rendered by J. Barbey D'Aurevilly, *Une Histoire sans nom*, ch. i.

[2] The inhabitants of the mountain village of La Valla believed that 'ces clubistes de la commune de St. Chamond prenaient des arrêtés et qu'après avoir dévasté leurs églises et les croix ils viendraient dévaster leurs maisons, que les commissaires qui étaient montés chez eux voulaient leur dicter des lois' (A.D.L., L 390, fol. 26).

of this section of the population,[1] it would appear that geographical factors combined with the common peasant mentality were more potent in forming mountain peasant opinion which, to all intents and purposes, was settled before the Terror. It is similarly tempting to associate the idea of a plain-based Terror with the existence of a large rural *menu peuple* in the plain, and especially in the vineyards of the first slopes where, in the case of the district of Montbrison, the towns lay. Yet, in practice, it is difficult to discern any particular spontaneous participation in the Terror by this poverty-striken element. As a working hypothesis it is reasonable to assume that the major towns of the district of Saint-Étienne, with their industrial population of artisans and companions, would produce militancy resembling that of the Parisian *sans-culottes*. Yet, such social and economic considerations do not help to explain the sustained terrorist activity in towns of the character of Montbrison, Saint-Galmier and Charlieu. On the other hand, the town of Roanne is one of the few cases where, in the most general terms, such arguments do have some validity. The unremitting moderatism of its authorities, including the administration of the district, came in part at least from the predominantly commercial, middle-class nature of its population. In any case, there was little to link this district geographically with the rest of the department, and the occupations of its leading citizens did nothing to compensate for this. Moreover, the mere physical fact of Roanne's position on a frequented major road to Paris helps to explain, on the one hand, the rapidity with which the inhabitants of the town were aware of national political developments,[2] and, on the other, the astonishing facility, when compared with the rest of the department, with which the revolutionary committees, the clubs, and the various administrative organs of the district as a whole corresponded with Paris, whether with the Convention, or with the Jacobins, or with the committees of government. In turn, this habit, born of geographical circumstance, redounded on the course

[1] Tomas, art. cit., p. 117, ascribes the different behaviour of the mountain and plain during the Revolution to the different social structures.

[2] A good illustration of the importance of the major road is given by the rev. com. of Saint-Martin-d'Estreaux, which knew about all issues affecting it before anyone else (A.D.L., L 424 *passim*).

of Javogues's mission. When the moderate authorities of the town and district of Roanne felt the menace of his personal visit to be imminent, they unhesitatingly embarked upon a campaign of denunciation directly to the Convention. The recall of Javogues in pluviôse was at least partly due to their protests.

II

THE FEDERALIST REVOLT

It is important to examine the federalist crisis of the summer of 1793 in some detail to understand the Terror of the Year II in the Loire. Although many other factors were involved, federalism was the most immediate cause of the Terror in the local context. It provoked the emergence of extra-ordinary institutions, the arrest of suspects, and the purge of the administrations. Moreover, the federalist crisis provided the local terms of reference for much of the Terror. It forced a clear political choice on the inhabitants of the districts of Montbrison and Saint-Étienne. Although that choice tended to be made on the basis of local problems and of class interests, and although it had often been largely formed, if not formulated, before the crisis, it was rapidly assimilated into the national political issues of those dangerous summer months. The counter-revolutionary overtones of federalism, particularly the association with the Lyon rebellion and the attacks on the *sociétés populaires*, automatically identified the victims of the federalists as the persecuted martyrs of the *République une et indivisible* and the federalists themselves as the enemies of the people seeking to undermine the resistance of the Republic to the onslaught of the tyrants of Europe. The former inevitably furnished the personnel of the Terror and the latter its victims. Finally, the rebellion gave a justification for terrorist measures against other categories of suspects, whose direct connection with it could not be established, for it provided concrete evidence of the sort of situation at which they seemed to aim. Up to a point, the intensity of the Terror was a function of the intensity of the federalist crisis: it was more violent at Montbrison, which had welcomed federalist troops, than at Boën, which had resisted them; it was more pervasive in the Loire, which was tainted with rebellion, than in the Puy-de-Dôme, whence had come the *levée en masse* to crush Lyon.

The federalist movement in that part of the Rhône-et-Loire that became the department of the Loire was grafted on to events at Lyon and waxed and waned with the fortunes of that city's revolt. It was an intrinsic part of the departmental revolt that grew in July and August out of the municipal revolution at Lyon on 29 May 1793.[1] This revolution was the reaction of the sectional assemblies, which were dominated by the moderates and incited by the administration of the department, against the Jacobin sectional clubs, *Club central*, and the Municipality. Tension had been building up during the winter as a result of local food problems and national political uncertainty. The food shortage was given a political hue by the popular conviction that it was part of a counter-revolutionary plot. Matters came to a head in the anguished months of March and April, when a deepening economic crisis was accompanied by the unrest caused by such factors as the *levée des 300000*, the news of the Vendée and of Dumouriez's treason, and persistent invasion scares from the near-by frontier. Paralysed by bankruptcy and by the unremitting obstruction of the Department, the Municipality came to adopt a terrorist programme, which had been finding increasing expression in the clubs since the previous autumn. The moderates in the sections rose in revolt, not because of the fiery speeches of men such as Chalier, but because the proposals of these men were being increasingly put into practice during April and May. The Jacobins had gained full control of the Municipality (which they had dominated since the elections of November 1792) by securing the election of Bertrand as mayor after the resignation of the moderate Nivière-Chol and by arresting his elected successor, Gilibert, on trumped-up charges. In the sections, revolutionary committees, not elected but designated by the *conseil général* of the commune, were gaining ever-increasing powers of arrest and domiciliary visit, and the right to seize arms, to issue *cartes civiques* and to establish lists of 'agioteurs, capitalistes et insouciants'. A 'Committee of Public Safety' composed of Jacobins had been set up; an attempt to create a revolutionary

[1] The parts of this chapter relating to the federalist movement at Lyon are based on C. Riffaterre, *Le Mouvement antijacobin et antiparisien à Lyon et dans le Rhône-et-Loire en 1793*, 2 vols.

tribunal had been foiled only by a decree from the Convention. Two events in May brought the crisis to a head. In the first place, on 14 May the *Représentants en mission* Albitte and Dubois-Crancé authorized the immediate organization of an *armée révolutionnaire* in Lyon: it was to be financed by a forced loan on the rich and the revolutionary committees were to disarm negligent or unpatriotic national guards. In the second place, on 24 May there were market riots and some pillaging, which the Municipality did nothing to stop and thus seemed to condone. The rising of 29 May was, therefore, essentially a conservative movement against anarchy to protect citizens whose property seemed threatened by disorder, by fixed prices, and by forced loans, and whose liberty seemed endangered by domiciliary visits, by arrest, by the seizure of their arms, and by extra-ordinary justice. It was a revolution about local issues; it was anti-jacobin; it was aimed at a Municipality which was establishing its political control over the city through extra-ordinary institutions and which was disarming citizens and handing their arms over to a force of *sans-culottes*.

The municipal revolution was transformed into an anti-parisian, anti-governmental rebellion during June and July. Lyon rapidly became the centre of a departmental revolt, which was part of the federalist protest against 'le degré progressif d'avilissement et de servitude où la représentation nationale est réduite par une faction scélérate et des tribunes insolentes'.[1] Events at Lyon, therefore, assumed a national political significance. During the second week in June the administration of the department accepted a federalist programme emanating from the Department of the Jura and began to correspond with the federalist authorities of other departments with a view to organizing a new legislature at Bourges and offering resistance to the system of anarchy now triumphant in Paris. The dismissal of Robert Lindet, who arrived at this point to investigate the situation, and, later, the execution of Chalier on 16 July, despite two decrees from the Convention forbidding it, marked Lyon's open defiance of the central government; the arrival of Biroteau and Chasset linked Lyon with the Girondins. The position was crystallized

[1] Resolution of the Depart. of the Jura, 24 May, quoted in É. Herriot, *Lyon n'est plus*, ii. 20.

by the decrees of 12 and 14 July, which declared Lyon to be in open rebellion, dismissed all officials, and ordered the *Armée des Alpes* to move against the city. But already early in July the federalist movement was beginning to disintegrate. An assembly of forty-two *sociétés populaires* at Valence at the end of June persuaded the Department of the Drôme to stay faithful to the Convention and, when General Carteaux captured Pont-Saint-Esprit on 14 July, a junction between the forces of Lyon and Marseille was no longer possible. Similarly, Montauban and Toulouse deserted the cause at the beginning of July, thereby cutting Marseille off from Bordeaux. Federalism in Normandy collapsed at Vernon on 13 July. The departments nearer Lyon, such as the Jura, the Ain, the Saône-et-Loire, and the Isère, which had dabbled in the movement, were defecting under pressure from the *Représentants en mission*. In addition, the plebiscite on the Constitution, which was being held in this area throughout July, encouraged many people to rally to the government. Thus, Lyon was becoming isolated and was forced to seek help from within the department of the Rhône-et-Loire.

The administration of the department had already sought to bring the Rhône-et-Loire as a whole into the revolt. It had summoned the primary assemblies to elect deputies to a *Commission populaire, républicaine et de Salut public* which met for the first time on 30 June 'pour prendre toutes les mesures de sûreté générale exigées par les circonstances'. But a significant number of cantons had refused to send representatives, while a great many deputies, specifically limited by their electors to a proper respect for the Convention, were extremely reluctant to countenance overt rebellion. From 7 July onwards a steady stream of deputies began to quit the assembly as they realized that the very existence of such a body constituted an act of rebellion in itself. The raising of a departmental force had been decided in principle as early as 19 June, and the federalists expected to be able to retain the services of many national guards who they hoped would attend the illegal federation of 14 July at Lyon. But this proved a complete failure, and it at once became evident that their allies in the department stood in need of more help from Lyon than they could supply to Lyon.

It was in these circumstances that, on 9 July, the *Commission populaire* decided to send a detachment of troops to Saint-Étienne. This was an act of political significance. It was aimed at curbing the important centres of Jacobin opposition at Saint-Chamond and Saint-Étienne and at supporting the federalists in the latter city, while at the same time controlling the arms industry in the event of a siege.[1] These troops occupied Saint-Chamond on 11 July and, with the connivance of Lesterpt-Beauvais, *Représentant en mission* to the arms industry, they were able to enter Saint-Étienne unopposed on the following day. The Jacobin Municipality of Saint-Chamond was replaced; the clubs in the two towns were ransacked;[2] the Jacobins fled into the mountains or into the neighbouring departments, and the more prominent of those who did not escape were arrested.[3] During the next few days, federalist sympathizers caused a great deal of unrest at Montbrison, and these troubles provided the pretext that the Municipality needed in order to ask for aid from Saint-Étienne.[4] After permission had been obtained from the *Commission populaire*, a detachment from Saint-Étienne arrived at Montbrison on 22 July.[5] The club was sacked, and those Jacobins who had not prudently withdrawn were put under arrest.[6]

Despite the fact that the republican army began to besiege Lyon on 8 August, the *muscadins* (federalists) remained in the Forez until early September, since the western approaches to the city remained open, whilst an imposing bevy of *Représentants en mission* slowly marshalled the resources of the surrounding departments for a protracted struggle which they had not foreseen. It was primarily to remove the last

[1] C.-J. Puy, *Expédition des Lyonnais dans le Forez, juillet–septembre 1793*, ed. L. Chaleyer *et al.*, p. 16.

[2] A.N., W 408, d. 939, a report of *commissaires* to estimate the cost of repairs at Saint-Étienne, shows that even the floorboards were torn up.

[3] For the federalist period in the dist. of Saint-Étienne, J. B. Galley, *Saint-Étienne et son district pendant la Révolution*, i. 525–696.

[4] A.D.R., 42 L 164, *reg. dél.* of Mun. of Montbrison, 18 July.

[5] For the early days of the occupation here, Thiollière *et al.*, *Compte rendu à ses commettants par le Conseil général du district de Montbrison.*

[6] There were thirty-seven arrests at Montbrison (A.D.R., 42 L 161, d. Peronin); 189 patriots of Saint-Étienne qualified for an indemnity after the crisis (Galley, op. cit. i. 570).

vestige of legality from the occupation of the Forez by the troops from Lyon that these *Représentants* decided on the creation of the new department of the Loire.[1] However, on 26 August the National Guard of Rive-de-Gier finally revolted and destroyed a detachment from Lyon;[2] on 28 August, in the face of an imminent popular explosion, the garrison at Saint-Étienne withdrew to Montbrison.[3] The *muscadins* were able to hold out there for another ten days, since, during the night of 31 August–1 September, they managed to surprise a detachment of republican troops under General Nicolas at Saint-Anthême, just over the border in the Puy-de-Dôme. But the net was being drawn round them. A column of troops, led by the *Représentant* Javogues, invaded the district of Saint-Étienne on 6 September, occupied the *chef-lieu* on the 7th, and marched on Montbrison on the 9th. On the same day, a large body of national guards from the district of Roanne, under the guidance of the *commissaire civil* Dorfeuille, occupied Boën. Simultaneously, the *levée en masse* of the Puy-de-Dôme, organized by the *Représentants* Couthon, Maignet, and Châteauneuf-Randon, entered the department. The federalist troops slipped away despite skirmishes at Montrond and Chazelles-sur-Lyon and retreated over the hills to Lyon, taking with them cartloads of food and refugees, and the mother and uncle of the *Représentant* Javogues as hostages.[4] Lyon was then fully invested and finally capitulated on 9 October.

But it would be wrong to see military occupation as the essential feature of federalism in the Forez. Just as the federalist movement in Lyon grew out of particular local issues, similarly in the Forez the movement was indigenous and had its own local origins. There was the same political struggle between the moderates and the Jacobins as at Lyon. The elements of this conflict were already visible in the Forez in 1792 when the members of the District of Roanne, who were later accused of federalist sympathies, publicly deplored the demonstration of 20 June at the very moment when, in

1 A.N., AF II 114 (860) 11, preamble to *arrêté* of 12 Aug.

2 E. Perrin, *Le Tombeau des muscadins, passim.*

3 For the expulsion of the *muscadins* from the Forez, Galley, op. cit. i. 715–56.

4 A.D.R., 1 L 381, Massol to Doppet, n.d.; A.D.R., 42 L 111, d. Noailly, declaration by Javogues's mother, n.d.

Saint-Étienne, the *sociétés populaires*, later to become centres of Jacobinism, were denouncing Marie-Antoinette and the Court.[1] But it was not until the winter of 1792–3 that the division of opinion became decisive.

The struggle was bitterest at Saint-Étienne, where the moderates had conquered the Municipality in the elections of 1792.[2] This was an exact reversal of the situation at Lyon, for the Jacobins of the clubs proceeded to take over the sections and to oppose the Municipality from this base. In February, leading Jacobins were being attacked in their homes, while on 9 March the clubs sent deputies to the *Représentants en mission* at Lyon in order to alert them to the fact that the town was in such a state of ferment that troubles might break out at any moment, and that the 'cabale aristocratique' had taken control of the administrative organs, especially the Municipality, with the express intention of harrying the patriots.[3] Throughout March there was incessant agitation in the sections and clubs against the Municipality, whilst the moderates retorted by demanding the arrest of Johannot, the most prominent of the Jacobins.[4] The division between the two groups was hardened by the exclusion of moderate *officiers municipaux* from the clubs and the resignation of one of the few Jacobins left in the Municipality.[5] The arrival of the *Représentants en mission* Reverchon and Pressavin at the end of March produced a temporary reconciliation, but from the beginning of May the agitation reappeared with renewed vigour. The sections began to set up revolutionary committees while the Municipality and the District counter-attacked by creating a *Comité central de Salut public*. The movement culminated in the arrest of Johannot by the Municipality on 30 May on his return from a visit to Lyon. In these circumstances it was natural that the moderates of Saint-Étienne, represented by the Municipality, should have put the local conflict into a wider perspective by sending a deputation on 12 June to congratulate the people of

[1] A.N., W 20, d. 1095, denunciation by Lapalus, 2 Nov. 1792; E.-M. Siauve, *Discours prononcé le 13 juin, l'an 4e de la Liberté, dans une assemblée de la Société populaire et fraternelle de Saint-Étienne, séante à Polignais.*

[2] Unless otherwise stated, this paragraph is based on Galley, op. cit. i. 397–499.

[3] Bibl. Lyon, Coste MS. 593.

[4] Bibl. Lyon, Coste MS. 601, no. 5.

[5] Ibid.

Lyon and to bring them financial support. The arrival of the troops from Lyon completed the moderates' control, for in the sections 'les citoyens . . . se sont retirés insensiblement sans vouloir délibérer, malgré les représentations faites par nous président et secrétaire'.[1] The attitude of the administration of the district was more tortuous than that of the Municipality. When the *muscadins* arrived, the administrators inscribed in their *registre des délibérations* their indignation at such illegality; henceforth the minutes of every meeting proclaimed this administration to be oppressed, and at every act of the counter-revolutionaries it noted: 'Considérant qu'il est sans force, que son autorité est méconnue, qu'il a lieu de craindre pour lui-même, [il] proteste contre tous ces actes de violence et de tyrannie et déclare à tous ses concitoyens qu'il n'est pas libre.'[2] But they carefully refrained from giving any public hint of these views, while, before the occupation, they had clearly shown that their sympathies lay with the moderates, and they actively collaborated with Lyon throughout the federalist period.[3]

The other great centre of political unrest was Montbrison, although at Saint-Chamond the Jacobin Municipality met with considerable opposition, while at Saint-Bonnet-le-Château there were disturbances and at Feurs there were squabbles within the Municipality.[4] The position at Montbrison is less well documented than that at Saint-Étienne, but it is clear that the Municipality in 1793 was controlled, as at Saint-Étienne, by moderates. Again, the club was clearly the centre of Jacobinism, for, later, the administration of the district was to protest about the insults to certain citizens who seemed to be the subject of systematic persecution for the simple reason that they were members of the club.[5] The first sign of open strife occurred in early February, when the families of Javogues and Dupuis, both Montagnard deputies,

[1] Resignation of the officers of the *section de l'Union*, quoted in Galley, op. cit. i. 549.

[2] A.N., D XLII 9, d. Loire, copies of the *reg. dél.* of the Dist. of Saint-Étienne.

[3] e.g. Bibl. Lyon, Coste MS. 603, deliberation of the Dist., 21 Mar.; A.D.R., 42 L 156, letter to Mun. of Saint-Héand, 11 Aug., urging armed support for Lyon.

[4] A.D.L., L 144; A.D.R., 42 L 163; A.C. Feurs, *reg. dél.*, 25 May.

[5] A.D.L., L 324, fol. 22, letter to Mun., 18 July. Their opponents met at the Café Suisse and 'y tenaient des conversations opposées au nouvel ordre des choses' (A.N., F1b II Loire 15, d. Montbrison, Dist. to Depart., 28 Feb.).

were insulted and the doors of Javogues's house were daubed with blood and red chalk.[1] In March the Municipality of Saint-Bonnet-le-Château identified Montbrison as being 'pour la chose publique et pour nous, le pays le plus redoutable et le plus inquiétant'.[2] The moderates of Montbrison were far quicker than those of Saint-Étienne to associate themselves with the municipal revolution at Lyon: it was on 1 June that the Municipality sent a delegation to congratulate the people of Lyon, and three days later opened a subscription list for the wounded.[3] When two *commissaires* from the Department, whose political attitudes were evidently out of line with the most recent developments, attempted to disperse the company of grenadiers, which, because of the cost of the uniform, tended to be the preserve of rich moderates, the members refused and threatened to attack the club, which no longer dared to meet.[4] On 16 July a crowd of young people sang seditious songs under the windows of each of its members; the next day, the club was broken into and 'un monument, emblème du Club et de la Constitution' was removed and burned in front of the Liberty Tree.[5] The summoning of troops to Montbrison on 18 July was the inevitable outcome, although there was no real need for them, in contrast to Saint-Étienne where the sections were largely Jacobin. Again, in contrast to Saint-Étienne, the district administration at Montbrison was sharply divided over the federalist crisis. Its conduct during the events of February had been most ambiguous,[6] but in July most of the members ceased to attend. Finally, the four who remained withdrew on 3 August to Roanne and thence into the Puy-de-Dôme, whilst still attempting to administer the district in spite of the *muscadins*.[7]

The situation in the Forez was similar in many respects to the situation elsewhere in France at the time, and more

1 Bibl. Lyon, Coste MS. 548, letter from Javogues, Dupuis, Dubouchet, Pressavin, Pointe, 18 Feb.; A.N., F^{1b} II Rhône 15, d. Montbrison, Depart. to Dist., 8 Mar.

2 Bibl. Lyon, Coste MS. 599, no. 13, letter to *Repr.* at Lyon, 12 Mar.

3 A.D.R., 42 L 164, *reg. dél.* of Mun. of Montbrison, 1 and 4 June.

4 Bibl. Lyon, Coste MS. 630, Valette and Mondon to Depart., 2 June.

5 Thiollière *et al.*, *Compte rendu à ses commettants par le Conseil général du district.*

6 Bibl. Lyon, Coste MS. 600, Dupuis to Achard, 18 Mar.

7 Thiollière, op. cit.; A.D.L., L 272, expense account of refugee administration.

particularly in neighbouring Lyon. It was merely one manifestation of the national unrest of the period, which was reflected in the struggles in the Convention. In common with other areas, the political struggle that developed in the Forez was essentially a contest between the socially and politically conservative elements, intent on maintaining the rule of law and the principles of the Constitution of 1791, and those, especially the members of the clubs, who demanded extraordinary measures for extraordinary circumstances. The mayor of Saint-Étienne, one of the most prominent of the future federalists, clearly expressed this division when he said of his enemies:

> Partout ils ont crié que le salut du peuple était la suprême loi, on ne devrait employer que des mesures révolutionnaires, que des moyens hors de la loi: bien convaincus qu'après avoir affaibli le corps politique par nos dissensions, ils le feraient expirer dans les convulsions de l'anarchie et qu'ils nous amèneraient insensiblement à ce point où l'excès de nos maux nous rendrait insensibles aux poids des nouveaux fers qu'ils veulent nous donner.[1]

As elsewhere, the agitation in the Forez had a background of economic crisis. Federalism coincided with a period of rising prices, which inevitably led to unrest. In August the high price of food caused disturbances at Roanne, which had held aloof from the federalist movement; at Saint-Étienne, the price of bread had almost doubled between January and July, while in August bread was costing 14 or 15 *sous* a pound in Montbrison.[2] Saint-Étienne, which was always prone to shortages, suffered particularly since her industry had declined with the development of the war. This explains why it was in Saint-Étienne that the Jacobins adopted the most extreme positions: the right of insurrection, the redistribution of the property of the rich, the rejection of the Constitution of 1791 and of the rule of law which compromised *le salut public*, the creation of an *armée révolutionnaire*, and the levying of forced taxes from the rich.[3] The Jacobins of Saint-

[1] A.D.R., 42 L 170, d. Boyer, draft of a speech by Praire-Royer, 14 July.

[2] A.D.R., 42 L 157, Mun. of Roanne to Mun. of Montbrison, 6 Aug.; Galley, op. cit. i. 413–16; A.D.R., 42 L 185, d. J. B. Monet, *mémoire*, n.d.

[3] This programme can be gathered from the denunciations against Johannot to the *Comité central de Salut public* in June 1793 (A.D.R., 42 L 42).

Étienne clearly connected the food shortage with counter-revolution, for they warned the *Représentants en mission* of the political dangers that arose out of the excessive price of food and that were daily nearer realization through the combined efforts of the rich *propriétaires* and the capitalist hoarders.[1] There was, therefore, in Saint-Étienne, as in Lyon, a direct link between the economic crisis and the general demands for extraordinary measures.

But it must be emphasized in this context that the pattern that developed in the Forez was not consciously part of a national movement before the federalist crisis. It is certainly true that there was some connection between Saint-Étienne and Lyon. The programme presented by the Jacobins of Saint-Étienne was clearly modelled on that of the Lyon clubs, while their leader, Johannot, proclaimed himself 'l'ami et le partisan de Chalier' and admitted that he had frequently travelled to Lyon during the six weeks preceding 29 May.[2] But the agitation at Saint-Étienne, like that at Montbrison, dated from well before Johannot's visits and was predominantly a response to local problems. Similarly, events outside the Forez obviously had an effect on the position there. For instance, the incidents at Montbrison in February were directly related to the execution of the King. More particularly, it is certain that developments at Lyon before 29 May served to alarm the moderates in the Forez considerably and to sharpen their resistance, because they could not avoid drawing the parallel between the realities in Lyon and the possibilities nearer home. The difficulties of communications can have done nothing to remedy the situation—slightly later in the year an inhabitant of Saint-Symphorien-de-Lay noted that only occasionally did the truth percolate through the thousands of absurd tales bandied about, so that one might believe whatsoever matched one's own hopes and fears.[3] The reluctance displayed by the Municipality of Montbrison in implementing the decree on revolutionary committees probably stemmed from what it heard about the way in which these

1 Bibl. Lyon, Coste MS. 593, letter of 9 Mar.

2 A.D.R., 42 L 40, provisional Mun. of Lyon to Mun. of Saint-Étienne, 17 June; A.C. Saint-Étienne, 1 D 10 (3), 30 May.

3 A.D.R., 42 L 181, d. D'Hauteroche, letter of 16 Aug.

bodies were being used in Lyon.[1] In the same way, the unrest at Saint-Étienne and Montbrison was bound to provoke anxiety in other communities in the Forez. Thus, when the Municipality of Saint-Bonnet-le-Château complained to the *Représentants en mission* at Lyon in March about the activities of a *notaire* from Usson, it attributed almost all the town's ills to its relations with Montbrison, the source of manifold rumours, 'cet antre féodal . . . ce cloaque de chicane [où] il va toutes les semaines aspirer les vapeurs fétides qu'il répand ici à son passage'.[2] But, again, it must be stressed that events in Paris or in Lyon would have provoked little response among the moderates if their fears had not been aroused already by local issues. It was not so much the garbled reports of noisy scenes in the *Club central* at Lyon that frightened the inhabitants of the Forez but the clear statements about insurrection made in the clubs at Saint-Étienne, such as the following: 'Cet abus des choses est devenu si dangereux dans ses conséquences que le peuple serait peut-être forcé de se livrer à l'insurrection pour se défendre contre l'oppression de ses magistrats.'[3] The moderates feared Jacobin talk of an *armée révolutionnaire*, primarily because the Jacobin Municipality of Saint-Chamond had sought to pay for its contingent of the *levée des 300000* by a forced loan on the rich: Albitte's and Dubois-Crancé's *arrêté* of 14 May merely confirmed their interpretation.[4] The disarming of nobles and suspects, undertaken by some Municipalities following the decree of 26 March, was a potent factor in mobilizing moderate opinion, for, as one victim of this measure said, 'l'on ne pourrait vous exprimer dans quelle agitation a vécu l'impétrant depuis qu'il est envisagé comme suspect'.[5] Can one wonder, then, that these men should have later been heard exhorting the *muscadins*, 'menez dur ces coquins de patriotes qui m'avaient volé mes armes', especially when, as was the case at Boën, it was to the club that the suspects felt they had to try to justify themselves?[6] The confiscations of

[1] A.D.L., L 324, fol. 24, Dist. of Montbrison to Depart., 4 May.

[2] Bibl. Lyon, Coste MS. 599, no. 13, letter of 12 Mar.

[3] Ibid., MS. 593.

[4] Pressavin and Reverchon, *Rapport des commissaires-députés, envoyés par la Convention dans les départements de Rhône-et-Loire et Saône-et-Loire*, 25 Apr.

[5] A.D.L., L 435, petition by Morel, n.d.

[6] A.D.L., L 390, fol. 12; A.D.L., L 435, petition by Morel, n.d.

arms in Lyon merely provided the moderates with a further element for appreciating events at home. Finally, the national instability of the *assignat* in this period was important in that it created uncertainty, adding to the hostility with which many conservative men of substance were likely to regard the political attitudes of the Jacobins. In January the steward of the Comte de Saint-Polgues reported that it was impossible to get the tenants to pay in anything but *assignats*; a few days later, his employer replied that specie was reported to be worth twice its value in *assignats* at Lyon and wondered, with evident concern, about the significance of such a sudden rise from the previous level of 28 per cent above.[1]

There were poor people in the ranks of the federalists and consequently among those arrested in the early days of the Terror. But, in most cases, their motives had little to do with the wider issues involved. Jean Girardon of Pouilly-lès-Feurs, who recruited for the *muscadins*, had worked as a carpenter for Rochefort, a leading federalist; similarly, one Faure was said to have been influenced into federalism by Chappuis Maubourg to whom he owed money.[2] The population of Saint-Étienne was subjected to a barrage of propaganda from the occupying forces—honeyed words, rousing speeches at the Town Hall and in the sections, posters, proclamations, *arrêtés*, and also harassment and incessant requisitions.[3] The case of Joseph Sagnolle of Saint-Chamond seems typical:

Mon mari est un malheureux ouvrier, sans fortune, ne sachant ni lire ni écrire, n'ayant d'autre ressource pour faire vivre et subsister ses trois enfants et sa femme que le métier de cylindreur de rubans, état précaire et subordonné aux caprices du goût et à l'inconstance du commerce. Depuis six mois il n'a presque rien fait, ce qui l'a mis hors d'état de pouvoir faire subsister sa famille. Un jour le chagrin l'ayant saisi il tâcha de le dissiper dans le vin; à cette occasion il eut du bruit avec sa femme, qui lui reprocha son infrugalité, ce qui échauffa la querelle. Et sur cela, il s'expatria et pris du service chez les lyonnais, qui lui offrirent 5 livres par jour. Ce fut pour lui une grande consolation de trouver par cet engagement le moyen de faire subsister sa famille.[4]

[1] A.D.R., 42 L 177, d. Dubourg de Saint-Polgues, letters of 8 and 25 Jan. 1793.
[2] A.D.L., L 411, fol. 1; A.D.R., 42 L 160.
[3] A.D.R., 42 L 178, d. Dulac, testimonial from club, n.d.
[4] A.D.R., 42 L 189, d. Sagnolle, petition to Javogues, 29 frim.

But, in general, the division between the moderates, future federalists, and the Jacobins, future terrorists, was one of class. The most important federalists in the area were the richest citizens: Chassain de Marcilly owned six estates; Dubourg de Saint-Polgues had bought 120,000 *livres*' worth of *biens nationaux*; when the woman Lesgallery and the woman Achard were arrested trying to flee, they were carrying more than 67,000 *livres* in *assignats*, coin, silverware, and promissory notes.[1] 'Il n'y a plus de riches que la République', rejoiced the *agent national* of the district of Boën (formerly that of Montbrison) in pluviôse as he pointed to the immense number of land holdings taken over as a result of the conspiracy.[2] The sectional assemblies at Saint-Chamond in June were disturbed by Jacobins, who complained that the sectional officers were all 'Gros'.[3] On the other hand the future federalists quite clearly identified their enemies as predominantly the lower strata of society. The moderates at Saint-Chamond declared that the club was made up of 'un tas d'ouvriers qui feraient bien mieux de s'occuper à travailler';[4] the troops from Lyon noted that at Saint-Étienne nearly all the numerous workers supported the Jacobins and that more than two thousand of them belonged to an organized resistance.[5] When the opposition between the moderates and the Jacobins was given expression it was essentially in terms of conflicting class-interests. The Jacobins' attacks were directed above all at the rich:

Se trouvant en la section d'Union de cette ville dans le courant d'avril dernier, il se présenta environ une douzaine d'ouvriers portant chacun un tablier de peau. Le citoyen Johannot, qui y était, prit la parole et dit d'une voix énergique: 'Voilà les vrais sans-culottes, ne recevons à l'avenir que de ces sans-culottes à tablier de peau. Méfions-nous des muscadins, des prêtres et des riches et n'en recevons aucuns dans la Société populaire . . .' Par un discours Johannot essaya ensuite de persuader au peuple assemblé qu'ils avaient le droit . . . sous leurs coups de chasser cette Municipalité, n'étant composée que de Riches qui ne cherchent qu'à abaisser les pauvres et à leur donner des entraves . . . Johannot parla pour démontrer au peuple que le bien, qu'avaient

[1] A.D.R., 42 L 189, d. Chassain, letter to Javogues, 2 pluv.; A.D.R., 42 L 177, d. Dubourg, *mémoire*, n.d.; A.D.R., 1 L 622.

[2] A.D.L., L 327, fol. 1, letter to *Repr.*, 26 pluv.

[3] A.D.L., L 144.

[4] A.D.R., 42 L 175, d. Coron.

[5] Puy, op. cit., pp. 26, 38.

les marchands, ne leur appartenait pas, parce qu'ils l'avaient usurpé aux ouvriers . . . Johannot a dit qu'il était plus difficile à un Riche d'être bon patriote qu'à un câble d'entrer dans le trou d'une aiguille . . . A la fin de son discours Johannot dit: 'Formons notre armée révolutionnaire toute de sans-culottes; nous irons chez les propriétaires et les forcerons bien à nous délivrer leurs denrées et s'ils ne veulent pas nous les pendrons car il faut que le pauvre vive comme le Riche.'[1]

Moderatism, and later federalism, were above all the reaction of the property-owners to this kind of talk: they insisted upon the authority of legally elected bodies and upon the supremacy of the law, because these guaranteed their material interests and their local predominance—Johannot remarked, with a certain insight, that 'avec la Constitution, rien que la Constitution, toute la Constitution, le tyran faisait égorger les patriotes . . . qu'il en était de même des autorités constituées qui, avec la loi, rien que la loi, toute la loi, compromettaient le salut du peuple'.[2] It is hardly surprising that the moderates considered a man such as Chana, the mayor of Saint-Chamond, to be, like Marat, an advocate of pillage and slaughter and accused the *clubistes* of intending to plunder all property.[3] This was the automatic reaction of all men of substance to outbursts of popular violence, such as those which tended at this time to lend reality to these speeches. The attitude of the Municipality of Saint-Bonnet-le-Château, which, however, remained aloof from the federalist movement, is typical:

La municipalité de Saint-Bonnet-le-Château représente que la garde nationale est peu sûre, qu'elle n'est composée en grande partie que d'ouvriers séditieux qui se sont portés dès le mois de mai dernier à de très grands attentats sur les propriétés les plus sacrées, qu'ils ont été dénoncés aux tribunaux et qu'aucun des coupables n'a été puni; que cette impunité jointe à la cessation de travail des manufactures de serrurerie porte ces ouvriers à annoncer hautement qu'ils n'attendent que la battue des grains pour (si on ne leur donne pas blé et argent gratis) faire une révolte complète, piller, tuer, mettre la ville à contribution et couper plusieurs têtes; que ces craintes font déserter les meilleurs citoyens, que le blé y est très cher, que sa circulation est interceptée.[4]

[1] A.D.R., 42 L 42, denunciations to *Comité central de Salut public*.
[2] Ibid.
[3] A.D.R., 42 L 175, d. Coron; A.D.L., L 390, fol. 13.
[4] A.D.R., 42 L 163, n.d.

One must, however, qualify this picture slightly. At Saint-Étienne and at Saint-Chamond the rich were chiefly merchants, as we have seen. Such men would inevitably tend to be sympathetic to the actions of their counterparts in Lyon, or at least would hesitate before dissociating themselves from them, for, as one moderate pointed out, Lyon was 'une ville qui a tant de part à l'activité du commerce de Saint-Étienne et sans laquelle nos manufactures peut-être languiraient'.[1] Thus, the federalist troops were well received at Saint-Chamond by the factors and agents of the principal trading-houses who were under orders to welcome them.[2] Moreover, the merchants were able to mobilize part of the population through their control of the silk industry. One *dévideuse* from Saint-Étienne was refused work throughout the federalist period on the grounds that her talk had set the whole of her street against Lyon; when the *muscadins* withdrew from Saint-Chamond, Dugas and Praire closed their warehouse saying that there would be no work until their return, when it would once again be plentiful.[3] The real centre of support for the Jacobins was in the workshops of the arms and metallurgical industry, among the 'sans-culottes à tablier de peau'. The federalists of Saint-Étienne said of their enemies that every time they wanted to attain some objective contrary to the principles of liberty, 'ils ont engagé le peuple à quitter ses ateliers'.[4] During the occupation, Bouillet, *commissaire* of the

[1] A.D.R., 42 L 40, a speech to the *section de la Liberté*, Saint-Étienne, 16 July.

[2] Puy, op. cit., p. 24.

[3] A.D.R., 42 L 181, d. Jacquet, evidence of Marie Monverne; A.D.R., 42 L 69, fol. 20.

[4] A.D.R., 42 L 40, speech in *section de la Liberté*, 16 July. There was, however, a great deal of discontent among those entrepreneurs working on government contract. In Oct. 1792 the *Reprs. en mission* Romme and Soubrany had made new regulations, which were confirmed by the decrees of 20 Mar. and 2 Apr. 1793. These fixed the price of labour and the price of sale before the execution of the contract and gave the Republic the sole right of purchase. The prices were fixed too low in respect of the cost of raw materials, while the large number of orders flowing in from the various Muns. for their volunteers would have brought about a price rise (cf. A.N., AF II* 128, no. 363, analysis of a letter from the mayor of Saint-Étienne to C.P.S., 12 May). Therefore, work for the Republic very largely stopped in April in favour of illegal private orders. The situation improved when Bouillet and Levayer, *commissaires du Pouvoir exécutif*, put the prices up in May, but there were still a great many 'sorties furtives'. It is significant that, as early as 8 July, the *Commission populaire* should have authorized a revision of the prices (Galley, op. cit. i. 426, 430–3, 532).

Minister for War, was able to organize a resistance movement in the arms industry, stopping the workers from attending the sectional assemblies, persuading them to hide arms, reading the newspapers to them, and enlisting the women to bring pressure to bear on the men.[1] When the federalist troops and the Municipality went to seize the books of the *Manufacture*, they felt it necessary to threaten to open fire if the workers formed a crowd.[2]

At Montbrison, however, the situation was somewhat different. As we have seen, this was a town of aristocrats, lawyers, and landlords. There was no common interest with Lyon. On the contrary, at the beginning of the Revolution there was a great deal of ill-feeling against Lyon, expressed in demands for a separate department for the Forez; these petitions claimed that there was nothing in common between this agricultural area and the commercial interests of Lyon and that an administration at Lyon had always sacrificed the Forez to Lyon and would always do so.[3] To a certain extent, the decision of the *Représentants* to set up a new department on these lines must be seen as an attempt to appeal to this sort of opinion. Yet Montbrison allied with Lyon before Saint-Étienne. The reason for this lies in the fact that the moderate movement at Montbrison, although drawing upon the same common fund of social conservatism as at Saint-Étienne, was probably of a slightly different stamp. Although there is no direct evidence of royalism, moderatism seems to have been always much more counter-revolutionary in character at Montbrison and to have represented much more the reaction of former privileged groups than at Saint-Étienne, where the moderates always remained basically republican. Certainly contemporaries tended to emphasize this aspect in the case of Montbrison. 'Montbrison est dans une contre-révolution ouverte', wrote the Forezian deputies in February, alleging that *émigrés* and refractory priests made no secret of their presence.[4] In April, Pressavin and Reverchon, both fairly

[1] A.D.R., 42 L 171, d. Bouillet, attestations for him by workers. [2] Ibid.

[3] e.g. *Adresse aux Foréziens*, n.d.; A.N., D IVbis 16, d. 270, resolution of the active citizens of Montbrison, 5 Mar. 1790; ibid., d. 271, 'Pétition des communes de la province du Forez et de partie de celles du Beaujolais', n.d.; D IVbis 84, d. Loire, 'Délibération de la ville de Saint-Germain-Laval-en-Forez', 24 Jan. 1790.

[4] Bibl. Lyon, Coste MS. 548, letter of 18 Feb.

sensible men, reported to the Convention that Montbrison was full of *aristocrates* and *fanatiques*, who had consistently and unequivocally demonstrated from the beginning of the Revolution their hatred of the new order, which injured both their pride and their interests.[1] Other observers found significance in the fact that, in the early days of the Revolution, affairs of state had been discussed there in a *Cercle*, whose social exclusiveness confined its membership to wealthy lawyers and bourgeois, to former nobles and privileged persons—'ou, pour mieux dire, aristocrates'.[2]

Finally, it must be noted that it is by no means sufficient to speak of the struggle between Jacobins and moderates and of federalism merely in terms of a class conflict. There was no sizeable *menu peuple* at Montbrison; yet the political struggle there was violent, however weak the Jacobins may in fact have been.[3] The peasants, who attacked the *muscadins* in a skirmish at Salvizinet near Feurs in September, were commanded by Jean-Joseph-Alexandre de Buronne, *chevalier de Saint-Louis*.[4] Although the richest federalists were for the most part considerably wealthier than the richest Jacobins, many active federalists were socially indistinguishable from the most militant of their opponents. The decision by men of this sort of wealth to become either moderate or Jacobin, federalist or terrorist, was essentially a political choice of what they thought right whether in local or in national terms. The administrators of the district of Montbrison evidently turned against the federalists because they felt that the call for troops and the actions of these troops were illegal and unjustifiable.[5] The federalist crisis split families: Pupier de Brioude's sister was the wife of the Montagnard deputy Dubouchet; Joseph Vissaguet denounced his second-cousins for ill-treating him as a patriot; Ardaillon *père*, *notable* of

[1] Pressavin and Reverchon, op. cit. Cf. J. L. Tallien, *Rapport et projet de décret sur les troubles arrivés à Lyon* (25 Feb.), accusing Montbrison of harbouring royalists; and also, during the federalist crisis itself, A.N., F7 4683, d. 1 (Dubois-Crancé), Dist. Ambert to Depart. Puy-de-Dôme, 3 Aug., relaying reports of royalist propaganda in Montbrison.

[2] A.D.R., 42 L 159.

[3] Pressavin and Reverchon, op. cit.: 'les patriotes, dont le parti est malheureusement très faible'; A.D.R., 42 L 160, testimony of Magnien: 'les patriotes de Montbrison auraient eu besoin d'un chef . . . mais ils n'en avaient pas.'

[4] Galley, op. cit. i. 729.

[5] Thiollière, op. cit., *passim*.

Montbrison, and his eldest son, *juge de paix* at Roanne, were federalists, but his second son had joined up as surgeon-major in the 8th Regiment of Artillery at Port-Malo and his third son acted as a *commissaire des subsistances* for the army besieging Lyon.[1] It was this situation that was reflected by the anxiety with which the officers commanding the volunteers from the Forez against Lyon watched the beleaguered forces and demanded reassignment as soon as their men began to recognize friends, with the resultant crop of rumours of impending fraternization.[2]

On the whole, the future department of the Loire held back from the federalist movement, which was confined to the major towns of the centre and south. Already in the elections to the *Commission populaire*, eighteen out of the forty-three cantons of these three districts had failed to send deputies, and in those primary assemblies which had met abstentionism had been high: only forty-four people attended the assembly at Charlieu as opposed to the 775 who voted for the Constitution on 28 July in the middle of the harvest season; at Montbrison, only eighty people appeared out of a total population of just over 6,000.[3] Both Boën and Feurs refused to associate themselves with the movement. Boën was particularly hostile. Its primary assembly had met only in order to protest against the illegality of the event.[4] On 3 August, after a period of increasing friction with the *muscadins* at Montbrison, the inhabitants of Boën gathered the national guards from the surrounding villages and marched on Montbrison; they were driven back in a brief skirmish and Boën was occupied for a short time.[5] The rural communities also mostly held aloof. When they did participate, with some hesitation, it was usually for the motives expressed by the mayor of Saint-Genest-Malifaux:

Prenons des moyens suffisants pour nous rendre conformes aux chefs-lieux de district et de département, qu'ils ont cent fois et que dis-je des mille [fois] plus d'esprit que nous. Si Saint-Genest n'est pour nommer deux députés il est fort à craindre que nous nous faisions

[1] A.D.L., L suppl. 64; A.C. Chazelles-sur-Lyon, *reg. dél.*, 14 Oct. 1793; A.D.L., L 80, fol. 54.

[2] A.D.R., 42 L 181, d. Hedde, petition of officers of *chasseurs*, 28 Sept.

[3] Riffaterre, op. cit. ii. 95–100.

[4] Ibid. ii. 107.

[5] Thiollière, op. cit.

prendre en horreur et en tête. Tous les cantons n'ont pas fait les mutins comme le nôtre.[1]

Religion does not appear to have been a potent factor in mobilizing the peasantry, even that of the hill country, behind a movement that remained republican until its last stages.[2]

But the attitude of the peasantry was not simply one of mere indifference. Even more than the Terror, federalism was an urban phenomenon, and it is during the summer of 1793 that we see clearly for the first time the antagonism between town and country, which was to be so characteristic of the Year II. Throughout the latter half of July and August the federalists of Saint-Étienne sought by repeated proclamations to overcome peasant hostility, which they imagined to be the result of the preaching of refugee Jacobins.[3] Montbrison was persistently troubled by rumours of peasants preparing to sack the town.[4] Much more than their collaboration with Lyon, it was this fear, combined with that of the traditional enemy, the Auvergnat, which caused many of the richer inhabitants to flee when the *muscadins* retreated from Montbrison.[5] Although the unsuccessful attack of 3 August on Montbrison was directed by the Municipality of Boën, it was basically a confused movement of the rural populations of the neighbouring cantons of the plain.[6] The *muscadins* never had any success in establishing themselves in the small centres of the Plaine du Forez: when they tried to persuade Sury to accept a garrison of Lyon troops to protect communications between Saint-Étienne and Montbrison, they finally had to

[1] A.D.R., 42 L 185, d. Monteux, letter to *procureur* of the commune, 26 June.

[2] We have only two examples: A.C. Amplepuis, *reg. dél.*, no. 2, fol. 14: 'Ils ont suivi cette armée rebelle, qui leur a fait entendre qu'ils se battaient pour la bonne cause et surtout pour défendre la Religion'; A. Portallier, *Tableau général des victimes et martyrs de la Révolution* . . ., article on Jean-Marie Croizier of Chevrières: 'J'ai combattu pour mon Dieu et pour mon Roi; j'ai combattu pour l'intérêt de la Religion Catholique.' On royalism in the Lyon federalist movement, Riffaterre, op. cit. ii. 1–96.

[3] Galley, op. cit. i. 607–11.

[4] e.g. A.D.R., 42 L 185, d. Morel *cadet*, letter to Javogues, 15 Oct.

[5] e.g. A.D.R., 42 L 178, d. Duperret, d. Durand, d. Dutroncy *père*; 42 L 186, d. Portier.

[6] A.N., F7 4683, d. 1 (Dubois-Crancé), appeal for help from inhabitants of the cantons of Boën, Feurs, and Saint-Georges-en-Couzan to Dists. and Depart. of Puy-de-Dôme, 4 Aug.: 'Toutes les campagnes des districts [*sic*] n'attendent que ce secours.'

agree to allow the local National Guard to do it; their earlier attempt to establish some sort of understanding with the peasantry by requesting one national guardsman from each canton to fraternize with them provoked no response at all.[1] At the beginning of September, one *muscadin* officer noted that almost all the communes in the canton of Feurs had taken up arms against the federalists, and on 4 September the Lyonnais had to send a detachment to disperse an armed crowd of peasants at Salvizinet near Feurs.[2] It is probable that the peasants of the Plaine du Forez hated federalism above all, because they thought that it was aimed at restoring the seigneurial regime of pre-revolutionary days. The fact that federalism was patronized by the great landowners must have seemed to justify this interpretation. But there was also much general hostility to the urban centres, where the landlords lived, which drained off much of the crops and ready cash and which, in the Plaine du Forez, gave little in return. After the skirmish at Salvizinet, peasants were talking of moving on Feurs, which was strenuously anti-federalist, and slaughtering the population.[3] The peasants were as reluctant to fight against Lyon for the Republic as they had been to fight for Lyon against the Republic, and the patriots had the same explanation for this as the *muscadins*.[4] It must be emphasized in this context that active peasant resistance was to be found especially in the lowlands within the economic and administrative orbit of the centres controlled by the federalists. The mountain people displayed the same mistrust of the affairs of the plain and the same reluctance to involve themselves in them as they were to show during the Terror. For instance, when an emissary arrived at the commune of Gumières, in the Monts du Forez, at the beginning of August with the news that the people were taking arms in the cantons of Moingt and Boën, the inhabitants decided after much hesitation to send an observer.[5] It was not until

1 A.D.R., 42 L 164, *reg. dél.* of Mun. of Montbrison, 23 and 5 Aug.

2 Galley, op. cit. i. 725–9.

3 A.D.R., 42 L 187, d. Relogue, petition, n.d.

4 A.D.L., L 382, fol. 7, *arrêté* of Javogues, 18 Sept.: 'Informés que cette classe d'hommes pervers ne cherchent qu'à égarer les citoyens de la campagne sous le prétexte des travaux de la terre . . .'

5 A.D.R., 42 L 43, *reg. dél.* of Mun. of Gumières, 4 Aug.

16 August that this commune got round to considering the Department's orders concerning the primary assemblies, which should have been held on 24 June to elect members to the *Commission populaire*, and then they were put off for another week.[1] Even in the Monts du Beaujolais, which had much closer economic links with Lyon, the peasants mistrusted both sides equally and saw the revolt primarily in terms of the damage that it did to the local cloth industry:

> La Convention ne cherchait qu'à s'enrichir et à faire égorger tout le peuple; . . . Dubois-Crancé était d'accord avec les lyonnais . . . ces derniers trouveraient plus de monde pour les secourir que pour les aller battre . . . et . . . cela mettait toute la montagne à la misère . . . les ennemis n'étaient qu'à 25 lieues de Paris et . . . il vaudrait bien mieux envoyer des forces de ce côté que contre Lyon.[2]

The district of Roanne was never directly implicated in the federalist crisis.[3] Half of the cantons abstained from electing deputies to the *Commission populaire*, which was a greater proportion than in any of the other districts.[4] Perhaps part of the reason lay in the fact that this area was relatively better informed about the realities of the national situation: it is significant that in June Saint-Symphorien-de-Lay and La Pacaudière, both on the main Paris–Lyon road, denounced the events at Lyon and declared their fidelity to the Convention.[5] But the inhabitants of Roanne itself, and the administrations there, pursued a very ambiguous policy and were reluctant to commit themselves to any side. On 4 June the administrations sent an address to the Convention, which denounced both Paris and Lyon.[6] In July, although the District was clearly favourable to Lyon, there was a considerable division of opinion within the Municipality, which made its attitude hesitant. Finally, when the *Représentants en mission* Rouyer

[1] A.D.R., 42 L 43, *reg. dél.* of Mun. of Gumières, 16 Aug.

[2] A.D.L., L 399, fol. 16, denunciation by Chavanon of Belmont against Marcus of Chandon.

[3] Unless otherwise stated, this paragraph is based on F. Pothier, *Roanne pendant la Révolution*, pp. 204–53.

[4] Riffaterre, op. cit. ii. 98–9.

[5] Ibid. ii. 104–5. Note that neither community was to show itself particularly enthusiastic during the Terror; so this attitude cannot have been due to the strength of local Jacobinism.

[6] A.N., AF II 114 (861) 15. It expressed basically federalist attitudes.

and Brunel visited the town late in July, the authorities officially adhered to the Convention. In August they attributed their previous ambivalence to commercial and family ties with Lyon, and it seems certain that this merchant oligarchy was intent throughout on protecting its wide trading interests against all political eventualities. There was indeed a strong moderate element with federalist sympathies. The town was one of the few in the whole department to send a detachment of national guards to the federation of 14 July at Lyon, despite the opposition of the *mariniers*, who tried to prevent them from crossing the Loire.[1] In the same month Lenoble, a *commissaire du Pouvoir exécutif* travelling south, was arrested by some citizens, who called him the successor and disciple of Marat because of some remarks he had made in an inn.[2] Even after their ostensible reconciliation with the Convention, the authorities were loath to take a positive stand. As late as 25 July, the District still had not distributed the Constitution to the communes;[3] Lenoble was kept in prison throughout August; the refugee administrators of the district of Montbrison left rather hurriedly for the Puy-de-Dôme when they learnt that the Municipality and District were going to ask them to do so after a few people had shouted abuse at the exiles.[4] Nevertheless, when Dorfeuille arrived at the beginning of September to organize the *levée* against Lyon, the people of Roanne responded with such alacrity that he was able to get the *Représentant* Reverchon to write a testimonial for the *société populaire*.[5]

The expulsion of the Lyonnais opened a period of uncertainty and confusion, which lasted until the fall of Lyon on 9 October, for the *Représentants en mission* at once left to direct the siege. Although the civil administrations remained in office, those in the major centres affected by federalism had been discredited, and arrests, which began immediately, thinned their ranks. At Saint-Étienne, the Municipality remained in control, but, directly after the retreat of the *muscadins*, the sections each delegated two *commissaires* to sit

[1] Riffaterre, op. cit. ii. 240.

[2] *Mission patriotique du citoyen Lenoble . . .*; A.N., F[1a] 551, d. Lenoble; A.N., F[1b] II Rhône 1, pp. 111, 116.

[3] A.D.R., 1 L 190, *arrêté* of Delaporte and Reverchon, Mâcon, 25 July.

[4] Thiollière, op. cit.

[5] A.C. Roanne, 1 D 1(2), fol. 184.

with it.[1] A large number of citizens were co-opted to act on committees and the authorities concentrated exclusively on the task of feeding and supplying the army besieging Lyon.[2] In the district of Montbrison the situation was rather different. At the *chef-lieu* there remained only the four patriotic members of the District and four very dubious members of the Municipality.[3] The *Représentants* Maignet and Châteauneuf-Randon set up a Committee of Public Safety which was composed at first exclusively of Auvergnats and which very rapidly assumed control of the whole area until the end of October. Its task was to supply the *levée en masse* of the Puy-de-Dôme, which had marched through the district and was now stationed in front of Lyon, and to protect its rear by arresting suspects. This Committee of Public Safety was characterized by a deep mistrust of the inhabitants of the Forez, and it proceeded to export the resources of the area in the direction both of the army round Lyon and of the Puy-de-Dôme. The remaining *officiers municipaux* ceased to have any significance, and they finally resigned on 5 October,[4] while the District, after attempting to maintain some sort of independent action, joined the Committee as a minority group of local patriots. At the same time, a garrison of 1,500 Auvergnats was installed in the town. Thus, Montbrison itself was firmly under the control of strangers who despised its inhabitants. At Feurs, Noirétable, and Boën, revolutionary committees composed of local patriots took over: the one at Boën corresponded directly with the Committee of Public Safety at Montbrison, while that at Feurs refused to be associated with the *chef-lieu*.[5] Thus, in the district of Montbrison, centralized civil authority had disappeared and the anarchical period of the Terror opened, for the area was run by extraordinary institutions.[6] In the meantime, the districts of Montbrison and Saint-Étienne were visited by *commissaires*

[1] Galley, op. cit. i. 700.

[2] Ibid. i. 767 n. 1.

[3] For the dist. of Montbrison Sept.–Oct. 1793 and the activities of this institution there, Colin Lucas, 'Auvergnats et Foréziens . . .', *Gilbert Romme et son temps*, pp. 129–37.

[4] A.D.R., 42 L 164, *reg. dél.* of Mun. of Montbrison, 5 Oct.

[5] A.D. P.-de-D., L 2784 and 2785.

[6] In frim. the Dist. of Boën requested the rev. com. of Boën to render its accounts, since 'il s'était chargé de la partie de l'administration [concernant] le canton de Boën pendant les troubles' (A.D.L., L 259, fol. 16, 2 frim.).

of every description, some specifically concerned with arrests, others engaged in the manifold tasks of obtaining supplies for the army but often undertaking arrests as well. There was virtually no co-ordination between these people, who often held their powers from quite different authorities.

Javogues reappeared at Saint-Étienne with his colleague, Bassal, on about 14 October, and between 21 and 29 October they proceeded to nominate the administration of the new department and to renew the Districts and Municipalities of Roanne, Montbrison, and Saint-Étienne. Javogues was content merely to change the personnel at Roanne and Saint-Étienne, in the latter case probably because of the resistance of the population to the federalist troops: the changing of the name of Saint-Étienne to Armeville or Commune d'Armes on 22 October seems to have been a reference to its patriotic mission in the Republic rather than a punitive measure.[1] But, for Montbrison, he reserved signal punishment, evidently modelled on that meted out to Lyon by the decree of 12 October.[2] Like Lyon, whose name was changed to Ville-affranchie, Montbrison became Montbrisé. As at Lyon, a column was to be erected with a similar inscription: 'LA VILLE DE MONTBRISON *fit la guerre à la Liberté*; elle n'est plus.' The town wall was to be razed. Finally, the *chef-lieu* of the district was transferred to Boën with the administration, the district tribunal, and the *bureau de conciliation*, while the *chef-lieu* of the new department of the Loire was attributed to Feurs.[3] Boën, indeed, already had a long history of patriotism during the Revolution, and this alone inevitably would have tended to oppose it to reactionary Montbrison over the federalist question. But one suspects that there was also a traditional underlying rivalry between two small urban centres, because Montbrison had always had a larger share than Boën in justice and administration and therefore in access to local sources of revenue. The Revolution reinforced these feelings by establishing a number of lucrative local

[1] A.D.L., L 123, fol. 338 (Saint-Étienne); A.N., AF II 114 (861) 15 (Roanne); A.C., Saint-Étienne, 1 D 10 (3), fol. 75.

[2] A.N., loc. cit., *arrêté* signed only by Javogues, as was the one relating to Roanne.

[3] The Dist. was transferred back to Montbrison by a decree of 11 prair. an II, and the Depart. was also established there by a decree of 6 fruct. an III.

administrations at Montbrison and giving Boën nothing. This rivalry was bound to make Boën choose a different path from Montbrison. The same was probably true of Feurs, whose inhabitants had pointed out to the National Assembly in 1789 that their town was the ancient capital of the Forez and had demanded the administration of a district and a tribunal.[1] In this sense, the decision of the *Représentants* to remove the District from Montbrison to Boën and to place the Department at Feurs appears to be as much a response to local interest groups as concern with the need to place administrations in a patriotic context and to meet geographical requirements.[2]

[1] Bibl. Lyon, Coste MS. 1255, no. 1, 'Ville de Feurs, ancienne Capitale du Forez, à Nosseigneurs de l'Assemblée nationale', n.d.

[2] Cf. A.D.R., 1 L 190, rev. com. of Boën to Couthon and Maignet, 23 vend., protesting about a rumour that Javogues and Bassal are considering leaving the *chef-lieu* at Montbrison and pointing out the advantages of Boën—Montbrison 'ne mériterait pas même une justice de paix'.

III

CLAUDE JAVOGUES

CLAUDE JAVOGUES was himself a native of the Forez. He was born on 19 August 1759 into an eminently respectable family of lawyers at Bellegarde-en-Forez.[1] Since the middle of the sixteenth century this family had been steadily improving its social position.[2] Antoine Javogues, who died in 1673, was a *notaire royal* and *capitaine châtelain* of Bellegarde; his son, Gaspard Javogues (1663–1741), purchased the hereditary right to these offices and added to them the *lieutenance du juge châtelain* throughout the *mandement* of the Marquis de Montrond (Magnieu-Cuzieu, Sury-le-Bois, and Montrond). Gaspard's elder son, Claude (1687–1763), great-uncle of the revolutionary, took a law degree at the University of Valence and became an *avocat en Parlement* at the *bailliage* of Montbrison, while his brother, the grandfather of the member of the Convention, succeeded to the legal posts at Bellegarde and Montrond. The two careers were united in the person of Rambert Javogues (1728–1808), the father of the deputy to the Convention. Rambert followed in the footsteps of his uncle by becoming *bachelier en droit canon et civil* of Valence and *avocat en Parlement* at Montbrison, while retaining the offices of *notaire* and *lieutenant du juge* at Bellegarde.[3] He consolidated this position further by securing the posts of *conseiller du roi* and *juge garde-marteau des Eaux et Forêts* at Montbrison. Meanwhile, his elder brother, a bachelor,

[1] Baptismal certificate in J. B. Galley, *Saint-Étienne et son district pendant la Révolution*, i. 556 n. 1.

[2] The details about Javogues's ancestors were supplied to me from the parish registers by M. André Peyron, genealogist at Saint-Étienne. Genealogies and biographical details also appear in Galley, op. cit. i. 556–8, P. Tézenas du Montcel, *Deux Régicides: Claude Javogues et Noël Pointe*, pp. 1–11, 19, and F. Gonon, *Un Forézien célèbre, Claude Javogues*, pp. 1–4. All these works, however, contain inaccuracies, especially Gonon. Except where indicated, these conclusions are based on a comparison of these four sources.

[3] The offices at Montrond and Sury-le-Bois seem to have been abandoned at this point, although Rambert remained *lieutenant du juge châtelain* of Magnieu (Tézenas du Montcel, op. cit., p. 11).

HATFIELD POLYTECHNIC LIBRARY

contributed to the reputation of the family by pursuing a military career as lieutenant in the *grenadiers royaux*.

At the same time as the professional status of the Javogues was improving, various members of the family had been contracting advantageous marriage alliances with the most prosperous inhabitants of the area round Chazelles. For instance, Antoine Javogues married the daughter of 'noble' Gaspard de Cellarier in about 1650; the great-grandfather of the revolutionary married the daughter of a *notaire royal* and *procureur* of Chazelles and his mother was the daughter of a *négociant* of Saint-Chamond.[1] From the financial point of view also, the family was solidly established by the end of the Ancien Régime. Already, in 1726, the marriage contract of Claude Javogues's grandfather indicated comfortable wealth in land, which was increased by his wife's dowry of a house at Chazelles.[2] In March 1793 Rambert Javogues's possessions were evaluated for tax purposes at 50,000 *livres* and included a house in the noble quarter of Montbrison and another at Bellegarde together with several properties in that parish.[3] In floréal an II, after the disappearance of the former *seigneur*, the Municipality of Bellegarde named Rambert Javogues without hesitation as one of the two most highly taxed inhabitants, but had to leave a space for the other name to be inserted later.[4] In 1812, one of Claude's brothers, Gaspard, was listed thirty-third of the hundred most taxed citizens of Montbrison with an estimated revenue of 4,500 *livres*.[5] Certainly, the Javogues could not rival some of the commercial fortunes of the large urban centres, nor even some of the landed wealth in the Plaine du Forez such as that of the Marquis de Poncins, who acquired *biens nationaux* to the tune of 330,550 *livres*;[6] nor did their prestige equal that of legal

[1] According to Galley, op. cit. i. 559, her uncle was a *prêtre-sociétaire* of Saint-Chamond, which gives some indication of the social position of her family. Note also the marriages of Fleurie Javogues with a *pharmacien* and *maître-chirurgien* at Chazelles (*c.* 1710) and of another Fleurie with a *négociant*, *marchand drapier*, and *bourgeois* of Saint-Symphorien-le-Château (1752). The sisters of the *conventionnel* continued this tradition by marrying a *marchand* of Chazelles and a *propriétaire* of Saint-Germain-Laval.

[2] Tézenas du Montcel, op. cit., p. 23.

[3] Ibid., pp. 9–10.

[4] A.D.L., L 53.

[5] *Liste des cent plus fort imposables de la commune de Montbrison.*

[6] Broutin, op. cit., p. 414.

families more anciently established at Montbrison. But, although not considerable by absolute standards, their fortune was far from negligible in an area where, as the *Représentant du peuple* himself was to point out, great wealth was rare.[1] Clearly, this was a family which was well connected with the more influential professional, commercial, and landed bourgeoisie of the Plaine du Forez and which was respected both at Montbrison and at Bellegarde, where Jean-Fleury Javogues, one of Claude's younger brothers, was elected *procureur de la commune* in 1790.[2] Several of the letters written by suspects to Javogues during his mission in the Loire confirm the extent of his family connections, friends, and acquaintances in these circles.[3]

The critical phase of this social development was undoubtedly the early eighteenth century when, with the *avocat en Parlement* Claude Javogues, the influence of the family ceased to be confined to the region round Chazelles and began to be felt at Montbrison. It was evidently in recognition of this achievement that the great-uncle of the revolutionary began to call himself 'noble Claude Javogues', and Rambert Javogues continued this practice. It is probable that, if there had not been a revolution at the end of the century, the Javogues would have imitated other families in the region by adding the name of a property with the particle and would eventually have bought an ennobling office.[4] Already they had adopted the habits of the wealthy landowners of the area to the extent of spending part of the year at Montbrison, the

[1] A.D.R., 42 L 141, d. Landine and Duvant, Javogues to Parein, n.d.: 'Si l'on considère que dans mon pays, quand on a 8000 livres de rente, on ne troquerait pas son sort contre celui d'un banquier de Paris.'

[2] A.D.L., L suppl. 356. Cf. also the type of godparent for Rambert's children—*conseillers du roi, procureurs du roi, marchands*.

[3] A.D.R., 42 L 158–42 L 186 *passim—notaires, avocats, procureurs, avoués, conseillers du roi, juges de paix, curés, marchands*, the *fermier* of several former *seigneurs* (estimated fortune 300,000 *livres*), the director of a coal business employing 300 workers, etc.; most of these people lived at Montbrison, but he had connections as far afield as Saint-Marcellin, Saint-Bonnet-le-Château, Firminy, Saint-Étienne, Maclas, and Saint-Chamond.

[4] Already at the time of the Revolution, two of Claude's younger brothers were being called Lafond and Duclos by their father, possibly the names of two family properties (A.D.R., 42 L 158, Javogues *père* to Claude Javogues, 28 Dec. 1793). Claude's brother Gaspard called himself Javogues de la Plagne at the time of his marriage in 1809.

local social centre, and the other part on their estates.[1] The Thermidorians themselves, adept at emphasizing the humble origins of terrorists, implicitly recognized Javogues's social respectability: as far as they were concerned, he was a class traitor, who exercised his cruelty 'dans son pays natal, au centre de ses liaisons, sur ses concitoyens, sur ses amis', and who 'manquant de moyens pour s'élever au-dessus de ses concitoyens . . . forma le projet sanguinaire de les détruire tous, et de ne conserver qu'une classe dont ses goûts et ses habitudes le rapprochaient'.[2]

The eldest of eleven children, Claude Javogues continued the family tradition by entering the legal profession. He obtained a law degree from Valence in 1785 and by 1788 he was practising as an *avocat en Parlement* at the *bailliage* of Montbrison.[3] The offices at Bellegarde seem to have been handed over to his brother, Jean-Fleury, who was *notaire* there at the beginning of the Revolution, while Claude pursued his career at Montbrison.[4] Similarly, it appears that at the time of the Revolution, Claude Javogues was preparing to make the traditional contribution to the social advancement of the family by marriage. In October 1792 he authorized the husband of one of his cousins to accept any marriage arrangements made for him by his parents.[5] The Thermidorians claimed that his suit was rejected by his proposed fiancée's brother, whom he consequently had executed, and one local historian reports an oral tradition to the effect that the person in question was the daughter of the Comte Lapierre de Saint-Hilaire.[6] Clearly, such a marriage would have been socially advantageous and is not improbable, since there seems to have been a superfluity of noble daughters at Mont-

[1] A.N., D III 349, d. Javogues, 'Tableau des crimes de Javogues dans le département de la Loire'.

[2] *Compte rendu de la gestion du directoire du district de Montbrison* (germ. an III), pp. 54–6.

[3] G. Javogues, *Un Conventionnel Forézien, Claude Javogues*, p. 4; *Almanach de Lyon*, 1789, p. 109.

[4] A.N., W 554, d. 10, Javogues *père* to Claude Javogues, 1 vent. an III. He must have preferred a military career in the *volontaires nationaux* since, in 1793, he called himself 'capitaine dans une compagnie du 5ème bataillon de Rhône-et-Loire' (A.D.R., 42 L 161). Another son was also a soldier since, in the Year III, he was in the military hospital at Saint-Jean-d'Angély (A.N., loc. cit.).

[5] Tézenas du Montcel, op. cit., pp. 18–19.

[6] A.N., D III 349, d. Javogues, Montbrison; Tézenas du Montcel, loc. cit.

brison at the end of the Ancien Régime; but it is impossible to verify this tradition.[1]

Very little is known about Javogues's activities before his election to the Convention. It is evident that he made very little impression as an *avocat*; only one printed brief, which he signed with a large number of colleagues, survives.[2] But this is not necessarily a judgement on his talent, for he had little enough time in which to establish his reputation. He appears to have been caught up in the excitement accompanying the abortive reforms of the courts in 1788, but there is no means of knowing whether this had the effect on him that it had on Bertrand Barère, for example.[3] The Thermidorians claimed that, at the outbreak of the Revolution, he was renowned for his drunkenness and that his application in late 1789 to join a literary circle at Montbrison which read the newspapers and discussed politics was rejected on these grounds.[4] Again, it is impossible to establish the truth of this statement, although the documents of the Year II are unanimous on his addiction to drink. In any case, in 1789 he enjoyed the esteem of his fellow-citizens sufficiently to be appointed to the rather disagreeable post of *commandant de la police nocturne* in the *milice bourgeoise*.[5] Their confidence was renewed in 1791 when he became an elector in the electoral assembly of the Rhône-et-Loire and was appointed, first of all, to scrutinize the credentials of the electors, and later a member of the *conseil général* of the District of Montbrison.[6] However, the fact that he was not chosen for the *directoire* of the District, despite his residence at Montbrison, shows that the confidence of his immediate colleagues, if not of the electors, had its limits. Since the *conseil général* only met between 18 and 26 October 1791, he had little to do. In the

1 In fact it was the count himself and not the girl's brother who was executed. It would have been difficult for Javogues to avoid arresting him, since his name had been mentioned in the Convention in July (*Procès-verbal de la Convention nationale*, xvi. 248).

2 *Mémoire à consulter pour Sieur Jacques-Marie Simon . . .*, 3 Mar. 1788.

3 A.D.R., 42 L 167, d. Mathon de Sauvin, letter to Javogues, 8 vent. an II; L. Gershoy, *Bertrand Barère*, pp. 44–60.

4 A.N., loc. cit.

5 *Almanach de Lyon*, 1789, p. 110.

6 *Liste des électeurs du département de Rhône-et-Loire*, 1791; G. Guigue, *Procès-verbaux des séances du conseil général du département de Rhône-et-Loire*, i. 410; Galley, op. cit. i. 560.

division of functions in the *bureaux* he received the cantons of Chazelles and Feurs for the upkeep of roads and for the investigation of communal affairs; he was present at only one deliberation, of a very moderate nature, on the political and religious conflicts of the period; in the summer of 1792, as a *commissaire* of the District, he investigated religious disturbances in the countryside, and it was perhaps at this time that his views on priests began to take form.[1] Similarly, we possess no information about the development of his ideas and political activity during this period. He was not given to expressing himself in print, while the disappearance of the records of the *Société des Amis de la Constitution* makes it impossible to evaluate his work in this body of which, apparently, he was one of the founders.[2] It is clear that his father, despite being old-fashioned enough to wear a wig in 1793,[3] was active in its debates.[4] Certainly, his friendships with local terrorists seem to have dated in many cases from before the Year II, while he was particularly close to Dupuy, deputy to the Legislative Assembly and future Montagnard in the Convention.[5] It seems probable, therefore, that in 1792 he was a Jacobin, but it is difficult to say what kind of Jacobin.

In these circumstances, the election to the Convention of a person politically so undistinguished remains something of a mystery. He was clearly not an obvious candidate, since he was elected in fourteenth position out of fifteen deputies with 480 votes out of 814 cast.[6] The meeting of the electoral

[1] Galley, loc. cit.; A.D.L., L suppl. 110, curé of Saint-Jean-Lavêtre to Dist. of Montbrison, 26 Jan. 1793.

[2] A.C. Montbrison, *reg. dél.*, no. 2, fol. 66.

[3] Tézenas du Montcel, 'Notes sur la famille de Claude Javogues', *Revue du Sud-Est illustrée*, July 1905, p. 72 n. 2: *laissez-passer* for Rambert Javogues, 28 June 1793, 'portant perruque'.

[4] A.D.L., L suppl. 356.

[5] e.g. A.D.R., 42 L 158, d. Despomets, letter to Javogues, 12 Oct. 1793: 'Vous êtes l'intime de mes parents les plus proches tels que le citoyen *Dupuy*, député, qui est mon cousin germain, ainsi que *Gaulne* . . . sans oublier mon ami *Thiolière*.' Similar references in ibid., d. Portier, 42 L 168, d. Prodon, 42 L 184, d. Mathon, 42 L 186, d. Pelardy. Dupuy was also a member of the *Société des Amis de la Constitution* of Montbrison (A.D.R., 42 L 185, d. Michon, Dupuy to the Jacobins of Montbrison, 24 Sept. 1792). Cf. also the fact that Javogues borrowed 2,205 *livres* from Richard (future member of the rev. com. of Montbrisé) in 1792 at the moment of his election (Tézenas du Montcel, *Deux Régicides*, p. 16).

[6] The minutes of the assembly are printed in Guigue, op. cit. i. 429 ff.

assembly, held at Saint-Étienne, was far from calm: Chalier reported that 'elle fait frémir par les cabales qui l'agitent et le nombre de vils aristocrates qu'elle renferme malgré l'affaire du 10 août'.[1] The most important divisions were those between Jacobins and political moderates (mostly adherents of Roland) and between the interests of Lyon and the Forez. These divisions were reflected in the results. The future Rolandists and men of the Plain gained the majority of seats (nine as opposed to six future Montagnards[2]), while the interests of Lyon were defeated by the interests of the Forez (six deputies as opposed to eight, with one stranger to the department[3]). At the same time, it is clear that within the Forez group there were divergences between the three districts. In the end, the district of Roanne gained three deputies, Montbrison three, and Saint-Étienne two. But Chalier noted that, for the twelfth place, 'il y a grand tapage dans la salle au sujet d'un *Verne*, aristocrate, qui veut absolument être député'. Verne was mayor of Roanne and, at this point, the district of Roanne already had three deputies as opposed to two for Montbrison and one for Saint-Étienne; eventually the seat went to Noël Pointe of Saint-Étienne. The election of Javogues must be placed in the context of these political and regional struggles. The most reasonable hypothesis is that he was a compromise candidate. He was Jacobin enough to be acceptable to that faction, yet sufficiently respectable socially and politically restrained enough to be acceptable to most of the moderates, who had lost the two previous seats

[1] A.N., F^{11} 217, d. Rhône, letter to Roland, 7 Sept. 1792.

[2] Chasset, Vitet, Fournier, Béraud, Moulin, Michet, Patrin, Forest, Lanthenas; Dupuy, Dubouchet, Pressavin, Pointe, Cusset, Javogues. Pressavin hovered continually on the edge of the Plain. Note that the Jacobins of the most important urban centres (Lyon and Saint-Étienne) had great difficulty in securing seats for themselves: Cusset was certainly less prominent than Chalier and Pointe less prominent than Desvernays or Johannot—cf. the similar situation in the elections of the Pas-de-Calais, L. Jacob, *Joseph le Bon*, i. 108.

[3] Chasset (Villefranche), Vitet (Lyon), Pressavin (Lyon), Patrin (Lyon), Cusset (Lyon), and Fournier (Millery), the *premier suppléant* who immediately replaced Dr. Priestly, who refused; Dupuy, Dubouchet, Javogues (Montbrison), Moulin, Michet, Forest (Roanne), Pointe and Béraud (Saint-Étienne). The Rolandist Lanthenas, elected last, was a stranger to the depart.; his election was probably a result of an alliance between the moderates and the electors of Lyon (predominantly moderate anyway), who despaired of getting their own candidate through against the combined opposition of men of the Forez and the Jacobins.

to the Jacobins Noël Pointe and Cusset.[1] He united both rural and urban votes through his connections at Montbrison and in the canton of Chazelles. He also united Saint-Étienne and Montbrison against Roanne: both were under-represented at that moment in proportion to Roanne, while Desvernays, mayor of Saint-Étienne and a leading Jacobin, who was presiding over the assembly, found Verne most obnoxious.[2] In these circumstances, Javogues received the organized vote of the district of Saint-Étienne: in the Year II, the mayor of Marlhes was to remind him that 'quand il fut question de vous porter aux scrutins, tous ceux, que j'avais en ma connaissance, vous portèrent, sinon Le Chambon'.[3]

Javogues's career in the Convention prior to his designation as *Représentant en mission* in July 1793 was as obscure as his time on the District of Montbrison. Before the debates on Lyon in mid July, he seems to have spoken only to express his votes during the trial of the King and to give a brief opinion on the impeachment of Marat. However, it is evident that he joined the ranks of the Montagnards fairly rapidly.[4] It is not known when he was admitted to the Jacobin Club, but he was an established member in prairial.[5] Moreover, Javogues's friendship with the other two deputies from Montbrison, Dubouchet and Dupuy, both of whom were Montagnards, would probably influence him in this direction; after a brief stay in lodgings in the Chaussée d'Antin, he moved in with them at rue Helvétius/Sainte-Anne, no. 1.[6] By February 1793 Javogues was clearly a Montagnard, for

[1] For Pointe's Jacobinism at this time, see Tézenas du Montcel, op. cit., *passim*; for Cusset's, his *Adresse aux vertueux électeurs de Rhône-et-Loire* (31 Aug. 1792).

[2] A.D.R., 42 L 160, interrogation of Verne.

[3] A.D.R., 42 L 174, Champagnat to Javogues, 14 niv. an II.

[4] Cf. A.C. Montbrison, *reg. dél.*, no. 2, fol. 66: 'Appelé à la Convention . . . il s'est fermement attaché aux principes révolutionnaires qui ont dirigé les grands travaux des immortels Montagnards.'

[5] F. A. Aulard, *La Société des Jacobins*, vi. 171 (*scrutin épuratoire*, 23 prair.); his name does not appear among the forty-three deputies admitted on 24 Sept. 1793 (ibid. iv. 331, 338). This would suggest (as does his change of address) that he did not immediately join the Montagnards, but arrived in Paris as something of an independent. It is impossible to establish how long this attitude lasted.

[6] *Almanach national*, 1793, p. 60, and ibid., an II, pp. 86, 92. On the friendship of Dupuy and Javogues, above, p. 66; on Dubouchet and Javogues, A.D.R., 42 L 184, d. Mathon, letter to Javogues, 9 pluv. an II. Cf. also the intimate tone of a letter to Javogues from Noël Pointe (A.D.R., 42 L 189, d. Sauzéas, n.d.).

he was included by the emissaries of the Lyon Jacobins among the 'députés sans-culottes du département de Rhône-et-Loire' to whom they addressed accounts of the Municipality's struggles with the moderates.[1] In any case, his vote on the fate of the King, when he demanded death within twenty-four hours, had already demonstrated his political allegiance.[2] Indeed, as a consequence of this vote, the royalists of Montbrison considered Javogues to be the most dangerous extremist of their three deputies; for in early February the relatives of Dubouchet were not touched and Dupuy's family was merely insulted, whereas not only was Javogues's family jeered at but their house at Montbrison was daubed with blood.[3] The letter in which Javogues, Dupuy, Dubouchet, Pressavin, and Pointe denounced this event leaves no doubt about their political convictions.[4] This impression is reinforced by an incident on the night of 1–2 June 1793, when, according to Marcellin Béraud (a deputy from Saint-Étienne), Collot d'Herbois and Javogues both rushed to the foot of the rostrum brandishing pistols at Guadet and Chambon of the Creuse, who stood firm with drawn swords.[5] His friendship with Collot, which is confirmed by Javogues's letters during his mission, further helps to place him politically.[6] Thus, Javogues's political position recommended him to the victors of 31 May–2 June; on 29 June, he was elected to the minor office of *suppléant* to the *comité des domaines*.[7] But he was in no way remarkable and, therefore, his appointment as *Représentant en mission* raises the same problem as his election to the Convention.

The debate of 12 July 1793 in the Convention, together with the changes in the membership of the Committee of Public Safety about this time, crystallized the government's

1 Bibl. Lyon, Coste MS. 345 and 546, letters from Achard and Gaillard, 11 Feb., and from Émery, 12 Feb.

2 E. Brossard, *Histoire du département de la Loire*, ii. 14–15, for the votes of all the deputies—Pointe and Javogues were the only ones to express themselves in this way.

3 Bibl. Lyon, Coste MS. 548 and 600, no. 7. Possibly this impression was given because Dubouchet and Dupuy did not qualify their vote as Javogues did.

4 Bibl. Lyon, Coste MS. 548, letter to Émery and Gaillard, 18 Feb.

5 M. Béraud, *Compte rendu à ses commettants*, ed. J. M. Devet, p. 12 n. 1.

6 A.N., AF II 58, d. 430, p. 2, and AF II 114 (861) 15.

7 *Procès-verbal de la Convention nationale*, xiv. 430.

hostile attitude to the Lyon federalists and saw the beginning of the organization of punitive measures and the extension of the military preparations against the rebels.[1] Among these measures was the appointment of Reverchon and Delaporte as *Représentants en mission* in the Saône-et-Loire, the Rhône-et-Loire, and the Ain.[2] Javogues was sent to join them on 20 July and the powers of the three *Représentants* were extended to the departments of the Isère, the Ardèche, the Haute-Loire, the Puy-de-Dôme, and the Drôme.[3] The mission of these proconsuls, although not stated in the decrees, was obvious: to stamp out the federalist contagion in the area and to organize and co-ordinate the resources of these departments against Lyon. For this latter task they would naturally have to work in conjunction with Dubois-Crancé, Albitte, Gauthier, and Nioche, *Représentants en mission* to the *Armée des Alpes*, who had been taking preliminary steps to contain the Lyon affair.[4] It is probable that Javogues was chosen for this mission largely because he was from the Rhône-et-Loire. Clearly, at a time when the mail was liable to interception[5] and many administrations had federalist sympathies, the Committee of Public Safety possessed little accurate information about the region and probably felt the need for a *Représentant* with local knowledge. Of the proconsuls already in the field, only Gauthier (Ain) and Reverchon (Saône-et-Loire) were local men and in any case came from areas situated on the periphery of the revolt. Certainly, Noël Pointe was in the region, but his mission related only to the arms industry and, in the state of communications, there was no guarantee that further orders would reach him. Moreover, although he had reported his escape from arrest by the federalists of Lyon, the government may have been uncertain about his ultimate fate.[6] Finally, the Committee

[1] É. Herriot, *Lyon n'est plus*, ii. 179–82, 188–92; *Procès-verbal de la Convention nationale*, xvi. 63–109.

[2] Ibid. xvi. 108–9.

[3] Ibid. xvii. 11.

[4] Cf. A.N., AF II 183, d. 1514, p. 12, C.P.S. to Reverchon and Delaporte, 30 July.

[5] A.N., AF II 183, d. 1513, p. 4, Dubois-Crancé, Gauthier, and Nioche to C.P.S. from Grenoble, 16 July, referring to interruption of all mails for Paris for the last month.

[6] *Procès-verbal de la Convention nationale*, xvi. 63, letter from Pointe read to the Assembly, 12 July; Pointe, *Compte rendu à la Convention nationale*.

needed to send out a man from Paris immediately with the latest instructions.

The selection of Javogues from among the deputies of the Rhône-et-Loire can also be explained. Only six were politically reliable.[1] Of these, Dupuy was a member of the Committee of General Security at this time and Cusset, Dubouchet, and Pointe were on mission.[2] The government probably preferred a man from the Forez to a man from Lyon, since the latter might be susceptible to blackmail through his relations and connections in the city; in any case, Pressavin was a dubious candidate since his nephew was secretary to the provisional Municipality.[3] In these circumstances only Javogues remained.[4] Moreover, he had emphasized his particular qualifications in respect of Lyon on 3 July, when, together with Pressavin, he had arrested and brought to the Committee of General Security a suspect from Mâcon, whom he accused of being a former *émigré* returned in order to foment trouble in Lyon.[5] In addition, it is probable that, at the Convention, he commented on the news from the Rhône-et-Loire during the discussions of the second and third weeks of July.[6]

Leaving Paris on 25 July, Javogues joined Reverchon and Delaporte at Mâcon three days later.[7] He assisted them in the mobilization of the Saône-et-Loire and took an active part in the direction of the military operations against Lyon,

[1] Above, p. 67.

[2] Cusset to the *Armée de la Moselle*, 29 June; Dubouchet to the Seine-et-Marne and Loiret, 15 July (*Procès-verbal de la Convention nationale*, xiv. 431, xvi. 287).

[3] A.N., F7 4775 (26), d. 1 (Teillard): note especially the highly suspect letter written to him by Pressavin, 21 July.

[4] Possibly Dupuy helped to determine the choice of the government as may have done Dubouchet, *suppléant* to the C.P.S. at this time, and Cusset, member of the C.P.S. (*Procès-verbal de la Convention nationale*, xv. 66). Similarly, if Collot d'Herbois already had influence at this time, he may have suggested his friend, since Collot was always interested in Lyon (e.g. A.N., D XL 23, d. Rhône-et-Loire, Jacob to the Convention, Lyon, 15 Jan. 1793: 'La semaine dernière Collot d'Herbois . . . vint en cette ville, au Club Central, pour déterminer la demande de la mort de Louis le dernier').

[5] A.N., W 285, d. 132, p. 17.

[6] Herriot, op. cit. ii. 229.

[7] A.N., W 554, d. 10, receipt given to Javogues by Lafaye *aîné*; AF II 411, d. 3308, p. 56, collective letter to C.P.S., 28 July; a letter written by Reverchon and Delaporte to the Committee on 27 July does not mention him (AF II 183, d. 1515, p. 17).

which began in earnest on 8 August with the arrival of the troops under the walls of the city.[1] Apart from the decision to divide the department of Rhône-et-Loire and general measures concerning the sequestration of goods from Lyon, both of which were above all tactical moves against the city itself, Javogues displayed no especial interest in the Forez until early September.[2] As we have seen, he participated in the expedition in the Loire which was made necessary by the destruction of General Nicolas's force at Saint-Anthême and which led him, between 5 and 17 September, via Saint-Chamond and Saint-Étienne to Montbrison, Feurs, and Chazelles, and back again.[3] Subsequently he directed operations against the south-west flank of Lyon, participated in the capture of the city, and personally released his mother and uncle from the prison where they had been kept as hostages.[4] But already after the campaign in the Forez, the other *Représentants* immediately recognized Javogues's special responsibility for the southern area of the Loire and they forwarded all business relating to this region to him.[5] Meanwhile, Javogues himself began the political purge of the district of Saint-Étienne through a series of *commissaires*. This responsibility was the natural consequence of the place occupied by Javogues in the disposition of the besieging forces round Lyon. The district of Saint-Étienne constituted the immediate hinterland of his command and it was inevitable that he should control this area in order to ensure his supplies of food and men and their security.[6] In the same way the Auvergnats of the *levée en masse*, stationed immediately to his north, were responsible for the district of Montbrison;

[1] Herriot, op. cit. ii. 314–16; A.N., AF II 252, d. 2139, p. 42, plan for the movement of troops, 4 Aug.

[2] His first major act concerning the Loire specifically is the order of mobilization for the dist. of Saint-Étienne, 1 Sept. (A.C. Saint-Étienne, 1 D 10 (3), fol. 52).

[3] Above, p. 40; A.N., AF II 184, d. 1521, p. 20, and ibid., d. 1522, pp. 44, 43, Javogues to C.P.S., 10 and 17 Sept.

[4] A.N., F7 4683, d. 1 (Dubois-Crancé), Châteauneuf-Randon to Dubois-Crancé, 15 Sept.; Couthon, *Première Partie du rapport sur le siège . . .*, pp. 8, 36; F. Mège, *Le Puy-de-Dôme en 1793 et le proconsulat de Couthon*, p. 237.

[5] e.g. A.D.R., 42 L 157, dispatches from Saint-Étienne forwarded by Gauthier to Laporte and by Laporte to Javogues, 23 Sept.; *Seconde Partie de la réponse de Dubois-Crancé*, p. 230.

[6] e.g. A.N., AF II 137 (1069), d. 30, p. 6, *arrêté* dated from Saint-Genis-Laval, 27 Sept., concerning deserters.

the *commissaires*, employed by Javogues, and the *commission des subsistances*, which he created at Saint-Étienne, were the counterpart of the Committee of Public Safety established by Couthon and Châteauneuf-Randon at Montbrison.[1]

It was not surprising, therefore, that Javogues, being a man from the Forez and already at work in the district of Saint-Étienne, should have returned to the department of the Loire after the fall of Lyon on 9 October. Indeed, this was the collective decision of the *Représentants en mission* at Lyon about the division of the labour that remained to be accomplished.[2] Javogues arrived at Saint-Étienne about 14 October, accompanied, for no apparent reason, by Bassal.[3] Javogues, at least, stayed until 10 or 11 brumaire/31 October or 1 November, when he moved to Feurs via Saint-Galmier.[4] He remained at Feurs until 15 or 16 brumaire/5 or 6 November.[5] Meanwhile, however, the decree of 9 brumaire/30 October, which sent Collot d'Herbois and Fouché to Commune-affranchie/Lyon, had also designated Javogues for the Saône-et-Loire.[6] After leaving Feurs, Javogues travelled to Commune-affranchie in order to confer with Collot d'Herbois.[7] It is evident that he was already thinking of extending his operations to the Ain, for it was at this point that he gave a general commission for arrest and sequestration to two administrators of that department and that Collot d'Herbois wrote to the Committee of Public Safety requesting powers for Javogues

[1] A.C. Saint-Étienne, 1 D 10 (3), fols. 54 and 59, 8 and 18 Sept.; A.D.R., 42 L 190, d. Yvon, *arrêté* of 15 Sept., authorizing the Mun. of Saint-Étienne to co-opt as many members as necessary; on the organization of supplies, see Galley, op. cit. i. 761–72. The Auvergnats had three C.P.S.s—Ambert, Montbrison, and Sainte-Foy-lès-Lyon.

[2] A.D. P.-de-D., L 2785, Maignet to committee at Montbrison, from Cne-aff., 17 Oct.: 'les nominations que nous lui avons confiées'. It seems, moreover, that this had already been decided at the time of the campaign in the Forez: A.N., AF II 184, d. 1522, pp. 44, 43, Javogues to C.P.S., 17 Sept.: 'lorsque j'irai établir, après l'expédition de Lyon, le département dont le chef-lieu provisoire est fixé à Feurs . . .'

[3] A.D.L., L 130, fol. 22, Bassal to Dist., 14 Oct.

[4] A.C. Saint-Étienne, 1 D 10 (3), fol. 80; A.D.L., L 130, fol. 30, L 79, fol. 9, L. 18, fol. 17.

[5] A.N., AF II 114 (861) 15; A.D.L., L 80, fol. 2.

[6] *Procès-verbal de la Convention nationale*, xxiv. 207.

[7] A.D.L., loc. cit.: 'Le citoyen Javogues va rejoindre à Lyon le Représentant du peuple Collot d'Herbois'; A.N., W 554, d. 10, receipts from Lafaye *aîné*, dated from Cne-aff., 23 brum.

for the Ain also.[1] Javogues arrived at Mâcon on 24 brumaire/14 November and he stayed in that town until 18 or 19 frimaire/8 or 9 December reorganizing the department on a revolutionary basis.[2] Nevertheless, he maintained an interest in the Loire and particularly in Montbrisé/Montbrison; he received a visit and later news from a militant of that town; he exchanged letters with the revolutionary Committee, wrote to the Municipality urging the execution of his earlier *arrêtés*, and sent denunciations against a number of Montbrisonnais to the *Commission Temporaire*.[3] But, on 18 or 19 frimaire/8 or 9 December, Javogues received two militants from the club at Bourg who recounted the difficulties encountered by the patriots in the Ain.[4] He immediately left Mâcon with a detachment of the Parisian *armée révolutionnaire* and arrived at Bourg on 20 frimaire/10 December, where he implemented a whole series of revolutionary measures.[5] The arrival of the *Représentant en mission* Gouly on 22 frimaire/12 December accelerated the departure which he was already planning.[6] From Bourg, he journeyed directly to Commune-affranchie, where he remained for a few days.[7] On 27 frimaire/17 December he returned to the department of the Loire via Saint-Chamond to Armeville/Saint-Étienne.[8] He stayed there for a month, leaving for Montbrisé on 25 nivôse/14 January.[9] On 19 pluviôse/7 February, he moved from Montbrisé to Feurs, and it was there, about midnight

[1] A.N., AF II 84 (623), *arrêté* dated 21 brum.; Courtois, *Rapport fait . . . au nom de la Commission . . .*, p. 291, letter dated 19 brum.

[2] A.N., AF II 58, d. 430, p. 2, Javogues to Collot, 28 brum.; AF II 186, d. 1539, p. 13, Javogues to C.P.S., 18 frim., giving a brief synopsis of his activities in the Saône-et-Loire.

[3] A.D.L., L 434 (1), fol. 66; A.D.R., 42 L 182, d. Lachasse, Chantelauze to Javogues, 12 frim.; A.D.L., L 434 (1) 7 frim.; A.C. Montbrison, *reg. dél.*, no. 2, fol. 13; A.D.R., 31 L 53, Bouvery-Fleury to the *Comm. Temp.* from Mâcon, 8 frim.

[4] *Vie révolutionnaire de Blanq-Desisles*, pp. 22–3; E. Dubois, *Histoire de la Révolution dans l'Ain*, iv. 77–86.

[5] A.N., AF II 186, d. 1540, p. 23, Gouly to C.P.S., 23 frim. Dubois places each event a day earlier, because he dates this letter, wrongly, as 22 frim.

[6] Ibid.

[7] A.D. S.-et-L., 1 L 3 (5), 28 frim., letter from Javogues, dated from Cne-aff., 25 frim.; A.N., AF II 138 (1075), p. 5, *arrêté* signed Fouché and Albitte, from Cne-aff., 26 frim., in consultation with Javogues.

[8] A.D.L., L 390, fol. 4, rev. com. at Saint-Chamond, session of 27 frim.; A.C. Saint-Étienne, 1 D 10 (3), fol. 101, arrival of Javogues, 27 frim.

[9] Galley, op. cit. ii. 393–8.

on 24 pluviôse/12 February, that he received the news of his recall.[1] For, on 20 pluviôse/8 February, in face of the mounting pressure of denunciations from the Loire, the Rhône, the Saône-et-Loire, and the Puy-de-Dôme, and after Javogues's reckless attacks on Couthon, the Convention had ordered that the proconsul should return within eight days and that his two collaborators, Lapalus and Duret, should be arrested.[2]

Claude Javogues was not the only *Représentant en mission* to have visited the department of the Loire during the Terror. But, despite the interlude of four *décades* spent away from the Loire, he was the only one to have remained in the area long enough to accomplish work in any detail.[3] Certainly, the department fell within the province of the super-proconsuls at Commune-affranchie/Lyon, but it is doubtful how much real authority they exercised as long as Javogues remained there. Although it was common practice for authorities and individuals to appeal to them, particularly during Javogues's absence, these proconsuls did not intervene very much in a direct manner in the Loire until after Javogues's departure in pluviôse. Although some of their more general *arrêtés* were implemented by the authorities in the Loire, Javogues pre-empted most of the political initiative from his neighbours at Commune-affranchie, and in any case of conflict, as, for instance, over the suppression of the *armée révolutionnaire* in nivôse, it was Javogues's decision which was the more important.[4]

During the trial of Carrier, the *Représentant* Sevestre remarked: 'Nous avons tous, dans nos missions, suivi l'impulsion de notre caractère; la latitude de notre liberté pour faire le bonheur ou le malheur du peuple n'a point eu de limites.'[5] For this reason it is important to consider Javogues's character. In their vindictive malevolence the Thermidorians were unanimous on this subject. For them, he was a bloodthirsty and cruel despot, an immoral and thieving sot.[6]

1 A.C. Montbrison, *reg. dél.*, no. 2, fol. 56; A.N., T 781, d. Marino, report.

2 *Procès-verbal de la Convention nationale*, xxxi. 98.

3 Girard de l'Aude stayed in the depart. from late frim. to early vent., but his mission was confined to the arms industry and he never operated outside Armeville.

4 Below, p. 173.

5 *Le Moniteur*, 7 frim. an III.

6 A.N., D III 349, d. Javogues, denunciations from Montbrison, Saint-Étienne, and Roanne.

Under the Directory, the Abbé Guillon, the historian of Lyon, endorsed this judgement, and their views have been adopted by most subsequent authors.[1] For Madelin, Javogues was 'le représentant peut-être le plus exagéré qui se fût vu, démagogue débraillé', and Herriot noted that he became famous for his cruelty.[2] The Thermidorians' hatred for Javogues was occasioned above all by his political principles and by the fact that he was associated with the period of repression. Much of their judgement on him, particularly their references to his lust for blood and his embezzlement, was therefore political comment and can be left aside as far as his personality is concerned. Nevertheless, other aspects need more careful attention, especially since they figure not only in the denunciations from the Forez, but also in those sent to the Thermidorian Convention by the inhabitants of the Saône-et-Loire and of the Ain, although this is not necessarily a guarantee of independence. For instance, Châlon-sur-Saône, which had a particular quarrel with him, spoke of 'l'insolence stupide, autant que féroce, et l'inaccessibilité cruelle, et les orgies dégoûtantes, et le langage révoltant, et les prédictions incendiaires du tyran', while Bourg-en-Bresse referred to 'ce Javogues, livré à la plus insigne crapule et toujours *plein de vin*'.[3]

C'était un homme d'environ trente-cinq ans, avec un commencement de ventre; carré des épaules, trapu, la voix cassante, la tête ronde à cheveux ras, les yeux clairs, gris et durs, sous des sourcils bourrus, la

[1] A. Guillon, *Histoire du siège de Lyon* . . ., ii. 57.

[2] This is hardly surprising on the part of frank anti-revolutionaries such as A. Balleydier, *Histoire . . . du peuple de Lyon pendant la Révolution*, ii. 201–2, 261, or J. M. Devet, *Dénonciation des stéphanois contre le Représentant Javogues*, etc., or F. Gonon, *Un Forézien célèbre, Claude Javogues*. L. Bauzon *et al.*, *Recherches historiques sur la persécution religieuse*, i. 473–6, display a similar attitude. M. Marion, 'La guerre aux riches en 1793 et le conventionnel Javogues', *Revue universelle*, 15 Apr. 1925, 129–46, whose appreciation of Javogues's character is more subtle, nevertheless reproduces almost word for word a comparison between Javogues and Carrier made by the Depart. of the Loire in mess. an III. G. Javogues, 'Une défense de Claude Javogues', *Ann. rév.* 1922, 417–19, etc., seeks to justify his ancestor and is perhaps too generous. Galley, op. cit. ii. 271–81, gives an accurate portrait, which tends to be marred, however, by his conviction that Javogues is ridiculous. Richard Cobb, *Les Armées révolutionnaires*, i. 240, etc., is the only historian both to have seen Javogues's political importance and to have found the man in the least attractive.

[3] A.N., D III 225, d. Châlon-sur-Saône; *Dénonciation des citoyens de la commune de Bourg . . . contre Amar, Javogues, Albitte et Méaulle* . . ., p. 5.

bouche largement fendue, aux lèvres minces et colériques; les joues bises encadrées de favoris broussailleux et mal plantés; enfin une de ces figures de dogue dont on dit: il ne doit pas être bon les jours![1]

The *commissaire-ordonnateur* of the *Armée des Alpes* also referred to the same animal in order to define his impression of the *Représentant*: 'Javogues . . . était un vrai butor, semblable à un dogue qui vient de rompre ses chaînes: il paraissait toujours prêt à se lancer sur le premier venu et à le déchirer à belles dents, toujours l'injure et la menace à la bouche, il ne respirait que le sang et le meurtre et brûlait de s'y plonger.'[2] On the whole, the contemporary documents confirm this portrait. Without doubt, Javogues was a violent, choleric, excessive man. Verbal violence was habitual among a great many of the revolutionaries of the Year II, particularly among those in sympathy with the Père Duchesne. In his memoirs, Fouché referred to 'ces phrases banales dans le langage du temps et qui, dans des temps plus calmes, inspirent encore une sorte d'effroi: ce langage d'ailleurs était, pour ainsi dire, officiel et consacré'.[3] Indeed, although the Thermidorians expressed indignation, this language was by no means the preserve of the terrorists: in the Loire, the *procès-verbaux* of the revolutionary committees frequently record the most obscene, if unimaginative, insults employed by suspects;[4] during the federalist crisis, one of the leading *muscadins* of Saint-Chamond appeared at the Municipality 'avec une paire de pistolets devant le ventre comme un brigand et le sabre nu à la main'.[5] Verbal violence was merely the expression of an age which, as Restif de la Bretonne attests, was a violent one below the philosophical urbanity of the wealthy; and the Thermidorians showed that the wealthy could be just as violent both verbally and physically as the *sans-culottes*. By

[1] Cited, without source, as a contemporary description, by Gonon, op. cit., p. 95.

[2] A. Birembaut, 'Javogues vu par C.-A. Alexandre', *A.H.R.F.* 1967, pp. 402–3. Cf. J. Godechot, *Fragments des mémoires de C.-A. Alexandre*, p. 11, establishing his reliability as a witness.

[3] Fouché, *Mémoires*, ed. L. Madelin, p. 44.

[4] e.g. A.D.L., L 382, fol. 10: 'La femme du dit Ronzi . . . a toujours dit et répété depuis plus de six mois, qu'elle s'en foutait, qu'ils étaient de la foutue canaille, que le maire était un bougre de gueux, qu'il n'avait pas pour deux liards pour répondre des bons qu'il signait, qu'elle s'en torcherait le cul, qu'elle l'écrasait ainsi que le foutu gueux de procureur de la commune.'

[5] A.D.R., 42 L 186, d. Perrussel.

itself, therefore, there is little significance in the fact that Javogues tended to greet unwelcome visitors with 'Foutez-moi le camp! Vous êtes tous entachés d'aristocratie! . . . Foutez-moi donc le camp, et dépêchez-vous!' or that he commonly used such terms as 'tout pour le pôt! tout pour le pôt!'[1]

Yet, with Javogues, verbal violence was not just a question of phraseology; it reflected the violence of his character. For with verbal violence went physical violence. He lashed out at people with the same ease as he heaped insults on them:

A menaci le geons qu'adusiant de requétes,
A parla de preysouns ou de coupa de tétes;
Ballie de cót de pün, de cót de pie au quió,
Vou-ère ce que Javogues saït faire lou mió.[2]

The Thermidorians had endless tales of his indiscriminate assaults. For example, when a soldier in the *armée révolutionnaire*, whose pay was slightly in arrears, was foolish enough to broach the subject with the proconsul in the street, he apparently received a blow which bloodied his nose and knocked him over at the feet of the *Représentant du peuple*, who, with cries of 'gueux' and 'coquin', called upon his companions to beat the man with their rifle-butts. Similarly, when some peasants presented him with a petition as he was mounting up to leave Armeville, he tore it to shreds and, trampling it under foot, turned on the petitioners with drawn sword.[3] The terrorists themselves confirm this picture. For instance, Marino and Delan, members of the *Commission Temporaire*, reported that he had seized the mayor of Feurs by the hair; one aggrieved *commissaire* wrote to him:

Tu napas conut que je voulait me moquer de ses chassuble en te dissant de man donner pour faire un paire de culote j'aures crut que

[1] *Extrait des registres des délibérations de la Société populaire de Châlon-sur-Saône*; A.N., D III 349, d. Javogues, Feurs. 'Pôt' ('expression qui lui était familière') was his name for the guillotine. Alexandre nicknamed him 'sacray coyon'—possibly an attempt to render Javogues's pronunciation of 'sacré couillon', which was perhaps another of his favourite phrases. This would suggest, then, that he spoke with a strong accent of the Forez.

[2] G. Straka, *Poèmes du XVIIIe siècle en dialecte de Saint-Étienne*, i. 635: 'Il menaçait les gens qui lui présentaient des requêtes / Il parlait de prison ou de couper les têtes,/ Lâcher des coups de poings, des coups de pied au cul, / C'est ce que Javogues sait faire le mieux.'

[3] A.N., D III 349, d. Javogues, Saint-Étienne.

tu aurait passer un moment joieux avec la compagnie, tu ma foutu un souflet, que jamais de ma vie personne mavait fait Venant de la pard de tois cest nest rien, jespere que a notre premiere [rencontre] tu ne serat pas aussy mechand, sans quoy je ne desirait pas de te revoir je te salue avec fraternite Champagnat ex commissaire.[1]

Representatives from the three villages of Lavalla, Saint-Martin-en-Coalieu, and Saint-Jean-Bonnefonds took the vain precaution of sending in an advance party and of putting on their Sunday-best before meeting the *Représentant*:

Il était midi sonné qu'il n'était pas encore levé. Je me présente [une] demi-heure après avec Bonnard-Chièze de Saint-Martin. La sentinelle nous dit: *Gare, il est de mauvaise humeur. . . .*

La chambre où il était logé était très vaste et pleine de monde: en grande partie des pauvres de la ville qui se plaignaient des riches. Il allait et venait de la cheminée à la fenêtre, prenant de temps en temps une poignée de pralines dans un gros paquet sur la cheminée. Il badinait parfois avec sa coquine nommée Merlasse, du Chambon, ou avec un enfant que tenait, vers le feu, cette Merlasse. Tantôt, il distribuait en allant ou venant quelques coups de poings ou de pieds aux assistants, toujours jurant et pestant contre quelqu'un.

Fontvieille lui fait sa demande en lui présentant les papiers soumis à sa signature. Celui-ci les prend et en bat les joues de Fontvieille. Et, comme son camarade Jean du Moulin Perrot avait bonne mine, Javogues le saisit des deux mains par le menton imprimant ses dix ongles dans sa figure et lui dit: *Ah! bougre de gueux, tu manges tout ton lard, ton fromage et tes poulets. J'ai un petit cœur de tigre, je te dévorerai!* Les ayant régalés, l'un et l'autre, de quelques coups de pieds et de poings, il les repoussa loin de lui.[2]

The excessive aspects of Javogues's character are also illustrated by his intemperance. In nivôse, one inhabitant of Armeville accused 'l'ivrogne Javogues' of debasing the august character of his rank by the extravagance of his behaviour and by his debauchery and drunkenness at every hour of the day—this denunciator's fury seems to have been aroused by the fact that, allegedly at least, Javogues had sat up until 5 o'clock in the morning with Dorfeuille quaffing the most exquisite wines seized in the cellars of a suspect and drinking

[1] A.N., T 781, d. Marino; A.D.R., 42 L 174, d. Champagnat, letter dated 14 niv. Cf. also A.N., D III 349, d. Javogues, contemporary denunciations by Lepoully of Armeville and the club at Ambert.

[2] Quoted by Galley, op. cit. ii. 279–80.

toasts out of a golden snuff-box.[1] A counter-revolutionary letter sent from Lausanne to the secretary of the criminal tribunal, in order to compromise him, suggested: 'Entretenez-vous toujours du Gros représentant, ne lui épargnez pas le Bourgogne.'[2] Moreover, the Thermidorian allegation that he lived quite openly with the *fille* Fourneyron (the 'Merlasse' mentioned above) and her mother is quite possibly accurate;[3] it is certain, at least, that the daughter was on terms of considerable intimacy with him, being admitted to his room while he was in bed, receiving presents from him, and following him from Armeville to Montbrisé.[4] In germinal an II, one denunciation from Armeville suggested that, not content with displaying 'une ivrognerie crapuleuse, . . . une violente colère, et . . . une débauche honteuse avec des femmes publiques qu'il avait constamment avec lui', Javogues went so far as to requisition (as he was supposed to have called it) a maiden who had brought him the sum that had been levied on her father.[5] It is difficult to estimate the truth of this accusation, which was a favourite one of the Thermidorians, and proto-Thermidorians. Nevertheless, it should be noted that, in this case, it was not taken up by the Thermidorians, nor did it appear in the other denunciations emanating from Armeville in the Year II.[6]

The Thermidorian allegations of dishonesty must be dismissed. On the contrary, all the evidence points to Javogues's scrupulous personal honesty. He was careful to give receipts for the gold and silver that he collected and kept detailed

[1] A.N., D III 349, d. Javogues, Lepoully (6 niv.).

[2] A.D.L., L 435.

[3] A.N., loc. cit., Saint-Étienne.

[4] A.D.R., 42 L 190, d. Veriselle, Marguerite Fourneyron to Javogues, n.d., and A.D.L., L 392, Joseph Cave to rev. com. of Armeville, n.d. Her maiden name was Merlat, which, in the Forez dialect, becomes Merlasse in the feminine. Born at Le Chambon, Marguerite Fourneyron, *cabaretière* and *rubanière*, was the wife of Claude Veriselle, with whom, apparently, she no longer lived; in the Year IV she was accused of being an accomplice in highway-robbery at Firminy, but was acquitted together with her mother and brother (A.D.L., L suppl. 45 (an IV), fols. 57 ff.). The stories associated with her are not based on documentary evidence and in many cases seem to be romance (mostly to be found in J. M. Devet, *Une Prison en 1793 et 1794*, pp. 23 n. 1, 25 n. 1).

[5] A.N., D III 349, d. Javogues, Lambert to C.P.S., 18 germ.

[6] A.N., loc. cit., particularly St. Étienne, Lepoully, and also Ambert, apparently based on information supplied from Armeville.

accounts.[1] He obliged his *commissaire* Jean Philippon to return the 20,000 *livres* that he had levied on the commune of Chevrières.[2] The Thermidorians were also prolific in their accounts of his cruelty. Their accusation that he intervened in the proceedings of the revolutionary tribunal urging the conviction of the accused can be refuted on internal evidence.[3] More disturbing, because they were already present in substance in a denunciation by the club at Ambert in pluviôse an II, are the suggestions of deliberate inhumanity in the treatment of prisoners.[4] It is impossible to verify whether Javogues did indeed requisition in front of a column of prisoners the quick-lime destined to consume their bodies, or whether he watched the convoy of the condemned from his window and drank to their good health in an orgy the same evening, or whether he refused bread to the suspects being transferred to Feurs, saying 'qu'importe? ils n'ont pas plus de deux jours à vivre'.[5] The death of the aged in the course of removal from one prison to another was not necessarily his personal responsibility, but might also have been the result of the literal execution of his blanket orders;[6] again, the fact that the prisoners waited two hours in the snow at Armeville before leaving for Montbrisé would have been the work of a zealous subaltern unable to predict the exact moment of the proconsul's departure;[7] the order to dig graves for the executed was not cruelty but an administrative detail.[8] Indeed, Javogues provided carts for the transfer of his prisoners instead of forcing them to make the journey on foot.[9] On the

[1] e.g. A.D.R., 42 L 189, d. Sauvade; A.N., AF II 186, d. 1539, pp. 15–16 (Saône-et-Loire); AF II 114 (861) 15 (Ain, Loire); Javogues, *Compte rendu . . . de ce qu'il a dépensé dans les missions*, 28 vent. an III.

[2] A.D.L., L 374, fol. 5, *arrêté* dated 28 Sept.

[3] A.N., D III 349, d. Javogues (Montbrison and Saint-Étienne). Note that there is no reference to this in the denunciation from Feurs. The Montbrisonnais claimed that the president was courageous enough to take the defence of the accused thus treated: this is most unlikely, since the only time at which both a tribunal and Javogues were at Feurs was in pluv. when the president was Lafaye, a pure terrorist.

[4] Ibid., Ambert.

[5] Ibid., Montbrison and Saint-Étienne. Note that, again, there is no reference to the second accusation in the denunciation from Feurs.

[6] Ibid., Montbrison and Feurs.

[7] Ibid., Saint-Étienne.

[8] Ibid., Montbrison, Saint-Étienne, and Feurs.

[9] A.D.L., L 124, fol. 23, payment by Dist. of Armeville to twelve carters 'pour conduire les équipages des prisonniers à Montbrisé et à Feurs'.

whole, it would seem that much of what appeared as cruelty to his enemies was in fact the product of the macabre humour and the extravagance of this violent man. One can see no more than this in his gloating over the ropes destined to bind prisoners during their transit[1] and in remarks such as 'ces bougres font les bégueules; il n'y a qu'à aller chercher la guillotine, cela les fera revenir' when supplicants fainted in his presence.[2] It was the verbal violence of an excessive temperament that led him to express his hatred of counter-revolutionaries by telling a judge of the revolutionary tribunal how much he would have liked to be in his position: 'Que je savourerais le plaisir de faire guillotiner tous ces B . . ., n'en laisse échapper aucun.'[3]

Javogues's violence, his excesses were not calculated: they produced neither systematic vindictiveness nor cruelty. His anger came in sudden outbursts. In a fit of passion he was quite capable of ordering arrest for relatively trivial motives. One *commissaire* was sent to gaol because he was unable to produce within twenty-four hours the shotgun which Marguerite Fourneyron had deposited at Brignais and which he had sent to Armeville along with all the others abandoned by the troops;[4] the Municipality of Montbrisé, which was ill advised enough to quibble about a requisition of cheese for Armeville, found itself faced with a warrant for its arrest *in toto*.[5] But these fits did not last long; in both cases, the proconsul repented fairly rapidly.[6] In other instances he showed moderation and clemency. A member of the revolutionary committee of Cervières visiting Javogues raised the question of Poyet *fils*, whom they had arrested for having said 'que les arrêtés de Javogues n'étaient pas des décrets et qu'il chiait dessus'; Javogues, who might justifiably have deemed the majesty of the sovereign people insulted, merely said that, since the matter was personal to him, he would order the man's

[1] A.N., loc. cit., Montbrison and Ambert. It is clear that ropes were purchased specifically for this purpose well in advance (A.D.L., L 130, fol. 64, payments made on 17 and 18 niv.).

[2] Bauzon, op. cit. i. 475.

[3] A.N., loc. cit., Montbrison and Ambert.

[4] A.D.L., L 392, petition by Joseph Cave, n.d.; Javogues refers decision on release to the committee of Armeville, 23 pluv.

[5] A.D.L., L 434 (1), fol. 37, *arrêté* dated 9 niv.

[6] Note how astonished the envoys of the *Comm. Temp.* were at the calm with which he accepted the news of his recall (A.N., I 781, d. Marino).

release.[1] After a skirmish in September, Javogues promptly placed under arrest two *chasseurs* accompanying him, who heaped abuse on a prisoner, cut open his head with a broad-sword, and shot him through the leg.[2] Even Lamartine, who showed no tenderness for Javogues elsewhere, recalled that his mother and he as a baby were received with sympathy and kindness by the proconsul.[3] It is quite probable that he could be pleasant when he wished: his colleague, Girard de l'Aude, noted that he received two envoys 'avec ses caresses ordinaires'.[4]

Moreover, one can distinguish in Javogues a certain love of the theatrical. Local patriots were shocked when he appeared at the club at Armeville brandishing a drawn sword, but it was a stage gesture of little significance.[5] He travelled in the 'belles voitures' of the suspects, 'lui que j'ai vu arriver ici à cheval avant la prise de Lyon'; 'nous l'avons vu paraître en public, entouré de licteurs'; 'ce sardanapale est arrivé . . . entouré d'une garde révolutionnaire à pied et à cheval . . .; il traînait à sa suite plus de deux cents malheureux chargés de chaînes . . .; et l'on a remarqué que d'un char de triomphe traîné par six chevaux, il repaissait à chaque instant son cœur du spectacle de ces victimes infortunées.'[6] Such striking of attitudes was by no means peculiar to Javogues among the terrorists: Euloge Schneider, for instance, was arrested by the puritanical Saint-Just for almost exactly the same behaviour as that just described of Javogues.[7] Indeed, few of

[1] A.D.L., L 430 (2), fol. 31: Poyet had added that 'quant à Javogues, il s'en foutait comme de son cul [et] il [lui] chiait et pissait dessus'—there is no indication of whether Javogues was aware of this (A.D.R., 42 L 170, d. Poyet).

[2] A.D.R., 42 L 160, interrogation of Monet, 22 brum.

[3] Lamartine, *Les Confidences*, p. 295; G. Javogues, 'Lamartine et Claude Javogues', *Ann. rév.* 1923, pp. 288–95. The authenticity of this reminiscence is debatable, especially since it was written in 1849. Lamartine situates the event in Dijon, where Javogues never worked, but may be confusing it with Mâcon, whence the family came. But he may also be confusing Javogues with another *Repr.*, Reverchon or Bernard de Saintes, for example.

[4] A.N., AF II 411, d. 3306, p. 58, letter to C.P.S., 6 niv. (pluv.).

[5] A.N., D III 349, d. Javogues, Lepoully, accusation no. 8; cf. also AF II 114 (861) 15, Javogues to Collot, 16 pluv.: 'Si la coquinerie triomphe plus longtemps à la Convention, je serai obligé de me faire justice moi-même et de leur brûler la cervelle.'

[6] A. Sée, *Le Procès Pache*, p. 42, Busson to Pache, 12 niv.; A.N., D III 349, d. Javogues, Feurs.

[7] J.-P. Gross, 'Saint-Just en mission', *A.H.R.F.* 1968, p. 45: accused of having appeared in Strasbourg 'avec un faste insolent, traîné par six chevaux et environné de gardes, le sabre nu'.

the more radical revolutionaries could resist a certain flamboyancy at appropriate moments—Saint-Just himself held his hand in an *auto-da-fé* of anti-revolutionary tracts when swearing the civic oath in 1790.[1] But, with Javogues, such gestures were not just occasional; they were habitual.

Javogues was, therefore, an unstable man, whom the Municipality of Feurs characterized as 'fougueux et emporté'.[2] There is little doubt as to the personal terror that he was capable of inspiring.[3] It is important to understand his excessive, intemperate nature since it inevitably influenced the course of his mission. He was above all a slave to his impulsiveness, and this clouded his judgement on many crucial occasions. Albitte remarked, with his usual penetration: 'J'aime et j'estime Javogues, mais je trouve qu'il ne calcule rien et que son tempérament l'empêche d'écouter toujours la raison.'[4] Despite the general political line discernible in his conduct, his most important decisions were often taken in reaction to other events and his reactions were always excessive. He always tended to exaggerate: in counter-revolutionary Montbrison 'le sang ruissellera un jour . . . comme l'eau dans les rues après une grande pluie', and 'Feurs serait traité comme Sodome et . . . pas un de ses habitants n'échapperait à la mort'.[5] He could claim without hesitation that more than 60,000 people in the department were dying of starvation.[6] Javogues was a man quite incapable of subtlety: people were either totally good or totally bad.[7] Although this was partly the consequence of his political manicheism, it was also an element of his personality. When the revolutionary tribunal at Feurs acquitted a noble, it automatically had 'le cœur orfèvre'; when the Municipality of Montbrisé

[1] Gross, *art. cit.*, p. 31.

[2] A.N., T 781, d. Marino, report.

[3] Cf. ibid.; the *commissaires* realized on leaving Javogues that the Mun., which had been supposed to escort them, had stayed fearfully in the antechamber during the interview.

[4] Bibl. Lyon, Coste MS. 1102, no. 2, letter to Repr. at Cne-aff., 4 pluv. Cf. Bibl. Clermont-Ferrand, MS. 357bis, fol. 80, Maignet to Convention, 29 pluv.: 'J'ai excusé constamment sa tête par son cœur.'

[5] A.N., D III 349, d. Javogues, Montbrison and Feurs.

[6] A.N., AF II 114 (861) 15, letter dated 16 pluv.

[7] Cf. in *Extrait des registres des délibérations de la société populaire de Châlon-sur-Saône . . .*, Julien Paillet to Javogues, 10 frim.: 'Tu enveloppes *tous* les Châlonnais dans une proscription générale; . . . tu les ranges *tous* dans la classe des Contre-révolutionnaires.'

failed to supply a small consignment of cheese to Armeville, he immediately saw this as evidence that the inhabitants of the town were unrepentantly continuing to hatch plots for the destruction of Liberty and Equality.[1] He was, therefore, easy prey for pressure groups which could strike the right attitude. This was especially true in the Saône-et-Loire and the Ain, but even in the Loire the highly dubious Lapalus was thus able to become his confidant,[2] while, after an energetic denunciation by the club at Saint-Chamond, an erstwhile drinking companion became 'le palliatif Dorfeuille' and the subject of an arrest-warrant for having established counter-revolution in Commune d'Armes.[3] In common with all terrorists, Javogues knew himself to be a true patriot and therefore he knew his enemies to be the enemies of the Revolution—when accused of having plundered the Loire he replied: 'Quoi, on ose m'accuser? N'ai-je pas tué le Roy?'[4] Yet, when coupled with his impulsive nature, this led him to disastrous political errors. It was doubtless in part his political evolution which led him to quarrel before the end of his mission with almost everybody from the other *Représentants en mission* to large groups of local militants. But his impetuosity is evident in such acts as the warrant for the arrest of his colleague Gouly,[5] the bitter and public denunciation of Couthon, Maignet, and the Puy-de-Dôme,[6] and the accusations that the Committee of Public Safety was planning counter-revolution.[7] Certainly, this last demonstrates courage, particularly when he exhorted Collot d'Herbois to show this letter to the Committee. Javogues's personal

[1] *Papiers inédits, omis ou supprimés par Courtois*, ii. 305–6, letter to the tribunal, 10 niv.; A.D.L., L 434 (1), fol. 37. Cf. also A.D.R., 42 L 184, d. Macabéo, petition to Javogues, 20 niv. (Macabéo, administrator of the Rhône, visited Armeville to inquire into the motives for the arrest of his brother and was himself arrested): 'Lorsque je fus traduit dans ton domicile, tu me traitas d'intriguant, tu me dis que je machinais dans cette commune un complot.'

[2] A.D.R., 42 L 183, d. Lapalus, letter to Javogues, 9 frim.

[3] A.D.L., L 237, letter dated 27 niv.; A.N., AF II 114 (861) 15, letters dated 16 and 22 pluv. Cf. Bibl. Lyon, Coste MS. 681, no. 7, Fouché, Méaulle, Laporte to Albitte, 1 pluv.: 'Ce mandat nous a doublement étonnés; Javogues, dans sa précédente lettre . . . faisait l'éloge de Dorfeuille.'

[4] Béraud, *Compte rendu à ses commettants*, ed. J. M. Devet, p. 9 n. 1.

[5] A.N., AF II 84 (621), *arrêté* dated 14 niv.

[6] A.N., AF II 137 (1069), d. 30, p. 22, proclamation dated 13 pluv.

[7] A.N., AF II 114 (861) 15, letter dated 16 pluv.

bravery cannot be impugned—at one point during the siege of Lyon, he advanced alone with Dubois-Crancé right up to the enemy lines—but his was the reckless courage of the extravagant.[1] Indeed, it is clear that during his time as a proconsul the traits of Javogues's character were progressively accentuated. By the end of his mission, his proclamations, *arrêtés*, and letters had become long tirades, without punctuation, in his inimitable and luxuriant style.[2] His sentiments in pluviôse were perfectly coherent as a political platform, but it is difficult to ignore a certain tone of frenzy in the terms in which he expressed them. By this time, he saw even Dupuy and Dubouchet as his enemies.[3]

The most lively portrait of Javogues is without doubt the one that emerges from Busson's account of the levying of the *taxe révolutionnaire* at Armeville.[4] Moreover, Busson is one of the most reliable sources that we possess on the personality of Javogues; a sincere Jacobin, although he disliked the politics of a *taxe révolutionnaire*, his indignation was above all moral:

> Il se rendit à six heures du soir dans la salle des séances de la Commune. Le corps municipal était assemblé, et il y avait un grand nombre de spectateurs. Il était gris comme un cordelier. Il fit asseoir, à côté de lui, une jeune et jolie fille qu'il avait appelée pour chanter une chanson patriotique. Il demanda de la bière et donna ordre qu'on en allât chercher dans la cave du citoyen Vincent qui est dans les prisons. On apporta d'abord huit bouteilles de bière. On fit plusieurs voyages, et il se but dans la salle environ trente bouteilles tant bière que vin. Javogues, les officiers municipaux, et ceux qui étaient *de nos amis*, mangeaient du saucisson avec du pain blanc qu'on avait saisi à un boulanger . . . buvaient de la bière et du vin à la barbe du peuple qui humait les sermons du représentant et qui disait dans son patois: *avisa, avisa que lous Bougres! ils se soulont bien, et nous nous avisons.* Les officiers municipaux et nos amis se jetaient de petites boules de pain blanc à la figure pour s'amuser.
>
> Un des spectateurs voulut faire des observations à Javogues sur les taxes arbitraires qu'il faisait, il cria au chef de la garde révolutionnaire: *sacré mille Foutre, arrêtez-moi ce bougre-là; que je le fasse fusiller.*

[1] *Troisième Partie de la réponse de Dubois-Crancé* . . ., p. 28.
[2] Especially A.N., AF II 114 (861) 15, letter dated 16 pluv. [3] Ibid.
[4] A. Sée, *Le Procès Pache*, pp. 42–6, Busson to Pache, 12 niv.; cf. also A.N., AF II 84 (622), Busson to Pache, 30 pluv.: 'Il n'y avait pas un enfant dans la ville qui ne sache que Javogues prenait les bains, qu'il avait avalé la médecine préparatoire, etc.'

La citoyenne Fressinette, vieille fille (qui a mené et mène une vie libre) étant instruite qu'on l'avait taxée à un taux qui excédait sa fortune, accourut à la séance pour faire des représentations à Javogues qui lui dit à haute voix: 'Tu es une garce, une sacrée putain, tu as plus t . . . de coups avec les abbés que je n'ai de cheveux sur ma tête; ton c . . . doit être si large que j'y entrerais tout entier.' Il ajouta ensuite par supplément: 'Toutes les femmes sont des sacrées garces, des sacrées putains; ce sont nos pots de chambre etc. etc. . . .'; il reprit ensuite: 'J'entends parler des Muscadines.'

Il dit à la fille du Maire qui a environ vingt ans: 'tu es une sacrée bougresse, une sacrée putain, mais bonne patriote pour cela.'

Il embrassa plus de cent fois la jeune fille qui était assise à côté de lui; il lui porta la main sur le sein, elle lui flanqua un bon soufflet en lui disant: 'Comment, toi qui es représentant du peuple, tu t'oublies à ce point-là?' Il lui répondit: 'Foutre, vois-tu bien, je ne ferais pas tant de mal en prenant cent tétons qu'en volant un sou de six liards.'

Je ne crois pas que de pareilles orgies soient bien propres à régénérer nos mœurs.

Il y a plusieurs *gueuses*, plus *gueuses* que ces filles qui raccrochaient autrefois sur le port au blé à Paris, qui vont voir le citoyen Javogues qui prend ses ébats avec elles; il y a une de ces gueuses dont la fille appelle Javogues son papa.

As early as the beginning of nivôse, Javogues's successor in the Ain and the Saône-et-Loire, the moderate Gouly, used the epithet 'ultra-révolutionnaire' to describe him.[1] Javogues accepted this designation for, according to the club at Ambert in pluviôse, he was saying that he could not care less about the denunciations reaching the Convention against him, and that, on the contrary, he himself would denounce 'ceux qui ont inventé le mot ultra-révolutionnaire et qui ne sont qu'une troisième faction de feuillants et de modérés'.[2] 'Javogues, digne sectateur des Hébert et des Chaumette,' echoed the Thermidorians, 'ne cessait de prêcher leur doctrine empoisonnée, et de vanter le patriotisme par excellence du Père Duchesne.'[3] Already, in germinal an II, a denunciation emanating from Armeville stigmatized him as 'l'hébertiste Javogues'.[4] Clearly, Javogues's political position in nivôse and pluviôse was akin to that of the Hébertists, but no direct link can be established between him and the various

[1] A.N., AF II 84 (620), *arrêté* dated from Belley, 5 niv.

[2] A.N., D III 349, d. Javogues.

[3] Ibid., Montbrison.

[4] Ibid., Lambert to C.P.S., 18 germ.

personalities normally included in this faction, despite the presence at Commune-affranchie/Lyon of a certain number of men close to them during the winter of the Year II.[1] If the term ultra-revolutionary is insufficient to describe him politically, it would be more accurate to characterize him as a neo-maratist of the type of Chasles or Collot d'Herbois than as an Hébertist. His revolutionary saints were Chalier and Marat: at Armeville he gave orders for the construction of a mausoleum to Chalier, while at Bourg he urged the club to cherish 'la mémoire glorieuse de Marat panthéonisé . . ., le bienfaiteur de l'humanité, . . . il n'est pas mort, il revit dans le cœur de tous les sans-culottes'.[2]

It is possible to debate how conscious an ultra-revolutionary Javogues was. One can argue that he was one above all by instinct, that his political extremism was simply another manifestation of the element of exaggeration in his character. One can portray him as the supreme individualist, acting out his impulses rather than implementing his beliefs, and temperamentally rather than ideologically incapable of accepting the directives of the Committee of Public Safety. Certainly, as we have seen, impulse and temperament were a very important feature of Javogues's behaviour, while his political effacement both before and after his mission might be taken to indicate lack of great conviction if it were not for his role in the Camp de Grenelle conspiracy. Such an argument, however, is not fully satisfactory. On the contrary, it is possible to detect in the detail of his work in the Loire, in his attitude to the law of 14 frimaire, in his relations with the central government, a consistent pattern which amounts to more than a simple sequence of instinctive reactions. Javogues never came nearer to explaining his political beliefs than in the lengthy preambles which he affixed as justification or exhortation to his *arrêtés*; yet one can discern here, beneath the flamboyant rhetoric, the repeated use of a number of political concepts that together make up a coherent political programme. One must hasten to stress immediately that these beliefs were

[1] e.g. the formal tone of a letter to Parein, n.d. (A.D.R., 42 L 141, d. Landine and Duvant).

[2] A.D.L., L 124, fol. 49; Javogues, *Discours prononcé à la Société de Sans-culottes républicains de Bourg . . .*

extremely summary and also that they were in no way original. All the ideas which Javogues displayed were familiar to the mass of the Parisian *sans-culottes*. Nevertheless, it is important to discuss them briefly for the comprehension of several aspects of Javogues's work which will be examined later. Furthermore, these ideas were probably typical of the attitudes of all the ultra-revolutionary proconsuls. These men still remain a rather shadowy group. Only Chasles's ideas have been analysed and they appear to have been formulated above all under the pressure of events during the Year III.[1] Fouché is usually dismissed, possibly quite wrongly, as a mere trimmer, while such men as Taillefer and Mallarmé are in danger of becoming an attractive, slightly inebriated band of anarchical *gais lurons*.

First and foremost Javogues was a democrat: he counted himself as one of those whose sole preoccupation had always been the happiness of the People.[2] He defined the People as those citizens who had suffered from the Ancien Régime[3] and predominantly as 'la partie industrieuse de la Société', including 'la classe agricole':[4] in other words, all those who, in town or country, worked and produced, the poor majority of Frenchmen. Poverty was an essential characteristic of the People: 'la misère' was 'le partage de la probité, de la simplicité et de la vertu'.[5] The enemies of the People were naturally 'l'aristocratie'. Just as the People were those who had suffered from the Ancien Régime, so 'l'aristocratie' referred to all those who had benefited from it, to all those who therefore regretted it—the *émigrés*, the nobles, the former privileged classes, the *procureurs*, and 'la horde des praticiens'.[6] But above all, the enemy of the People, by definition poor, was the Rich. 'Ces misérables reptiles'[7] were felt by Javogues to oppress the People just as surely as the privileged had done during the Ancien Régime: great wealth

1 C. Pichois and J. Dautry, *Le Conventionnel Chasles et ses idées démocratiques*.

2 A.N., AF II 138 (1077), p. 15, *arrêté* against Châlon, 13 frim.

3 A.N., AF II 138 (1077), p. 28, *arrêté* issued at Arme-Commune, 16 frim.

4 A.N., AF II 114 (861) 15, *arrêté* issued at Armeville, 8 brum.

5 A.N., AF II 114 (861) 14, *arrêté* of 6 niv. Cf. Chasles's definition of the People as 'tout ce qui ne peut pas exister sans les secours et le produit du travail . . . la masse ouvrière et peu aisée' (Pichois and Dautry, op. cit., p. 76).

6 A.N., AF II 114 (861) 15, *arrêté* issued at Armeville, 8 brum.

7 Ibid., letter to Collot, 16 pluv.

testified to the secular oppression, slavery, and misery of the People.[1] After making an initial distinction between 'prêtres réfractaires fanatiques' and ordinary priests[2]—but a distinction which he tended to forget[3]—Javogues soon added the whole 'caste sacerdotale' to the list. For the priests were intimately connected with all the other antagonists of the People:

> Le fanatisme [est] absolument vendu à la cause des Riches et des Rois. . . Lorsque le Peuple éprouvait les horreurs de la disette, les Prêtres et les Riches, au lieu de lui donner du pain, le consolaient par l'ostentation de quelques signes éblouissants, lui promettant un avenir fortuné dans les espaces imaginaires et le faisaient mourir à petit feu sur la terre.[4]

Indeed, as the winter of the Year II progressed, the other categories of enemies took second place to 'ces rhinocéros connus sous le nom de *Riches* et de *Prêtres*' who were in league with the hoarders to assassinate 20,000,000 people.[5] The antithesis of the People was, therefore, the

> ramassis le plus impur et . . . l'écume la plus sale de la société . . ., toute classe qui, regrettant les anciens abus, voulaient ressusciter le régime de la tyrannie, prêtres, ci-devant nobles, procureurs, avocats, usuriers, accapareurs, gros marchands, financiers, en un mot tous les grugeurs de l'espèce humaine, . . . seigneurs, . . . nobles, . . . évêques, . . . la sainte pratique, . . . fripons de négociants en gros et en détail et . . . tous ceux qu'on appelait *messieurs les honnêtes gens*; banquiers, . . . égoistes, . . . agioteurs; gros Propriétaires.[6]

Naturally, the Republic was the political system designed for the People;[7] but the Republic envisaged by Javogues was 'la République démocratique'. In the Democratic Republic, 'le peuple doit exister seul'.[8] Therefore, its establishment

[1] A.N., AF II 114 (861) 14, *arrêté* of 6 niv.

[2] e.g. commission for arrests given on 14 brum. mentions only 'prêtres réfractaires, fanatiques' (A.D.L., L 18, fol. 26).

[3] e.g. A.N., AF II 114 (861) 15, *arrêté* issued at Armeville, 8 brum.: 'une conspiration générale de la part des . . . privilégiés . . . et des prêtres'.

[4] A.N., AF II 114 (861) 14, *arrêté* of 6 niv.

[5] Ibid., A.N., AF II 137 (1069), d. 30, p. 8, *arrêté* of 26 frim.

[6] Javogues, op. cit.; A.N., AF II 138 (1077) 3, *arrêté* issued at Mâcon, 6 frim.; AF II 114 (861) 14, *arrêté* of 6 niv.

[7] 'Le Peuple' and 'Républicains' were interchangeable terms (e.g. A.N., AF II 137 (1069), d. 30, p. 22).

[8] Javogues, op. cit.

involved the destruction of all the enemies of the People, the pruning of 'toutes ces branches parasites [qui] étaient autant de sangsues qui cherchaient à dessécher le tronc de l'arbre social planté pour l'édifice de la prospérité publique'.[1] For, to date, Liberty and Equality had been but vain words: 'il est temps que les sans-culottes jouissent en réalité du bonheur dont les hommes pervers et assassins de la société ne lui laissent entrevoir que la peinture.'[2] This Democratic Republic was bound to be atheistic, since 'les restes antiques d'une superstition et d'un simulacre religieux' were merely agents of oppression.[3] Reason and Philosophy were to replace Christianity—Deism had no place in Javogues's scheme, he never mentioned the Supreme Being. The Thermidorians accused him of preaching the worship of the sun and the stars: in fact, this was Dorfeuille's idea and there is no sign that Javogues adopted it.[4] They also accused him of advocating free love and the abolition of marriage; certainly, this idea was being aired by some of the Parisians at Commune-affranchie, but, again, there is no evidence that Javogues held this opinion.[5] But, more important than the elimination of priests was the destruction of the Rich. For the Rich were nothing more than monstrous embezzlers whose wealth rightfully belonged to the *sans-culottes* and to the poor who had sweated to produce it.[6] Already, the confiscations of property consequent upon the revolt of Lyon had started to return this wealth to its rightful owners, since it now belonged to the *sans-culottes* by right of conquest; but this process had to be completed by an act of restitution.[7] This view led Javogues to proclaim that 'l'édifice de la prospérité publique ne sera consolidé que sur la destruction et le cadavre du dernier des honnêtes gens'.[8]

[1] A.N., AF II 114 (861) 15, *arrêté* issued at Armeville, 8 brum. 'Prospérité publique' means 'prospérité du Peuple'.

[2] A.N., AF II 137 (1069), d. 30, p. 22.

[3] A.N., AF II 138 (1077), p. 20.

[4] *Compte rendu de la gestion du Directoire du district de Mont-Brison*, p. 55; Dorfeuille, *Discours . . . après la lecture du décret sur les hommes de couleur*, Cne-aff., 20 vent.

[5] A.N., D III 349, d. Javogues, Montbrison; *Journal de Commune-affranchie et des Départements de Rhône-et-Loire*, 6 frim.

[6] A.N., AF II 114 (861) 14, *arrêté* of 6 niv.

[7] A.N., AF II 137 (1069), d. 30, p. 17.

[8] Javogues, op. cit.

The Democratic Republic was certainly built upon the twin pillars of Liberty and Equality, but the operative word was Equality, 'cette égalité sublime, base de la vraie liberté'.[1] All men were equal and society owed to all of them bread and work.[2] Property owners, therefore, had the obligation to preserve each man in his natural rights and his liberty, and to furnish him with the means of existence.[3] Hence, the ownership of property must be associated with social virtue: 'l'aliment de la société, le bonheur de ses frères, la bienfaisance et l'humanité: voilà les titres les plus recommendables de la propriété.'[4] But the Rich man was incapable of such virtue, since, by definition, his wealth was the product of the inhuman exploitation of the People. Inevitably, therefore, the Rich man had 'le cœur d'acier' and was an enemy of the People.[5] But Javogues never questioned the principle of private property. It was great wealth that he detested: he did not denounce the *propriétaires* but the *gros propriétaires*, he rarely attacked the *marchand* but always the *négociant* and the *gros marchand*.[6] The Democratic Republic, therefore, was a Republic of small property-owners: 'Nous avons fait séquestrer beaucoup de biens. En les divisant pour la vente, le peuple pourra devenir propriétaire, et ce ne sera qu'alors que dans notre pays nous pourrons nous flatter d'avoir la république de nom et d'effet.'[7] But Javogues never envisaged equality of property. He admitted inequality of fortune. His *taxe révolutionnaire* fixed the limit of wealth at 100,000 *livres*, that is twice the declared fortune of his own family; the fact that he entrusted the education of an abandoned child to Richard, a retired *marchand* of Montbrisé, whom some accused of being too rich to be allowed to remain on the revolutionary committee, shows that he accepted that

[1] Quoted by A. Guillon, *Histoire du siège de Lyon*, ii. 123.

[2] A.N., AF II 114 (861) 14, *arrêté* of 6 niv.

[3] A.N., AF II 137 (1069), d. 30, p. 8. Javogues makes a distinction between material property and veritable property—the latter consists of 'les droits imprescriptibles et impérissables de la nature', of which liberty is the most precious (Javogues, op. cit.).

[4] Ibid. Cf. 'Ils disaient: je suis propriétaire. Mais cette qualité te donne-t-elle le droit d'être assassin de la société ? te donne-t-elle le droit d'ôter à la société tous les moyens d'exister?' (ibid.).

[5] Ibid.

[6] Above, p. 90.

[7] A.D. P.-de-D., L 322, Javogues to Couthon, 22 Sept.

wealth and patriotism were compatible within certain limits.[1]

Thus, Javogues's idea of the new society to be produced by the Revolution was a republic of small property-owners, delivered from all the deadly social parasites and living in some ideal brotherhood of man—'Plus de pusillanimité; justice, impartialité: voilà la conduite des Républicains, humanité, bienfaisance, amitié, fraternité, destruction de tous les ennemis de la patrie.'[2] It was to be the reign of natural rights, which he considered to be *liberté*, *égalité*, and *le bonheur du peuple*. He believed that all this was contained in essence in the Constitution of 1793.[3]

We have already emphasized that nothing that Javogues said was original. To cite comparisons only from the areas adjacent to the Loire, Albitte and Fouché both had very much the same attitude to priests as Javogues,[4] while Fouché stated that the wealth of the Rich was only a deposit made by the nation and which the nation could seize for the relief of the poor if it was not used voluntarily for this end.[5] The *Instruction* of the *Commission Temporaire*, circulated at the end of brumaire with the express approbation of Collot d'Herbois and Fouché, contained in a concise form most of Javogues's views; it was, however, more circumspect on the question of the Rich and more reticent on religion. There was no great difference between Javogues's view of the rights of the People and the belief expressed by Collot, Fouché, and Albitte, that all citizens should have an equal right to the advantages of society and that their rewards should be proportionate to their labour, their productivity, and the zeal with which they devoted themselves to the service of the nation.[6] None the less, Javogues does appear as the most extreme ultra-revolutionary of all the proconsuls in the region, with the possible exception of

[1] A.N., AF II 114 (861) 14, *arrêté* of 6 niv.; A.C., Montbrison, *reg. dél.*, no. 2, fol. 53; A.D.L., L 434 (2), fol. 40.

[2] Javogues, op. cit. In the Democratic Republic, the People become 'l'immense famille des Français' (A.N., AF II 137 (1069), d. 30, p. 22).

[3] A.N., AF II 138 (1077), p. 20.

[4] L. Meunier, 'Albitte, conventionnel en missions', *A.H.R.F.* 1946, pp. 264–73; Madelin, op. cit. i. 67, 100–2, 104.

[5] Ibid. i. 68.

[6] A.N., AF II 137 (1060), d. 4, p. 8, *arrêté* issued at Cne-aff., 24 brum. Cf. Fouché's *arrêté* of 19 Sept. at Clamecy (Madelin, op. cit. i. 68).

Collot d'Herbois.[1] Albitte was basically far too moderate in his attitudes.[2] As for Fouché, he always made the distinction between the *mauvais riche* and the *bon riche* and never seems to have had an organized programme for the redistribution of property.[3] It is significant that none of the *Représentants en mission* in the Ain, where Javogues spent a mere three days, was as violently attacked by the Thermidorians as he was.[4] Finally, he was poles apart from Couthon and Maignet, who instituted a *taxe révolutionnaire* in order to finance educational establishments in the belief that it was only by education that the wealthy could bring the propertyless to understand why they should respect the property of others.[5]

Nevertheless, although Javogues's notions about the ultimate goal were summary, his view of the immediate measures to be taken was clear. The destruction of the enemies of the People was not merely the *sine qua non* of the achievement of the Democratic Republic. It was also the most urgent and primordial element in the preservation of the Revolution and of the advantages that it had already won for the People. For, 'n'avez-vous pas vu, comme un et un font deux, que dans l'espoir de faire un auto-da-fé des républicains, les malveillants, lorsqu'ils avaient la force, ne s'en sont servis que pour réduire le peuple à la misère ?'[6] The Revolution must progress without pause forward towards the Democratic Republic; there could be no halt, for that would be to slip backwards. The importance that Javogues attached to the arrest of suspects derived from this attitude: the slightest indulgence was a retrogressive act in revolutionary terms.[7] It also dictated his emphasis on the role of revolutionary tribunals, which he established at Mâcon and Bourg, not to mention

[1] In the absence of a competent biography of Collot d'Herbois, it is difficult to assess his views exactly.

[2] Meunier, art. cit., pp. 62–3, quotes Albitte's views on the need to be less harsh on minor counter-revolutionaries.

[3] Madelin, op. cit. i. 94, 97.

[4] E. Dubois, *Histoire de la Révolution dans l'Ain*, iv. 86.

[5] F. Mège, *Le Puy-de-Dôme en 1793 et le proconsulat de Couthon*, pp. 590–7.

[6] Javogues, op. cit.

[7] A. D. P.-de-D., L 322, Javogues to Couthon, 22 Sept. Cf. A.N., D III 349, d. Javogues, Montbrison alleges that he claimed that one only became a patriot by denouncing and that another 2,000,000 heads were needed to complete the Revolution.

his dealings with the tribunal at Feurs. For Javogues, the Terror was undoubtedly the next and final step forward into the Democratic Republic. And it was this idea that inspired his attitude to the governmental decisions of the winter of the Year II, such as the law of 14 frimaire and the *liberté des cultes*. They impeded the progress of the People towards the Democratic Republic—more, they allowed the Rich and the Priest to reassert their position. Such measures were, therefore, counter-revolutionary and their authors were the allies of all the parasites of the human race. He lamented, therefore, his inability to destroy the confidence that the *sans-culottes* had in Robespierre and Couthon, whom he disparagingly entitled 'Messieurs', and thundered: 'Ah! Barère, Couthon, Prieur de la Côte d'Or, Saint-Just et d'autres que je ne connais pas, quels supplices pourront jamais expier les maux que le peuple éprouve?'[1]

[1] Ibid., Ambert; A.N., AF II 114 (861) 15, Javogues to Collot, 16 pluv.

IV

THE *SOCIÉTÉS POPULAIRES*

THE great majority of the *sociétés populaires* of the Loire were founded during the Terror. Only seventeen out of fifty-nine were in existence before September 1793 and, except for two in the industrial villages round Saint-Étienne, they were in the more important urban centres.[1] The creation of these early clubs took place in two distinct phases. The first was at the very end of 1790 and during the first few months of 1791. It was at this time that five clubs were formed in Saint-Étienne and others at La Ricamarie, Outrefuran, Saint-Chamond, Montbrison, Saint-Bonnet-le-Château, Charlieu, and Perreux. These foundations were part of the general movement throughout France. The second phase was at the end of 1792 and during the early months of 1793, and represented a patriotic response to the national political tensions and to the increasing religious ferment locally. This phase was of relatively minor importance, concerning only four or five clubs: Boën, Feurs, Saint-Germain-Laval, Roanne, and possibly Rive-de-Gier. The revolutionary movement in this area appears, therefore, to have been backward at this time in relation to France as a whole, since the majority of the pre-Terror provincial clubs were already founded before the last two months of 1790.[2] This situation is another illustration of the physical isolation of the region and of its influence upon the political consciousness of the inhabitants.

With the exception of Roanne, where there is evidence of a meeting on 21 August,[3] all these clubs broke down at the time of the federalist crisis. The club at Charlieu had already

[1] See Map 5. The registers survive for Charlieu and Régny (A.D.L., L 402, 403, 416), and those for Saint-Chamond have been published by G. Lefebvre, *Registre des procès-verbaux de la Société républicaine de Saint-Chamond*. The remainder of the documentation is provided by incidental references and individual procès-verbaux.

[2] J. Godechot, *Les Institutions de la France sous la Révolution et l'Empire*, p. 66.

[3] *La Société populaire de la ville de Roanne à la Convention* . . . (Sept. 1793).

MAP 5. *Sociétés populaires*

ceased to function as early as 14 April, because the members failed to pay their subscriptions.[1] The clubs in the district of Saint-Étienne and those at Montbrison and Boën were dispersed and their meeting-places ransacked by the federalist troops from Lyon. The club at Saint-Bonnet-la-Montagne/-le-Château took fright and held no reunions after 22 July.[2] Indeed, it is open to question whether most of these clubs were ever very resolutely active before the summer of 1793. The collapse of the club at Charlieu in April was due basically to the apathy of its members. Already it had slumbered undisturbed between 10 July 1791 and 30 September 1792, and the meetings during the winter of 1792–3 were apparently only concerned with the election of officers, apart from a few discussions on the distribution of bread to the poor and on clothing for the troops.[3] The fact that in pluviôse an II the *agent national* of the district of Boën (formerly Montbrison) thought that only the clubs at Boën and Montbrisé were not of recent origin must be taken to reflect the atrophy of the early clubs at Saint-Bonnet-la-Montagne/-le-Château and at Feurs.[4] The clubs at Saint-Étienne, however, show signs of continuous activity. The Municipality headed by Antoine Desverneys (November 1791–December 1792) doubtless represents the success of their electoral action. A petition of May 1792 to the Legislative Assembly, denouncing the administration of the department of Rhône-et-Loire, collected 606 signatures and said that as many again would have signed if they had known how.[5] The denunciations laid against the Jacobin leader Johannot in June 1793 reveal that during the spring of 1793 these clubs were discussing much the same proto-terrorist programme as that advocated by Chalier and his followers at Lyon.[6] The club at Saint-Chamond also appears to have been busy. In February 1792 its members marched on the Capucin monastery because the non-juror inmates were keeping the constitutional churches empty, an event which moved one scandalized priest to bad verse:

[1] A.D.L., L 399 (1), fol. 25.
[2] A.D.L., L 327, fol. 5, L 436, fol. 29.
[3] A.D.L., L 401, fol. 9 ff.
[4] A.D.L., L 327, fol. 1, letter to *Repr.*, 26 pluv.
[5] A.N., F^{1b} II (Rhône), d. Saint-Étienne.
[6] Above, p. 48.

Au club tout est égal, y bavarde qui veut,
Chacun dit ce qu'il sait, on s'entend comme on peut
. . . . . .
on résout à son aise
Mille difficultés qu'on croyait autrefois
Être la mer à boire au conseil de nos rois.
Le club de Saint-Chamond ne le cède à nul autre
Du vrai patriotisme il est l'ardent apôtre.[1]

Most of the old clubs reappeared fairly rapidly after the expulsion of the federalists from the Forez during the first fortnight of September and with the prospect of the imminent defeat of Lyon. At Charlieu, a group of Jacobins started meeting again at the house of one of the members on 30 August and the club was properly reorganized on 15 September.[2] At Montbrison, Maignet, *Représentant du peuple* marching with the *levée en masse* of the Puy-de-Dôme, reinstalled the club on 17 September.[3] Although the nonchalant club at Saint-Bonnet-la-Montagne did not open its doors again until 20 brumaire/10 November, the one at Saint-Germain-Laval was operating before 11 October.[4] In the district of Saint-Étienne, the patriots experienced some difficulty in recommencing their activities due to the massive departure of so many militants for the republican army besieging Lyon. The club was re-established at Saint-Chamond on 28 September, but the Municipality had to agree to act as its officers until the return of the militants.[5] The clubs at Saint-Étienne were not officially reopened until 10 October, their place having been filled since the retreat of the *muscadins* by the sectional assemblies purged of their federalist elements.[6]

The unsatisfactory nature of the documentary evidence makes it difficult to establish any clear chronological pattern for the creation of clubs during the Terror. It is evident that the real impulse to the formation of clubs came from the *Représentant en mission* Javogues, whose *arrêté* of 5 brumaire/26 October invited 'les citoyens des cantons du département de la Loire . . . à se réunir en sociétés'.[7] It is equally evident

[1] Bibl. Lyon, Coste MS. 1073, (Abbé Combry), 'La Capucinade'.
[2] A.D.L., L 402 and L 399 (1), fol. 25. [3] A.D.R., 42 L 181, d. Jamier.
[4] A.D.L., L 436, fol. 29, and L 196 (denunciation against Verdellet).
[5] Lefebvre, op. cit., p. 15. [6] A.C. Saint-Étienne, 1 D 10 (3), fol. 71.
[7] A.N., AF II 114 (861) 15.

that this *arrêté* provoked only a slow response. Only three new clubs appeared during the rest of brumaire.[1] The majority were formed in frimaire and nivôse: eleven certainly and five probably in frimaire, four certainly and two probably in nivôse. Only one dates certainly from pluviôse, and of the six to which we have references only from pluviôse, it seems probable that one or two were founded earlier.[2] A few clubs were created even later, after the departure of Javogues, being for the most part in isolated mountain communities. Thus, although the establishment of clubs continued for a long time, those in the more important centres were generally in existence by the end of frimaire.

By inviting the citizens of the cantons to form *sociétés populaires*, Javogues indicated the character of these clubs. Established in the *chefs-lieux* of the cantons, they were not communal but cantonal and drew their members from the population of the canton as a whole, although the majority came from the *chef-lieu* for obvious reasons of population density and distance. The inhabitants of Renaison, for example, went to the club at Saint-Haon-le-Châtel, while of the sixty-three members at Moingt, fifteen came from other communes of the canton.[3] There were, however, exceptions to the rule. On the one hand, the system of clubs was never complete: none was established at Parigny (*chef-lieu* of a canton in partnership with le Coteau), nor at Villemontais, Saint-Polgues, Belmont, La Fouillouse, Saint-Genest-Malifaux, or Maclas. On the other hand, some were founded in villages which were not *chefs-lieux* of cantons, although these usually had some specific *raison d'être*. Sansnizier/Saint-Nizier formed one in pluviôse because it was difficult to get to the *chef-lieu* in the evening.[4] Arduous communications also dictated the decision to create six separate clubs from the outset in the mountain canton of Saint-Jean-Soleymieux, one for each commune except for the four communes forming the

[1] See Map 5.

[2] Although one can accept that Marlhes, (Saint-)Just-la-Pendue, and Crémeaux were late-comers, given their geographical position, it is unlikely that, e.g., Le Coteau, just across the river from Roanne, should have been so behindhand.

[3] A.D.L., L 237 and L 433. Many underlined their character in their titles, e.g. 'la société populaire des neuf communes du canton de Néronde' (L 411, fol. 1).

[4] A.D.L., L 237.

parish of Saint-Jean and La Montagne-en-l'Advieux, which all met together.[1] The clubs at Usson and Panissières doubtless owed their existence to the high population of these communes. Cervières and Noirétable each established a club as another move in their struggle to be recognized as the *chef-lieu* of the canton, and this in itself is significant, because each evidently thought that a club was an important element of the character of a *chef-lieu*. The one at Crémeaux was probably formed to remedy the absence of one at the *chef-lieu*, Roche-Libre/Saint-Polgues.[2] But there is no very obvious reason for the existence of clubs at Déome/Saint-Sauveur, (Saint-)Julien-la-Vêtre, and Fourneaux: perhaps the latter two cases are evidence of the role of the major roads as vehicles of ideas for the populations through which they passed.

The cantonal character given to the *sociétés populaires* of the Loire was deliberate policy. It was often difficult, especially in the mountains, to assemble enough people of goodwill to form a club. For example, when the Jacobins of Ville-Fontfort/Saint-Galmier sent *commissaires* at the invitation of four inhabitants of Chevrières to investigate the possibility of creating a club there, they found that in fact these four citizens represented the sum total of those willing to join.[3] These institutions could become dangerous if dominated by enemies of the Revolution, because, by denouncing the patriots and by misinforming the people about the laws and about the true nature of their rights and duties, they could mobilize the ignorant mass against the *gouvernement révolutionnaire*. Thus, when one militant proposed in frimaire that the club at Armeville/Saint-Étienne should send out members to found them in each commune, the influential Pignon immediately insisted that they be confined to the *chefs-lieux* of cantons, emphasizing that

> les lumières n'étant pas suffisamment propagées dans toutes les communes de la campagne, il serait dans ce moment impolitique ou du

[1] A.D.L., L 439: Saint-Jean and La-Montagne; Soleymieux; Chazelles-sur-l'Advieux; Margerie; Gumières; Lavieu. Only Margerie and Chazelles appear to have functioned.

[2] Cf. A.D.L., L 426, fol. 16; it is the club at Crémeaux that elects the rev. com. of the canton.

[3] A.D.L., L 374, fol. 11. This is the only case recorded of one club attempting to found another.

moins très inutile d'y établir des Sociétés populaires qui ne pourraient faire aucun bien et qui, peut-être, feraient beaucoup de mal.[1]

The cantonal system had distinct advantages. In those areas where the patriots were few and far between in the villages, it grouped the scattered militants, strengthened their zeal, which might otherwise have wilted in isolation, and rendered their action more powerful by giving it a collective rather than an individual character. Moreover, the system gave the clubs a wider field in which to exercise their authority; the benefits of this were especially visible in their efforts to obtain a suitable food supply for the urban centres from the surrounding countryside. Finally, it gave the clubs a wider audience, especially among those persons in authority in the villages, thus facilitating the education of the citizens, the diffusion of a proper knowledge of the laws, and the collection of information.

It is clear that Javogues intended that the clubs should be spontaneous creations, since he merely invited the citizens to form them, whereas, in the same *arrêté*, he specifically ordered the establishment of revolutionary committees. In fact, however, few of the clubs about which we possess any precise information were the result of the spontaneous association of local militants. This is true even of the re-establishment of some of the old clubs after the federalist crisis. At Charlieu, for example, the Jacobins only made desultory efforts to regroup since they only met twice (30 August and 1 September); the real initiative came from the Municipality, which, considering that *le salut public* made its re-establishment imperative, invited the citizens to put their names down on a register opened by the secretary of the revolutionary committee.[2] Similarly, it was the Municipality that took upon itself to reopen the club at Saint-Chamond, and even then only after it had been reprimanded by Javogues.[3] As for Saint-Étienne, despite the departure of so many militants for the army, it is curious that the town should not have seen its

1 A.N., AF II 114 (860) 8.

2 A.D.L., L 402 and L 399 (1), fol. 25. In any case, the club only properly got under way on 1 brum. after an initial meeting on 1 Oct.

3 Lefebvre, op. cit., p. 15; A.C. Saint-Chamond, *reg. dél.*, 19 Sept., letter from Javogues, n.d.

clubs in renewed activity until Pignon arrived on 10 October with express orders from Javogues.[1] The majority of the clubs founded during the Terror owed their existence either to the Department or their District, represented by a member on a tour of inspection, or else to the Municipality of their commune or the local committee. All these authorities appear to have taken the invitation of Javogues as an order.[2] Thus, the first meeting of the club at Régny was called by the Municipality, although the presence of an administrator of the department suggests that the real initiative came from him.[3] In the district of Boën (formerly Montbrison), the *agent national* later claimed that most of the clubs had been formed 'par les soins de l'administration';[4] certainly those in the south-west of the district (Saint-Rambert, Saint-Bonnet-la-Montagne, Saint-Georges-en-Couzan, Usson, Saint-Jean-Soleymieux, and Saint-Marcellin) were all created by Plagnieu, administrator of the district, during his two missions there in brumaire and frimaire. Similarly, it was an administrator of the district of Commune d'Armes/Saint-Étienne who was responsible for the establishment of one at Saint-Paul-en-Jarez.[5] The clubs at Moingt and Sury were formed by decisions of their Municipalities, and at Saint-Martin-d'Estreaux the local revolutionary committee took the initiative.[6] There were few exceptions to this pattern: only those clubs founded before the date of Javogues's *arrêté*—Néronde, Saint-Haon-le-Châtel, and Saint-Just-en-Chevalet—appear to be undoubtedly spontaneous in origin; except for Usson, the same was probably true of those formed in places which were not *chefs-lieux* of cantons. However, it is difficult to say with any certainty whether those clubs which owed their existence to a Municipality or a committee were spontaneous in origin or not. For the most part, Municipalities and committees tended to contain the most politically conscious and active members of the community. They were the men who would form the core of the club. In effect, therefore, this

[1] A.C. Saint-Étienne, 1 D 10 (3), fol. 68, *arrêté* of 27 Sept.

[2] e.g. A.D.L., L 439, creation of the clubs of the canton of Saint-Jean-Soleymieux 'conformément à l'arrêté du Représentant du peuple'.

[3] A.D.L., L 416, fol. 1.

[4] A.D.L., L 327, fol. 5.

[5] Lefebvre, op. cit., p. 111.

[6] A.D.L., L 433, L 422, fol. 3, L 424, fol. 11.

type of foundation merely meant that the future leaders of the club were acting in the official capacity that they already had in order to give a more official basis to their new association.

In theory at least, the clubs brought the local terrorists together and excluded from their ranks all those who, by their words and deeds during the federalist crisis or during the early years of the Revolution, had shown themselves to be hostile to the new order. Most were purged of their unreliable elements, although, as we shall see, considerable reservations must be made as to the revolutionary commitment of those who remained.[1] Generally the purge was undertaken spontaneously by the club and usually followed the same pattern—a number of members of impeccable political antecedents were designated to verify the political virginity of the rest.[2] Apart from the *scrutin épuratoire*, a number of other checks existed to prevent the infiltration of undesirable elements. At Saint-Étienne and at Saint-Chamond new members were admitted only after their nomination by an established member had been publicly announced and their record discussed by the club. A majority vote of seven-eighths of those present was necessary for admission.[3] At Charlieu a *certificat de civisme* was obligatory for all postulants, and at Saint-Chamond for all those who had resided in the commune for less than a year.[4]

Although the president of the club at Saint-Chamond suggested in nivôse that, for the good of the Republic, the patriots of all these bodies should be as one,[5] the clubs made relatively little effort to rise above local preoccupations and form a network of affiliated societies throughout the department maintaining a regular correspondence with each other. Certainly, they occasionally exchanged letters with other clubs or sent *commissaires* to them. The one at Charlieu,

[1] e.g. Charlieu was purged twice (A.D.L., L 402 (18 brum.) and L 403 (27 niv.)); at Saint-Chamond the *scrutin* took four days, 16–19 Oct. (Lefebvre, op. cit., p. 36).

[2] Lefebvre, op. cit., p. 36, and A.D.L., L 416, fol. 14 (Régny, 10 niv.); only Saint-Étienne (A.N., loc. cit.), Saint-Germain-Laval (A.D.R., 42 L 157), and Roanne (A.D.L., L 81) appear to have been purged by outside agents.

[3] Galley, op. cit. i. 190; Lefebvre, op. cit., p. 33. Voting at Saint-Chamond was done with coloured and white dried peas.

[4] A.D.L., L 402 (18 brum.); Lefebvre, op. cit., p. 62.

[5] Lefebvre, op. cit., p. 114.

for instance, distributed copies of a speech on the *calotins* by one of its members to all the clubs of the district and in turn received a parcel of similar documents from Feurs.[1] Saint-Chamond, which showed itself to be the most advanced in this respect, established regular contact with neighbouring Commune d'Armes/Saint-Étienne and Valdorlay/Saint-Paul-en-Jarez in nivôse and made overtures to Commune-affranchie/Lyon at about the same time.[2] But, for the most part, the few links of affiliation that were established took place in the spring and summer of 1794.[3] It is evident, therefore, that the clubs of the department of the Loire were never likely to participate in the great regional movement of association in late 1793, which the government branded as a new federalism and rendered illegal by the law of 14 frimaire.[4]

Thus their activity was essentially local. They constituted a sort of clearing-house where local problems could be solved in the proper spirit of the *gouvernement révolutionnaire*, either directly by the immediate and collective action of the club, or indirectly by reference to the competent authority, whether regular or revolutionary, whether local, departmental, or national. They acted as a sort of forum, where a patriotic citizen could air his views on public affairs, however ridiculous they might be:

> un membre a dit que la Patrie ayant plus que jamais besoin de secours et d'hommes pour sa défense, il fallait à l'avenir s'opposer de tout son pouvoir à la fréquence des mariages et en interdire l'usage, alléguant pour toutes raisons que les garçons pour se soustraire à la réquisition s'empressaient trop de se marier. L'assemblée a éclaté de rire.[5]

[1] A.D.L., L 402 (29 brum.) and L 403 (30 niv.).

[2] Lefebvre, op. cit., pp. 115, 125.

[3] Saint-Chamond associated with Millery and Beaujeu in the Rhône in vent., with Feurs in prair., and with neighbouring Rive-de-Gier as late as mess. (Lefebvre, op. cit., pp. 159, 165, 212, 223); Régny associated with Lay at the end of prair. and with Perreux and Thizy (Rhône) at the end of mess., but the envoys sent to Charlieu for this purpose in therm. never made the journey (A.D.L., L 416, fols. 13, 17, 18); Charlieu associated with Mâcon (Saône-et-Loire) and Perreux in pluv., but neighbouring Roanne had to wait until germ. (A.D.L., L 403, 13 pluv. and 4 germ.).

[4] Only Saint-Chamond decided to send a delegate to a republican congress announced by Marseille, and this was never implemented, as far as can be seen (Lefebvre, op. cit., p. 16).

[5] Lefebvre, op. cit., p. 52.

To the club came all those who had complaints to make, as, for example, a citizen of Charlieu who protested that his wife had had her thumb cut off by a sword.[1] At the same time, they were the elementary channel through which knowledge of the objectives of the Terror was disseminated to the general public and through which the terrorists attempted to mobilize their fellow citizens in support of the *gouvernement révolutionnaire*.[2] Furthermore, they constituted a reservoir of patriots. It was to them that the authorities, both regular and revolutionary, applied for occasional *commissaires* at the local level, upon whom they could rely without knowing them personally. For example, in nivôse, the Department ordered each club to nominate four *commissaires* to enforce an *arrêté* prescribing a general inventory of grain.[3] The Districts of Roanne and Armeville/Saint-Étienne both handed over the actual establishment of these inventories to the clubs.[4]

These institutions also embodied the sum total of the knowledge of individual patriots about their fellow citizens, and therefore it was to them that the authorities applied for information of this kind. For example, the District of Boën consulted the clubs about the civic spirit of petitioners, while Javogues used the club at Saint-Chamond to get at the truth about the alleged federalist sympathies of Boiron, who had recently been admitted to the Convention as first *suppléant* for the Rhône-et-Loire.[5] Furthermore, their political purity and their detailed knowledge encouraged the authorities to consult them about the nomination of officials. Indeed, the law of 14 frimaire stipulated that the *Représentants en mission* should seek the advice of the clubs when purging the administrations. Although Javogues appointed the new administrations of the department and of the districts of Boën and Roanne without reference to the clubs, he did consult the one at Commune d'Armes/Saint-Étienne over the

[1] A.D.L., L 402 (20 brum.).

[2] All the clubs attempted to mobilize the population in support of the national war effort: for example, they opened a subscription list to equip a *cavalier jacobin* and another to provide a ship for the Mediterranean fleet; they sent shirts to the local regiment and bought flags (A.D.L., L 403 (10, 21 frim., 1, 5, 17, 19 niv.); Lefebvre, op. cit., pp. 30, 75, 120).

[3] A.D.L., L 18, fol. 137.

[4] A.D.L., L 403 (11 pluv.); L 123, fol. 345 (26 Oct.) and L 124, fol. 20 (21 pluv.).

[5] A.D.L., L 259, fol. 22; A.N., F7 4444, d. 5, p. 394.

renewal of the District and the Municipality of that town in brumaire,[1] and in nivôse the club approved his nominations to a few vacancies in that District.[2] Méaulle and Reverchon both consulted the clubs about the readjustments that they made to the administrations later in the Year II.[3] Similarly, the administrations themselves consulted the clubs on eventual replacements and on the nomination of minor officials. The District of Boën, for instance, handed over the nomination of the *agents du salpêtre* to the clubs.[4]

The clubs offered the patriots an opportunity for collective action in three spheres at a local level, all essential to the smooth working of the *gouvernement révolutionnaire*: firstly, the surveillance of suspects and the supervision of the local regular authorities; secondly, the civic education of the population; thirdly, the care for public welfare. Although Javogues was rather laconic on this subject in his *arrêté* (merely stating that the citizens should meet 'pour maintenir l'esprit public, lire les décrets de la Convention, s'éclairer mutuellement sur leurs droits et leurs devoirs'), Pignon, in his inaugural speech at the renewal of the clubs at Armeville/Saint-Étienne, was more expansive about their functions:

> Sentinelles sans cesse vigilantes, elles scrutent sans cesse la conduite des administrations gangrénées et perverses, elles surveillent les gens suspects, elles dénoncent les abus d'une arbitraire autorité, elles font exécuter les lois populaires que l'on jette dans l'oubli et elles ne cessent d'éclairer le peuple sur ses vrais intérêts et sur les pièges de ses ennemis qui veulent le rejeter dans les fers; elles sont, enfin, le foyer ardent, où le génie public vient sans cesse puiser une nouvelle chaleur et retrouve sans cesse une nouvelle énergie.[5]

In theory at least, their task in the sphere of surveillance was twofold. On the one hand, their vigilance was directed towards uncovering the hidden machinations of the

[1] A.N., AF II 114 (861) 15: all four *arrêtés* were signed at Commune d'Armes before Javogues had visited other parts of the department. Only the appointments for Commune d'Armes, therefore, can have been made in consultation with a club —and, indeed, this *arrêté* mentions the club's role in the decision specifically. He also consulted the club at Feurs over the nomination of a new mayor (A.D.R., 1 L 201).

[2] A.D.L., L 123, fol. 370.

[3] e.g. A.C., Montbrison, *reg. dél.*, 8 vent. (Méaulle); A.D.L., L 262, fol. 85 (Reverchon).

[4] A.D.L., L 260.

[5] A.N., W 408, d. 939.

counter-revolutionaries, which, through the daily contact of their members with the population as a whole, they were well placed to perceive. On the other, their attention was alerted to ensure that the civil administrations did not, either by malice or by ignorance, hinder the prompt execution of the decrees of the Convention and the *arrêtés* of the *Représentants en mission*, thus damaging the *gouvernement révolutionnaire*. Pignon, as we have seen, laid more stress upon this than on their other functions. Similarly, the Municipality of Moingt was moved to form a club above all else by the possibilities that it offered for the surveillance of suspects.[1]

In fact, however, the activity of the clubs in the Loire in relation to suspects appears to have been relatively unimportant, despite the character of the region as an area of intensive repression. Indeed, it was this character itself that limited their role, for the multiplicity of the organs of repression in the area largely catered for the suspects. Repression was primarily the business of the revolutionary committees and the *commissaires*, especially those of the *Représentant*. The clubs do not appear to have infringed in any significant manner upon the functions of other bodies in this field. They seem to have occupied a position in the background, concentrating on supplementing the efforts of others and on supplying information. They undertook tasks of a general nature, usually those requiring a considerable amount of time. For example, the club at Saint-Chamond checked the registers of the sections during the federalist crisis for suspect material, and it also read through the printed list of suspects and pointed out some omissions.[2] They also passed on such denunciations as were presented to them rather than directly to the revolutionary committees.[3] They supplied details about suspects wherever necessary. Plagnieu, administrator of the district of Boën, for instance, visited the clubs at Rambert-Loire/Saint-Rambert and Saint-Bonnet-la-Montagne/-le-Château specifically for that purpose, while the administration of this district wrote to all the clubs for the answer to the request of the *Commission Temporaire* for the names of the

[1] A.D.L., L 433, referring to the danger of rebellion by friends and relatives of arrested suspects.

[2] Lefebvre, op. cit., pp. 50, 51, 53.

[3] e.g. ibid., pp. 43, 66, 138, 180.

jurés d'accusation on the Rhône-et-Loire criminal tribunal during summer 1793.[1] Similarly, since the support of a club was an important guarantee, the clubs, solicited on all sides by suspects, exercised considerable influence upon the ultimate fate of arrested persons. Such power had to be used with discretion: at Saint-Chamond, the club agreed to intercede on behalf of young men involved in the federalist affair by error rather than wickedness, but the petition of one citizen on behalf of his brother was met with stony silence.[2] At Charlieu, *commissaires* from the club at Villefranche, seeking attestations in favour of Lapalus's victims, provoked a frankly hostile reaction.[3] On the other hand, the clubs had the duty of protecting patriots from slander, since to render a patriot suspect was a victory for the counter-revolution; thus, when a cabal of moderates denounced the revolutionary committee of Charlieu to the *Commission Temporaire* in pluviôse, the club sent out a whole series of testimonials and petitions and even nominated *commissaires* to follow one arrested patriot wheresoever he might be sent until his release was obtained.[4] Finally, the members of the clubs also had an individual role to play. For example, following troubles at the market, the mayor of Armeville/Saint-Étienne proposed that each member should help the police by dealing personally with troublemakers.[5] As for the members of the one at Saint-Chamond, they undertook to impose the tricolour cockade on the womenfolk and to keep a weather eye open for those who did not respect the *décadi*.[6] Nevertheless, the relative unobtrusiveness of their activity did not prevent the clubs from occasionally taking the initiative over matters of surveillance, if they felt that the circumstances demanded it: for instance, it was the *société populaire* that took charge of the inquiry into a religious demonstration in the parish church at Charlieu in early frimaire.[7]

As far as the supervision of the regular authorities was concerned, the clubs do not appear to have played the part of hostile vigilantes that Pignon assigned to them. This again

[1] A.D.L., L 378, fol. 12, L 441, fol. 4, L 259, fol. 22.
[2] Lefebvre, op. cit., pp. 101, 43.
[3] A.D.L., L 403 (6 pluv.).
[4] Ibid. (1, 11, 20 pluv.).
[5] A.C. Saint-Étienne, 1 D 10 (3), fol. 85.
[6] Lefebvre, op. cit., pp. 75, 114.
[7] A.D.L., L 402 (2 frim.).

was due, to a large degree, to the circumstances prevailing in the department at the time. At the beginning of the period under review, Javogues reformed all the major administrations with terrorist personnel of impeccable political virtue. As for the Municipalities of the smaller urban centres and the humbler officials, the organs of repression rapidly weeded out the suspects, and those who remained had either proved their patriotism during the federalist crisis or else were sufficiently responsive to the atmosphere to avoid reprehensible activity. It is true that the club at Charlieu harshly censured the Municipality there for its negligence in brumaire over the question of the indemnities due to the relatives of soldiers,[1] and the one at Saint-Chamond complained bitterly about the non-attendance of the Municipalities of La Valla and Saint-Jean-Bonnefonds at the *fête de Chalier*.[2] But by far the most normal relationship between the local regular authorities and the clubs was a state of cordial co-operation, in which the club sought to supplement the action of the Municipality, to bring to its notice matters that might have escaped its attention, and to stimulate its zeal over questions that it might have neglected.[3] Nevertheless, in the relationship between the Municipalities and the clubs, there was never any real doubt as to which was the more important partner. The president of the club of Saint-Chamond, who praised the vigilance of the Municipality and observed that 'pour entretenir la bonne intelligence, il fallait qu'à l'avenir la Société travaillât de concert avec la municipalité', happened to be also the mayor.[4] The club at Charlieu clearly manifested its primacy when, after censuring the Municipality, it requested Lapalus and Évrard, *commissaires* of the Committee of General Security, to inspect the registers and examine the conduct of that body.[5] Moreover, whenever a Municipality appeared incapable of dealing with the situation, as, for example, in the case of food

[1] A.D.L., L 402 (20 brum.). [2] Lefebvre, op. cit., p. 95 (13 frim.).

[3] e.g. the replacement of unworthy officers in the National Guard; the securing of the indemnity due to the wives of those who marched on Lyon; having the church bell rung on the eve of the *décadi*; the enforcement of market regulations; the confiscation of false grain declarations; the execution of the law on the draining of ponds; keeping the streets clear of ice, etc. (A.D.L., L 402, 403, *passim*, and Lefebvre, op. cit., *passim*).

[4] Lefebvre, op. cit., pp. 23, 76. [5] A.D.L., L 402 (20 brum.).

supplies, a club had no hesitation about bypassing it, either by appealing to higher authority or by acting on its own initiative. Similarly, the clubs tended to take command whenever the urgency of the situation demanded immediate action, as, for instance, when the one at Charlieu without reference to the Municipality ordered the destruction of all dogs with twenty-four hours on account of an epidemic of rabies.[1]

One of the most important functions of the clubs was to undertake the civic education of the community. Their task was to bring the citizens to a proper consciousness of their rights and duties. Such a programme had a triple objective. First, to enable the citizen to protect himself and also the community from the attacks of the malevolent, whose intentions he might not otherwise perceive. Second, to protect the Revolution from damage caused by the ignorance, the errors, or the indifference of the citizens. Third, to direct the activity of the people in the interests of the *gouvernement révolutionnaire* by explaining its nature and its aims. Javogues recognized this educative importance when he insisted that all the *commis de bureau* of the administration of the department should be required to attend the club regularly.[2]

The clubs acted as purveyors of precise information about political events and legislation. The revolutionary committee at Saint-Martin-d'Estreaux, for example, was moved to create a club because panics were being caused when citizens, in their ignorance, took as decrees motions that had been rejected as quite contrary to the principles of liberty.[3] At La Pacaudière, where people were always pleading ignorance of the law, the committee finally ordered the head of each family to attend the club every *décadi* at two o'clock when the laws would be read out and explained.[4] The newspapers were read aloud at every meeting of the club at Saint-Chamond, which also appointed a member to read out and expound the articles of the Constitution after an administrator from the Department had urged it to devote itself especially

[1] A.D.L., L 402 (15 brum.).

[2] A.D.L., L 18, fol. 32.

[3] A.D.L., L 424, fol. 11—the main road was, of course, a channel for false news as much as for accurate news.

[4] A.D.L., L 412, fol. 23.

to the study of this text and of the laws in general.[1] In addition to commentaries on legislation and on the news, frequent speeches stimulated the political consciousness and the civic zeal of the citizens—'un membre a parlé avec beaucoup de véhémence de la ferme et constante générosité des bons patriotes, des mauvaises intentions, des indignes procédés et des projets désastreux des rebelles'.[2] Moreover, the clubs enabled the more important terrorist personnel from the administrations of the districts or of the department to instruct the local militants on their duties and thus to mobilize them as intermediaries through which to galvanize the population into action. The *agent national* of the District of Boën wrote in his *compte décadaire* of the end of pluviôse:

> Je regarde comme une mesure très avantageuse et nécessaire, celle d'envoyer des bons sans-culottes visiter les sociétés populaires et y prêcher les vrais principes. Le peuple est susceptible de toutes sortes d'impressions; il faut saisir avec soin les moyens de lui en donner de bonnes. Il est avide des nouvelles, il faut profiter de cette disposition pour l'instruire.[3]

Almost all the administrators and other personalities, when on tours of inspection, made a point of visiting the clubs, where they delivered harangues.[4]

Beyond these purely didactic preoccupations, the clubs also turned their attention to forms of propaganda of a more general nature. They encouraged the singing of patriotic hymns and the recitation of texts such as the Declaration of the Rights of Man, especially by the young *citoyennes*, and gave a favourable audience to the efforts of local poets on republican themes, while the club at Saint-Chamond even created a separate organization for the young citizens.[5] They arranged impressive ceremonies to commemorate Lepeletier, Marat, and Chalier and to celebrate victories such as the capture of Toulon; they set up republican inscriptions and statues of liberty, they hung pictures of the republican martyrs in their

[1] Lefebvre, op. cit., p. 32 and *passim*; at Moingt, the Mun. undertook to furnish the club with the decrees and *arrêtés* that it received (A.D.L., L 433).

[2] Lefebvre, op. cit., p. 26.

[3] A.N., AF II 35 (287) 25.

[4] e.g. A.D.L., L 416, fol. 1; L 441, fol. 4.

[5] A.D.L., L 403 (11 niv.); Lefebvre, op. cit., pp. 68, 136; ibid., p. 16; ibid., p. 172 (26 vent.).

meeting-places, they planted Liberty Trees, they replaced the crosses on the steeples by pikes, they saw to the obliteration of remaining insignia of the seigneurial past and destroyed in solemn ceremony evidence of the inequality of the Ancien Régime.

Despite the reservations expressed by many individual members, the more important clubs exploited the field of civic education to campaign against the Church. The District of Armeville/Saint-Étienne informed the Convention in frimaire that 'les Sociétés populaires ont démasqué l'hypocrisie des apôtres de la Superstition, combattu leur erreur et dissipé les ténèbres mystérieuses dont ils s'enveloppaient'.[1] The celebrations organized by the clubs to commemorate the republican martyrs, for example, had a strong antichristian undertone. The club at Charlieu, which gave more unanimous support than most to dechristianization, demanded that a general assembly of the inhabitants be called to vote the dismissal of the curé and passed resolutions inviting the Municipalities of the canton to enforce the *repos décadaire* and to destroy all the *signes fanatiques* (wayside crosses, shrines, etc.).[2] Similarly, it was to the club that the parish priest of Saint-Chamond presented his resignation, at the end of brumaire, while, a month later, a motion that all those priests who had not resigned should be arrested was much applauded.[3] Saint-Chamond also demanded that pikes and liberty caps should be placed on the church steeples and on the crosses and decided that all those who did not celebrate the *décadi* should be considered suspect.[4]

A discussion of the work of the clubs in civic education also raises the question of the sort of audience they had. As far as the actual meetings were concerned, although only the members, selected for their political purity, had the right to participate in the debates, the more important clubs at least were also attended by a large crowd of non-members, usually predominantly women, upon whom the speeches and motions were designed to have a stimulating effect. The club at Saint-Chamond had to set up barriers to keep the crowd out of the precinct and also made several rules concerning the noise

1 A.D.L., L 156, fol. 91.
2 A.D.L., L 402 (29 brum.).
3 Lefebvre, op. cit., pp. 74, 107.
4 Ibid., pp. 96, 115.

made by children.[1] But basically, the meetings preached to those already converted in the sense that, except for poor people seeking warmth in midwinter, only those came who wanted to come. The revolutionary committee at La Pacaudière was conscious of this when it ordered a representative from each family to attend the meetings of the club.[2] In order to reach the rural population, the societies could send out individual members to act as 'apôtres civiques'. As far as one can see, only Saint-Chamond and Feurs organized such proselytism on a regular basis.[3] But it is more than likely that both the *commissaires* sent out on other missions and some individual members, whether rural members of the cantonal clubs or others travelling on private business, never missed an opportunity to preach the cause.[4]

In addition to surveillance and civic education, the clubs expended considerable energy in looking after the welfare of the community at large, although this assignment was never clearly expressed either in the governmental directives or in the statements of the more important militants about the functions of the clubs. They were always ready to spring to the defence of the reputation of the commune: for example, in nivôse the one at Saint-Chamond angrily denounced Dorfeuille, who had suggested in a newspaper article that religious fanaticism had held their town in thrall until his visit.[5] They also sought to foster institutions beneficial to the commune. The club at Saint-Chamond campaigned to retain the criminal tribunal, wrote to the Jacobins to gain support for the local hospital's petition to the Convention for a subsidy, and also debated at length the possibilities of establishing an arms industry in the town.[6] The clubs also strove to solve the small problems of detail in the smooth working of communal life. The one at Charlieu, for example, asked the Municipality to make sure that the streets were kept clear of ice and

[1] Lefebvre, op. cit., pp. 138 and 107, 138, 143. [2] Above, p. 111.

[3] A.D.L., L 156, fol. 101; A.D.R., 1 L 190.

[4] e.g. destruction of a wayside cross by two members from Saint-Chamond travelling on business (A.D.L., L 390, fol. 26).

[5] A.D.L., L 237; at the beginning of Oct. they sought to protect the town from the anger of the nation by sending an address to the Jacobins of Paris justifying the behaviour of the inhabitants during summer 1793 (Lefebvre, op. cit., p. 116).

[6] Lefebvre, op. cit., pp. 103, 117, 143. Javogues had established the tribunal at Saint-Chamond, but the decree creating the new department placed it at Feurs.

agitated for the establishment of a post-office, promulgating in the meantime a number of regulations concerning the person who went to collect the mail at Roanne.[1]

But the action of the clubs reached well beyond these matters of relatively minor importance. They appear to have undertaken a mission of maintaining social harmony within the community and of upholding social justice. The revolutionary committee at Saint-Martin-d'Estreaux expected that personal enmities and mean passions would wilt away in so respectable an institution, with the result that 'les hommes se verraient tous comme des hommes, s'estimeraient davantage et se traiteraient plus fraternellement'.[2] At Saint-Chamond, one orator 'déclame, gronde et tonne contre la gent aristocratique et fanatique . . . ajoutant que, si le sort de ces scélérats était à sa disposition, il le rendrait pire que celui des bêtes de somme et qu'il les exterminerait tous'. Instead of approving such an evidently patriotic intention, the president gave him a long lecture to bring him back to less austere projects, saying that he knew the speaker too well not to think that he would take real pleasure in sharing his loaf of bread with the most dangerous aristocrat or his own worst enemy if he saw either going hungry.[3] Moreover, victims of blatant social injustice could expect the clubs to come to their aid, as, for instance, in the case of a citizen of Saint-Chamond who had been evicted from his house by the former *seigneur*, because underneath it there was coal on which the *seigneur* had the monopoly.[4]

More particularly, the clubs were all constantly attentive to the material situation of the poorer sections of the community, whose circumstances deteriorated during winter 1793–4 owing to the industrial crisis.[5] The club at Saint-Chamond, for instance, declared categorically at the beginning of the period that its sole objective was the public weal and the relief of the unfortunate, while the revolutionary committee at Saint-Martin-d'Estreaux hoped that in the

[1] A.D.L., L 403 (17, 15 niv., 3 pluv.).
[2] A.D.L., L 424, fol. 11.
[3] Lefebvre, op. cit., p. 55.
[4] Ibid., p. 101.
[5] The amount of time spent by each club in this field depended, of course, upon the importance of the problem. Thus Saint-Chamond, a highly populated industrial centre, was considerably more preoccupied with it than Charlieu, a small market town.

club indigent citizens would be able to reveal their needs with dignity, so that those in easier circumstances might experience the real joys of sharing their comforts.[1] Although some individual cases came to the attention of the clubs, as, for example, the sad case of the *menuisier* Paran at Saint-Chamond, who was too old and too infirm to earn his living any more, the clubs usually expressed themselves in more general terms.[2] Saint-Chamond carried on a long campaign from the end of October to the middle of nivôse in order to obtain the indemnity due to the wives of those who had joined the republican army against Lyon, but it showed itself extremely reluctant to intervene in the actual sharing out of the sum in accordance with the individual circumstances of the beneficiaries.[3] Charlieu and Saint-Chamond had a *bureau de secours* and a *comité de bienfaisance* respectively and opened subscription lists for the poor, and both were prepared on occasion to give help in kind, witness, for instance, the suggestion at Saint-Chamond that the candles of the churches should be distributed to the poor instead of being left for the rats to eat.[4] In practice, however, except in the case of old people and the physically incapable, the clubs much preferred to exercise charity indirectly by procuring work for the destitute. Thus, for example, when the one at Régny decided to lend money to the poor, it was simply because, by buying the cotton, they would earn more than by doing piece-work, and the same society sent *commissaires* to Commune-affranchie/Lyon to buy the raw materials in the name of the club.[5] At Saint-Chamond, the Jacobins petitioned the Municipality to occupy the unemployed with repairing local roads, while the insistence with which they demanded the demolition of the castle would appear to have been inspired as much by a vision of a source of employment as by a hatred of the Ancien Régime.[6]

But it is the question of food supply that best illustrates all these various aspects of the activities of the clubs, for it touches upon all of them. And, indeed, it was to the problem

[1] Lefebvre, op. cit., p. 22; L 424, fol. 11.

[2] Lefebvre, op. cit., p. 128.

[3] Ibid., pp. 49, 68, 82, 85, 101, 107, 113, 120.

[4] Ibid., pp. 151 and 107; A.D.L., L 403 (10 frim., 19 and 22 niv.).

[5] A.D.L., L 416, fols. 1 and 3.

[6] Lefebvre, op. cit., pp. 106, 141.

of obtaining sufficient food for the community that the clubs devoted most time. Their action in this sphere consisted above all in supervising and supplementing the Municipalities. In the first instance, this involved merely such activities as passing on complaints, pointing out necessary measures, providing additional personnel, and collecting information. Thus, for example, the club at Saint-Chamond urged the Municipality to set up public weighing-machines, and in return responded to the Municipality's request for it to collect denunciations of offences against the *maximum*; and at Armeville/St.-Étienne, the club appointed *commissaires* to distribute potatoes at the market on behalf of the Municipality.[1] The clubs sought to attenuate the hardship caused by the shortage: 'Le président a proposé une recette pour faire une bonne soupe avec une livre de farine suffisante pour douze personnes. Sa proposition a été goûtée, mais pas encore la soupe.'[2] They were the places where individual citizens could come to make their suggestions, good or bad: 'Un orateur propose un moyen infaillible . . .'; 'Un autre membre a dit que, pour faire circuler et refluer les subsistances en tous genres et de première nécessité, il n'y avait pas de moyen plus prompt et plus sûr que. . . .'[3] But the urgency of the problem in most urban communes during the Year II soon led the local extra-ordinary bodies to take command. At Saint-Chamond, for instance, the club came to the forefront in late brumaire when, after the Municipality had been shown to be quite incapable of preventing the maltreatment of country women, it proceeded on its own initiative to post the National Guard at the market, to fix the opening time, and to appoint *commissaires de police*.[4] Once this point had been reached, the initiative lay largely in the hands of the extraordinary institutions. All the major decisions at the communal level emanated from them, and the fact that the urban

[1] Lefebvre, op. cit., pp. 89, 101; A.N., AF II 114 (860) 8. The club at Fontfort decided to send *commissaires* to all the communes of the canton to verify all inventories, to come to an agreement with the villages on their needs, and to take the rest (A.D.L., L 18).

[2] Lefebvre, op. cit., p. 98.

[3] A.D.L., L 403 (20 niv.); Lefebvre, op. cit., p. 75.

[4] Ibid., pp. 66, 77. The club at Charlieu took over in much the same way on 10 frim. (A.D.L., L 403).

centres were adequately supplied during the winter of the Year II, despite a constant state of alarm, was very largely due to the co-operation between the clubs and the revolutionary committees, whatever the contribution of the *Représentant en mission* and of the higher regular authorities may have been.

In the beginning, the clubs attempted to obtain supplies by persuasion. For example, members of the club at Charlieu visited neighbouring Vougy amid the celebrations for the planting of the Liberty Tree and, profiting from such a favourably patriotic atmosphere, invited the Municipality to send off some grain that very evening to Charlieu where the *sans-culottes* had been without for several days.[1] Later, the same club sent a proclamation to all the communes of the canton reassuring them about the general grain situation, but inviting them to bring butter and eggs and so forth to the market.[2] Attempts at persuasion were always short-lived, and the clubs turned to the administrations of the districts for permission to use force. The higher regular authorities invariably acquiesced, since they recognized the competence of the clubs in this field and indeed used them for such operations as the establishment of inventories.[3] Thus, the club at Charlieu blamed the shortage on the egoism and indifference of the neighbouring communes, especially Vougy which had failed to comply with any requisitions, and consequently demanded the right to use armed force.[4] In pluviôse, the District of Roanne authorized it to undertake a general inventory in the whole canton, to make house-to-house searches, to use force, and to confiscate false declarations.[5] This was, in effect, to hand over the responsibility for food supply at the cantonal level to the club of the *chef-lieu*. Earlier, this club had petitioned the District for a detachment of the *armée révolutionnaire* to enforce the threshing of grain, and the club at Saint-Chamond was using this weapon to conduct house-to-house searches at about the same time.[6]

[1] A.D.L., L 402 (13 brum.). [2] A.D.L., L 403 (22 pluv.).

[3] The clubs never took major coercive measures without the authorization of the higher regular administrations, which reveals the limits in practice to their revolutionary independence and authority. For a fuller discussion of the revolutionary functions of the regular authorities, see below, Ch. VIII.

[4] A.D.L., L 403 (5 niv.). [5] Ibid. (11 pluv.).

[6] A.D.L., L 402 (13 brum.); Lefebvre, op. cit., p. 56.

But the food shortage was due more to the general penury within the department than to the ill will of the rural population. Again, it was the clubs that took upon themselves the task of attempting to obtain additional supplies for their commune from outside the area and of protecting local interests in the distribution of supplies imported by the administrations of the districts. The club at Charlieu sent repeated petitions through *commissaires* to the Convention and to the *Comité des Subsistances* asking for help, others to the *Représentants en mission* at Ville-affranchie/Lyon and to Javogues requesting powers to buy grain in the neighbouring departments, and others to the District to get local requisitions in favour of Roanne changed to the benefit of Charlieu.[1] The club at Saint-Chamond also sent *commissaires* to Paris, and it was directly to the club that the *Représentant* Boiron, a citizen of the town, wrote with the news of his successful intervention on their behalf.[2] Noting that delivery was going to be made to the District, the club immediately sent *commissaires* to that administration to make sure that the town and its canton did indeed get all that it had been promised.[3]

The more articulate of the local militants were agreed upon the fundamental importance of the clubs. Plagnieu, administrator of the district of Boën, for example, termed them 'le palladium de notre Constitution', while Pignon considered them to be 'les colonnes les plus inébranlables de la République'.[4] It is, however, difficult to make generalizations about the action of the clubs in the department as a whole. Despite the lack of precise documentation, it is apparent that the effort made by individual clubs varied enormously and that many never succeeded in shaking off a persistent lethargy. Indeed, one can argue that the absence of documents is due as much to the inaction of the majority of clubs as to the vicissitudes of political events and of the passage of time. For instance, the clubs of the canton of (Saint-) Jean-Soleymieux were founded on 11 frimaire/1 December, but only two had actually begun to function

[1] A.D.L., L 403 (1, 20, 29 niv.; 6, 16, 17, 18, 24 pluv.).

[2] Lefebvre, op. cit., pp. 103, 128.

[3] Ibid., p. 131.

[4] A.D.L., L 378, fol. 12; A.N., W 408, d. 939 (inaugural speech at Saint-Étienne, 10 Oct. 1793).

before mid pluviôse.[1] At Régny the club manifestly made very little impression on the citizens, at least in its early days, since the meeting of 25 frimaire/15 December was attended by a great throng of people of all ages 'qui croyaient que c'était une assemblée de commune et que l'on s'assemblait pour d'autres motifs que ceux dont on s'entretient dans les sociétés populaires, la plus grande partie d'entr'eux ne connaissant pas ce que c'est que ces sociétés'.[2] Similarly, only the major clubs held enough meetings to be able to pursue a constructive action on anything other than the most elementary questions. Charlieu assembled every Monday, Wednesday, and Saturday and Saint-Chamond met regularly every two or three days, but (Saint-) Bonnet-la-Montagne/-le-Château and Régny confined themselves to two meetings in the *décade*, while Moingt met only on the *décadi*.[3] Some clubs appear to have had difficulty in accomplishing even the relatively simple task of civic instruction: at Ville-Fontfort/Saint-Galmier, for example, the remonstrances of one citizen on this subject were applauded by 'tout le societte criant at auote voj ce just nous avont etabli une cociette pour ce instruire attendut que nous avo paie pour la bonemant de novele ja me nous recevon rien a leurs le presidan il voule leve la ciance an disant cilance'.[4] Equally, the extent to which the clubs made any impact upon the rural population through their *commissaires* and *apôtres civiques* is questionable, especially in the mountains during the winter.

Moreover, the revolutionary purity of the majority of the clubs is highly debatable, despite the purges to which they submitted themselves. For the most part, they were far too large to represent simply an active minority of pure citizens—Saint-Chamond, 394 members; Marcellin-la-Plaine/Saint-Marcellin, 234 members; Montbrisé, 167 members; (Saint-) Bonnet-la-Montagne/-le-Château, 147 members; Chazelles-sur-l'Advieu, 109 members; Gumières, 94 members; Usson, 91 members; Régny, 65 members; Moingt, 63 members; Chazelles-sur-Commune-affranchie, 52 members knowing

[1] A.D.L., L 439, fol. 10.

[2] A.D.L., L 416, fol. 1.

[3] A.D.L., L 403 (7 frim.); Lefebvre, op. cit., *passim*; A.D.L., L 436, fol. 29, L 416, fol. 2, L 433.

[4] A.D.R., 42 L 180, d. Sarely. Read phonetically.

how to sign, etc.[1] In some of the smaller communities there cannot have been much difference between a club and the general assembly of the inhabitants. When the club at Fontfort/Saint-Galmier was purged by a group of zealots, its membership was reduced from over 200 to forty.[2] The club at Charlieu appears exceptionally active in support of the Terror: it took the initiative in getting rid of the curé, organized the recruiting of the *armée révolutionnaire* in the area, and sent *commissaires* 'chez tous les égoïstes, insouciants et modérés aristocrates et fanatiques' to levy subscriptions for the poor, for a *cavalier jacobin*, and for shirts for the troops.[3] What can have been the attitude of the club at (Saint-Symphorien-de-) Lay, which proposed as the new *juge de paix* the son of a former *secrétaire du roi*?[4] The club at Saint-Chamond showed itself to be much more reticent than that of Charlieu, despite the fact that the District of Armeville/Saint-Étienne considered it to be the purest in the area.[5] The political immaturity of some of its members is revealed by the regulation adopted at the end of brumaire forbidding applause until the president had given the lead in order to avoid further repetition of some embarrassing mistakes.[6] The campaign of dechristianization provoked enough reservations here for one *officier municipal* to think it necessary at the beginning of frimaire to make a speech aimed at calming the disquiet caused by the resignation of local priests.[7] Three weeks later, a spokesman for a group of members petitioned the club for the free exercise of their religion in a 'maison nationale' (i.e. church).[8] Indeed, dechristianization troubled an important group in a majority of the clubs. At Montbrisé, a motion to

[1] Lefebvre, op. cit., *passim*; A.D.L., L 440, L 434 (4), L 403, fol. 10, L 436, fol. 29, L 439; ibid., L 443, L 416, fol. 2, L 433; A.D.R., 42 L 40, d. Pupier. It is impossible to say whether this number actually attended the meetings: whereas Charlieu promptly struck off the list all those who failed to appear at three consecutive assemblies (L 403, 8 pluv.), at Régny it was suggested that fifteen constituted a quorum (L 416, fol. 2). Similarly, it is impossible to say whether the number of adherents increased or diminished in relation to the pre-Terror situation: Boën had sixty members at the end of 1792, which suggests that numbers tended to remain about the same (Bibl. Roanne, 3 L (1) 4).

[2] A.D.L., L 327, fol. 19, *agent national* of Dist. of Boën to *Repr.*, 29 flor.

[3] A.D.L., L 402 (29 brum.) and 403 (10 frim.).

[4] A.D.L., L 18, fol. 60.

[5] A.D.L., L 156, fol. 101, Dist. to C.P.S., 8 pluv.

[6] Lefebvre, op. cit., p. 76. [7] Ibid., p. 86. [8] Ibid., p. 104.

close the churches caused such a division of opinion that the Municipality and the revolutionary committee were obliged to publish a reassuring proclamation.[1] It seems likely that the religious demonstration at the club at Armeville/Saint-Étienne in frimaire, which was described as the work of women not belonging to the club, found sympathy with some sections of the club itself: the administration of the district was guarded in its comments on this society, merely remarking that it had incurred the hatred of the enemies of the People through the energy of some of its members.[2] Similar incidents over the religious question took place in the clubs of (Saint-) Bonnet-la-Montagne/-le-Château and Ville-Font-fort/Saint-Galmier, while the revolutionary committee at Montmarat/Saint-Just-en-Chevalet recorded disapprovingly the fact that the club sent *commissaires* to the Municipality to inquire 'qui, après avoir pris les croix, les avaient vendues à leur profit', and others to discuss with the Department the whole question of freedom of worship.[3]

It is extremely difficult to define exactly the role of the clubs. Since they never operated as a co-ordinated system across the department, the influence of each one was strictly limited to the immediate vicinity, and the energy displayed by each varied considerably. The activities of the more lively clubs were multifarious, but their total commitment to all the various aspects of the Terror remains doubtful. Ultimately, the intensity and the nature of the activities of a club depended upon the militancy of its members. It was, therefore, only in the more important revolutionary centres, where the most militant terrorists were to be found, that the clubs played a really effective role, although the lack of registers from Armeville/Saint-Étienne and Montbrisé/Montbrison prevents us from properly documenting this assertion. Thus they attained their fullest development only in those places where the exponents of the Terror were already most powerful, where the regeneration of the regular administrations was already most complete and the activities

[1] A.C. Montbrison, *reg. dél.*, no. 2, fol. 10.

[2] A.D.L., L 123, fol. 360, L 156, fol. 101.

[3] Richard Cobb, 'Un comité révolutionnaire du Forez: le comité de surveillance de Bonnet-la-Montagne (Loire)', *A.H.R.F.* 1957, p. 300; A.D.R., 42 L 180, d. Sarely; A.D.L., L 421, fol. 8.

of the other organs of the Terror were most effective. In the countryside and in the mountains, where religious fanaticism, ignorance of the laws, apathy, immobilism, and even open hostility flourished, i.e. precisely those abuses it was the clubs' mission to combat, they were of relatively late foundation and their activities were very limited.

Two lessons can be drawn from this conclusion. In the first place, the variety that we perceive in the militancy of the clubs was in part a cause and in part an illustration of the elementary fact that the Terror in the Loire was an urban, plain-based phenomenon, certainly not native to the countryside and affecting it only intermittently and feebly, especially in the mountains. The clubs in the mountains were largely stagnant or hostile to the principles of the Terror.[1] The clubs in the plain, confined to the *chefs-lieux* of cantons, were for the most part intent on imposing the interests of these towns, and especially of the urban consumer, on the surrounding countryside.[2] In the second place, this general conclusion reveals the real position of the clubs—by themselves, they could not be effective organs of the Terror; they were merely one element of a whole structure of terrorist institutions and only within the structure could they play an effective role.

Within this structure, however, the clubs occupied an important place. They were the organ through which the local militants acted collectively in the defence of the Revolution; with the revolutionary committees they were the basic component of the extra-ordinary institutions of the Terror. Dealing with every aspect of local life, their role was above all that of auxiliaries to all the other revolutionary or regular authorities which had more specific functions. They acted as a sort of catch-net at the lowest level for all matters that escaped the attention of more specialized

[1] Cf. Galley, op. cit. ii. 31, who, basing his conclusion on a register which has since disappeared, says of the club at Bourg-Argental: 'Rien de moins jacobin: cocarde jacobine, mais sentiments plus que modérés.'

[2] The club at Charlieu expressed this attitude in a particularly clear fashion, when it told the Mun. to deliver no grain to inhabitants of the neighbouring communes unless they presented a certificate from their Mun. dated from the previous day stating that they had no grain, had not harvested any, and were in possession of no *bon d'approvisionnement* (A.D.L., L 402, 10 frim.).

bodies. Moreover, they represented the basic link between the *gouvernement révolutionnaire* and the citizens. On the one hand, as far as the revolutionary and regular authorities were concerned, the clubs constituted one of the major channels through which instruction was diffused to, and pressure brought to bear on, the population at large. But on the other hand, they also represented the interests of the citizens *vis-à-vis* the authorities and were the channel through which the community could defend itself. The moderate club at Roanne was doing no more than this when it participated in the denunciations against Javogues and Lapalus. The clubs represented the people seeking, through the intermediary of the most politically conscious members of the community, to protect its interests and the Revolution, with which those interests were identified. In so far as the militants of the Year II accepted that the Terror was the best means of defending the Revolution, the clubs inevitably became agents of the Terror. It was this sentiment that the club at Charlieu was expressing when it declared that it was 'transportée de joie de la pétition faite à la Convention nationale par la société mère des Jacobins de Paris de mettre la Terreur à l'ordre du jour'.[1] But most clubs, exclusively preoccupied with local questions, tended to see the Revolution and the Terror only in the context of their particular community. They served the Terror only in so far as they felt that it served the interests of the community. Their support, therefore, was selective—whole-hearted where such matters as food supplies were concerned, but qualified in relation to religious and social problems.

[1] A.D.L., L 402 (29 brum.).

V

THE *COMITÉS DE SURVEILLANCE*

THE revolutionary committees were both the most widespread and the most indispensable of the extra-ordinary institutions of the Terror. Endowed with the right to arrest suspects, they were the corner-stone of the edifice of repression, while they also in practice exercised supervision over a large number of matters of public interest in communal affairs. Together with the clubs, they represented the permanence and the reality of the repressive and coercive aspects of the Terror at a local level.

At one time or another during 1793–4 there were at least ninety-two of these committees in existence in this department, which comprised 237 parishes.[1] Their geographical distribution was, however, most uneven: the district of Roanne contained fifty-eight, whereas the districts of Boën and Armeville/Saint-Étienne contained only fourteen and nineteen respectively. This proliferation in a predominantly rural district, where the authorities of the *chef-lieu* remained steadfastly moderate, is apparently a paradox when the other two districts, which were subjected to a much more intensive programme of Terror, were so thinly provided for. There is no simple explanation for this complex phenomenon. It certainly shows the importance of roads and rivers as vehicles for political impulses: of the committees set up in the district of Roanne before the federalist crisis, Saint-Martin-d'Estreaux, La Pacaudière, Roanne, Parigny, Saint-Germain-Laval, and Saint-Just-en-Chevalet were all on or

[1] Changes of membership are not counted as separate committees. We possess the complete registers from fourteen, the *reg. dél.* only from twenty-six, and the *reg. des dénonciations* only from another two. Although neither Roanne nor Armeville has left anything but incidental records, the committee at Montbrisé is fully documented, while there is a solid body of documents for secondary centres such as Charlieu, Saint-Chamond, Saint-Galmier, and Saint-Bonnet-la-Montagne. This last one has been the subject of an article: Richard Cobb, 'Un comité révolutionnaire du Forez: le comité de surveillance de Bonnet-la-Montagne (Loire)', *A.H.R.F.* 1957, pp. 296–315.

close to major highways, while Briennon, Vougy, and Villerest were all on or close to the river Loire, which carried considerable traffic. It also followed from the way in which the early committees were set up before the Terror, which gave the district of Roanne a head start. Lastly, it was a result of local pressures during the Terror: it was doubtless the proselytism of the energetic patriots of Charlieu that incited all the villages of that canton to form committees (except for Saint-Denis-de-Cabanne 'à cause du peu de population'),[1] while the activities of Lapalus, *commissaire* of the Committee of General Security in brumaire and frimaire, must have provided a powerful stimulus east of the Loire.

The spontaneous creations that appeared in quite a few towns throughout France after August 1792, and especially during the period of mounting tension in the early spring of 1793, found no echo in the Forez. The first revolutionary committees were formed as a direct response to the law of 21 March 1793. There were twenty-two in existence before September and the majority were founded during the month of May.[2] In most cases, these early creations can be attributed to definite factors. Apart from the geographical considerations, which have been mentioned, local political factors conditioned the appearance of these committees. Charlieu, Saint-Germain-Laval, and Saint-Étienne all had active Jacobin colonies, while the formation of village committees in the east of the district of Roanne was connected with the agitation in the Monts du Beaujolais during this period when the Jacobins, in a minority, saw these committees as a means of self-defence.[3] The committee at Chavanay was possibly set up under the influence of that militant Jacobin from Saint-Étienne, Pignon, who was courting the daughter of one of the local landowners.[4] Above all, however, it was the political circumstances of the early summer that dictated the peculiar distribution of these first committees—fifteen in the district of Roanne, seven in the district of Saint-Étienne, and none

[1] A.N., W 20, d. 1095, *certificat de civisme* for Alesmonière, 12 flor.

[2] See Map 6.

[3] Colin Lucas, 'La brève carrière du terroriste Jean-Marie Lapalus', *A.H.R.F.* 1968, pp. 497–8.

[4] A.N., W 408, d. 939, letters from Dorothée Jourdan to Pignon, Dec. 1792–Oct. 1793.

MAP 6. *Comités de Surveillance*

in that of Montbrison. The law of 21 March was properly promulgated only in the district of Roanne, whose central authorities always insisted on legality, to the detriment both of federalism and of the Terror. The administration of the district of Montbrison made no reference at all to the decree in its registers, and it did not include it among the revolutionary laws emphasized as being important in a circular sent out to the communes on 24 May.[1] When, on 26 May, the two sections of Montbrison each attempted to elect a committee, the moderate Municipality refused to proclaim the results on the grounds of irregularities and finally the District annulled the elections.[2] As far as the district of Saint-Étienne was concerned, the moderate administration of the district noted the reception of the law on 20 April, but does not seem to have done anything about it.[3] Revolutionary committees were formed in the four sections of Saint-Étienne during the first half of May, because the sections were dominated by the Jacobins of the clubs who saw the committees as a means of acting against the moderate Municipality.[4] The regular authorities' riposte took the same form with the *Comité central de Salut public du district de Saint-Étienne*.[5] But when this body attempted to persuade other communities to establish committees, there was no response, for it was evidently a political manœuvre which the Jacobins would not countenance and which left the uncommitted rural population indifferent.[6]

Like the clubs of the same period, the early committees do not appear to have been particularly active. The terms of the decree of 21 March did not give them much real scope and in most places the political threat was not sufficiently immediate

[1] A.D.L., L 335 *passim* and L 324, fol. 13; the Mun. of Moingt, for instance, received the decree of 30 Mar. interpreting that of 21 Mar., but not this latter (A.C. Moingt, *enregistrement des lois*).

[2] E. Brossard, *Notes sur l'histoire du département de la Loire*, ii. 80.

[3] A.D.L., L 169.

[4] Two sectional committees were in activity at Saint-Chamond in July when they were helping to run municipal affairs after the majority of the Mun. had fled (A.D.L., L 144). They were federalist, but since the Mun. had been Jacobin, it is possible that they had originally been formed before the crisis.

[5] Above, p. 41.

[6] Bibl. Saint-Étienne, MS. 310, notes by Pupil; A.D.R., 42 L 42, petition to Dist., 31 May, urging it to enforce the decree of 21 Mar. without delay, especially in the industrial villages round Saint-Étienne.

to warrant the sort of extension of their activities that was occurring in Paris.[1] At Saint-Étienne, where the situation might have given them some opportunities, they did not have the Municipality behind them, as did their counterparts in Lyon; moreover, the appearance of militant federalism so soon after the establishment of the sectional committees prevented them from ever really getting off the ground. Even Charlieu was not particularly assiduous in its activities until the end of the federalist period; indeed it ceased to function altogether between 20 June and 6 September, that is at the very time when the crisis was at its height.[2] The committee at Coutouvre appears to have been typical of the small rural ones at this time: elected on 12 May, it met once on 20 June to nominate its officers and then went into abeyance until 22 September.[3] Only the committees on the main Paris–Lyon road (Saint-Martin-d'Estreaux, La Pacaudière, and Parigny) seem to have been really active before the Terror, for their location brought them a good deal of business within the terms of the decree of 21 March.[4] But even they lapsed towards the end of the summer: Saint-Martin-d'Estreaux did not meet between 22 August and 21 October, La Pacaudière between 26 August and 11 brumaire/1 November, with a brief meeting on 10 October to elect a vice-president, and Parigny between 28 September and 20 frimaire/10 December.

As far as the committees of the Terror are concerned, twelve certainly, and four probably, were founded in

[1] J. B. Sirich, *The Revolutionary Committees in the Departments of France*, p. 37, makes the distinction between 'elected' committees, which rarely went beyond the routine functions laid down by the law, and the more active 'nominated' committees, which were set up by the *Repr. en mission* or higher authorities, who delegated to them their own vaguely defined powers of general security. The early committees of the Loire fall into the former category and clearly run true to type.

[2] A.D.L., L 399 (a), fols. 1–17.

[3] A.D.L., L 408; cf. L 407, Combre—first meeting 9 June, second meeting 3 Nov.; L 410, Montagny—elected 12 May, first meeting 3 Nov. It is not clear what happened at Saint-Just-en-Chevalet (elected 26 May), for the first three pages of the register have been torn out (L 421).

[4] A.D.L., L 424, 412, 417; e.g. La Pacaudière—orders to innkeepers to keep a register for travellers and to send it to the committee every day; several visits to the inns to see if this was being done properly; debates concerning the arrest of deserters. This collapse of committees during the summer of 1793 was a widespread phenomenon (Sirich, op. cit., p. 23).

September–October; frimaire saw the creation of sixteen committees with seven appearing for the first time during this month; four were formed in nivôse and two in pluviôse, while the first references to another five and thirteen also date from nivôse and pluviôse respectively, but in these latter cases they may well have been in existence before those dates. Only one was definitely set up after pluviôse, while the other six, whose activities have left traces only after pluviôse, may again have been in existence before that time. Thus, for the most part, these committees came into being during the months of September–frimaire, the most active period of formation being in frimaire. The development of the revolutionary committees in the Loire was, therefore, parallel to that of the clubs.

The events of the summer marked numbers of people as suspects and proved the reality of the machinations of the internal enemies of the Republic. Moreover, in September and October the possibility of counter-revolutionaries escaping from Lyon made the task of checking on strangers a real necessity. In principle, we might expect the expulsion of the federalist troops from the Forez during the first fortnight of September to stimulate the revolutionary committees to renewed activity and to provoke the creation of new ones. In fact, however, the immediate reaction was very uneven. In the districts of Roanne and Saint-Étienne, where the central authorities remained in office until late October, the patriots were as slow as they had been in the clubs. Charlieu, which met regularly from 6 September in order to receive denunciations, was the exception.[1] It was only in the district of Montbrison, where the central authority had collapsed, that there were any immediate developments. Between 11 and 19 September, Committees of Public Safety were formed at Saint-Bonnet-la-Montagne/-le-Château, Noirétable, Boën, Feurs, and Montbrison. The committee at Montbrison was founded by the *Représentants en mission* and was composed

[1] A.D.L., L 399 (a), fol. 17. Mably, the first to appear in the district of Roanne after the federalist crisis, was not formed until 29 Sept. (A.D.L., L 237); in the district of Saint-Étienne, it was not until 15 Oct. that a new committee was formed at Saint-Chamond, while the first reference to the new single committee at Saint-Étienne itself dates from 21 Oct. (G. Lefebvre, *Société républicaine*, p. 34; A.C. Saint-Étienne, 1 D 10 (3), fol. 74).

exclusively of Auvergnats.[1] Similarly, the committees at Noirétable and at Boën were formed by *commissaires* of the *Représentants*, but were composed of local men.[2] That at Saint-Bonnet-la-Montagne was created by the Municipality and contained equal numbers of men of the Forez and officers of the troops from the Auvergne.[3] Only the one at Feurs was both completely spontaneous and indigenous.[4]

Except for Montbrison's Committee of Public Safety, whose papers have survived, these committees are almost totally undocumented.[5] But this pattern tends to suggest that in the Loire the committees created immediately after the federalist crisis were much more a response to the absence of properly constituted regular authorities and to the technical problems arising out of the mobilization of forces against Lyon, than a response to the counter-revolution, and that they were much more administrative bodies than organs of combat against the internal enemies. Noirétable, Montbrison, and Saint-Bonnet were evidently created primarily to deal with the details of the passage and maintenance of the troops from the Puy-de-Dôme. The committee at Saint-Bonnet was never anything more than the executive of the Municipality, and the question of suspects never appears to have been raised.[6] The committee at Montbrison rapidly took over the administration of both the commune and the district, although its interest in most of the district was desultory, and the surveillance of suspects was never more than a part of the whole job of protecting and organizing the rear of the army besieging Lyon. The canton of Boën seems to have been entirely administered by its own Committee of Public Safety,[7] while it is more than possible that the

[1] A.D. P.-de-D., L 2781, 19 Sept.

[2] A.D.L., L 430 (1), fol. 1, 13 Sept.; A.D.L., L 429, 14 Sept. Founded probably by Dulac and Limet, *commissaires* of Couthon (A.D.R., 42 L 159).

[3] A.D.L., L 377, fol. 12, 11 Sept., 20 members.

[4] A.C. Feurs, *reg. dél.*, 19 Sept.; A.D. P.-de-D., L 2785.

[5] A.D. P.-de-D., L 2781–94.

[6] A.D.L., L 377, fol. 12: 'pour seconder la municipalité dans toutes ses dispositions et opérations . . . ils auront toutes facultés et pouvoirs pour l'exécution des délibérations . . . de la municipalité et pour transmettre tous rapports et observations aux autorités constituées de la ville'; A.D.L., L 378, fol. 6: all those in prison on 3 Oct. had been arrested by *commissaires* from the army.

[7] A.D.L., L 259, fol. 16, Dist. to rev. com. of Boën, 2 frim.

committees of both Boën and Feurs were above all manifestations of local particularism and were designed to protect local interests, especially over questions of food resources, against the raids of *commissaires* from the army, who could only aggravate the effects of the depredations wrought by the Lyon federalists.[1]

But these Committees of Public Safety of the district of Montbrison do not appear to have long outlived, at least in their primitive form, the circumstances that had given them birth. The one at Noirétable, for instance, apparently lapsed as early as 25 September.[2] The majority of the revolutionary committees of the period of the Terror were organized, either directly or indirectly, by higher authorities. At root, two impulses can be distinguished. On the one hand, Javogues's *arrêté* of 5 brumaire/26 October ordered the establishment of a revolutionary committee in the *chef-lieu* of each canton; on the other, on 7 brumaire/28 October, the newly formed administration of the department sent a circular to the Districts, for reprinting and distribution to the communes, reminding them of the laws of 21 and 29 March.[3] On 30 October, the District of Armeville/Saint-Étienne backed this up by ordering all Municipalities to conform without delay to the law of 21 March, while, two days previously, the Committee of Public Safety of Montbrisé/Montbrison had responded to the Department's circular by having large numbers of copies of the laws of 21 and 29 March printed for distribution.[4] Most of the new committees can be traced back to these directives in one way or another. The creation of some committees was more directly provoked by higher authorities than that of others. Thus, for example, Javogues

[1] e.g. A.D. P.-de-D., L 2785, letters from C.P.S. of Boën and of Feurs to that of Montbrison, 3 and 8 Oct.

[2] A.D.L., L 430 (1).

[3] A.N., AF II 114 (861) 15; A.D.L., L 18, fol. 10. The law of 29 Mar. ordered names of inmates to be displayed outside every house. The *arrêtés* of the Depart. and Javogues were complementary in the sense that whereas the law of 21 Mar. prescribed the formation of committees in each commune by general assemblies of the inhabitants, Javogues modified this by placing them in the *chefs-lieux* of cantons and prescribing the choice of members from the clubs.

[4] A.D.L., L 130, fol. 29; A.D. P.-de-D., L 2781, 28 Oct. The Dist. of Roanne doubtless considered that its communes were already sufficiently informed. Cf. also A.C. Chazelles-sur-Lyon, unclassified papers: Dist. of Boën to Mun., 7 frim., announcing Javogues's *arrêté* and ordering it to notify the clubs of the canton.

encouraged the club at Saint-Galmier to set one up when he passed through the town, and he presided over the meeting of the club at Feurs that chose the committee there; at Saint-Jean-Soleymieux, it was an administrator from the District who gathered the citizens of the canton together in order to elect their committee.[1] But even those committees whose establishment appears more spontaneous were nevertheless usually expressly motivated by some reference either to Javogues's *arrêté* or to that of the Department: for instance, the Municipality of Rambert-Loire/Saint-Rambert called a general assembly for the election of a committee by announcing Javogues's *arrêté* in the market and by displaying copies of it on the Liberty Tree.[2] This seems to be true also of the less carefully supervised institutions in the district of Roanne.[3] Similarly, the original committees set up in the second half of October by the clubs at Saint-Chamond and Montbrisé were quickly modified by these clubs in order to conform with Javogues's *arrêté*, and, in the case of Montbrisé, the list was submitted to the *Représentant* for ratification.[4]

Moreover, the regular administrations exercised a strict control over the composition of the committees. Javogues's *arrêté* made no allusion to the relations between the committees and the regular authorities, but the Department's arrangements for its implementation stipulated that the Districts were to appoint the members from lists of candidates drawn up by the clubs.[5] In practice the District of Roanne merely ratified the choice made by the clubs, whereas the District of Boën chose the twelve men directly from the membership lists of the clubs, while the District of Armeville chose from thirty candidates presented by the clubs and also

[1] A.D.L., L 79, fol. 9; L 432, 12 brum.; L 381, fol. 53. Note that Javogues did not appoint the committees of the three *chefs-lieux* of districts when he renewed the authorities there at the end of Oct.

[2] A.D.L., L 441, fol. 1, 1 frim. (*arrêté* received on 29 brum.).

[3] e.g. Perreux (A.D.L., L 413), Néronde (L 411, fol. 3), Saint-Polgues (L 426), Villemontais (L suppl. 565).

[4] Saint-Chamond: A.D.L., L 390, fol. 4 (27 Oct.); Montbrisé: L 434 (1), fols. 1, 2. At Montbrisé the original committee had comprised sixteen members and was probably reformed because the *arrêté* prescribed twelve.

[5] A.D.L., L 18, fol. 19. In the middle of frim., the Depart. sent out *commissaires* to see if the committees had been re-established by the Dists. in conformity to this *arrêté* (L 18, fol. 81).

drew up a list of *suppléants*.[1] Similarly, when, as from pluviôse, many members began to resign because of the incompatibility of their various posts or of family ties one with another, it was again the Districts that appointed their successors,[2] while in cases where committees were proved to have made improper use of their powers, these same administrations saw to their renewal.[3] At the same time, both the District of Boën and that of Armeville pursued a policy of making the subordination of the committees to themselves a uniform reality. The policy became distinct from the beginning of frimaire, but as early as 30 October the District of Armeville made it clear that the committees were answerable to it for any infringement of the law in their activities.[4] On 12 frimaire/2 December, the powerful committee at Montbrisé complained to Javogues, then in the Saône-et-Loire,

> que le district séant à Boën méconnaît son institution et ne veut point correspondre ni communiquer avec ce dit comité sous prétexte d'illégation [*sic*], que cependant sa formation eut lieu avant l'arrêté du département à cet égard et que ce serait donner par là une rétroactivité à ses opérations permanentes.[5]

In this case, the regular administration won a tactical victory by compromising to the extent of renominating officially the same members.[6] But many of the smaller of the more spontaneous committees were also of faulty composition and they were not able to offer any resistance to a reform by the District. In many cases, the administrations seem to have used the excuse that the committee was not composed of members taken from the whole canton. The District of Armeville, for instance, claimed that since Javogues had ordered the establishment of committees composed of good republicans from the whole canton, 'il résulte donc de l'arrêté du citoyen

[1] Dist. of Roanne: e.g. A.D.L., L 176, fols. 57, 84, Perreux and Ambierle; Dist. of Boën: e.g. L 259, fols. 31, 80, Chazelles and Moingt; Dist. of Armeville: e.g. L 393, fol. 1, Saint-Genest-Malifaux, and L 156, fol. 113, letter to Mun. of Pélussin, 23 vent.

[2] e.g. A.D.L., L 261, fol. 13, Saint-Rambert, and L 260, 12 germ., Sury.

[3] A.D.L., L 18, fol. 74, *arrêté* of Depart., 14 frim., concerning the renewal of the committee at Roanne.

[4] A.D.L., L 130, fol. 28.

[5] A.D.L., L 434 (1), fol. 21.

[6] Ibid., fol. 34, 28 frim. The committee at Armeville was similarly renewed on 9 frim. (A.D.L., L 156, fol. 89).

Javogues que l'administration était autorisée à recréer tous les comités pour les organiser d'après ce nouveau mode'.[1] In fact, neither Javogues nor the Department ever specifically stated that this should be the case, but merely said that they should be chosen from the clubs set up by all the inhabitants of the canton. Even such committees as the one at Feurs, which had been appointed in the presence of Javogues himself, and the one at Saint-Chamond, which had been modified by the club in response to the *arrêté* of 5 brumaire/ 26 October, were renewed in this way.[2]

Thus, in the districts of Boën and Armeville at least, the committees were clearly hierarchically subordinated to the Districts even before the law of 14 frimaire/4 December. This situation should be contrasted with that in the department of the Landes, where a long struggle by the Department for control over the revolutionary committee at Dax was resolved in favour of the committee by the provisions of the law of 14 frimaire.[3] In the Loire this law only ratified an existing state of affairs when it conferred on the Districts the power of 'la surveillance de l'exécution des lois révolutionnaires et des mesures de gouvernement, de sûreté générale et de salut public', and to the revolutionary committees and Municipalities their application. Henceforth, the Districts continued to intervene, going so far as to reverse arrest warrants and decisions made by the committees.[4] Similarly, from the beginning the Department and the Districts of Boën and Armeville used the committees not only to implement purely repressive measures but also to supervise the execution of their administrative *arrêtés*. The District of Armeville, for instance, invariably ordered the committees to be present at all *levées de scellés* and sales of sequestrated goods.[5] In many cases, the clubs and the committees were

[1] A.N., F[1b] II Loire 7, d. Bourg-Argental, Dist. to the *Commission des administrations civiles* . . ., 15 mess.

[2] A.D.L., L 261, fol. 6, 25 niv., and L 390, fol. 5, 28 frim.

[3] A. Richard, 'Le comité de surveillance et les suspects de Dax', *A.H.R.F.* 1930, pp. 27–30. In the Loire, it was unthinkable that a committee should have as much power as that of Nancy, which the *Repr. en mission* themselves authorized to reform the administration of the department (J. Godechot, 'Le comité de surveillance révolutionnaire de Nancy', *R.f.* 1927, p. 256).

[4] e.g. A.D.L., L 261, fol. 11, 3 pluv., and L 260, 12 germ.

[5] A.D.L., L 130 *passim*. Cf. Dist. of Boën, L 259, fol. 58.

specifically associated in this capacity, as, for example, when the Department ordered them both to enforce its *arrêté* concerning the requisition of all miners supplying the arms industry.[1]

In the district of Roanne, however, the situation of the committees was somewhat different. Here, beyond exercising a general control over appointments, the District did not intervene at all. Indeed, its moderatism made it fundamentally suspicious of such bodies and its contacts with them were minimal. When, on 12 September, it took measures to ensure that the rebels did not take refuge in the area under its jurisdiction, it made no mention at all of the revolutionary committees; it was the Municipalities and the *juges de paix* who were competent in the matter: 'invitons en outre tous les bons citoyens à surveiller les malveillants, donner d'activité aux insouciants et réprimer tous perturbateurs du repos public.'[2] Even as late as 16 prairial/4 June and in an *arrêté* concerning food hoarding, which was a matter in which the committees were especially competent, although the Municipalities were told to denounce offenders to the committees, it was the ordinary and not the extra-ordinary authority that was specifically entrusted with the enforcement of the economic regulations.[3] Thus, in this area, the committees preserved a greater independence and a greater spontaneity in their action, while, with the exception of Roanne itself, their membership remained on the whole much more static than those of the other two districts. One consequence of this situation was, of course, that the authorities tended to be unaware of the existence of the smaller ones. Even the committee at Saint-Martin-d'Estreaux, despite its geographical position, complained, at the beginning of frimaire, that it seemed to be totally unknown since the *commissaires* of the various higher authorities always went to the Municipality.[4]

[1] A.D.L., L 18, fol. 98, 29 frim. Cf. Dist. of Boën, L 259, fols. 41, 60.

[2] A.D.L., L 176, fol. 8.

[3] A.D.L., L 176, fol. 191. Note that, in pluv., the Dist. of Boën asked the committees to supply information about the purge of regular and extra-ordinary authorities that had been requested by the *Comm. Temp.*, whereas the Dist. of Roanne asked the Muns. (A.D.L., L 328, fol. 1, and L 237).

[4] A.D.L., L 424, fol. 14, 4 frim.

As with the clubs, Javogues imposed a cantonal pattern on the committees.[1] Only Belmont (district of Roanne) and Maclas (district of Armeville) failed to comply. There was nothing in his *arrêté* to prohibit the formation of committees elsewhere, but the Districts of Boën and Armeville did not encourage exceptions to the rule. The creation of a committee at Valbenoîte was doubtless justified by the large peripheral population round the *chef-lieu*, while the committee at Malleval was probably unknown to the District and was perhaps formed in connection with the struggle between the mayor of (Saint-Pierre-de-)Bœuf and the *juge de paix* of the canton.[2] Cervières and Noirétable naturally both set up committees as part of their quarrel over the siting of the *chef-lieu* of the canton, but, significantly enough, decisions by the Department and the District of Boën between brumaire and nivôse established the *chef-lieu* at Cervières and expressly dissolved the committee at Noirétable for this reason.[3] The cantonal nature of the committees was further emphasized in the districts of Boën and Armeville by their composition, for, as we have seen, the administrations of these areas insisted that the members should come from all parts of the canton. As far as the district of Roanne was concerned, although the multitude of small committees in the cantons obviously diminished the practical necessity for such a procedure, and although some of the older committees were exclusively composed of inhabitants of the *chef-lieu*,[4] nevertheless several of those set up in the *chefs-lieux* of cantons during the Terror contained representatives from the whole area.[5] Moreover, in practice, the cantonal committees exercised their authority and action throughout the canton whenever

[1] The most normal pattern adopted by the *Repr.* seems to have been the dist. committee: e.g. Roux-Fazillac in the Charente or Lacoste and Peyraud in the north-eastern departments (Sirich, op. cit., pp. 56, 61). However, Ysabeau seems to have encouraged the cantonal pattern in the Gironde, and Borie used it in the Gard (ibid., pp. 55, 127). It was not until 7 vent. that Fouché and Méaulle adopted it for the dist. of the Campagne de Cne-aff. by suppressing all the committees except those in the cantonal *chefs-lieux* (Bibl. Lyon, 111 107).

[2] For the struggle at Bœuf, see A.D.L., L 355, *reg. des dénonciations*.

[3] A.D.L., L 18, fol. 44, and L 259, fols. 24, 59.

[4] e.g. Charlieu, Saint-Germain-Laval, Saint-Just-en-Chevalet.

[5] e.g. Saint-Symphorien-de-Lay, Perreux, Villemontais, Néronde, Parigny (renewal).

they were of a mind so to do. The activity of the committee at Saint-Genest-Malifaux, for instance, consisted primarily in watching over the Municipalities of its canton; the one at Bonnet-la-Montagne issued warrants for the arrest of inhabitants of the whole area, while the members of the one at Saint-Marcellin/Marcellin-la-Plaine claimed later to have constantly travelled round their canton.[1] The same was largely true of the district of Roanne, although here the existence of village committees tended to complicate matters: for example, as late as germinal, the committee at Montmarat/Saint-Just-en-Chevalet complained that the Municipalities were unwilling to recognize its right of supervision over the whole canton.[2] For the most part, however, the committees of the *chefs-lieux* seem to have occupied a position of superiority *vis-à-vis* their lesser colleagues within the canton: thus, for instance, the one at Charlieu upbraided the other committees of the canton for their passivity, while, as was also the case at Bel-Air/Saint-Haon-le-Châtel, it frequently issued warrants for the arrest of inhabitants of villages where there was a revolutionary committee.[3]

At the local level the committees were naturally closely identified with the clubs. Some stressed this connection in their title: 'le comité de surveillance de la société populaire' of Roanne, for instance.[4] The committee at Néronde used the seal of the club for its business, while the one at Montbrisé, as did doubtless many others, used the club's meeting-place.[5] Indeed, in a sense, the committees were emanations of the clubs. In the first place, their importance obviously made it imperative that their power should remain in trustworthy hands, and it was inevitable that the members should come from the clubs, which alone, ostensibly at least, could guarantee their impeccable character in this difficult period. This was already the case before Javogues officially

[1] A.D.L., L 393 *passim*, L 436 *passim*, L 440, petition to Dist., 22 therm.

[2] A.D.L., L 421, fol. 23. Cf. refusal by committee of Saint-Victor to co-operate with that of Régny (A.D.L., L 414, fol. 6).

[3] A.D.L., L 399 (1), 1 pluv. and *passim*; note especially the arrest of the president of the rev. com. at Vougy, 2 niv., L 419 *passim*. Committees would not in general issue arrest warrants against inhabitants of another canton, but would write to the committee or to the Dist.

[4] A.D.L., L suppl. 377, letter to Dist., 1 brum.

[5] A.D.L., L 411, fol. 3; A.D.R., 42 L 157, letter to rev. trib., 30 brum.

prescribed it in his *arrêté* of 5 brumaire/26 October; the clubs at Roanne, Saint-Chamond, and Montbrison had all set up committees to receive denunciations.[1] In many cases, the members tended to be the most influential figures in the club, the arch-priests of this local tabernacle of patriotism. The president of the committee at Néronde was also the president of the club; at Charlieu, it was the committee, together with the Municipality, that had prompted the club back into activity; at Bonnet-la-Montagne and at Fontfort/Saint-Galmier, the committees comprised the pure minority of the clubs, the mass of whose members were moderate.[2] In the second place, the two bodies were complementary in that, although the club was the watch-dog of the community, it was the committee, with its powers of search and arrest, which had the means of making the vigilance of the patriots an effective element in the regulation of the internal order of the Republic. In practice, the preoccupations of both the committees and the clubs were very much the same, whether it be in the search for suspects or in the defence of local interests, particularly over food questions; but, whereas the club could only denounce, exhort, and intimidate, the committee could act in a much more concrete manner. Although Montbrisé is an important exception since there appears to have been practically no formal contact between the two here, it was usual for the committees and the clubs to work in concert over most questions.[3] At Néronde, for instance, the committee employed members of the club for domiciliary visits, while, whenever the club sent out *commissaires*, one of them was nearly always a member of the revolutionary committee; at Firminy, the committee asked the club for information about all the people under arrest and consulted it on the best way to avoid gatherings on Sundays, while the club, after debating on the dangers of abandoned

[1] Bibl. Roanne, 3 L (1) 19, 11 Sept. (probably parallel with the original rev. com.); Lefebvre, op. cit., p. 34, 15 Oct., a committee of seven; A.D.L., L 434 (1), fol. 2, Oct., a committee of sixteen.

[2] A.D.L., L 411, fol. 1; L 399 (1), fol. 25; Cobb, art. cit., p. 298; A.D.L., L 327, fol. 19, *agent national* of Dist. of Boën to *Repr.*, 29 flor. Cf. even Saint-Chamond, where, on 16 frim., the club sent *commissaires* to Cne-aff. in order to plead for citizens who had taken arms for Lyon, and, on the next day, the rev. com. protested against this illegal act (A.D.L., L 390, fol. 3).

[3] A.D.L., L 434 (1) *passim*.

mine-shafts, turned to the committee to see that they were filled in; at (Saint-Pierre-de-)Bœuf the club forwarded all the denunciations that it gathered to the committee and at Valdorlay/Saint-Paul-en-Jarez the committee decided that it would deliver *certificats de civisme* only to members of the club.[1] The committees and the clubs enjoyed parity of status. Only in rare instances did a club make a decision that was binding on the committee or vice versa:[2] normally they merely issued requests to each other. Certainly, a committee would arrest members of a club for suspect activity in the club if the occasion warranted it, as was the case at Bonnet-la-Montagne where *commissaires* from the Department and the District were opposed over the religious issue in pluviôse; on the other hand, at Bel-Air/Saint-Haon-le-Châtel the club regularly renewed the members of the committee *ex officio*, although when the club at Commune d'Armes/Saint-Étienne did the same thing in germinal, the *Représentants en mission* annulled it as being contrary to the principles of liberty.[3] On the whole, however, there was an identity of membership and of interest between the two and they tended to follow common policies: this was particularly evident in the case of Roanne, where both bodies were unanimous in their attacks on Lapalus and Javogues.[4]

Legally, the revolutionary committees and the Municipalities were supposed to be very much on equal terms. The law of 14 frimaire/4 December gave them parity of status for the application of revolutionary laws, and decrees on 30 frimaire/20 December and 18 nivôse/7 January sought to emphasize the collaboration that should characterize the relationship between the two. In practice, however, the Municipalities tended to find themselves subordinated to the committees in most questions.[5] On the one hand, this was largely because

[1] A.D.L., L 411 *passim*, L 385 *passim*, L 395 *passim*, L 146, 11 pluv.

[2] e.g. Lefebvre, op. cit., p. 121: decision by the club at Saint-Chamond, 11 niv., that a member of the committee shall visit the inns every night to check passports.

[3] Cobb, art. cit., pp. 299 ff.; A.D.L., L 419 *passim*, L 124, fol. 136.

[4] *Mémoire adressé au Comité de Sûreté générale de la Convention nationale le 9 nivôse dernier . . .*

[5] This was nearly always the case: note how quickly even a pre-Terror committee like the departmental rev. com. of the Loire-et-Cher asserted its control over the Muns. (H. Calvet, 'Les rapports du Comité de surveillance et les autorités constituées du département de Loire-et-Cher', *A.H.R.F.* 1928, p. 433).

the interests of the committees extended beyond 'la police de sûreté générale' to a great many sectors of the business of communal administration. But it was also because the coercive powers that the revolutionary committees possessed, and also, in many cases, the greater political commitment of their members, led them on from supplementing to directing the efforts of Municipalities, which had neither the weapons nor often the conviction to fulfil all the obligations of local government in this period.[1] Roche-libre/Saint-Polgues and Jars-la-Montagne/Saint-Martin-d'Estreaux, where the committees were reformed by the Municipalities on grounds of irregular composition, were unique cases.[2] It is significant that both communes lay in the district of Roanne, where the administration displayed such a total lack of interest in the committees, and in both cases it was the committee itself that noted its illegality and turned to the Municipality for help; Roche-libre even prescribed the manner of its replacement. Much more typical of the relationship between the two was La Pacaudière, where, in early frimaire, the committee, considering the slowness with which laws were being applied, organized the detailed procedure of regular meetings of the Municipality, with which it was obliged to comply under penalty of being declared suspect.[3] Throughout nivôse and pluviôse, the committee at Saint-Genest-Malifaux maintained a running war with the Municipalities of the canton and particularly with that of the *chef-lieu*, frequently ordering them to come to the committee to render an account of themselves and to receive directives.[4] The committee at Bourg-Argental quarrelled venomously with its Municipality, arresting three members, including the *agent national*, in pluviôse: tension reached such a pitch that the District was obliged to intervene and finally reformed the committee:

nous sommes bien étonnés de l'irrégularité de votre conduite et du scandale que vous causez à tous ceux qui sont instruits de votre

[1] Sirich, op. cit., pp. 144–7, emphasizes that the *agents nationaux* and the Muns. voluntarily handed over a good deal of business to the committees, but, in the Loire, the initiative seems to have come very largely from the committees.

[2] A.D.L., L 426, 21 and 24 pluv., L 425, 5 germ.

[3] A.D.L., L 412, fol. 12, 5 frim. Cf. A.D.L., L 393, 9 pluv., the committee at Saint-Genest-Malifaux sends instructions to the Muns. on how to hold their meetings and to keep their registers.

[4] A.D.L., L 393 *passim*.

désunion; que voulez-vous que l'on pense d'un comité qui ne met aucune harmonie entre les corps constitués et qui [sont] continuellement opposés les uns aux autres. . .?[1]

Similarly, the committee at Cervières arrested the whole Municipality of (Saint-) Julien-la-Vêtre in pluviôse for failing to seize a suspect, and here again the District had to intervene to annul the order.[2] Bourg-Argental and Cervières were, however, extreme examples and illegal in any case, for, as the District of Boën said, the law of 14 frimaire 'ne donne aucun droit sur les corps constitués aux comités de surveillance'.[3] For the most part, relations between committees and Municipalities displayed that degree of harmony advocated by the District of Armeville and were very similar to those between the clubs and the Municipalities. In general, the committees acted as overseers, calling the attention of the Municipality to some matters, stimulating its zeal over others, and providing information and advice.[4] There was naturally a great deal of variation in this from place to place. At Montbrisé the committee ignored the Municipality almost totally, but the committees at Saint-Martin-d'Estreaux and Valdorlay/Saint-Paul-en-Jarez did most of their work through it, inviting it to act on each question.[5] At Marcellin-la-Plaine/Saint-Marcellin and at Bonnet-la-Montagne collaboration was particularly close, while at Rambert-Loire/Saint-Rambert and Sury the arrest warrants issued by the committees were almost exclusively based on information supplied by representatives sent to them by the Municipalities of these two cantons.[6]

It is thus clear that the revolutionary committees were from the outset part of a definite structure of authorities. But the degree to which they contributed to the efficient functioning of that structure throughout the department as a whole is debatable. Throughout the period under review, and even after the law of 14 frimaire/4 December had entrusted them

[1] A.D.L., L 156, fol. 105, Dist. to rev. com., 23 pluv.; the *agent national* 'a fait tout son possible pour avilir la surveillance et l'autorité révolutionnaire . . . il s'est torché le derrière en assemblée des réquisitions faites aux termes de la loi par le comité révolutionnaire' (A.D.R., 42 L 187, d. Robert).

[2] A.D.L., L 261, fol. 23, 17 pluv.

[3] A.D.L., L 261, fol. 23.

[4] Good examples are Rive-de-Gier and Saint-Chamond (A.D.L., L 389 and 390 *passim*).

[5] A.D.L., L 434, L 424, L 384 *passim*.

[6] A.D.L., L 382 *passim*; Cobb, art. cit.; A.D.L., L 441 and 442 *passim*.

with the application of the revolutionary laws, most of the committees remained unacquainted with those laws and often unsure of their own functions.[1] The committee at La Pacaudière, very conscious of the habitual ignorance of certain countryfolk, always insisted with justification that it was only by making the people aware of the laws that one could ensure that the guilty alone were brought to punishment; but it was more important that the committees should themselves know the laws.[2] As late as 9 pluviôse/28 January, the committee at Charlieu, certainly the most lively of the whole district of Roanne, complained that it was not receiving the laws and the *arrêtés* of the proconsuls—'cependant nous sommes tenus de veiller à leur exécution'.[3] At the beginning of frimaire, Saint-Martin-d'Estreaux still did not possess even the decrees concerning its own functions.[4] Within the department there was no automatic process for informing the committees. Some worked by hearsay, others wrote to their colleagues at the *chef-lieu* of the district who they supposed were more experienced, and there were others who requested the District or the Municipality for the loan of laws.[5] But the regular administrations do not appear to have been particularly eager to respond to the complaints of the committees. Valdorlay/Saint-Paul-en-Jarez spent nearly a month pestering the District of Armeville for decrees and finally, on 11 pluviôse/30 January, decided to write to the Committee of General Security.[6] Personal contacts appear to have been hardly more successful: members of the committee at Rambert-Loire/Saint-Rambert travelled to the Department, but it was not until 2 pluviôse/21 January that this committee officially received the decree of 27 vendémiaire/18 October obliging it to inform suspects of the reasons for their arrest.[7] Even the

[1] This was a universal problem (Sirich, op. cit., pp. 62–3). Even the Minister of the Interior's circular of the end of September saying that he would send all relevant decrees directly to the committees was not received at Régny until the beginning of vent. (A.D.L., L 413, 3 vent.)

[2] A.D.L., L 412, fol. 22.

[3] A.D.L., L 399, fol. 23.

[4] A.D.L., L 424, fol. 14.

[5] e.g. A.D.L., L 424, 18 frim.: the president of the committee at Saint-Martin-d'Estreaux says that 'il a lu dans les papiers publics que la Convention nationale . . .'; L 393, fol. 2, Saint-Genest-Malifaux to 'le comité central de Commune d'Armes', 4 niv.: 'point central, guidez la marche de vos rayons'; L 411, fol. 4, Néronde to Mun.

[6] A.D.L., L 394, fols. 19 ff.

[7] A.D.L., L 441, fols. 4, 18.

more important of these bodies laboured under the same disadvantages. As late as the end of pluviôse, the District of Commune d'Armes found it necessary to inform the committee at Rive-de-Gier that it did not need permission to search a house; throughout brumaire and frimaire, the committee at Montbrisé repeatedly solicited the Department and the revolutionary tribunal at Feurs for advice and guidance.[1] Moreover, Javogues had emphasized that the committees belonged to a structure of organs of repression when he directed that the suspects arrested by the committees should be sent to the district prisons, whence they were to be forwarded to the revolutionary tribunal at Feurs for trial. Yet, here also, quite apart from the vicissitudes of the tribunal itself, the system functioned badly since, for most of the period, the committees were very lax about sending reasons for arrest with the suspect.[2] For the most part, suspects from the rural areas languished in the prisons without anybody knowing anything about them. It was not until 13 pluviôse/1 February that Javogues finally defined the conduct of relations between the tribunal and the committees, but the suppression of the tribunal ten days later effectively stifled the development of any co-ordinated machinery. Finally, the provisions of the law of 14 frimaire/4 December, which aimed at making the revolutionary committees agents of the government, were not followed in the Loire to any significant extent, at least before germinal. With the single exception of Roanne,[3] the presidents of the committees did not send *comptes décadaires* either to the Committee of General Security or to the Districts; indeed, it is rare to find any committee in the districts of Boën and Armeville writing to the Committee of General Security other than in exceptional circumstances, although some of those in the district of Roanne were more willing to do so.[4]

[1] A.D.L., L 156, fol. 106; e.g. L 18, fol. 24; A.D.R., 42 L 19, 42 L 156.

[2] e.g. A.D.L., L 156, fol. 105, Dist. of Armeville to rev. com. at Bourg-Argental, 23 pluv. Bonnet-la-Montagne, which sent its suspects directly to the tribunal, was exceptionally efficient (Cobb, art. cit., pp. 301–2).

[3] *Papiers inédits, omis ou supprimés par Courtois*, i. 235–43.

[4] The major committees in the dist. of Roanne corresponded quite actively with the committees of government in pluv. and vent. during the tension surrounding the end of Javogues's mission.

As far as Paris and a few other major towns were concerned, legislation lagged behind the practice of the revolutionary committees. Originally, they had only had the right of receiving the declarations of foreigners, and it was not until the Law of Suspects, 17 September 1793, that the Convention legalized what was already happening in Paris and elsewhere to the extent of entrusting them with drawing up lists of suspects, the arrest of suspects, and the sealing of their papers.[1] In the Loire, however, the early committees had adhered to the letter of the law for the most part: although the committee at Charlieu started to collect denunciations conscientiously from 6 September onwards, it only ordered the arrest of one person before 14 October, when a *commissaire* of the Committee of General Security arrived and informed the committee of the terms of the law of 17 September—up to that point, it had usually forwarded all business to the Municipality or to the District.[2] The committees set up in the Loire during the period under review, therefore, functioned on the basis of the Law of Suspects. In his *arrêté* of 5 brumaire/26 October, Javogues referred them specifically to it, while the Department, in an *arrêté* of 17 brumaire/7 November, recalled these legal limits to their functions:

Les fonctions des comités de surveillance se bornent à la recherche des émigrés, des prêtres réfractaires, des complices de la rébellion lyonnaise et de tous ceux qui sont déclarés suspects par la loi du 15 [*sic*] septembre 1793, [à] recevoir les dénonciations des citoyens, à faire constituer en état d'arrestation les personnes et à requérir les

[1] Cf. the committee at Nancy, which, from the moment of its foundation in March, had the right of arrest and which drew up a list of suspects on the basis of which the *Repr. en mission* arrested 200 people in mid April (Godechot, art. cit., pp. 249–51). In one or two cases, the Convention had already accorded the right of arrest to individual committees as, e.g., to Melun in June (E. Campagnac, 'Le comité de surveillance de Melun', *Ann. rév.* 1908, p. 469).

[2] A.D.L., L 399 (1) *passim*. Note that the small committee of Vougy declared on 19 June that it existed 'pour surveiller à l'exécution des décrets de la Convention nationale et à établir le bon ordre et veiller à ce qu'il ne se passe rien de contraire aux principes révolutionnaires' (A.D.L., L 427, fol. 1). This shows that militants in the area already conceived of a wider role for the committees, but the corresponding actions were rare: e.g. during the summer Saint-Martin-d'Estreaux kept an eye on grain supplies and held an inquiry into the 'Vive Louis XII' (*sic*) scrawled on the walls of the sacristy (A.D.L., L 424). The C.P.S. at Montbrison and Boën, however, both made quite a number of arrests in Sept. and Oct. (A.D. P.-de-D., L 2781 and A.D.R., 42 L 159).

municipalités de faire séquestrer les propriétés de ceux qui sont déclarés rebelles par la loi, la police des maisons de justice appartenant aux municipalités, l'élargissement aux tribunaux.[1]

It was only with the law of 14 frimaire/4 December that the committees were given widely extended powers over the execution of revolutionary laws at the local level. But, in this case, the committees in the Loire were well in line with national developments, for most of the energetic ones had already extended their activity to embrace all aspects of local life and in practice supervised the enforcement of all laws. Indeed, in this respect as in others, the law of 14 frimaire made very little real difference, and it did not infuse new life into the more lethargic committees. On the contrary, apart from the problems created by the exclusion of members holding other official posts, its most noticeable effect was to throw into confusion some bodies which did not properly understand the article prohibiting the association of revolutionary committees.[2] Only the committees at Montmarat/Saint-Just-en-Chevalet and Régny appear to have complied with this law to the extent of sending out *commissaires* specifically to inquire into the execution of the laws and measures of general security.[3]

If the dominant theme of the committees' activity always appeared to be the surveillance and the arrest of suspects, up to a point this was due to the fact that their power came from their right to issue arrest warrants and that therefore their most concrete actions tended to be expressed in this form. But the term suspect, both as defined in the law of 17 September and in practice in the department of the Loire, covered a multitude of sins ranging from politically subversive words and deeds and economic offences to political apathy and, increasingly as the winter wore on, religious opposition. It is hardly meaningful, therefore, to estimate the achievements of the committees simply in terms of warrants of arrest. This is especially true, moreover, since whatever

[1] A.D.L., L 18, fol. 24.

[2] e.g. Parigny (A.D.L., L 176, fol. 82), Saint-Martin-d'Estreaux (A.D.R., 42 L 163), and Villemontais (A.D.L., L suppl. 565, 29 niv.). This was a fairly common reaction since the *Repr.* at Cne-aff. were obliged to issue an *arrêté* to counteract it (A.N., AF II 137 (1062), d. 6, p. 7, 26 frim.).

[3] A.D.L., L 422, 21 pluv.; L 414, fol. 6.

interpretation any particular committee put on the concept of suspects, the issue of warrants for their arrest was proportionately only a small part of its activity relating directly to them. The committees also accomplished a considerable amount of work which extended from countersigning and, in some cases, delivering *certificats de civisme* to finding out about property belonging to people arrested elsewhere, checking on travellers and on letters, and undertaking house-to-house searches for counter-revolutionaries in hiding, etc.[1] All this constituted the daily routine of the committees against suspects. The effectiveness of the revolutionary committee at a local level, not merely in respect of suspects but in every field of its activity, resided not so much in the use of the arrest warrant as in the permanent threat of its use. The wide variety of definitions of suspect allowed for a wide variety of practice among the committees. Most committees acquitted themselves competently enough of the straightforward task of political repression arising out of the federalist crisis. But some of them, particularly the smaller rural ones, were not prepared, or perhaps not sufficiently politically conscious, to go beyond this, so that, in the case of a mountain canton like that of (Saint-)Georges-en-Couzan, which had remained aloof from the federalist movement, the committee did not make a single arrest for political crimes or others.[2] Except in the centres of disaffection, such as the eastern Seuil de Neulize, the committees were generally willing to ensure the departure of the young men of the *première réquisition*, but such questions as the enforcement of the *repos décadaire* and the destruction of *signes fanatiques* received attention only from the committees of the larger urban centres.

It is important to stress the diversity of the activities of the revolutionary committees. Certainly the supervision of the political orthodoxy of the population, at least to the extent of preventing a recrudescence of the disastrous events of summer 1793, remained a central preoccupation. But the

[1] e.g. A.D.L., L 397, 23 niv. and 20 pluv., L 399, 28 brum. and 15 frim., L 385, 9 vent., L 386, 18 and 25 mess., L 411, 12 frim., L 417, 4 vent., L 393, 19 pluv., L 394, 12 niv., etc.

[2] A.D.L., L 438 *passim*. Cf. A.D.L., L 418, fol. 25, Chartre's commission from rev. trib. to prompt committees to forward documents and to arrest suspects still at liberty, 'connaissant l'innocence de la plupart des comités'.

emphasis on the type of crime most likely to lead to dangerous unrest and disaffection varied naturally from committee to committee in proportion to the relative urgency of the problems confronting the population. Thus, for instance, the repression of federalism and counter-revolution dominated the activities of the committee at Montbrisé—it was not until 2 ventôse/20 February that a reference to economic questions appears with a discussion concerning the infringement of the *maximum*; at Bonnet-la-Montagne, it was the religious issue which furnished the most important work; but at Charlieu, Saint-Chamond, and Rive-de-Gier, while the strictly political aspect of their work was pursued conscientiously, the committees displayed a more lively interest in the regulation of economic matters.[1] In any case, food supply constantly claimed the attention of the vast majority of urban committees, as it did that of the clubs.[2] The action of the committees consisted, in the first place, of ensuring that the resources of the canton were exploited to the fullest extent: they ordered the assessment of available stocks; they sent *commissaires* round the *chef-lieu* as well as the villages to check declarations and to search houses and farms for hoards of food; they threatened or arrested recalcitrant farmers; they watched for clandestine exports; and sometimes they took over the business of requisitioning supplies for the *chef-lieu*. In the second place, their vigilance was unremitting over the sale of food: this was particularly evident in their efforts to enforce the application of the *maximum*, but it also extended to such questions as weights and measures, the quality of food (particularly bread and meat), the good order of the market, and the prevention of bulk buying for resale and of purchase from the peasants before they reached the market.

Furthermore, the activities of the revolutionary committees covered a whole spectrum of matters of communal interest, and in this they again resembled the clubs, of which, as we have stated, they were often the *bras agissant*. Quite apart

1 A.D.L., L 434 (1), L 436, L 399, L 390, and L 389 *passim*.

2 For examples of the activity of the committees in the economic sphere, see especially Charlieu (A.D.L., L 399), La Pacaudière (L 412), Saint-Chamond (L 390), and Rive-de-Gier (L 389).

from keeping an eye on obvious problems such as illegal felling in the National Forests or dishonesty in the sales of *biens nationaux*, we find the committees devoting their attention to questions like the depth of graves, local communications, the damage done by goats and pigs 'par la faute des petits bergers qui ne les gardent pas ou très mal', late-night drinking, 'les jeux de billards où très souvent des citoyens passent les nuits', and so on.[1] It was to the committee as much as to the club that the poor people of Régny turned to get raw cotton which was being drained off by the non-application of the *maximum* in neighbouring centres.[2] In some cases, people seem to have considered the committees as substitutes for the court of the *juge de paix*, as, for example, those citizens who denounced a pig merchant to the committee at Saint-Chamond for having broken a contract of sale because he was offered more.[3] Indeed, some committees encouraged this by interfering in the maintenance of ordinary law and order, which was the province of the Municipality (*police municipale*). They issued warrants for the arrest not merely of such dangerous people as counter-revolutionaries, economic offenders, *fanatiques*, and deserters, but also of local rowdies like Jean Chalon of Sury 'qui n'a jamais rien su respecter de sa vie', or Julien Beauvoir and Jean Despercieux of Saint-Julien-Lavêtre, arrested by the committee at Cervières for insults, threats, and assault and battery on the high road.[4] Therefore, the committees, with their local knowledge, often performed a usual function of social regulation which had little to do with the *gouvernement révolutionnaire*.

Generalizations about the action of the revolutionary committees must be subjected to very much the same qualification as those about the clubs. There was a great deal of variation not only in the type of activity but also in the intensity of activity, as with the clubs. Javogues's *arrêté* of 5 brumaire/26 October stipulated that the committees should meet every day, but, except for the major towns and a particularly scrupulous one like Rambert-Loire/Saint-Rambert, this was

[1] These examples are taken from Firminy and La Pacaudière (A.D.L., L 385 and 412).

[2] A.D.L., L 414, pluv., especially 27 pluv.

[3] A.D.L., L 390, fol. 14.

[4] A.D.L., L 442, 12 niv., L 430 (2), 28 niv.

never the case.[1] Moreover, the mere fact of meeting was not in itself an indication of activity: Chérier met regularly every *décadi*, but of eight meetings between 20 frimaire/10 December and 30 pluviôse/18 February, there was no business in five and another two were marked only by the renewal of the *bureau*.[2] As we have seen, the action of the committees against suspects was never of uniform energy—and this after all was their prime function in the terms of Javogues's *arrêté*. Indeed, these were the characteristics of the majority of rural committees throughout France. In the villages, the efficacy of the revolutionary committees as instruments of the Terror was severely handicapped at the outset by problems of literacy and of peasant caution,[3] while in these small, inbred, xenophobic communities, committees of twelve local men were unlikely to be active terrorist agents. Certainly, in some cases, such as Coutouvre, the religious schism distinguished the local terrorists from their victims.[4] But beyond this there would be little to occupy the members of a committee in villages immersed in the unchanging routine of peasant life and insulated from most of the provincial and national events of the Revolution,[5] while they could scarcely be expected to implement directives from the towns, particularly over food supplies. In addition, there was always the likelihood of a certain complicity between the members of a small committee and minor offenders.[6] In these circumstances there was theo-

[1] For Saint-Rambert, A.D.L., L 441, fol. 2, 8 frim. The more active village committees usually met between three and six times a month: e.g. Bœuf and Le Chambon (A.D.L., L 395 and 384). But many of the smaller bodies in the dist. of Roanne were, one suspects, like Combre which met precisely ten times between 9 June 1793 and 9 fruct. an II (A.D.L., L 407).

[2] A.D.L., L 406. Romain-les-Vergers more often than not recorded that there was no business or else spent its time countersigning attestations (A.D.L., L 396); finally, the *agent national* of the Dist. had to exhort it: 'sortez de ce sommeil léthargique: vous êtes en révolution, c'est-à-dire en insurrection contre la tyrannie et les bas valets' (A.D.L., L 156, fol. 114).

[3] e.g. A.D.L., L 124, fol. 3, petition by Saint-Genest-Malifaux to be allowed to keep its secretary because it cannot find anyone else.

[4] A.D.L., L 400, fols. 5–10, 22.

[5] Note that when the committee at Saint-Genest-Malifaux arrested a man for 'insultes et voies de fait sur le receveur de la commune', one senses that this was an affair of extraordinary importance: fourteen pages of the register are devoted to orders, interrogations, witnesses, and correspondence relating to it (A.D.L., L 393, 18 pluv.).

[6] e.g. A.D.L., L 409, fol. 1, denunciation to committee at Saint-Symphorien-de-Lay, 24 niv., against eight members of the committee at Vendranges for suppressing a *procès-verbal* concerning illegal wood-cutting.

retically everything to be said for cantonal committees which could rise above an *esprit de clocher*: by germinal the District of Roanne had come to this conclusion, pointing out that

dans les campagnes ces comités se rassemblent seulement une fois tous les quinze jours et n'ont rien à faire. Les membres sont souvent éloignés d'une lieue les uns des autres et il arrive souvent que la plupart ne savent pas écrire. L'Administration pense qu'il serait suffisant d'établir des comités révolutionnaires dans les chefs-lieux de canton seulement.[1]

In practice, however, the cantonal committees in the rural areas, and especially in the mountains, were liable to the same disadvantages. Some of these cantonal committees, like those at Montchalier/Saint-Germain-Laval, Néronde, Cervières, Régny, Marcellin-la-Plaine/ Saint-Marcellin, and Valdorlay/ Saint-Paul-en-Jarez, appear reasonably competent, but they were either centres of some importance or relatively well situated geographically. Other cantonal committees, such as Villemontais, Romain-les-Vergers/Saint-Romain-en-Jarez, and La Fouillouse, stagnated,[2] while at Saint-Just-la-Pendue, *commissaires* from the District were obliged to nominate the members themselves on the grounds that most of the inhabitants had such a history of religious and political dissidence that they would have chosen people more adept at breaking laws than at enforcing them—even so, the committee was very circumspect and merely denounced people to the Municipality or else to the revolutionary committee at Roanne for behaviour which, elsewhere, would have brought immediate arrest.[3]

But these lesser committees were not the only ones whose revolutionary zeal could be questioned. In frimaire, the revolutionary tribunal at Feurs wrote angrily to the committee at Armeville:

Il est étonnant de voir votre peu de zèle pour la chose publique. Tandis que des gens plus égarés que coupables gémissent dans les

[1] A.D.R., 1 L 190, letter to *Repr.* at Cne-aff., 16 germ.

[2] A.D.L., L suppl. 565, L 396, L 386.

[3] A.D.L., L 423, 25 Oct.; L suppl. 565, e.g. 20 Nov., denunciation of an inhabitant for speaking against the Convention and the *prêtres constitutionnels*; the only arrest was when a *commissaire des Repr.* demanded it after a requisitioned horse had been stolen back by its owner. Cf. ibid., list of suspects, etc., 6 germ., showing three suspects still at liberty in the commune.

cachots, vous laissez jouir de la liberté à des scélérats qui souillent la terre qui les porte . . . Que votre conduite à l'avenir dissipe la complicité dont on peut vous taxer.[1]

The committee, which had recently been reformed, was able to shift the blame on to its predecessor, but, at the beginning of pluviôse, complaints were again voiced at the *conseil général* of the commune about the nonchalance with which the committee delivered *certificats de civisme* to anybody who asked for one.[2] As for the committee at Roanne, it proved to be consistently moderate. Although Civeton reported in November that the committee had purged itself of 'les membres gangrenés' and that 'ça a pris du nerf', in frimaire it came to light that the committee had liberated on its own initiative several counter-revolutionaries and nobles, with the result that the Department dismissed all the members.[3] Their successors were no better. For instance, they arrested a local militant for having demolished a cross on his own initiative, which elsewhere would have been a laudable action, while they participated actively in the campaign against Lapalus and Javogues.[4] In pluviôse, five of them were arrested and another was dismissed by the *Représentant* Méaulle in germinal.[5] Despite this, the committee at Roanne was the one that, with approximately 159 warrants, made by far the largest number of arrests; moreover, its warrants covered the whole of the Plaine du Roannais, whereas in the rest of the department, it was extremely rare for a committee to act outside its canton. It is probable that this activity must be attributed at least in the beginning to the quasi-permanent presence at Roanne or in the neighbourhood of particularly energetic *commissaires*, men like Civeton and Lapalus, who designated suspects to the committee as well as arresting them themselves.[6]

[1] A.D.R., 42 L 163, 10 frim.

[2] Ibid., 17 frim.; A.C. Saint-Étienne, 1 D 10 (3), fol. 117, 5 pluv.

[3] A.D.L., L 81, letter to Depart., 5 Nov.; L 18, fols. 58–74.

[4] A.D.L., L suppl. 3, 17 Dec.; Lucas, art. cit., pp. 523–30.

[5] A.D.L., L 176, fols. 107, 141.

[6] For the figure, below, p. 154. Some committees also developed the habit of forwarding their suspects to the committee at Roanne for arrest (e.g. A.D.L., L 412, La Pacaudière), which, again, was almost unknown in the rest of the depart. Lapalus spent a whole day with the committee (A.D.R., 42 L 157, committee to rev. trib., 12 frim.); at the beginning of Nov., Civeton was spending as much time there as he could (A.D.L., L 81, letter to Depart., 5 Nov.). By the time of the withdrawal

On a different level, it is clear that the energy shown by the committees at Fontfort/Saint-Galmier and Bourg-Argental was much more the product of local factional strife than of revolutionary zeal. The one at Fontfort was dominated by the friends of Jean Phillipon, former *commissaire* of Javogues and member of the *conseil général* of the Department, who called themselves 'Les Amis chauds de la Liberté' and 'traitaient le reste de la commune de faction', although the *agent national* of the District did not find them more republican than the population in general.[1] The two *registres des dénonciations* of this committee are almost exclusively composed of evidence against about a dozen people, mostly prominent members of the Municipality and the *juge de paix*.[2] The committee at Bourg-Argental managed to impute an impressive range of crimes to its Municipality, but was itself guilty (at least according to the District of Armeville) of a wide variety of *abus d'autorité*, including tyrannizing neighbouring villages (some of which were not even in the department), fraudulent requisitions, fabricated evidence, protection of the young men of the *première réquisition*, etc.[3]

However, despite these reservations about the quality and the quantity of their activity, one must not underrate the contribution of the revolutionary committees to the Terror. Although, as was the case with the clubs, they tended to remain parochial and often intent above all on protecting the interests of urban consumers against the surrounding countryside, they played a primordial part in regulating local life according to the principles of the revolutionary laws. Again, although they also closely resembled the clubs, in that their commitment to each of the various aspects of the Terror was determined by the degree to which they accepted them as the best solutions to the local community's problems, it

of *commissaires* on the recall of Javogues, the committee would already have got into the habit of operating in this way.

[1] A.D.L., L 327, fol. 19; letter to *Repr.*, 29 flor.

[2] A.D.L., L 437. This committee falsified evidence unscrupulously: one illiterate denunciator took a copy of his denunciation and discovered, when he had it read to him by a friend, that it was completely different from what he had actually said (A.D.L., L suppl. 110).

[3] A.N., F^{1b}II Loire 7, d. Bourg-Argental, Dist. to *Commission des administrations civiles*, 15 mess. A similar situation at the committee at Bœuf, exclusively devoted to attacking the *juge de paix*.

nevertheless remains true that they undertook the fundamental business of repression at the communal and cantonal level. However unsatisfactory the system may appear in practice and whatever the contribution of other authorities and bodies involved in repression, they did furnish the revolutionary tribunal with a considerable amount of raw material. At least 535 arrest warrants were issued by the committees throughout the department, although we have already pointed out the limitations of such a calculation as a realistic image of their activity.[1] In fact, this figure would seem rather low for an area of intensive repression,[2] but it must be emphasized, on the one hand, that this is a minimum, since there is no means of establishing the exact total for such committees as Armeville, Rive-de-Gier, Fontfort/Saint-Galmier, and Roanne, and, on the other, that a number of other authorities, particularly the *Représentant* and the various *commissaires*, were actively engaged in repression.[3] It was the committees which accomplished the minutiae of clearing up after the federalist crisis and of attempting to ensure that all citizens got a fair share of local food resources at a reasonable price.

The utility and the strength of the committees resided in their intimate knowledge of local affairs and people, which

[1] This figure is calculated from the *reg. déls*, various fragmentary *registres d'écrou*, and individual *procès-verbaux*.

[2] The committee at Montbrisé issued only ninety-one warrants, whereas the one at Charolles (Saône-et-Loire), which was not in an area of intensive repression, delivered ninety-seven between 1 brum. and 20 frim. (A.D. S.-et-L., 4 L 7). There is nothing in the Loire to compare with the 300 to the credit of the committee at Dax or with the 787 or more arrests made by the committee at Nancy, although the authority of that at Dax extended to the whole district and that of Nancy momentarily covered the whole department (Richard, art. cit., p. 25; Godechot, art. cit., pp. 249–62). However, in these two cases these were frontier regions, and the arrests were continued right up to therm., whereas in the Loire arrests very largely ceased after vent.

[3] There is no means of approximating the amount by which the total varied from this minimum. Rive-de-Gier must have noted warrants on another register, which has since disappeared; for Fontfort, there is only the *registre des dénonciations*, while the *tableau des détenus* (prair.) shows twenty-one people under arrest but does not indicate on whose authority (A.D.L., L 437). A figure of 159 arrests for Roanne may be fairly accurate, since the *registres d'écrou* seem complete (A.D.L., L 199 and L suppl. 3), not to mention the list drawn up by the committee and published in Courtois supplementary papers (i. 235). But at Armeville, where there were five lock-ups, only one *registre d'écrou* survived (J. M. Devet, *Une Prison en 1793 et et 1794*) and gives the evidently unrealistic figure of fourteen arrests by the committee.

allowed them to distinguish between the harmless and the dangerous and which gave them the insight necessary for the day-to-day functioning of the *gouvernement révolutionnaire* at a local level. Not only did this enable them to discover disaffection invisible to a stranger and to know where to look for hoarded food, but it also contributed to preventing the rigour of the Terror from becoming abusively harsh. The committee at Coutouvre was not displaying political naïveté but a sense of proportion and a grasp of the tactics of village politics when it summoned all those declared suspects to embrace the Liberty Tree in its presence and to swear their civic oath once again or else be sent to the revolutionary tribunal as rebels. After this ceremony the committee felt able to state that blame could only be attached to two people who had exploited the ignorance of all 'les petits peuples' and that these latter now recognized their error.[1] In this type of community they would indeed find it difficult to retreat from such a public acknowledgement. Similarly, the committee at La Pacaudière, when faced with a man who had given his neighbour's servant the anti-revolutionary advice that he should refuse to work on Sundays, instructed him to tell the neighbour 'qu'il lui parlait en ami'. Certainly, the crime appeared grave, but the committee felt such lenience justified since it knew that the two men had had a quarrel about a thicket of bushes.[2] To sum up, the vigilance of the revolutionary committees appears to have been fundamental in the preservation of the internal security of the Republic and in the enforcement of the revolutionary laws in the communes. Whatever their practical limitations, the committees in the department of the Loire, in common with those in France as a whole, seem to have adequately achieved the purpose of their foundation without inordinate *abus de pouvoirs*.

[1] A.D.L., L 408, fol. 10, 15 and 21 Nov.

[2] A.D.L., L 412, fol. 5, 16 and 30 vent.

VI

THE *ARMÉE RÉVOLUTIONNAIRE*

THE *armée révolutionnaire* of the Loire was created by an *arrêté* of the *Représentants en mission* Javogues and Bassal issued at Armeville/Saint-Étienne on 20 October 1793.[1] Chronologically, therefore, although the formation of these armies was already well under way throughout France as a whole, this decision was taken before the peak period in brumaire.[2] But, although it appeared later than Fouché's army in the neighbouring Allier (20 September), this army was the first of its kind in the Lyonnais and in the vast province of the super-proconsuls of Commune-affranchie/Lyon.[3] The formation of this body in the Loire was in no way surprising. The department was an area of intensive repression and chronically short of food, one or both of which conditions were always present wherever an *armée révolutionnaire* was created. Moreover, such a body represented the common ground of the ideas of both the violent, insubordinate terrorist Javogues and the governmental, Montagnard terrorist Bassal (Bassal was to create another one at Besançon).[4] It is possible that it also corresponded to the demands of local patriots, since Armeville, where the *arrêté* was signed, was an urban centre more preoccupied by food problems than any other in the department; Johannot, the new mayor appointed by Javogues, had argued in the clubs of the town as early as May 1793 for the formation of an *armée révolutionnaire*.[5]

Javogues and Bassal both soon left the department, and with Javogues went Duret, the new army's commander-in-

[1] A.N., AF II 114 (859) 6.

[2] Richard Cobb, *Les Armées révolutionnaires*, i. 302–6.

[3] The Parisian *armée rév.* did not arrive at Cne-aff. until 5 frim.; it was only on 9 brum. that the proconsuls in that town decided to levy these armies in the ten departs. under their jurisdiction (Richard Cobb, *L'Armée révolutionnaire parisienne à Lyon*, p. 7; A.N., AF II 114 (859) 1).

[4] It is not clear whose was the initiative: the original of the *arrêté* is in Bassal's handwriting.

[5] Above, p. 49.

chief. After their departure the *armée révolutionnaire* of the Loire came into being only slowly: it was not until 15 frimaire/5 December that the first review took place.[1] The *Représentants* had ordered Descombes Montmellieu, *dit* Plume de Fer, the *commissaire des guerres* of the army, to organize the companies, while the task of equipping the battalion was handed over to the Department. In practice, however, it was difficult to dissociate the two functions, and the regular administration finally took charge of the whole organization. On the one hand, the clubs and the revolutionary committees played very little part in raising the force—and this is a distinguishing feature of the *armée révolutionnaire* of the Loire—since they themselves were only in the process of formation at this time. On the other hand, Descombes was remarkably inefficient. From time to time he exceeded his powers as defined by the *Représentants*, as, for example, when he tried to organize the equipment of the companies of Roanne.[2] At other times, nobody could find him when needed: one of the captains from Roanne complained that Descombes not only failed to appear in order to organize the companies, but even omitted to reply to the letters written to him.[3]

There was a distinct pause before the regular authorities began to organize the battalion.[4] This was partly the result of their uncertainty about the activities of the *commissaire des guerres*.[5] It must also be attributed to the fact that the new regular administrations had only just been appointed (the Department did not start its meetings until 3 brumaire/24 October) and the links between the renewed Districts and the entirely new Department were not yet functioning properly.[6]

[1] A.D.L., L 18, fol. 62.

[2] A.D.L., L suppl. 377, letter to Dist. Roanne, 7 Nov.

[3] A.D.L., L 81, Civeton to Depart., 27 brum. and 5 Nov.; a *commissaire* from the Depart. was obliged in early frim. to travel to Cne-aff. before he found Descombes (A.D.L., L suppl. 419, Gelas to Depart., 5 frim.).

[4] The Depart. finally took control on 23 brum. by sending two *commissaires* to the Dists. to supervise the organization (A.D.L., L 18, fol. 36).

[5] Descombes failed to meet the Depart. for the consultations that it had demanded (A.D.L., L 18, fol. 3), and the Depart. justified its take-over as being necessary to repair the damage done by his inactivity.

[6] One must also remember the effect of the lack of a well-informed *état-major*, owing to the departure of Duret—e.g. a *commissaire* from the Depart. was told at

Although from the very first day of its existence the Department promulgated a number of *arrêtés* concerning the mobilization of resources to equip this army, not until 16 brumaire/6 November did the District of Roanne circulate the *arrêté* of the *Représentants* to the Municipalities under its jurisdiction. It directed them to publish the *arrêté* on the following Sunday after mass and vespers and to take the names of volunteers.[1] This appears to have been the basic method of recruitment throughout the department. For instance, both at Bonnet-la-Montagne and at Rambert-Loire/Saint-Rambert it was the Municipality that opened the enrolment registers.[2] In the larger centres, however, it seems that the officers did a considerable amount of recruiting, since there were already men enrolled at Armeville before the Department came into existence and at Roanne before the District published the constitutive *arrêté*.[3] Moreover, Descombes sent a couple of captains to recruit in the district of Boën, while Javogues appears to have appointed a special recruiting officer.[4] Finally, the various *commissaires* on missions for the regular administrations also took a hand in recruiting.[5]

However, the first review on 15 frimaire/5 December did not mark the inauguration of the *armée révolutionnaire*. It is true that on 12 frimaire/2 December, Archimbaud, captain at Rambert-Loire, had still not taken up his post of judge at the *Commission militaire* at Feurs because the organization of his company was incomplete.[6] But Descombes was in a posi-

the end of brum. that there was no point in his going to Saint-Rambert because no recruiting was being done there, although the Mun. had been recruiting since 6 brum.

[1] A.N., F7 4648, d. Civeton. [2] A.D.L., L suppl. 419.

[3] A.D.L., L 81, Descombes to Depart., Armeville, 23 Oct.; above, p. 157, n. 3. In the absence of the registers of the clubs of Roanne, Montbrisé, and Armeville, it is difficult to tell whether they recruited, but the complete absence of incidental reference to this (especially in the loquacious Thermidorian documents) suggests that they did not.

[4] A.D.L., L 81, Descombes to Depart., Armeville, 23 Oct.; A.D.L., L 69, Contamine to Depart., 15 frim.

[5] e.g. Plagnieu at Saint-Bonnet-la-Montagne, Costalin at Saint-Symphorien, Chartre at Roanne (A.D.L., L 378, fol. 12 and L 81).

[6] A.D.R., 42 L 163, Archimbaud to *Comm. mil.*, 12 frim. In fact, this company was already partially active well before that date, since on 4 Nov. it executed an arrest warrant (A.D.R., 42 L 182, d. Labarre).

tion to dispatch fifty men from Commune d'Armes to Feurs only three days after the *arrêté* of the *Représentants*.[1] Already on about 6 brumaire/27 October a detachment was at work searching the Château de Saint-Polgues for hidden treasure and incriminating documents under the direction of a *commissaire* from the Department.[2] The three companies of the district of Roanne had their full quota of men by 27 brumaire/17 November; at Montbrisé only the second company had a few vacancies at the end of brumaire.[3] The delays in the organization of the *armée révolutionnaire* arose not from any difficulty in finding soldiers but rather in equipping them.

On 9 brumaire/30 October the Department ordered each District to see to the arming, equipping, and clothing of the companies raised in the area of its jurisdiction and directed that these objects should, in the first instances, be taken from the sequestrated goods of arrested *marchands*; should this prove insufficient, the remainder was to be purchased at the price prescribed by the *maximum*. Each soldier was to be provided with a coat, a jacket, two pairs of trousers, two pairs of stockings, two pairs of gaiters, two pairs of shoes, two bags (one in leather and one in cloth), one hat, three shirts, and two collars. The armourers of Armeville were to provide 1,200 muskets and 1,200 swords. The equipping of the army was to be completed within two *décades*, that is before 29 brumaire/19 November.[4] Such a programme was, however, quite impracticable. In the first place, it coincided with demands made on the department to equip and arm not only the *Armée des Alpes* but also the *première réquisition* and the 5th Battalion of the Puy-de-Dôme, hastily raised during the *levée en masse* against Lyon and stationed in the Forez since the middle of September. In the second place, the reserves of the department had been seriously depleted during the siege of Lyon, particularly by the Auvergnat Committee of Public Safety of Montbrison which had set about ruthlessly supplying the *levée en masse* and restocking the department

[1] A.D.L., L 81, Descombes to Depart., 23 Oct.
[2] A.D.L., L 79, fol. 2, Chana and Chartre to Depart.
[3] A.D.L., L 83, fol. 4, Costalin to Depart., 27 brum.; A.C. Montbrison, *reg. dél.*, no. 2, fol. 9 (30 brum.).
[4] A.D.L., L 18, fol. 13.

of the Puy-de-Dôme. As far as the essential item of muskets was concerned (and there was never any question of supplying the swords referred to by the Department), the District of Armeville noted in early November that the total of requisitions already amounted to 22,000 muskets, and had to request the local gunsmiths of Saint-Chamond to furnish the soldiers being enrolled in that town.[1] On 27 brumaire/17 November the Department wrote to the *Représentants* at Ville-affranchie to obtain ammunition, but on 9 frimaire/29 November it was obliged to admit that the detachment at Feurs not only did not have any ammunition, but did not even have any muskets.[2] It was not until 11 nivôse/31 December that Descombes was able to complete the arming of the garrison at Roanne.[3] As for the clothing of the troops, it soon became apparent that the problems were just as great. Only forty-three men of the 306 raised in the district of Roanne could be fully equipped from local resources, and the District was obliged to send *commissaires* to ask the *Représentants* at Ville-affranchie for cloth.[4] The situation was much the same in the other districts. The District of Commune d'Armes, having bought up all the available cloth in the area, was also forced to apply to the *Représentants* at Ville-affranchie for additional supplies, including 532 dozen large buttons and 1,596 small ones, for lack of which the preparation of uniforms was paralysed.[5] The District of Boën adopted a different solution by simply ordering the Municipalities of Boën, Feurs, Rambert-Loire, Fontfort/Saint-Galmier, Chazelles-sur-Commune-affranchie, and any other community where this army would eventually be established to take the necessary measures.[6] A few days later one member, exasperated by the pressure from the Department, suggested in open meeting that the text of Javogues's *arrêté* made the Department

[1] A.D.L., L 130, fol. 32.

[2] A.D.L., L 18, fols. 44, 65.

[3] A.D.L., L 176, fol. 82 (by that time the detachment at Roanne probably no longer existed).

[4] A.D.L., L 196, 'État du recrutement de l'armée révolutionnaire' (dist. of Roanne); A.D.L., L 176, fol. 44 (27,319*l.* 5*s.* was spent at Cne-aff. on cloth—fol. 53).

[5] A.D.L., L 130, fol. 34 (10 Nov., requisitions and searches); ibid., fol. 44 (15 frim., *commissaires* to Cne-aff.); ibid., fol. 46 (16 frim., payment of 2,053*l.* 10*s.* to *frères* Fournal for 'fournitures à l'armée révolutionnaire').

[6] A.D.L., L 259, fol. 25 (10 frim.).

responsible for this job and that the District was obliged to deal only with the clothing of the *première réquisition*.[1] But in the end it too was forced to send out a *commissaire* to purchase cloth at Annonay and Vienne.[2] Thus, although the enrolment was for the most part finished at the end of brumaire, the equipment was far from complete long after 15 frimaire/5 December. On 17 frimaire/7 December one member of the *état-major* was urging the District of Roanne to take action on this matter because the soldiers were now on continual service in harsh weather;[3] on 21 frimaire/11 December, the Municipality of Rambert-Loire had just got together enough beds for a detachment of only forty men;[4] the leather bags, for which a contract had been approved by the District of Roanne on 27 brumaire/17 November, were not delivered until 7 pluviôse/26 January;[5] the *commissaire* of the District of Boën was still buying cloth at Vienne on 25 pluviôse/13 February;[6] a contract for hats handed out by the Department was only fulfilled on 26 nivôse/15 January, and the consignment was not officially inspected until 4 ventôse/22 February, when nearly a third were rejected.[7]

As in the case of most *armées révolutionnaires*, it is difficult to establish the social composition of the army of the Loire. Although we possess the complete enrolment lists, they mention neither the profession nor the marital status of the members; in the case of only two companies is any indication of the birth-place given, while the age of the soldiers is stated for only three companies.[8] It is impossible, with a few exceptions, to identify more precisely the 1,200 soldiers known to us only by their name and forenames, even when we know exactly where they came from: in the case of smaller communes, there were often only a few names for the whole community, representing an inextricable tangle of family branches; in towns like Armeville and Saint-Chamond sheer

[1] Ibid., fol. 45 (24 frim.). Cf. A.D.L., L 81, Gelas to Depart., Armeville, 1 frim.: refusal by Mun. to provide shoes.

[2] A.D.L., L 261, fol. 1, 23 niv.

[3] A.D.L., L suppl. 419, letter from Prénat.

[4] Ibid., Mun. to Depart.

[5] A.D.L., L 196 (315 bags at 14*l*. apiece = 4,410*l*.).

[6] A.D.L., L 329, fol. 11, Dist. of Boën to *Repr.*, 5 vent.

[7] A.D.L., L 18, fols. 139, 193.

[8] A.D.L., L suppl. 419. Birth-places noted for two companies from Roanne and age given for two companies from Montbrisé and one from Roanne.

numbers make any precise identification among the *petit peuple* impossible. Some of the officers are more easily identified in that we possess their signatures,[1] which can be compared with other documents, and there are more incidental references to them, while a few at least have past histories of which we have some knowledge.

For the most part, however, it seems that the *armée révolutionnaire* of the Loire conforms to the general pattern.[2] Essentially it was composed of urban dwellers, middle-aged and in many cases married. Its soldiers were mostly the poorest artisans, workers, *journaliers*, *locataires*, etc., while its officers belonged socially to a somewhat superior élite, often with a more or less tenuous military background. Although politically immaculate, if not always militant, the army had its sprinkling of deserters, counter-revolutionaries, young men of the *première réquisition*, and even some swindlers, but this in no way made it an army of the socially maladjusted. In short, it was a typical microcosm at departmental level of a national phenomenon.

The recruiting ground of the army was predominantly, though not exclusively, the towns. The distinction made at the time between the four companies of Armeville and the two companies of Saint-Chamond indicates that they were recruited in these towns rather than in the district as a whole. The small urban centres of Rambert-Loire, Bonnet-la-Montagne, and Fontfort/Saint-Galmier each provided a solid contingent, while we can identify men from Feurs, Boën, and Montchalier/Saint-Germain-Laval.[3] Civeton remarked that two hundred citizens of Roanne had enrolled.[4] He went on to say that he was counting on the countryside to make up the complement. But on the whole the rural population seems to have been reluctant to join. This was not necessarily out of mistrust for a body essentially urban in character and justification. The terrorist *procureur* of Sail gave quite a different explanation for the fact that no volunteers registered with the Municipality: agriculture was particularly arduous in this

[1] On reports and receipts for pay.

[2] Cobb, op. cit. i. 307–61.

[3] For Saint-Galmier, A.D.L., L suppl. 419, reply to a letter announcing the enlistment of thirty men (20 frim.).

[4] A.D.L., L 81, letter to Depart., 20 brum.

area and all farmers attempted to retain as many labourers as possible, large families being far from a burden on them.[1] He added, as a decisive factor, the experience of the *levée* against Lyon during the previous summer, for all those whom he contacted personally protested that they had been swindled too often by the N.C.O.s at that time. Nevertheless, there were individual soldiers from the country areas, such as Jean Girard of Grézieu, André Tamain of Saint-Rirent, André and Charles Bourrin from Valdorlay, seven volunteers from Saint-Maurice-en-Gourgois, etc.[2] Two of the companies at Roanne contained large numbers of men who were born outside the town, although in this case it may well be that many of them lived there.[3] At all events, whether these soldiers in the Roanne companies represent actual recruitment in the rural areas or merely migration of population, the places of origin of those of them born in the department underline the fact that the rural minority in the army of the Loire came from the villages of the immediate hinterland of the towns (for example, patriotic Moingt): we can identify no soldier from the mountain areas, apart from the group from Bonnet-la-Montagne which was an industrial area.[4]

The average age for the three companies for which we possess statistics is thirty-seven, although a distinction must be made between the Company Chantelot (Roanne), where the majority are aged between twenty-six and thirty-five, and the two companies from Montbrisé, where there is a much more even spread between twenty-six and fifty.[5] Thus, in

[1] A.D.L., Chaleyer MS., no. 354, Game to Dist. of Roanne, 10 Nov.

[2] A.D.L., L suppl. 194, fol. 5, debt proceedings against Girard suspended because of his absence with the *armée rév.*; L suppl. 3, fol. 56, arrest for desertion; L 146, sick-leave; A.D.R., 42 L 156, denunciation. Cf. A.D.L., L 81, letter to Depart., 2 frim., referring to recruitment in the villages round Saint-Symphorien-de-Lay by Costalin.

[3] As far one one can see, the army was recruited entirely within the depart., although Contamine 's'est rendu utile dans la dite armée depuis cette époque en recrutant dans divers départements de la république' (A.D.L., L 18, fol. 76, 15 frim.). The designation 'natif de', which is given for the two companies of Roanne, usually refers to the birth-place, and some of the soldiers of these companies were natives of places as far afield as Mantes, Paris, Limoges, and La Charité-sur-Loire.

[4] A similar emphasis on the peripheral villages is present in the rural element of the army of Versailles (Cobb, op. cit. i. 351).

[5] A.D.L., L suppl. 419. Company Chantelot: average age, 34·9; Company Martin: average age, 38·7; Company Phalippon: average age, 37.

general, the *armée révolutionnaire* in this respect is like the typical armies raised at Moulins and Nantes.[1] Certainly there were young men in the battalion: there were at least two youths (not counting the drummers), while there was a sufficient number of young men of the *première réquisition* to incite the Department to write to the *état-major* demanding their exclusion.[2] It is impossible to establish what proportion of these men was married, but it is clear that a good many were. At the time of the temporary dissolution of the army in nivôse, the Department claimed that to a large extent it consisted of family men; earlier on, an administrator recruiting round Saint-Symphorien-de-Lay thought that most of those who had signed up with him had jobs, wives, and children, while, at the end of nivôse, it was said of a detachment from Vallée-Rousseau/Saint-Chamond that not only was every man in it married but the majority had a large number of children.[3] A list of men returning home from Ville-affranchie at the final dissolution in ventôse indicates a ratio of one to three.[4] But it is likely that the proportion was higher: on the one hand, only a few companies went to Ville-affranchie at this time, and married men may have tried to avoid being included in that number, while, on the other hand, many of them probably omitted to join up again in the reorganization in nivôse, considering that the illegality of the army made it too dangerous. In this case the ratio of one to three may be applicable to the army *after* nivôse.[5] We can identify very few soldiers as definitely not married. Indeed, although there was nothing in the original *arrêté* of the *Représentants* on the subject, the civil administrations seem to have understood quickly that married men were the best material: in its circular on recruitment, the District of Roanne emphasized that the battalion would not be serving outside the department and

[1] Cobb, op. cit. i. 346.

[2] For the drummers, see A.C. Saint-Étienne, 1 D 10 (3), fol. 98, complaint to the Mun. that many of the drummer-boys of the National Guard had left to join the *armée rév.* (21 frim.); A.D.L., L 79, fol. 22, Depart. to second-in-command, 15 frim.

[3] A.D.L., L 18, fol. 130; L 81, Costalin to Depart., 2 frim.; A.N., D III 335, *compte décadaire* of 28 niv.

[4] A.D.R., 1 L 804. Cf. A.D.R., 31 L 54, petitions by family men to be allowed to go home, early vent.

[5] Below, p. 176.

that this was yet another reason why good patriots with families should join.[1]

The *armée révolutionnaire* of the Loire was no exception to the general rule in offering high pay and easy conditions of service. In its recruiting propaganda the Department made much capital out of this 'service doux et momentané', pointing to the maximum of fifteen days activity in every sixty and recalling that dependants of men serving here qualified for subsidies as much as those of men at the frontiers.[2] But the presence of large numbers of middle-aged married men had its disadvantages, since it accentuated the latent localism of companies, whose members in many cases were likely to consider their primary task to be to help solve the food problems of their home town.[3] The *agent national* of Vallée-Rousseau/Saint-Chamond reported grumbling among the detachment that had marched for eleven days through the snow to escort the pay chest without receiving any special indemnity, and acknowledged that 'ils préfèrent de rester dans leurs foyers, où ils ont plus d'aisance pour entretenir eux et leurs familles'.[4] A rumour in brumaire, sparked off by an *arrêté* of the proconsuls at Ville-affranchie ordering the exchange between departments of these *armées révolutionnaires*, played havoc with recruiting, and for a time there were fears in responsible circles of a wave of desertions also.[5] When, during the temporary suppression of the force following the law of 14 frimaire, the *Représentants* at Ville-affranchie ordered its amalgamation with the Parisian *armée révolutionnaire*, the Municipality of Parigny, for instance, reported the obstinate refusal of several soldiers living there to comply.[6] It was not merely a question of leaving the department; some

1 A.N., F7 4648, d. 4 (Civeton).

2 A.D.L., L 18, fol. 28 (address to *armée rév.*, 20 brum.). Between 20 Oct. and 4 niv. the army cost the Depart. 119,817*l.* 18*s.* 4*d.* (A.D.L., L 18, fol. 44), which was paid out of the ordinary tax income, although the *arrêté* of 20 Oct. said that this was to be refunded by the revenue from sequestrated property. Although the basic idea of Javogues and Bassal was, therefore, akin to that of most *Reprs.*—an *impôt sur l'incivisme*—they never went as far as most in prescribing the direct financing by *taxes rév.* (Cobb, op. et loc. cit.); the *taxe rév.* at Armeville in niv. was earmarked for the poor and for the encouragement of industry.

3 Cf. Cobb, op. cit. i. 289.

4 A.N., D III 335.

5 A.D.L., L 81, Costalin to Depart., 2 frim.

6 A.D.L., L 373, fol. 118, 7 pluv.

detachments were reluctant to travel within it. Even Phalippon, an officer and a pure patriot, persuaded the Municipality of Montbrisé to send part of the 5th Battalion of the Puy-de-Dôme to Feurs instead of the 100 men of the *armée révolutionnaire* demanded by the Department, alleging that, 'par ordre du Représentant', their job was to guard the town's gaols.[1] In pluviôse the commander-in-chief was obliged, when ordering the company at Rambert-Loire up to Montbrisé, to recommend to the local revolutionary committee the use of armed force to secure obedience.[2]

The accent was naturally on patriotism: 'trouver de bons sans-culottes pour l'armée', 'formée parmi les patriotes les plus chauds', 'pères de famille bons Patriotes', 'bons sans-culottes des campagnes'.[3] Although the clubs apparently took no part in recruiting and although there was no *scrutin épuratoire*, members of the clubs undoubtedly enlisted.[4] Nevertheless, as in the case of the revolutionary battalion of Bordeaux,[5] it included men with a distinctly dubious past, such as those recognized by one arrested suspect at Montbrisé as having marched with the *muscadins* from Saint-Étienne in the summer.[6] Typical of this type of man was Jean-Marie Reynaud, a *huissier* from Bonnet-la-Montagne and sergeant-major of the company at Rambert-Loire, who had been arrested in September after a suspicious absence of two months, but had been released for lack of evidence, although he was already known to be hostile to the Revolution and despite 'la haine particulière du peuple contre lui'.[7] Deserters and those on sick-leave from the frontiers were also seduced by such a lucrative haven.[8]

[1] A.C. Montbrison, *reg. dél.*, no. 2, fol. 9.

[2] A.D.L., L 441, fol. 21. People evidently suspected that the *armée rév.* was a camouflaged recruitment for the frontier armies (A.D.L., L 18, fol. 28, proclamation refuting such rumours).

[3] e.g. A.C. Saint-Rambert, *reg. dél.*, 27 Oct.

[4] e.g. A.D.R., 42 L 186, d. Pupier, testimonial from club at Montbrisé, 30 pluv., noting the absence of many members with the *armée rév.*

[5] Cobb, op. cit. i. 312, 357–8.

[6] A.D.R., 42 L 185, d. Monot, defence, n.d.

[7] A.D.R., 42 L 187, d. Reynaud; A.D.L., L 377, fol. 11. In germ. an III he became *commissaire* of the Dist. of Montbrison for disarmament (A.C. Feurs, *reg. dél.*, 30 germ.). During the Terror he was finally arrested on Javogues's orders (n.d.) (A.D.R., loc. cit.).

[8] e.g. A.D.L., L 390, fol. 2, and A.D.R., 42 L 156.

But, without going to these extremes, it is clear that the motives that induced many of the ordinary soldiers to enlist had little to do with politics, while the social composition of the rank and file was, as far as we can see, biased towards a much humbler type of person than the respectable artisans and shopkeepers who sat in the clubs.[1] The prosperous citizens composing the Municipality of Feurs, smarting under the gratuitous insults of one Sergeant Masson, spoke disdainfully of these 'jeunes gens sans éducation'.[2] Patriotism was undoubtedly the determining factor in cases like that of the *cafetier* Brat *dit* Saint-Just, who was a member of the club at Montbrisé from the time it reopened in October and who became a *notable* of the town in messidor an II;[3] Private Pierre Decelle was an assiduous denunciator to the revolutionary committee at Montbrisé and was beaten up in floréal an III—his father was a long-standing Jacobin whom Javogues appointed to the administration of the department.[4] But both Brat, who paid 30 *livres* 6 *sous* in *taille* and *subsidiaire*,[5] and Decelle, whose father had been *procureur* of the commune of Moingt in 1792–3,[6] appear to be rather exceptional from the point of view of social origins among the rank and file of the *armée révolutionnaire*. The same is true of François Gonnard, *vigneron* at Montbrisé, paying 13*l.* 1*s.* in taxes, and of Dominique Pinatel, *huissier audiancier* at the district tribunal of Armeville, for *huissiers*, although in many cases the proletariat of the legal profession, were still rich enough to be officers and higher N.C.O.s. Much more typical of the recruits from urban centres were others from Montbrisé, whom we can identify, such as Bourguignon, a small *serrurier* and *locataire* rue Neuve paying only 12*s.* in *taille* and *subsidiaire*; Barthélémy Roche, *tanneur*, paying 2*l.* 7*s.* in taxes; Maligot, *locataire* in the faubourg de la Croix, paying 12*s.*; Jean Chauve *dit* Tissot, *locataire* in the faubourg

[1] Cf. Cobb, op. cit. i. 343.

[2] A.D.L., L 81, letter to Depart., 26 brum.

[3] A.D.L., L 262, fol. 85.

[4] A.D.R., 42 L 186, d. Pugnet; A.N., BB^{18} 690.

[5] For all tax figures cited for Montbrison in this chapter, 'Registre de la thaille, subsidiaire et vingtième de Montbrison, année 1789', *Bulletin de la Diana*, 1941, pp. 227–443.

[6] A.C. Moingt, *reg. dél.*, *passim.* He was also always present in the municipal assemblies and in those of the principal inhabitants from 1789 onwards.

d'Écotay, who paid 1*l*. 16*s*.; the carpenter Jacques Langlois of the rue Saint-Jean, paying 1*l*. 1*s*.; Pierre Lombardin, *cordonnier* and *locataire*, paying 12*s*.; Jean Richard and Annet Pradet, stonemasons, who do not even figure on the tax rolls.[1]

The country recruits probably came from the same social stratum. Jacques Berthollet, who signed the minutes of the meeting at which the deputies from Moingt drew up the *cahier de doléances*, was an exception by virtue of his social importance, though not necessarily of his fortune since Moingt was a particularly poor community.[2] The *procureur* of the commune of Sail evidently assumed that the recruits would not be the *cultivateurs* but the *manœuvres*.[3] The seven volunteers from Saint-Maurice-en-Gourgois were all *journaliers laboureurs*, while Jean Girard was a *locataire* at Grézieu.[4] These men enrolled more for material reasons than for political reasons. 'L'homme étant sans travail s'engagea.'[5] The six companies raised in the district of Armeville reflect as much the readiness to enlist of the *menu peuple* affected by economic crisis (e.g. Raspart, *ferblantier*; Claude Gabe, *coutelier*),[6] as the size of the largest urban centres in the department.[7] It is significant in this context that the river workers at Roanne, the *menu peuple* of that town, refused to a man to join: brumaire was one of their periods of seasonal over-employment owing to river conditions, and they found the

1 A.D.L., L 289, adjudications for the demolition of the town wall at Montbrisé, which was done by the indigent artisans (11 frim.). The other names come from the lists (A.D.L., L suppl. 419) correlated with isolated *procès-verbaux* and the tax rolls. There were also numbers of *garde-séquestre*, usually a post for the honest poor (A.C. Montbrison, *reg. dél.*, no. 2, fol. 47, 30 niv.).

2 A.C. Moingt, *reg. dél.*, 8 Mar. 1789.

3 Above, p. 162.

4 A.D.R., 42 L 156; A.D.L., L suppl. 194, fol. 5. One or two richer peasants are distinguishable in the *cavalerie rév.* in pluv., and had probably enlisted in order to keep an eye on their requisitioned horses: e.g. A.C. Feurs, *reg. dél.*, 8 pluv.

5 A.D.R., 42 L 174, d. Chalançon (of Lésigneux), petition concerning his substitute in the *levée des 300,000*. The commune's contingent was never called up, and finally the man joined the *armée rév.*

6 A.D.L., L suppl. 419; A.D.L., L 441, fol. 22 (Gabe cannot sign his name).

7 We can identify very few soldiers connected with the arms industry, which of course was expanding at that time. This would appear to be true even of the artillery company, for its officers called the death of one of the *canonniers* 'la suite funeste de de l'inexpérience de divers sujets dans la manœuvre du canon' (A.D.R., 1 L 190, letter to Javogues, 11 niv.).

rates of pay too low as well as fearing that they would be obliged to serve out of reach of their work.[1] One should not overstress the importance of the unemployed element, for in a well-documented case like Lille[2] it is clear that those completely out of work showed no alacrity to join; but, for those living on small incomes, rendered even more precarious by economic crisis, the pay was an appreciable supplement, especially since the easy conditions meant that in the larger towns one could combine one's *métier* with the service, provided that the detachments did not move about too much (and we have seen that the soldiers had a marked aversion to such moves).

It is uncertain what criterion was applied to the selection of officers and, indeed, whether they were elected or appointed. Most of these men could claim some sort of military background. But only Escoffier, second-in-command, appears to have had any link with the professional army: he had organized the *levée des 300 000* in the district of Saint-Étienne in his capacity as 'agent militaire et officier'.[3] There were a few *gendarmes*,[4] but for the rest, their claim rested on their position, often an important one, in the National Guard. For instance, Captain Archimbaud, also a retired *gendarme*, was the *adjudant-général* of the Guard at Saint-Rambert, while Lieutenant Aulagnier and Second-Lieutenant Dubois had been adjudant and sergeant-major respectively of the Moingt battalion since its inception.[5] Both Captain Phalippon and Lieutenant Chaux held positions in the National Guard at Montbrison and, after the dispersal of the *armée révolutionnaire*, became its commanding officer and its second-in-command respectively.[6] As for Duret, his rank of *adjudant-général* in the *Armée des Alpes*, although recognized by the *Représentants* at Ville-affranchie,[7] was never officially recognized

1 A.D.L., L 81, Civeton to Depart., 20 brum. Cf. G. Lefebvre, *Études orléanaises*, ii. 260, citing a statement by the rev. com. at Orléans, 19 pluv., that the Loire had been navigable for several months.

2 Cobb, op. cit. i. 347–9.

3 A.D.L., L suppl. 388.

4 e.g. Second Lieutenant Vimord, *brigadier* of the *gendarmerie* of Noirétable (A.D.L., L 430 (1)).

5 A.N., F7 3686, d. 6 (Archimbaud)—he became a *gendarme* again after the suppression of the army (A.D.L., L 260); A.D.R., 42 L 95, d. Aulagnier.

6 A.D.L., L 434 (1), A.D.L., L suppl. 64.

7 A.N., W 193, d. 1, order by Fouché for cloth for his general's uniform.

and was probably conferred on him by Javogues.[1] His military training appears to have been solely in the National Guard, where he had reached the rank of 'major' in the battalion of the Grande Côte in 1791 when living in Lyon.[2] But the officers of the National Guard who entered the *armée révolutionnaire* of the Loire had a distinct advantage over their numerous colleagues with a similar background in other battalions,[3] for they had mostly seen active service against the rebel town of Lyon either as fugitive volunteers in the *compagnies lyonnaises* or as commanders of detachments in the *levée en masse* in September. Thus Captain Égalon Élie was captain of the *chasseurs de Saint-Étienne* there in late September, and his subordinate Mourgues became a second lieutenant of artillery in the *armée révolutionnaire*.[4] Petré, captain of the National Guard of one of the sections at Rive-de-Gier, was appointed by Javogues commander of the *levée en masse* of that town; Descombes Montmellieu was an *officier volontaire* against Lyon, and one of his relations addressed him, though with what degree of accuracy is uncertain, as 'citoyen général de la cavalerie nationale'.[5]

Socially and professionally, these men were a very diverse group. Their civilian occupations ranged from the *fabricant en coton* and the *chirurgien* to the *tailleur d'habits* and the *tailleur de pierres*. Their fortunes varied considerably: whereas the *huissier* Benoit Fayolle *fils* of Saint-Germain-Laval paid 86*l*. 6*s*. in taxes and had been *consul* of the town in 1785,[6] the *cordonnier* Antoine Chaux only paid 2 *livres* and rented his house.[7] Perhaps it is significant that Chaux started as a sergeant and only later was promoted lieutenant, doubtless on account of his outstanding patriotism. Nevertheless, the officers and the higher N.C.O.s (sergeants and sergeant-majors) represented both a social and a political élite when compared with the ordinary soldiers. Although the clubs did

1 He has no dossier in the Archives de la Guerre at Vincennes.

2 A.N., W 193, d. 1, officer's commission, 30 July 1791.

3 Cobb, op. cit. i. 329–42.

4 A.D.R., 42 L 181, d. Jacquet.

5 A.D.R., 42 L 83, d. Petré; 42 L 187, d. Rey.

6 A.D.L., C 69 (2), 'Tableau des propriétaires et habitants de Saint-Germain-Laval', 1788.

7 'Registre de la thaille, subsidiaire et vingtième de Montbrison, année 1789', *Bulletin de la Diana*, 1941.

not participate in the organization of the battalion, it is quite clear that their members dominated its command structure, as was the case in the armies of Lille and Bordeaux.[1] These men were militants and they will therefore be included in the discussion on the terrorists.[2]

The law of 14 frimaire/4 December, which suppressed all the departmental and communal *armées révolutionnaires*, was officially received by the Department on 3 nivôse/23 December and by the lower administrations within the next three days.[3] But the terms of the decree were already known: at Roanne, for example, both individual soldiers and officers on behalf of their companies handed in their resignations to the District on the day before the official notification.[4] As early as 22 frimaire/12 December, the Department got wind of it and, being composed of ardent patriots, was stunned. It immediately wrote to the *Représentants* at Ville-affranchie contending that all the true patriots in the department were agreed that such a measure would make it extremely difficult to achieve the final eradication of the previous summer's counter-revolution.[5] But Fouché was too experienced a politician to allow his views to be made public at such a juncture, and carefully omitted to reply, despite the arrival in Commune-affranchie of a member of the Department.[6] The result was that, when the administration received the decree officially, it had little option but to execute it, although it still attempted to obtain a clear directive from Commune-affranchie.[7] It also attempted to contact Javogues, recently arrived at Commune d'Armes, but, characteristically, he neglected to reply and then proceeded to vent his wrath on the unfortunate administration, when the harm was done:

> Si quelque chose a dû nous causer de la surprise [protested the Department on 11 nivôse/31 December], c'est la lecture de ta lettre d'hier. Nous ne savons ce qui peut justifier les reproches amers dont tu

[1] Cobb, op. cit. i. 453, 735.
[2] Below, p. 316.
[3] A.D.L., L 79, fol. 32 (Depart.); A.D.L., L 176, fol. 74, Dist. Roanne (5 niv.) and A.C. Roanne, 1 D 1 (2), fol. 235; A.C. Montbrison, *reg. dél.*, no. 2, fol. 31 (6 niv.).
[4] A.D.L., L 176, fol. 73.
[5] A.D.L., L 80, fol. 8.
[6] A.D.L., L 18, fol. 109.
[7] A.D.L., L 79, fol. 32, letter to *Repr.* at Cne-aff., 3 niv., asking for advice on how to avoid breaking the law.

nous accables et nous ne croyons pas avoir cessé de mériter de ta confiance et celle de nos administrés. Tu nous fais un crime de la dissolution de l'armée révolutionnaire créée par Bassal et toi. . . . Lorsque nous eûmes reçu le décret nous en transmîmes un exemplaire purement et simplement à l'état-major de l'armée révolutionnaire et au même instant nous t'écrivîmes pour savoir quel parti il y avait à prendre dans cette circonstance. Nous savons même que [Descombes] Montmellieu t'écrivit sur le même sujet. Nous as-tu fait réponse? Quoique l'armée révolutionnaire ne se soit dissoute qu'au dernier moment, avons-nous reçu avant sa dissolution l'arrêté que vous avez pris, Girard et toi, pour la conserver? Quoique nous sentissions parfaitement la nécessité de sa conservation, pourrions-nous raisonnablement prendre sur nous une pareille mesure, quand les Représentants du peuple ne le faisaient pas? Avons-nous provoqué cette dissolution? Pouvions-nous soustraire les chefs et les soldats à la soumission d'un décret et à la crainte des peines qu'il prononce? Quelle force avons-nous pour les retenir à leur poste? Hé! où est donc notre crime?[1]

Javogues's reaction to this part of the decree of 14 frimaire had in fact been prompt: within three days of its arrival in the department he had inveigled the naïve and inoffensive Girard de l'Aude, *Représentant en mission* to the arms industry of Commune d'Armes, into signing with him an *arrêté* maintaining the *armée révolutionnaire*.[2] Javogues's thinking in this matter ran very much along the same lines as those of the administration of the department, which had questioned whether the decree was applicable to the situation in the Loire, where the prisons were overflowing with counter-revolutionary scoundrels whom nothing would prevent from escaping and carrying the torch of civil war through the countryside if the *armée révolutionnaire* were disbanded. Javogues argued that the department of the Loire was a 'pays en révolte'. The *armée révolutionnaire* should, therefore, be maintained on the evidence of the decree itself, whose section III, article 20, made an exception for rebel areas—or so he professed to believe. The raising of such a force had been 'une mesure de salut public, d'un ordre supérieur', designed to stamp out the brands of civil war lit by the horrible

[1] A.D.L., L 80, fol. 10.

[2] A.N., AF II 114 (861) 14, *arrêté* of 6 niv., Commune d'Armes. Cf.: 'mon collègue Javogues, dont j'ai signé avec plaisir les écrits qu'il m'a présentés' (A.N., AF II 114, d. 3306, p. 58, Girard to C.P.S., 6 pluv.).

conspiracy of the villains at Lyon; the coalition between the rich and the priests to starve the people was the most recent evidence of the fact that the emergency was far from being at an end. But, on the one hand, the maintenance of the army was not a permanent but a temporary measure 'jusqu'au rétablissement complet de l'ordre', while, on the other, in order to preserve a semblance of respect towards the decrees of the Convention, it was forbidden to call itself 'armée révolutionnaire'—'elle ne sera considérée que comme garde nationale requise pour la détention des conspirateurs'.

This *arrêté* posed a difficult problem for the patriots with their intimate experience from the previous summer of what happened to people who disobeyed the Convention. Its illegality became increasingly apparent with the notification on 17 nivôse/6 January of the decree of 27 frimaire/17 December concerning those *armées révolutionnaires* that refused to disband.[1] This impression was reinforced when, on 20 nivôse/9 January, the proconsuls at Ville-affranchie ordered the battalion to be incorporated into the Parisian *armée révolutionnaire* at Commune-affranchie and made arrangements to station the 3rd Battalion of the Jura in the Loire for the maintenance of public order (thereby invalidating the arguments advanced by Javogues for maintaining the *garde nationale requise*).[2] Only the moderates of the District of Roanne knew their own mind—on 27 nivôse/16 January, they ordered the three captains of the detachments in their district to comply with the orders of the *Représentants* at Ville-affranchie and proceeded to use Javogues's infringement of the law of 14 frimaire as a powerful argument in their offensive against him.[3] Indicative of the dilemma in which most patriots found themselves was the statement that the *huissier* Pointier, with his legal background, was careful to make to the Municipality of Montbrisé before resuming his duties:

... qu'ayant été adjudant-sous-officier de la cidevant Armée Révolutionnaire il avait cessé toutes fonctions militaires et s'était conformé au décret de la Convention du 18 frimaire [*sic*] et qu'il n'entendait point porter les armes en cette qualité; que comme bon citoyen il croit qu'il est de son devoir de se conformer à l'arrêté des Représentants du peuple

[1] A.D.L., L 120. [2] A.N., AF II 114 (859) 4. [3] A.D.L., L 176, fol. 94.

Javogues et Girard qui le requièrent comme garde nationale requise et que ce n'est qu'en cette qualité qu'il servira la République.[1]

As for the Department, it attempted to tread a middle path between the choleric Javogues, whose proximity made nominal obedience imperative, and the powerful proconsuls of Commune-affranchie. After receiving the *arrêté* of 20 nivôse/ 9 January from Commune-affranchie on 21 nivôse/10 January, the Department had it printed for circulation but omitted to register its reception formally until 24 nivôse/13 January.[2] Meanwhile it immediately sent a copy to Javogues and tried to obtain some sort of policy statement from him by hinting at the difficulties under which it was labouring in providing adequate provisions and quarters, because it did not know how many soldiers were to be grouped at Feurs 'soit par tes ordres ou ceux de tes collègues [pour] le rassemblement de l'armée révolutionnaire'.[3] At the same time, it wrote to the *Représentants* at Ville-affranchie explaining that the *armée révolutionnaire* had been dissolved according to the decree of 14 frimaire; a couple of days later, it forwarded to them the printed version of the *arrêté* of 20 nivôse/9 January, with a letter assuring them of the vigour with which the administration would prosecute its execution.[4] As late as 9 pluviôse/28 January the Department was still attempting to maintain a position of legality. While carefully stressing that the troops at Feurs were companies of the former *armée révolutionnaire* assembled there prior to incorporation as prescribed by the Lyon proconsuls' *arrêté* of 20 nivôse, it resolved at the same time that, since the 3rd Battalion of the Jura had not yet arrived, it would ask Javogues to provide for the prisons to be guarded either by the absent Jura battalion or, more realistically, 'par les volontaires incorporés dans la quatrième division de l'Armée Révolutionnaire'—that is to say the former *armée révolutionnaire* of the Loire.[5]

[1] A.C. Montbrison, *reg. dél.*, no. 2, fol. 43 (18 niv.).

[2] A.D.L., L 18, fol. 130; A.D.L., L 120.

[3] A.D.L., L 80, fols. 16 and 17 (21 and 22 niv.). Cf. ibid., fol. 18, letter to Mun. of Feurs, 24 niv.: 'cette troupe qui doit incessament se rendre dans vos murs de passage ou autrement.'

[4] A.D.L., L 18, fol. 130 (letter of 21 niv.); A.D.L., L 80, fol. 18 (letter of 23 niv.)

[5] A.D.L., L 18, fol. 163.

Javogues's and Girard's *arrêté* was signed on 6 nivôse/26 December, that is to say at the very moment when the companies were being officially ordered to disband. Javogues must have prevented this happening at Armeville, where he was at the time, for there is no trace of any disbandment there.[1] But, on the same day, the Municipality of Montbrisé passed the order on to the commanding officers in that town, while the moderate District of Roanne implemented the decree more vigorously, warning the detachment 'au son de la caisse qu'ils aient à s'y conformer afin que nul individu de la dite armée révolutionnaire caserné à Roanne n'en puisse prétendre cause d'ignorance'.[2] It is questionable whether the *arrêté* of Javogues and Girard in fact maintained the battalion intact. It seems likely that this was only partially the case and that the *garde nationale requise* was smaller than the *armée révolutionnaire* and also contained some new elements, although under the same *état-major*. The quarter-master closed his accounts and sent them to the Department on 28 nivôse/17 January, in other words at a time when it was clear that the *armée révolutionnaire* as an institution was not going to be suppressed in the department.[3] Therefore, substantially, it must have been a second army that came into existence. The enrolment lists in the departmental archives of the Loire were also probably deposited there in nivôse and represent the state of the battalion at that time. Many soldiers were slow to return to their posts.[4] Although Javogues was able to order a company from Montbrisé to Feurs on 30 nivôse/19 January, on 12 pluviôse/31 January the commander-in-chief was still having great difficulty in assembling the company from Rambert-Loire.[5] It seems certain that the three companies of the district of Roanne disappeared completely. One of the captains—an enthusiastic protagonist of the *armée révolutionnaire*—officially opted on 27 nivôse/16 January for the post

[1] The *arrêté* was notified to the Dist. of Commune d'Armes on the same day, 6 niv. (A.D.L., L 130, fol. 58). But see below for possible changes in the artillery company.

[2] A.C. Montbrison, *reg. dél.*, no. 2, fol. 31; A.D.L., L 176, fol. 74.

[3] A.D.L., L 18, fol. 160.

[4] e.g. A.D.L., L 441, fol. 22, 15 pluv., rev. com. of Rambert-Loire arrests a dozen soldiers from Armeville travelling without papers to join their company at Montbrisé.

[5] A.C. Montbrison, *reg. dél.*, no. 2, fol. 47; A.D.L., L 441, fol. 21.

of *commissaire des Représentants* rather than that of captain in the *garde nationale requise*, and later appeared as a lieutenant in the *cavalerie requise*.[1] As from 5 nivôse/25 December, it was the ordinary National Guard that provided the sentinels at the prison in Roanne.[2] At the time of its dispersion in ventôse, the battalion only consisted of six companies as opposed to the twelve existing at the beginning of nivôse,[3] and the mission given by Duret on 15 pluviôse/3 February to 'Chataing, lieutenant de la compagnie de Rive-de-Gier' suggests that at least one of these companies was entirely new, for in the lists of the old *armée révolutionnaire* there is neither a company from Rive-de-Gier nor a Lieutenant Chataing.[4] Similarly, the officers of the company of *canonniers* from Armeville, who signed a petition to Javogues on 11 nivôse/31 December, were not those whose names figure as the officers of that company on the enrolment lists.[5] Lafaye *le jeune*, promoted departmental *commissaire des guerres* after the law of 14 frimaire ended his office as *procureur général syndic*, also indicated that the *garde nationale requise* was, in part at least, composed of different recruits from the old army when he complained that Javogues had admitted more than 700 men who had no equipment at all.[6]

Moreover, the army of the Loire was changing its character, for large numbers of *jeunes gens de la première réquisition* were in its ranks in pluviôse, which had not been the case before nivôse.[7] This was a development which brought it much more into line with the armies formed by Chasles, Isoré, and Paganel and which also emphasizes the reluctance of many older men, politically militant or not, to go along with Javogues on his revolutionary adventure.[8] The army was also changing its character in that, whereas previously it had been scattered throughout the department in garrisons (Roanne, Montbrisé, Feurs, Rambert-Loire, Armeville, Saint-Chamond), Javogues now started to gather it together in one

1 A.D.L., L 176, fol. 94, this date reveals the long-lasting chaos in the army; A.N., F7 4648, d. 4 (Civeton), requisition of 6 vent.

2 A.D.L., L 176, fols. 89, 104.

3 Cobb, op. cit. ii. 762.

4 A.C. Feurs, *reg. dél.*, 15 pluv.; A.D.L., L suppl. 419.

5 A.D.R., 1 L 190.

6 A.D.R., 1 L 216, 'Observations' (11 pluv.).

7 Ibid.

8 Cobb, op. cit. i. 286–8.

battalion at Feurs, as a single unit under the direct command of the *Représentant*.[1] Another innovation was the formation of a cavalry unit.[2] The mobility of such a force had obvious advantages as well as being an effective substitute for the men now absent from the original quota of 1,200. Javogues seems to have considered it to be the core of his army. On the one hand, Duret undertook its equipment with unusual urgency by requisitioning *chevaux de luxe* and by removing saddles, harnesses, etc. from sequestrated properties, whereas the other recruits, according to Lafaye, were hardly provided for.[3] On the other hand, the ablest officers of the former *armée révolutionnaire* and even outstanding patriots not previously connected with the force were incorporated into it—the former second-in-command, Escoffier, and Civeton both accepted demotion by becoming, respectively, captain and lieutenant; Costalin, former member of the *Conseil général* of the Department, and Chevallier, *juge de paix* of Thizy (Rhône) and an old friend of Javogues's confidant Lapalus, both became lieutenants.[4] Finally, part of the Parisian *armée révolutionnaire* appeared in the department. Javogues brought a detachment with him from Commune-affranchie at the end of frimaire,[5] while a second detachment under the *commissaire civil* Marcellin came about 10 nivôse/30 December, apparently at the invitation of Javogues.[6] In all, the group comprised about 400 men drawn from the 3rd, 5th, and 7th Companies of the 3rd Battalion, and was commanded by Captain Macquart and Captain Fauveau.[7] This was to be the

[1] A.D.L., L 80, fols. 16, 18, 19 (third *décade* of niv.).

[2] A.D.L., L 176, fol. 81.

[3] e.g. A.C. Feurs, *reg. dél.*, 8 and 15 pluv.; A.N., F^{1c} III Loire 5, dists. of Boën and Armeville; A.C. Roanne, 1 D 1 (2), fol. 272. There may have been three companies (A.D.L., L 124, fol. 27).

[4] A.D.L., L 124, fol. 27; A.N., F^7 4648, d. 4 (Civeton); A.D.R., 42 L 168, d. Bresson, Chevallier to Javogues, 6 pluv.; A.D.L., L 418, fol. 23. Civeton was probably first lieutenant, since in late pluv. he called himself 'chef de la compagnie de cavalerie établie par Javogues' (Vingtrinier, op. cit. i. 216, no. 4984); Escoffier probably went prudently out of circulation as soon as Javogues was recalled.

[5] A.D.L., L 390, fol. 4.

[6] A.N., D III 355, *compte décadaire* of Saint-Chamond, 28 niv.; Lefebvre, op. cit., p. 120 (10 niv.); *Les Soirées de la campagne ou le voyageur révolutionnaire*, 16 niv., article entitled 'Coup d'œil sur Commune d'Armes'.

[7] Scattered references identify some soldiers and their companies: Galley, op. cit. ii. 183; A.D.L., L 281; A.C. Montbrison, *reg. dél.*, no. 2, fol. 49. On Macquart and Fauveau, see Cobb, op. cit. i. 164, 173, ii. 507–14, 664, 973.

most active element of the *armée révolutionnaire* in the Loire during the rest of Javogues's time there, and he relied heavily upon it. Under the general direction of Duret, it was primarily the Parisians who enforced the *taxe révolutionnaire* at Armeville, who satisfied the demands of the *Représentant* for precious metal, who escorted the prisoners as he moved from Armeville to Montbrisé and Feurs, and who appear as the instrument of his campaign of dechristianization at this point much more than the native *garde nationale requise*.[1]

Adopting the distinction made by Richard Cobb, one may say that the action of the *armée révolutionnaire* of the Loire was almost exclusively 'administrative' as opposed to 'révolutionnaire', i.e. it was predominantly an executive instrument of the extra-ordinary, and more especially of the regular institutions of the department.[2] The insignificant Descombes Montmellieu in no way resembles men such as Griois, Seigneur, or Peyrend-d'Herval; the shadowy figure of Duret appears only fleetingly in a purely administrative capacity, which made no impression on the political orientation of the battalion.[3] The most striking personality is undoubtedly Civeton, *commissaire* of Javogues, *commissaire* of the proconsuls at Ville-affranchie, and a captain in the *armée révolutionnaire*; but Civeton always acted either as a *commissaire des Représentants* or as the captain of a company, never embarking on the unbridled forays that marked the career of a real *commissaire civil* such as Le Batteux or Vauquoy.[4] Even Marcellin and the detachment of the Parisian *armée révolutionnaire* did not have any independent existence. Although they were not subjected to the local authorities as the indigenous army was, the Parisians acted essentially on the orders of Javogues; their participation in the *taxe révolutionnaire* at

[1] e.g. A.C. Saint-Étienne, 1 D 10 (3), fols. 103, 112; A.D.L., L 124, fol. 16; Galley, op. cit. ii. 396–8; A.D.L., L 345, fol. 456.

[2] Cobb, op. cit. ii. 365.

[3] Like most of the military commanders of these companies (ibid. i. 329 ff.).

[4] A clear example of Civeton's methods is the case of the expedition against Saint-Just-la-Pendue at the end of frim.: 'J'ai requis le commandant de l'armée révolutionnaire à Feurs; il m'a fourni 50 hommes, Roanne 60, Saint-Symphorien 40, Tarare 50 et la compagnie de grenadiers de Neulize' (A.D.L., L 81, Civeton, 'commissaire des Représentants' to Depart., 1 niv.)—i.e. despite his rank, he acts solely as a *commissaire* by formal requisition to the *armée rév.* and the National Guard, without calling even upon his own company directly.

Armeville and in the dechristianization campaign was no more than the reflection, albeit on a willing instrument, of the policies of the *Représentant*. The Thermidorians claimed that Javogues urged his soldiers to shoot down former nobles, priests, lawyers, and pettifoggers like wild beasts;[1] certainly, his *arrêté* of 6 nivôse/26 December drew the attention of the recreated *garde nationale requise* particularly to the rich and the priests who, he alleged, had allied in order to starve the People. But there is no indication that the *armée révolutionnaire* itself took any initiative in translating such sentiments into action. Javogues was the Taillefer of the Loire, but there was no Viton.[2]

In the case of many *armées révolutionnaires*, it is their participation in the dechristianization movement which is the hallmark of their terrorist conviction and independence. In the Loire there were three major strands in the action of the *armée révolutionnaire* in this field. Firstly, the search for precious metals in the churches of the district of Armeville and the accompanying desecration undertaken by the Parisian *armée révolutionnaire*: but the soldiers were directed by *commissaires du Représentant*—it was Renard who emptied the churches of Commune d'Armes, and Voytier who visited the churches of the neighbouring villages and burned the altar, the statues, and the crucifix at La Ricamarie and at Planfoy.[3] Secondly, the damage wrought in certain parishes in the district of Boën under the orders of Fusil, member of the *Commission Temporaire*, during his brief visit to the department in early nivôse: here again the *armée révolutionnaire* was merely the executant.[4] Thirdly, the destruction of wayside crosses in a limited area around Montbrisé during the first half of frimaire: although there is nothing to link this positively with orders from above, such an action was perfectly in line with the policy at that time of most of the patriots in

[1] A.N., D III 349, d. Javogues, Montbrison.

[2] Viton, commander-in-chief of the *armée du Lot* (Cobb, op. cit. ii. 587–90, 713–19).

[3] A.D.L., L 124, fol. 16, L 345, fol. 456; Q 50, Mun. of Chuyers to Dist., 26 vend. an III.

[4] De la Chapelle, *Histoire des tribunaux révolutionnaires de Lyon et de Feurs*, pp. 29–31; A.D.L., Q 414 (Virigneux, Viricelle); A.C. Saint-Rambert, *reg. dél.*, 14 niv.; Jean Cerisier, *Reg. dél. de la commune de Savigneux*, pp. 9–10.

the local administrations, while there is no evidence of the soldiers going beyond attacking the crosses to more significant excesses on statues, holy books, etc. and to propaganda.[1] When detachments of the army visited villages in connection with food supplies or on expeditions such as that to Saint-Just-la-Pendue, there is never any sign that they wreaked havoc on 'les hochets du fanatisme'. This is a slender balance-sheet for an institution which, in other areas, became the symbol of militant atheism.[2]

Since the army lacked a political or military command capable of directing it independently, it was inevitable that it should become the instrument of the local authorities. In any case, Javogues's and Bassal's constitutive *arrêté* prescribed that it should obey orders from the Municipalities and the higher administrations. In fact, it was predominantly controlled by the Department and the Districts, and only to a lesser extent by the Municipalities, the clubs and the revolutionary committees. From the outset, it was the Department—already largely responsible, as we have seen, for the successful implementation of the proconsuls' *arrêté*—which organized the practical details of its service and prescribed its use to the subordinate regular administrations.[3] The Department's *arrêté* of 12 brumaire/2 November clearly stated the relationship between the latter and the *armée révolutionnaire* when it ordered the Districts to take all measures rendered necessary by the present circumstances in concert with the commanders of the detachments in their area.[4] Essentially, the role of the *armée révolutionnaire* in the Loire was to provide the necessary force for the execution of the orders of the regular and extra-ordinary institutions. The detachment garrisoned at Feurs, 'pour le service près le département', was symbolic of the position of the whole battalion, and when the Department issued a proclamation to the citizens of that town

[1] A.D.L., L 81, Decelle to Depart., 14 frim.; A.D.R., 42 L 169, d. Bouarde, evidence of Daphaud.

[2] e.g. Chaix in the canton of Lormes (Cobb, op. cit. ii. 676).

[3] e.g. A.D.L., L 18, fol. 28, *arrêté* of 20 brum. establishing the rotation of service of the companies; ibid., fols. 3, 9–10, 11, 20, various *arrêtés* of 3–13 brum. prescribing the use of this force for enforcement of *maximum*, threshing of grain, guard of prisons, etc.

[4] Ibid., fol. 19.

after religious strife in the club, characteristically the *armée révolutionnaire* was detailed to accompany the administrator who published the address.[1] Under these conditions, it is evident that class considerations did not influence its conduct: it was an instrument of government, equally adept at arresting an individual who was preaching a grain riot at Roanne as at guarding the nobles of the canton of Bourg-Argental.[2]

Javogues and Bassal gave wide terms of reference to the *armée révolutionnaire*. It was to search for suspects and conspirators and to guard the gaols where they would be kept; to protect the supply of food; to enforce the requisitions of the administrations, to break up suspect gatherings, to pursue men of no fixed abode, to demolish *châteaux* and any other buildings liable to harbour dangerous assemblies; to keep order at markets, to escort administrators during domiciliary visits, to keep watch on estates and forests belonging to the nation; to enforce the recruitment laws and the *maximum*.[3] These objectives resemble those invoked by the majority of *Représentants* when creating these armies.[4] Apart from incidental questions such as the threat of its use in order to provoke the immediate payment of the backlog in taxes,[5] the activity of the *armée révolutionnaire* essentially fell into two categories: repression and food supply.

Its routine repressive activity did not differ from that of the majority of these armies: to execute arrest warrants, to escort prisoners travelling within or, eventually, outside the department, and to guard the prisons.[6] Nearly all the arrests ordered by the regular administrations were effected by this army, while the various *commissaires*, whether of the administrations or of the *Représentants*, called upon its services whenever a detachment happened to be within reach.[7] Similarly, in the major centres where companies were stationed, the

[1] Ibid., fol. 94 (26 frim.).

[2] A.D.L., L suppl. 3, fol. 43 (13 Dec.); A.D.L., L 130, fol. 60.

[3] A.N., AF II 114 (859) 6.

[4] Cobb, op. cit. i. 263–73.

[5] A.D.L., L 130, fol. 29 (Dist. of Armeville). It never took part in the demolition of *châteaux*; the only reference to the National Forests was when it was used to escort groups of prisoners accused of *délits forestiers* (ibid., fol. 40).

[6] Cobb, op. cit. ii. 547, 560–73 (especially p. 564).

[7] e.g. A.D.R., 42 L 182, d. Labarre, 42 L 186, d. Philippon; A.D.L., L 80, fol. 7, L 259, fol. 20, L 130, fol. 30.

revolutionary committees, with the exception of moderate Roanne, invariably preferred to use the patriotic force rather than the more unreliable National Guard.[1] Before the disruption of the battalion in nivôse, all the major prisons of the department were guarded by these soldiers, while the larger convoys of prisoners were entrusted to them, as were important individual suspects.[2] Occasionally, it was called upon to participate in repressive operations of a wider scope. This was the case at the end of brumaire, when the revolutionary committee at Fontfort/Saint-Galmier used a minor brawl as a pretext to persuade the Department to send a *commissaire* with a detachment of the *armée révolutionnaire* against the Municipality and the *juge de paix*.[3] Similarly, it was a mixed detachment of the *armée révolutionnaire*, the 5th battalion of the Puy-de-Dôme, and the National Guard under Civeton that went at the end of frimaire to clear the hills round Saint-Just-la-Pendue of their fugitive counter-revolutionaries, refractory priests, and deserters, and the *armée révolutionnaire* remained stationed there for a while.[4] Finally, it is possible that it was the *armée révolutionnaire* that undertook the executions by firing-squad at Feurs. There is no direct evidence of this, and the Thermidorian writers fail to mention a subject which, one imagines, would have suited their purposes admirably. Nevertheless, when the Department complained to the tribunal at the end of frimaire about the inefficiency of the firing-squad, it wrote that it had just delivered a quantity of ammunition to Escoffier.[5] Since Escoffier was the second-in-command and, at this time, the effective commander of the army, this would suggest that the *armée révolutionnaire* was, in some capacity, associated with these executions: in any case,

[1] e.g. A.D.L., L 441 *passim* and L 434 (2) *passim*. The rev. com. of Roanne did not always disdain the army: A.N., F7 4648, d. 4 (Civeton), warrant of 8 frim.

[2] e.g. A.D.L., L 176, fols. 89, 104 (Roanne), L 79, fol. 16 (Feurs); A.D.R., 42 L 169, d. Bouarde (Montbrisé); A.D.L., L 130, fol. 60 (Armeville); A.D.L., L 55, fol. 4, and A.D.R., 42 L 182, d. Labarre.

[3] A.D.L., L 81, letter to Depart., 28 brum.; A.D.R., 42 L 157 and 168.

[4] A.D.L., L 81, Civeton to Depart., 1 niv.; A.D.R., L 190, ibid. to Javogues, n.d.; A.D.L., L 176, fol. 74.

[5] A.D.L., L 79, fol. 26. If this were established, it would be a characteristic peculiar to the *armée de la Loire*, for, discounting the actions at Nantes and in the Morbihan, even the *armée parisienne* only participated very indirectly in legal executions (Cobb, op. cit. ii. 548).

the men used must have been taken either from the *armée révolutionnaire* or the 5th Battalion of the Puy-de-Dôme, since these were the only two bodies of troops available in the department at the time.

'Du moment de notre activité naîtra celui de l'abondance dans nos marchés et boutiques', wrote Civeton at the end of brumaire.[1] Although this optimism was misplaced, it reflects the assumption made by all patriots that the *armée révolutionnaire* was the indispensable agent in obtaining a proper distribution of food through the protection of markets, the search for hoarded stocks, and the enforcement of the *maximum*. As with all these bodies, the *armée révolutionnaire* became the instrument of the urban centres against a rural population increasingly unwilling to supply the markets under the double menace of over-all shortage and fixed prices.[2] But this was due less to a control of the army by communalist-minded regular and extra-ordinary institutions at a local level, as was the case with the smaller armies organized by individual towns, than to the simple fact that the feeding of the large urban population in this agriculturally poor department was the major preoccupation of all the authorities at every level. Thus, at its very first meeting, the Department ordered the Districts to send *commissaires* with detachments of the *armée révolutionnaire* to all communes to discover which had not implemented the laws on the *maximum*;[3] the District of Armeville went further by sending four detachments throughout the whole district in order to check the accuracy of the declarations of grain reserves by house-to-house searches.[4] Of the three districts, that of Roanne, despite its food problems, was the least affected by the *armée révolutionnaire* in this respect, because of the reluctance of the moderate administrations.[5] Even the relatively fertile district of Boën was worked over by this force because the events of the summer had depleted the harvest; the authorities of the town of Montbrisé employed it several times to obtain food from the surrounding countryside.[6] Characteristically, it was in the

1 A.D.L., L 81, letter to Depart., 27 brum.

2 Cf. Cobb, op. cit. ii. 451–6.

3 A.D.L., L 18, fol. 3 (3 brum.).

4 A.D.L., L 81, letter to Depart., 2 niv.

5 No mention at all.

6 A.C. Montbrison, *reg. dél.*, no. 2, fols. 4, 9, 47.

district of Armeville, the poorest area in the department, that the *armée révolutionnaire* was most active. The Municipality of Commune d'Armes, for instance, frequently sent it, with or without the express permission of the District, to the rural communes to obtain additional grain and flour for the town, and used it to mount guard at the bakers' shops and at the market.[1] In some areas of France the *armées révolutionnaires* were used to thresh the grain during the autumn of 1793, and this was prescribed in brumaire by the *Représentants* at Commune-affranchie when they created armies in the departments under their jurisdiction. The action of the army of the Loire, however, does not appear to have gone as far as this, despite the fact that the Department authorized the Municipalities to employ it to this end and that the District of Armeville even organized three companies of 'batteurs révolutionnaires' for use in the Forez if necessary.[2]

Thus, the activity of the *armée révolutionnaire* of the Loire reflects in essentials the fundamental preoccupations of all its sisters in the Republic and is characterized by its complete subordination to the local authorities and more especially to the regular administrations. The position of the army was clearly revealed when, after a number of cases of insubordination had occurred at Montbrisé, the army's second-in-command wrote to the Department begging it to help the officers maintain discipline: the Department immediately reduced one of the corporals to the ranks.[3] Similarly, the revolutionary committee at Montbrisé wrote to the revolutionary tribunal for a ruling concerning the negligence of the commander of the detachment in the town, who had failed to report on the execution of a number of arrest warrants, thereby implying that, although the committee had no dis-

[1] e.g. A.C. Saint-Étienne, 1 D 10 (3), fols. 76, 77, 84. Cf. A.D.L., L 371, fol. 59 (Mun. of Valbenoîte, 24 frim.): 'L'armée révolutionnaire venait dans cette commune et leur empêchait d'acheter les denrées menues qui leur sont nécessaires pour substanter leur famille . . .'. At Saint-Chamond, on 13 brum., the club, ordered house-to-house searches with the *armée rév.* in view of the shortage (Lefebvre, op. cit., p. 57).

[2] A.D.L., L 18, fols. 20, 54 (*arrêtés* of Depart., 13 brum. and 3 frim., directing its use for sequestrated and confiscated grain)—significantly enough, only the Dist. of Armeville seems to have implemented this directive (A.D.L., L 130, fol. 38); A.D.L., L 18, *comité des subsistances* of Armeville to Depart., 5 brum.

[3] A.D.L., L 81, letter to Depart., n.d.; A.D.L., L 18, fol. 71 (13 frim.).

ciplinary powers over the *armée révolutionnaire*, the latter was at least obliged to render account to it.[1] The army that existed after nivôse was equally subservient and differed only in that it came more directly under the control of the *Représentant*. In any case, the Department had lost many of its powers by the law of 14 frimaire. There were very few exceptions to this rule. In the case of food, we can see none; in the case of repressive measures, the arrest by Sergeant Granjon of one of the federalists of Armeville, whom he met while travelling to Saint-Chamond, is remarkable for its unique nature—a much more normal attitude was that of Captain Mathieu Égalon, who heard that Jean-Pierre Maccabéo had tried to recruit for the federalist forces, but merely drew up a report of the fact without arresting him.[2] Equally unique was the really very minor incident when Rochat, the Jacobin *juge de paix* of the canton of Saint-Jean-Soleymieux, arrested after his denunciation by the assembly of the inhabitants and refused certain documents by the Municipality for this reason, returned with the *armée révolutionnaire* in order to obtain them.[3]

Naturally, the soldiers of the *armée révolutionnaire* were prone to bad behaviour in the execution of their duties, and petty theft and rough treatment were not uncommon. The rich and the counter-revolutionaries, in whose houses they tended to be billeted or whom they guarded under house arrest, could expect little leniency. The detachment in the house of Salichon *jeune* at Armeville kept an open table for seventeen days and got through 300 bottles of fine wine and several hectolitres of ordinary wine.[4] The ex-curé of Chazelles-sur-l'Advieu complained, admittedly in the Year III, that during a domiciliary visit he lost at least two hundredweight of salted pork, a couple of donkey-loads of ordinary wine, 160 bottles of matured and imported wines, as well as thirty

[1] A.D.R., 42 L 188, d. Lachaize, *procès-verbaux* of 6 and 10 frim. Cf. also A.D.R., 42 L 95, fol. 24, Aulagnier and Dubois, officers arrested in niv., to *Comm. rév.*, 3 vent.: 'Ils se sont fait représenter par devant le Représentant Javogues pour savoir le fait de leurs arrestations, mais il a répondu que c'était les affaires du comité mais non les siennes, et s'étant fait représenter au comité ils ont fait réponse que c'était les affaires de Javogues.' If it was not clear to whom the *armée rév.* was subordinated, it was at least evident that it was not a free agent.

[2] A.D.R., 42 L 190, d. Yvon (21 Oct.); A.D.L., Q 218 (4 Nov.).

[3] A.D.L., L 381, fol. 56 (3 niv.).

[4] A.N., loc. cit.

couples of pigeons, a great quantity of small objects and pieces of furniture, and as much linen as the soldiers wanted.[1] The seventy-four-year-old Praire Durey was harshly handled by the Parisians looking for precious metal on Javogues's orders. Suspecting him of having a hoard hidden away, they threatened first of all to keep him in prison without any of the essentials of life; then they waved murderous weapons at him in the most ferocious manner; finally, in full view of his family, they took him out into the courtyard of his house, tied him to a tree in front of a firing-squad, blindfolded him, and said that he would be executed unless he revealed his cache:

> J'avais déclaré et livré tout ce que je possédais, je ne pouvais rien ajouter et m'écriai 'J'ai dit la vérité, vous pouvez tirer.' A cette réponse l'on suspendit et l'on me détacha. Une personne qui me dit à l'oreille: 'avoue, malheureux, ou tu vas périr'; même réponse de ma part et j'attendis l'instant fatal.[2]

But, as with the vast majority of these armies, these incidents in no way mean that the *armée révolutionnaire* of the Loire was a band of thieves as the Thermidorians claimed.[3] There were only two clearly criminal characters in it: Lieutenant Aulagnier and his second lieutenant, Dubois, who were arrested in nivôse for the theft of 16,000 *livres* together with gold and silverware from the persons whom they were guarding under house arrest.[4] Indeed, the soldiers appear remarkably restrained in comparison with some of their colleagues in other areas who, without being in the least criminal, were given to much more licentious activities. The *armée révolutionnaire* committed no more than the minor misdemeanours characteristic of all troops which were grossly exaggerated by the Thermidorians in exactly the same way as the patriots of the Forez themselves exaggerated out of all proportion the excesses of the 5th Battalion of the Puy-de-Dôme. The soldiers treated their lodgings at Feurs in the manner in which so many troops from time immemorial have treated their billets, breaking into wardrobes, fouling beds, removing

[1] A.D.L., L 281, fol. 11.

[2] A.D.R., 42 L 186, d. Praire, petition to *Comm. rév.*, 29 pluv.

[3] A.D.L., L 384 (Égalon Élie): 'Ceux qui avaient posé les scellés chez les riches pour voler leurs portefeuilles et ne demandaient qu'à voler.'

[4] A.D.R., 42 L 167, d. Aulagnier.

water-taps, mattresses, and linen, burning doors, bedsteads, and floor-boards, etc.[1] Even the incidents of indiscipline at Montbrisé, where they stopped peasants coming to market outside the town and paid at a rate well below the *maximum*, were only serious in so far as they were prejudicial to the continued supply of the market.[2]

In general, therefore, the *armée révolutionnaire* of the Loire, the third largest of the departmental and communal armies, is a typical example of them.[3] It displays almost all the basic characteristics emphasized by Richard Cobb in his study of this phenomenon, without ever illustrating the independence or the excesses of some formations, such as the *armée révolutionnaire* of the Lot. It was one of the 'armées discrètes', which formed the majority.[4] Its soldiers were as unenterprising as those of all provincial armies, and it lacked a *commissaire civil* of calibre.[5] Javogues was taking it in hand after his return to the department and, if his mission had not been interrupted, it might have developed along the lines of its more radical fellows. Within the context of the department, it was, in common with the greater number of the armies, an important weapon in the hands of the local authorities for translating their decisions into acts, whether by carrying out arrests, enforcing food requisitions, or simply escorting important convoys of prisoners, money, or archives. More than that, its mere existence was a powerful argument in securing obedience: the Department was exploiting an oft-used manœuvre when, in nivôse, it threatened to send the troops to collect the silver in the churches of those communes that failed to surrender it within three days.[6] But we cannot, on this evidence, endorse the view that leads Richard Cobb to include the Loire in the areas where 'des forces

1 A.C. Feurs, *reg. dél.*, 17 frim., 13 and 17 niv.

2 A.D.L., L 81, Escoffier to Depart., n.d.

3 The *armée du Lot* had 3,200 men and the *Légion de la Montagne* had 2,200 (Cobb, op. cit. i. 299–300). Javogues and Bassal ordered the levy of 12 companies of 100 men each, including officers, i.e. 1,200 men. An *arrêté* of the Depart. of 9 frim. (A.D.L., L 18, fol. 62) talks of 11 companies and 1,148 men, while the enrolment lists (mid frim.?) show 12 companies plus a company of *canonniers* plus the *état-major*, in all 1,273 men (A.D.L., L suppl. 419).

4 Cobb, op. cit. ii. 552.

5 Ibid. ii. 553, on the character of the rank and file of provincial armies.

6 A.D.L., L 80, fol. 18, circular to Dists., 25 niv.

révolutionnaires ont . . . momentanément régné en maîtres, se comportant comme en pays conquis, destituant, arrêtant, mettant en liberté, remplaçant à tour de bras, balayant autorités constituées et objections juridiques', and to say that 'dans la Loire l'armée créée par Javogues sera la principale pourvoyeuse de la Commission militaire de Feurs et de celles qui siègent à Lyon'.[1]

The maintenance of an *armée révolutionnaire* in the Loire by Javogues despite the law of 14 frimaire was illegal and indeed contributed to his recall at the end of pluviôse. It was therefore inevitable that it should rapidly disappear after his departure. Its last task was to escort the prisoners awaiting trial at Feurs to Commune-affranchie.[2] The *Représentant* Méaulle, who went to the Loire in order to clear up after Javogues, sent a letter explaining the situation to his colleagues Laporte and Fouché, who, on 7 ventôse/25 February, disbanded the army.[3] All the soldiers were to be sent home, except for the young men of the *première réquisition*, who were ordered to join the depot regiments. The horses (700 according to Javogues),[4] which this *Représentant* had requisitioned, were to be valued and sent to the service for which they were best suited, except those unsuitable for any service and those indispensable to agriculture.[5] The companies were formally dismissed by the *commissaire des guerres*, Lafaye, on 13 ventôse/3 March.[6] The *armée révolutionnaire* of the Loire was, therefore, the last but one of these communal and departmental armies to be dissolved and the last one in France to have been operative outside the context of the Parisian *armée révolutionnaire*, for the army of the Allier, which outlived it by about fifteen days, had already been absorbed into the Parisian detachment at Commune-affranchie.[7]

[1] Cobb, op. cit. ii. 548, 549.

[2] A.D.L., L 261, fol. 47, detachment under Civeton, 25–29 pluv.

[3] A.N., AF II 114 (860) 13, 'vu la lettre du Représentant du peuple Méaulle', 'considérant que cet ordre des choses est irrégulier'.

[4] A.N., AF II 114 (861) 15, Javogues to anon., 22 pluv.—probably one of his habitual exaggerations.

[5] This had already been undertaken by Civeton, game to the last, on the orders of Méaulle during the first *décade* of vent. (A.N., F7 4648, d. 4 (Civeton)).

[6] A.D.L., L 124, fol. 72. There was in fact a certain amount of confusion over the dissolution. Some companies, obeying the *arrêté* of the *Reprs.* of 20 niv., went to Cne-aff.

[7] Cobb, op. cit. ii. 762.

VII

THE *COMMISSAIRES*

JACQUES GODECHOT has already emphasized the importance of the 'agents de liaison' in the functioning of the Terror.[1] But he was speaking only of the *Représentants en mission* and of the various itinerant agents of the *Conseil Exécutif* and the committees of government, whose purpose was to impose unity of action on the diversity of ordinary and extra-ordinary institutions throughout the Republic. It is essential to elaborate this theme for a proper understanding of the Terror at a regional level, since, in the context of a department, the minor *commissaires* in many ways performed the same functions as did their more spectacular counterparts in the national context.

The *commissaires* were the agents employed by any institution or authority for the execution of tasks falling within its jurisdiction and for the implementation of policies and decisions made by it. Every regular and extra-ordinary authority in the department, from the *Représentant en mission*, himself a *commissaire* of the government, down to the local revolutionary committees and clubs, used large numbers of them. Moreover, the *commissaires* of authorities from outside the department pursued their missions in the area. Some *commissaires* were employed by more than one authority at once; many passed successively from the service of one to that of another.[2] Their powers varied immensely both between *commissaires* of different institutions in respect of the varying competence of each institution, and also between *commissaires* of the same institution in respect of the differing objects of their particular missions. Certainly, *commissaires* were no new phenomenon;

[1] J. Godechot, *Les Institutions de la France sous la Révolution et l'Empire*, pp. 304–9.

[2] e.g. Civeton employed by Javogues and the *Comm. Temp.* (A.N., F7 4648, d. 4 (Civeton), and A.D.L., L 176, fol. 64); André Béraud, employed by Javogues and then taken on by the Dist. of Armeville (A.C. Saint-Étienne, 1 D 10 (3), fol. 68, and A.D.L., L 130, 31 Oct.).

they were an important feature of administration just as much under the Ancien Régime as during the early years of the Revolution. But their multiplication is one of the distinctive characteristics of the Terror and they therefore merit a separate place in a discussion of the structure of terrorism. At the same time, their multiplicity renders it extremely difficult to make any statement about them which is more than the barest generalization.

The authority of the *commissaire* came from the body employing him. For the purposes of his mission he *was* that body, which had delegated the whole or a part of its authority to him. Similarly, when a *commissaire* used a *sous-commissaire* to help him in part of his mission, he delegated to him for the execution of his task that authority which he himself had received from his employer. 'Tu es le pouvoir exécutif', wrote one *sous-commissaire* in the district of Roanne to an agent of the *Conseil Exécutif*, 'je suis, ainsi que tu l'as bien voulu, ton Représentant.'[1] The *commissaires* of the more important authorities, particularly those of the central government and of the *Représentants en mission*, usually received a written statement of the terms of reference of their mission and of the powers delegated to them; they were supposed to register these powers with the administrations in the area of their mission, but in many cases they omitted to do so.[2] If the *commissaire* was authorized to use armed force for the achievement of his mission, it would also be stated in his powers, although in practice this was only written into the powers of those who were not also members of the administrations of the districts or of the department, since, presumably, the latter would have an *ex officio* right to do so.[3] This right to call on the National Guard (or the *armée révolutionnaire* whenever convenient) was only accorded to those with repressive missions, whether arrest or sequestration, and occasionally for tasks likely to encounter some hostility such as the massive

[1] A.N., F^7 4394 (2), d. 3, p. 29, Charles Guyot to Moinaux, 3 Oct. Cf. Vauquoy said: 'Je suis délégué d'un représentant du peuple, je suis donc pariel à un représentant du peuple' (Richard Cobb, *Les Armées révolutionnaires*, ii. 627).

[2] e.g. complaint by Dist. of Armeville that Jourjon never registered (A.D.L., L 124, fol. 45), and failure of Malboz, Teyssier, etc., active in the dist. of Boën since 14 brum., to register before 18 frim. (A.D.L., L 259, fol. 34).

[3] e.g. A.D.L., L 176, 22 pluv.; L 130, 12, 23, and 31 Oct., 11 Nov., and 26 pluv.

requisitions of cavalry equipment for the *armée révolutionnaire* ordered by Javogues in pluviôse.[1]

The importance of the *commissaires* resided fundamentally in their mobility. All the ordinary and extra-ordinary authorities (even, in the case of Javogues, the *Représentant en mission* himself to a large extent) were rooted to one spot. All institutions, even the most informal revolutionary committee gathering at the house of one of its members, needed a meeting-place where the necessary quorum could carry on business; the busiest authorities were tied down by archives and clerks and by practical problems of transport, lodging, and time involved in a move.[2] *Commissaires* were, therefore, indispensable to every authority. They were the mechanism which reconciled the isolation of immobile administrative bodies from the mass of the population and from subordinate authorities with the increasing demands for omniscience and omnipresence imposed by the circumstances of the Year II. They were the eye and the arm of institutions which otherwise had to rely upon independent organs for information and for the implementation of their decisions.[3] For instance, the *Commission Temporaire* at Commune-affranchie, a body that functioned as the *commissaire* of the *Représentants* there, was, significantly enough, divided specifically into two sections, one of which was *permanente* and always resided at Commune-affranchie, while the other was *ambulante*, with its members journeying round the departments under the jurisdiction of the proconsuls at Commune-affranchie.[4]

Another major advantage of using *commissaires* was that in delicate matters they allowed the authorities to rely only on men whose commitment to the Terror was unqualified. This was particularly important, since many aspects of the *gouvernement révolutionnaire* were bound to meet with passive

[1] e.g. A.D.L., L 130, loc. cit.; e.g. A.D.L., L 124, fol. 18, and L 382, fol. 45, powers of Gelas, Gaye, and Duplain.

[2] Cf. the law of 14 frim., sect. II, art. 13, which made this a statutory obligation: 'Toutes les autorités constituées seront sédentaires, et ne pourront délibérer que dans le lieu ordinaire de leurs séances . . .'

[3] Note how, when one commune announced an error in its *recensement des grains*, the Dist. of Roanne decided that it could not verify the claim since so many administrators were already away on mission (A.D.L., L 176, 16 frim.).

[4] A.N., AF II 137 (1063), d. 13, p. 24, *arrêté* of Collot, Fouché, and Delaporte, 20 brum.

resistance from minor local authorities. For example, all three Districts set up a whole system of *commissaires* to draw up tables of reserves of grain: villages could be expected to make false returns in order to protect their resources.[1] As for the *commissaires* appointed for repressive measures, it was even more essential that they should be men who would show no sympathy for the suspects. For routine problems which required a large number of *commissaires*, such as the *recensement des grains* or the requisition of cattle for the army, local personalities were employed.[1] But, whenever possible, the Districts and the Department tended to use their own members, particularly the *conseillers généraux*.[2] Vial spent fifty-four of the sixty-four days of the life of the *conseil général* of the department absent on various missions;[3] in nivôse, after the suppression of the *conseil général* by the decree of 14 frimaire/4 December, the *directoire* of the department twice found that it did not have a quorum for its deliberations because so many members were absent on mission.[4] Similarly, the local committees and clubs nearly always delegated their own members: the club at Saint-Chamond, for instance, gave 215 missions to its members between 28 September and 30 pluviôse/18 February.[5] Javogues for the most part used eminent patriots —in the early days men such as Pignon, Civeton, Jean Philippon, François Guyot, and Perier, many of whom would soon move on to posts in the administrations; when he returned to the department, he used officers of the *armée révolutionnaire*, such as Phalippon and Fayolle, or members of the Department whose functions had been suppressed by the law of 14 frimaire, such as Chana, Lafaye, and Vial. Not unnaturally a few mistakes were made in the confusion at the beginning of the period immediately following the federalist crisis, especially by the Auvergnat Committee of Public Safety of Montbrison, which had no personal knowledge of

1 A.D.L., L 130, 26 Oct. (Armeville), L 259, 3 frim. (Boën), L 176, 12 Oct. (Roanne).

2 A.D.L., L 259, 19 brum., 3, 7, and 25 frim., 15 and 19 niv.

3 A.D.L., L 18, 3 brum., order by Depart. to Dists. to send *commissaires* taken from their *conseils généraux* into the villages to enforce the laws relating to the *maximum*.

4 A.D.L., L 18, 8 niv.

5 Ibid., 22 and 29 niv.

6 G. Lefebvre, *Société républicaine*, *passim*.

the background of its servants.[1] Nevertheless, the essential quality of the *commissaire* was that he was a politically reliable man to whom such dangerous subjects as food, repression, dechristianization, etc. could be entrusted. Thus, *commissaires* were often used when a reply was urgently needed from a higher authority or when it was imperative to defend certain interests.[2] The authorities of Roanne sent a series of *commissaires* to Paris and to Commune-affranchie in their struggle against Lapalus and Javogues; if the Department had sent a *commissaire* to Javogues as well as to the *Représentants* at Ville-affranchie at the end of frimaire, the misunderstanding over the suppression of the *armée révolutionnaire* might have been largely avoided.[3]

Most of the manifold *commissaires* operating in the department exercised purely executive functions, that is to say they were given a limited mission concerned with a specific object or objects of administration. These ranged from buying leather for the requisition of shoes for the army to the sale of perishable sequestrated goods, from the installation of a revolutionary committee to the adjudication of fishing rights on national property, from supervising the collection of taxes to enforcing the departure of the young men of the *première réquisition*.[4] Some missions would require a great deal of travelling, such as those concerned with the purchase of grain in other departments, whereas others were purely local, such as the drawing up of an inventory for a particular property.[5] Some tasks were relatively more important than others, as, for example, draining ponds to raise the river level for the mills as opposed to the removal of bedding for troops from suspects' houses.[6] Similarly, *commissaires* were used from time to time by the higher administrations in order to obtain

[1] e.g. A.D. P.-de-D., L 2781, 11 Oct., complaints that some *commissaires* for placing seals 'sont aristocrates et peut-être plus muscadins que ceux chez qui ils devaient exercer leur mission'.

[2] e.g. A.D.L., L 176, 15 frim., Dist. of Roanne sends Vally to *Repr.* and Depart. to obtain food; L 259, 1 frim., Dist. of Boën sends Plagnieux to carry the administration's defence to the Depart.

[3] A.D.L., L 176, 5, 24, 25, and 26 frim., 8 pluv.; L 18, 4 niv.

[4] e.g. A.D.L., L 176, 17 Sept., L 130, 13 niv., L 259, 25 frim., L 261, 21 pluv., L 438, 16 pluv., L 390, 18 niv.

[5] e.g. A.D.L., L 176, 22 vent. and 24 brum.

[6] e.g. ibid., 20 Oct.; L 259, 21 frim.

first-hand information, like, for instance, the two sent by the District of Boën to inquire into the dispute between Noirétable and La Chamba, or the one employed by the District of Armeville to collect the details about mines asked for by the Committee of Public Safety.[1] In some cases, a *commissaire* would have only one task, while in others he might have several.[2] But beyond emphasizing the variety of their business and their importance as a mechanism for the efficient administration of the *gouvernement révolutionnaire*, we can largely ignore these men for the purposes of this chapter.

Equally, there is no need to dwell in detail upon most of the agents of authorities outside the department who appeared in the Loire during this period. Such men as Joseph and Louis Caillet, *commissaires* of the Minister of the Interior for the confiscation of all goods belonging to the inhabitants of Lyon, or Bourgeois and Hubert, sent by the Minister for War to regulate the arms industry, or Bataillard and Jacob, *commissaires* of the *Commission des subsistances* to supervise the mines, were again mere executives.[3] More important were Dorfeuille and Millet, *commissaires* of the *Représentants en mission*. Dorfeuille was first employed in September by the *Représentants* directing operations against Lyon in order to mobilize the national guards of the district of Roanne against the federalist troops in the Forez, as well as to enlighten public opinion about the real nature and causes of the troubles and to publicize the measures adopted by the Convention, together with the means used by the *Représentants* to implement them.[4] After a brief spell on the revolutionary tribunal of Commune-affranchie, the *Représentants* there sent him to Commune d'Armes in late frimaire to direct the arms industry and with more general powers to destroy *fanatisme*, to co-ordinate the various authorities, and to maintain 'l'esprit public à la hauteur de la Révolution' in the whole district.[5] But during his

[1] A.D.L., L 261, 1 pluv., L 130, 12 frim.

[2] e.g. ibid., 4 niv., mission of Bajard.

[3] A.C. Roanne, 1 D 1 (2), fol. 188; A.D.L., L 130, fol. 14 and L 18, fol. 30; L 123, fol. 390.

[4] A.D.L., L 176, fol. 5, powers dated 27 Aug., signed Dubois-Crancé, Gauthier, and Reverchon.

[5] A.D.L., L 130, fol. 52, powers dated 22 frim., signed Albitte, Fouché, Laporte, and Collot d'Herbois.

time in the Loire this former *acteur tragique* from Toulouse, who had spent most of the early years of the Revolution touring the clubs to propagate the revolutionary spirit by reading his own works,[1] exercised his talents ('son maintien noble et assuré, son ton gracieux, son air modeste, sa voix sonore')[2] almost exclusively in the realm of propaganda. In the district of Roanne, he sent *sous-commissaires* round the villages to read and distribute to the assembled people an address he had written;[3] in the district of Armeville, he harangued the population of Rive-de-Gier, Saint-Chamond, and Armeville, and in the latter town he organized two grandiose *fêtes civiques* full of allegories denouncing superstition, one of them culminating in the mock execution of the tyrants of Europe.[4] As for Millet, he visited the department in late brumaire and early frimaire with a wide mandate from the *Représentants* at Commune-affranchie which combined powers of arrest with these same functions of propaganda and the supervision and co-ordination of authorities.[5] But he only worked very briefly in the district of Roanne and in the northern part of the district of Boën, soon returning to Commune-affranchie as secretary and 'investigateur de pièces relatives aux coupables' at the revolutionary tribunal.[6] The only representatives of this type of *commissaire* who merit any special attention are Lapalus, *commissaire* of the Committee of General Security to the district of Roanne, and the various emissaries of the *Commission Temporaire*. They must be considered in connection with the part played by *commissaires* in repression.

[1] A.D.R., 1 L 208, contains a few biographical hints and details of his journeys.

[2] Bibl. Lyon, Coste MS. 681, no. 2, minutes of the club at Angers, 29 May 1701.

[3] A.N., F7 4648, d. 4 (Civeton).

[4] *Journal de Commune-affranchie et des départements de Rhône et Loire*, 2 niv.: these speeches contained mostly exhortations on 'fanatisme', the *maximum*, and suspects—he claims a speech of two hours at Saint-Chamond in the open air (on 25 frim./15 Dec.!); ibid., 5 niv.; *Journal républicain des deux départements de Rhône et de Loire*, supplement to 26 niv.

[5] A.D.L., L 18, fol. 56, powers for districts of Campagne de Lyon, Roanne, Montbrison, and Saint-Étienne, dated 7 brum., signed Couthon, Delaporte, and Maignet.

[6] A.D.L., L 176, fol. 47, L 259, fol. 19; A.D.R., 42 L 157, letter to *soc. pop.* of Montchalier-Laval, 3 frim.; A.D.R., 42 L 10, letter to Dorfeuille, 1 frim.; ibid., list of members of the rev. trib. Millet was a former engineer of the *Ponts et Chaussées* (A.N. T 566 (1)).

The role with which the *Représentants* had entrusted Dorfeuille and Millet was the same one played by all the *commissaires* who had functions extending beyond the purely administrative field—they supervised the Terror and its humbler institutions; they supplemented the efforts of these institutions wherever necessary and also acted as the propagandists of the *gouvernement révolutionnaire*. For example, in frimaire, Gay of the Department visited several parishes of the district of Roanne 'pour y connaître l'esprit public, propager les principes de la Constitution, y ramener l'ordre et les mettre à la hauteur de la Révolution, y prêcher les droits de l'homme, l'exécution des lois et tout ce qui sera jugé convenable et enfin tout ce que les vrais républicains doivent s'empresser de faire'.[1] Plagnieux of the District of Boën, who appears to have been a particularly able *commissaire*, carefully wrote a few basic principles in the *registre des délibérations* of the Municipalities of Rambert-Loire/Saint-Rambert, (Saint-) Marcellin-la-Plaine, and (Saint-) Jean-Soleymieux and gave judicious encouragement to the Municipality of Bonnet-la-Montagne by writing praise for its patriotism and for the accuracy of its *recensement des grains* in its register.[2] Between frimaire and pluviôse the revolutionary committee of Valdorlay/Saint-Paul-en-Jarez was visited by two *commissaires* of the Department and two from the District of Armeville, who checked its registers, resolved a few problems for it, and encouraged it;[3] another *commissaire* of the Department felt so strongly that the feebleness of the District of Roanne made it imperative for him to keep a careful eye on the conduct of affairs in the town, that he held long meetings with both it and the Municipality about the revolutionary and repressive measures.[4] At a lower level, one should note the action of *commissaires* like those sent throughout the canton of Néronde by the committee and the club jointly to expound the great principles of the Constitution and to inquire into the implementation of the *première réquisition* and the confiscation of suspects' possessions; simi-

[1] A.D.L., L 176, 11 frim.: Gay cannot be connected with the similar general mission given by the Depart. on 18 frim., mentioned below.

[2] A.C. Saint-Rambert, *reg. dél.*, 19 brum.; A.D.L., L 382, fol. 18, L 381, fol. 51, L 378, fol. 13.

[3] A.D.L., L 394, fols. 9, 11, 13, 20.

[4] A.D.L., L 81, letter from Dubessey, 2 niv.

larly, the club at Saint-Chamond appointed *commissaires surveillants* to travel round the canton supervising food supply.[1]

Occasionally, the functions of supervision, co-ordination, propaganda, and repression were all specifically outlined in the powers delivered to *commissaires*: those sent by the Department into each district in frimaire were ordered to check that the revolutionary committees were properly organized and had the right attitudes, to issue all proclamations deemed necessary, to arrest all suspects still at large, and finally to reveal to the people all the ills that result from *fanatisme*.[2] More normally, however, a *commissaire* would carry out most of these tasks without being expressly directed to do so. Fusil's request to the *Commission Temporaire* is significant: 'Envoyez-moi des imprimés, des chansons, des mandats d'arrêt et de la cire';[3] Chartre, delegated by the Department to search the estate of a rebel, spent his time, while waiting for a colleague at Roanne, purging the club; Plagnieux seized every opportunity of making rousing speeches:

> Le citoyen Plagnieux est monté dans la chaire de la dite église . . . Il nous a fait amplement connaître quels étaient les devoirs des vrais républicains. Son discours a duré [une] demi-heure et pendant ce temps l'on aurait entendu voler une mouche dans l'assemblée. Son discours fini, les claquements de mains se sont fait entendre jusque dans les maisons les plus éloignées de ce bourg. Lorsque le commissaire est descendu de la chaire le citoyen Rochat, juge de paix du canton, l'a embrassé en versant des larmes de joie. Le citoyen Meygrat, procureur de la commune, en a fait autant et à cet exemple tous les citoyens se sont jetés en foule sur ce commissaire pour lui donner le même baiser fraternel. Après quoi ils se sont donnés mutuellement le même baiser en criant Vive la République une et indivisible, Vive la Convention nationale, et Vive le citoyen Plagnieux commissaire. . . .[4]

[1] A.D.L., L suppl. 101, 6 frim.; Lefebvre, op. cit., p. 137, 9 pluv.

[2] A.D.L., L 18, 18 frim. By virtue of this commission, Potey, for example, on his first day at Montbrisé, visited the rev. com. to check on its work and attitude, issued a warrant against a trouble-maker in the mountains, broke up a fight in the guardroom, and denounced a number of emblems of feudalism to the Mun. (A.D.L., L 81, letter from Potey, 25 frim.).

[3] De la Chapelle, *Histoire des tribunaux révolutionnaires de Lyon et de Feurs*, pp. 29–31, Fusil's report on his mission, 15 niv. The members of the *Comm. Temp.* invariably made speeches wherever they went: e.g. Perrotin at Roanne and Dessirier at Amplepuis (A.D.L., L 176, fol. 86, and A.C. Amplepuis, *reg. dél.*, no. 2, fol. 23).

[4] A.D.L., L 81, letter from Chartre, 28 brum.; L 381, fol. 53, also L 382, fol. 21, and L 378, fol. 12.

Indeed, although the *commissaires* were never consciously organized as a system, it would not be an exaggeration to refer to them, from the greatest, the *Représentant en mission* himself, down to the obscure envoy of a revolutionary committee, as a system of supervision and co-ordination at every level from the regional to the local, with wider or narrower terms of reference and larger or smaller geographical areas of jurisdiction.

The most influential *commissaires* were those whose principal activity was repression. Their basic objective was to supplement the inadequacies of the repressive institutions. Endowed with powers of arrest, their task was to ensure that the laws concerning suspects and rebels were uniformly applied throughout the area and to achieve an ideal situation where no suspect remained at liberty. Civeton said that he had powers 'pour purger le département de la Loire'.[1] Their activity was characterized by the few formalities attached to it; the federalist crisis had rendered the problem of suspects acute and it needed to be dealt with rapidly and comprehensively. Lapalus admitted that he had arrested without distinction all those on whom there lay the slightest suspicion, and he protested 'je me suis conduit, dans mes opérations, en révolutionnaire'; an observer of the work of Javogues's *commissaire*, Pignon, related that he had worked 'révolutionnairement'; the agents of the *Commission Temporaire* were always authorized to take whatever 'mesures révolutionnaires' the circumstances demanded.[2] Acting as travelling inquisitors, they usually intervened directly, issuing and executing their own arrest warrants or else delegating their execution to a *sous-commissaire*. In some cases, however, and especially in the later months of the period, they would have recourse to the revolutionary committees: thus, for instance, Fusil and Lefranc, *commissaires* of the *Commission Temporaire*, visited the committee at Montbrisé in nivôse

[1] A. Vingtrinier, *Catalogue de la bibliothèque lyonnaise de M. Coste*, i. 216, no. 4984, letter to *Reprs.*, 28 pluv.

[2] Ibid. i. 212, no. 4911, letter to *Comm. Temp.*, 16 niv., and A.D.R., 42 L 183, d. Lapalus, letter to Dorfeuille and Millet, 16 niv.; A.N., W 408, d. 939, investigation of 3–6 prair., evidence of Nesme; e.g. A.D.L., L 176, fol. 112, powers of Grimaud, and A.D.R., 42 L 21, 28 frim., powers of Lemoigne and Michel.

and suggested that a house-to-house search would be *à propos*.[1] At the same time, *commissaires* ordered committees and Municipalities to draw up lists of suspects wherever this had not been done.[2] Moreover, nearly all these *commissaires* devoted considerable attention to making certain that the various decrees ordering the sequestration of the possessions of suspects and rebels were implemented, and to sealing arrested persons' papers, which was an essential measure if plots were to be uncovered and suspects convicted.[3] It is extremely difficult to make any accurate assessment of the work of these *commissaires* in terms of arrests, largely because, on the one hand, their *procès-verbaux* were written on loose sheets and therefore much more liable to destruction than the registers of the revolutionary committees, and also because, on the other hand, many of them appear to have been most negligent about recording their activities. From diverse sources we have been able to count 363 arrest warrants issued on their own initiative, that is to say excluding arrests carried out on the orders of an employer.[4] But it must be stressed that this is a minimum figure. It is impossible to attempt to calculate the amount of property that they sequestrated: Pignon and Béraud, for example, claimed to have seized well over 5,000,000 *livres*' worth in the district of Armeville.[5] These *commissaires* were, then, just as important as the revolutionary committees in organizing, stimulating, and implementing repression.

Leaving aside those employed by the local revolutionary committees who were usually designated to make a number of specified arrests and can therefore be included in the category of executive *commissaires*, the *commissaires* for repression can for convenience be divided broadly into four types according to the source of their powers: first, the

[1] A.D.L., L 434 (1), fol. 40.

[2] e.g. Lapalus at Charlieu (A.D.L., L 399 (1), 24 vend.) and Pignon at Saint-Chamond and Saint-Étienne (A.C. Saint-Chamond, *reg. dél.*, 6 Oct., and A.C. Saint-Étienne, 1 D 10 (3), fol. 68, 5 Oct.).

[3] In some cases missions were given exclusively for sequestration: e.g. Javogues's order to Deville to seize Lyonnais cloth in the bleach-crofts of the dist. of Roanne, 3 Sept. (A.D.L., L 176, fol. 15).

[4] The most important figures are: Lapalus, 112; Pignon and *sous-commissaires*, 90; Civeton, 73; *commissaires* of *Comm. Temp.*, 39.

[5] A.D.R., 42 L 186, d. Pignon, letter to Javogues, 9 Oct.

members of the *Commission Temporaire*; second, Jean-Marie Lapalus who, as *commissaire* of the Committee of General Security, is in a class of his own; third, the *commissaires* of the proconsuls; and finally, the *commissaires* of the regular administrations.

The *Commission Temporaire* had jurisdiction over the department of the Loire since it was the agent of the regional proconsuls based at Commune-affranchie.[1] In the middle of nivôse, Lemoigne, Michel, Boissière, and Perrotin all appeared briefly at Roanne in order to investigate vociferous complaints from the people of that town against Lapalus.[2] At the end of frimaire, Dubois and Copette, members of the club at Ville-affranchie and employed by the *Commission* to remove precious metal from the churches, were at work in the canton of Chazelles-sur-Commune-affranchie.[3] At some time in late nivôse, Sadet was active in the department, since Javogues arrested him for unknown reasons and the *Commission* had to delegate two members to intercede on his behalf.[4] But the only one of its *commissaires* to have done work in any detail was Fusil. With his assistant Lefranc and a detachment of the Parisian *armée révolutionnaire*, he travelled round the districts of Boën and Armeville during the whole of nivôse.[5] They visited Feurs, Montbrisé, and the neighbouring small villages, Bonnet-la-Montagne, Rambert-Loire, Sury, and Armeville.[6] Their work consisted above all in dechristianization—clearing out churches, prohibiting the celebration of mass, enforcing work on Sundays, and celebrating *fêtes civiques*—but in the course of this work they arrested a number of priests and other suspects.

[1] Richard Cobb, 'La Commission temporaire de Commune-affranchie', *Terreur et Subsistances*, pp. 55–94. This article is very incomplete on the work of the *commissions ambulantes*.

[2] A.C. Roanne, 1 D 1 (2), fols. 238, 240 (13 and 17 niv).

[3] A.C. Chazelles-sur-Lyon, *reg. dél.*, 26 and 30 frim., 3 niv.

[4] A.D.R., 31 L 50, 3 pluv.; A.C. Montbrison, *reg. dél.*, no. 2, fol. 51, *arrêté* signed Fouché, Laporte, Méaulle, and Javogues, 4 pluv., releasing him. There are no details of this mission.

[5] Fusil was at Feurs on 2 niv. (A.D.L., L 18, fol. 115); he was recalled on 28 niv. (A.D.R., 31 L 54).

[6] Feurs, A.D.L., L 18, fols. 115 and 117; Montbrisé, A.C. Montbrison, *reg. dél.*, no. 2, fol. 36; Bonnet-la-Montagne, De la Chapelle, op. et loc. cit.; Rambert-Loire, A.C. Saint-Rambert, *reg. dél.*, 17 niv.; Sury, A.D.L., L 329, fol. 3; Armeville, A.D.R., 31 L 50, 15 niv.

Jean-Marie Lapalus was appointed as a *commissaire* by the Committee of General Security at the end of September.[1] With his companion Évrard, whose effective role was, however, negligible, his mission was to arrest 'les tyrans de leur pays . . . les conjurés . . . les députés fugitifs et conspirateurs' who, it was said, had fled into the Monts du Beaujolais, and also to conduct an inquiry into the behaviour of all the district administrations in the Rhône-et-Loire. In fact, Lapalus's activity affected the three departments in which the Monts du Beaujolais stood—the Rhône, the Loire, and the Saône-et-Loire (districts of Villefranche, Roanne, and Marcigny). As far as the department of the Loire is concerned, Lapalus was one of the dominant figures in the history of the Terror, since, for a time, he *was* the Terror in the eastern half of the district of Roanne. He arrived at Roanne on 24 vendémiaire/15 October and ceased to work as a *commissaire* of the central government in about the middle of nivôse. The period of his most intense activity was the month of frimaire, for he appears to have fallen ill during brumaire. He was himself a native of the Haut-Beaujolais and had originally gone to Paris at the end of July 1793 in order to obtain the intervention of the government on behalf of the local patriots who were then having a difficult time. He was therefore concerned with repression primarily in the mountains and only secondarily in the Plaine du Roannais. Similarly, the nature of his previous experiences there, when he had seen that dissensions centred above all on the religious problem, dictated the character of his activities. Under his direction repression took predominantly, though not exclusively, the form of arresting *fanatiques* and priests. At the end of his mission the area was completely *déprêtrisé*, if not *déchristianisé*. But Lapalus very rapidly ran into the virulent hostility of the inhabitants of Roanne, while his arrests provoked increasing agitation in the countryside towards the end of frimaire. He had incarcerated several members of the club at Roanne, and when the club sprang to their defence, he threatened to have it walled up. From the beginning of frimaire the regular and extra-ordinary authorities of Roanne launched a campaign

[1] For a detailed survey of Lapalus's activity, Lucas, art. cit. This paragraph is based on this.

against him at Paris and Commune-affranchie, which culminated in the middle of nivôse in the issue of a warrant for his arrest by the *Commission Temporaire*. Lapalus was able to escape and placed himself under the protection of Javogues, whose confidential assistant he became.[1] In pluviôse he was appointed to the revolutionary tribunal at Feurs.

As far as the *commissaires* of the *Représentants en mission* and those of the regular administrations are concerned, one must make further distinctions according to the period at which they were employed. The *commissaires*, whose powers were the widest and whose activity was the most developed, were those appointed during the few weeks following the expulsion of the federalist troops from the Forez until just after the fall of Lyon. As we have seen, this was a period of near anarchy, when most of the major regular authorities in the districts of Montbrison and Saint-Étienne were discredited. It was vital to mobilize the resources of the area for the siege and it was essential to seize all the sympathizers with the rebels, both to secure the rights of national vengeance and to prevent any rising to the rear of the army.[2] One of Javogues's *commissaires* in the district of Saint-Étienne reported at the beginning of October that the legislation and the *arrêtés* concerning the rebellion were completely unknown there, with the result that he had found everything very quiet and the large number (as he believed) of guilty men quite unmolested.[3] The dearth of trustworthy administrators and the absence of any system of revolutionary committees led not only to the establishment of the Committees of Public Safety in the district of Montbrison, but also to the appointment of a large number of *commissaires* throughout the department. Quite apart from the plethora of purely administrative missions,[4] a variety of authorities delegated wide powers for

[1] A.N., W 408, d. 939, investigation of 13–26 flor. an II, evidence of Vernoy, ex-secretary to Javogues: 'Le citoyen Lapalus était . . . auprès de Javogues, chargé de vérifier les différentes accusations et pétitions des détenus pour d'après en faire son rapport.'

[2] Above, p. 57.

[3] A.D.R., 42 L 157, Pignon to Javogues, 8 Oct.

[4] The C.P.S. of Montbrison largely confined its repressive activities to that town: seals placed on 144 people's papers in Montbrison compared with 3 outside, 44 arrest warrants for Montbrison compared with 9 for elsewhere; its *commissaires* were almost all employed for requisitions for the army (A.D. P.-de-D., L 2781–2).

the area. One can cite as examples the Auvergnats Dulac and Limet, *commissaires* of Couthon, Maignet, and Châteauneuf-Randon, who organized Committees of Public Safety, arrested suspects, and collected food for the army;[1] Pinaud of Saint-Marcellin, to whom Javogues gave powers expressed as limitless in order to make all the national guards of the district of Montbrison march against Lyon;[2] Joseph Reynard, employed by Javogues for the arrest of deserters;[3] Liogier, member of the Department of the Haute-Loire and *commissaire* of Couthon, Maignet, and Châteauneuf-Randon in the south-west corner of the department, 'chargé de la surveillance dans cette partie de la République';[4] Forest of Moingt, who was busy sequestrating property round Montbrison on the flimsy pretext of a 'commission pour affaires militaires' signed by General Nicolas;[5] the *commissaires* sent out by the Municipality of Saint-Étienne to search for suspects and those employed by the District for the sequestration of property, and many other examples.[6]

The largest single group of *commissaires* during this early period were those who held their powers from Javogues. In this case one must distinguish further between, on the one hand, those appointed at the time of the expulsion of the federalists and during the siege of Lyon, and, on the other, those appointed immediately after the fall of Lyon when Javogues returned briefly to the department. As long as the siege lasted, Javogues was directly concerned only with the southern part of the department, for the *Représentants* with each of the units besieging Lyon were primarily interested in

[1] A.D.R., 42 L 159, 42 L 176, d. Desnoyelles; 42 L 179, d. Debigny and d. Fauget; 42 L 181, d. Jacquet d'Arthun; A.D.L., Chaleyer MS. 283, *reg. dél.* of Mun. of Fontanès, 9 Oct. They had been Couthon's *commissaires* for the *levée en masse* in the dist. of Thiers (A.N., T 566 (1), letters to Couthon, 5 and 8 Sept.).

[2] A.D.R., 42 L 163, 170, d. Caire, powers dated 8 and 17 Sept.; probably only active in the south of the dist.

[3] A.D.L., L 130, fol. 16, powers dated 26 Sept.; probably only active in dist. of Saint-Étienne.

[4] A.D.L., L 382, fol. 10, and L 378, fol. 5, registered with Mun. of Saint-Marcellin and Saint-Bonnet-la-Montagne, 24 and 25 Sept.

[5] A.D. P.-de-D., L 2783, p. 6, powers dated 29 Aug.

[6] A.D.R., 42 L 179, d. Praire Neyzieu, *procès-verbal* of 2 Oct.; A.D.L., L 130, fols. 12, 16, 22, *commissaires* of Dist., Sept.; A.D.R., 42 L 174, d. Chabanes, petition to Dorfeuille, 8 niv., recounting his activity as *commissaire* of the Dist. for arrests and sequestration immediately after the fall of Lyon.

ensuring control over the area on which they were based.[1] It was only after the siege that Javogues began to employ *commissaires* for the whole department.[2]

Of all Javogues's *commissaires* in this period the lawyer Pignon was undoubtedly the most important. In late September he received from Javogues the normal commission to arrest all suspects and to sequestrate and place seals upon their belongings throughout the district of Saint-Étienne.[3] In principle, this was a joint commission with André Béraud, mayor of Saint-Pierre-de-Bœuf, but Béraud seems to have been as completely dominated by Pignon as Évrard was by Lapalus. Pignon was remarkable for the thoroughness with which he organized his mission. As far as the business of repression was concerned, he ruled as absolute master over the whole of the district of Saint-Étienne. The other direct *commissaires* of Javogues there made very little impression compared to him, or else they worked in close collaboration with him, as did, for example, Saint-Didier, whose especial interest seems to have been Saint-Chamond and who reported his activities to Pignon.[4] Pignon was the only *commissaire* in this early period to have attempted to make repression at all systematic. The Municipalities that he visited drew up lists of suspects;[5] he kept a careful record of all those people whose property had been sequestrated, made lists of property to be sequestrated, and issued a general proclamation ordering the confiscation of all goods belonging to the inhabitants of Lyon;[6] he even appears to have purged some of the smaller Municipalities and to have provisionally appointed substitutes in consultation with an assembly of

[1] e.g. Philippon (powers dated 7 Sept. for cantons of Saint-Galmier and La Fouillouse, A.D.L., L 130, fol. 16); Perier (active round Saint-Chamond mid Sept.–mid Oct., A.D.R., 42 L 167, d. Bruyas, 42 L 170, d. Terrasson and d. Trainet); Saint-Didier (active at Saint-Chamond and Saint-Étienne, early Oct., A.C. Saint-Étienne, 1 D 10 (3), fol. 67); etc.

[2] e.g. Raymond (powers dated 12 Oct. for dist. of Montbrison, A.D.R., 42 L 186, d. Prodon, A.D. P.-de-D., L 2781, 27 vend.); Civeton, Broa, and Chantelot (powers dated 21 Oct. for dist. of Roanne, A.N., F7 4648, d. 4 (Civeton)); Malboz and three others (powers dated 14 brum. for dist. of Boën, A.D.L., L 18, fol. 26).

[3] A.C. Saint-Étienne, 1 D 10 (3), fol. 68, powers dated 27 Sept.

[4] A.N., W 408, d. 939, Saint-Didier to Pignon, 6 Oct.

[5] e.g. ibid., 'État et liste des citoyens suspects' (Saint-Romain-les-Atheux).

[6] Ibid., 'Liste de ceux dont les biens ont été séquestrés dans le district de Saint-Étienne' (in Pignon's hand) and other such lists; A.D.L., L 390, fol. 12.

the inhabitants.[1] Beyond this, he devoted attention to such matters as the *levée en masse*, the requisition of saddle-horses, and the *maximum*.[2]

But the most significant aspect of Pignon's career was his use of *sous-commissaires*. He organized a complete system of *sous-commissaires* to cover the whole district, and thus his supervision and intervention became automatically much more of a uniform reality throughout the area than they ever would have been if he had relied on his own efforts alone. In some cases powers were delegated to *sous-commissaires* for the whole district, as, for instance, Jean-Claude Gauthier, authorized to search for refractory priests, suspects, and trouble-makers throughout the area.[3] More normally *sous-commissaires* were assigned to one section of the district, and Pignon developed a pattern of one or two of them per canton.[4] Beyond this, there were *sous-commissaires* with missions relating to specific persons, while in some cases Pignon entrusted a Municipality with the execution of a warrant for the arrest of a suspect whom he had not been able to seize personally at the time of his visit.[5] The precise nature of the functions of these *sous-commissaires* is rarely altogether clear. A few were certainly endowed with full powers of arrest, as, for example, Jean-Claude Gauthier. Yvon, on the other hand, was authorized only to get reports from the Municipalities about the sequestrations they were supposed to have undertaken.[6] The Municipality of Outre-Furan was ordered to seize a suspect and to sequestrate his property, while Charles Démolis was sent to supervise this with powers to requisition armed force if the situation demanded it and to file an official denunciation of the Municipality should it refuse to comply.[7]

[1] A.N., loc. cit., investigation of 3–4 prair., witnesses from Bœuf and Malleval, and investigation of 13–26 flor., evidence of Antoine Fromage.

[2] Ibid., notes entitled 'moyen pour opérer la levée des jeunes gens', 'chevaux de selle', 'impositions', 'municipalités', 'gardes nationales', 'sœurs de Saint-Joseph', 'renouvellement des municipalités', 'loi qui taxe les denrées de Ière nécessité', 'esprit public'.

[3] A.D.L., Q 92.

[4] A.N., loc. cit., list of cantons and corresponding names of *sous-commissaires*.

[5] e.g. ibid., investigation of 13–26 flor., evidence of Thivet; e.g. ibid., *procès-verbaux* dated 29 and 30 Sept. at Saint-Pierre-de-Bœuf and Chavanay.

[6] A.D.R., 42 L 190, d. Yvon, powers dated 19 Oct. for cantons of Maclas, Pélussin, and Bœuf.

[7] A.D.L., L 130, fol. 20, powers of 9 Oct.

Ducros and Champagnat, *sous-commissaires* in the canton of Marlhes, sequestrated property and collected denunciations which they forwarded to Pignon without making any arrests;[1] but Jean Coste claimed that he had powers both to place seals and to search for suspects.[2] As for Jourjon, on 17 October at Saint-Romain-en-Jarez he called himself *commissaire* 'pour faire la visite des gens suspects', and on 18 October at Cellieu *commissaire* 'pour s'informer des gens suspects'.[3] In any case, a number of these *sous-commissaires*, including Jourjon, clearly did make arrests on their own initiative.[4] However, there is no evidence that any of them were particularly independent of their employer: on the contrary, some referred problems to him in great detail.[5]

Although Pignon was the man who developed the idea to its greatest extent, he was not the only one to have used sub-delegates. François Guyot employed his colleague Jean Lacour from the Municipality of Saint-Germain-Laval, while throughout his mission Lapalus constantly relied upon them.[6] But neither Guyot nor Lapalus ever gave them more than executive powers for specified arrests, although Lapalus occasionally ordered his *sous-commissaire* to decide on the utility of incarceration according to information gathered on the spot. But the delegation of powers in this way was dangerous in that it created an element of confusion. Some *sous-commissaires* did not trouble to indicate their real status: Ducros and Champagnat were not the only ones to call themselves 'commissaires chargés de pouvoirs des Représentants du peuple', which naturally gave them an appearance of greater authority than they actually possessed.[7] Although Pignon himself was careful to register his powers with every

1 A.D.R., 42 L 175, d. Crouzat.

2 A.D.L., L 130, fol. 31.

3 A.N., loc. cit., *procès-verbaux* of these dates. Cf. ibid., declaration by Jourjon to Dist. of Armeville, 16 pluv., that Béraud and Pignon gave him powers 'pour accélérer le séquestre'.

4 e.g. ibid., *procès-verbaux* of 17 Oct. at Chagnon and letters from Chol to Pignon, 10–12 Oct.

5 e.g. A.D.L., Q 92, Girodet and Coste at Bourg-Argental, 14 Oct., and A.N., loc. cit., Chol to Pignon, 10 and 12 Oct.

6 A.D.L., L 418, fol. 18; Lucas, art. cit.

7 A.D.R., 42 L 183, d. Lardon. Note also how ordinary *commissaires* sometimes used each other as *sous-commissaires*, e.g. 'sur la réquisition du citoyen Perier, commissaire, d'après la réquisition du citoyen Tardy, le cidevant minime Gauthier a été arrêté' (A.D.R., 42 L 180, d. Gauthier).

Municipality that he visited, his *sous-commissaires* were very much more negligent about publicizing the nature of their functions.[1] In some cases, the delegation of powers reached absurd lengths: for instance, the execution of one arrest warrant issued by Lapalus was delegated four times.[2] Indeed, the profusion of ordinary *commissaires* in the early period was already conducive to a muddled situation which a proliferation of *sous-commissaires* of ambiguous authority could only aggravate. Although some *commissaires* were able to work in harmony,[3] others interfered with each other. Chol, *sous-commissaire* of Pignon, complained that one of the very few patriotic curés of the Monts du Pilat had been arrested by *commissaires* with powers from the *Représentants du peuple*.[4] The activities of Forest, an *aubergiste* from Moingt, who was marching around the countryside with some armed men seizing and carrying off foodstuffs and movables, brought an angry denunciation from the Committee of Public Safety at Montbrison. The committee itself hesitated to arrest Forest, who made no secret of his bitter resentment of its interference, because he profited from the confusion of the early days by vehemently claiming a verbal commission from the *Représentants*. Indeed, within three days, the committee found itself enlisting him as its own *commissaire*, although it did try to insist that he behave calmly and without noisy display.[5]

In the powers that he gave to them, Javogues had expressly authorized Pignon and Béraud to use *sous-commissaires*,[6] but it is evident that he quickly became worried by the proportions this had assumed. On 23 October he suppressed all the

[1] e.g. A.N., loc. cit., certificates dated 29 Sept., 1 and 5 Oct., given by Muns. to acknowledge the registration of Pignon's powers.

[2] A.D.R., 42 L 120, d. Jean Thomas.

[3] e.g. A.D.R., 42 L 163, *commissaires* of proconsul with those of Dist. of Boën.

[4] A.N., loc. cit., Chol to Pignon, 10 Oct.

[5] A.D. P.-de-D., L 2782, p. 1, and L 2783, p. 6, 21 Sept.

[6] 'Autorisent les citoyens Béraud et Pignon à s'adjoindre telles personnes qu'ils jugeront à propos pour exercer la plus active surveillance et pour empêcher qu'aucune personne puisse échapper à la peine portée par la loi du 12 juillet dernier.' This does not give any clear indication of the functions that he intended the *sous-commissaires* to have: the decree ordered the dismissal and arrest of all officials implicated in the rebellion, but the authorization in Javogues's *arrêté* is inserted after the powers of sequestration and before the powers of arrest delegated to Pignon and Béraud.

commissions he had given for the district of Armeville on the grounds that he had only appointed *commissaires* as a temporary substitute for the regular authorities whose conduct had been counter-revolutionary; now that these administrations had been renewed and were able to exercise the function of active supervision, *commissaires* had become not merely redundant but positively dangerous on account of the great opportunities for abuse arising out of the difficulties in accurate accounting. 'Il importe', he continued, 'de resserrer les pouvoirs dans les corps administratifs, afin d'éviter toute confusion, d'assurer la fidélité des opérations et d'empêcher la fraude'; the District of Armeville alone was competent for arrests, the sealing of papers, and sequestration, but it could delegate its powers to the Municipalities provided these rendered an exact account of their operations.[1] Certainly, this *arrêté* did not in any way mean the end of the use of *commissaires* for repression in the department. The attitude of mind that inspired this decision had not prevented Javogues from commissioning Civeton, Broa, and Chantelot two days previously with wide powers of arrest in the district of Roanne, while Malboz and his three companions were not given their mission by him until 14 brumaire/4 November.[2] But neither group was authorized to use *sous-commissaires*. Moreover, the District of Armeville soon discovered the impossibility of dispensing altogether with *commissaires* for repression, and on 31 October delegated powers of arrest and sequestration in certain areas to André Béraud and Gabriel Girodet, a former *sous-commissaire* of Pignon.[3]

Nevertheless, Javogues's *arrêté* of 23 October is important because it marked the end of a period of confusion. The numbers of *commissaires* in charge of repression declined sharply. Malboz and his colleagues continued to be active round Bonnet-la-Montagne until the end of frimaire, while Civeton, who operated with quiet efficiency west of the Loire in the district of Roanne, was still making arrests there in mid pluviôse, although, in the latter case, the fact that he received powers of arrest from the *Commission Temporaire*

[1] A.D.L., L 123, fol. 343, signed at Armeville. [2] Above, p. 204, n. 2.

[3] A.D.L., L 130, fols. 29, 30: Béraud for the cantons of Pélussin and Bœuf, Girodet for the canton of Bourg-Argental.

must have helped him to continue.[1] But henceforth those with the widest powers and geographical areas of jurisdiction were almost exclusively those employed by the higher regular administrations, such as the five members of the District of Boën sent by their colleagues on 15 brumaire/5 November throughout the district to carry out arrests, to sequestrate property, to inquire into 'le patriotisme des citoyens', and to draw up lists of suspects, or else the three members of the Department who received a similar mission for the department on 18 frimaire/8 December.[2] The development of the regular administrations as the most important employers of *commissaires* meant that the missions were much more clearly organized. There was no continuation of the practice of sub-delegation: on the contrary, on 22 brumaire/12 November the Department deplored the fact that several *commissaires* for the purchase of grain on behalf of the towns and the army were extending the area of their activity by delegation, and it ordered that no *commissaire à subsistances*, whoever his employer, might operate before his powers had been counter-signed by the Department; earlier, it had already appointed one of its members to supervise the *commissaires* sent from Armeville to buy food in the district of Boën.[3] Those of their agents who were not themselves administrators were subjected to far greater restrictions than their predecessors had been. Thus, the powers of arrest that the District of Armeville gave to André Béraud on 31 October were only valid until the Municipalities received the *arrêté* of 30 October prescribing the execution of the Law of Suspects; then, 'il ne sera plus que surveillant des municipalités', entitled merely to denounce.[4]

But Javogues's *arrêté* and the increasing assertion of the authority of the regular administrations were not the only factors in clearing up the confused situation of the early period. The fall of Lyon naturally meant the withdrawal of the multiple *commissaires* employed to deal with the needs

[1] A.D.R., 42 L 167, d. Rony; Bibl. Roanne, 3 L (1) 18, multiple arrest warrant, dated 12 pluv., signed Civeton and Costalin: they were at that moment Javogues's *commissaires* for the requisition of cavalry equipment, but had no repressive powers in that capacity (Bibl. Roanne, 3 L (1) 20, powers dated 7 niv.). A.N. F7 4648, d. 4 (Civeton), powers from *Comm. Temp.*, dated 13 frim.

[2] A.D.L., L 259, 15 brum., L 18, 18 frim.

[3] A.D.L., L 18, 22 and 14 brum.

[4] A.D.L., L 130, fol. 29.

of the army and its protection. The development of a system of revolutionary committees obviated the necessity for such a large number of *commissaires* assigned to direct the work of repression, with their consequently wide powers. Furthermore, the appointment of so many of the more important of the early *commissaires* to other posts removed them from their functions: thus, for example, François Guyot became secretary-general and Jean Philippon and Perier became *conseillers généraux* of the Department, Raymond, Tardy, and Pinaud were appointed administrators of the district of Boën, and Saint-Didier became secretary of the District of Armeville. Finally, the fact that Javogues was absent from the department between mid brumaire and the end of frimaire removed one of the most fertile sources of commissions. But even after his return Javogues only very rarely gave to his *commissaires* the wide repressive powers which their predecessors had had.[1] Now they were habitually employed for specified arrests, however many there may have been in any one mandate: for instance, having received a list of nearly a hundred suspects in the district of Armeville, Javogues empowered Pignon to arrest all those mentioned on it.[2]

Apart from the question of *sous-commissaires* and the difficulties produced by large numbers of *commissaires* of differing origins, one of the greatest problems raised by the use of *commissaires* for anything more than limited executive tasks was the ease with which they were able to commit *abus de pouvoirs*, because there was in reality very little means of controlling a *commissaire* in the field. An *abus de pouvoirs* must be taken to mean an action either beyond the terms of reference of the particular *commissaire* or altogether beyond the competence of the authority that had delegated powers to him, or else an abuse of those powers, especially on the part of *commissaires* employed for repression when they made

[1] The only one we have found is Fayolle, authorized *c.* 8 pluv. to arrest and to transfer to Feurs all the suspects and counter-revolutionaries he might discover throughout the depart. (A.D.R., 42 L 156); this mission was only executed at Montchalier-Laval and Roanne (A.D.L., L 414, fol. 16, L 176, fol. 105).

[2] A.D.R., 42 L 163, powers dated 2 pluv. Cf. A.D.R., 42 L 176, d. Martinon, on verso of a letter denouncing a number of suspects, powers for the arrest of 'ceux désignés dans la lettre'.

arrests without sufficient cause.[1] In some areas of France there were spectacular cases of this, such as the careers of Vauquoy, Dolle or Viton. In the Loire, however, while there certainly was a number of *abus de pouvoirs*, it never reached the same proportions.[2] Many *commissaires* were careful to respect the limits of their functions. One, who had been ordered to make an arrest by Javogues but who had run into opposition from the villagers, applied to the *Représentant* for the right to use force and for extended powers of arrest, instead of adopting them at once; Vial, *commissaire* of the Department in brumaire, wrote back for 'des pouvoirs que je mette tous ceux ci-devants dans la gage' after a suspect noble had started to insult him, demanding his powers and saying that they were quite insufficient and contrary to a law that prohibited his arrest and the sequestration of his effects.[3] As for arbitrary arrest, one *commissaire* insisted to the *procureur* of a village Municipality, who was complaining about an inhabitant, that he could only make an arrest on the basis of a formal denunciation, while even Fusil reported that, in order to remain within the bounds of legality when arresting priests, he had adopted the technique for getting two patriots to make any sort of denunciation: 'alors je ne l'arrête point comme prêtre, mais bien comme dénoncé.'[4] Not all, however, were quite so punctilious under the pressure of circumstances, nor did they always give any clear reasons for the arrests they made.[5] Naturally, *commissaires*, were accused of using

1 Cf. law of 14 frim., sect. III, art. 15: 'Il est expressément défendu . . . d'étendre l'exercice de leurs pouvoirs au-delà du territoire qui leur est assigné; de faire des actes qui ne sont pas de leur compétence; d'empiéter sur d'autres autorités, et d'outrepasser les fonctions qui leur sont déléguées, ou de s'arroger celles qui ne leur sont pas confiées.'

2 e.g. the case of Forest of Moingt: 'les actes arbitraires qu'il se permettait en établissant des gardes de 12, 15, 18 et 20 hommes dans différentes maisons et en enlevant et faisant transporter chez lui des bestiaux, vins, grains et autres objets' (A.D. P.-de-D., L 2783, p. 6, C.P.S. of Montbrison to *Reprs.*, 21 Sept.).

3 A.D.R., 42 L 169, d. Thévenet, letter to Javogues, Sept.; A.D.L., L 81, letter of 24 brum.

4 A.D.L., L 81, Palley to Depart., 29 brum.; De la Chapelle, op. et loc. cit. Note how, when one suspect at Maclas refused to open the door because Pignon had omitted to bring the Mun. with him, Pignon preferred to wait for the Mun. rather than break down the door, and thus the suspect had time to destroy all incriminating evidence (A.N., W 408, d. 939, *procès-verbal* of 1 Oct.).

5 e.g. A.D.L., L 434 (1), fol. 16, arrest of Maisonneuve *cadet* for 'des excès de despotisme' in the arbitrary arrest of Couturier.

their powers for satisfying old grudges: thus, for instance, one man arrested by Champagnat and Ducros, *sous-commissaires* of Pignon, alleged that they had vowed him undying hatred because he had supported their opponent in a court case.[1] Such statments are impossible to verify, but are perfectly credible since the opportunity was certainly there.

In this context, Pignon presents a complicated case. Like Lapalus, Pignon devoted much of his repressive energy to religious trouble-makers in the villages, whom he considered the source of all ill. The preamble of his powers referred to the negligence of the Municipalities over implementing article 2 of the decree of 12 July, thus leaving unpunished those guilty men, 'qui ont porté les armes contre la patrie ou qui ont participé aux complots des contre-révolutionnaires de Lyon', and he was authorized to arrest 'toutes personnes suspectes'.[2] The decree of 12 July concerned only officials who had connived at the revolt of Lyon, and therefore Javogues had already considerably extended its terms of reference; but it is not clear whether 'toutes personnes suspectes' were a category on their own or whether they were those mentioned in the preamble. If the latter was the case, Pignon exceeded his powers.[3] Clearly, Javogues intended to designate above all those directly implicated in the rebellion, since he remonstrated with Pignon: 'Je t'approuve très fort de détruire le fanatisme, mais des muscadins et à force . . . persuade-toi bien qu'il nous faut des muscadins et au lieu de nous envoyer la canaille, envoie-nous du gros.'[4] But he never called Pignon to order for *abus de pouvoirs*. Nevertheless, immediately after the recall of Javogues, Pignon and two of his *sous-commissaires* were bitterly attacked and arrested.[5] They were accused of unwarranted arrests, embezzlement, theft, and extortion of money by threat of arrest:

[1] A.D.L., 42 L 183, d. Lardon, letter to *Reprs.*, n.d. Cf. A.D.R., 42 L 189, d. Seguin, Teyssier to Javogues, n.d., denying accusations of personal vengeance in the arrest of Seguin.

[2] A.C. Saint-Étienne, 1 D 10 (3), fol. 68.

[3] Note that he twice requested 'des ordres précis pour les fanatiques' from Javogues, but there is no trace of any specific response (A.D.R., 42 L 157, letter of 8 Oct., and 42 L 186, d. Pignon, letter of 9 Oct.).

[4] A.N., W 408, d. 939, letter of 10 Oct.

[5] Ibid., Pignon, Jourjon, and Démolis were acquitted by the rev. trib. on 18 mess.

> L'abus que le nommé Pignon a fait de ces pouvoirs a révolté tous les citoyens du district . . . il n'y a pas de despote sur terre qui fut autant redouté . . . une quantité de personnes préférant la tranquillité achetaient à tout prix leur liberté . . . de pauvres malheureux sans ressources et sans moyens pour acheter leur liberté étaient détenus sans autre crime que d'avoir déplu à Pignon ou à ses adhérents . . . les sous-commissaires de Pignon contraignaient les municipalités où ils passaient à leur donner 24 livres par jour pour étape en qualité de capitaine.[1]

The vast majority of the accusations were completely without foundation. An inquiry by the district tribunal disproved the cases of theft and extortion: there is a great difference between pocketing money and suggesting a *don patriotique* to the Municipality.[2] Pignon may have acted in a somewhat cavalier fashion: in at least one case, for example, he refused to show the *procès-verbal* to a suspect before signing it, as he was obliged to do by law, and coerced the mayor into countersigning.[3] Only the question of the 24 *livres étape* was proved against Pignon's secretary and *sous-commissaire*, Jourjon, but this appears to have been a genuine misunderstanding and Jourjon had refunded the Municipalities in nivôse.[4] Apart from this, all we can say for certain is that flocks of petitioners and relatives haunted the houses of Pignon and Jourjon and inevitably offered gifts, which the needy Jourjon in particular may have been tempted to accept.[5]

The only real case in the department that might amount to extortion was when Jean Philippon made the commune of Chevrières pay 20,000 *livres* in September because so many of the young men of the *première réquisition* had disappeared rather than march against Lyon.[6] But this does not appear

[1] Ibid., 'Observations relativement à la conduite qu'a tenue le nommé Pignon'.

[2] Ibid., investigations of 13–26 flor. and 3–6 prair.: see particularly the evidence of the *femme* Poidebard.

[3] A.D.R., 42 L 170, d. Mathivet, letter 'au général Javogues', Oct.

[4] A.N., W 408, d. 939, interrogation of Jourjon, 25 germ., and receipts from Muns.

[5] Ibid., extracts of denunciations to rev. com. at Armeville, 2–6 vent.; A.D.R., 42 L 84, fol. 22, 'adresse . . . de la Société populaire de Commune d'Armes . . . en faveur de Pignon', 28 vent.: 'Jourjon, sans en faire part à Pignon, sans doute a reçu de ses propres parents très riches des secours dus à sa misère.' Jourjon clearly had quite a few distant relatives among those arrested (A.N., loc. cit., investigation of 13–26 flor., *passim*). The most acceptable gifts appear to have been wine, coal, hares, bedding, and clothes.

[6] A.D.L., L 374, fol. 5.

to have been criminal in any way, although Javogues made him pay it back: the moderate District of Roanne treated the communes of Violay and Saint-Just-la-Pendue in the same way and at about the same time,[1] while Philippon continued to enjoy Javogues's esteem, since he was appointed to the Department. Of all the *commissaires* active in the department, Lapalus was certainly the most careless in the conduct of his mission. Although his powers were not well drafted, he was clearly not intended to arrest so many villagers, whose sole crime was to be *fanatiques*, while he entered into conflict with the regular and revolutionary authorities of two districts as well as with the *Commission Temporaire*, whose decisions he defied.[2] When requested by the club at Roanne to exhibit their powers, Lapalus's companion Évrard replied that they had secret powers and would communicate them at the appropriate time and place. Their *sous-commissaires* adopted much the same attitude, and Deville, for example, when asked by the curé of Ambierle for proof of his powers, stated that, whether he had any or not, he was not the sort of man to show them.[3] Nevertheless, even Lapalus does not compare with some of his colleagues elsewhere in France: he did not invest his *sous-commissaires* with the plenitude of his own powers, nor did he undertake *randonnées révolutionnaires* through the countryside at the head of a detachment of the *armée révolutionnaire*, closing churches and levying *taxes révolutionnaires*.

The central government in Paris understood that the unbridled use of *commissaires* was an important factor in maintaining the 'anarchical' Terror, and they occupy, therefore, a prominent place among the provisions of the law of 14 frimaire/4 December.[4] But, as far as the department of the Loire is concerned, this law had very little influence upon the situation. Certainly, Lapalus claimed that he had ceased his mission because the decree excluded the Committee of General Security from those authorities entitled to employ *commissaires*, but in reality he was compelled to withdraw much more by the growing opposition.[5] The practice of subdelegating powers disappeared well before this date, while

1 A.D.L., L 176, fol. 10. 2 Lucas, art. cit.

3 *Mémoire adressé au Comité de Sûreté générale*, pp. 10, 23.

4 Sect. III, arts. 12–15. 5 Lucas, art. cit., p. 522.

all the *abus de pouvoirs* that we have cited, except those of Lapalus, date from the early period. The regular administrations continued to use *commissaires* without interruption, despite the restriction of this right to the Committee of Public Safety, the *Représentants en mission*, the *Conseil Exécutif*, and the *Commission des subsistances*. The only significant point was the article which stipulated that the powers of all the *commissaires* of a *Représentant* lapsed at his recall. But it seems unlikely, given the circumstances surrounding Javogues's recall, that his agents would have survived in any case.

Despite the tendency of the *commissaires* to cause confusion when operating in large numbers with few limitations on their powers, they were an essential element of the repressive and administrative aspects of the Terror. Although their action is most evident in the matter of repression, it is true nevertheless that it was only the use of *commissaires* in general that provided the multiple institutions of the Terror with a direct link with much of the population. They were an instrument which allowed these institutions to exert constant pressure on, and to maintain extensive supervision over, the inhabitants of an area, while providing higher authorities with a realistic means of co-ordinating the work of subordinates. It was largely the *commissaires* who ensured that the Terror was in any degree at all 'à l'ordre du jour' in the villages. Naturally, there were practical limits to their effectiveness. We have already indicated the way in which geographical factors affected the dissemination of political impulses within the department.[1] Occasionally a *commissaire* might run into open hostility, particularly if he was unaccompanied by force.[2] But, usually villagers had recourse to much more subtle weapons for dealing with this type of visitor:

Nous vîmes arriver un jour le nommé Chavannes, maître-maçon d'Ocharra, avec deux manœuvres, le 27 novembre, munis qu'ils étaient de tous les instruments nécessaires pour descendre nos cloches et les briser, ainsi qu'ils en exhibèrent l'ordre qui leur en était donné, et voulaient de suite se mettre à l'ouvrage! Avec Rivet, du Pinay, qui

[1] Above, p. 30.

[2] e.g. A.D.R., 42 L 169, letter to Javogues, Sept., report by two *commissaires* that they had lost an important suspect to a mob of armed villagers.

avec moi représentions la municipalité, nous nous avisâmes aussitôt de proposer à nos briseurs de cloches un bon petit déjeuner qui fut accepté de suite; nous nous rendîmes chez moi, près de mon poêle, vu le grand froid qu'il faisait, nous eûmes soin de verser de larges rasades à nos hôtes, et le petit vin capiteux que Chapard tirait de Malleval ne tarda pas à produire de l'effet. Le chef et l'un de ses ouvriers étaient dans une humeur à satisfaire nos projets, mais le troisième voulait encore aller travailler seul au clocher. Nous fîmes alors venir des filles, avec Giraudet, le joueur de violon. La danse et la bouteille finirent par nous montrer que notre plan réussissait assez bien; la veillée était grande, on finit par parler affaires. Chavannes, le chef, était un jeune veuf qui voulait se remarier. Je lui proposai alors Anne Malaure, nièce de Marie Préher, qui était logée chez nous à cette époque; il approuva fort mon offre de service et je devins vite son confident. Pendant que je négociais, Rivet avait soin des bouteilles. Enfin, je réussis finalement à obtenir de Chavannes que nous descendrions nos cloches nous-mêmes pour bien montrer aux autres communes que nous étions aussi patriotes qu'elles. . . .[1]

None the less, as far as the rural population, which made up the majority of the inhabitants of the department, was concerned, it was only the experience of the unheralded appearance of *commissaires* that could begin to reverse the pattern of peasant immobilism and passive resistance to the Terror. The visit of a bullying *commissaire* with a few soldiers, or even without any, accompanied by dire threats of future wrath and an occasional judicious arrest, inevitably made a great impression on naturally timorous peasants, passionately anxious for their careful hoards of money and knowing full well that the seasons do not wait upon a man in prison. Deville, one of Lapalus's *sous-commissaires*, who arrived at Ambierle with one assistant, found that all the priests there had escaped before he could arrest them. He threatened the village with reprisals, and said that if the five priests were not in Roanne gaol the next day, the Municipality would be sent to the revolutionary tribunal: the mayor went down on his knees to beg for mercy and Deville was heard to say, as he left, 'Est-il possible! Deux hommes font trembler une paroisse!'[2] Fusil complained sadly, that, although their arms were itch-

[1] MS. memoirs of Jean-Louis Barge of La Valla, quoted by F. Gonon, *Un Forézien célèbre, Claude Javogues*, pp. 142 ff.

[2] *Mémoire adressé au Comité de Sûreté générale*, p. 23.

ing to be at work for the Republic, 'nous n'avons trouvé que des agneaux dans notre route'.[1] The extent to which such communities would execute orders depended upon the degree to which they could be made to fear further visits from these inquisitive men.[2] Even those same villagers who had dealt so successfully with the men sent to take down their bells felt obliged, after receiving written orders and the inspection of another *commissaire*, to send in the bell-ropes, to explain with a complete absence of good faith that the icy roads prevented transport, and even to lay plans for stealing a bell from a neighbouring hamlet if necessary.[3]

But the significance of *commissaires* in the Terror was not merely that of an indispensable mechanism of administration and repression. The more important *commissaires* were men who possessed considerable power, momentarily at least, at a local level. As such, their personality in many ways influenced the pattern of the Terror in the sense that, in the last resort, their ideas dictated the order of priorities that they imposed on the tasks with which they were entrusted. This is particularly evident in respect of those who were in charge of repression.[4] We have seen that both Pignon and Lapalus were convinced that religion was the greatest source of danger to the Republic, and that this led them to place the emphasis of their repressive action on the arrest of *fanatiques*, thereby giving their activity a form which neither the Committee of General Security nor Javogues had envisaged. On the other hand, Vial, operating in the district of Armeville on behalf of the Department in brumaire, considered at that time that nobles and federalists were the most important suspects.[5] Potey demonstrated the character of his preoccupations when he suggested a public bonfire of all playing-cards in the main square of Montbrisé, arguing that it was essential to eradicate

1 De la Chapelle, op. et loc. cit.

2 Cf. A.N., W 408, d. 939, Mun. of Saint-Romain-les-Atheux to Pignon, 18 Oct.: 'exposent que, malgré les menaces, qui ont été faites de la part des commissaires des Représentants du peuple, les rebelles ou fanatiques semblent augmenter leur orgueil et leurs discours liberticides.'

3 Gonon, op. et loc. cit.

4 Cf., e.g., G. Sangnier, *La Terreur dans le district de Saint-Pol*, i. 276–91, who shows the immense differences between the repressive activities of the various *commissaires* employed in the cantons by the rev. com. of Saint-Pol.

5 A.D.L., L 79, fol. 14, letter from Depart., 26 brum.

totally all signs of royalty and feudalism and to deprive those who liked card-games of the opportunity to utter proscribed names. One of his colleagues was so impressed by his zeal in this respect that he wrote urging his home commune to remove anything that might shock the 'œil républicain' before Potey arrived.[1] Similarly, the extent and reality of dechristianization were very much dependent on the attitude of itinerant *commissaires* passing through the villages. Fusil devoted most of his attention to this question, while two *commissaires* visiting La Valla gave ample proof of their personal convictions on the matter when they discovered that some of the gold and silver objects in the church had been hidden: 'Les deux envoyés du district, mécontents, sabrèrent les saints et les corniches des autels, déchirant les livres, puis ouvrant le tabernacle, ils jetèrent à terre et foulèrent aux pieds les hosties, en proférant d'horribles blasphèmes.'[2]

Moreover, on points of detail a *commissaire* could make decisions that could help to further the spirit of the *gouvernement révolutionnaire*: for instance, Vial ordered the Municipality of Chuyers to send all the vestments of the church to the District except what was too worn, which should be distributed to the poor.[3] Finally, in the speeches he made and in the instructions he gave to local authorities, a *commissaire* was bound to express above all else his own ideas, and these were bound to influence his audience in so far as it was seeking guidance:

> La République est proclamée [said Dorfeuille], ce n'est plus le règne des damoiseaux; c'est le règne des hommes. Plus d'or, plus de mollesse, plus de vices; du fer, du travail, des vertus. . . Il ne doit plus y avoir ni pauvres ni désœuvrés; tous les républicains doivent le tribut de leurs bras ou de leurs talents . . . Alors nous sentons plus vivement qu'ils sont nos frères et le fruit de notre travail doit être partagé avec eux. Le superflu de l'opulent, si mal employé dans l'ancien régime, va devenir le patrimoine et le soulagement du pauvre et du malheureux . . . Si un riche n'est nommé à aucun emploi, c'est une preuve qu'il est

[1] A.D.L., L 81, letters of 30 and 25 frim.

[2] Gonon, op. et loc. cit. Cf. A.C. Noailly, *reg. dél.*, 13 pluv., visit from Civeton, who orders the *marques du fanatisme* in the church and on the square to be replaced by those of Reason, and all crosses, statues, and holy pictures to be burnt.

[3] A.D.L., Q 50, Mun. to Dist., 26 vend. an III.

suspect; c'est qu'il manque de républicanisme . . . Travaillons donc, citoyens, travaillons pour la patrie et la liberté . . . chaque jour de décade nous livrant au repos, nous livrant à la joie.[1]

[1] *Journal de Commune-affranchie* . . ., supplement to 9 niv., speech at Armeville.

VIII

THE REGULAR ADMINISTRATIONS

THE activity of the regular administrations (the Department, the Districts, and the Municipalities) and their relations with the extra-ordinary institutions have already been considered indirectly in the preceding pages. The purpose of this chapter, then, is merely to place their contribution to the Terror in perspective. Originally, the regular administrations were the bodies responsible for executing the decrees of the National Assembly and the decisions of the central government. Despite the growth of extra-ordinary authorities during the Terror, they continued to fulfil this role in the Year II. Inevitably, therefore, they had an important part to play in the *gouvernement révolutionnaire*, since the decrees of the Convention and the *arrêtés* of the *Représentants en mission*, which they implemented, were concerned with the elaboration of that system of government. The law of 14 frimaire/4 December recognized this, for, although it drastically reduced the competence of the Departments, it clearly emphasized that the Districts and the Municipalities were an integral element in the execution of revolutionary laws and of measures of government at a local level. Throughout the Terror, the regular administrations organized and directed the *gouvernement révolutionnaire* in the departments, and the success of this system was, to a large extent, dependent on the degree of efficiency and conviction of these authorities. But, beyond the functions that they had by virtue of their position in the hierarchy, the more important administrations in the Loire (with the exception of those at Roanne) must be counted as agents of the Terror because, in the second half of October, Javogues appointed most of the leading militants of the area to them.[1] The zeal that these

[1] A.N., AF II 114 (859) 6 and (861) 15; AF II 137 (1069), d. 30, p. 5; A.D.L., L 123, fol. 338; A.C. Saint-Étienne, 1 D 10 (3), fol. 75. Apart from the effect of 14 frim. on the Depart., the composition of these administrations remained largely

administrations displayed in the prosecution of the *gouvernement révolutionnaire* sprang naturally from the personal commitment of their members to it.

The importance of the Department and of the Districts resided in the first instance in their activity as organizers of the Terror. Although many of the initiatives originally came from the *Représentant en mission* (the beginning of repression, the creation of an *armée révolutionnaire*, the establishment of clubs and revolutionary committees, etc.), the successful realization of these measures was above all the work of the local authorities. We have seen that the energy of the Department was largely responsible for the organization of the *armée révolutionnaire* and that the details of its equipment were dealt with by the Districts.[1] Similarly, both the Department and the Districts of Boën and Armeville prescribed the execution of the decree of 21 March concerning revolutionary committees, either independently of Javogues's *arrêté* or else in response to it, and they vigorously pursued the enforcement of these decisions.[2] The formation of many of the committees and clubs was inspired directly by these administrations or by their *commissaires*. The activity of the Department and the Districts in this respect was encouraged by the fact that Javogues was absent from the area between late brumaire and late frimaire. Again, in the absence of the *Représentant*, it is clear that before 14 frimaire/4 December the higher regular administrations occupied a dominant position within a definite hierarchy of ordinary and extra-ordinary institutions, and that this hierarchy owed its coherence to the assertion of control over it by the higher administrations. The Department stood at the apex of a structure of authority, distributing to the Districts the decrees and *arrêtés* of its immediate superiors and its directives on their implementation. The Districts in turn passed them on to the Municipalities with their own

unchanged throughout the period of Javogues's mission. In vent. Méaulle recomposed the Dist. of Armeville and made a few changes in the Muns. of Montbrisé and Roanne and in the Depart. In mess. Reverchon completely reformed the Dist., the Mun., tribunals, etc. at Montbrison and made substantial alterations to the Depart. and the Mun. of Roanne. The personnel of the major administrations were totally replaced finally by Charlier and Pocholle at the beginning of frim. an III.

[1] Above, pp. 157–61.

[2] Above, pp. 132–3.

instructions. Both the Department and the Districts instructed the *comités révolutionnaires* and checked on their activities, while the Districts, as we have seen, exercised a very real control over them.[1] The *armée révolutionnaire* was entirely subordinated to the direction of these administrations.[2] Only the revolutionary tribunal was independent.[3] Naturally, in the pre-frimaire/4 December period, the regular administrations did not always function together smoothly. The Department suffered from the teething troubles of an entirely new institution: in the middle of frimaire it did not yet possess a treasurer or funds, and at the beginning of pluviôse it was still having difficulty in finding printing equipment.[4] The District of Boën was also initially thrown into confusion by the move from Montbrison.[5] As late as 27 frimaire/17 December, the Department was upbraiding the District of Armeville for failing to make any report on its activities,[6] while the Districts always had great difficulty in getting any response from the smaller Municipalities.[7]

Once the structure of terrorist institutions was established the higher regular administrations continued to be active as part of it. Before the law of 14 frimaire/4 December, there was little difference between the preoccupations of the Department and those of the Districts, and the only distinction that can be made is in terms of the nature of their immediate subordinates and of the geographical area of their jurisdiction. Their function was essentially to decide on methods of applying the *gouvernement révolutionnaire* and to supervise and co-ordinate their execution, while attempting to instil the principles of the Year II into inferior authorities and the population at large by proclamations and instructions. We have already referred to their activity in this respect in the

[1] Above, pp. 133 ff. [2] Above, pp. 180 ff.

[3] Below, pp. 249 ff.

[4] A.N., D IVbis 84, d. Loire, letter to Convention requesting a treasurer, funds, a seal, a courier service, and authorization to acquire buildings for offices; A.D.L., L 18, 7, 12, and 21 brum., 13 frim., similar demands to *Reprs.*; ibid., 4 pluv., interview with departmental printer.

[5] Ibid., 2 and 11 frim. [6] A.D.L., L 79, fol. 28.

[7] The Dist. of Boën attempted to solve some of the problems by hiring 4 couriers to distribute laws and *arrêtés* twice per *décade* (A.D.L., L 259, fol. 29), but the Dist. of Armeville merely tried to insist that the villages send in someone each week to pick up their packet (L 156, fol. 105).

discussion of their *commissaires*.[1] Since, in the absence of the *Représentant en mission*, the Department and the Districts were the only authorities whose competence was not narrowly limited either to a locality or to a particular task, they automatically held a dominant position. Faithful to their role as administrations, they administered the Terror in the Year II: their *arrêtés* were above all administrative decisions, whether they regulated the delivery of *certificats de civisme* or enforced the *repos décadaire*.[2] At no point did they take initiatives that were not, in some way or another, authorized by a decree or by an *arrêté* of the *Représentants en mission* having jurisdiction over the department.[3] Indeed, in many cases, the methods of government of the Terror were inherent in the administrative measures they had to take. This is especially evident in the case of food supply, which occupied a considerable proportion of their time. The use of requisitions, the enforcement of the *maximum*, the recourse to the *armée révolutionnaire* and to the legislation concerning hoarding were essential in order to ensure a proper distribution of the department's meagre resources and to overcome the recalcitrance of the peasantry.[4] Similarly, such problems as contributing to the war effort, collecting precious metal from the churches, and removing church bells could only be resolved in the last resort by revolutionary and coercive methods.[5] The administrations accepted this: for instance, the Department recognized that in a revolution the movements of the people 'doivent dépasser le cours tranquille et calme . . . des lois déjà assises et consolidées', and that 'l'application des lois doit être révolutionnaire'.[5]

The strictly administrative character of the business of the Department and of the Districts was qualified, again with the exception of Roanne, by the terrorist convictions of the administrators. The *procureur-général-syndic*, for example, proclaimed the need to be pitiless for the sake of humanity, to use the laws to shed blood in order to spare it—'plus de

1 Above, pp. 196–7.
2 e.g. A.D.L., L 18, fol. 77, L 123, fol. 360.
3 e.g. A.D.L., L 79, fol. 35, 'nos arrêtés émanés de la loi même'.
4 e.g. A.D.L., L 18, 3 frim.; L 123, 26 Oct., 1 frim.; L 124, 21 pluv. and 17 vent.
5 e.g. A.D.L., L 130, 6 frim.; L 18, fol. 137; L 156, fol. 86.
6 A.D.L., L 18, fol. 77.

relâche, que le sommeil fuye nos paupières; que les ris et les jeux aillent chercher ailleurs les idolâtres du plaisir; liberté et repos sont incompatibles, jusqu'à ce que la République soit purgée du dernier des suppôts de l'aristocratie . . .'[1] Such sentiments led these authorities to adopt a more positive attitude to the Terror than that of ordinary executives. For example, both the Department and the Districts of Boën and Armeville displayed considerable energy in attempting to implement Collot d'Herbois's and Fouché's *arrêté* of 24 brumaire/14 November prescribing the levy of a *taxe révolutionnaire* in each commune, and were only thwarted by the dilatoriness of the smaller Municipalities in drawing up lists of rich and poor.[2] More particularly, the terrorist principles of the administrations are visible in the policies that they developed on the religious problem. Although they were careful not to act illegally and although they emphasized in the early period that the pure Catholic religion was in no way jeopardized,[3] they clearly used such matters as the collection of precious metal and church bells as opportunities for attacking 'cette religion intolérante et persécutrice qui ne fut jamais celle du sans-culotte Jésus'.[4] Early in frimaire, they were enforcing with alacrity measures for the demolition of the *signes du fanatisme* and were saying that the Supreme Being had no other temple than the universe and no other cult than that of Reason.[5] In nivôse, when the dechristianization campaign reached its zenith in the Loire after Javogues closed the churches, the Department reported that it had sent out *commissaires* with orders to destroy Christian altars and to replace them with ones dedicated to Reason.[6] As we have seen, the individual administrators attended to all these points themselves when out on mission.[7]

Finally, the higher regular administrations also made an important contribution to repression. They organized not only the system of revolutionary committees, but also the sequestration of property and the apposition of seals. They

[1] A.D.L., L suppl. 565, speech of 12 brum.
[2] A.D.L., L 79, fols. 22, 29; L 18, 29 frim.; L 259, fols. 26, 45, 64; L 130, 26 Oct.
[3] e.g. A.D.L., L 18, fol. 81.
[4] A.D.L., L 18, fol. 40, L 123, fols. 33, 360, L 156, fols. 86, 91, etc.
[5] e.g. A.D.L., L 18, fol. 64, 9 frim.
[6] A.D.L., L 79, fol. 35.
[7] Above, p. 218.

collected lists of suspects and published the names of *émigrés*, of refractory priests, of conspirators, and of the convicted or suspected;[1] the District of Armeville issued a definition of suspect appropriate to the particular circumstances of the region.[2] Their *commissaires* looked for incriminating evidence, requested denunciations from assemblies of inhabitants, and sounded out the political attitudes of the population.[3] Beyond this, the administrations intervened directly both by giving *commissaires* general powers of arrest and also by issuing arrest warrants: the Department delivered 35 warrants before the end of frimaire, while the District of Armeville issued four, that of Boën one, and that of Roanne one before the end of pluviôse.[4] To some extent, their repressive activity was implicit in the functions that had been given to them at the beginning of the Revolution. For instance, before 14 frimaire/4 December, the Department's functions included the maintenance of order,[5] while the competence of the Department and the Districts in the matter of *biens nationaux* naturally forced them to deal with the sequestration of property, especially since the decree of 19 October declared that the possessions of rebels should be treated like those of *émigrés*. Moreover, early in the period, Javogues recognized the authority of the regular administrations over the system of repression, for when he suppressed his *commissaires* in the district of Armeville in October, he gave the supervision of arrests and sequestrations to the District with the right to delegate to the Municipalities, provided that they reported back to the District and that the District in turn reported to the Department.[6]

The consistent moderatism of the District of Roanne forms a complete contrast with the Department and the other two Districts. Although Javogues replaced the authorities situated

[1] e.g. A.D.L., L 374, fol. 11, order by Dist. of Boën to Chevrières to send in list of suspects; L 18, fols. 67, 83, arrangements for the publication of lists.

[2] A.D.L., L 130, fol. 28.

[3] Above, p. 209.

[4] A.D.L., L 18, *passim*, and L 437, 3 frim.; L 130, 12 Oct., 7 Nov., and 28 pluv.; L 259, 5 frim.; L 176, 7 pluv. Note that, before its renewal, the Dist. of Roanne arrested 12 people between 1 and 23 Sept. (ibid.).

[5] Note how it is the Depart. which takes measures to quell the religious troubles that break out at Saint-Germain-Laval, late frim. (A.D.R., 42 L 157, and A.D.L., L 18, fol. 100).

[6] A.D.L., L 123, fol. 343, *arrêté* of 23 Oct.

at Roanne at the same time as he purged the other major administrations, it is likely that his *arrêté*, signed at Armeville, was not based on any first-hand information. Javogues had not visited the district since the federalist crisis and indeed did not go there at any time during his mission. He had probably not met many militants from the area recently other than François Guyot, who in any case came from Saint-Germain-Laval.[1] His knowledge of the state of the district, therefore, was gained from such sources as Dorfeuille, who was unreliable since he was blindly enthusiastic about the obviously dubious administrators in office during the summer,[2] or from the hearsay of the patriots gathered at Armeville, or else from his own observation of the Roanne delegates to the electoral assembly for the Convention in 1792.[3] It does not necessarily follow that the new administrators constituted a positive political danger, although the president of the District was arrested by the *Commission Temporaire* at the end of pluviôse 'comme suspecté d'incivisme et prévenu de fanatisme'.[4] But, clearly, they were not a good choice, for several *commissaires* noted that 'les nouvelles autorités sont dans les principes mais trop faibles en moyens'.[5] As a result of their inadequacy, they relied upon the advice of their predecessors.[6] This seems to have been specifically countenanced by Javogues, but it was inevitable that they should in this way fall under the influence of these men, whose attitude to the federalist crisis had been so suspiciously hesitant. Moreover, this administration was highly inefficient. It appears to have existed almost exclusively for the benefit of the town of Roanne, devoting only slight attention to the rest of the

[1] Patriotic *procureur de la commune*, 1793; refugee to army besieging Lyon; reinstated by Javogues, 3 Sept., and made *commissaire*; appointed *secrétaire général* of Depart. by Javogues.

[2] A.C. Roanne, 1 D 1 (2), fol. 184; A.D.R., 42 L 10, Millet to Dorfeuille, frim.

[3] A.D.R., 42 L 160, interrogation of Verne, former judge of Roanne dist. tribunal: denounced by Desvernays (patriot of Armeville, appointed president of Depart. by Javogues) for a squabble in the electoral assembly. Note that even the authorities appointed at Armeville itself contained several people soon revealed to have been federalists (Galley, op. cit. ii. 27).

[4] A.C. Roanne, 1 D 1 (2), fol. 273, arrest warrant signed Marino and Delan, Feurs, 26 pluv.

[5] A.D.L., L 81, letter from Chartre, 28 brum.; ibid., letter from Dubessey, 2 niv.

[6] A.D.L., L 232, fol. 25, Dist. to *Repr.*, 2 niv.

district and being preoccupied above all by the problem of feeding the *chef-lieu*.[1] Whereas the Department had organized its subcommittees on 4 brumaire/25 October, it was not until 2 nivôse/22 December that the District of Roanne followed suit: on 19 pluviôse/7 February the president had to bring his colleagues' attention to the fact that they still had not implemented that decision.[2] Finally, relations between the District and the Department were always bad, and Roanne was intent on acting as independently as possible. In frimaire the Department complained that the District was usurping the functions of the higher authority by printing laws and decrees directly without forwarding them to the Department for this purpose; the *commissaire* sent from Roanne to inform the Department of the decree of 18 frimaire/8 December suspending all legal proceedings against public officials at Roanne, categorically refused to allow the Department to keep his copy of the decree; in floréal, the District protested that the Department was upbraiding it almost daily in the most violent and insulting terms.[3]

Since the administrators of Roanne were under the influence of their predecessors, they naturally accepted the values current in the early years of the Revolution. They inherited the sort of attitude that had prompted their predecessors, when faced by the religious strife of 1791, to formulate a policy described as 'nous avons mandé, caressé, menacé . . . nous allons donc encore temporiser', and, when faced by a grain riot and popular demands, to reject price-fixing, stating that 'nous devons, au contraire, assurer et donner protection aux marchands et leur laisser la liberté dans leurs ventes, liberté qui est l'âme du commerce, en les invitant seulement, et de gré, à considérer la misère publique et se contenter du plus médiocre profit'.[4] In the Year II, although the chronic food shortage at Roanne obliged the administrators to multiply their requisitions, they always showed themselves to be extremely uneasy about this and later, in their published report on their administration, they took

[1] A.D.L., L 176, *passim*.
[2] A.D.L., L 18, fols. 3, 4; L 176, fols. 70, 109.
[3] A.D.L., L 80, fol. 5; L 18, fol. 91, L 231, fol. 50.
[4] F. Pothier, *Roanne pendant la Révolution*, pp. 91, 48.

great pains to stress the inevitability of this method and its legality.[1] Despite the situation at Roanne, they never discussed any infraction of the *maximum* or any problem arising out of its application.[2] Although, in September, the former administration had taken a number of elementary steps to organize repression, that of the Year II revealed itself to be much more reluctant and appointed very few *commissaires* in this sphere when compared with the other similar authorities.[3] On the contrary, we have seen how suspicious it was of the revolutionary committees and how it made no effort to foster them.[4] It had an intense dislike of the 'moyens révolutionnaires' which the other administrations accepted as normal, and only began to use them in ventôse when the food situation became critical and the market had only a quarter of normal supplies despite requisitions.[5] When, at the end of frimaire, there was a religious insurrection at Belmont, it simply directed the *juge de paix* to gather the necessary evidence, while its instructions to him to 'renvoyer les dites prévenues par devant les tribunaux si le cas y échoit' were carefully non-committal on the type of justice within whose competence these deeds fell.[6] Indeed, it was remarkably friendly towards suspects. It did not feel that those who had refused to march against Lyon were tainted, but rather that it was their business that had kept them at home. It had no hesitation in acceding to the request of three dangerous suspects to be allowed to live at home with two guards and to receive their friends; the *jury d'accusation* appointed in nivôse contained a large number of people whose political purity was highly debatable.[7] One of the judges of the district tribunal, arrested for federalism, had good reasons, then, for writing to his friends, urging them to get the District to demand his transfer back to his home town under house arrest.[8] Moreover, it made no move to

[1] A.D.L., L 185, mess.

[2] A.D.L., L 176, *passim*.

[3] A.D.L., L 176, fol. 8 (12 Sept.); only 7 and 22 pluv. (ibid.).

[4] Above, p. 136.

[5] A.D.L., L 176, fol. 118 (3 vent.).

[6] Ibid., fol. 79. It was not until 2 germ. that the Dist. directed that someone should be sent to the rev. trib. (ibid., fol. 136).

[7] Ibid., fols. 64, 20; A.D.R., 42 L 168, d. Chartre, Guyot and Chartre to Javogues, 4 pluv.

[8] A.D.L., L 196, letter from Verdellet.

intervene when the revolutionary committee at Roanne arrested militant terrorists, and it took no steps to punish the commander of the town's National Guard, who refused to execute Lapalus's general warrant against more than two of the former Municipality on the grounds that he did not think that the law of 17 September could be applied to the others.[1] It is not surprising, therefore, that the District should have played a leading part in the campaign against Lapalus and Javogues.

The law of 14 frimaire/4 December was received officially by the Department on 3 nivôse/23 December and by the Districts and the Municipalities of the major towns within the next three days.[2] Its most obvious immediate effect was naturally to destroy the position of the Department as an agent of the Terror.[3] As far as the Loire was concerned, the attitude of the decree towards this administration was unjustified, for if anything it appears to be, of all the regular administrations, the most committed to the Terror. On 5 nivôse/25 December the president, the *procureur-général-syndic*, and the *conseil général* left, declaring that 'rentrés dans leurs foyers, ils continueraient d'électriser les campagnes'.[4] Henceforth the Department scrupulously observed the provisions of the decree that limited its competence to taxation, industry, communications, and *biens nationaux*. It even went as far as to refuse to direct food supplies since this was not mentioned in the decree, but rapidly rescinded its decision when Javogues furiously accused it of 'tiédeur et d'insouciance et presque aussi d'aimer l'or'.[5] Indeed, Javogues does not appear to have taken much notice of the law of 14 frimaire in this respect as in others: for instance, he continued to entrust the distribution of his *arrêtés* on revolutionary matters to the Department, and at the beginning of pluviôse ordered it to carry out his warrant for the arrest of the mayor of Feurs.[6] For its part, this administration continued to watch out for

[1] e.g. A.D.R., 42 L 180, d. Game, *mémoire justificatif*: 'Roanne . . . me fait un crime de ce que je n'ai pas fait ou n'ai pas laissé faire sur son exemple'; A.D.L., L 327, fol. 8, warrant against Chartre, vent.; A.N., F7 4423, d. Rhône-et-Loire, *procès-verbal*, 6 frim.

[2] Above, p. 171, n. 3.

[3] Sect. II, art. 7; sect. III, arts. 5 and 6.

[4] A.D.L., L 18, fol. 108.

[5] A.D.L., L 80, fol. 11, Depart. to Javogues, 11 niv.

[6] A.D.L., L 120, *passim*; L 18, 1 pluv.

enemies of the Republic as far as it was now legal for it to do so, assuring Javogues that it would not fail to report to him anything that came to its attention; for example, when it received reports of religious strife at Montmarat/Saint-Just-en-Chevalet and Montchalier/Saint-Germain-Laval, it hastened to request prompt action from the *Représentants* at Armeville.[1]

It was above all the Districts that benefited from the provisions of the law that abolished their subordination to the Department.[2] They became the most powerful regular administrations, depending directly on the committees of government in Paris and entrusted with the supervision of all revolutionary laws and 'mesures de gouvernement, de sûreté générale et de salut public'. This decision was merely the logical consequence of the decree of 10 October 1793 and of Billaud-Varenne's report of 28 brumaire/18 November.[3] In fact, however, the practical effect of the law of 14 frimaire on the activity of the Districts was negligible during the period under review, since they already exercised all the functions that it attributed to them. The decree modified their relationship with the Department, but it did not affect the range of their preoccupations, nor their control over the lower organs.

The system of *agents nationaux* and *comptes décadaires*, designed to bring the hierarchy of Municipalities and Districts more immediately under the direction of the central government, seems to have come into operation only slowly.[4] Certainly, there was no difficulty about the appointment of *agents nationaux* since, with very few exceptions, they were the former *procureurs* and *procureurs-syndics* as the decree directed that they should be.[5] In most cases, the *agents nationaux* of the smaller communes underwent the *scrutin épuratoire* in pluviôse.[6] But this was merely to change their

1 A.D.L., L 79, fol. 35, letter of 15 niv.; L 18, 14 niv.

2 Sect. II, art. 6; sect. III, art. 5.

3 Decree of 10 Oct., art. 4: 'Le gouvernement correspondra immédiatement avec les districts, dans les mesures de salut public.' Billaud-Varenne proposed to increase the powers of the Dists. and to subordinate them directly to the Convention.

4 Sect. II, arts. 14–22.

5 Ibid., art. 15.

6 A.D.L., L 237, *épurations* in the dist. of Roanne; L 260, *passim*, late niv.—vent., Dist. of Boën ratifying choices made by small communes; L 438, fol. 4, rev. com. of Georges-en-Couzan to Dist., 21 vent., reporting completion of *épuration* of all *agents nationaux* in the canton.

title and did not, *per se*, make them agents of the central government. That could only be achieved by the enforcement of the *compte décadaire*. Although the District of Armeville corresponded regularly with the Convention and the committees of government after 16 nivôse/5 January, these letters were not specifically presented as *comptes décadaires*;[1] the *agent national* of the District of Boën did not send his first report until 28 pluviôse/16 February.[2] The *agents nationaux* of these two Districts did not make the tour of inspection suggested by the decree until the second half of pluviôse.[3] Similarly, although one or two Municipalities started to send in *comptes décadaires* to the District as from the end of nivôse, it was not until the third *décade* in pluviôse that the measure began slowly to be implemented more generally, while some did not comply until as late as prairial or messidor.[4]

At the base of the structure of regular administration stood the Municipalities. From the beginning of the Revolution they had exercised considerable powers, for they were able to proclaim martial law and to direct the National Guard for the maintenance of order, while economic regulation at the communal level was at their discretion. On the whole, their patriotic record had been good before the Year II, and the period following the fall of the King had seen an extension of their functions to the *police de sûreté générale*, *certificats de civisme*, and the disarmament of suspects.[5] The law of 14 frimaire confirmed this pattern by conferring on them, simultaneously with the revolutionary committees, the enforcement of revolutionary laws and 'mesures de sûreté générale et de salut public' under the supervision of the Districts.[6] Shortly afterwards, the Committee of Public Safety defined them as 'en quelque sorte les bras qui meuvent le levier révolutionnaire, les lois mouvant ces bras'.[7] In practice, however, as far as the department of the Loire is concerned,

1 A.D.L., L 156, fols. 95, 102, etc.

2 A.N., AF II 35, d. 287, p. 25: we have not found those of Roanne.

3 Ibid.; A.D.L., L 130, 12 pluv.

4 e.g. A.D.L., L 146, Valbenoîte (29 niv.), Valdorlay (1 pluv.), Martin-la-Plaine (end of prair.), Saint-Julien-en-Jarez (26 mess.); L suppl. 106, Saint-Nizier (pluv.), Arcinges (pluv.). Most communal *agents nationaux* sent reports only once a month.

5 Decrees of 10 Aug. 1792, 21 and 26 Mar. 1793.

6 Sect. II, art. 8.

7 Quoted by Godechot, op. cit., p. 288.

the Municipalities of the Terror period clearly appear to be the least important of all the ordinary and extra-ordinary institutions. As we have seen, they were generally distinctly subordinate to the revolutionary committees and subject to pressure from the clubs.[1] The higher administrations tended to consider this to be the proper relationship.[2] Nevertheless, it would be a mistake to underrate the action of the Municipalities. The whole range of communal administration, whether ordinary or revolutionary, lay within their competence and, although in very many cases the initiative resided with the local extra-ordinary institutions, it is noticeable that these nearly always worked through the regular administration except in the matter of repression.[3] The Municipalities were the executive agents as much of the committees and the clubs as of the Districts. The enforcement of the *maximum* and the organization of food supplies remained their province, and the role of the extra-ordinary organs was to inform them and to support them with their coercive powers.[4] Similarly, its representatives were always present at domiciliary visits;[5] it was the Municipality that the revolutionary committee at Charlieu invited to sequestrate the possessions of suspects and that the committee at Cervières ordered to destroy the *signes du fanatisme*.[6] Before committees were established in their communes, several Municipalities participated in repression by sequestrating property and by arresting suspects.[7] Later, they retained and continued to exercise their powers of *police municipale* covering minor disorders.[8]

Basically, one must make an elementary distinction between the Municipalities of the small rural communes and those of the urban centres. The most common picture of the small rural administration was a reflection of the immobilism of the peasant population: the District of Armeville com-

[1] Above, pp. 110, 140–2.

[2] e.g. A.D.L., L 259, fol. 61, measures by Dist. of Boën to enforce the removal of church bells, including orders to committees and clubs to supervise the Muns. closely.

[3] Above, loc. cit.

[4] e.g. A.D.L., L 385, 22 pluv., and L 412, 11 and 26 Aug., 14 Nov., 21 pluv.

[5] e.g. A.D.L., L 389, 27 niv. and 3 pluv., L 417, 19 pluv., L 434 (1), 13 niv.

[6] A.D.L., L 399, 9 pluv., L 430 (2), 11 niv.

[7] e.g. A.C. Chazelles-sur-Lyon, *reg. dél.*, 10 and 16 Oct., 21 and 25 brum.: 4 arrests and 3 sequestrations.

[8] A.D.L., L suppl. 3, *registre d'écrou* of the *maison d'arrêt* of Roanne, *passim*.

plained that many Municipalities under its jurisdiction were like 'des montagnes que le levier de l'opinion publique ne peut soulever'.[1] They suffered from the same problems of illiteracy and administrative incapacity as the rural committees.[2] As late as floréal, the committee at Firminy discovered that the Municipality of Ça Loire/Saint-Paul-en-Cornillon did not have a *registre des délibérations*; the *agent national* of Saint-Jodard protested to the District of Roanne, admittedly at the beginning of the Year III:

> Citoyen comme etant cultivatur de nessance et [un] pu insturit du [dès le] commansemant des municipalite lon mavait nomme procurur magre que je nais jammais rien connus dant les loy . . . Ile suffisay que je fu bon republiquin mais apresant que de procurur on ma change an ageant [national] je comprant ancor moins le loy que auparavant de plus vous mave anvoye des tablau a ramplir viavi [vis-à-vis] des Buttin [Bulletins] de Loy de la Republique ces toutafait ce qui [me] met a la derniere misaire je ni comprant dutous rien je ne pu pas vous anvoye des barbouillage ou vous ne conaitre rien je ne trouve perssonne dant notre commune pour le faire ceux qui ni sont pas oblige ne sy prese pas nous avont bien un citoyen greffier qui et comme moi pu instruit et pu fortune aussi bien que mois et malade ilsia [il y a] lontam et hor deta [d'état] de le faire.[3]

The natural consequence of such a situation was that the most intelligent inhabitants of the village could gain a dominant and—if their attitudes were hostile to the *gouvernement révolutionnaire*—a pernicious influence. For example, Antoine Ray, arrested by the revolutionary committee at Charlieu for preventing the supply of grain to Charlieu's market, was commander of the National Guard of Vougy, president of its revolutionary committee, and a *notable*: he directed the Municipality according to his whim and claimed disdainfully that nothing was accomplished if he did not do it himself.[4]

[1] A.D.L., L 81, letter to Depart., 2 niv.

[2] In the normal course of events and without any outside pressures, little enough business arose out of the administration of a small village: 'Il n'y a rien arrivé d'extraordinaire pendant cette décade . . . la municipalité n'a pris aucune délibération', reported Arcinges for the first two *décades* of pluv. (A.D.L., L suppl. 106).

[3] A.D.L., L 385, fol. 18; L 194, letter dated 12 brum. Cf. A.D.R., 42 L 175, d. Coste, Bourg-Argental's plea for the release of their secretary, 9 niv.

[4] A.D.L., L 399, fols. 10, 17, 18; cf. Cherblanc *père* of Balbigny—*notaire*, deputy to primary assembly at Montbrison 1789, elector until 1792, mayor until 1792, then *officier municipal*, then *agent national* mid 1794 in place of his son appointed *uge de paix*, also *assesseur du juge de paix* (A.D.L., L 194).

But one must not assume that this was the only feature of rural Municipalities, for that would be to accept the generalizations made by the militants in urban revolutionary committees, preoccupied by food shortages which they attributed to the maliciousness of the peasants, and the opinions of overworked administrators, exasperated by the slowness and parochialism of village officials. Quite apart from the deep-rooted reciprocal mistrust between town and country and the evident peasant resistance over religious and economic issues, there was a major problem of communication between the rural population and the urban revolutionaries. The failure of the traditionally-minded peasants to adopt the superficial manifestations of republicanism current in the Year II, which sprang essentially from the habits of the urban *sans-culottes*, gave the impression to the townspeople, sometimes quite falsely, that they were therefore opposed to the whole revolutionary movement. The club at Saint-Chamond had no very tender feelings for the rural population, but when a detachment of the Parisian *armée révolutionnaire* complained that some people had lifted their hats to them, it hastened to defend these countryfolk as pure patriots none the less, who would not have dreamed of raising their hats to *aristocrates*.[1] It is certainly true that the majority of small Municipalities offered passive resistance to all orders relating, however tenuously, to the religious issue, and that they did their best to avoid grain requisitions. It is also true that, by the Year II, the Municipalities of certain areas were as frankly anti-revolutionary as the majority of the inhabitants of their communes.[2] The religious schism had plunged the villages of the Seuil de Neulize, for instance, into a state of endemic disturbance, which the levy of troops, grain requisitions, and further measures against priests and churches could only aggravate.[3] At the end of frimaire, an armed expedition had to be sent against Saint-Just-la-Pendue, whose Muni-

[1] G. Lefebvre, *Registre des procès-verbaux de la Société républicaine de Saint-Chamond*, p. 120.

[2] e.g. A.D.R., 42 L 157, denunciation against the Mun. of Saint-Jean-Lavêtre for being under the influence of refractory priests.

[3] e.g. Bibl. Lyon, Coste MS. 1261, no. 1, 'adresse des patriotes de Nulize aux administrateurs du district de Roanne', 23 Mar. 1793; A.D.L., L 232, fol. 11, L suppl. 424, L 176, fols. 10, 31.

cipality was protecting deserters and refractory priests.[1] The Municipalities of Neulize, Pinay, and Saint-Jodard all gave passports and certificates to a counter-revolutionary from Montbrisé, which allowed him to flee to Switzerland.[2] On the other hand, certain Municipalities scrupulously executed the law: between 21 frimaire/11 December and 30 pluviôse/18 February, 30 communes of the district of Roanne sent in their bells; the Municipalities of Saint-Julien-d'Odde and Verrières volunteered to hand over the precious metal in their churches; Chandon and Saint-Hilaire removed all crosses other than those in the church; the Municipality of Saint-Julien-en-Jarez closed the church on orders from Saint-Chamond.[3] But the Municipality of the small village of (Saint-Laurent) La Conche was exceptional in going so far as to state that it wished to substitute 'le culte de la raison et de la vérité à celui de l'erreur et de l'imposture, ne voulant plus être les dupes des prêtres, qui sous le prétexte de la religion abusaient de la crédulité des vertueux habitants des campagnes'.[4]

Indeed, the militant terrorists were only a small minority in the rural areas. It was fairly rare for them to be members of the Municipality, since, in very many cases, the composition of these lesser administrations did not alter very much between the early years of the Revolution and the Year III, for the villages tended to be dominated by a few relatively wealthy men.[5] It was more normal for them to find their way into a revolutionary committee, which was of more recent creation and whose members, in the Year II, were nominated by the Districts on the recommendation of the clubs. Some Municipalities, such as Jonzieu, were split into

[1] Above, p. 182; cf. A.D.L., L 176, fol. 80, 9 niv., alleging 130 deserters living openly and without interference from the Mun. in these villages.

[2] A.D.R., 42 L 178, d. Dubruc.

[3] A.D.L., L 189, Q 50, 16 niv.; E. Brossard, *Notes sur l'histoire du département de la Loire*, ii. 33 (early frim.); A.D.L. Q 50, 1 frim.

[4] Ibid., 5 niv.

[5] A.D.L., L 194 and 277, resignations in frim. an III: e.g. La Côte-en-Lavalla, the whole Mun. since 1791; Chalmazet, the mayor, three *officiers municipaux*, and all the *notables* since 1792, the *agent national* and two *officiers* since 1791; Balbigny, mayor and one *officier* since 1791, *agent national* (formerly mayor) and one *notable* (previously *procureur*) since 1790. The curé would often be a member: e.g. the curé of Gumières was mayor from 1790 until his arrest in Oct. 1793 (A.D.R., 42 L 43, *passim*).

two factions;[1] others, which did fall into the hands of militants, often found themselves opposed by the inhabitants: Saint-Romain-les-Atheux had to call in a *sous-commissaire* of Pignon in order to consolidate its hold over the commune, while the Municipality of Crémeaux complained that it had been unable to arrest two people who had abused it in the most shocking fashion because not one of the bystanders would lift a finger to help.[2] This sort of situation was liable to lead to much disturbance as the Municipality used its powers to attack its political enemies: for instance, the mayor, the *agent national*, and one *officier municipal* of Saint-Germain-la-Montagne visited several houses with a large crowd of people under their influence, broke one person's arm, cut down another's trees ('le justifiant en disant qu'ils appartenaient à une aristocrate et que les bons citoyens avaient le droit d'en disposer'), and then, having wreaked havoc on the latter's household, broken the furniture, emptied the larder, and devastated the poultry-yard, they carried off some sheep which were slaughtered and eaten.[3] But, in any case, even among those country people who were prepared to accept the *gouvernement révolutionnaire*, few were enthusiastic about all its aspects, as we noted when studying the rural committees. By far the most divisive issue in the villages was the religious question. The fact that the advocates of the constitutional clergy tended to become ostensible supporters of the Terror was largely a reaction against the increasing identification of the refractory priests with counter-revolution; it did not necessarily mean that they ever saw the Terror as anything other than an element in their struggle against *fanatisme*. The politically isolated mayor of Neulize was perfectly prepared to seek outside help in order to arrest the rebels and enemies of the Republic hiding in his commune, yet, at the same time, he was hoarding grain in a small house in neighbouring Pinay and refusing to declare it.[4]

The urban centres of the department can be divided into two types according to their size: in the first place, the four

[1] A.D.L., L 124, fol. 113, denunciation by *agent national* and two *notables* against the mayor and three *officiers municipaux*.

[2] A.N., W 408, d. 939, 'État et liste des gens suspects . . .', 22 Oct.; A.D.L., L 176, fol. 83.

[3] A.D.L., L 194, denunciation to Dist. of Roanne, 18 frim. an III.

[4] A.D.L., L 18, fols. 5, 9, 12, L 409, fol. 4.

major towns (Saint-Chamond, Saint-Étienne, Montbrison, and Roanne), and in the second place, the small market-towns (Saint-Galmier, Feurs, Charlieu, etc.). The Municipalities in the latter towns represented politically an intermediate stage between the villages and the large towns in that, although the militant terrorists were more numerous and more conscious than in the villages, the pattern of the work done by Municipalities reproduced some of the themes that we have noted for the rural communities.[1] Thus, for example, Saint-Galmier was sharply divided between the terrorists, who controlled the revolutionary committee, and their opponents in the Municipality; the battle-ground was the club.[2] But at Charlieu the Municipality shared the republican fervour of the club and the committee, although its contribution was less positive than theirs.[3] At Feurs and at Saint-Germain-Laval, the Municipality had been split into factions before the Terror, and the fall of Lyon marked the victory of the Jacobins over the moderates.[4] Unlike the situation in the villages, the terrorists of these small towns counted among their number personalities of more than local stature, such as, for example, Guyot of Saint-Germain-Laval, or Jean Philippon of Saint-Galmier. The action of these Municipalities was, therefore, more frequently in harmony with the developments of the Terror: for instance, Rambert-Loire/Saint-Rambert not only emptied the church of all its ornaments 'comme tableaux, Christ et autres', including those on the altar, and collected devotional books from the citizens, but also ceremonially burned them all.[5]

Javogues renewed the Municipalities of Armeville, Montbrisé, and Roanne at the same time as the three Districts, while he appointed a new mayor at Saint-Chamond and sent a certificate of good conduct to the town.[6] Therefore, except for Roanne, where the choice suffered from the same

[1] Note that there tends to be a stability of municipal personnel here also: e.g. Charlieu, one *officier* and one *notable* 1790–4, ditto 1791–4, *agent national* and one *notable* 1792–4; Saint-Germain-Laval, one *officier* 1790–4, mayor and two *officiers* 1791–4, two *officiers* 1792–4 (A.D.L., L 194).

[2] Above, pp. 121, 153.

[3] Above, p. 102.

[4] A.C. Feurs, *reg. dél.*, 25 May; A.N., AF II 114 (861) 16, *arrêté* of *Reprs.*, 3 Sept.

[5] A.C. Saint-Rambert, *reg. dél.*, 14 niv.

[6] Above, p. 220, n. 1; A.C. Saint-Chamond, *reg. dél.*, 25 Oct. and 17 Sept.

disadvantages as that of the District, these administrations contained men whose dedication to the Terror was recognized. One *commissaire*, sent to Armeville to make some arrests, noted that the mayor displayed such great zeal for the good of the Republic that he went round pointing out those on the list.[1] Saint-Chamond and Armeville had the most energetic Municipalities in the department despite the fact that the committee and clubs pre-empted many of their functions. The Municipality at Montbrisé, however, where the problems of food and work were less urgent, was less active.[2] But all three rigorously enforced economic regulations and used the *armée révolutionnaire* to secure food supplies, while Armeville and Montbrisé also employed it to keep public order.[3] The Municipality of Saint-Chamond not only took the initiative in closing the churches, but also wrote to the neighbouring communes urging them to emulate this 'mesure de sûreté générale'.[4] Similarly, the Municipality of Armeville presided over the desecration of the churches.[5] Indeed, the latter administration appears to have been more committed than any other Municipality to the more radical aspects of the Terror, both because of the personal convictions of the mayor Johannot and because of the gravity of the food shortages and of the industrial crisis.[6] It affirmed its attitude by prescribing that 'le Conseil général de la Commune . . . dira *toi* au lieu de *vous*, au singulier', and that members would not be admitted to meetings without the *bonnet rouge*, and by using its powers of *police municipale* against all citizens who scandalized the patriots by indecently walking abroad without cockades.[7] As a more profitable response to the urgent problems of the day, some members advocated a *taxe révolutionnaire* as early as

[1] A.D.R., 42 L 176, d. Gonin-Desvernays, report by Goutard, 1 pluv.

[2] A.D.L., L 434 (1), fol. 27, complaint to committee by members of Mun. that *Conseil général* fails to meet every evening as had been decided.

[3] Above, pp. 183–4; A.D.L., L 123, fol. 360, L 434 (1), fol. 23.

[4] A.C. Saint-Chamond, loc. cit., 9 frim.; A.D.L., Q 50, *procès-verbal*, 1 frim.

[5] Galley, op. cit. ii. 175–6.

[6] It is difficult to calculate how much popular pressure was brought to bear directly on the Mun.: on 17 Oct., it requested permission from the Dist. to take a wrought-iron balustrade from a former convent 'pour le faire de suite placer dans le lieu de ses séances pour éviter que la foule des auditeurs ne se jette sur l'enceinte occupée par les membres' (A.D.L., L 130, fol. 24).

[7] A.C. Saint-Étienne, 1 D 10 (3), fols. 85, 94, 109.

4 September, while in brumaire the Municipality drew up lists of destitute citizens and took active steps to enforce Bassal's and Javogues's *arrêté* ordering all employers to give work to their employees.[1] Javogues's *taxe révolutionnaire* at Armeville at the beginning of nivôse was in accordance with, if not inspired by, the desires of the Municipality, and it was to the Municipality that Javogues gave the task of levying it.[2]

As for the Municipality of Roanne, one *commissaire* visiting the town thought that its basic defect was incapacity and lack of education.[3] But its attitudes clearly showed it to be on the side of the moderates. When Civeton ordered it to seal the houses of all arrested persons, it protested that this was impossible because it would take too long: the majority of the houses belonged to merchants and would need inventories; there were the wives and the children to be thought of; no decree had been received and it had far too much to do anyway.[4] At the beginning of nivôse, it received an angry reprimand from the Department for delivering *certificats de civisme* to men unworthy of them.[5] The parish church remained open after all those in the surrounding countryside had been closed; it was not until 21 pluviôse/9 February that the Municipality ordered that the 'cidevant autel' should be destroyed.[6] The mayor was remarkably mild in the exercise of his police powers, rarely sending to prison for more than twenty-four hours people who had assaulted him, showered abuse on him, or tried to provoke a riot by fiery speeches.[7] It was this moderatism that caused the Municipality to support the denunciations against Lapalus and Javogues.

The *Représentant du peuple* Albitte defined the *gouvernement révolutionnaire* as

> un gouvernement qui détruit jusqu'au dernier germe du fanatisme, qui anéantit tous les restes détestables de la royauté et de la féodalité, qui

1 Ibid., fols. 53, 83.

2 Ibid., fols. 107–10; on 14 frim. it had written to congratulate Collot and Fouché on their *arrêté* of 24 brum., and on 2 niv. it had petitioned Javogues for permission to ignore the formalities imposed by the Depart. for levying the tax (J. M. Devet, *Une Taxe révolutionnaire*, pp. 7, 11).

3 A.D.L., L 81, letter from Dubessey, 2 niv.

4 A.C. Roanne, 1 D 1 (2), fol. 216.

5 A.D.L., L 18, fol. 102.

6 A.D.R., 42 L 180, d. Game, Game to Javogues, n.d. (after 4 niv.); A.C. Roanne, 1 D 1 (2), fol. 268.

7 A.D.L., L suppl. 3, *passim*, especially 13 and 31 Dec., 11 pluv.

ôte aux ci-devant tous les moyens de nuire, qui écrase les contre-révolutionnaires, les fédéralistes et les coquins, qui ranime les patriotes, honore les sans-culottes et fait disparaître l'indigence . . .[1]

To this end the regular administrations of the Loire contributed in varying degrees. Although the District of Roanne is a case apart, the higher administrations, including the Department itself until the beginning of nivôse, were clearly essential to the direction and co-ordination of terrorist measures. But, although most of the Municipalities of the more important urban centres were 'dans les principes', they were overwhelmed by the problems of food supply and public order and lost much of their initiative to local extra-ordinary institutions. The majority of the lesser Municipalities, whose members had often been elected for the first time in the days of limited suffrage, were, like most peasants, either hostile or indifferent to the Terror or, at best, highly selective in their adoption of some of its weapons. The Municipalities did not justify the confidence that the law of 14 frimaire placed in them. In the last analysis and regardless of the orders issued by the Department, the *Représentant en mission*, and the Convention, it was the degree of political commitment of the administrators themselves combined with the degree of urgency of local problems that dictated the detailed policies of these institutions. The contrast between the Districts of Roanne and Armeville or between the Municipalities of those two towns, both of which enjoyed exactly the same powers, is sufficient illustration of that point. It was the moderatism of the Roanne authorities that made the activity of Lapalus and other *commissaires*, such as Civeton, so important.

[1] Quoted by Godechot, op. cit., p. 258.

IX

THE *TRIBUNAL RÉVOLUTIONNAIRE*

THE succession of revolutionary tribunals that sat at the *chef-lieu*, Feurs, from the middle of brumaire to the end of pluviôse an II completed the repressive elements of the extra-ordinary institutions of the Terror within the department of the Loire. The revolutionary tribunal at Feurs was a section of the tribunal sitting at Commune-affranchie, although it had a briefer existence than the latter and always acted autonomously. The two tribunals were designed to cope with repression arising out of the federalist revolt of the former department of Rhône-et-Loire, the section at Commune-affranchie dealing with the rebels of that town and of the area that became the department of the Rhône, while the section at Feurs judged those who were implicated in the rebellion's ramifications in the Forez. The earliest of the tribunals, the *Commission de justice populaire*, was created on 12 October 1793 (two days after the fall of Lyon) by an *arrêté* of the *Représentants en mission* Couthon, Maignet, and Laporte, and the section at Feurs was installed on 17 brumaire/7 November 1793.[1] Although the *Commission populaire* at Commune-affranchie was confined to dealing with rebels who were either captured unarmed or had never taken arms, leaving the *Commission de justice militaire* (constituted during the siege) to judge combatants, an *arrêté* of Couthon and Maignet dated 15 brumaire/5 November extended the competence of the Feurs tribunal to all types of prisoner.[2] This *arrêté* appears, however, to have gone unnoticed in the typical

[1] A.N., AF II 137 (1064), d. 14, p. 3; A.C. Feurs, *reg. dél.*, 17 brum. Both contemporaries and historians use the terms *Commission révolutionnaire* and *tribunal révolutionnaire* as synonyms. Indeed, one *arrêté* issued at Cne-aff. officially gave the name of *trib. rév.* to the *Comm. pop.* (S. de la Chapelle, *Histoire des tribunaux révolutionnaires de Lyon et de Feurs*, p. 104). There was, however, a slight difference in that the *trib. rév.* (Paris, Rochefort, Brest, etc.) used a jury, whereas the *Comm. rév.* (Lyon, Feurs, Marseille, Orange, etc.) did not. The *arrêté* of 12 Oct. provided for the nomination of a jury, but this was never put into effect.

[2] A.N., AF II 114 (860) 10.

confusion arising out of the transfer of authority at Commune-affranchie from Couthon and Maignet to Collot d'Herbois, Albitte, and Fouché, for a few days later these proconsuls appointed a section of the *Commission militaire* at Feurs, including three members from the *armée révolutionnaire* of the Loire in order to give it a military tone. It started work on 1 frimaire/21 November.[1] But on 7 frimaire/27 November the *Représentants*, seeing that this division of labour between four tribunals was in fact slowing down their work, provisionally suspended them all pending the creation of a more effective system.[2] As far as Feurs was concerned, this resulted in the suppression of the original *Commission populaire* in favour of the recent *Commission militaire* on 16 frimaire/6 December.[3] This tribunal was replaced, in turn, by a *Commission de justice révolutionnaire* created by Javogues on 13 pluviôse/1 February 1794.[4] But on 23 pluviôse/11 February, the revolutionary tribunal at Feurs was finally dissolved by the *Représentants en mission* at Commune-affranchie as part of the general clearing-up process connected with the recall of Javogues.[5]

Quite apart from these changes of personnel and name, the revolutionary tribunal at Feurs had a very chequered career. The *Commission populaire* experienced many initial difficulties in getting under way. The first problem arose out of the refusal of the president, Lafaye *le jeune*, to serve since he had just been appointed *procureur-général-syndic* of the department of the Loire. To Javogues's urgent inquiry whether the tribunal was functioning, the Department replied regretfully on 4 brumaire/25 October that they were awaiting Lafaye's replacement.[6] It was not until 9 brumaire/30 October that Couthon and Maignet got round to appointing his successor, Bonarme, judge at the district tribunal of Clermont-Ferrand, and a further pause ensued whilst the *arrêté* was transmitted

[1] A.N., AF II 114 (859) 2, 25 brum.

[2] A.D.R., 42 L 11. It appears that this *arrêté* was never enforced at Feurs, since the *Comm. pop.* organized executions on 13, 16, and 19 frim., while the *Comm. mil.* did likewise on 16 frim. (de la Chapelle, op. cit., pp. 272, 289).

[3] A.D.R., 42 L 163 (received at Feurs on 21 frim.). Taillant and Meyrand, members of the old *Comm. pop.*, were appointed to the *Comm. mil.*

[4] A.N., AF II 137 (1069), d. 30, p. 13.

[5] A.N., T 781, d. Marino. The tribunal effectively ceased work on 25 pluv.

[6] A.D.L., L 80, fol. 1.

to him from Commune-affranchie.[1] Meanwhile, additional delay ensued from the fact that the same *Représentants* had had to authorize the treasurer of the *Armée des Alpes*, in Commune-affranchie, to release some funds for heating, pay, and clerical expenses and for the purchase of uniforms for the judges.[2] The installation of the tribunal on 17 brumaire/7 November did not mean that its difficulties were at an end. The establishment of the rival *Commission militaire* and the ensuing dissolution of the *Commission populaire* were only of marginal importance, for the former inherited not merely the latter's prisoners but also its problems. Money was short at the beginning when so many things had to be organized.[3] Of more immediate concern was the problem of disposing of the convicted. Doubtless in reply to another of Javogues's impatient inquiries, the tribunal wrote on 26 brumaire/16 November that the only evidence of its zealous activities that it could offer was the minutes of its installation, since, in default of an executioner and a guillotine, it had no accounts of promptly executed death-sentences to forward.[4] The Department, to which the judges addressed similar remonstrances, assured them that, on the very day of the tribunal's installation, an administrator had been sent to order a guillotine at Ville-affranchie. But the arrival of the instrument at Feurs on 2 frimaire/22 November only brought new problems. On the same day, the Municipality was obliged to petition the Department to be allowed to requisition part of the vicarage garden in order to enlarge the Place d'Armes which was too small for *le Rasoir National*. It was only on 9 frimaire/29 November that four rebels could finally be executed in the presence of what officials described as a huge crowd chanting 'Vive la République'. Nevertheless, the machine was not functioning properly, and *le Vengeur du Peuple* was, moreover, seriously out of practice, since he had had no work to do for the last three years. On 19 frimaire/9

[1] A.D.R., 42 L 155.

[2] Ibid. (*arrêté* of 6 brum. concerning uniforms) and A.N., AF II 137 (1064), d. 3, p. 6 (*arrêté* of 6 brum. concerning the other points).

[3] e.g. A.D.L., L 80, fol. 5, *procureur-général-syndic* to *Reprs.*, 3 frim., demanding funds and a treasurer.

[4] For the rest of the paragraph, see Colin Lucas, 'La guillotine à Feurs en l'an II', *A.H.R.F.* 1965, pp. 216–17.

December, the *procureur-général-syndic* remonstrated with the Municipality of Feurs about the complaints he was receiving because the guillotine had that same day, as on a previous occasion, missed its stroke through being either improperly sharpened or misaligned. The Municipality replied with disarming ingenuousness that not only had it been receiving the same complaints, but even some of the members had noticed the fact; they had interviewed the executioner, who had said that he was very distressed by the situation because he did not know how to put it right. It assured the Department that workmen were at that instant engaged in taking the guillotine apart and had promised to make it work properly. They can have had little success, however, for the authorities were obliged to use a firing-squad. But even then there were initial difficulties, and the Department, out of all patience, acidly reproved the tribunal on 27 frimaire/17 December for allowing the dignity of the People to be so compromised by that day's execution when several volleys were needed and those sentenced had to wait whilst the soldiers ran around looking for cartridges.

These technical problems were, however, soon superseded by difficulties of a more political nature. Preoccupied by legal considerations of evidence, the *Commission militaire* acquitted some nobles, thereby incurring the wrath of Javogues, for whom, in the context of the federalist revolt, the rank of noble was a sufficient indictment in itself. The *Représentant* wrote a furious letter from Armeville on 10 nivôse/30 December ordering that the revolutionary tribunal be suspended:

Je vous défends de juger aucun criminel jusqu'à ce que je sois arrivé à Feurs. J'ai vu avec la plus vive douleur que les ennemis nés de la révolution, qu'un Comte, commissaire de la commune pour la Commission Populaire, un noble, tel que Magneux, qui possède des richesses immenses, ont été relâchés et déclarés innocents. Il faut que vous ayez perdu toute honte et toute pudeur pour aller blanchir des aristocrates aussi gangrenés. Je sais qu'il y en a parmi vous qui ont *le cœur orfèvre*, et qui aiment l'or. Des êtres aussi méprisables ne sont pas faits pour le gouvernement républicain. Vous veillerez seulement à la garde des prisons jusqu'à mon arrivée, et vous me répondrez sur vos têtes de tous les prisonniers qui sont chez vous, et de la tranquillité. Je croyais que votre conduite vous donnerait quelques droits à la reconnaissance publique; mais vous n'êtes que des lâches et des injustes. Tenez-vous à votre poste sans juger, pour que mes oreilles ne retentissent plus de vos iniquités.[1]

In fact, Javogues did not arrive at Feurs until late in the second *décade* of pluviôse. Revolutionary justice in the department of the Loire was therefore interrupted between 10 nivôse/30 December and 19 pluviôse/7 February, when the new tribunal, set up by Javogues's *arrêté* issued at Montbrisé, started its operations.[2]

But the dispute between Javogues and the *Commission militaire* was really a conflict between two concepts of justice. In the opinion of all terrorists, revolutionary justice was both the vengeance of the people and the proof of its power; it was the earnest of the Revolution and the ultimate coercive force in obtaining the acquiescence of the nation in the methods of government imposed by the national emergency. The vital characteristic of the justice dispensed by the revolutionary tribunals was its inexorable speed: there was no appeal from them and, because of the rapidity with which their decisions were reached and carried out, they furnished an example which cowed potential counter-revolutionaries and rid the country of rebels, whilst at the same time securing the release of the innocent upon whom error or malice had laid the taint of suspicion. All the proconsuls in this region were unanimous in the trouble they took to emphasize this feature in *arrêtés* establishing or modifying these tribunals. Collot and Albitte, for instance, decided to abolish the original tribunals on the grounds that their terms of reference made them too ponderous, and ordered the new tribunal 'de ne conserver dans ses formes que celles qui s'accordent avec les prompts effets de la volonté du peuple'.[3] Javogues, who always tended to think in specific if not realistic terms, felt that twenty-four hours between a suspect's arrival and burial were ample.[4]

1 *Papiers inédits omis ou supprimés par Courtois*, ii. 305–6.

2 During the suspension, the old tribunal went on collecting evidence (A.D.R., 42 L 155).

3 A.D.R., 42 L 11, *arrêté* of 7 frim. Cf. A.N., AF II 137 (1064), d. 14, p. 3; ibid. (1069), d. 30, p. 13; AF II 114 (859) 2.

4 A.D.R., 42 L 18, letter to *trib. rév.*, 5 brum.

Most of the members of the first two tribunals at Feurs, however, shared the much more orthodox concept of justice that prevailed in the civil courts of the Ancien Régime and the Revolution with their natural insistence on the rule of law and on judicial standards of culpability and innocence. All the judges of the *Commission populaire* were either professional lawyers, taken from the district courts of the Puy-de-Dôme, or members of the regular administrations of the same department. The attitude underlying the operations of this tribunal was clearly expressed by two of its members at the moment of its dissolution:

> Nous prenions le parti de faire des notes abrégées des dispositions des témoins; il en résultait un peu de longueur. Il est bien assuré que nous n'aurions pas condamné à mort trente ou quarante individus par jour. La Commission militaire, qui nous remplace . . . adoptera peut-être des formes plus promptes et satisfera mieux l'impatience nationale. Ce qu'il y a de certain, cher ami, c'est qu'on ne pouvait nous demander compte du sang que nous aurions versé et des motifs de la mort de tel ou de tel.[1]

Although the *Commission militaire* was certainly rather less formal and although it contained three officers of the *armée révolutionnaire*, two of the judges of the previous tribunal were also members, while the president, Bardet, was a lawyer from Commune d'Armes. It seems that by and large the more terrorist-minded but less educated military element allowed itself to be dominated by the legal expertise and scruples of the professional element.[2] It was only with the establishment in pluviôse of the *Commission révolutionnaire* that revolutionary justice began to function satisfactorily according to the norms of the Terror.

[1] A.N., T 566 (1), Bonarme and Bouscarat to Couthon, 22 frim. The revolutionary section of the criminal tribunal at Nantes, which was presided over by an Ancien Régime judge from Rennes, displayed very much the same characteristics, and Carrier had the same reaction as Javogues and the *Reprs.* at Cne-aff., although he never reformed the tribunal on this account (G. Martin, *Carrier et sa mission à Nantes*, pp. 320–1).

[2] The domination of the professional element may have been in part due to the fact that, although the tribunal started its operations on 1 frim., Phalippon did not take his seat before 13 or 14 frim. because of gout (A.D.R., 42 L 158, letter to Bardel, 11 frim.), and Archimbaud did not appear before 14 frim. because of difficulties in organizing his company (A.D.R., 42 L 163, letter to Bardel, 12 frim.).

During the execution of 22 pluviôse/10 February, which was the only one to take place during the six days that the *Commission révolutionnaire* was active (19–25 pluviôse/7–13 February), twenty-eight people were put to death; during the forty days of its activity (1 frimaire–10 nivôse/21 November–30 December) the *Commission militaire* had condemned only twenty-one, while the *Commission populaire* had had executed a mere fifteen during the thirty-five days of its existence (17 brumaire–21 frimaire/7 November–11 December).[1] More striking than the executions was the sheer number of suspects with which the *Commission révolutionnaire* dealt in a day. During the five days 19, 21–24 pluviôse/7, 9–12 February, the tribunal interrogated 207 prisoners, of whom seventy-two were seen on 19 pluviôse alone.[2] The *Commission militaire* certainly had a far quicker turnover than the *Commission populaire*, but its highest figure for any one day was sixteen (4 nivôse/24 December), and in fourteen days spent on interrogations it only managed to deal with a total of eighty-one suspects.[3] It was, therefore, only with Javogues's *Commission révolutionnaire* that revolutionary justice at Feurs achieved some degree of parity with that dispensed at Commune-affranchie, where, for example, 208 people were executed on 15 frimaire/5 December.[4]

The accelerated pattern developed by the *Commission révolutionnaire* could be achieved only by sacrificing all procedural formalities. The deterioration of the standard of interrogation from the *Commission populaire* through the *Commission militaire* to the *Commission révolutionnaire* is an interesting reflection of the different attitudes of successive panels of judges.[5] The interrogations undertaken by the *Commission populaire* covered on average three folio pages of manuscript; the judges allowed the accused to develop in detail his defence and they carefully laid out the grounds of their judgement. At first the *Commission militaire* imitated this procedure, but from about 2 nivôse/22 December its technique

[1] Figures from De la Chapelle, op. cit., pp. 272, 289–91.

[2] A.D.R., 42 L 161.

[3] Ibid., 15, 19, 26, 28, 29 frim., and 1–9 niv.

[4] Another indication of the progression of the tribunals towards more revolutionary forms is to be found in their changing composition: whereas the *Comm. pop.* had both an *accusateur public* and a *greffier*, the *Comm. mil.* had only a *greffier* and the *Comm. rév.* had neither.

[5] For all this paragraph, A.D.R., 42 L 160–1.

became much briefer, consisting often only in establishing the identity of the accused, and in asking him whether he knew the reasons for his arrest and whether he had taken up arms against the Republic. But this tribunal showed a marked tendency to leniency: the decision of the judges appeared to depend largely on whether a witness could be found against the accused or not. When there was neither witness nor strong suspicion against the prisoners, they were acquitted—especially deserters, people arrested without passport, and even those who protested vigorously enough that they had only taken up arms under duress. The interrogations of the *Commission révolutionnaire*, averaging between two and eight lines of manuscript and rarely concerning anything but identity and the ritual question 'Pourquoi as-tu été arrêté?', were even more summary; so much so that one arrested lawyer protested indignantly against the 'laconisme' of his interrogation.[1]

Moreover, the tone adopted in the interrogations of this tribunal was quite distinct from that of its predecessors.[2] Whereas the judges of the *Commission populaire* had been ready to listen to the accused, those of the *Commission révolutionnaire* were aggressive and forced the accused to defend himself rather than to explain. 'Pourquoi as-tu blamé le jugement de Capet?', they would ask; the accused would have to protest that he had not said a word about it. Thus, when two butchers from Armeville charged with selling tainted liver appeared before them, the judges assumed that they had intended to poison the patriots. The judges of the earlier *Commission populaire* appear to have been largely concerned with the behaviour of suspects during the federalist crisis. The grounds invoked to justify their verdicts included, for example, the fact that the convicted man had enrolled with the *muscadins*, had shot at patriots, or had been seen at a skirmish; or else that he had attended a celebration banquet, had danced the *farandole* amid shouts of 'À bas la Convention', or had sent his grain to Lyon; as for those who claimed coercion, they were said to have had countless opportunities to quit or else public opinion was decidedly against them. In

[1] A.D.R., 42 L 95, fol. 15 (Verne of Roanne).
[2] For this paragraph, A.D.R., 42 L 160–1.

contrast, the judges of the *Commission révolutionnaire*, as far as one can infer from the summary interrogations, were more concerned with the standards of political and social orthodoxy peculiar to the Year II. They wanted to know about a man's opinion of the execution of the King, about his religious beliefs, about his connections with refractory priests; they wanted to know whether he corresponded with aristocrats and how much money he had. As far as the federalist revolt was concerned, the earlier tribunals were preoccupied essentially with those who had taken an active part in the rebellion. But the *Commission révolutionnaire* regarded material contributions to the federalist cause, whether voluntary or not, and also indifference to or passive acquiescence in the rebellion, as being just as treasonable as open revolt. Thus, in its ultimate stages under the inspiration of Javogues, the revolutionary tribunal at Feurs became the weapon of a much wider concept of the Terror than implied in the purely repressive functions given it at the time of its inauguration.

The business of the revolutionary tribunal was to try suspects: only on five occasions did it overstep this role by issuing arrest warrants on its own initiative.[1] This did not mean, however, that it was a body apart from the structure of ordinary and extra-ordinary institutions within the department. On the contrary, it was the end of a chain of denunciation and surveillance, of arrest and trial; the disposal of suspects either by acquittal or by conviction was as essential a part of repression as their arrest. But the nature of the relationship of the tribunal to the other institutions illustrates the complexity of the Terror. It was only very belatedly, with Javogues's *arrêté* which created the *Commission révolutionnaire* in pluviôse, that any specific procedure was established regulating contacts between the body responsible for judging suspects and the bodies responsible for arresting them. The *Représentant* ordered the revolutionary committees to forward to the tribunal all the information, documents, and

[1] A.D.L., L 434 (2), 21 brum.; A.D.R., 31 L 60, 22 brum.; A.D.R., 42 L 179, d. Flichet, 16 frim.; A.D.R., 42 L 155, 16 frim.; A.D.R., 42 L 183, d. Boissenet, 19 frim. In this respect the tribunal at Feurs differed radically from the one at Orange (P. Vaillandet, 'Le procès des juges de la Commission révolutionnaire d'Orange', *A.H.R.F.* 1929, p. 146).

denunciations in their hands within three days, and there immediately followed a flood of documents or letters explaining the absence of documents from some, though by no means all, of the committees.

Prior to that date, however, this vital link was far more tenuous. The tribunal possessed no means of coercing the local authorities until Javogues declared in his *arrêté* that recalcitrant or negligent committees would be deemed accomplices of the Lyon rebellion. Indeed, the tribunal always remained very restricted in its sphere of activity (whatever the changing attitude of the successive *Commissions* may have been) and was unable to influence in any significant manner the character of repression as a whole. It could only work with the suspects brought before it and arrested by authorities outside its control, although it was able, up to a point, to give priority to one aspect of the Terror rather than another by selecting certain categories of suspects for trial before others: for instance, it specifically excluded two individuals from a group of prisoners called up from Montbrisé because it wanted to try crimes of hoarding first, but instructed that all 'domestiques et journaliers non contre-révolutionnaires' be included.[1] The tribunal exercised absolutely no authority over the repression: it could act only when a suspect had been arrested. It could only seek to stimulate in a general way the zeal of the local bodies and of the population at large. To the revolutionary committee at Rambert-Loire/Saint-Rambert, for example, the *Commission militaire* wrote that much more than 'une surveillance contemplative' was needed, and suggested that it would be better to send in the suspects rather than just their names; the public prosecutor of the *Commission populaire* circulated a printed proclamation throughout the department expressing his profound dismay at the lack of enthusiasm shown by his fellow citizens for helping the tribunal endow the nation's vengeance with that signal thoroughness befitting it—'quelques dénonciations, quelques détails nous sont parvenus; mais qu'ils sont insuffisants!'[2] From time to time a revolution-

[1] A.D.R., 42 L 155, letter of 2 niv.

[2] A.D.R., 42 L 155, letter of 28 frim.; Bibl. Saint-Étienne, C X p. 29, s.d. (end brum.). Cf. also A.D.R., 42 L 157, the circular (28 brum.) sent out with this

ary committee, lacking in self-confidence, turned to the tribunal for advice or sought its support against a powerful authority sheltering suspects. On such occasions the tribunal might hope to extend its influence, although it appears never to have tried to do so.[1]

To a great extent, therefore, the tribunal had to rely on the co-operation of the revolutionary committees or, in their absence, of the Municipalities in its search for evidence of crimes and of plots known and unknown, and it was constantly writing letters to them asking for documents, transcripts of denunciations, etc.[2] However, few of these authorities, essentially local in their preoccupations as we have seen, appear to have shown in this context much enthusiasm for tasks other than making arrests.[3] On the one hand, the revolutionary committees and the Municipalities of the major centres were overburdened with work and had little time for the lengthy

to all the rev. coms.: 'Pénétrés comme je pense que vous l'êtes de l'importance et de l'étendue de vos fonctions, vous vous êtes assurément occupés du travail dont la Convention vous a chargés; assurément votre registre de dénonciations est ouvert; assurément vos concitoyens ont couru au comité et vous ont donné sur chaque individu ou détenu suspect les renseignements propres à éclairer sa conduite; assurément encore vous allez et dans le plus bref délai me donner toutes ces dénonciations, tous ces renseignements . . .' Note how carefully the tribunal, by using the word 'assurément', has avoided any suggestion that it might be attempting to give orders. Again, when the tribunal appointed its own *commissaires* to hurry things up in pluv., it was unable to give them powers of arrest: e.g. the commission to Chartre only told him to urge the rev. coms. to arrest those still at liberty (A.D.L., L 418, fol. 25).

[1] e.g. A.D.R., 42 L 187 and 179, (Saint-)Jean-Soleymieux and Montbrisé ask for guidance; A.D.R., 42 L 188, Montbrisé denounces a soldier in the 3rd Battalion of the Isère.

[2] Note that the tribunal had almost no contact with the clubs, which one might consider the obvious source of information. This reflects the legalistic preference of the earlier *Commissions* for tangible proof as opposed to hearsay or to witnesses whose patriotism was not always easy to establish. The purest Jacobins had fled from the *muscadins* and those who had remained were for that very reason possibly untrustworthy, while the Auvergnat *Comm. pop.*, already ill-disposed towards the people of the Forez in general, had no personal acquaintance with them. Both the *Comm. mil.* and the *Comm. rév.* did, however, use a few outstanding patriots as witnesses (A.D.R., 42 L 161; A.D.L., L 18, fol. 181, and L 44). Even the *Comm. rév.*, however summary its procedure, wanted documentary evidence, as is shown by Javogues's *arrêté*.

[3] Montbrisé was the only one to have responded at all willingly to the demands of the tribunal and to have kept up an active correspondence with it (A.D.L., L 434 (1), *passim*).

business of searching through masses of papers and copying out denunciations. The committee at Montbrisé explained that the evidence was so diffuse that it did not as yet form a sufficiently coherent corpus of documents to satisfy judges of integrity; in another letter, it said that it would have sent all the necessary information much earlier if it had not been obliged to make three copies of everything.[1] The committee at Armeville made less effort to mask its desire to procrastinate when it replied to the exhortations of the tribunal by saying that, since it believed that the case of the prisoners in question was not due to come up immediately, it had thought itself justified in putting the matter off for a few days.[2] On the other hand, the authorities of the larger towns, where arrested suspects were collected together, were not always in a position to supply any information. The majority of lesser local authorities did not follow any consistent policy of sending explanations along with the prisoner and, when applied to for these, would neglect to reply.[3] Moreover, especially in the early days of repression, there was such a diversity of *commissaires*, Municipalities, and committees carrying out the arrests that the Terror's left hand did not know what its right hand was doing: revolutionary committees, which had been set up rather late in the day, hardly knew the reasons that had prompted the Municipality to make arrests; and the local authorities did not always understand why an itinerant *commissaire* had dispatched certain members of the community under guard to the district prisons.[4] In fact, before the response to Javogues's *arrêté* in pluviôse, the tribunal had relatively little success in getting the local committees to send in the documents that it considered necessary for the accomplishment of its task. With few exceptions, the direct contacts of the first two *Commissions* were largely confined to the more important urban centres such as Montbrisé, Saint-Chamond, Boën, Commune d'Armes, and Roanne. In any case, the tribunal was bound to concentrate on these towns since they were centres of

[1] A.D.R., 42 L 188 and 42 L 163, letters of 13 Nov. and 14 frim.

[2] A.D.R., 42 L 188, letter of 8 frim.

[3] e.g. A.D.R., 42 L 156, rev. com. at Montbrisé to tribunal, 3 niv.

[4] e.g. A.D.R., 42 L 163, letter from committee of (Saint-)Jean-Soleymieux, 20 pluv., and A.D.R., 42 L 188, letter from committee of Armeville, 8 frim.

repression and had prisons where arrested suspects were brought from the surrounding countryside.[1]

At the same time as it sought the co-operation of the committees, the tribunal also turned to the regular administrations for help. Such collaboration was clearly imperative since the regular authorities administered all sequestrated possessions and could break the seals. As early as 11 brumaire/1 November the public prosecutor appealed to the Department to organize the search for incriminating letters, etc., and this administration prescribed that each District should nominate *commissaires* to visit every commune under its jurisdiction and, in the presence of the Municipality, remove and send to the Department relevant material. A central committee was to be set up at the Department, which would make a selection and forward it to the tribunal.[2] It is not at all clear how effective this measure was.[3] The District of Roanne appears merely to have passed on the *arrêté* to all the communes, where, since the district had not been directly involved in federalism, there was little response.[4] Similarly, the District of Armeville, feeling that its own members were too busy, contented itself with appointing *commissaires* for Armeville, Saint-Chamond, and Rive-de-Gier only, and authorized 'les municipalités des cantons' (*chef-lieux*?) of the rest of the district to deal with the matter.[5] The District of Boën went as far as to nominate three of its members, but they only went to Boën itself, Montbrisé, and Saint-Jean-Soleymieux.[6] However, this development did set up another channel

1 A.D.R., 42 L 155–7, *passim.*

2 A.D.L., L 18, fol. 17. In fact no central committee was created and such documents as were collected in this way were dealt with either by the *bureau des contentieux* or by the *bureau des séquestres* (ibid., fols. 50, 76).

3 Quite independently of this system, travelling administrators or *commissaires* took it upon themselves to look through suspects' papers or to direct local authorities to do so (e.g. A.D.L., L suppl. 290, fol. 3, Vial to Depart., *c.* 27 frim.), while occasions involving the breaking of seals, but not directly concerned with the search for evidence, were exploited for this purpose (e.g. A.D.L., L 130, fol. 53, order by Dist. of Armeville to *juge de paix* of Saint-Paul-en-Jarez to look for papers when selling cows belonging to a suspect).

4 A.D.R., 42 L 156, committee of Coutouvre to Dist. of Roanne, 21 pluv.

5 A.D.L., L 130, fol. 33; cf. also A.D.L., L 18, fol. 140, secretary of Dist. to Depart. sending twenty parcels of incriminating letters.

6 A.D.L., L 259, fol. 9; A.D.R., 42 L 157, letter from *procureur-syndic* of Dist., 24 brum.; A.C. Montbrison, *reg. dél.*, no. 2, fol. 6 (38 documents taken); A.D.R., 42 L 185, d. Mollin.

of information through the ordinary regular authorities alongside the direct contact between the extra-ordinary institutions. Thus when, for example, the revolutionary committee at Rive-de-Gier sought to obey Javogues's *arrêté* of 13 pluviôse, it did not send its information directly to the tribunal as prescribed, but personally to Chana, administrator of the Department, then visiting Commune d'Armes, and it suggested that all documents be sent in future either to the District or to the Department.[1] This is a typical illustration of the parallelism of function between ordinary and extra-ordinary bodies in matters arising out of the Terror.

Thus, before the establishment of the *Commission révolutionnaire* by Javogues in pluviôse, the link between the tribunal and the basic elements of the terrorist organization, so essential to the rapidity and the success of repression, remained tenuous and inefficient. To a large extent the use of *commissaires* would have overcome the laxity of this system by establishing direct and personal communication and by affording the tribunal a means of exerting pressure. Certainly, the *Commission militaire* resorted tentatively to this method on three occasions, sending a member of the revolutionary committee at Feurs to Montbrisé and Armeville.[2] But it was not until the *Commission révolutionnaire* was set up that *commissaires* began to be used as a matter of policy, and it is probable that, had this *Commission* had a longer life, the system would have been extended to cover the whole department.[3]

It is clear, therefore, that it was only during the brief career of the *Commission révolutionnaire* that the tribunal became a fully integrated part of the structure of terrorist institutions in the Loire, capable of making repression effective. While it is certainly true that the changes of personnel and the interruptions of their activity hindered their long-term development, the first two *Commissions* remained singularly unrevolutionary in character. For it was essential that revolutionary justice should be swift and implacable and, above all, that it

[1] A.D.R., 42 L 180, d. Gauthier.

[2] Commissions to Chatelard, 1, 10, and 16 frim. (A.C. Montbrison, *reg. dél.*, no. 2, fol. 10; A.D.R., 42 L 188; A.D.R., 42 L 155).

[3] Commissions to Chartre and to Philippon (A.D.L., L 418, fol. 25, L 421, fol. 9, L 441, fol. 22).

should be seen to be so. This could not possibly be achieved by affixing verbose verdicts on a few isolated individuals to the Liberty Trees.[1] One solution would have been to have made the tribunal move round the department, thereby accelerating the process of trial and giving it the necessary publicity.[2] In frimaire, the *Représentant du peuple* Châteauneuf-Randon suggested to his colleagues at Ville-affranchie that the tribunal and the guillotine be sent to Armeville in order to deal with the large number of suspects detained there, and, indeed, these *Représentants* did include instructions to that effect in their *arrêté* of 16 frimaire/6 December, which set up the *Commission militaire* as the sole tribunal at Feurs.[3] But the tribunal never moved from Feurs, and the only time that the guillotine was seen at Commune d'Armes was when it was borrowed by Dorfeuille for the symbolic execution of the effigies of the tyrants of Europe 'et tous les chefs de la canaille anti-populaire' in a patriotic *fête* that he organized there.[4] For most of its existence the tribunal remained slow-moving, pettifogging, and dependent upon the reluctant collaboration of local authorities, whom it did not know how to rouse to activity. Suspects rotted long months in prisons, waiting to be called up to Feurs in two or threes when the tribunal finally got round to their cases,[5] until Javogues cleared out the cells as he moved up from Armeville through Montbrisé to Feurs in late nivôse and early pluviôse.[6] Repression could not be said to have achieved its object as long as suspects were merely arrested and not tried. At the time of its dissolution, the tribunal transferred 168 prisoners and 279 dossiers to its counterpart at Ville-affranchie.[7]

[1] e.g. A.D.R., 42 L 163, Dist. of Armeville acknowledges receipt of 100 copies each of judgements on six people (10 niv.).

[2] Cf. the effect of the use of a travelling guillotine by the *armée rév.* of the Moselle (Richard Cobb, *Les Armées révolutionnaires*, ii. 552), and also the visits of the *Commission extraordinaire* of Bayonne to Saint-Sever and Dax (A. Richard, 'Le comité de surveillance et les suspects de Dax', *A.H.R.F.* 1930, p. 33).

[3] A. Vingtrinier, *Catalogue de la bibliothèque lyonnaise de M. Coste*, i. 207, no. 4837, letter of 13 frim.; A.D.R., 42 L 163.

[4] *Journal de Commune-affranchie et des départements de Rhône-et-Loire*, 10 niv.

[5] e.g. A.D.R., 42 L 155, letters to the authorities of Montbrisé.

[6] J. B. Galley, *Révolution*, ii. 393; A.D.L., L suppl. 64, petition of Verd.

[7] A.D.R., 42 L 20 and 163.

Moreover, the tribunal's inability to dispense justice promptly was positively harmful in that, on the one hand, poorer suspects were ruined by being cut off from their means of livelihood, while on the other, the prolonged detention of rich employers produced hardship for the workers dependent on them. As early as 28 brumaire/18 November, the revolutionary committee at Montbrisé was suggesting that the tribunal might try the least guilty first—'ceux-ci sont bien malheureux par le déficit des subsistances dans leurs familles . . . Ce sont seulement quelques petits chiens des tables des ci-devant riches.'[1] Châteauneuf-Randon thought it essential to try the prisoners at Armeville immediately, above all because most of them were 'gros manufacturiers' whose release was demanded by the workers.[2] In this respect the *gouvernement révolutionnaire* in the Loire, designed in part to alleviate the condition of the *sans-culottes*, in fact added to their problems. Finally, the inadequacy of the tribunal compromised the work of Javogues and the Terror in this department. In the last resort, the failure to deal efficiently with the suspects after the flood of arrests produced an atmosphere of anguished expectancy and of uncertainty as to future developments which the fulminations of the *Représentant* against the Puy-de-Dôme and his infringements of the law of 14 frimaire did nothing to resolve. Too many people had been in prison for too long; too many families had been unable to dispose of their possessions; too many employees were beginning to see in the repression a suspended threat to their income. Such a situation cannot have been unconnected with the growing unrest that can be dimly perceived in the department towards the end of Javogues's mission; it certainly had a bearing on the attempts made by the inhabitants of Roanne to bring about Javogues's recall.

[1] A.D.R., 42 L 188 and 172. [2] Vingtrinier, op. et loc. cit.

X

THE *REPRÉSENTANT EN MISSION*

As a body, the *Représentants en mission* constituted the most important single element in the structure of the provincial Terror. Delegated in increasing numbers by the Convention as the problems of national defence and of internal dissidence grew over 1793, they had become generalized throughout the country by the time of Javogues's appointment. Jacques Godechot has rightly characterized them as 'agents de liaison'.[1] They were intended to link the departments firmly to the central direction of the Convention and to cure the impotence of the legislative body to enforce the implementation of its policies and decisions by the local executive. 'Tout bon gouvernement', said Billaud-Varenne, 'doit avoir un centre de volonté, des leviers qui s'y rattachent immédiatement et des corps secondaires sur qui agissent ces leviers, afin d'étendre le mouvement jusqu'aux dernières extrémités...'[2] At least until the creation of *agents nationaux*, the *Représentants en mission* were the most important of these *leviers* designed to achieve uniformity of administration behind the national government. In late 1793, after the incipient disintegration of France with the federalist rebellions, this task involved above all the imposition of political uniformity on both regular and extra-ordinary institutions and on the population, and the enforcement of administrative uniformity to co-ordinate resources for the war effort. The separation of powers, which 1789 had held so dear, could not survive in the crisis of 1793–4, and the *Représentants en mission* were one of the elements in its abrogation, which was achieved as a system by the *gouvernement révolutionnaire*. Members of the legislative body, they supervised, reformed, and directed the executive at its lower levels just as the

[1] J. Godechot, *Les Institutions de la France*, p. 304.

[2] *Rapport fait . . . sur un mode de gouvernement provisoire et révolutionnaire*, 28 brum. an II.

committees of the Convention were increasingly doing at its higher levels. The *Représentants en mission* were indispensable to the committees for the edification of the *gouvernement révolutionnaire*, for, as the experience of the *Comité de Défense générale* had revealed, it was insufficient for the Convention to control the central organs of the executive without dominating its local organs.

Nevertheless, it is difficult to speak of a system of *Représentants en mission* before early 1794. The absence of rational organization and the hesitations of national policy permitted conflicts of jurisdiction and clashes of temperament and of political conviction. This early confusion arose naturally from a situation in which, until the emergence of the great Committee of Public Safety in the summer of 1793, the central government was itself still in the process of evolution. Moreover, until late 1793, the government was preoccupied above all with the armies and the frontiers. To mention only the area round Lyon, Albitte reported in October on the lack of co-ordination between proconsuls: new *Représentants* were being sent without the old ones being recalled and they were not co-operating with each other, while the same department was being assigned to several *Représentants* so that one, residing forty leagues away, was destroying the arrangements of another.[1] Moreover, many proconsuls, of whom Javogues was a typical example, showed themselves strikingly independent of the central government, failing to report their activities and flouting the decrees of the Convention and the orders of the Committee of Public Safety. This was the negation of the purpose of the *Représentants en mission*. Instead of acting as an *agent de liaison* between the Convention and the departments, this type of proconsul, from being himself a *commissaire*, was becoming a regional Convention and his own *commissaires* were becoming *Représentants en mission*. The abolition of the separation of powers had gone too far; the proconsul was thus legislature and executive. It was really only with the law of 14 frimaire/4 December and with the efforts of the Committee of Public Safety to enforce it during the succeeding months that the practice of *Représentants en mission* came to resemble an organized system able to fulfil

[1] A.N., AF II 185, d. 1526, p. 10, letter of 2 Oct.

its original objective. But the system could never be entirely free from the blemish of the personality and political attitudes of these men, whose status made them too powerful; in a sense, the creation of the *agents nationaux* should be seen as an attempt to counterbalance the *Représentants* by another system easier to control and check.

Within a department, the *Représentant en mission* was by far the most powerful of the institutions of the Terror. His attributions were all-embracing. Although the earliest proconsuls had been given specific powers for specific tasks, by the time of Javogues's appointment their authority was unlimited and their decisions subject only to the ratification of the Convention itself. Already, the eighty-two proconsuls sent out on 9 March 1793 for the *levée des 300 000* had been accorded the right to take any measure they might deem necessary for the re-establishment of order and for the reform and arrest of administrative personnel. The decree of 30 April, reorganizing the missions to the armies, had also stated that the *Représentants* had unlimited powers for the tasks delegated to them. The decree of 17 July gave their *arrêtés* the force of law until endorsed or annulled by the Convention, while that of 16 May had already obliged the local authorities to obey these *arrêtés*. Indeed, the decrees which nominated Reverchon, Delaporte, and Javogues as *Représentants en mission* (12 and 20 July) did not bother to define their powers or even their mission; the resolution of the Committee of Public Safety, which sent Javogues into the Saône-et-Loire in brumaire, merely said 'pour les mesures de sûreté générale qu'il croira nécessaires'.[1] Thus, the proconsuls, members of the Convention, were invested with all the authority of the Convention. And this was not simply a situation achieved by the decision of that body; the proconsuls were *Représentants du Peuple*, they were the repositories of the will of the sovereign people. Their authority, therefore, came not merely from a government but directly from the people; to resist a *Représentant en mission* was to resist the will of the sovereign people, and this was, *ipso facto*, counter-revolution. If, as Barère suggested, it

[1] Cf. L. Jacob, *Joseph Le Bon*, i. 250, C.P.S. to Le Bon, 24 brum.: 'vos pouvoirs sont illimités, tout ce que vous jugez convenable au salut de la chose publique, vous pouvez, vous devez le faire sur-le-champ.'

was through the Convention that 'la Nation exerce sa dictature sur elle-même',[1] by extension it did so also through the *Représentants en mission*.

It is clear, therefore, that any study of a *Représentant en mission* during the 'anarchical' Terror must be divided into two broad themes. Not only must one discuss the proconsul as an institution of the Terror within the context of the department, but it is also essential to consider his relations with the central government and with his neighbouring colleagues in order to illustrate the state of the *gouvernement révolutionnaire* at that time. The first of these forms the subject of this chapter; the second will be discussed in the final chapter.

As far as Javogues's action within the department of the Loire is concerned, a preliminary distinction can be made between two phases of his work, although certain aspects were common to both. These two phases correspond with the two periods of his mission there. During the early period, from the campaign in the Forez to his departure for the Saône-et-Loire, Javogues was principally concerned with the purge or the construction of the institutions of the Terror and with the repression of federalist elements generally; the second period, during nivôse and pluviôse, was more markedly devoted to revolutionary measures for the foundation of the Democratic Republic. Although Javogues's activities in the Saône-et-Loire lie outside the scope of this study, it must be emphasized that he underwent a distinct change of attitude between his two periods in the Loire. This was not so much an evolution of his ideas but rather a fuller realization of the potentialities of his position. Many of the more important *arrêtés* of the second period were in fact merely reproductions of those already published in the Saône-et-Loire in frimaire.[2] On the other hand, his *arrêté* of 6 frimaire/26 November from Mâcon, establishing revolutionary committees and clubs, added a long preamble defining and denouncing the enemies

[1] Speech to the Convention, 5 Apr. 1793.

[2] e.g. demolition of castles (A.N., AF II 138 (1077), p. 38, Mâcon, 16 frim., and ibid., p. 36, Commune d'Armes, 1 niv.), secularization of churches (ibid., p. 20, Mâcon, 15 frim., and AF II 114 (861) 15, Commune d'Armes, 1 niv.), threshing and declaration of grain (AF II 138 (1077), p. 4, Mâcon, 12 frim., and ibid., p. 8, Commune d'Armes, 26 frim.).

of the People, which had been entirely absent from the similar text issued at Armeville in brumaire.[1] Moreover, the *arrêté* of 20 October creating the *armée révolutionnaire* of the Loire was a baldly administrative document containing none of the political justifications that figured in the *arrêté* of 6 nivôse/26 December maintaining the body.[2] It was in the Saône-et-Loire and the Ain that Javogues first began to take indiscriminate punitive measures against priests.[3] It is difficult to determine the cause of this development: it was probably a combination of the discussions with Collot d'Herbois in mid brumaire, the influence of the particularly alert militants of Mâcon and Bourg, and his first contact with the Parisian *armée révolutionnaire*.[4] Therefore, on his return to the Loire at the end of frimaire, Javogues clearly had a plan of campaign and experience in its execution.

In the second half of 1793 the work of all the *Représentants en mission* centred on the purge of the administrations and the construction of terrorist institutions. As far as the regular administrations were concerned, Javogues's task was in a sense easier than that of most of his colleagues. He did not have to resort to the laborious business of checking the conduct of each individual administrator: he was organizing a completely new Department, while the previous Districts and major Municipalities had been implicated more or less overtly in the rebellion. Thus, a comprehensive reform between 21 October and 8 brumaire/29 October installed a new personnel in the most important posts in the department.[5] Similarly, before his departure in mid brumaire, Javogues had made the necessary arrangements for the complete organization of extra-ordinary terrorist institutions.[6] The *armée révolutionnaire* of the Loire was established by his joint *arrêté* of 20 October with Bassal, while his *arrêté* of 5 brumaire/26 October contained a master-plan for a system of

1 A.N., AF II 138 (1077), p. 3; AF II 114 (861) 15, 5 brum.

2 A.N., AF II 114 (859) 6; AF II 114 (861) 14.

3 A.N., AF II 84 (622), report by Marino and Bonnerot on their mission to the Ain, 25 niv.

4 The Parisian *armée rév.* was at work in the Saône-et-Loire in early frim.; Javogues took a detachment with him to Bourg, where it immediately started emptying the churches (A.D.R., 1 L 622, receipts given by Davril); the same detachments accompanied him to the Loire.

5 Above, p. 220.

6 Above, pp. 99, 132, 156.

revolutionary committees and clubs in the *chefs-lieux* of the cantons. A revolutionary tribunal had already been provided by the proconsuls at Ville-affranchie. Clearly, therefore, Javogues had accomplished the basic groundwork for the administration of the Terror before the end of his first period in the Loire. He could safely leave the implementation of his instructions concerning the extra-ordinary institutions to the reliable personnel of the higher regular authorities.

Nevertheless, Javogues never properly completed his work in this sphere. As far as the regular administrations were concerned, apart from the higher bodies (Department, Districts, and tribunals), his reforms affected only Roanne, Montbrisé, and Armeville. In these towns, the reorganization was thorough, including the *juges de paix*, the *bureaux de conciliation*, the trade tribunals, and even, in the case of Montbrisé, the steward and surgeons of the hospital.[1] Hardly any of the previous incumbents retained their posts, for the faithful minority was promoted or, occasionally, released on personal grounds.[2] Elsewhere, however, Javogues made practically no changes at this or any other time. At Saint-Chamond, which he visited thrice, no arrangements appear to have been made to replace the federalists in the Municipality except for the appointment of a new mayor—the patriotic members returned and their opponents in their turn either fled or were arrested;[3] the *procureur de la commune* was never questioned and continued his zealously bureaucratic activity throughout the Year II as *agent national*. Similarly, Javogues passed through Saint-Galmier in brumaire, but left unreformed a Municipality which was soon to be attacked bitterly by the revolutionary committee for its alleged federalism. The only alterations made at Feurs were to fill places vacated by promotions.[4] During his second period in the Loire, Javogues made a few adjustments to the District of Armeville and was

1 A.D. P.-de-D., L 2781, 14 brum.

2 A.D.R., 42 L 76, fol. 80, Fromage to *Comm. rév.*, n.d.: he was removed from office because of age.

3 G. Lefebvre, *Souvenirs de cent ans*, p. 25, n. 1; J. B. Galley, *Révolution*, i. 796; A.C. Saint-Chamond, *reg. dél.*, 25 Oct.

4 A.C. Feurs, *reg. dél.*, 13 and 14 brum., replacement of *juge de paix* and mayor; cf. A.C. Chazelles-sur-Lyon, *reg. dél.*, 19 brum., replacement of *juge de paix* deceased.

clearly intending to do the same to those of Boën and Roanne,[1] but he never evinced the slightest interest in any other administration beyond the occasional arrest.[2] The minor administrations, even of *chefs-lieux* of cantons which could be towns of some importance, remained therefore substantially unpurged, purified only incidentally by the activities of *commissaires* or revolutionary committees. Thus, the penetration of Javogues's reforming action to the lower levels of administration was inadequate and his work compares unfavourably in intention if not in practice with that of Joseph Le Bon, for example.[3] When yet another of his tirades showered it with abuse which it deemed better directed at the Municipalities, the Department rather pointedly suggested that he might care to reform the vast majority of them that hindered the forward march of the Revolution.[4] Indeed, his attitude towards the personnel of minor Municipalities seems to have been careless: he reinstated the mayor of Saint-Genest-Malifaux, for example, whose infamy was notorious enough to move a member of the Convention for the Haute-Loire to fury when the news reached him in Paris.[5]

The same weakness is discernible in his dealings with the structure of extra-ordinary organs. The only revolutionary committee whose composition he personally supervised appears to have been that of Feurs, although the absence of documents from Armeville prevents any general conclusions on this subject.[6] Certainly, the organization of these bodies was largely undertaken during his absence from the department, but he does not seem to have intervened significantly in the extra-ordinary institutions even after his return. There is no positive evidence that he ever vetted the membership of the revolutionary committees, or exhorted the clubs to purge themselves or issued general instructions to that effect. The only specific alteration that he made was to the revolutionary

[1] A.D.L., L 123, fol. 370; L 329, fol. 6, Dist. Boën to *Repr.* at Cne-aff., 21 pluv.: 'le citoyen Javogues se propose quelque changement parmi nous'; below p. 365.

[2] e.g. A.N., AF II 114 (861) 15, dismissal of mayor of Feurs, 1 pluv.

[3] Jacob, op. cit. i. 292. Le Bon visited all the major towns of the Pas-de-Calais and was only prevented from extending his investigations even further by pressure of business.

[4] A.D.L., L 80, fol. 11, letter of 11 niv.

[5] A.D.R., 42 L 96, fol. 36, Lemoigne to a colleague, n.d.

[6] A.D.L., L 432.

tribunal. Here again, Javogues contrasts unfavourably with Le Bon, who carefully scrutinized clubs and committees, although, admittedly, the *nouveau fédéralisme* of the former was a crucial problem in the Pas-de-Calais.[1]

The limitations of Javogues's activity in this context were inherent in his technique. The standard pattern, of which Laplanche provides perhaps the clearest example, was for the *Représentant en mission* to purge all the local authorities in a public meeting of the population or of the club.[2] Moreover, the proconsuls usually worked in close conjunction with the clubs, in some cases to the exclusion of the regular administrations, and indeed were expressly recommended so to do by the Committee of Public Safety.[3] Despite the paucity of the documentation relating to the clubs, it is evident that Javogues did not follow this practice consistently.[4] Except for the adjustments made to the District of Armeville in nivôse, the purge of the administrations appears to have been undertaken without either the advice or the ratification of the clubs. Indeed, a number of suspects among the administrators appointed for Armeville in brumaire were almost immediately pointed out to Javogues.[5] Apart from Armeville, the only club that he undoubtedly did visit was that of Feurs in brumaire, while he possibly also appeared at the one at Saint-Galmier at about the same time.[6] On the other hand, he did not visit either the club or the committee at Saint-Chamond when he passed through there on his way to Armeville in late frimaire. The committee was obliged to go to his lodgings to consult him.[7] There is no trace of a visit on the registers of the committees at Rambert-Loire/Saint-Rambert and Montbrisé.[8] When he did hold a public meeting, Javogues appears

[1] Jacob, op. cit. i. 254–73, 310.

[2] T. Lemas, 'La Mission de Laplanche . . . dans le Cher', *R.f.* 1895 (28), pp. 496–529.

[3] Circular to *Repr. en mission*, n.d. (F.-A. Aulard, *Actes du Comité de Salut public*, ix, 161).

[4] Possibly he had been influenced by an unfortunate experience at Mâcon where he found that, when he wanted to renew the administrations with the advice of the club and the rev. com., 'c'était un compérage et un commérage qui ne finissaient pas' (A.N., AF II 58, d. 430, p. 2, Javogues to Collot, 28 brum.).

[5] Galley, op. cit. ii. 27.

[6] A.D.L., L 432; L 79, fol. 9, rev. com. at Saint-Galmier to Depart., 7 brum.

[7] G. Lefebvre, *Société républicaine*, pp. 106–10; A.D.L., L 390, fol. 4.

[8] A.D.L., L 441, L 434 (1 and 2), *passim*.

to have preferred to do so elsewhere than in the club; for instance, the one in which the *taxe révolutionnaire* was drawn up at Armeville was held in an assembly of the *conseil général* of the Municipality.[1] This is not to suggest that Javogues altogether neglected the virtues of public oratory and propaganda. There is not necessarily any truth in the allegation made by a contemporary that Javogues never tried to inspire a love of the Revolution in the people and never harangued the population; there is no reason why a man who had spoken to the clubs at Bourg and Ville-affranchie should refrain from doing so in the Loire.[2] On the contrary, at the levy of the *taxe révolutionnaire* he made a long and vehement speech, and he also gave a civic address at the installation of the new District and Municipality of Armeville.[3] Moreover, the long preambles of his *arrêtés* amounted to essays designed for the political education of the people. Nevertheless, contacts with the clubs and their inevitable concomitant of inflammatory speeches cannot have formed an important part of his technique. There are too few references to such contacts and, at a time when the orations of local personalities were abundantly reproduced, no speech by him in the Loire was ever printed; it was the speech at Bourg that was read out to the club at Charlieu.[4] He certainly participated in the patriotic celebration organized by Dorfeuille at Armeville, but he does not appear to have grasped this opportunity to harangue the crowd.[5]

Javogues preferred to surround himself with men whose patriotism he felt he could rely upon. He was not, of course, unique in this respect: Albitte, for instance, behaved in the same way in the Ain.[6] The most important figures in the second period were Lapalus and Duret, but this pattern can be seen from the very beginning. These men, most of whom Javogues placed in positions of authority, brought the

[1] A.C. Saint-Étienne, 1 D 10 (3), fol. 103.
[2] A.N., D III 349, d. Javogues, Lepoully.
[3] A.C. Saint-Étienne, loc. cit.; Galley, op. cit. ii. 16, and A.D.L., L 123, fol. 338.
[4] A.D.L., L 403, fol. 19, 21 pluv.
[5] *Journal républicain des deux départements de Rhône et de Loire*, supplement to 26 niv.
[6] L. Meunier, 'Albitte conventionnel en missions', *A.H.R.F.* 1946, p. 238.

higher administrations to which they belonged into harmony with the attitudes of the *Représentant*. This helps to explain why Javogues was on the whole far less suspicious of the regular administrations than many of his colleagues. One visitor to Feurs found Javogues in the company of Dumas, Thiolière, Gaulne, and Berthuel, all members of the Department; when the District of Armeville warned the communes against a rumour about an attempt on the life of the *Représentant*, it cited the fact that he had dined with the administrator Chorel Laplagny on the previous evening.[1] Since the original purge of the administrations in brumaire was accomplished without the advice of the clubs, it was presumably based on that of Javogues's group of intimates. Certainly a few days later Javogues informed the Department of the arrest of one of their colleagues 'que vous aviez fait nommer à l'administration de [la] Loire'.[2] His confidants channelled information to him and, one supposes, influenced him at least in his judgement on individuals if not in the formulation of policy, although this is difficult to substantiate. One suspect wrote plaintively to David, *greffier* of the criminal tribunal, that rumour had it that he had persuaded Javogues to change his mind about granting the man's petition; in frimaire, the same David wrote to the revolutionary committee at Saint-Rambert that he had not indicated Gérentet, the former canon, as a suspect but his namesake, the former monk.[3] Towards the end of his mission, a great deal of the proconsul's work appears to have been done by Lapalus and, to a lesser degree, by Duret, although the extent to which they took decisions on their own initiative cannot be established.[4]

Such a situation did not necessarily insulate Javogues from the affairs of the department. It did mean, however, that his contacts with the lesser institutions were confined to deputations or to conversations with individual members. Large

1 A.D.L., L 430 (2), fol. 30; L 156, fol. 94.

2 A.D.L., L 79, fol. 4, letter of 15 brum. Note that he took the trouble to recount the patriotic record of the replacement who was presumably unknown to the group who had been placed in the Depart.

3 A.D.R., 42 L 186, d. Portier; A.D.L., L 441, fol. 1.

4 e.g. A.D.L., Q 191, inventory of Lapalus's effects at Feurs, 28 pluv.: 'nous n'y avons trouvé que des paperasses ainsi que quelques registres appartenant à Bonnet-la-Montagne'; A.N., W 408, d. 939, evidence of Vier of Rive-de-Gier that Pignon told him that he was being arrested on Lapalus's orders.

numbers of deputations consulted the *Représentant* or drew his attention to particular questions. Thus, for instance, an assembly of the inhabitants at Montbrisé attempted to solve some of the problems facing the town at the end of October by sending four representatives to discuss them with Javogues; the two members of the committee at Perreux, who had been sent to Saint-Claude in the Vosges to identify a suspect, finally abstained from completing their journey when Javogues told them that they could ask for the suspect to be sent.[1] Individual members of minor institutions travelled to meet the proconsul, while in many more cases the authorities would write to him.[2] In turn, Javogues often instructed the committees to deal with specific questions, particularly in matters arising out of repression.[3] Contact with the general public was also maintained by the accessibility of the proconsul's chambers, which contrasts with the seclusion in which Carrier, for instance, lived.[4] The report of one observer of the throng in Javogues's apartment has already been quoted.[5] Naturally, however, Javogues's temperament must have reduced the effectiveness of this contact.

This method of operation had one basic defect. The initiative lay, in the last resort, with the local institutions or with local patriots. This gave more opportunity, which was only partially overcome by fear of the might invested in a *Représentant en mission*, to those who wished to hide or to distort facts. Javogues, already temperamentally, was also technically, an easy prey for faction. Pignon forwarded information gathered by one of his *sous-commissaires* pointing out that 'elle te fera voir qu'il est bien essentiel pour toi de bien placer ta confiance. Les Odrax et autres de cette espèce t'ont trompé et les sans-culottes sont vexés.'[6] No credit can be given to Javogues for the way in which faction struggles in the Loire did not reach the proportions they assumed in other areas. The situation was aggravated by Javogues's comparative immobility, for the local authorities did not always have the energy or the

[1] A.D.R., 42 L 182, d. Labarre; A.D.L., L 413, fol. 2.

[2] e.g. A.D.L., L 430 (2), fol. 30; ibid., fol. 11, committee at Cervières to Javogues, requesting replacement for arrested *juge de paix*; L 400, fol. 2, committee at Charlieu to Javogues, denouncing the refuge of a local noble at Paris.

[3] Below, pp. 273–4.

[4] G. Martin, *Carrier et sa mission à Nantes*, p. 347.

[5] Above, p. 79.

[6] A.D.R., 42 L 157, letter dated 8 Oct.

inclination to send deputations obliged to travel some distance, while the poor with grievances could not possibly do so. Moreover, his disinclination to travel prevented Javogues from accomplishing his important tasks of supervising and stimulating the administrations. Joseph Le Bon, for example, was always on the move, counselling, reproving, exhorting, directing.[1] The most obvious gap in Javogues's work in this respect is his total failure to visit the district of Roanne and to verify the political attitudes of the authorities in the *chef-lieu*, although he was proposing to do so when he was recalled. But he never showed any signs of intending to visit Boën. Much more serious was the fact that Javogues apparently never checked the records of the higher administrations, let alone those of the Municipalities and committees, in the towns that he did visit. Clearly, he considered that since he had appointed the members of most of these administrations, they were inevitably trustworthy. But even trustworthy personnel could adopt inopportune policies or make faulty decisions. Certainly, Javogues would write stormy letters to the administrations that displeased him and even occasionally issue arrest warrants against them for disobedience, but this hardly amounted to proper supervision.[2]

If a *Représentant en mission* was unable to travel sufficiently, there were two major remedies. The one, which was adopted by Le Bon in the later stages of his mission, consisted in calling together the *agents nationaux* in order to give them instructions and combine their activity; the other, which was preferred by Laplanche and Dubouchet, consisted in delegating wide powers to mobile *commissaires*.[3] Javogues had recourse to neither of these methods: he did not even employ *commissaires* to investigate important problems on which he could not get satisfactory information from local sources, as Maignet did, for example.[4] As has already been emphasized,

[1] Jacob, op. cit. i. 178–84, 247–69.

[2] e.g. A.D.L., L 80, fols. 10 and 11, Depart. to Javogues, 11 niv.; e.g. the wholesale arrest of the Mun. of Montbrisé, 9 niv. (A.D.L., L 434 (1), fol. 37).

[3] Jacob, op. cit. i. 317; E. Campagnac, 'Les délégués du représentant Laplanche en mission dans le Cher', *R.f.* 1902 (43), pp. 300–46; T. Lhuillier, 'Laurent le Cointre', *R.f.* 1895 (28), p. 243.

[4] P. Vaillandet, 'La mission de Maignet en Vaucluse', *A.H.R.F.* 1926, 168–78, 240–63.

Javogues only gave limited powers to his *commissaires* for specific issues, apart from a brief period at the beginning of his interest in the Loire. Javogues preferred to leave the business of supervision and stimulation to the higher regular authorities. As far as the Department and the Districts of Armeville and Boën were concerned, this confidence was largely justified. But it was misplaced and had dire consequences for Javogues in the case of Roanne.

It is clear, therefore, that generalizations about the impact of Javogues's work on the department as a whole must be made with caution. The image of an omnipresent, suspicious proconsul coercing administrators and population alike into patriotism by his scrutiny cannot be applied in this case. On the other hand, it would be false to suggest that his influence was hardly felt at the lower levels. Javogues transacted a great deal of business through the medium of the higher administrations, especially the Department.[1] To them he referred petitions and decisions; they in turn consulted him and sought decisions from him. It was to them that he entrusted the execution of his political and administrative directives. Similarly, it was the Municipality of Armeville that he ordered to levy and administer the *taxe révolutionnaire*.[2] Indeed, in no case did Javogues ever entrust the enforcement of his *arrêtés*, except those relating to individuals, to the extra-ordinary institutions.[3] Thus, for example, it was the whole hierarchy of regular administrations that was ordered to proceed to the threshing of grain and the assessment of resources, it was the Municipalities which were ordered to draw up lists of rich and poor and to relieve the indigent.[4] By relying in this fashion on the regular administrations, Javogues in fact ensured the penetration of his directives down the hierarchy, at least in so far as the rural Municipalities could be made to comply with any orders at all. Furthermore, he was indirectly mobilizing the extra-ordinary resources of the Terror as well, for, as we have seen, the Department and the Districts combined regular and extra-ordinary attributions. The revolutionary

1 A.D.L., L 18, L 123, L 130, L 176, L 259–62, *passim*.

2 A.C. Saint-Étienne, 1 D 10 (3), fols. 103, 108, 113.

3 Cf. the arrest of the Mun. of Montbrisé was entrusted to the patriot Ravaud, captain of *gendarmerie*, and not to the rev. com. (A.D.L., L 434 (1), fol. 37).

4 A.N., AF II 137 (1069), d. 30, p. 8; AF II 114 (861) 14.

committees and the *armée révolutionnaire*, controlled by the Department and the Districts, were thus brought in to support the policies of the *Représentant* in a much broader spectrum of matters than his own direct use of these bodies would suggest at first sight. Therefore, in so far as the majority of the more important administrations of the Loire were zealous and reliable, Javogues did fulfil his function of co-ordinator of effort and resources within the department.

Nevertheless, Javogues's refusal to delegate his powers and his reliance on the regular administrations did have at least one practical advantage. As has been suggested elsewhere, the use of powerful *commissaires* tended to provoke an anarchy of conflicting authorities. After the confusion during the last stages of the siege of Lyon, this was never a feature of the Loire. On the contrary, Javogues strengthened the Department and the Districts as elements of order by implicitly giving them primacy. Indeed, his *arrêté* of 23 October revoking the powers of his *commissaires* in the district of Armeville clearly indicates that he was determined to prevent such a situation from arising; similarly, the order to Philippon to refund the 20,000 *livres* levied at Chevrières shows a conscious attempt to restrain those *commissaires* that he did employ.[1] Whatever Javogues's contribution to the disruptive elements in the 'anarchical' Terror, it was certainly not the introduction of disunity and anarchy into the area under his control. As far as he was able, he brought order and authority to the legacy of confusion from the federalist crisis.

As a *Représentant en mission* Javogues was not in the same class as for example, Maignet, who, assisted by three secretaries and eight scribes, wrote 2,000 letters and issued as many *arrêtés* during his time in the south-east.[2] Nevertheless, the sheer amount and the diversity of business transacted by Javogues, as by all proconsuls, is striking. His work ranged from trying to procure funds for the departmental treasury to authorizing administrators to lodge in sequestrated houses; from appealing to the population to pay taxes regularly to annulling sales of national lands made by the federalist administrations; from finding a successor to the *pharmacien* of a hospital to providing for the care and education of an

[1] Above, p. 213. [2] Vaillandet, art. cit., pp. 170–1.

abandoned child.[1] Since he was the highest authority in the department, it was inevitable that many questions of detail, upon which no other authority cared to make a decision, should end up before him. Some he would merely reject as none of his business; others he would refer to the appropriate body; but many more clamoured for his attention.[2] Beyond this, many individuals would appeal directly to the *Représentant*, either before or after other channels were exhausted, in the hope of obtaining his rapid intervention. His word could achieve much; it was therefore normal that much should be asked of him. Incarcerated suspects were especially prolific in this respect: the dossiers of the revolutionary tribunal of Feurs contain 223 letters addressed to him by or on behalf of suspects and another twenty to people close to him.[3] Although most, asking for release or proclaiming innocence, were the business of the tribunal, some required attention, for they requested money for prison costs or made denunciations.[4] Suspects were not alone in petitioning the proconsul: a musket-maker requested a loan for the purchase of metal, to be paid back when the weapons were completed; a baker wanted to be allowed to sow a drained pond belonging to a suspect without interference from the Municipality, etc.[6] Disabled soldiers and widows of those killed by the *muscadins* wanted relief while waiting for their indemnities.[6] Occasional agents employed for various jobs had to be rewarded, and overdue salaries paid.[7] Patriots had to be satisfied—a gold watch here 'pour les bons et agréables services' rendered to the Republic, a job there for the deserving unemployed.[8]

[1] A.D.L., L 18, 6–19 brum., L 156, fol. 85; A.N., F^1c III Loire 5, *compte décadaire* of Saint-Chamond, 5 pluv.; A.N., AF II 114 (861) 15, proclamation of 11 Sept., ibid., *arrêté* of 15 brum.; A.C. Montbrison, *reg. dél.*, no. 2, fol. 55; ibid., fol. 53.

[2] e.g. A.D.L., L 390, fol. 6, petition forwarded to rev. com. at Saint-Chamond; Lefebvre, op. cit., p. 121: 'a l'égard des étapes, le citoyen Représentant Javogues a dit que cela ne le regardait pas.'

[3] A.D.R., 42 L 167–90, *passim*.

[4] e.g. A.D.L., L 79, fol. 8, Javogues to Dubourg, Saint-Polgues, 15 brum.; A.D.R., 42 L 158, Despomet to Javogues, n.d.

[5] A.D.R., 42 L 175; d. Chometon; A.D.L., L 260, 13 vent.

[6] e.g. A.D.L., L 55, fols. 2, 4, 5.

[7] e.g. A.D.L., L 260, 2 pluv., L 55, fols. 3 and 4, L 130, fol. 56.

[8] A.D.L., L 130, fol. 67; L suppl. 29, fol. 2, Javogues's secretary to dist. tribunal of Boën, 20 brum.: 'Je dois vous prévenir que l'intention du citoyen Javogues . . . est que le citoyen Varennes soit placé, qu'il le soit au moins comme huissier audiancier.'

There were even letters from his own family seeking his sympathy for an arrested relative, stable situations for his brothers, and advice on whether to sell the house at Montbrisé.[1] However, Javogues ignored his family: he made no attempt to intervene when one brother was sent to the revolutionary tribunal at Feurs for stirring up trouble at Fonfort/Saint-Galmier—not unnaturally, the tribunal promptly sent him back to the *juge de paix*, as one judge hastened to reassure Duret.[2]

Javogues's most constant preoccupation was with repression. This interest was partly a direct response to the situation created by the rebellion and partly an elementary step towards the Democratic Republic: 'nous devons tous aller d'un pas ferme au même but, celui de purger le sol de la Liberté de tous les traîtres et de tous les contre-révolutionnaires qui l'infectaient: toute pusillanimité retarde le bonheur du peuple et devient un crime.'[3] It is clear that, in the Loire, the achievements of the Terror in the sphere of repression must be largely attributed to the work of the *Représentant en mission*. It was Javogues who set the repressive mechanism in motion during the latter days of the siege of Lyon by his system of *commissaires* and by his orders to Municipalities and to the National Guard in the southern part of the department.[4] At Montbrison, he did not wait for the establishment of the appropriate authorities, but issued arrest warrants against 148 people on 14 September during the expulsion of the *muscadins*.[5] Similarly, he had ordered a much smaller number of arrests at Saint-Étienne on 7 September.[6] But the arrests at Saint-Étienne were made only slowly; it is evident that the local authorities, whether patriots or survivals from the

[1] A.D.R., 42 L 168 d. Maussier, 186, d. Perrochias, letters from his sister; 158, letter from his father ('si tu plumes tant de différents particuliers, tu peux bien faire quelque chose pour tes proches; première nécessité, suivant un ancien proverbe, doit commencer par soi-même').

[2] A.D.R., 42 L 161, interrogation (much longer than that of his co-defendants); 42 L 177, d. Dubourg, Phalippon to Duret, 3 niv.

[3] A.D. P.-de-D., L 2785, p. 53, Bassal and Javogues to C.P.S. of Montbrisé, 20 Oct.

[4] Above, p. 72.

[5] A.D.L., suppl. L 11; cf. A.C. Feurs, *reg. dél.*, 13 Sept., warrant for sixteen suspects.

[6] A.C. Saint-Étienne, 1 D 10 (3), fol. 55, no figure given; Tézenas du Montcel, *Deux Régicides*, p. 26, says seventeen; Galley, op. cit. i. 735–6, says seven.

federalist era, were reluctant to proceed against suspects in competition with the business of supplying the *levée en masse*, and managed to prevent Javogues's *commissaires* from operating effectively in the town. Further evidence of the importance of the proconsul in stimulating repression may, therefore, be gathered from the fact that the arrest of federalists only really began at Armeville from mid October, that is to say after the arrival of Javogues.[1] Although the largest numbers of arrests were made during the first period of Javogues's mission, he continued to order them throughout the whole of his stay in the department. Since he was the highest authority in the area, denunciations were often made directly to him, especially by patriots who felt that local authorities were not energetic enough to act, while denunciations received by authorities outside the department were forwarded to him as a matter of course.[2] Javogues always reacted by ordering the arrest of the person incriminated; any investigation of the facts came after the suspect had been secured and was usually left to the revolutionary tribunal or referred to a revolutionary committee.

Javogues's direct activity with regard to the arrest of suspects was exceptional, even for a *Représentant en mission* in an area of intensive repression. Carrier at Nantes, for example, only ordered two arrests himself, while, during the eighteen months that he was on mission, Châteauneuf-Randon only issued warrants against fifteen suspects.[3] Excluding those arrests operated by *commissaires* endowed with general repressive powers during the early period, at least 530 arrests were made on the orders of Javogues; given the state of the documentation, this must be considered as a minimum figure.[4] In a very few cases, he gave way to local pressures for the release of suspects. For the most part, this happened in the early days when he was not

[1] Ibid. ii. 61.

[2] e.g. A.D.R., 42 L 167, d. Mathon de Sauvain; 42 L 176, d. Martinon, *Comm. Temp.* to Javogues, 22 niv.

[3] Martin, op. cit., p. 340; *Rapport des missions remplies par Châteauneuf-Randon.*

[4] Based on incomplete *registres d'écrou*, references in registers of rev. coms., lists of arrested persons made by Muns. in germ., the *Liste générale des dénonciateurs et terroristes* (Montbrison), the *Liste générale des dénonciateurs et dénoncés* (Lyon), and scattered papers, especially in the dossiers of the tribunal of Feurs.

perhaps fully aware of the problems involved.[1] Later, he occasionally returned a suspect to the revolutionary committee for examination and release if justified.[2] Six suspects at Saint-Chamond just happened to be lucky that the committee pressed their case when the proconsul visited the town and were able to obtain his favour.[3] More generally, Javogues would leave the decision to the tribunal, although he would be prepared to support claims of innocence.[4] Even when he did order release, he tended to do so rather casually: he got very angry when the Municipality of Saint-Chamond not unnaturally wanted written confirmation of verbal instructions given to a deputation.[5]

Javogues also devoted considerable energy to the other aspects of repression. His continued interest in the revolutionary tribunal reveals his preoccupation with the liquidation of the corrupted elements of society, while the cortège of prisoners that he brought with him to Feurs from Armeville and Montbrisé in pluviôse shows his determination to reach a final solution.[6] Apart from keeping an eye on the attitudes and composition of the tribunal, he centralized information for it until his arrangements in mid pluviôse for the direct transmission of evidence from the committees.[7] Many of the documents in the dossiers of the tribunal are annotated by the *Représentant* or his secretary. In important cases, he requested information from local authorities and directed the tribunal to reliable witnesses.[8] Similarly, he took steps to tighten up the considerable laxity of prison security and to stop the widespread practice of house-arrest.[9] Finally,

[1] e.g. A.D.L., L 130, fol. 15, *arrêté* of 20 Sept. releasing *procureur de la commune* of Saint-Genest-L'erpt in response to petition of population but under its collective responsibility.

[2] A.D.L., L 435, 16 and 17 pluv., five cases referred to Montbrisé; L 430 (1), fol. 4, 18 pluv., two cases to Cervières.

[3] A.D.L., L 390, fol. 4.

[4] A.D.R., 42 L 96, d. Verd, 42 L 182, d. Dufresne.

[5] A.D.L., L 390, fol. 8.

[6] Above, p. 178.

[7] e.g. A.D.L., L 390, fol. 6, copies of denunciations sent by rev. com. of Saint-Chamond to Javogues, 3 niv.; L 392, Julliard to rev. com. of Armeville, n.d.: 'on a remis au citoyen Javogues . . . par vos ordres mes papiers.'

[8] e.g. A.D.R., 42 L 172, d. Achard, Mun. of Brignais to Javogues, 3 brum.; 42 L 181, d. Villemalet, Javogues to public prosecutor at Feurs, 5 brum.

[9] A.N., AF II 138 (1077), p. 28, *arrêté* of 16 frim. (*sic*), Arme-Commune; A.C. Feurs, *reg. dél.*, 10 pluv., commission to Chavanis.

throughout his mission he pursued the sequestration of the property of suspects, which was often neglected by the overworked administrations. During the expedition in the Forez in September, he ordered the execution of the decree of 12 July concerning rebel property and personally directed the sequestration of more than two hundred houses.[1] In brumaire, he drew the attention of the Department to this matter and ordered the establishment of a central administration for sequestrated property together with the circulation of printed lists to enable local authorities to identify non-resident suspect landowners.[2] In nivôse and pluviôse he made detailed arrangements for the inventory of sequestrated property and himself appointed the *commissaires* for this job.[3] His arrest warrants never failed to prescribe sequestration as well.[4]

Food supply was a problem which exercised all the *Représentants en mission* during the winter of the Year II. This is particularly true of those proconsuls in an area of intensive repression, for it is axiomatic that the intensity of the Terror was intimately associated with the gravity of the food shortage. The power of the *Représentants* made them best fitted to deal with the emergency in which many areas lived constantly at this time; an energetic proconsul could be the saviour of a large population by his requisitions, apportionment, and co-ordination of resources. Javogues had a further advantage in this respect since his powers, which included eight departments adjacent to the Loire, could have enabled him to direct a combined effort to alleviate misery in this latter department. However, his activity in this sphere was disappointing when compared with the size of the problem. To a degree this can again be imputed largely to his technique. Since Javogues left the initiative in the relations between *Représentant* and local authorities to the latter, he could only act as petitions were presented to him and without

[1] A.N., AF II 184, d. 1521, p. 20 and d. 1522, pp. 43–4, Javogues to C.P.S., 10 and 17 Sept.; A.C. Chazelles-sur-Lyon, *reg. dél.*, 10 Oct.; A.D.R., 1 L 187, Javogues to Mun. of Longe and Treyve, 21 Sept.

[2] A.D.L., L 79, fols. 1, 4, Javogues to Depart., n.d. and 24 Oct.

[3] A.D.L., L 434 (1), fol. 43, *arrêté* of 16 niv.; L 18, fol. 132; A.C. Montbrison, *reg. dél.*, no. 2, fol. 56, *arrêté* of 13 pluv.

[4] e.g. A.C. Feurs, *reg. dél.*, 13 Sept., and A.C. Saint-Chamond, *reg. dél.*, 19 Sept.

a comprehensive knowledge of the geographical distribution of scarcity and abundance. The authorities in the district of Roanne, for instance, for the most part ignored Javogues and appealed directly either to the proconsuls at Commune-affranchie or to the central organs of government in Paris.[1] As a result, Javogues made practically no provisions for supply to this area, in which the larger towns suffered considerable distress. It was not until 21 pluviôse/9 February that the District of Roanne approached him for permission to appropriate sequestrated grain as an interim measure, which he immediately granted despite the bad state of his relations with that District.[2] The club at Régny was exceptional in petitioning him for supply in nivôse; even Jacobin Charlieu preferred to rely upon its own coercive weapons and upon its representatives in Paris until the situation became really critical at the beginning of pluviôse.[3] Similarly, Javogues's reliance on the regular administrations maintained the Department as the co-ordinator and distributor of supplies. His anger over the Department's hesitation about its competence in matters of food supply after the law of 14 frimaire is ample evidence that this system was of his own choosing.[4] Thus, when faced by the food crisis at Armeville at the end of frimaire, he merely directed the Department to deal with it.[5] In return the Department bothered the *Représentant* very little with food problems: only when the Committee of Public Safety ordered it to supply the *armée des Alpes* did it turn to him for support.[6] The only major contribution that he did make towards a solution of food problems on a departmental basis was an *arrêté* in late frimaire, which laid down detailed provisions for the immediate threshing of the previous harvest, for the centralization of accurate inventories of resources, and for severe punishments for hoarders.[7] This *arrêté* ordered the Department to forward a general table of reserves to the government and to the 'Représentants du peuple près l'armée des Alpes'—presumably the latter referred to Javogues rather than to the proconsuls at Commune-affranchie,

[1] e.g. A.D.L., L 176, 28 frim.; A.C. Roanne, 1 D 1 (2), 5, 8, 20 Oct., 1, 16 niv.

[2] A.D.L., L 188, *arrêté* of 24 pluv.

[3] A.D.L., L 416, 30 niv.; L 402, *passim* and 29 niv., 15, 20 pluv.

[4] A.D.L., L 80, fol. 11. [5] A.D.L., L 18, 3 niv. [6] Ibid., 11 pluv.

[7] A.N., AF II 137 (1069), d. 30, p. 8, *arrêté* dated 26 frim.

for they both used the title. But, even if such a table did reach him, it does not appear to have inspired any subsequent food policy from him. Moreover, despite the fact that the non-application of the *maximum* was used to justify the maintenance of the *armée révolutionnaire* in nivôse, Javogues never used his authority to attempt to enforce the uniform observance of this measure.[1]

It would, however, be untrue to say that Javogues made no effort to intervene in the food crisis. When appeals were made to him, he did not fail to respond promptly. But his interventions were in practice confined to the district of Armeville; it was here that the crisis was at its most acute, and it was here that he established his closest contacts by the length of his visit and by his reliance on the area for supply during the siege of Lyon. In September, he had established a provisioning committee at Saint-Étienne, which was able to feed the town as well as the army when Javogues permitted it to requisition grain in the Plaine du Forez.[2] In early brumaire, he authorized Commune d'Armes to purchase grain throughout the former provinces of Burgundy, Franche-Comté, and Bresse as well as in the Loire and the Haute-Loire.[3] Saint-Chamond was given a similar authorization for Burgundy.[4] A permit to buy, however, could only obtain what these areas were prepared to sell. The departure of Javogues for the rich Saône-et-Loire was a godsend for Commune d'Armes, as the Department did not hesitate to point out, for he could supplement the efforts of the buyers from that town.[5] As early as 2 frimaire/22 November, the Municipality of Commune d'Armes, 'considérant que le citoyen Claude Javogues . . . a toujours manifesté pour le peuple d'Armeville un zèle paternel', appealed to him to employ on their behalf his wide powers in whatever manner his zeal for the Republic might suggest.[6] His efforts tided Armeville and Saint-Chamond over frimaire—Saint-Chamond was given requisitions on the district of Châlon-sur-Saône and on the departments of the Côte-d'Or and the Haute-Saône; a boat-load of grain was sent

[1] A.N., AF II 114 (861) 14, *arrêté* of 6 niv.
[2] A.C. Saint-Étienne, 1 D 10 (3), fols. 54, 59; A.D.R., 1 L 190.
[3] A.D.L., L 123, fol. 347.
[4] A.C. Saint-Chamond, *reg. dél.*, 26 Oct.
[5] A.D.L., L 80, fols. 2, 5, letter to Dist. of Armeville, 16 brum. and 2 frim.
[6] A.C. Saint-Étienne, 1 D 10 (3), 2 frim.

directly to Armeville from the Saône-et-Loire.[1] Javogues continued to help after his return to the district. Armeville was authorized to send *commissaires* to get grain from the Haute-Saône and soap, oil, etc. from Vienne; Saint-Chamond received further requisitions on Châlon-sur-Saône and the Ain.[2] Indeed, it was doubtless his action over the food shortage which prompted the club at Saint-Chamond to send addresses of thanks 'pour l'intérêt qu'il a toujours pris à cette commune' to Javogues on 2 and 10 nivôse/22 and 30 December.[3] Moreover, although the large urban centres naturally received most of his attention, Javogues did not neglect to accord requisitions both on the districts of Boën and on other departments to smaller communities—particularly the industrial satellites of Armeville, such as Valbenoîte and Saint-Genis-Terrenoire.[4] Nevertheless, it is questionable to what extent some of Javogues's efforts were realistic and therefore productive. The boat-load of grain sent from the Saône-et-Loire to Armeville contained 1,396 quintals;[5] it seems unrealistic in comparison to accord requisitions of 3,000 and 5,000 quintals on the Isère to the much smaller populations of Saint-Genest-Malifaux and Valbenoîte.[6] In any case, these communes were only able to obtain 200 and 125 quintals respectively.[7] Similarly, Javogues's lack of information on resources within the Loire led him, in at least one case, to give supply on a commune which could deliver nothing, even after the *commissaires* of the beneficiary, who had a vested interest in discovering grain, had conducted a house-to-house search.[8]

The district of Armeville also preoccupied Javogues by the gravity of unemployment and poverty there. The most immediate problem was that provoked in September by the

[1] A.D. S.-et-L., 1 L 8/26, frim., *passim*; 2 L 199, fol. 189, Dist. of Châlon to Javogues, 16 frim.; A.D.L., L 156, fol. 90, Dist. of Armeville to C.P.S., 14 frim., and fol. 96, to *Commission des Subsistances*, 18 niv.

[2] A.C. Saint-Étienne, 1 D 10 (3), 13 niv.; A.N., AF II 114 (861) 14, *arrêté* of 20 niv.; A.C. Saint-Chamond, *reg. dél.*, 8 and 18 niv.

[3] Lefebvre, op. cit., pp. 113, 121.

[4] A.D.L., L 18, fol. 151 (Saint-Genis-Terrenoire), L 374, fol. 13 (Saint-Christo-Val-fleury and Lachaud), L 371, fol. 63 (Valbenoîte), L 124, fol. 22 (Doizieu), L 146, 1 pluv. (Valdorlay), L 393, fol. 9 (Saint-Genest-Malifaux); A.D.R., 1 L 190 (Rive-de-Gier).

[5] A.D.L., L 156, fol. 96.

[6] A.D.L., L 393, fol. 9, L 371, fol. 63.

[7] Ibid.

[8] A.D.L., L 374, fol. 13.

departure of large numbers of bread-winners in the *levée en masse* against Lyon. Javogues sought to alleviate the hardship by ordering the District to pay through the Municipalities to each family a daily allowance of three *livres* for the wife and twenty *sous* per child.[1] Saint-Rambert was ordered to set up a provisioning committee to distribute relief proportionate to their needs to the most impecunious only.[2] In Armeville itself, lists of the destitute had quickly been drawn up, and throughout the period the Municipality and the District either found small jobs for them or gave them direct help.[3] Indeed, immediately after the siege, Javogues sought to maintain some sort of system of payments by ordering the District of Armeville to forward 6,000 *livres* to that Municipality for distribution to the unemployed and especially those with a large family.[4] For the essential problem in the area was the lack of employment. As has already been emphasized, stagnation was general and federalism merely aggravated it, especially in the silk industry, where the most important employers were rapidly imprisoned. Javogues attempted to provide both immediate relief and a solution in depth. On the one hand, he ordered all the *marchands* to give work to the unemployed or to pay the equivalent wage if the Municipality considered them unjustified in refusing.[5] On the other hand, he provided alternative sources of work by opening a credit of 50,000 *livres* for a month's wages for all the unemployed of the luxury trades who wished to convert to the simplest jobs in the arms industry.[6]

Most of these measures in favour of the poor lacked realism. Only the arrangements to facilitate redeployment in the arms industry were an unqualified success. Large numbers of workers were absorbed into this branch, which expanded rapidly during the Terror.[7] But, the success of the

[1] A.N., AF II 137 (1069), d. 30, p. 3, *arrêté* of 15 Sept.

[2] A.D.L., L 53, *arrêté* of 2 Oct.

[3] A.C. Saint-Étienne, 1 D 10 (3), fol. 80, 11 brum.; e.g. ibid., fol. 83, 19 brum. the destitute to supervise and distribute food to the prisoners.

[4] A.D.L., L 123, fol. 343, *arrêté* of 24 Oct.

[5] A.C. Saint-Étienne, 1 D 10 (3), fol. 80, *arrêté* of 11 brum.

[6] A.N., AF II 114 (859) 6, *arrêté* of 22 Oct. In application, this measure benefited only the silk workers (A.C. Saint-Étienne, 1 D 10 (3), fol. 81, 17 brum.).

[7] A.D.L., L suppl. 434–8, 448, 454, apprentice indentures, an II; Galley, op. cit. ii. 226.

conversion was probably due more to sheer necessity than to Javogues's efforts to underwrite it. For chronic lack of finance crippled the attempts at direct relief: Saint-Chamond did not obtain the money to pay the siege subsidies until 3 pluviôse/22 January; in nivôse, the Municipality of Armeville decided that the subventions to the destitute should be made in kind rather than in cash.[1] In any case, the grant made towards the relatives of the *levée en masse* appears highly unrealistic and out of proportion to normal wage levels. It caused considerable friction between Javogues, his colleagues, and the authorities at Saint-Étienne;[2] the District was at pains to point out that Javogues was involving them in a daily expenditure of 80,000 *livres*.[3] As for the attempt to force the employers to find work for the unemployed, this was a total failure.[4]

It must be emphasized that there is an apparent paradox here. In respect of poverty and of food supply Javogues was quite remarkably inert for someone who was verbally such an explicit and energetic democrat. One can only resolve the paradox by realizing that, as far as Javogues was concerned, the measures to which we have referred were merely interim arrangements. He only used them during his first period in the Loire, at a time when he was preoccupied with the urgent question of the political security of the Republic. They were temporary expedients designed to alleviate symptoms. For Javogues saw poverty and food shortage essentially as symptoms of social injustice aggravated for the present by the machinations of social parasites—'Les fortunes énormes', he proclaimed, 'attestent depuis un temps immémorial l'oppression, l'esclavage et la misère du peuple'; 'les Riches coalisés avec les Prêtres ont conçu le criminel dessein d'affamer le Peuple par les subsistances.'[5] During the second period of his activity in the Loire, Javogues sought to strike more directly at what he considered to be the root causes of the social problems of the Year II by a series of revolutionary measures. These measures can be divided into five component parts:

[1] A.N., F1c III Loire 5, *compte décadaire* of Saint-Chamond, 14 pluv.; A.C. Saint-Étienne, 1 D 10 (3), fol. 111.

[2] A.C. Saint-Étienne, 1 D 10 (3), fols. 55, 67; A.D.L., L 156, fols. 82, 87.

[3] A.D.L., L 156, fol. 76, letter to *Repr.* at La Pape, 18 Sept.

[4] A.N., AF II 114 (861) 14, *arrêté* of 6 niv.

[5] Ibid.

arrest and sequestration, the *taxe révolutionnaire*, the collection of precious metal, the demolition of castles and *châteaux*, dechristianization. Naturally, these types of activity were the general stock-in-trade of most *Représentants en mission*. Arrest, sequestration, and collection of precious metal were patronized, if not practised, by every proconsul, while quite a broad spectrum of differing brands of militant terrorist worked in all five of these spheres simultaneously. The fundamental difference between proconsuls was the way they used these weapons, in the goals they pursued through them. A *taxe révolutionnaire*, for instance, could be levied in radically different ways for profoundly different purposes. In Javogues's hands these measures became a coherent programme of social regeneration aimed at the abolition of inequality and at the elimination of dangerous, parasitic elements. The destruction of its parasites alone brought society closer to the Democratic Republic; at the same time, the proceeds of this destruction were immediately distributed to the People.

The demolition of castles and *châteaux de luxe*, ordered by an *arrêté* of 1 nivôse/21 December, needs little discussion. This measure is a clear illustration of the dual quality of Javogues's programme. On the one hand, 'ces colosses, monuments de l'orgueil et de l'oppression' were an insulting testimony to inequality and should therefore be destroyed; on the other, the stones were to be distributed to the poor to help them build their houses.[1] Similarly, Javogues's repressive activities have already been discussed. It is impossible to decide where repression ceased to be political and became social, for no clear distinction can be drawn between the political and social enemies of the People. Many of those arrested for federalist crimes were in fact the rich, the social enemies of the People. Javogues's extensive personal commitment to repression and the continuation of repressive activity throughout the mission indicate that he considered arrest as a weapon to purge society. Nevertheless, although his writings repeatedly identified the rich as suspects, as enemies, it is rare to find him justifying an arrest warrant solely on these grounds. Certainly, various categories of people were suspect: late in the mission, there was a general

[1] A.N., AF II 138 (1077), p. 36.

warrant against priests; early in the mission, the *avoués* of Montbrison, with three specific exceptions, were classed as suspect.[1] But in the great majority of cases, when Javogues did enter motives on an arrest warrant, they included concrete counter-revolutionary acts. The sequestration of property, however, was clearly intended to constitute a reservoir of property to be transferred to the People on conviction of the owner.

Javogues's most positive contribution towards reshaping society took the form of a *taxe révolutionnaire*. These levies, made by the *Représentants en mission* and other extra-ordinary authorities, were common in the autumn of 1793. To mention only the area adjacent to the Loire, both Fouché and Albitte, for instance, raised them in the Nièvre, Allier, Rhône, and Ain, while the itinerant members of the *Commission Temporaire* practised what they had preached in the *Instruction*.[2] The purpose of these taxes was usually to relieve the poor with the superfluous wealth of the rich. The authorities of Armeville clearly felt that such a tax was the only solution to their problems: the idea had been aired by militants in early 1793 and was raised with increasing urgency during the autumn.[3] It was at Armeville, soon after his return, that Javogues made his arrangements for a revolutionary levy. An *arrêté* of 6 nivôse/26 December ordered all the Municipalities of the department of the Loire to draw up two lists, the one containing the names of the indigent, the other the names of the 'riches et gros propriétaires'. In the latter category fell all married men worth more than 100,000 *livres* and all bachelors worth more than 50,000 *livres*. The residue of their wealth above these sums was to be allotted to the destitute according to the degree of their capacity for work and according to their needs.[4] Already on 3 nivôse/23 December Javogues had personally imposed this tax on the rich of Armeville in a somewhat orgiastic public assembly of the Municipality. The assembled people, counselled by Desvernays, who was rich enough to have a fair idea of the wealth of his more respectable

[1] Below, p. 289; A.D. P.-de-D., L 2781, letter to C.P.S. of Montbrison, 19 Oct.

[2] L. Madelin, *Fouché*, i. 95, 102, 132; Meunier, art. cit., p. 250; A.D.R., 4 L 27, Boulot and Dessirier to *Comm. Temp.*, 15, 19, 20, 30 frim.; 31 L 50 (15 frim.), Dessirier to *Comm. Temp.*

[3] Above, p. 44.

[4] A.N., AF II 114 (861) 14.

compatriots, decided who should be taxed and estimated the size of each fortune; the *Représentant* then fixed the amount of tax, usually being the total excess over 100,000 *livres*.[1] It is quite evident, therefore, that what was involved was not merely a forced contribution, but a definite attempt to transfer wealth from the rich minority to the poor majority. It is indicative of Javogues's attitude to the *taxe révolutionnaire* that, in nivôse, he made none of the direct moves to help the poor that had characterized his action in brumaire.

The *taxe révolutionnaire* was never levied outside Armeville. It was doubtless under the influence of Javogues, then in the town, that in early pluviôse the Municipality of Montbrisé drew up a provisional roll for poor relief bearing the names of wealthy people, who were to be taxed in proportion to their ability to pay, with the euphemistic consideration that 'les inviter . . . c'est prévenir leurs désirs'.[2] But this appears much more as an interim, Ancien Régime-style reaction to food shortage than as an application of the *taxe révolutionnaire*. In any case, the decision had no recorded consequence. Similarly, the voluntary contributions from the rich of Saint-Chamond that Bourgeois, president of the criminal tribunal, hoped to inspire with the 60,000 *livres* that he had obtained from the imprisoned Dugas brothers do not appear to have materialized.[3] Elsewhere in the department, a certain activity was displayed in drawing up the lists of rich and poor. However, in the majority of cases, this was a response to Fouché's and Collot's order of 24 brumaire/14 November, containing similar provisions for the relief of the poor, rather than to Javogues's directives.[4] Some authorities, particularly those at Roanne, opposed the measure bitterly; in general, it was the revolutionary committees rather than the Municipalities that showed enthusiasm for it.[5] Few of the lists were complete before late pluviôse, and some were only drawn up

[1] A.C. Saint-Étienne, 1 D 10 (3), fol. 103 ff.; see J. M. Devet, *Une Taxe révolutionnaire*.

[2] A.C. Montbrison, *reg. dél.*, no. 2, fol. 51.

[3] A.D.R., 42 L 178, d. Dugas, Bourgeois to Javogues, 10 pluv.

[4] e.g. A.D.L., L 390, fol. 13 (Saint-Chamond, 24 niv.), and L 146, *compte décadaire* of Valbenoîte, 29 niv.

[5] This was possibly because the execution of Collot's and Fouché's tax was entrusted to them (A.N., AF II 137 (1060), d. 4, p. 8).

in germinal and floréal when it was decided to assign the proceeds to the payment of the committees.[1] But the work never advanced beyond the lists—the multiple declarations made in the Year III concerning revolutionary taxation in the district of Boën in fact referred to requisitions and to 'gifts' of precious metal.[2] In Armeville itself, however, the levy was pursued vigorously, although Javogues rapidly handed over the responsibility to the Municipality.[3] The *armée révolutionnaire* was used to enforce the tax by the blackmail of threatened arrest and by release on payment.[4] Certainly, the original figure was soon found to have been far too optimistic, and Javogues had to agree on 13 nivôse/2 January to a general reduction in estimates. Nevertheless, on 23 nivôse/12 January, the Municipality was able to present to the *Représentant* the lists of the poor and on the next day the accounts of the levy.[5]

The collection of precious metal forms a link between the themes of wealth redistribution and dechristianization in Javogues's programme. Gold and silver were symbols of oppression, he said. Some of these precious objects had been gathered to satisfy the avarice of priests and the over-credulity of this generation's ancestors, while others had been collected at tremendous cost to flatter the vanity of opulent aristocracy; but both were equally insults to the distress of the poor.[6] But, as was the case with the demolition of the *châteaux*, this was more than the destruction of a symbol. First, the confiscation of coinage would protect the republican *assignat* against the speculation of the rich, who were increasing the misery of the People by depreciating its currency.[7] Second, the confiscation of precious metal was in fact a direct reduction in the fortune of the wealthy, for whom, in the absence of banks, plate represented investment and coinage both a reserve and now, increasingly, an invest-

[1] e.g. Sury, 23 pluv. (A.D.L., L 442, fol. 3), Montmarat, 10 pluv. (L suppl. 536), Le Chambon, 1 flor. (L 438, fol. 8).

[2] A.D.L., L 281, *passim*.

[3] Devet, op. cit.

[4] A.D.R., 42 L 182, d. Journet, 42 L 185, d. Mourgues *fils*; A.N., D III 124, d. Saint-Étienne, petitions from Clémençon, Penel, and Paradis (an III).

[5] A.C. Saint-Étienne, 1 D 10 (3), fol. 113.

[6] A.D.L., L 259, fol. 28, Dist. of Boën to Convention, 15 frim.

[7] Cf. A.D.R., 31 L 50, discussion in *Comm. Temp.*, 7 frim.

ment also. Third, this measure was at the same time an integral part of dechristianization, since it deprived the Church of the consecrated vessels essential to the celebration of the sacraments. Finally, the centralization of precious metal in the hands of the government would further stabilize the *assignat*, by giving it a metal guarantee as well as a landed one and hence alleviate the situation of the People. The collection of precious metal differed from the *taxe révolutionnaire* in one important respect; whereas the latter was aimed at producing a redistribution of wealth, the former was merely a corrective to comparative levels of wealth. Wealth was removed from the rich, but it was not, except for a few cases of copper coinage, distributed to the poor. Gold and silver were 'base' metals to be despised in the Democratic Republic.

The confiscation of gold and silver was a universal feature of the winter of the Year II throughout France. The *Représentants* at Commune-affranchie, for instance, set up a special commission to deal with the influx at the former mint, while the *Commission Temporaire* employed agents specifically for searches both at Commune-affranchie and in the surrounding area.[1] As far as the Loire was concerned, Javogues was certainly neither the instigator nor the sole participant in this activity. From the beginning of the Terror, the national emergency had produced the same searches here as elsewhere. The *commissaires* in charge of sequestration or inventories forwarded the metal that they had found to the administrations; the Comte de Saint-Polgues's country house was ransacked in a successful hunt for his treasure.[2] A few patriotically minded citizens exchanged their cash or their plate for *assignats*.[3] By 22 frimaire/12 December, the Department had 450,000 *livres*' worth in its possession.[4] Similarly, the removal of the sacred vessels from the churches had already begun before Javogues returned to the department at the end of frimaire.[5] Nevertheless, it is clear that Javogues's return corresponded with an increase of activity in this sphere and

[1] A.N., AF II 114 (859) 3, *arrêté* of 10 frim.; A.D.R., 1 L 622.

[2] e.g. A.D.L., L 18, fols. 51, 79, L 55, fol. 7, L 394, fol. 8; A.D.L., L 79, fol. 2, Chana and Chartre to Depart., 6 brum.

[3] e.g. A.D.L., L 130, 19, 21, 29 frim.

[4] A.D.L., L 80, fol. 8, Depart. to *Repr.* at Cne-aff., 22 frim.

[5] A.D.L., Q 50 and L 130, *passim*.

that he himself displayed a keen personal interest in it. The emptying of the churches was accelerated in the district of Armeville largely, it seems, by the *commissaires* whom Javogues employed specifically for this purpose.[1] The levy of the *taxe révolutionnaire* was accompanied by a thorough search for hidden treasure, often with some brutality: the ageing *veuve* Borne, for example, was tied to the banisters in her home and roughly handled.[2] In both the districts of Boën and Armeville, the administrations now sent *commissaires* to check through sequestrated property; the *Représentant* employed a number of agents for the same purpose; denunciations of hidden treasure were carefully followed up.[3] It is indicative of the general atmosphere that prevailed after Javogues's return that it was not until 4 nivôse/24 December that the former seigneur of the village of Fontanès, under house arrest there, surrendered his silverware to the Municipality for dispatch to the District; the Comte Charpin de Feugerolles attempted to placate the proconsul's fury at his acquittal by handing over his plate.[4] Some of the metal that came into Javogues's hands was the product of voluntary gifts, while the amount of voluntary exchange of metal into *assignats* increased during his presence in the Loire; but it is clear that by far the majority of receipts stating that someone 'm'a remis pour faire hommage à la Convention nationale ...' were in fact euphemisms for coercion. In the Year III, citizen Perrussel of Saint-Étienne remarked bitterly: 'Après m'avoir arbitrairement et sans motifs fait incarcérer, Claude Javogues m'a emporté plusieurs effets sous le prétexte d'en faire hommage à la Convention; le tout pendant mon injuste détention et sans aucune participation de ma part.'[5]

But Javogues acted above all as a central collecting agency. Many communes sent their metal directly to him, while the administrations forwarded what they received.[6] His aim was

[1] e.g. A.D.L., L 124, fol. 16, 11 niv.; L 130, fol. 66, 22 niv.; Q 50 (Bourg-Argental, Saint-Julien-Molin-Molette, Saint-Pierre-en-Colombaret).

[2] A.D.L., L 281, declaration by *veuve* Borne.

[3] e.g. A.D.L., L 124, fol. 6; A.C. Saint-Rambert, *reg. dél.*, 9 pluv.; A.C. Feurs, *reg. dél.*, 11, 21, 23 pluv.; A.D.R., 42 L 174, d. Challaye, 42 L 176, d. Dubouchet.

[4] A.D.L., Chaleyer MS. 283, 4 niv.; Tézenas du Montcel, op. cit., p. 50.

[5] J. M. Devet, *Une Prison en 1793 et 1794*, p. 79.

[6] e.g. A.D.L., Q 50 (Outrefuran, Valbenoîte, Marlhes, Commune d'Armes).

evidently to purge the department. When passing through Saint-Chamond he removed all the metal that had been amassed.[1] There was a note of urgency in the Department's circular of 25 nivôse/14 January by which it informed the Districts that the imminent arrival of Javogues, to whom they were obliged to hand over the precious metal of the churches, now made the use of coercive methods imperative.[2] Already in early nivôse, he had sent a wagon-load to the mint at Commune-affranchie; when he left the department, some twenty-seven chests full of precious metal remained behind at Feurs, while another eight were waiting for him at the District of Boën.[3] He later reported to the Convention that he had collected over 4,425 *marcs* of silver, more than a *marc* of gold, 649,643 *livres* in specie, and 123,853 *livres* in *assignats*.[4]

Javogues's thinking on dechristianization evolved during the autumn of 1793. On 10 October, he wrote to his *commissaire* Pignon: 'Tu t'amuses, mon cher, à m'amener de vieilles bigotes... Tu parles de foutaises; c'est toi qui fais les foutaises. Tu t'amuses à de vieilles ensorcelées au lieu des muscadins et de Riches ci-devant.'[5] By the beginning of his second period in the Loire, however, he had come to consider priests as enemies in the same class as the Rich. Here again, Javogues was certainly not the only agent of dechristianization. The attack on the Church was well under way throughout the department during frimaire. Already in brumaire Pignon's repressive activity had been largely related to priests and *fanatisme*; Lapalus displayed very much the same preoccupations in the district of Roanne. Most of the higher civil administrations encouraged the destruction of crosses and statues. Priests had already begun to abandon their status formally before the end of frimaire. Nevertheless, as was the case with the collection of precious metal, Javogues's return to the department gave a new impetus to dechristianization. His programme for the Democratic Republic coordinated disparate expressions of dechristianization into an avowed policy under the patronage of the *Représentant*.

1 A.C. Saint-Chamond, *reg. dél.*, 29 frim.
2 A.D.L., L 80, fol. 18.
3 A.D.R., 31 L 55 (8 niv.); A.N., T 781, d. Marino, and A.D.L., L 61, fol. 35.
4 Javogues, *Compte rendu*.
5 A.N., W 408, d. 939.

'C'est Javogues, Représentant Montagnard,' wrote the District of Armeville, 'qui a donné le coup de massue à l'hydre de la superstition.'[1]

The central measure in Javogues's action was the *arrêté* of 1 nivôse/21 December which converted all the churches of the department into clubs and Temples of Reason where the people could read the official papers and laws, learn their rights and duties, and exercise the civic virtues; the presbyteries were to be made into schools and to serve as *mairies* wherever none already existed; a public fire was to be maintained there during the winter for the relief of 'l'humanité souffrante'.[2] There could be no clearer proclamation of the abolition of religion—priests were only referred to incidentally as the 'ci-devant prêtres'. It is doubtful whether Javogues employed *commissaires* to enforce this *arrêté*. But he certainly launched a dechristianization offensive in the southern area of the department through the *commissaires* whom he employed for the collection of ecclesiastical plate, especially since many of these men extended their confiscations to vestments.[3] Moreover, these agents inspired priests to renounce their status and, in some cases, arrested them.[4] Javogues's own attitude to the question of *déprêtrisation* was obviously well known: for example, between 18 and 22 nivôse/7 and 11 January, ten priests handed over their *celebret* to the Municipality of Montbrisé—three of them wrote to Javogues specifying that they had done so because he apparently desired the abolition of the priesthood.[5] The immediate consequence of this campaign was to make the priesthood more suspect than ever. By 12 nivôse/1 January the revolutionary committee at Montbrisé was able to issue an arrest warrant on the sole grounds that a man was suspect because he was a curé.[6] On 17 nivôse/6 January, Lefranc, delegate of the *Commission Temporaire* but showing powers from Javogues, ordered the arrest of all priests and canons at Rambert-

[1] A.D.L., L 156, fol. 102, letter to C.G.S., 8 pluv.

[2] A.N., AF II 114 (861) 15.

[3] e.g. A.D.L., L 130, fol. 66.

[4] e.g. A.D.L., L 392, Ginet of Malleval to rev. com. at Armeville; A.D.R., 42 L 172, d. Vial, Vial to Javogues, 19 niv.

[5] A.C. Montbrison, *reg. dél.*, no. 2, fol. 42, et seq.; A.D.R., 42 L 179, d. Épailly, petition to Javogues, n.d.

[6] A.D.L., L 434 (1), fol. 39.

Loire/Saint-Rambert.[1] On 27 nivôse/16 January, Javogues took this progression to its logical conclusion: Lieutenant Berneton of the *gendarmerie* received orders to arrest all the priests in the district of Boën.[2] Berneton executed this measure at Bonnet-la-Montagne and at (Saint-) Jean-Soleymieux; other *commissaires* were active in the cantons of Cervières, Rambert-Loire, Fontfort/Saint-Galmier, Mont-chalier/Saint-Germain-Laval, and Montmarat/Saint-Just-en-Chevalet.[3] Contamine's orders, dated 13 pluviôse/1 February, extended the measure to the whole of the district of Roanne.[4] Meanwhile, Javogues had given a collective order at Montbrisé to arrest all priests without discrimination.[5]

Dechristianization was, relatively, the most successful of the various parts of Javogues's democratic programme. Naturally, it would be inaccurate to say that the area was dechristianized, since the population remained predominantly religious. Similarly, on a more limited level, many priests did remain at liberty, particularly those who formally renounced their status. But in nivôse and pluviôse most churches did close and religious ceremonies were reduced to a minimum, at least in the more accessible areas of the department. This was not wholly Javogues's work. In the district of Armeville, Pignon had done a considerable amount of the groundwork, particularly by arresting priests on the pretext of federalism. This was the only measure of Javogues's programme that was ever thoroughly applied in the district of Roanne, but that was a result of Lapalus's independent activity.[6] Nevertheless, Javogues played a dominant role in dechristianization and the decisive impulse came from him. Moreover, Javogues's measures were more revolutionary than those of any other authority, with the exception of the members of the *Commission Temporaire*, who did not however work in any detail in the Loire. Javogues sought to

1 A.D.L., L 441, fol. 16.

2 A.D.L., L 381, fol. 61.

3 A.D.L., L 436, fol. 20; A.D.R., 42 L 190, d. Valette; A.D.L., L 430 (2), fol. 26, L 441, fol. 3, L 260 (24 vent.); A.D.R., 42 L 178, d. Durand; A.D.L., L 421, fol. 8; J. Cohas, *Saint-Germain-Laval pendant la Révolution*, p. 99.

4 A.D.L., L 430 (2), fol. 66.

5 A.D.L., L 435, Mougin to *Repr.* at Cne-aff., 14 vent.

6 C. Lucas, 'La brève carrière du terroriste Jean-Marie Lapalus', *A.H.R.F.* 1968, pp. 508–12.

purge society of parasitic, deceiving priests by comprehensively arresting them all; Lapalus was satisfied if they surrendered their *celebret*.

On the whole, however, Javogues never came near to founding the Democratic Republic in the department of the Loire. The failure of the *taxe révolutionnaire* outside Armeville is a good example of the practical difficulties facing the implementation of such a programme. Such measures could only be enforced to the extent that local regular and extraordinary authorities either were willing or could be forced to execute them. The tax was levied at Armeville both because the Municipality was favourable to it and because the proconsul was residing there with a considerable revolutionary force. Even where attempts were made to execute the various directives concerning a *taxe révolutionnaire*, they were either half-hearted or ran into difficulties. In several places the poor refused to be placed on the lists, thereby destroying the whole object of the levy—at (Saint-) Maurice-en-Gourgois the wealthy landowners spread the rumour that anybody on the list of poor would indubitably be transported to the Vendée or some such place.[1] Elsewhere, the discordance between the ideas of the *Représentant* and those of the local authorities produced modifications that completely undermined the social significance of the tax—thus, the committee of Saint-Genest-Malifaux transformed this confiscation of excess wealth into a tax on revenue.[2]

But even at Armeville the *taxe révolutionnaire* was only a theoretical success. And this illustrates another aspect of Javogues's democratic programme, its repeated lack of realism. The total levy imposed on 3 nivôse/23 December was 16,495,000 *livres* on eighty people of which 1,000,000 was to be paid within twenty-four hours. It is debatable whether it was realistic to assess the fortune of these eighty people at over 24,000,000, but it was certainly unrealistic to suppose that so much could be produced in cash at such short notice. When the taxes were readjusted on 13 nivôse/2 January, the total levy fell sharply to the figure of only 940,000 *livres*, that is to say less even than the deposit demanded within twenty-four hours. Of this sum, only

[1] A.D.L., L 441, fol. 24. [2] A.D.L., L 393, fol. 11.

453,150 *livres* had actually been paid before 24 nivôse/13 January; the remainder had been made up in promissory notes, of which only two were redeemed.[1] Moreover, Javogues's general *arrêté* of 6 nivôse/26 December was characterized by a similar fundamental lack of realism. There was no provision for any central agency of distribution; the superfluity of the rich was supposed to be transmitted to the poor within each commune. Yet in the vast majority of rural communes the number of inhabitants with a total fortune of more than 100,000 *livres*, even taking into account a natural reluctance to volunteer such information, was nil, while the numbers of poor were high. Without any co-ordination on the departmental level, therefore, the *taxe révolutionnaire* would have remained useless, even if levied, because of the geographical distribution of wealth which, although mostly in the form of land, was gathered into the hands of urban dwellers.

But Javogues's programme was not merely crippled by lack of realism. It was also incomplete. The *taxe révolutionnaire* was ineffective as a social panacea without the distribution of capital in land. In the first place, Javogues made no attempt to accelerate the sale of national lands and sequestrated property, nor did he take measures to enforce the division of communal lands. Yet these were at least as important steps on the road to the Democratic Republic of small holders as dechristianization, for example. In this respect, the delay in dispatching arrested suspects was fatal, for their execution would have released their property. However, Javogues was dealing with this aspect at the time of his recall. In the second place, the attempt to use the *taxe révolutionnaire* to operate a permanent transfer of wealth reflected the contradiction between an instinctive respect for property and the practical readjustment of wealth in the interests of social justice. At root, it was not sufficient to force property on to the market by taxing the rich landowner. It was unlikely that the poor, the People, would ever have enough money as individuals to buy property at whatever price. The revolutionary authorities would have to seize the sources of excess wealth and distribute them directly themselves. Although men like Javogues clearly

[1] These brought an additional 6,000 *livres*.

did not hold property to be altogether inviolable, such direct action would certainly have been repugnant to them. Therefore, in order to achieve this result, the *taxe révolutionnaire* needed completing by a revolutionary tribunal that was much more directly a social weapon than the one at Feurs ever allowed itself to be. In the circumstances, the property of the rich could only be liberated for redistribution by the execution of the rich. This could only be done at all comprehensively if wealth were to become a sufficient motive by itself for the death sentence. But the tribunal at Feurs never considered it as anything other than highly suspect. In any case, in a society dominated by landed wealth, how could the urban poor benefit from plots carved out of estates lying some distance away? It would have been more effective, in immediate terms, to imitate the *Commission Temporaire* which instructed the Municipalities of the district of Villefranche to search the houses of the rich in order to remove all excess belongings for distribution to the *sans-culottes*.[1] The social significance of the collection of precious metal suffered from exactly the same contradiction. For full effectiveness, the gold and silver of all the rich should have been confiscated; but, in practice, only the metal of suspects was taken.

Finally, Javogues did not always implement his own programme thoroughly. The most striking illustration of this is again the *taxe révolutionnaire*. When the Municipality of Armeville presented Javogues with the list of the poor and with the proceeds of the tax, he promised to make arrangements for the distribution before leaving the town.[2] On 17 ventôse/7 March, the Municipality informed the *Représentants* at Commune-affranchie that Javogues had never sent them his promised decision.[3] He had merely distributed 904 *livres* to various needy individuals and had given verbal orders to use these funds to provide bread for the poor, which, to date, had cost 15,000 *livres*. It pointed out that the town was crowded with paupers in direst straits, yet, for lack of this authorization, it could not touch the money that had been expressly designated for their relief. In the end, only 70,904 *livres* out of the cash total of 459,150 *livres* went

[1] A.D.R., 31 L 53 (6 niv.). [2] A.C Saint-Étienne, 1 D 10 (3), fol. 153.
[3] Devet, op. cit., pp. 57–8.

directly to the poor.[1] The *taxe révolutionnaire* was devoted to incidental expenditure—some was used to refund the district treasury for certain expenses such as the subsidy for the conversion of silk workers to the arms industry and the cost of the Chalier monument; the revolutionary committee was paid with it and grants were made to the club. But most of it went towards financing the expansion of the arms industry and the waterworks to increase the flow of the river Furan. This was a long way from the democratic objective preached by Javogues.

Therefore, Claude Javogues's activity as *Représentant en mission* in the Loire suffered in every respect from limitations both in conception and in practice. Nevertheless, it must be remembered that his work was left incomplete above all because it was interrupted by his recall. Javogues attempted some sort of final solution in each area as he visited it—the train of prisoners collected at Armeville and Montbrisé, the *taxe révolutionnaire* imposed at Armeville and probably suggested at Montbrisé, the *commissaires* for dechristianization, the confiscation of gold and silver during his stay at Armeville, and a house-to-house search in Montbrisé on 17 pluviôse/5 February for the same purpose.[2] It is for this reason that the district of Roanne, which he intended to visit after Feurs, was left largely untouched. With revolutionary justice at last functioning correctly, it is possible that Javogues might have made a much more profound impact on the Loire than he did, if he had been allowed to complete his programme. Indeed, whatever his limitations—and the regular administrations did much to compensate for them—he played a fundamental role in orientating the Terror in the Loire. Javogues was the most powerful authority in the department; he organized the Terror and he patronized the terrorists. There was a good deal of truth in the statement that 'les soins du citoyen Javogues terrassent continuellement l'aristocratie, abattent la superstition et le fanatisme et établissent partout le meilleur esprit'.[3] His direct personal contribution was more or less marked according to the issue, but, in the last resort,

[1] E. Brossard, *Histoire du département de la Loire*, ii. 478; A.D.L., L 124, fol. 77, *arrêté* of Fouché and Méaulle, 25 vent.; A.D.R., 1 L 190, *arrêté* of Reverchon, 11 therm.

[2] A.D.L., L 281, *passim*.

[3] A.D.L., L 329, fol. 6, Dist. of Boën to *Repr.* at Cne-aff., 21 pluv.

the major initiatives came from him—or, at least, it was his adoption of certain attitudes and practices which gave them force. For Javogues favoured a particular brand of Terror; this inevitably gave a particular character to the period. Javogues's mission was essentially political. The frontier was far away, and it was only incidentally that the Loire fell into the orbit of the armies. The arms industry at Armeville did not concern Javogues, for it had its own *Représentant* in the person of Girard. Clearly, the original impulse to the Terror came from the federalist crisis. But the Terror was prolonged and transformed by Javogues. In many areas of intensive repression, such phenomena as *taxes révolutionnaires*, the collection of precious metal, and even dechristianization were more or less directly measures provoked by the war crisis. For Javogues, however, these measures were a programme of social regeneration. Although this attitude cannot be said to have penetrated very deeply in the Loire, the measures dictated by the attitude were implemented more or less widely, thus giving its particular character to the Terror in the Loire. Whatever practical imperfections can be discerned in Javogues's programme and activity, it none the less remains true that the churches were closed, and the assets of the wealthy severely damaged—their complaints in the Year III are ample testimony to this.[1] It also remains true that, however attenuated and transformed his directives became in the course of their transmission, the *Représentant en mission* was the most important political figure in the department; he could, as he chose, accelerate or retard the processes of the Terror. The state of the Loire after Javogues's departure, when the personnel of the institutions remained unchanged, is substantial proof of this. Almost immediately the urgency fell out of the Terror. Arrests by the revolutionary committees dwindled rapidly after pluviôse, even in large centres such as Montbrisé; the meetings of the clubs began to decline in frequency and content; the collection of precious metal was replaced during ventôse and germinal by gifts of *assignats* and clothing for the troops.[2] The *agent national* of the district

[1] e.g. A.D.L., L 281, *passim*.

[2] e.g. rev. com. at Montbrisé (A.D.L., L 434 (1)), twelve warrants 30 pluv.–30 therm., of which three were for suspects in hiding since federalism; Charlieu

of Commune d'Armes summed up the role of the *Représentant en mission* in the Terror when he declared

que le nommé Marcoux remit ses lettres de prêtrise à l'administration, signa lui-même sa remise et que, quelques jours après le départ du citoyen Javogues, Représentant du Peuple, il vint les redemander et que, trouvant une résistance invincible, il nous dit qu'il nous ferait signifier sa demande par huissiers, ajoutant qu'il n'avait pas été libre en nous les donnant et que maintenant . . . il était libre.[1]

(L 399), only three warrants after 30 pluv. and marked decline in business; Changy (L 398), only deliberated twice after pluv., etc. . . .; club at Charlieu (L 402), only ten noteworthy meetings after pluv. (L 260, *passim*).

[1] A.D.R., 42 L 150, d. Marcoux.

XI

THE TERRORISTS

CONSIDERABLE emphasis has been laid in the preceding chapters on the importance of the individual militant's contribution to the evolution of the Terror at a local level. The discrepancies between the activity of similar institutions in different localities must be explained, at least in part, in terms of the varying energy, preoccupations, and political commitment of their members. Any study of the institutions of the Terror is, therefore, unconvincing without some discussion of the terrorists themselves. However, although the terrorists are distinguished by certain common characteristics, the character of their terrorism was the product of factors whose nature and influence are not always easy to determine in the case of each individual. The men of the Year II came from a background of social and political experience during the late Ancien Régime and the early Revolution. The nature of the documents and the practical limits on this study render it impossible to describe this experience, in both its collective and its personal aspects, in any very meaningful terms. In many cases the terrorists are more than names but, for the most part, they are less than individuals.

The terrorists were an extremely disparate group of men. It is consequently difficult to formulate any lapidary definition of them. They are most obviously identifiable as the men who participated more or less directly in the implementation of the Terror. By this definition, they would comprise the members of all the various regular and extra-ordinary institutions of the Terror including the *armée révolutionnaire* and the clubs. Such a definition, however, implies an unrealistically large number of people, despite a certain amount of common membership between institutions. The revolutionary committees alone account for about 1,200 men and the *armée revolutionnaire* for nearly 1,300; as for the clubs, working from the purely arbitrary basis of the average of those whose membership is known, they furnish perhaps as many as another 7,500, excluding those people who were also members of the committees. The definition of terrorist must include a certain degree of militancy, although it would be a mistake to be too exacting in the application of this standard. Clearly, membership of an institution of the Terror was not necessarily a guarantee of even attenuated militancy. The personnel of the minor rural Municipalities must be largely eliminated from the ranks of the terrorists because their preoccupations were often foreign to the Terror when they were not at variance with it. Some of the lesser revolutionary committees must also be rejected both on the same grounds and also because of their inactivity. With individual exceptions, the ordinary soldiers of the *armée révolutionnaire* may be ignored, for their motivation and their behaviour as individuals seem predominantly 'non'-terrorist.

Between the two extremes of militants and non-terrorists, however, there were large numbers of men who were more or less sincere in their terrorism and whose commitment to the Terror was more or less selective. The clubs pose a particularly delicate problem in this respect. Although their proliferation was largely justified by the Terror, the members were by no means automatically terrorists. As has already been emphasized, there is little evidence to suggest how rigorous were the conditions of entry. Membership of the club was an obligation for many types of person. For example, the club afforded a certain amount of necessary publicity to tradesmen, while it provided some measure of protection for those engaged in the highly dangerous business of selling food; similarly, former *commissaires feudistes*, *huissiers*, *procureurs*, and people from the other hated professions of the Ancien Régime would scarcely hesitate to take the indispensable precaution of going through the motions of terrorism if they were given the opportunity. It would, therefore, be unrealistic to regard all the members of the clubs as terrorists, but, in the state of the documents, it is difficult to distinguish between them. One can only make what is at best a rather intuitive selection of those clubs whose members were likely on the whole to be more terrorist. But one must not forget to emphasize that only a proportion of these men would be terrorists and that a minority in other clubs would have some terrorist conviction. Much the same sort of selection must be made with regard to the revolutionary committees of the lesser centres. Apart from some committees, which appear predominantly terrorist, there would be a larger or smaller proportion of terrorist individuals in them.

At root, a distinction has to be drawn between the militants, of whom there were only a limited number, and the ordinary terrorists of varying degrees of energy, of whom there were a relatively large number. The militants are reasonably easy to identify because they held the most important posts during the Terror. One can estimate their numbers in rather generous terms as being about 500. The ordinary terrorists provided the militants with their political basis and were employed in minor capacities, particularly as *commissaires* for local jobs of little importance. They formed a more amorphous group, which it would be hazardous to attempt to evaluate in terms of numbers. For the most part, they are distinguishable only by their membership of the clubs, but some indication of the political merit of individuals can be gleaned from their appearance as *jurés d'accusation*, *dénonciateurs*, *suppléants* to the revolutionary committees, etc.

The Terror was an urban, plain-based phenomenon. Consequently, the terrorists were predominantly townsmen from the lowlands. The militant terrorists themselves considered that certain urban groups were by definition terrorist: the leather-aproned workers at Armeville were obviously *sans-culottes*, as were the watermen at Roanne.[1] But there is little concrete evidence to suggest that such groups made a more marked contribution to the ranks of the terrorists than others. The professions and *métiers* of the militant and ordinary terrorists represent the whole spectrum of urban occupations. Indeed, there are few more misleading ways of assessing social status during the Ancien Régime and the Revolution than to describe a man by his profession. This tells us nothing of his fortune or his social and family relationships. The dominant feature of the eighteenth century on almost all levels of society was the diversity of sources from which each

[1] Above p. 48; A.D.L., L 18, 9 brum.

individual drew his livelihood.[1] Therefore a man was not necessarily either solely or principally occupied in the profession to which he claimed to belong in any one document. Many extraneous factors could dictate the choice made between several occupations in such descriptions. Moreover, one *épicier* or *notaire* was not necessarily the equal of another: social reality depended much more on such questions as where a man's shop was in the town, for whom he transacted legal business, how many debts he had contracted, how many children he had to provide for, and even how many of them were girls. Furthermore, even when all these things were more or less equal, the differences in social importance between men living in communities of different sizes were immense, while it is impossible to equate men living in industrial communities with those living in predominantly commercial or administrative centres. Although calculations of fortune, such as appear in the succeeding pages, do help to situate an individual socially, they are only of relative value and must be taken in conjunction with other types of evidence. A discussion of the social status of the terrorists must, therefore, be imperfect and impressionistic. The case of Claude Phalippon of Montbrisé, a captain in the *armée révolutionnaire* and a judge on the *Commission militaire*, illustrates some of these difficulties. He was normally described as an *aubergiste*,[2] but in fact he derived a mixed income from innkeeping, market gardening, and dealing in wood. He was the main supplier of firewood to the District of Montbrison before the federalist crisis,[3] while he rented quite a sizeable piece of land in the market gardens near Montbrison which cost him nearly 21 *livres* in tax.[4] Indeed, at first sight, Phalippon seems a very prosperous citizen. At the end of the Ancien Régime, he was taxable at 68*l.* 6*s.*;[5] he was able to purchase the buildings of the Capucins in Montbrison at the beginning of the Revolution, and it was later suggested, doubtless with

[1] For an admirable demonstration of this point see Olwen Hufton, *Bayeux in the Late Eighteenth Century*, pp. 41–112.

[2] e.g. A.D.R., 42 L 185, d. Montet, Montet to Javogues, 13 Sept.

[3] A.D.L., L 272.

[4] 'Registre de la thaille, subsidiaire et vingtième de Montbrison, année 1789', *Bulletin de la Diana*, 1941, pp. 227–443.

[5] Ibid.

exaggeration, that he had made bids totalling 100,000 *livres* for *biens nationaux*;[1] his elder brother was a well-to-do landowner at Boisset-Saint-Priest, whose fortune placed him on the list of the *notables* of the department for the Year X.[2] But from 1793 to 1795, Phalippon was in fact in chronic financial difficulties. These were considerably aggravated by the federalist crisis and the Thermidorian Reaction,[3] but, before the rebellion, he was already being hounded by his creditors.[4] His period of service in the *armée révolutionnaire* would appear, therefore, to be a case where patriotism and gainful employment were married harmoniously.

In general terms, it is clear that those terrorists who served in the regular and extra-ordinary institutions were usually men with some financial resources of their own. This can easily be realized by considering the cost to the individual of occupying a post that demanded more than intermittent activity. The *armée révolutionnaire* is, of course, a case apart, since its members received regular pay. The most important single fact in this matter is that salaries were always well in arrears. For instance, the members of the *conseil général* of the department, which was abolished by the law of 14 frimaire, were paid off individually between nivôse and floréal, mostly in late pluviôse and early ventôse.[5] The sums owing to them were about 200 *livres*. Similarly, despite the law of 5 September 1793, the members of the revolutionary committees were not paid until germinal and some not until fructidor.[6] Inevitably, therefore, these men had to pay their expenses out of their own pockets. The cost of being a member of the higher regular administrations could be sizeable since it involved travel and renting a room at the *chef-lieu*.[7] A *commissaire*, often a member of an institution as well, was also a man who needed some personal resources since he was normally paid afterwards. For instance, Malboz and Lacour,

[1] A.C. Montbrison, *reg. dél.*, no. 2, fol. 156; Méaudre *et al.*, *Mémoire sur le département de la Loire*, p. 27.

[2] A.N., BB[18] 690; *Liste des notables du département de la Loire*, 12 vend. an X.

[3] A.C. Montbrison, loc. cit., fol. 157; A.D.L., L suppl. 47, judgement of the dist. tribunal of Montbrison, 27 germ. an III.

[4] A.D.L., L 324, Dist. of Montbrison to the Minister of War, 14 June 1793.

[5] A.D.L., L 44, *passim*.

[6] e.g. A.D.L., L 55, *passim* (dist. of Boën).

[7] There was a tendency to provide lodgings for some, though not all, administrators in sequestrated houses.

who had been Javogues's *commissaires* round Bonnet-la-Montagne, were claiming 1,011 *livres* in nivôse: Malboz, at least, could afford this sort of outlay, since he was one of the four rich men whom the Municipality of his home town ordered to furnish beds for the *armée révolutionnaire*.[1] Moreover, the members of the revolutionary committees in particular had to pay for the incidental expenditure of the institution itself. In ventôse the members of the committee at Montbrisé claimed nearly 300 *livres* as reimbursement for clerical and other expenses since late October, while one member of the committee at Feurs had spent over 250 *livres* of his own money for this purpose during the same period.[2]

Militancy was, therefore, a luxury available only to those with some funds. Naturally, there were exceptions, and there were great differences between the fortunes of individual militants. But, in general, the *menu peuple* saw the Terror in terms of employment and concentrated on such jobs as *garde-séquestre* or sentries or else became soldiers in the *armée révolutionnaire*.[3] It was dangerous to attempt to militate without sufficient personal funds. Montellier met with disaster, for his *petit commerce* was ruined, with the help of the *maximum*, during his time on the revolutionary committee at Saint-Chamond.[4] Mondon, who owned only his house and had no source of income other than his own labour, was much more sensible about reconciling the claims of the Republic and those of his family: he felt that, quite apart from the hours spent sealing suspects' belongings, his membership of the Municipality of Rambert-Loire took up enough of his time to justify his refusing any other call, even to such an unexacting job as that of *officier public*.[5]

In the smaller localities, lack of business meant, of course, that membership of the Municipality or the committee was not necessarily incompatible with the need to earn a living, especially since neither body would meet every day. But this was largely compensated for by the fact that the socially

[1] A.D.L., L 18, fol. 117, L 377, fol. 20.

[2] A.D.L., L 434, 13 vent., L 55, fol. 30.

[3] Cf. A.D.L., L 403, fol. 23; the club at Charlieu received complaints from the sentries about the non-payment of wages and the refusal of prisoners to pay.

[4] A.D.L., L 390, Montellier to rev. com. at Saint-Chamond, n.d.

[5] A.C. Saint-Rambert, *reg. dél.*, 14 pluv.

predominant would normally be selected in any case in a small community.[1] When the committee at Saint-Genest-Malifaux decided to fine absentees *5 livres*, it was in fact commenting on its own conception of the value of money.[2] In the late summer of 1793, the commune of Coutouvre was continually troubled by a group of malcontents; matters came to a head in October when Franchon, president of the committee, was accompanying the tax-collector on his rounds:

> Dans le moment est intervenu Claude Petel, qui, à sa manière ordinaire, a pris à la gorge le dit Franchon avec des jurements exécrables en disant que [ni] les grangers ni les locataires et généralement tous les petits ne devaient point de contribution mobilière, en sorte que personne d'eux ne veut payer. . . . Nous comité nous avons observé qu'ils sont une troupe de libertins qui se sont coalisés ensemble pour ne pas payer les contributions mobiliaires ni obéir directement ni indirectement à leurs supérieurs.[3]

In larger centres, the committees and Municipalities would meet every day and the volume of business was greater. The committees at Saint-Chamond and Rive-de-Gier, which were not such wealthy communities as some, both made significant attempts to reduce the work load of individual members. Saint-Chamond instituted a rota of four members for each morning who reported to the others assembling in the afternoon; Rive-de-Gier only met at 4 o'clock, that is to say when the light was fading.[4] Nevertheless, it was still a considerable burden for a poor man to bear, particularly when one considers that at Rive-de-Gier the committee worked until at least 10 o'clock in the evening.[5] Moreover, whatever formal arrangements were made, there was always an amount of additional time-consuming business. The members of the committee at Marcellin-la-Plaine hotly contested the conclusion of the *agent national* that they had done only fifty-four days' work, claiming that the formal records could not show all the continuous incidental occupation in their office and

[1] The committee at Saint-Jean-Soleymieux was composed entirely of men who had been *citoyens actifs* (A.D.L., L 381, fols. 5–20). Note also the way in which men still holding offices to which they had been elected before the Terror appeared in the committees—even at Bonnet-la-Montagne, eight members held other official posts, mostly in the Mun. (A.D.L., L 260, 17 prair.).

[2] A.D.L., L 393, fol. 10.

[3] A.D.L., L 408, fol. 4.

[4] A.D.L., L 390, fol. 15, L 389, fol. 5.

[5] A.D.L., L 389, fol. 31.

around the canton; a full house-to-house search by the Municipality and committee at Montbrisé always lasted eight hours, usually starting at either 8 o'clock in the morning or 8 o'clock in the evening.[1]

The clubs displayed the same characteristics. Most had both an entrance fee and a monthly subscription which tended to restrict membership to men with a little money to spare. At Roanne and Régny, the new member paid three *livres*, and at the latter club the monthly payment stood at ten *sous*.[2] The members at Charlieu paid five *livres* initially and thereafter ten *sous* monthly.[3] Saint-Chamond's figure of 25 *sous* monthly without any entrance fee was only a marginal concession towards admitting a poorer type of member.[4] Saint-Martin-d'Estreaux appears to have been alone in making the rich pay for the poor.[5] But it justified this decision, significantly enough, as being 'afin d'ôter au pauvre ce nouveau sujet de gémir sur son indigence'. The paternalism of this remark reflected the tone of most of the debates in the clubs, even in the one at Saint-Chamond, about the problems of the poor. As far as one can see, and keeping in mind the lack of documents from Armeville, the deliberations of the clubs in the Loire showed few of the more radical preoccupations of their Parisian counterparts. Although the members were sincerely afflicted by the plight of the poor and were determined to come to their aid, their action was conducted in a paternalistic spirit.[6] It merely prolonged and extended the activity of the clubs of the earlier years—the pre-Terror club at Charlieu, for instance, organized a regular distribution of bread to the poor.[7] The behaviour of the clubs appears very much as that of *possédants*. The *menu peuple* were those against whose intrusion into the precinct the clubs had to erect barriers.[8] Moreover, the dominant figures in the clubs tended to be not merely those with the most fervent convictions but also the most eloquent. And a prosperous background was a marked advantage for the development of

[1] A.D.L., L 400, letter to Dist. of Montbrison, 22 therm.; L 434 (1), fols. 36, 40.
[2] A.D.L., L 419 and L 416, fol. 4.
[3] A.D.L., L 403, fol. 7.
[4] G. Lefebvre, *Société républicaine*, p. 34.
[5] A.D.L., L 424, fol. 11.
[6] Above, p. 115.
[7] A.D.L., L 401, *passim*.
[8] Above, p. 113.

this talent. Literacy also was an important asset, since much of the clubs' business consisted in reading out the newspapers and writing letters. Poor Joseph Sarely, who certainly had a tendency to state his views forcefully but who could read no other writing than his own tortured fist,[1] stood little chance of becoming influential. Militancy in the clubs was as time-consuming as membership of other institutions and demanded a certain number of basic skills not available to all. Above all, money was once again indispensable, for the preponderant voices were those of the men who collected the information, presented the clubs' case, and travelled on their behalf. The four *commissaires* who undertook the journeys to Commune-affranchie and the lobbying of the *Représentants en mission* in defence of the *patriote opprimé* Perraud, which was a political case of some importance at Charlieu, magnanimously waived their claim to expenses; the two *commissaires*, who were sent from Régny to buy cotton at Commune-affranchie in order to alleviate the desperate unemployment, financed the whole operation out of their own pockets to the tune of nearly 400 *livres*.[2]

The club at Montbrisé may be used as a case study. However, it must be emphasized that this amounts to no more than an illustration. On the one hand, the political situation in which the club was reformed meant that its members were likely to be more carefully selected than in places less affected by federalism; on the other hand, there is no evidence that permits the application of detailed conclusions drawn from Montbrisé to industrial Armeville. A list of the members drawn up in late frimaire contains 167 names, but 22 members belonged to the battalion of the Puy-de-Dôme and another 15 were inhabitants of neighbouring communes.[3] Therefore the sample consists of 130 people of whom 100 have been identified on the tax roll of 1789.[4] The results are illustrated in the accompanying diagram. The preponderance of

[1] A.D.R., 42 L 180, d. Sarely; A.D.L., L suppl. 110.

[2] A.D.L., L 403, fol. 24, L 416, fol. 3.

[3] A.D.L., L 434 (4).

[4] 'Registre de la thaille, subsidiaire et vingtième de Montbrison, année 1789', *Bulletin de la Diana*, 1941, pp. 227–443. The fact that thirty members cannot be identified in this way is not necessarily an indication of their poverty. Some may still have been living with their parents in 1789 and would not therefore be listed separately from their fathers; for others, the list of the club does not give sufficient

medium-sized fortunes, taxed at between 20 and 100 *livres*, is striking. Although just over a third of the members paid less than 15 *livres*, only three paid less than 1 *livre*, while,

THE TERRORISTS MONTBRISÉ

Total *taille, subsidiare,* and *vingtième* paid in 1789.

(1) gives the percentage of members in each of the tax brackets shown on the right of the column.

(2 a,b,c) gives the number of members in each tax bracket and is designed to permit comparison between the three bodies.

1

Société populaire (100 members identified out of 130)

2

(a) *Comité révolutionnaire* (10 members identified out of 12)

(b) *Officiers municipaux* (9 out of 10)

(c) *Notables* (12 out of 18)

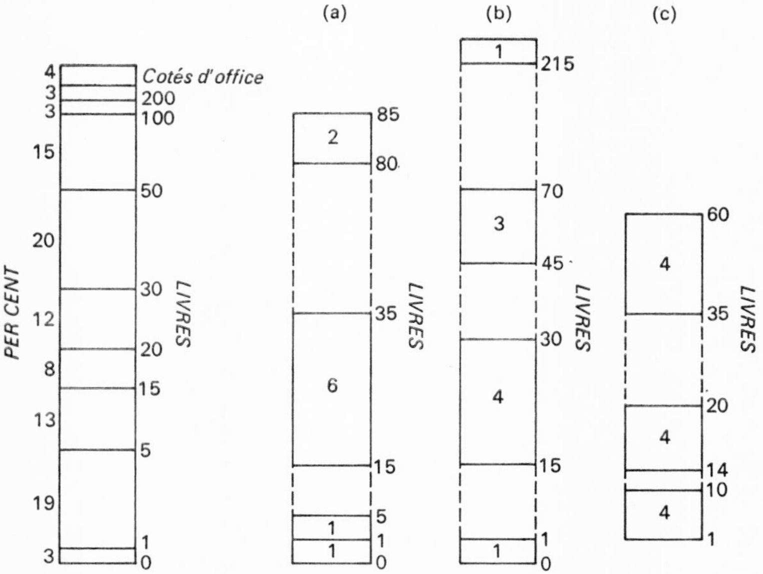

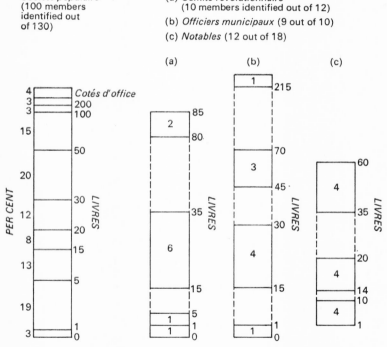

at the other end of the scale, six members paid over 100 *livres*. Four were *cotés d'office* during the Ancien Régime because of their rank: Claude-Henri Dupuy, for instance,

information to permit identification; in a few cases, a nickname may have been used, for example, Bourbonnais whose real name was Pethiot; finally, some members may have lived in hamlets not included in the tax roll.

who was the father of the deputy to the Convention, had been *trésorier de France* and was described in 1789 as 'un gentilhomme vivant noblement'.[1] But Dupuy was not typical of the club as a whole. In so far as the principal occupation of each member can be determined, the club seems to have reflected fairly accurately the economic structure of the town. The presence of twenty-two people from the legal professions still suggested the importance of the courts in late eighteenth-century Montbrison, despite the fact that the lawyers had been predominantly federalist—only seventeen *avocats*, *notaires*, *procureurs*, and *avoués* found their way into the club, compared with the fifty-four practising in the town in 1789.[2] Six teachers were another indication of the character of the town, while Montbrison's isolation from the minor industries of the central area of the department was emphasized by the small number of artisans of this kind.[3] The bulk of the membership of the club was made up of people who provided the services necessary for this sort of community. Four *tailleurs d'habits*, two *horlogers*, two jewellers, an *architecte-sculpteur*, two *perruquiers*, two *confiseurs*, and a well-to-do doctor[4] reflected the type of clientele whose needs had to be satisfied. Three *aubergistes*, a *cafetier*, a printer, and a *libraire* demonstrated the administrative character of the town. The *boulangers* were, naturally, present in force, while a group of *jardiniers* represented the most profitable suburban occupation for an inhabitant of Montbrison.[5] For the rest, the members were drawn from all the normal urban service trades—a *serrurier*, a *sellier*, a *charron*, a *maréchal*, a *maçon*, *menuisiers*, *charpentiers*, a *drapier*, a *quincaillier*, and so on, together with a group of unspecified *marchands*. However, one must draw attention once again to the limitations of this type of analysis: Ballandrod *père*, for example, was variously described as a *notaire*, a *commissaire feudiste*, a *commissaire aux rentes nobles*, and a *géomètre*;[6] Joseph Levet, a

[1] *Bulletin de la Diana*, art. cit.

[2] *Almanach de Lyon*, 1789, p. 109.

[3] 9 *cordonniers*, 3 *tanneurs*, 5 *chapeliers*, 5 *tisserands*, 2 *teinturiers*, 1 *blanchisseur* (the latter two served both the hat-makers and the weavers).

[4] Durand, paying 119*l*. 19*s*. in taxes; the *conventionnel* Dubouchet was another prosperous doctor in the town (*Compte-moral du citoyen Dubouchet*).

[5] 5 *boulangers* and 4 *jardiniers*.

[6] *Bulletin de la Diana*, art. cit.; A.D.L., L 277, *Almanach de Lyon*, 1789.

chirurgien, was paying 5*l.* 19*s.* in taxes in 1789, but bought part of the buildings of Notre-Dame convent in 1791 for 4,500 *livres*.[1]

Apart from those in high office, Montbrisé's most militant terrorists were to be found in the revolutionary committee and in the Municipality, which was appointed by Javogues. This was natural since, on the one hand, the proconsul had a personal knowledge of his nominees and, on the other, the violence of the federalist crisis and the importance of the task of repression separated the wheat from the chaff. Montbrisé presents, therefore, an excellent sample for a study of the militants as opposed to the ordinary terrorists. Ten of the twelve members of the committee can be identified on the tax roll of 1789,[2] as can nine of the ten *officiers municipaux*, including the mayor and the *procureur de la commune*, and twelve of the eighteen *notables*.[3] The results are again illustrated in the accompanying diagram (p. 305). Clearly, both the members of the committee and the *officiers municipaux* were drawn especially from the more affluent section of the club. Although men from the higher levels of wealth as expressed in taxation were not properly represented in proportion to their numbers in the club, men paying between 15 and 40 *livres* kept the smaller income group in a minority considering the relative distribution of wealth in the club. To a lesser extent, the same is true of the *conseil général*, although the preponderance of the prosperous was slightly less marked than in the other two bodies. Indeed, with exceptions, the

[1] A. Huguet, *Le Cloître de Notre-Dame de Montbrison en* 1791, p. 16. Perhaps he was a relation of Levet, *avoué*, who was arrested in the Year II, and was buying for him.

[2] Only Eustache Cayeux, *marchand*, is an unknown quantity, since the *cordonnier* Personnier received some votes in the municipal elections in 1790 and must, therefore, have been a *citoyen actif* (A.C. Montbrison, *reg. dél.*, no. 1, fols. 112–19). Bernard, who paid less than 1 *livre*, was a recent immigrant from the Auvergne, who probably had few assets in the commune as yet, but who was possibly related to an important paper-maker at Ambert (A.N., F7 3681 (4); R. Estier, 'La crise de la papeterie auvergnate au 18e siècle', *Cahiers d'histoire*, 1966, p. 191).

[3] As far as the unidentifiable *notables* are concerned, Arthaud purchased *biens nationaux* worth 1,900 *livres* on behalf of a fellow citizen, while Chabreriat's father paid 21*l.* 8*s.* in taxes in 1789 and he himself was claiming 1,205 *livres* during the Terror for goods supplied to counter-revolutionaries (Huguet, op. cit., p. 18; A.D.L., L 263, fol. 49). Both were *notables* of the department in the Year X (*Liste des notables du département de la Loire*, 12 vend. an X).

most important posts were occupied by the more prosperous. The members of the committee were marginally more solid citizens than the *officiers municipaux*, and the latter were, as a group, somewhat wealthier than the *notables*. The mayor and the *procureur de la commune* were socially more impressive figures than the majority of their colleagues—the latter paid nearly 70 *livres* in taxes, and the former paid 215 *livres* jointly with his father, owned at least two houses in the town, and, in frimaire, delivered up his 'titres, terriers et autres livres féodaux' to the Municipality for destruction.[1] Finally, the most interesting feature of these institutions is the predominance of men from the service trades: in the committee, the liberal professions supplied only the *notaire* Ballandrod and Gras, *président du Collège*,[2] while an *officier municipal*, who was a well-to-do *huissier*, but, therefore, from the lowest of the legal professions, was their sole representative in the Municipality, apart from the *secrétaire-greffier*, who was naturally a schoolmaster.

No other centre in the department is as well documented as Montbrisé from this point of view. Tax assessments are presented in the tables of 'propriétaires et habitants' drawn up in 1788. But the details given in them are not always sufficient to identify individuals, particularly in the larger communities, while we have not found those relating to the *département* of Saint-Étienne. Moreover, the figures from these tables, which ostensibly give the total taxes paid by the inhabitants of the commune (*taille*, *accessoires*, *capitation*, and *vingtième*), should not be equated with the figures for Montbrisé, and the figures for one community should not be compared with those for another. The scribes followed no uniform practice as to the taxes they included, and different scribes omitted in an arbitrary fashion different categories of inhabitant.[3] Therefore, this information can only be used to render an impression of relative levels of wealth, and nothing can be deduced from the fact that a man is not to be found in these documents. It is clear, however, that the militants of the

[1] A.D.L., L suppl. 59; A.C. Montbrison, *reg. dél.*, no. 2, fol. 26. He was not a *notaire*, and therefore the papers must have been his own.

[2] A.D.L., L 259, fol. 54.

[3] Cf. F. Tomas, 'Géographie sociale du Forez en 1788', *Bulletin de la Diana*, 1965, pp. 83–6.

smaller Jacobin towns were as prosperous as at Montbrisé. As far as the revolutionary committee of the canton of Boën is concerned, details are available for seven of the nine members who lived in the *chef-lieu*.[1] Apart from one man who paid 27*l.* 15*s.*, they were all taxed at between 50 and 110 *livres*. Even allowing for the discrepancies in the documentation, Boën seems a special case. At Feurs, figures have been found for nine of the eleven original members of the committee.[2] Apart from one man, whose father paid over 250 *livres*, they were divided equally between those who paid between 11 and 15 *livres* and those who paid between 25 and 40 *livres*. At Charlieu, one can supply this information for twelve of the fifteen members of the committee.[3] Here the payments ranged from 154*l.* 4*s.* to 6*l.* 16*s.* But the weight was very clearly towards the upper end of the middle of the scale: two paid nearly 75 *livres*, five paid between 38 and 50 *livres*, and three paid about 20 *livres*. It is obvious, therefore, that as far as the districts of Boën and Roanne are concerned, one must treat with the utmost caution such statements as 'presqu'aucun d'eux ne jouit d'une aisance qui leur permette de remplir avec autant de désintéressement qu'ils le souhaiteraient les fonctions, dont ils ont été honorés'.[4]

The information available for the terrorists of Armeville, Saint-Chamond, and Rive-de-Gier is much more fragmentary. The size of these towns makes it considerably more difficult to identify individuals. In general terms, the documents suggest, with one notable exception, a rather poorer type of militant in the south of the department than elsewhere. This is not necessarily a comment on their social status within these communities. For example, incomes seem to have been relatively low at Saint-Chamond, where wealth was concentrated in the hands of a few men, particularly the silk merchants: of the 588 people listed as *notables* in the department in the Year X, only seven came from Saint-Chamond.[5] As for Armeville, one of the Parisians at Commune-affranchie noted in nivôse that 'ses habitants sont ou des sans-culottes ou des millionnaires: il n'y a, pour ainsi

[1] A.D.L., C 82. [2] A.D.L., C 69 (1). [3] A.D.L., C 82.

[4] A.D.L., L suppl. 102, rev. com. of Marcellin-la-Plaine to *Repr.*, 11 flor.

[5] *Liste des notables du département de la Loire*, 12 vend. an X.

dire, point de nuance'.[1] Moreover, the deepening industrial crisis of the Revolution makes it difficult to apply to the Year II indications of wealth drawn from earlier years. During the winter of the Year II, Armeville was constantly troubled by the repeated and violent demands not only of the poor but also of the *fabricants* and workers whose clients were increasingly falling in arrears.[2] The District calculated in nivôse that there were at least 2,000 *rubaniers* without bread and without any form of work in the city.[3] In these circumstances *commissaires*, for instance, were not necessarily men of substance prepared to wait for their indemnity. They could equally well be men deprived of all other sources of income, who saw an opportunity for revenue no matter when it was actually paid. However, one should not take this argument too far. The *coutelier* Pierre Chapelle, who was paid 400 *livres* in early nivôse for 47 days spent requisitioning grain, was described by his colleagues on the *Conseil général* of the commune of Armeville as a 'brave sans-culotte', who had only his daily labour with which to feed his family.[4] In fact he was sufficiently respected in his trade to be appointed director of the *Commission des armes et des ateliers* in messidor an II.[5]

The revolutionary committee at Rive-de-Gier seems to have conformed to the general pattern of the rest of the department. Seven members had been electors in 1789 and one of them had been a member of the Municipality set up in 1787.[6] At the other end of the scale, Philibert Raisin was the only *domestique* who can be identified in any of the committees of the department, and he was certainly a poor man: an inventory of his effects in ventôse listed two sheets, two barrels of wine, one tin candlestick, one frying-pan, one empty pinewood writing-desk, etc.[7] However, Rive-de-Gier began to petition for payment at the end of nivôse, which was relatively

[1] *Les Soirées de la campagne ou le voyageur révolutionnaire*, 16 niv.
[2] A.D.L., L 123, fol. 376.
[3] Ibid.
[4] A.C. Saint-Étienne, 1 D 10 (3), fol. 108.
[5] J. B. Galley, *Révolution*, ii. 225 n. 4.
[6] G. Lefebvre, *Souvenirs de cent ans*, pp. 52–7, list of electors.
[7] A.D.L., L 389, fol. 34, and Q 315. He had been the servant of a counter-revolutionary and was arrested in ventôse for having taken his master's horses to Lyon during the federalist crisis.

early.[1] The members of the committee at Saint-Chamond also began to feel the financial pinch of being in office at about the same time. On 17 nivôse/6 January they petitioned the District for an indemnity on the grounds that committee work took all day and that they were finding onerous the time and more especially the expenses involved in travelling as *commissaires* in order to maintain an adequate supervision over the whole canton.[2] The club obviously considered their complaints to be justified since, on 2 pluviôse/21 January, it opened a subscription list for them.[3] Nevertheless, both of these committees had been prepared to wait for some time before making representations. Since the club at Saint-Chamond decided to pay both old and new members from the subscription,[4] it seems that the poorer element there just dropped out, leaving the committee to men like Mosnier, Preynat, Dervieux, and Berne, and to *suppléants* like Villemagne and Granjean, all of whom had been among the electors in 1789.[5] The *teinturier* Berne,[6] in any case, was quite an important figure in Saint-Chamond, since he employed a number of *compagnons* and his wife had been promised 1,000 *livres* in her marriage contract by a future counter-revolutionary.[7] Berne had been one of the electors from Saint-Chamond for the Convention.[8]

The first revolutionary committee of the Terror at Armeville, the names of whose members are not recorded, may have been composed of men whose small resources hindered them from devoting continuous attention to their duties. Certainly, the new committee set up in mid frimaire remarked that its predecessors had been able to devote to the committee only such time as their personal affairs had allowed.[9] This, however, was far from being the case with the new committee. The outstanding figure was Guy Boissieux. He was a *marchand de rubans* and was described in the early years of the

[1] A.D.L., L 81, letter to Depart., 29 niv.

[2] A.D.L., L 390, fol. 11.

[3] G. Lefebvre, *Société républicaine*, pp. 132, 136.

[4] Ibid., p. 137.

[5] G. Lefebvre, *Souvenirs de cent ans*, pp. 36–8, list of electors.

[6] On a 'Tableau de la population de Saint-Chamond', 14 pluv. an IV (A.D.L., L suppl. 172), he is described as a *négociant*.

[7] A.D.L., L 390, fol. 1; A.D.L., Q 244.

[8] A.D.L., L suppl. 325.

[9] A.D.R., 42 L 163, letter to *Comm. mil.*, 17 frim.

Revolution as a 'bourgeois'.[1] In 1789 he had been the delegate from Montaud to the electoral assembly of the *bailliage* of the Forez.[2] In brumaire an II, he became treasurer of the commune;[3] and there was good reason for this appointment, for in 1791 he and a fellow citizen had spent jointly nearly 20,000 *livres* on two houses from the *biens nationaux* at Saint-Étienne.[4] In the Year II Boissieux declared a revenue of 700 *livres* derived from them and from another house at Latour, from land at Montaud, a *rente* at Malleval, and an annuity from a fellow citizen; he was a creditor for nearly 36,000 *livres*, while his debts amounted to only 7,000 *livres*.[5] Most of the other members were of the same sort of standing, although they were probably not all quite as prosperous as Boissieux. Catelan, the son of another *marchand de rubans* who paid 200 *livres* into the *contribution patriotique* of 1789, lived in the centre of the town, where only the wealthy could afford houses.[6] Antoine Ancelin paid 100 *livres* to the *contribution patriotique*, while Benoît Sauvage lived in the very middle-class rue Roannel and bought a *bien national* at Valbenoîte for the sum of 41,200 *livres* in 1791.[7] Claude Trouillet's father paid 150 *livres* into the *contribution patriotique* and he himself had been an elector in 1789.[8] Louis Philibert donated 36 *livres* to the *contribution patriotique*, Richard paid 30, and Jean-Baptiste Serre gave a silver snuff-box worth 13*l.* 15*s.*[9]

The Municipalities of Saint-Chamond and Armeville, however, apparently contrasted with the committees. The *officiers municipaux* of Saint-Chamond presented their grievances to the club at the remarkably early date of 13 brumaire/3 November. They demanded to be replaced or else to receive

[1] J. B. Galley, *Ancien Régime*, p. 222; id., *Révolution*, i. 37. [2] Ibid.

[3] A.C. Saint-Étienne, 1 D 10 (3), fol. 79. [4] Galley, op. cit. i. 218.

[5] A.C. Saint-Étienne, 2 G 66, declaration of 27 niv. an II.

[6] J. M. Devet, *La Contribution patriotique de 1789*, p. 33; Galley, *Ancien Régime*, p. 225. The *contribution patriotique* was supposed to represent a quarter of the revenue before tax.

[7] Devet, op. cit., p. 27; Galley, *Ancien Régime*, p. 238, and *Révolution*, i. 225. Sauvage's *contribution patriotique* was for 96 *livres* (Devet, op. cit., p. 41).

[8] Ibid., p. 33; Galley, *Révolution*, i. 35, 83.

[9] Devet, op. cit., pp. 61, 37, 7. Brunon-Soviche, another member, subscribed only 24 *livres*, but managed to buy in partnership a house worth 8,700 *livres* from the *biens nationaux* (ibid., p. 25; Galley, *Révolution*, i. 220).

a reasonable indemnity, for, they said, they were not rich enough to live off *rentes* and the great volume of municipal business prevented them from going to their workshops, 'leur unique ressource', so that they had no chance to work to feed their families.[1] Only four of them had been electors in 1789,[2] while promotions had removed their richer colleagues such as Chana and Paret. Certainly, the club does not appear to have responded to this plea and the men continued in office. But one should perhaps relate it to the ascendancy gained by the club and the committee in municipal affairs at precisely this time.[3] As far as the Municipality of Armeville is concerned, few of the members appointed by Javogues can be identified with certainty. Three of the *notables* made quite substantial payments to the *contribution patriotique* ranging from 72 to 130 *livres*; three *officiers municipaux* made more modest contributions of between 18 and 24 *livres*.[4] Another *officier municipal*, Joseph Reynard, who was director of the *épreuve des canons de la manufacture*,[5] won the auction of the lead from the churches of Armeville in ventôse with a bid of 2,430 *livres*.[6] But the general aspect of the Municipality seems to have been reflected more truly by the mayor Johannot. He had rich relations in the Vivarais, whence he had emigrated to Saint-Étienne in about 1785,[7] but his paper-making business employed only his wife and his daughter, apart from help offered occasionally by his friends.[8] From the beginning of the Revolution he had been pursuing a ruinous lawsuit in order to get possession of a paper-mill and an estate, which alone could provide him with some assets.[9]

[1] G. Lefebvre, *Société républicaine*, p. 60.

[2] G. Lefebvre, *Souvenirs de cent ans*, pp. 36–8.

[3] Above, p. 117.

[4] Coulet, Grangeonnet, Berthéas (Devet, op. cit., pp. 22, 39, 53); Merley, Larderet, Dupré (ibid., p. 60).

[5] A.D.L., L 156, fol. 111.

[6] A.D.L., L 124, fol. 50. Javogues called Chovet-Peyronnet 'un ouvrier qui aime mieux un plat de poissons que des pommes de terre' (A.N., AF II (861) 15, letter of 22 pluv.). His name appeared on the 100 millions loan in 1815 along with Boissieux, Catelan, and Guillermin of the rev. com. (A.C. Saint-Étienne, 2 G 66). Puyforcat, another *officier municipal*, handed over some silver knives and forks in the Year II (A.D.L., L 130, fol. 54).

[7] Galley, *Révolution*, i. 483.

[8] A.D.R., 42 L 42.

[9] A.D.L., L 68, Johannot to Depart., 25 niv. an II.

Three *officiers municipaux* and two *notables* petitioned Javogues, alleging that

ils sont au dernier moment auquel ce sont des sans-culottes, auquel ils désirent un secours de toi [*sic*]. Nous voulons faire le bien du peuple; c'est notre désir, mais tu ne prétends pas laisser les sans-culottes sans ressources et leur famille à mourir dans leur maison point de ressources pour les entretenir [*sic*].[1]

Despite the fact that the well-to-do *notable* Grangeonnet was one of the signatories, this can be accepted as being the position of many of the members of the *conseil général* at least. At the beginning of nivôse a petition was sent to the *Représentants du peuple* to obtain a salary for the *officiers municipaux* and the *notables* after one member had stressed the fact that the *notables* could not leave their work in order to transact the business of the commune without an indemnity.[2] In mid pluviôse, the mayor complained to his colleagues that local counter-revolutionaries had profited from these petitions to demand the replacement of their authors by wealthier men:

...ne vous dissimulez pas [he continued] c'est ici la lutte de l'aristocratie contre le patriotisme. De deux choses l'une, ou la municipalité restera composée comme elle l'est actuellement de vrais sans-culottes ... ou elle sera composée de gens riches, qui rejetteront cette commune dans les mauvais principes.[3]

A new petition for salaries was immediately addressed to the *Représentant* Girard, and yet another was sent to him and to his colleagues at Commune-affranchie a few days later.[4]

Therefore, leaving aside comparative levels of wealth between the two towns, much the same pattern apparently pertained at Armeville as at Montbrisé. The revolutionary committee was again wealthier than the Municipality and the *officiers municipaux* were probably more affluent than the *notables*, since the emphasis was on the poverty of the latter. At Saint-Chamond also the committee appears to have attracted a rather more well-to-do type of citizen than the Municipality. Moreover, as was the case at Montbrisé, the

[1] A.D.R., 1 L 190, Gauché, Pupil, Grangeonnet, Lusier, and Vernay-Vial to Javogues, n.d.

[2] A.C. Saint-Étienne, 1 D 10 (3), fol. 101, 1 niv.

[3] Ibid., fol. 120, 10 pluv.

[4] Ibid., fol. 125, 22 pluv.

professional composition of the local authorities in these two towns reflected above all the character of the economy. All the documents referring to Saint-Chamond spoke of 'artisans' who had abandoned their 'ateliers'.[1] The Municipality of Armeville was also described in the same way.[2] However, there was a marked professional difference between the committee and the Municipality at Armeville. The *négociant* Coulet and the *papetier* Johannot were not typical of this latter body, whose members, in so far as they can be identified, were predominantly drawn from the metallurgical and the arms trades.[3] The service trades only appeared as a minority at the end of the list of *notables*.[4] Although the committee did contain three *armuriers* and a *forgeur*, the strongest element in numerical terms was six *marchands*, of whom only a *marchand fourbisseur* was clearly connected with the metallurgical industry.[5] Finally, despite the difficulties in evaluating the social reality behind the name of a profession, it is noticeable that neither the notoriously low revenue specialities of the metallurgical industry (the *limeurs de boucles*, the *faiseurs de fourchettes*, the *forgeurs de fiches*, etc.) nor the multitude of miserable owner-operators of the mines seem to have been represented anywhere.

Some reference to public positions held before the Terror has been made in the discussion of the militants in the district of Armeville. This is a useful indication of the social importance of the individual concerned. Whereas appointment to office during the Terror required merely that an individual's political purity should be known to the authority responsible for the appointment, it relied much more in the preceding years on a man's prestige. This was especially true

[1] A.D.L., L 124, fol. 161, the members of the rev. com. 'sont presque tous des pères de famille qui ont abandonné leurs ateliers'. Ten of the twelve members of the rev. com. can be identified on a list of the names of all the inhabitants of Saint-Chamond drawn up on 14 pluv. an IV (A.D.L., L suppl. 172); the professions of eight are marked on that list: 5 *passementiers*, 1 *cloutier*, 1 *tanneur*, 1 *négociant*.

[2] A.C. Saint-Étienne, 1 D 10 (3), fol. 101.

[3] 1 *chaudronnier*, 2 *couteliers*, and 4 *forgeurs*; 9 *armuriers*, 2 *canonniers*, 1 *éprouveur*, and 1 *doreur*—this last would be employed on the *armes bourgeoises*.

[4] A *tonnelier* (whose business would come above all from the packaging needs of the arms and metallurgical industries), a *tailleur d'habits*, and a *cabaretier*.

[5] 2 *marchands de rubans*, 1 *marchand papetier*, 1 *marchand fourbisseur*, 2 'marchands'. The other two members were a *maître teinturier* and a *perruquier*.

of elective office which demanded that a candidate be known to a fairly wide section of the population, not to mention the suffrage qualifications of the period. Quite a large number of militant terrorists at a local level had this kind of background. At Armeville, for instance, both the committee and the Municipality contained men who had represented their trade in assemblies in 1789 and others who had been members of the Municipalities of the first years of the Revolution.[1] Both Berthéas and Merley-Bontemps, members of the Municipality of the Year II, represented the *canonniers* on the *contrôle des armes* of the *Manufacture* from early 1793 onwards.[2] The situation was the same at Montbrisé where, in 1790, several leading terrorists received votes in the municipal elections. Although only a few actually obtained office, many more took an active part in local life, since their signatures appear on the minutes of the meetings of the *citoyens actifs* during the early years of the Revolution.[3] This pattern was even more marked in the smaller communities. At Moingt, for example, most of the militant terrorists were important figures before the Year II—six of the members of the committee, the terrorist mayor, and two of the founder members of the club had all been on the municipal assembly of 1788 and subsequent Municipalities or else had participated in assemblies of the 'principaux habitants'.[4]

The command structure of the *armée révolutionnaire* was dominated by militant terrorists whose social and political background was no different from that of the other terrorists. Indeed, they were very often the same men, who left other

[1] Trouillet, deputy for the *maîtres teinturiers*, 1789; Ancellin, deputy for the *forgeurs;* Berthéas, deputy for the *canonniers*; Tournier, *syndic* of the *forgerons* in 1788; Brunon-Soviche, Bérardier-Merley, Chovet-Peyronnet, *officiers municipaux* in 1791, and Ancellin, Sauvage, and Philibert, *notables*; Reynard, *officier municipal* in 1792, and Sauvage, Philibert, Guillermin, Chovet-Peyronnet, and Perset, *notables* (Galley, *Révolution*, i. 24, 35, 83, 270, 399, and Bibl. Lyon, Coste MS. 601, no. 5).

[2] Galley, op. cit. i. 423 n. 2, 601.

[3] A.C. Montbrison, *reg. dél.*, no. 1, fols. 1, 2, 112–19: Plaisançon, *officier municipal*, in 1790; Fricour in 1791 and Thomé, Faure, and Durand, *notables*. Curtil, Chabreriat, Guinard, Chaux, Phalippon, Griot, etc., also received votes. Guinard, Thomé, Chantelauze, Fricour, Thévenon, and Durand were members of the electoral assembly at various times between 1790 and 1792 (A.D.R., 1 L 335; *Liste des électeurs du département du Rhône-et-Loire*, 1791; A.D.L., L suppl. 325).

[4] A.C. Moingt, *reg. dél.*, *passim*.

institutions to join the army and returned to them after the army was disbanded. Some even pursued simultaneous careers during the Terror. Captain Pierre Marcet, for example, was a member of the revolutionary committee at Armeville in October and joined it again in pluviôse; Sergeant Pagnon held the office of postmaster at Montbrisé throughout the Terror, while Captain Civeton was also a *commissaire des Représentants*.[1] The officers and the N.C.O.s were both men of proven political excellence and reasonably prosperous citizens. Bassal and Javogues evidently considered that this would be the case as far as the officers were concerned, since they ordered them to buy their own uniforms and arms.[2] The officers were perhaps in general a slightly wealthier group than the N.C.O.s, but there were exceptions in both cases. Duret, the commander-in-chief, married into the family of Dupuy, member of the Convention, and, when he was executed, had at least one creditor who owed him 22,000 *livres*; the wives of three rich counter-revolutionaries, two of whom had had pretensions to nobility before the Revolution, addressed him as 'citoyen parent'.[3] But the *plâtrier* Civeton paid only 4*l*. 12*s*. in taxes, although he was definitely an employer and an entrepreneur.[4] On the other hand, Sergeant Pagnon paid 42*l*. 5*s*. in taxes in 1789, had been able to buy the prebend of Germanieu for his son in the 1780s, and owned more than one house in Montbrisé.[5] Corporal Daphaud was also somewhat exceptional among the N.C.O.s, but his case provides a convenient illustration of the local militants. He ran a business as a *menuisier* with his father at Montbrisé.[6] They owned their house and rented a couple of depots in town and also held a small garden in *fermage* from the Cordeliers. In all they paid 21*l*. 1*s*. in taxes in 1789 and the son was a *citoyen actif* during the early years of the

[1] Galley, *Révolution*, ii. 32–3; A.C. Montbrison, *reg. dél.*, no. 2, fol. 28; above, p. 192.

[2] A.N., AF II 114 (859) 6, *arrêté* of 6 Oct.

[3] A.D.R., 42 L 186, d. Pelardy, A.D.L., L 234, Depart. to Dist. of Roanne, 8 flor. an II; A.D.R., 42 L 186, d. Pupier de Brioude.

[4] A.D.L., C 69 (1), Roanne; A.D.L., L suppl. 317, judgement by *juge de paix* against him, 25 Oct. 1792, A.C. Roanne, 1 D 1 (2), fol. 190, contract for repairs to the parish church, early 1793.

[5] *Bulletin de la Diana*, art. cit.; Huguet, op. cit., p. 164; A.D.L., L 263, fol. 12.

[6] *Bulletin de la Diana*, art. cit.

Revolution.[1] The Daphaud family was, therefore, a typical case of artisans who had prospered; they were not quite well enough established to own much property, although they were beginning already to conform to the normal urban pattern by obtaining some agricultural land in the near vicinity to live off (a small garden would be the cheapest and the nearest and thus the first stage in this development). By the Year III, Daphaud *fils* was able to take another step up the social ladder, calling himself a 'cultivateur' and paying 4,000 *livres* for a house that was probably worth more.[2] His political career coincided with the Terror: he had had to flee from the *muscadins* and, in addition to service in the *armée révolutionnaire*, he was a member of the club, a *garde séquestre*, a *notable* of the Municipality, a denunciator to the revolutionary committee, and was appointed director of the *atelier du salpêtre* in germinal an II.[3]

The men appointed by Javogues to the Department and the Districts were, in the main, both politically and socially militants of the greatest prestige. Although the composition of the *conseil général* of the Department was obviously dictated in part by the desire to include representatives from the widest possible geographical area, it was an impressive collection of local personalities. There was a large group of men who held office in their community. For example, Jean Phalippon, the brother of Claude Phalippon of Montbrisé, had been mayor of Boisset-Saint-Priest since 1790 and was still mayor in the Year X, quite apart from having been a member of the electoral assembly for both the Legislative and the Convention.[4] The *marchand* Prud'homme-Lacroix of Armeville paid 100 *livres* into the *contribution patriotique*;[5] the *charpentier en bateaux* Popelain of Roanne was an *officier municipal* in 1791, paid nearly 100 *livres* in taxes in 1788, and in germinal an II loaned 1,000 *livres* to the District for the purchase of grain;[6] Michel Portier, a *chapelier* from

[1] A.C. Montbrison, *reg. dél.*, no. 1, fol. 2.

[2] A.D.L., L suppl. 47, lawsuit in fruct. an III demanding the revision of the sale 'pour cause de lézion'.

[3] A.D.R., 42 L 172, d. Belfond; A.D.R., 42 L 178, d. Durand; A.D.L., Q 136; A.N., AF II 114 (861), 14, maintained in office by Reverchon in mess. (A.D.L., L 262, fol. 85); A.D.L., L 434 (2), *passim*; ibid., 3 prair.

[4] A.D.L., L 362, fol. 2; *Liste des notables*.

[5] Devet, op. cit., p. 59.

[6] A.D.L., L 206, C 69 (1), L 189.

Montbrisé, bought 30,000 *livres'* worth of *biens nationaux* during the Revolution.[1] Even members like the *serrurier* Bernuizet and the *grammairien* Durand, who appear rather poorer than the rest, were nevertheless men of some repute locally: despite the fact that he paid only 3*l.* 17*s.* in taxes, Bernuizet was a *notable* and an *assesseur* of the *juge de paix* at Saint-Germain-Laval in 1792 and called himself a *propriétaire*;[2] Durand, whose taxes were assessed at 10 *livres*, was a *notable* of Montbrison at the early date of 1790.[3]

This tendency was even more marked in the *directoire* of the Department. The president, Antoine Desvernays of Armeville, had been mayor of that town in 1791; he possessed a country house in addition to his town house and had given 288 *livres* to the *contribution patriotique*; at the end of the Ancien Régime, he had been an *associé libre* of the select *Société royale d'agriculture* of the *généralité* and also a member of the *noble jeu de l'arc en mains*, which was a privileged company for Saint-Étienne's high society.[4] The former *avocat en Parlement* Jean Gaulne came from a similar background: during the Ancien Régime he had called himself 'noble Jean Degaulne' and had land in the village of Sainte-Colombe at least; he had been a member of the municipal assembly at Feurs in 1787, and was an *officier municipal* from 1789 to 1791 and the *juge de paix* of the canton in 1792.[5] His compatriot Jacques Berthuel had also been a member of the municipal assembly at Feurs in 1787 and, after continuing as an *officier municipal* from 1789 to 1791, he became mayor in 1792; his tax assessment stood at 112 *livres* and he bought vineyards from the *biens nationaux* worth over 30,000 *livres*, not to mention a whole series of presbyteries in parishes that had been abolished.[6] Also from Feurs was Jean-Claude Thiolière,

[1] A. Broutin, *Histoire des couvents de Montbrison avant 1793*, ii. 69.

[2] A.D.L., C 69 (2); A.N., AF II 114 (861) 16, *arrêté* of 3 Sept.; A.D.R., 42 L 180, d. Gubian.

[3] *Bulletin de la Diana*, art. cit.; A.C. Montbrison, *reg. dél.*, no. 1, fols. 112–19.

[4] Galley, *Révolution*, i. 270, 465, 565; id. *Ancien Régime*, pp. 236, 300, 316; Devet, op. cit., p. 31.

[5] A.C. Feurs, *reg. dél.*, *passim*; A.D.L., L 81, Mun. of Sainte-Colombe to Depart., n.d.

[6] A.C. Feurs, loc. cit., *passim*; A.D.L., C 69 (1); A. Broutin, *Histoire de la ville de Feurs*, pp. 513–14; A.N., AF III 298 (1181), Gaulne to Minister of Interior, 1 germ. an IV.

who had been president of the District of Montbrison in 1792–3.[1] He only paid 21 *livres* in taxes in 1788, but his wife came into quite a substantial inheritance from her father in 1790.[2] Moreover, he was obviously a man of considerable importance: he was a former president of the *élection* of Saint-Étienne, he sat in the assembly of the Third Estate of the *bailliage* of Montbrison in 1789, and he had bought the Château de Pellussieux just before the Revolution.[3] Dubessey had also been a member of the assembly of the *bailliage* and had subsequently been Chalier's colleague on the district tribunal of Lyon in 1792–3.[4] The *cordonnier* and *tanneur* Chana had been elected mayor of Saint-Chamond in 1792 and, in 1812, was listed among the hundred most highly taxed inhabitants of that town with a declared annual revenue of 1,000 *livres*.[5] As for the *procureur-général-syndic*, Lafaye *le jeune*, either he or his brother had been a *notaire* at Rive-de-Gier and *lieutenant du comté ecclésiastique* of Lyon there and in several surrounding villages before the Revolution.[6] The *secrétaire général* of the Department, François Guyot, had been elected *procureur de la commune* at Saint-Germain-Laval in 1792 and was paying 130 *livres* in taxes in 1788.[7]

The social position of the members of the *directoire* of the Department was exceptional. But most of the administrators of the districts of Armeville and Boën were also obviously more influential members of society than the average militants in office in the communes. Again, many were mayors or *officiers municipaux* in their home towns: Bourges, for example, was mayor of Saint-Georges-en-Couzan.[8] Again, some had held public positions before the Revolution: Fontvielle-Dufay, for instance, had been *syndic* (mayor) of Saint-

[1] Thiolière, *Compte rendu à ses commettants*.
[2] A.D.L., C 69 (1); A.D.L., L suppl. 47, lawsuit arising out of the legacy, an III.
[3] A.D.L., C 62; Broutin, op. cit., p. 436.
[4] A.D.L., loc. cit. and L 18, fol. 118.
[5] A.N., F^{1b} II Loire 10, d. Objets généraux, Gaulne to the Directory, 24 germ. an IV; *Liste des cent plus forts contribuables de la commune de Saint-Chamond en 1812*.
[6] Galley, *Ancien Régime*, pp. 519, 523; id. *Révolution*, i. 773. His brother, Lafaye *l'aîné*, represented the section du Plâtre of Lyon together with Bertrand, the future mayor of Cne-aff., at the electoral assembly for the Convention (A.D.L., L suppl. 325).
[7] A.N., AF II 114 (861) 16, *arrêté* of 3 Sept.; A.D.L., C 69 (2).
[8] A.D.L., L 438, fol. 1.

Jean-Bonnefonds and Jacquemont had been a member of the Municipality of Boën in 1788.[1] They were men whose social predominance had already been recognized by their fellow citizens before the Terror: the *notaire* and former *procureur fiscal* Pinaud had been one of the members of the assembly of the *bailliage* of Montbrison and was *juge de paix* of the canton of Saint-Marcellin in 1790; Tardy was an *officier municipal* of Saint-Rambert from 1790 to 1793, and Misson was elected to the Municipality of Saint-Étienne in 1791.[2] They were men of substance. Nicolas Desvernays, probably related to the president of the Department, called himself a 'bourgeois' when he gave 100 *livres* to the *contribution patriotique*;[3] Voytier entitled himself an 'ouvrier armurier' in the Year II, but earlier in 1793 he had claimed to be a 'négociant' and his colleagues on the District described him as a 'marchand fabricant d'armes';[4] Bajard owned the barracks at Rive-de-Gier, which he rented to the *gendarmerie*, and was appointed supervisor of the administration of the Canal de Givors in late 1793;[5] Justamont of Cervières described himself as a 'phisitien [*sic*] et philosophe' and built *montgolfières* when he was not valuing the *biens nationaux* on behalf of the District of Montbrison;[6] Joseph Bouchet had been one of the five royal prebendaries at Montbrison before the Revolution, Jean-Antoine Fontvieille owned a coal-mine at Saint-Étienne although residing at Saint-Julien-en-Jarez, Bruel was in sixteenth position on the list of those inhabitants of Saint-Héand who paid enough taxes to be eligible for the Department in 1790, Jacquemont paid 160 *livres* in taxes and so on.[7] As was the case with the Department, there were only a few representatives in the Districts from the trades that predominated in the lower institutions.[8] These men were

1 Galley, *Ancien Régime*, p. 562; A.D.L., C 82.

2 A.D.L., C 62; A.D.L., L 362, fol. 3; A.C. Saint-Rambert, *reg. dél.*, *passim*; Galley, *Révolution*, i. 270.

3 Devet, op. cit., p. 13.

4 *Discours du citoyen Voytier, ouvrier armurier* . . .; Galley, op. cit. i. 567 n. 1; A.D.L., L 130, fol. 57.

5 A.D.L., L 124, fol. 161, L 130, fol. 30.

6 A.N., D XXXVIII 3, d. 31; A.D.L., L 271, Aug. 1792.

7 Huguet, op. cit., p. 13; A.D.L., L 68, 25 niv.; A.C. La Fouillouse, unclassified papers; A.D.L., C 82.

8 A *sellier*, an *aubergiste*, a *boulanger*, an *armurier*, etc.

above all *marchands* and urban and rural *propriétaires*. Moreover, it was in the higher regular administrations that were to be found some lawyers and men from the liberal professions as well as a few priests, all of whom were noticeably absent from the inferior institutions.[1]

It is evident, therefore, that despite a wide diversity of fortune, the terrorists cannot be equated with the Parisian *sans-culottes*.[2] The *menu peuple*, whose political consciousness is in any case open to debate,[3] were entirely excluded. The wage-earners, who constituted an important element of the militant *sans-culottes*, were also absent. Indeed, the social basis of the militant terrorists as distinct from the ordinary terrorists was the opposite of the position in Paris: the clear correlation between wealth and militancy has been demonstrated by the differences both between institutions at the communal level and between communal and higher authorities. Although the artisan and *boutiquier* element was much in evidence in the communes, it appears both distinctly wealthier and socially more influential than its counterpart in the Parisian sections. On the other hand, however, the terrorists were by no means the richer members of society. Javogues *père*, who paid nearly 370 *livres* in taxes,[4] and the former *trésorier de France*, Dupuy, represented the upper limit of the terrorists on the social scale. Neither could be termed leaders of society in absolute terms, even in the Loire; both were accepted as terrorists above all because of their Montagnard sons. Dupuy's terrorism was highly dubious —when asked to supply evidence about federalism in Montbrison, he replied evasively that he had remained hidden in his house throughout the occupation of the town.[5] The Year II saw the arrival in power of men who were at one and the same time both a new class and not a new class politically. They were men who had already participated in public life

[1] Lawyers: Depart.—1 *avocat*, 2 *notaires*, 1 *homme de loi*; Dist. of Boën—1 *procureur*, 1 *notaire*. Liberal professions: Depart.—3 teachers, 1 *chirurgien*; Dist. of Boën—1 teacher; Dist. of Armeville—1 *ingénieur-architecte*. Priests: Depart.—1; Dist. of Boën—2; Dist. of Armeville—2.

[2] A. Soboul, *Les Sans-culottes parisiens en l'an II*, pp. 439–51.

[3] Cf. *Les Soirées de la campagne ou le voyageur révolutionnaire*, 16 niv.; the *sans-culottes* of Armeville 'ne méritent ce nom que sous les rapports de la pauvreté'.

[4] *Bulletin de la Diana*, art. cit., pp. 245, 354.

[5] A.D.R., 42 L 178, d. Dupuy.

and had received the votes of their fellow citizens, but they had never dominated local public life or had undisputed access to office. At Montbrison, for instance, although a number of future terrorists had received votes in the municipal elections, only seven of them held municipal office in 1790 and 1791.[1] Before 1793 the representatives of the *noblesse de robe* and the rich lawyers controlled the Municipality and even more clearly the District, even though they did not hold every seat in these bodies. The disappearance of the lawyers as a predominant group in the regular and extraordinary authorities of the Year II in Montbrisé and the district of Boën is symptomatic of this development. Similarly, in the south of the department, the great *négociants* of the silk industry, the directors of the *Manufacture*, and the investors in the coal-mining *concessions* were, with rare exceptions, out of power during the Terror. Indeed, although the votes in their favour testify to a certain local influence, the election in 1791 to municipal office at Saint-Étienne of Bardet (president of the *Commission militaire* of Feurs), Misson (president of the District of Armeville), and Pointe (the member of the Convention) was contested on the grounds of insufficient taxes.[2] The case against Bardet was accepted. The Terror, therefore, was characterized at Montbrisé and in the industrial towns by the transfer of power at the local level towards the lower end of the ruling class of the previous years.

It is important to remember in this context, however, that the protection of the interests of the poorer sections of the community and the identification of those interests as the interests of the nation were an essential feature of Jacobinism. In fact, the support of the urban labouring classes for the Terror was never very explicit in the Loire during the Year II, partly because the Terror, triumphant, did not need to solicit popular approbation and partly because it encountered popular reticence on several points of practice. Much clearer evidence of such support for the Jacobins as a political group

[1] A.C. Montbrison, *reg. dél.*, no. 1, *passim*: Plaisançon (club), Pommier (club), Fricour (rev. com.), Thomé (club), Durand (rev. com.), Bouchet (Dist.), Colardet (club). Therefore only three could be called militants. In 1790, Guinard (*officier municipal*), Desormes (club), and Chabreriat (*notable*) were among the *proxime accesserunt* in the elections.

[2] Galley, *Révolution*, i. 270.

is to be found both during the federalist crisis and during the struggles under the Directory. Whatever their social situation, the militant terrorists were democrats and distrusted great wealth. Later, some of them were to explain the policies they pursued in the municipal administration of Saint-Étienne under the Directory in terms that characterize their constant preoccupation throughout the period: 'ils ont craint que *les Gros n'écrasassent les Petits*, ils ont agi d'après cette idée, et ont fait tout pour donner dans toutes circonstances la prépondérance aux *Petits*.'[1] None the less, it would be dangerous to assert that their terrorism was born out of a class antagonism. It may be legitimate to argue that, in local terms, the Terror represented the seizure of power by a politically frustrated group and that some individuals understood it as such. This thesis, however, presumes a degree of parity in social status and political background between militants throughout the department which is hard to document. It is significant in this respect that even at Montbrisé the newly reopened club sprang unanimously to the defence of the federalist mayor, crying 'oui, il est patriote; il est vraiment ami du peuple', despite the fact that he was quite an extensive landowner and had been an *officier du point d'honneur* and a member of the Constituent Assembly.[2] Much more apparent is the fact that the social group which produced the terrorists also produced counter-revolutionaries and moderates. The *chapelier* Michel Portier of Montbrison, a member of the *conseil général* of the Department in the Year II, was the brother of two leading federalists, although their political differences did not prevent them from coming to his aid when he was attacked by the *muscadins*;[3] both Berthuel and Thiolière had as relatives and friends a number of counter-revolutionaries;[4] Chorel-Laplagny was arrested in July 1793 on the orders of the mayor of Saint-Paul-en-Jarez, who was his relation by marriage;[5] Rochat, the terrorist

[1] A.N., BB18 434, Capt. Fangeroux to General Caneul, 24 germ. an V.

[2] A.D.R., 42 L 181, d. Jamier; Broutin, op. cit., p. 400; A.D.R., 42 L 160.

[3] A.D.R., 42 L 164, *reg. dél.*, of Mun. of Montbrison, 23 July.

[4] A.D.R., 42 L 158, Despomeys to Javogues, 12 Oct.; A.D.R., 42 L 160, evidence given by Thiolière against his nephew by marriage, Lachaize; evidence by Berthuel against his relatives Lesgallerie and Latanerie.

[5] A.D.L., L 394, fol. 22.

juge de paix of Saint-Jean-Soleymieux, was the uncle of an *émigré*.[1]

More striking than these individual cases is the fact that, as far as one can see, the members of the District, Municipality, and committee at Roanne did not contrast with their colleagues at Montbrisé and Armeville socially in the way that they did politically. Information on Roanne is fragmentary because of the difficulties of identification inherent in unsatisfactory material, while it has already been emphasized that no comparison of detail can be made between tax figures here and those drawn from other sources. Nevertheless, the composition of the District, with its mayors, *propriétaires*, and *marchands*, presents no anomaly. The Municipality also conforms to the established pattern. Eight of the ten *officiers municipaux*, including the mayor and the *procureur de la commune*, can be identified on the table of 'propriétaires et habitants' of 1788, as can twelve of the eighteen *notables*.[2] The *officiers municipaux*, like those of Montbrisé, seem to have come from the middle range of fortune and were characterized by being slightly wealthier as a group than the *notables*, although the gap seems more pronounced than at Montbrisé.[3] There were also the same few men, who had held public office in the previous years, as were to be found in similar institutions elsewhere.[4] In professional terms, the Municipality of Roanne reflected the same predominance of the service trades that was to be found at Montbrisé.[5] But, while there was also a group of five *mariniers*, doubtless included on the specious grounds that they represented a politically reliable element by definition, the presence of five *marchands* and a *fabricant en coton* meant that the predominant economic interest at Roanne maintained a share in local

[1] Forest et al., *Sur les élections du département de la Loire*, an VI.

[2] A.D.L., C 69 (1).

[3] *Officiers municipaux*: five pay between 40 and 92*l.*, two pay between 20 and 25*l.*, one pays 8*l.*; *notables*: five pay between 25 and 41*l.*, two pay between 18 and 23*l.*, five pay between 4 and 12*l.*

[4] Three *officiers municipaux* had been respectively deputy of the *maîtres boulangers* in the assembly of the *département* in 1788, an *officier municipal* in 1792–3, and a *notable* in 1790, 1791–2 (F. Pothier, *Roanne pendant la Révolution*, pp. 19, 151, 37, 74).

[5] 3 *boulangers*, 2 *cordonniers*, 1 *aubergiste*, 1 *cabaretier*, 1 *tailleur*, 1 *jardinier*, 2 *charrons*, 2 *maréchaux*, 1 *doreur*, 1 *chaudronnier*, 1 *cordier*.

power much more clearly than was the case at Montbrisé and Armeville. One cannot prove, however, that it was this group which formed the political attitudes of the Municipality by supporting the moderate *procureur de la commune*, who was the curé of Roanne. Indeed, the *farbicant de coton*, Chantelot, was one of Roanne's few militant terrorists and he rapidly left his colleagues to join the *armée révolutionnaire*. The revolutionary committee presents a more difficult problem because one can establish no certain list of its members.[1] It may have contained as many as twenty people.[2] As a sample, one can take the nine men who, in frimaire, were expelled from the committee by the Department and the eleven (including two assistants) who were appointed by the District to replace them.[3] An examination of the tax assessments of those who can be identified in this way reveals that the first group, which had been proved moderate, was in fact somewhat less well-to-do than the second group, which was going to manifest exactly the same political attitudes. But both groups conformed to the position elsewhere in the department, in the sense that a combination of wealth and previous public position made them socially rather more influential than the members of the Municipality.[4] On the other hand, they also resembled the terrorists in that, on the whole, they were not men who had controlled public life before the Terror, while their urban land-holding, in so far as they can be identified on the *contribution foncière* of 1791,[5] was medium-sized and did not include the most highly valued real estate in the town.

In these circumstances, it is evident that terrorism, and more particularly militant terrorism, was not so much a phenomenon of class as a phenomenon of the individual. Why

[1] See, e.g., the different signatures of documents in A.D.R., 1 L 984, 42 L 157, 42 L 185, d. Michon, A.N., W 20 d. 1095, and also the resignations in niv. and pluv. (A.D.L., L 176, fols. 88–110).

[2] Cf. A.D.L., L 176, fol. 61, which seems to suggest a rev. com. of 18 full members and 8 assistants.

[3] A.D.L., L 18, fol. 74, L 176, fol. 61.

[4] First group: three deputies of the Third Estate in the assembly of the 'département' in 1788, two *notables* 1792–3; second group: one member of the municipal assembly in 1788, one *notable* 1792–3 (Pothier, op. cit., pp. 19, 37, 74, 151, and A.D.L., C 69 (1), Meguin *père*).

[5] A.C. Roanne, 1 G 1—the best property was in the sections of the Marais and of Matel.

did Jean-Baptiste Ferrand, *notaire* at Boën, member of the municipal assembly in 1788, member of the *conseil général* of the Department of the Rhône-et-Loire in 1791–2, member of the *directoire* of that Department in 1792–3, become president of the anti-federalist Committee of Public Safety of Boën and the 'dénonciateur de quarante personnes dont plusieurs, et deux de ses parents entre autres, sont morts sur l'échafaud'?[1] Why did Jacques Raymond, former *Régent du Collège de Boën* and constitutional curé of Trelins, become a militant terrorist, when Louis Vignon, *professeur au Collège de Roanne* and constitutional curé of the town, became a leading moderate?[2] What made a *déchristianisateur* and a supporter of Lapalus out of François-Gilbert Game, a landowner at Saint-Martin-d'Estreaux and *procureur de la commune* of Sail, who was capable of quoting Plato and Virgil in support of an argument about the pagan origins of the Christian doctrine of the after-life?[3] Suspicion of federalism brought prison for his brother, who was also a landowner at Saint-Martin-d'Estreaux, a lover of fine Aubusson carpets and gilded mirrors and chandeliers, and a member of the District of Roanne from 1790 to 1793.[4] Why did the *marchand ferblantier* Costalin, whose real estate at Roanne was valued for taxation at 250 *livres*, become such a convinced terrorist that he joined the *armée révolutionnaire* when the *conseil général* of the Department was abolished?[5] The real estate of the *marchand drapier* Dusauzey was also valued at 250 *livres* in the same *section du Centre*, but he was an active moderate in the revolutionary committee.[6]

In general terms it is clear that the terrorists were not predominantly unstable, violent men. Certainly, there were individuals of this kind. Jean Philippon of Saint-Galmier, for instance, seems to have had much the same character as Javogues: 'un esprit aussi inquiet que le sien', remarked the

[1] A.D.L., C 82; Galley, *Révolution*, i. 272, 402; Méaudre et al., *Mémoire sur le département de la Loire* p. 25.

[2] A.D.L. L suppl. 356, A.D.R., 42 L 164, *reg. dél.*, of the Mun. of Montbrison, 16 June; A.D.L., L suppl. 511; Pothier, op. cit., p. 87.

[3] Bibl. Roanne, 3 L (1) 20, Game to Lapalus, n.d.; A.D.L., Q 202; A.D.L., Chaleyer MS. 354, Game to Dist. of Roanne, 10 Nov. 1793.

[4] A.D.L., Q 202; Pothier, op. cit., pp. 38, 113.

[5] A.C. Roanne, 1 G 1; above, p. 177.

[6] A.C. Roanne, loc. cit.; A.D.L., L 176, fol. 61.

agent national of the district of Boën, 'n'est pas fait pour habiter une petite commune'.[1] Pignon had a certain fondness for playing cards and for failing to pay his debts afterwards;[2] Desvernays *aîné* apparently had a deplorable background of marital strife, and his refusal to return his wife's dowry after their divorce landed her in jail for debt;[3] as for Chana, his favourite evening relaxation was said to be getting drunk on spirits and then going to make a speech at the club.[4] But for one bitter, officious terrorist like David of Montbrisé, called 'le petit Requin de Javogues',[5] there was another more amiable like Lafaye *le jeune*, about whom, in a moment of enthusiasm, one of his colleagues scrawled on the back of a dossier 'Lafaye le jeune est un B[on] B[ougre]';[6] for one rather shady terrorist like Michel Gelas, who omitted to return objects that he borrowed,[7] there was another rigorously honest one like 'l'austère' Chorel-Laplagny, who indignantly refused the gift of a bottle of choice wine which he suspected, wrongly, had been removed without payment from a sequestrated property.[8] Although information about the age of the terrorists is scarce, it is certain that youth was not a major characteristic. There were a few young men, like the twenty-one-year-old Claude Fauriel,[9] and there were a few old men, like the sixty-year-old Desvernays. But, for the most part, they came from an age span from the late twenties to late forties. The average of the known ages of ten members of the revolutionary committee at Saint-Chamond was thirty-five;[10] the average age of fifty victims of the Thermidorian Reaction at Montbrison and in the neighbourhood who gave evidence in the Year VI, was thirty-nine in the Year II.[11] The terrorists were married men with children: of the ninety-eight mem-

[1] A.D.L., L 327, fol. 19, 29 flor. an II.

[2] A.N., W 408, d. 939, Molle to Pignon, 25 Mar. 1793.

[3] Galley, op. cit. i. 274.

[4] A.D.R., 42 L 168, d. Callet, letter to Callet *père*, 26 Mar. 1793.

[5] A.D.L., L 259, fol. 69; A.C. Feurs, *reg. dél.*, 30 germ. an III.

[6] A.D.R., 42 L 178, d. Duperret.

[7] A.D.L., L 389, Chana to rev. com. of Rive-de-Gier, 17 flor. an II.

[8] A.D.R., 42 L 187, d. Ravarein, letter from Girard, 4 vent.; A.D.L., L 156, fol. 97, L 394, fol. 20.

[9] *Officier municipal* of Armeville: he became a famous writer and historian. Johannot was the grandfather of the philologist Littré.

[10] Figures taken from A.D.L., L suppl. 172, 'Tableau de la population de Saint-Chamond' (14 pluv. an IV), and corrected for the Year II.

[11] A.N., BB^{18} 690.

bers of the club at Montbrisé, for whom this information is available, only eight were bachelors and two were widowers who had not remarried; only nineteen of the married men did not have any children living with them in the Year II, while the average number of children still living with their parents at that time was three.[1]

The factors that made these ordinary, respectable citizens into terrorists were diverse and mostly incalculable. Although terrorism was predominantly an urban phenomenon, not all urban centres produced the same numbers of terrorists or the same degree of militancy. It is quite possible that common experiences may have helped to predispose some groups to terrorism more than others. It is evident that the violence of the federalist crisis at Montbrison and in the industrial centres of the south made active militants out of a number of people. We have already referred to the way in which secular antagonisms probably incited Boën and Feurs to take a political line opposed to the one chosen by Montbrison. Similarly, rivalry between Roanne and Charlieu may have confirmed the inhabitants of the latter town in their adherence to the Terror; their struggle during the eighteenth century against the stranglehold of the local Cluniac monastery over their communal affairs had possibly already inclined them to adopt the radical rejection of the Ancien Régime implied in the Terror.[2] Mere accident should also be taken into consideration: for example, the efficiency of the revolutionary committee at Néronde may well be attributable to the fact that one of its leading members, Mondon, had been living in rented accommodation at Montbrison and had had to flee back to Néronde in the summer of 1793, presumably taking with him his political attitudes and experience.[3] Similar

[1] Figures based on A.D.L., L suppl. 59, an inventory of the inhabitants of each house at Montbrisé dated 29 pluv. an II. Since this survey was presumably conducted for food distribution, there is apparently no age-limit on those classed as children; but naturally, there is no concrete evidence that these figures represent the whole family.

[2] M. Dumoulin, *Charlieu au XVIIIe siècle*, pp. 51–62. Note that Charlieu had only one sort of bread before the federalist crisis and at a time when Montbrison had two and Saint-Étienne three (L.-J. Gras, *Histoire du commerce local*, p. 319), while, in prair. an III, the Dist. of Roanne noted that the rev. com. of Charlieu was the only one in the dist. to have been in league with the tyrant Robespierre and his confederates (A.D.L., L 236).

[3] A.D.L., L 411, fol. 10.

arguments can be applied to individuals. There is quite possibly a considerable basis of truth for the typical Thermidorian accusation that a terrorist's first victims were his personal enemies.[1] Animosities between individuals were naturally fertile ground for political opposition. For instance, Pignon's associate, Béraud of Saint-Pierre-de-Bœuf, had a long-standing quarrel with the future suspect Richard, against whom he was planning to publish a pamphlet in late 1792.[2]

Moreover, although there were tensions between the terrorists, as will be demonstrated later, they were men who were often linked to one another by ties of blood, marriage, and friendship. In the smaller communities, blood and marriage relationships were almost inevitable: most of the lesser committees lost members after the decree of 7 frimaire/27 December excluding men related up to the fourth degree. But in some places the situation was quite remarkable—one suspect called the committee at Noirétable a 'tribunal de famille' because so many members were related to each other.[3] This was not a phenomenon that was confined to small communities; at Saint-Chamond, six members, including two brothers, were within the prohibited limit.[4] At Montbrisé, Fricour of the revolutionary committee was married to the sister of his colleague Curtil, while Antoine Chaux, a lieutenant in the *armée révolutionnaire* and a judge on the last two revolutionary tribunals at Feurs, was the brother-in-law of the *marchand* Claude Meynard, a member of the club; Drouillet of Moingt, a second lieutenant in the *armée révolutionnaire*, was the nephew of Bouarde of the Department; Chorel-Laplagny was the uncle of the *procureur-général syndic* Lafaye *le jeune*; at Perreux, the *agent national* was the brother-in-law of one of the members of the committee and they were the only supporters of Lapalus in the commune.[5] These are far from being the only examples of

[1] A.N., F^{1b} II Loire 17, d. Saint-Galmier, citizens of Saint-Galmier to General Montchoisi, n.d., denouncing Jean Philippon.

[2] A.N., W 408, d. 939, Béraud to Pignon, 7 Dec. 1792.

[3] A.D.R., 42 L 170, d. Poyet.

[4] A.D.L., L 390, fol. 19.

[5] A.N., BB^{18} 690; A.D.L., L 434 (2), fol. 32; A.D.R., 42 L 187, d. Ravarein, letter from Girard, 4 vent.; A.D.L., L 413, 16 flor. Richard (rev. com. of Montbrisé) had married into the family of Chavassieu (club and appointed to the Dist. by Reverchon) (Huguet, op. cit., p. 174).

such family connections. There were also business relations between the terrorists. For instance, Deville of the Department and Palley of the District of Boën, who were both *marchands* at Saint-Galmier, were in litigation with another *marchand* of the town in 1793, while Barbant, a member of the club at Montbrisé, was given power of attorney by Chantemerle *fils aîné*, who was president of the club in early brumaire.[1] Friendship between terrorists is much more difficult to document, since it was normal that they should address each other with some degree of familiarity during the Year II. However, the letters that they wrote to each other were full of requests to be remembered more particularly to certain individuals—'mon collègue Chaux te salue', 'J'embrasse de toute mon âme David et Montmellieux', etc.[2] Some letters were far more affectionate than was warranted by political alliance and republican formulas: 'Mon très cher ami, Je t'écris pour m'informer de l'état de ta santé. Il y a fort longtemps que je n'ai pas eu de tes nouvelles. . . . Je finis en t'embrassant.'[3] There were few better recommendations for a suspect than friendship with an established terrorist—one official, making a report on the suspects at Armeville, did not know what Lenoir was accused of, but thought he should mention that he was a friend of Avanturier's.[4] Obviously, friendships were mostly confined to inhabitants of the same commune, but the terrorists came from a social and political background that transcended local limits. One militant in the district of Roanne was advised to send the mayor of La Pacaudière, in order to obtain satisfaction from Javogues, since they knew each other and, moreover, he also had friends from whom he could get support among those close to the proconsul; Raymond of Boën called Chantelauze of Montbrisé 'frère et ami' rather than the 'citoyen' which he habitually employed in correspondence; Pignon's *sous-commissaires* seem to have been for the most part his personal friends; Maccabéo, who was a member of the Department of the Rhône, told Javogues

[1] A.D.L., L suppl. 60; A.D.L., L 263, fol. 25; A.D.R., 42 L 181, d. Jamier.

[2] A.D.R., 42 L 177, d. Dubourg, Phalippon to Duret, 3 niv.; P. Donot and L. de Neufbourg, *Le Forez pendant la Révolution*, p. 163, Chantelauze to Javogues, 27 Sept. 1793.

[3] A.D.R., loc. cit.

[4] A.D.R., 42 L 159.

that, when he visited Armeville, he had seen nobody but Jourjon and Misson with whom he was already acquainted.[1]

Naturally, this argument must not be taken too far. As has been emphasized already, the terrorists had friends and relations in the other camp. Palley of Saint-Galmier was not merely the business associate of Deville; his son was the *procureur de la commune* whom Philippon denounced.[2] As far as marriages are concerned, Habram of Montbrisé was married to Antoinette Latanerie, who came from a family of counter-revolutionaries, while in the Year IV Barbant married the widow of a man who had been executed during the Terror.[3] It is impossible to establish whether friends influenced each other to adopt the same political position or whether friendship developed out of similar political views. While accepting the latter as a common occurrence, one must not discount the former as a factor in producing terrorism. The terrorists were men who walked out with, drank with, and visited each other before, during, and after the Terror. On the day that the club at Montbrison was pillaged by the *muscadins*, Chantelauze was strolling with Bruyas, one of the patriotic administrators of the district; when Michel Portier was insulted for being a *clubiste*, he was walking with Pagnon, Morel, Just, and Billard among others.[4] The café was a meeting-place and, although the patriots tended to frequent one and the suspects another, it does not necessarily follow that a man went to one or the other originally because of his political convictions: a petition for one suspect from Montbrisé, signed by several terrorists, alleged as a weighty argument in his favour that he usually went to Simonin's *café* rather than to the *café des Suisses*.[5] Most of the witnesses of an argument 'au café de Montbrisé'

[1] *Papiers inédits omis ou supprimés par Courtois*, ii. 310–11; A.D.L., L 326, fol. 7; A.N., W 408, d. 939, letters to and from Pignon; A.D.R., 42 L 184, d. Maccabéo.

[2] A.D.L., L 81, Philippon to Depart., 7 frim.

[3] Huguet, op. cit., pp. 147, 125. François Guyot's father-in-law owned the house where the refractory priests held services during the Terror (J. Cohas, *Saint-Germain-Laval pendant la Révolution*, p. 120).

[4] A.D.R., 42 L 182, d. Lametherie; A.D.R., 42 L 164, *reg. dél.* of the Mun. of Montbrison, 23 July: Pagnon, *soc. pop.*; Morel, appointed *greffier* of the *juge de paix* by Javogues; Just, father-in-law of Brois, *notable*; Billard, *notable*. Cf. a similar situation at Saint-Chamond (A.D.L., L 390, fol. 14).

[5] A.D.L., L suppl. 96.

in ventôse were terrorists.[1] Finally, in fructidor, Lafaye *le jeune* and David were still meeting at Phalippon's house of an evening despite certain temperamental differences between them.[2]

Indeed, the Terror appears in many ways as a system of acquaintances and friendships at a local level. The terrorists were men who did not merely rely upon their political affinities with other terrorists, but also had a claim upon their affections at difficult moments. When Chavassieu heard a rumour that he had been appointed mayor or *agent national* of Montbrisé, he immediately went round to see Lafaye and Lapalus to get them to tell Javogues that he would not be any good at either of these jobs. He need not, however, have been quite so apprehensive of an outburst of rage from the proconsul over such unpatriotic diffidence. At about the same time as this incident, without any prompting from Chavassieu, Javogues decided to release an ageing canon of his immediate family. Unfortunately, when the old man got home he found that his gold and his silverware had been seized for the Republic and that two soldiers from the *armée révolutionnaire* had been stationed in his house. When he began to abuse them, Chavassieu, patently anxious to avoid a confrontation with some sergeant, hurried off to get Phalippon himself, the commander of the whole detachment in the town. The trouble was that the soldiers demanded to be paid, as was the rule. The old canon not only categorically refused to do so, but even demanded compensation, and eventually began to insult Phalippon also, saying, with a fine innocence of the facts of life in the Year II, that he would take him to court. In a letter relating the whole business to his son, Chavassieu admitted that he fully expected at that point to see the old man back in prison again. However, the next morning, the canon went to see Javogues who received him with great gentleness, indeed embraced him, and took his great age into consideration, and got him both to recognize Phalippon for an honest man and also to pay the required sum to the guards.[3] There can be no doubt whatever that it

1 A.D.L., L 433.

2 A.D.R., 1 L 190.

3 A.D.R., 42 L 147, d. Chavassieu, letter to his son, 11 pluv. It is possible to read this document as saying that Javogues paid; but that seems extravagant.

was personal friendship that averted a disaster here, a disaster not merely with the choleric Javogues who acted so completely out of character in this situation, but also with Phalippon, a man of sound terrorist views about wealthy clerics notwithstanding his easy-going personality. For Pignon, too, friendship was an important element in at least one terrorist partnership. When questioned later by his detractors about his *sous-commissaire* Jourjon, he replied that Jourjon was his friend and visited him daily as a friend and for no other reason.[1] They were practically neighbours: Pignon lived at No. 8, rue Neuve and Jourjon at No. 12.[2] Neighbourliness is, indeed, another factor which should not be discounted too lightly in the formation of a terrorist personnel. A house-to-house survey in Montbrisé, drawn up during pluviôse an II probably in order to help in the distribution of food, gives the names and addresses of all the inhabitants of the town.[3] Certainly, there were quarters of the town that were inhabited predominantly by the rich and the noble, such as, for example, the rue de la Croix and the rue de la Magdeleine. It is also evident that the terrorists came predominantly from one part of the town—the Quartier Sainte-Anne and the extension of these streets into other quarters, together with the Grande Rue. Possibly this reflects the concentration of the service trades in this area, or at least the concentration of the sort of level of wealth in them from which the terrorists were recruited. But the terrorists did not merely live in the same streets, they also tended to form distinct groups of neighbours or near neighbours. However, one cannot attribute any particular influence to the militant terrorists in the creation of this structure, since the distribution of their domiciles does not reveal any significant pattern. On this basis, it is not too exaggerated to suggest that terrorism may have been partly the result of a man's influence on his neighbours, that a man may originally have gone to the club because he was invited to do so by his neighbour on an idle evening, that men may have been recruited into the personnel of the Year II because of recommendations by neighbours who had the ear of the *Représentant* and of the other revolutionary authorities.

1 A.N., W 408, d. 939, interrogation of 25 germ. an II.

2 Ibid.

3 A.D.L., L suppl. 59.

But, since the terrorists came from a social background which produced all brands of political attitude, militant terrorism must be deemed to have been above all the product of a political choice to which all these factors were merely contributory. This choice was the cumulative result of a whole series of successive choices made during the preceding years of the Revolution. By the middle of 1793, a man was in many ways predestined to become a terrorist because his political attitude at that time had emerged progressively from his reactions to such issues as the Flight to Varennes, the religious question, the fall and execution of the King, the September Massacres, the economic crisis, popular misery, military defeat, and the Fall of the Girondins. It is difficult to explain in any other terms the fact that the perfectly respectable lawyer from Saint-Étienne, Pignon, who delivered a funeral oration for Simmonneau in 1792,[1] became, in 1793, a leading Jacobin and later one of the most important terrorists in the department. Naturally, the issues that had a formative influence on each individual varied according to which problem he deemed to be crucial. Johannot, for example, was obviously affected above all by the popular misery engendered by the deepening economic crisis; this led him to formulate economic terrorist demands in early 1793 and to reject the policies of economic liberalism and the rule of law cherished both by the Girondins and by the future federalists.[2] Brunon-Soviche's opinion on the execution of the King demonstrated the emergence of a future terrorist from a political preoccupation with the fragility of the new republic:

> Citoyen, vous connaissez mon caractère; vous savez combien je suis éloigné du sang et du carnage. Eh bien! je ne vous dissimule pas que je regarderais comme un malheur nécessaire l'anéantissement de quelques individus que les lois ne peuvent atteindre et dont la perversité raffiné nuit autant à la République qu'une armée innombrable. Soyez-en sûr, ces scélérats n'attendent que notre départ sur la frontière pour égorger nos femmes et nos enfants ou pour les réduire par la faim.[3]

Matters of purely local interest could also be instrumental in the development of a terrorist. It is perhaps not too

[1] Pignon, *Discours . . . en l'honneur de Simmonneau.*

[2] Above, p. 48.

[3] Letter of 28 Jan. 1793, quoted by Galley, op. cit. i. 417.

exaggerated to say that the terrorist in André Béraud of Saint-Pierre-de-Bœuf began to be formed in 1790 when, as *procureur de la commune*, he championed the population's claims to communal rights on the islands in the Rhône, which had been assimilated into the private property of a local noble, and was promptly dismissed from office by the Department for allowing the inhabitants to invade them.[1] Similarly, Archimbaud of Saint-Rambert, a future captain in the *armée révolutionnaire*, became a popular hero when he led a riot in April 1792 over communal rights to private property in the town moat and was arrested: 1,200 national guards from the area round Saint-Rambert and even from Saint-Étienne marched on Montbrison to release him from prison and there were demonstrations in his favour as far afield as Saint-Chamond.[2] But, above all, it was the religious issue that was the first catalyst in separating the moderates from the future terrorists. It was a problem that united both those preoccupied by the internal dangers to the Revolution and those primarily concerned with popular misery and the difficulties in obtaining adequate food supply at reasonable prices.[3] Village terrorists, particularly in the north of the department, were men whose terrorism was almost exclusively confined to the religious issue; Bouchet and Raymond, both members of the District of Boën, had attempted unsuccessfully to be constitutional curés in the most troublesome parishes of the whole district;[4] Pignon's activities as a *commissaire* demonstrate without a shadow of doubt that religion was the formative influence in his terrorism.[5] In the opposite direction, one should note that the political attitudes of the future federalist mayor of Saint-Étienne were already in the process of development in 1790 when, as president of the District, he allowed refractory priests to officiate in a chapel of the 'béates' at Marlhes: when the Municipality ordered the National Guard to destroy the chapel because ten

[1] A.D.L., L suppl. 140.

[2] A.N., F7 3686, d. 6 (Archimbaud).

[3] Note how in 1791 the village of Trelins reacted against pressure in favour of the constitutional church by refusing to supply the market at Boën (J. Palluat de Bessat, 'La résistance à la constitution civile dans le district de Montbrison, 1791–1792', *Les Amitiés foréziennes et vellaves*, 1926, p. 405).

[4] Ibid., pp. 400–10.

[5] Above, p. 217.

parishes were meeting there on Sundays, he arrived with a detachment of dragoons to punish those responsible for this decision and authorized the priests to use the chapel of his château.[1]

This succession of issues had brought the future terrorists to reject the rule of law and to admit the primacy of *le salut public* even before the federalist crisis. Federalism was the last of the catalysts in this development. Almost all the militants of the Year II suffered at the hands of the *muscadins*—Duret and David, for instance, fled into the Puy-de-Dôme; Berthuel was tied over the mouth of a cannon before being arrested; Curtil, Clément, Personnier, Thévenon, Griot, Chana, Chorel-Laplagny, Decelle, Johannot, etc. were all imprisoned.[2] Indeed, maltreatment by the *muscadins* was a passport to office during the Terror: almost all the members of the Municipality of Armeville, for example, can be identified on the indemnity lists.[3] But, as has already been emphasized elsewhere, the militants of the Year II were a distinct political group before the federalist crisis; it was for this reason that they were attacked by the federalists. Despite the absence of documents from the pre-Terror clubs, it is clear that what was being said in them foreshadowed the Terror and that it was being said by the men who were to become militant terrorists. It was the *clubistes* whom the federalists attacked—men like Pagnon and David were obviously known political figures by the summer of 1793, since the *muscadins* clamoured for their heads; the federalist Dutroncy recognized Raymond, the curé of Trelins, as his enemy because the motions he proposed in the club at Boën were publicly notorious.[4] The political opinions of many of these men were already sufficiently formed by the second half of 1792 to bring them into conflict with the moderates. It was quite obvious, for example, in which direction lay the sympathies of Armelin of Saint-Chamond at that time,

[1] A.D.R., 42 L 175, d. Crouzat.

[2] A.D.L., L 272; A.D.R., 42 L 160, interrogation of Lachaize, 42 L 157, list of those arrested at Montbrison, A.D.R. 42 L 190, d. Vielle; A.D.L., L 394, fol. 22; A.D.R., 42 L 186, d. Pugnet.

[3] A.C. Saint-Étienne, 2 D 12, fol. 16.

[4] A.D.R., 42 L 161, interrogation of Monet, 42 L 164, *reg. dél.* of the Mun. of Montbrison, 16 June.

. . . patriote à grands mots,
Orateur intrépide, éventeur de complots;
Son poitrail est orné d'un ruban tricolore,
Quand sa bouche a fini, son sourcil parle encore.[1]

Guyot of Saint-Germain-Laval frequented the *Club central* at Lyon as early as 1791; the signatures of many of Armeville's leading terrorists were on a petition sent to the Legislative Assembly in May 1792 demanding the dismissal of the Department of the Rhône-et-Loire for having countenanced *fanatisme*; Game had a violent quarrel with another member of the electoral assembly of 1792 who told him that he was a thorough scoundrel and a disgrace to the assembly, to which Game retorted by vilifying several of its most respected personalities.[2] By the spring of 1793 the militants of the Year II were leading agitators—it was Guyot (future *secrétaire général* of the Department) who was mainly responsible for the large number of suspects disarmed at Saint-Germain-Laval; Chana (future member of the Department), Conord (appointed *juge de paix* by Javogues), and Saint-Didier (future secretary of the District of Armeville) were seen as ringleaders by the moderates of Saint-Chamond as early as March 1793; Decelle (future member of the Department) was threatening his political enemies in the same month; as for Costalin (future member of the Department), his soldiers were refusing to serve under him in the National Guard at Roanne in July.[3] It was these militants who led the resistance to federalism in places like Boën,[4] it was they who organized the vote on the Constitution and who carried the result to the Convention.[5] The collapse of federalism

[1] Bibl. Lyon, Coste MS. 1073, [Abbé Combry], 'La Capucinade'.

[2] A.D.R., 42 L 168, d. Chartre; A.N., F¹ᵇ II Rhône 16, d. Saint-Étienne; A.D.L., L suppl. 317.

[3] G. Guigue, *Procès-verbaux des séances du conseil général du Rhône-et-Loire*, ii, 4 July; A.D.R., 42 L 168, d. Callet, 42 L 186, d. Pugnet; Bibl. Roanne, 3 L (1) 20, 21 July. Quite a number of militants may have frequented the *Club central*: this was certainly true of Johannot (above, p. 41), while Vial of Rive-de-Gier was able to recognize a bust of Chalier as 'parfaitement bien imité' (A.D.L., L 79, fol. 10).

[4] e.g. A.D.R., 42 L 164, signatures on a letter from Boën calling the communes to arms, 12 Aug.

[5] e.g. A.D.R., 42 L 164, all the officers of the section des Pénitents at Montbrison for this vote were future terrorists, and Martin, a future captain in the *armée rév.*, was chosen to take the result to Paris (A.D.R., 42 L 186, d. Prodon).

inevitably meant their emergence as the new political leaders. At Saint-Étienne, for example, they immediately took over the sections and the Municipality and began to organize supplies for the army and the town.[1] It was from this position that they found their way into office with the organization of the Terror under Javogues.

Henceforth the Terror provided these men with careers. There was a considerable amount of movement between institutions, and once a terrorist had held even minor office, it was rare for him not to find further employment in the Terror. Almost all the members of the *conseil général* of the Department, for example, were given other jobs when that institution was abolished by the law of 14 frimaire: Lacroix and Clair immediately joined the District of Armeville; Javogues employed Bouarde, Decelle, Portier, and Chartre as his *commissaires* for the investigation into the Committee of Public Safety of Montbrison; Philippon found his way on to the District of Boën in messidor after a period on the revolutionary committee at Fontfort/Saint-Galmier, etc.[2] The *secrétaire général* of the Department moved to be a judge of the *Commission révolutionnaire* and then to be *agent national* of the District of Boën; Lafaye *le jeune*, the *procureur-général-syndic*, was appointed *commissaire des guerres*.[3] Reverchon's reform of the Municipality and committee of Montbrisé in messidor consisted very largely of exchanges between the two bodies.[4] On a different level, Démolis, who had been one of Pignon's *sous-commissaires*, was taken on as a clerk by the Department.[5] There were many other kinds of opportunity available in the Terror. Bouarde, Desarnaud, Goguelin, and Chavassieu all managed to get their sons on to the Department's office staff;[6] Fricour and Bouarde prevailed upon their friends in the Department to nominate their sons for the École de Mars.[7] Claude Phalippon of Montbrisé, who always

[1] Galley, op. cit. i. 699–734. At Montbrison, large numbers of future terrorists were employed in subordinate capacities by the C.P.S. (A.D. P.-de-D., L 2781, *passim*).

[2] A.D.L., L 130, fol. 370; A.N., AF II 137 (1069), d. 30, p. 22; A.D.L., L 262, fol. 85.

[3] A.N., AF II 137 (1069), d. 30, p. 13; A.D.L., loc. cit.; A.D.L., L 18, fol. 193.

[4] A.D.L., L 262, fol. 85.

[5] A.D.L., L 18, fol. 7.

[6] Ibid.

[7] A.D.L., L 327, fol. 21.

had an eye for the main chance, offered his services for repairs to the apartments of the revolutionary committee and turned his house into a depository for sequestrated furniture and other movables;[1] Fonlup obtained the contract for supplying wine to the troops of the *levée en masse*;[2] it was always the *marchand cordier* Gayet-Lacroix who provided the District of Roanne with all the ropes that it needed;[3] and other militants from Montbrisé and Armeville were able to make a little on the side by giving evidence to the revolutionary tribunal.[4]

Before the Terror, the Jacobin militants had been under considerable pressure from their opponents. This produced an apparent unity among them which until the Year II obscured the fact that their political attitudes were by no means uniform. The contrasts between them were not merely confined to the differences in preoccupation and emphasis that were visible among the *commissaires* during the Terror. There was an immense political gulf between a man like Civeton, who felt that a noble who had derogated from his rank before the Revolution by trading could reasonably be considered a patriot, and a man like Chana, who deemed that those who allowed themselves to be seduced by the counter-revolutionaries were more guilty than the counter-revolutionaries themselves.[5] Decelle was so scandalized when the commander of a force that manhandled the curé of Champs claimed to be acting on the orders of Javogues, that he protested to the proconsul that he could not believe that a man as just as he would wish to violate the sacred rights of the individual and his property.[6] Yet Lafaye *le jeune* advocated the *taxe révolutionnaire* in violent terms.[7] Two members of the club of Marcellin-la-Plaine proclaimed 'Liberté, Égalité, mort aux tyrans et aux riches, tyranneaux rebelles, et les ennemis irréconciliables du peuple souverain', but Justamont of the

1 A.D.L., L 434 (1), fol. 1; A.C. Montbrison, *reg. dél.*, no. 2, fol. 156.

2 A.D. P.-de-D., L 2783, p. 6.

3 A.D.L., L 197, *passim*.

4 e.g. A.D.L., L 18, fol. 181. The payment was 6 *livres* per day and witnesses usually spent between five and twelve days at Feurs.

5 A.N. F7 3056, Civeton to Pouilloux, 30 flor. an II; G. Lefebvre, *Société républicaine*, p. 72.

6 A.D.R., 42 L 168, d. Bouarde.

7 A.C. Saint-Étienne, 1 D 10 (3), fol. 103. His brother, Lafaye *aîné* had been vice-president of the Jacobins of Paris in June 1793 (A.N., W 6, d. 252, signature on a letter) and was a member of the *Comm. Temp.* at the time of the *Instruction*. This may account for the attitudes of the younger brother.

District of Boën was quite prepared, when he was a member of the committee of Noirétable in October, to release a highly suspect priest on the grounds that a momentary error could not be considered a crime, especially when it had not harmed the Republic in any way.[1] Only the Parisian Jean Bourgeois had clear affiliations with the Hébertists,[2] but contemporaries evidently considered some men, like Chana and Philippon, to be 'exagérés',[3] while the fact that a few terrorists were able to continue in office during the Year III, whereas a few others subscribed to *L'Ami du Peuple* and *Le Tribun du Peuple*, testifies to radical differences in attitude which must already have existed in the Year II.[4]

It is not surprising, therefore, that increasingly bitter divisions should have emerged during the Year II. After nivôse the terrorists began to fall apart under the pressure of personal antagonisms. At Moingt, for example, an obscure quarrel set Decelle, Bouarde, and the committee at each other's throats during pluviôse and ventôse. Both Decelle and Bouarde had been members of the *conseil général* of the Department and, after the dissolution of this body, Bouarde joined the committee at Moingt. It was his son whom Decelle denounced for the violence employed in the arrest of the curé of Champs and for the curious disappearance of a number of objects from the church. After some hesitation, during which time Bouarde *fils* tried to intimidate Decelle, the committee ordered his arrest. This decision was probably connected with the fact that, a couple of weeks earlier, Bouarde's nephew had denounced two of the members of the committee for embezzlement. There followed a series of petitions and counter-petitions, accusations of despotism, and finally a brawl in the café at Montbrisé.[5] The situation at Moingt

[1] A.D.R., 42 L 187, d. Robert; A.D.L., L 430 (1), 23 Oct.

[2] Bibl. Lyon, Fonds général MS. 3706, Bourgeois to Parein, 18 frim.; A.N. F7 4394 (2), d. 1, pp. 50–1, Bourgeois to Vincent, 3 and 9 niv.

[3] A.N. F1b II Loire 10, d. Objets généraux, Gaulne to the Directory, 24 germ. an IV.

[4] e.g. four of the five members of the Dist. of Montbrison appointed by Charlier and Pocholle, 7 frim. an III, were former terrorists (Bibl. Lyon, Coste MS. 1246, no. 3); Thiolière, Thivet, Bardet, Chana, Delhorme (A.N., F7 4771, d. 3, Lebois), and Chovet-Peyronnet (A.N., F7 3056)—according to Forest et al., *Sur les élections du département de la Loire*, an VI, Chana corresponded with Babeuf.

[5] A.D.R., 42 L 168, d. Bouarde; A.D.L., L 434 (2), fol. 32, L suppl. 513, L 433.

was typical of similar incidents in many places in the department. At Armeville, hostility built up against the mayor Johannot from frimaire onwards. Even before the Terror he had insulted various militants including the *officier municipal* Reynard, who had given him shelter at one time.[1] He was on very bad terms with the powerful Pignon; he quarrelled with Javogues, with the District, and with individual militants.[2] At the end of frimaire, members of both the committee and the Municipality denounced him to the *Représentant du peuple* Girard in the club, and matters reached a climax when Méaulle visited the club in ventôse, for, after a series of denunciations, Johannot was rejected from office by the assembled people.[3]

These quarrels testified to a growing demoralization of the militant terrorists in face of popular lassitude and revulsion against the Terror which, by nivôse, was also beginning to affect them as well in various ways. Despite the *maximum*, the Terror, particularly in its repressive aspects, affected the poor adversely rather than favourably. The case of Berry Labarre, who was the largest shipper of coal out of Rambert-Loire, was typical. After his arrest, petitions flooded in from the *marchands de bois* of the mountain villages round Bonnet-la-Montagne, from the *marchands de charbon*, *voituriers*, and *ouvriers* of the villages round Armeville, from the *marchands de cloux* of Firminy, from the *ouvriers* and *charpentiers en bateaux* of Rambert-Loire, and from the *mariniers* of Saint-Just-sur-Loire.[4] They all pointed out that this one arrest was an economic catastrophe. Yet it was not until 26 ventôse/16 March that a *conseil d'administration* was appointed to carry on his business.[5] Similarly, the inhabitants of Chazelles-sur-Commune-affranchie were complaining vociferously in pluviôse that the arrest of the *marchands chapeliers* of Commune-affranchie had brought their workshops to a

[1] A.D.R., 42 L 42, evidence of Long.

[2] A.N., W 408, d. 939, Johannot to Pignon, 2 Nov. 1793; A.D.R., 42 L 187, d. Revier, Revier to Javogues, 12 pluv.; A.D.L., L 156, fol. 104.

[3] A.D.L., Q 50; A.C. Saint-Étienne, 1 D 10 (3), fol. 135.

[4] A.D.R., 42 L 182, d. Labarre. Cf. the similar situation caused by the arrest of Calemard of Firminy (A.N., W 393, d. 911), also the effect of the arrest of a generous local magnate (A.D.R., 42 L 169, d. Gonin-Larivoire).

[5] A.D.L., L 260, 26 vent.

standstill.[1] The extreme slowness of payment on government contracts and of the distribution of indemnities to the victims of federalism only aggravated the situation.[2] Moreover, the large numbers of lengthy imprisonments without trial were causing resentment. As one militant pointed out to Javogues:

> Le cri particulier réclame contre tant de détentions presque sans fondement. L'intérêt général exige aussi qu'on en dévoile au peuple les motifs. Il ne voit pas de meilleur œil une arrestation dont on ne lui dit pas la raison que nous n'avons regardé dans le temps les lettres de cachet. Ces détentions de quatre mois sans donner aux prévenus des moyens de justification ne lui font pas trouver le gouvernement plus expéditif que celui qu'ils ont secoué. . . . La disette nous entoure de toutes parts . . . cependant l'on retient beaucoup de personnes très utiles à l'agriculture . . . Tu sens bien que les gens gardés et leurs gardiens sont des citoyens perdus à la société. . . . Les campagnes effrayées fuyent les villes et le laboureur tremble dans sa chaumière.[3]

In other words, even some militants were beginning to see the Terror as a tyranny and to consider it responsible for the continuing economic crisis. This sentiment was widespread among the population: at Régny, for example, a small crowd with a violin gathered one night in pluviôse singing: 'vive les pétitionnaires, ils mangeront des bonbons; les autres sont des couillons avec leurs commissaires et ils mangeront de la m . . . .'[4] Towards the end of Javogues's mission public hostility was already beginning to focus on a few militants regarded as mainly responsible for the situation. There was evidently a slander campaign against Duret, for example, in late nivôse and early pluviôse, since he went round various Municipalities collecting testimonials to prove that he had not been implicated in the federalist rebellion.[5] Pignon was under considerable pressure as early as frimaire, when one of his *sous-commissaires* was arrested; he himself was arrested immediately after the recall of Javogues and was never out of trouble again. The District led the attack on him in ventôse,

[1] A.D.L., L 431, collective petition of the local authorities to the Dist. and the Depart., 4 pluv.

[2] e.g. the indemnities were not paid at Armeville until 29 vent. (A.C. Saint-Étienne, 2 D 12, fol. 16).

[3] A.D.R., 42 L 180, d. Game, Game to Javogues, 19 pluv.

[4] A.D.L., L 413, 23 pluv.

[5] A.N., W 193, d. 1.

which is more proof of the deep rifts existing among the militants by then.[1]

The resumption of large-scale arrests after the return of Javogues in late frimaire, the weight of requisitions, the lingering economic depression, and the development of dechristianization made many ordinary terrorists more and more uneasy. There is little doubt that the majority of them participated in the evolution of public opinion at a local level. The members of the club at Feurs must have been increasingly irritated at the way in which Javogues's *commissaires* solved the difficulty of finding horses for the *cavalerie requise* by simply appearing on market-day, when it was already a delicate enough matter to get the peasants to market at all;[2] the arrest of one of its leading members by Javogues brought unanimous protest from the club at Saint-Chamond in pluviôse, while Sibert, of the committee of that town, probably expressed the feelings of many terrorists and militants in the south of the department when he said that, although Javogues was constantly saying that his sole preoccupation was with the happiness of the people, in fact the people had never been in such a bad situation, being completely deprived of all essentials.[3] Terrorist opinion developed during nivôse into a rejection of the repressive aspects of the Terror and led consequently to the increasing isolation of the *Représentant du peuple*, who was identified with them, from the personnel. Even the Department, where Javogues had placed his most trusted men, was affected by this development. Thiolière and Berthuel, together with Lafaye, the former *procureur-général-syndic*, were the first to bring his activities in the Loire to the attention of Reverchon, one of the leaders of the attack on him in the Convention.[4] Two of their colleagues, on the other hand, complained to Javogues in mid pluviôse that at Feurs 'tes amis, qui sont ici en petit nombre

[1] A.N., W 408, d. 939; A.D.R., 42 L 170, d. Pignon, Pignon to Javogues, 25 niv.: 'C'est en vain, cher ami, que l'on cherche à t'atténuer mon patriotisme.'

[2] e.g. A.C. Feurs, *reg. dél.*, 8 pluv.

[3] A.N., loc. cit. (Vier, 12 pluv.); A.N., D III 349, d. Javogues, denunciation dated 7 pluv. Note that, in the middle of pluv., the coal industry of Saint-Chamond was practically paralysed by the requisition of horses for the *cavalerie rév.* (A.N. F1c III Loire 5, 21 pluv.).

[4] A.N., AF III 298 (1181), MS. notes by Reverchon on analysis of a denunciation by Méaudre, Duguet, and Praire, fruct. an IV.

et qui sont étrangers, comme on nous appelle, sont détestés'.[1] Indeed, the Department as a whole had been under fire from at least the beginning of pluviôse.[2] The movement of opinion in the town of Feurs itself, however, seems to have been simply a case of moderate reaction discernible in many areas of France, which was given fuel by Javogues's order of 1 pluviôse/20 January for the arrest of the mayor.[3] The club, apparently prompted by the committee, supported the petitions of a number of detainees, crying, significantly enough, that if such a situation was tolerated they would all end up in prison or even worse.[4] Marino and Delan's account of the public rejoicing in Feurs at the news of Javogues's recall leaves little doubt as to the reality of popular resentment against the proconsul and his policies.[5] By ventôse, matters had reached the point at Feurs where the *ultra* Chana was expelled from the club.[6]

At Montbrisé the local terrorists had always been reluctant to envisage the implementation of any really intensive repressive policies. As early as 9 October, the Auvergnat Committee of Public Safety had encountered hostility to measures of sequestration affecting people other than those designated in Javogues's massive arrest warrant of September.[7] By the beginning of frimaire many terrorists felt that repression had gone as far as local pride, economic welfare, and public tranquillity would allow, and this argument began to be heard in the club. On 5 frimaire/25 November, for instance, Chantemerle *fils aîné* said that it had been most unjust to call the town Montbrisé when it had never been counter-revolutionary but simply a victim of the Lyon conspiracy; it was, therefore, equally an injustice to have deprived the town of the District and the tribunal when it had done no more to forfeit the confidence of the Republic than had Feurs, Boën, and so on.[8] Chantelauze took the same line a few days later in a letter to Javogues, stating that the town had been

[1] A.D.R., 42 L 163, d. Chavassieu, Chavassieu and Potey to Javogues, 17 pluv.
[2] A.D.L., L suppl. 290, fol. 9, Depart. to Javogues, 2 pluv.
[3] A.N., AF II 114 (861) 15. [4] A.D.R., loc. cit.
[5] A.N., T 781, d. Marino, report.
[6] A.D.R., 42 L 149, d. Chappuis de Maubourg, Guyot to Dubessey (vent.).
[7] A.D. P.-de-D., L 2783, p. 6.
[8] A.D.R., 42 L 168, d. Chantemerle *fils*.

purged of its suspect elements and expressing the hope that, now that it was worthy of its *Représentant*, he would once again invest it with his confidence.[1] These were by no means the unauthorized statements of a moderate minority. On 5 frimaire/25 November, the Municipality and the committee issued a joint statement calling for calm (which in itself reveals the extent of public feeling), saying that the proconsuls and the Convention were about to receive an address 'à l'effet de justifier ta conduite et de dissiper tes craintes. Encore un instant et tu goûteras les douceurs de la paix'.[2] It is clear, therefore, that the series of arrests, allied with the current revolutionary rhetoric and the economic disruption, had brought the population of this town as a whole to view the Terror as a kind of sword of Damocles hanging over them: just as garbled versions of events at Lyon had served to aggravate the federalist crisis, so doubtless now did stories of the purging of Commune-affranchie give substance to rumours in a town of which Javogues had spoken so publicly in exactly the terms used of Commune-affranchie. It is equally clear that the local terrorists were far from immune to this decline in public morale. Montbrisé was, however, in a very delicate situation in this respect, for there was no denying that counter-revolution had been more of a reality there than anywhere else in the department. Relief from the Terror depended upon the willingness of the *Représentant* to stop the Terror, a leniency in which Javogues had no inclination to indulge. In mid nivôse, one local terrorist noted that the town was still in a state of extreme nervousness.[3] At this point the inhabitants of Montbrisé turned on the old enemy, the Auvergnats. It was on 18 nivôse/7 January that the revolutionary committee began to hold an inquiry into the embezzlements allegedly made by the *levée en masse* and the Committee of Public Safety.[4] The Auvergnats had become

[1] A.D.R., 42 L 182, d. Lachasse.

[2] A.D.L., L 434 (1), fol. 11; A.N., D IVbis 84, d. Loire, the Jacobins of Paris to the *Comité de Division*, 23 frim., summarizing a letter from the institutions at Montbrisé.

[3] A.D.R., 42 L 147, d. Chavassieu, Chavassieu to his son, 15 niv.

[4] A.D.L., L 434 (5). For the rest of this paragraph, see C. Lucas, 'Auvergnats et Foréziens pendant la mission du conventionnel Javogues', in *Gilbert Romme et son temps*, pp. 137–47.

the paragons of republican virtue as a result of their contribution to the capture of Lyon, which Couthon and Maignet had carefully publicized. The development of the theory of their culpability and its successful presentation to Javogues represented the attempt by the inhabitants of Montbrisé to shift opprobrium off themselves on to someone else guilty of an even more heinous crime in the terrorist scale of values than federalism. It was in this way that they sought (with quite accidental success) to put an end to intensive repression and to return to normality. The selection of *l'étranger* as the scapegoat was typical of the Terror—this tactic was also visible in a primitive form at Feurs;[1] it reached its greatest extent with the attack of the inhabitants of Commune-affranchie on the Parisians between pluviôse and germinal.[2]

As far as the terrorists of Armeville are concerned, it was essentially economic motives that originally led them to demand the end of repression. In early nivôse the revolutionary committee sent to the Convention a petition countersigned by the District in which it demanded the abrogation of the law of 12 July 1793 in so far as it applied to Armeville.[3] It explained in great detail that the citizens of Armeville were indeed patriots and not rebels since they had resisted the *muscadins* and expelled them from the city; but above all, it predicted that the application of this law at the present time would cause irreparable damage, because it would throw into prison not merely wayward countryfolk but also a great number of both employers and workers in the arms industry. Although the basic problem was exactly the same as that at Montbrisé, the inhabitants of Armeville found a different solution. Salvation came with the *Représentant* Girard de l'Aude in late frimaire. Faced with the contrast between Girard and Javogues, who were both in Armeville at the same time, the inhabitants and the terrorists gave their allegiance to the former and viewed the latter with growing suspicion. In the first place, Girard's mission was

[1] Above, p. 345.

[2] E. Herriot, *Lyon n'est plus*, iii. 402 ff. Note also a similar development at Nantes (G. Martin, *Carrier et sa mission à Nantes*, p. 385).

[3] A.N., D III 124, d. Saint-Étienne. The law of 12 July declared traitors all public officials who had participated in or tolerated the existence of the federalist *Commission populaire*.

confined to the arms industry. He was, therefore, actively engaged in remedying the economic crisis, whereas Javogues was preoccupied with political matters which the inhabitants of Armeville increasingly considered to be past history, and not merely irrelevant but positively harmful to the crucial problems of the day. In the second place, Armeville found Girard to be a much more realistic and approachable man than Javogues. An incident involving Salichon and his son, both of whom were under arrest at the time, illustrates the contrast between Girard and Javogues as it must have appeared to the inhabitants of Armeville. The father was called in before the *Représentants* first. As soon as Girard learned that he had been arrested because a large amount of soap had been found on his premises, his attitude relaxed and, when Salichon informed Dorfeuille that he was neither rich nor a noble, Girard told him that he could go. But when the younger Salichon appeared:

> Le Représentant Javogues me dit: Comment, coquin, tu oses te présenter devant moi? Tu crois donc que j'ignore tes crimes et tes forfaits contre la Représentation nationale? Je te réponds que tu peux dormir ce soir d'où tu viens, car, sans ceux qui sont présents, je t'aurais déjà expédié pour l'autre monde. . . . Après quelques instants de délibération, mon sort fut remis entre les mains du Représentant Girard, qui m'élargit vingt-quatre heures après.[1]

By early pluviôse, Javogues was aware that his policies had ceased to find a response at Armeville. It was partly for this reason that he turned on Dorfeuille, who had been helping Girard to organize the arms industry, and accused him of having established counter-revolution; and that he attacked Pignon and Chovet-Peyronnet and said that the club was made up solely of 'Riches'[2]—in this case an epithet describing a political attitude which refuses to destroy all the enemies of the People. When Javogues retaliated by refusing to release money for essential payments, popular resentment against him in Armeville was so great that the National Guard wanted to march on Montbrisé; the club sang Girard's praises to the Convention and the committee denounced Javogues.[3]

[1] Quoted in J. M. Devet, *Une Prison en 1793 et 1794*, p. 111.

[2] A.N., AF II 114 (861) 15, letter of 22 pluv.

[3] Below, p. 362.

This rejection of all that Javogues stood for by so many terrorists in the major centres of the department explains why, although the same personnel continued in office for the rest of the Terror, the recall of the *Représentant* marked the end of repression and the rapid transformation of the Terror into a comparatively benign system of governmental *dirigisme*. Certainly, the terrorists felt obliged to forward a few testimonials to Paris in the wake of the proconsul. But they were brief and had a suspicious flavour of the obituary about them. The club at Armeville only sent a short paragraph of the vaguest generalizations.[1] At Montbrisé, it was the Municipality that made the effort, but after devoting most of its address to his career before the Terror and to his part in the siege of Lyon, it concluded that, if Javogues had dealt harshly with all who appeared to have been connected with the conspiracy, 'ce n'a été sans doute que parce que les circonstances l'exigeaient pour le salut de la République'.[2] As for the club at Saint-Chamond, it decided that 'il serait injurieux de vouloir justifier la conduite du citoyen Javogues'.[3]

1 A.N., D III 349, d. Javogues, 10 vent.
2 A.C. Montbrison, *reg. dél.*, no. 2, fol. 66 (14 vent.).
3 Lefebvre, op. cit., p. 155 (25 pluv.).

XII

THE END OF THE MISSION

THE decree of 20 pluviôse/8 February, which recalled Javogues, was the culmination of a long series of incidents which had set him at odds with the central government and with his colleagues. Although his activities within the department of the Loire reveal a preoccupation with order and hierarchy, his relations with the Committee of Public Safety and other *Représentants en mission* provide a case study of the confusion of the 'anarchical' Terror. Javogues displayed precisely that fractious insubordination that the law of 14 frimaire was designed to eliminate. His impenitent indifference to the provisions of that law illustrates the limits on the government's control over the Terror even in nivôse. His recall must be placed alongside that of such men as Taillefer, Mallarmé, and Dartigoëyte as an integral part of the extension of that control. Moreover, these incidents took place against the background of a mounting unison of recrimination against the proconsul. In this, Javogues again illustrates a theme of national history, for many of these denunciations were part of the moderate offensive of the mid winter of Year II, of which Chasles and Carrier, for example, also fell foul.[1]

The function of a *Représentant en mission* as an *agent de liaison* was twofold. On the one hand, he had to inform the central government of conditions in the departments, and on the other, he had to supervise the execution of the government's policies there. Javogues failed altogether to accomplish either task. Clearly, however, it was not really until frimaire that relations between him and the Committee of Public Safety began to deteriorate, since the Committee's decision to send him into the Saône-et-Loire in brumaire

[1] C. Pichois and J. Dautry, *Le Conventionnel Chasles et ses idées démocratiques*, pp. 59–65; G. Martin, *Carrier et sa mission à Nantes*, pp. 347–70. Carrier was recalled on the same day as Javogues.

shows that it had no complaint against him at that time. Javogues was never a model of assiduity in keeping contact with the central government. Nevertheless, during the siege of Lyon he had written four letters, and in October he wrote from Armeville hinting briefly at his actions in the Loire.[1] Rapidly, however, any eagerness to inform the central government dwindled. It was only in response to two inquiries on points of detail that in mid frimaire he was moved to forward to the Committee of Public Safety a succinct account of his activities in the Saône-et-Loire together with copies of his *arrêtés*.[2] At the beginning of nivôse the Committee received two letters from Girard and Javogues jointly. But one was merely countersigned by Javogues, while the other, which sent a copy of the *arrêté* maintaining the *armée révolutionnaire*, was possibly also written by Girard in order to cover himself in respect of the law of 14 frimaire.[3] The letter which Javogues requested Collot d'Herbois to communicate to the Committee in pluviôse was not a report but a challenge.[4] Finally, a brief account of his latest actions addressed formally to a 'citoyen collègue' on 22 pluviôse/10 February was possibly intended for the president of the Convention, given Javogues's mistrust of the politics of the Committee of Public Safety by that time.[5] Throughout his mission, the government's knowledge of Javogues's activities was very rarely gleaned directly from the proconsul himself. He stands in complete contrast to Carrier and Joseph Le Bon, for example. Both these men kept the central government constantly informed of their decisions and policies, while Le Bon at least was always seeking the advice and direction of the Committee of Public Safety.[6] Some of the most striking misdeeds of the 'anarchical' Terror are associated with the name of Carrier, while in the Year III

[1] A.N., AF II 184, d. 1521, p. 20, 10 Sept.; ibid., d. 1522, p. 44, 17 Sept.; AF II 150, d. 1213, p. 35, 30 Sept.; *Papiers inédits omis ou supprimés par Courtois*, ii. 302, 10 Oct.—excluding his signature on collective letters. A.N., AF II 411, d. 3308, p. 35, 21 Oct.—letter also signed by Bassal but in Javogues's hand.

[2] A.D.L., L suppl. 95 and L 18, C.P.S. to Javogues, 19 brum. and 3 frim; A.N., AF II 186, d. 1539, p. 13, Javogues to C.P.S., 18 frim.

[3] A.N., AF II 411, d. 3306, p. 56, 2 niv.; AF II 186, d. 1543, p. 3, analysis of a letter of 6 niv.

[4] A.N., AF II 114 (861) 15, 16 pluv.

[5] Ibid., 22 pluv.

[6] Martin, op. cit., p. 48; L. Jacob, *Joseph Le Bon*, i. 273.

both he and Le Bon became symbols of all that was excessive and horrible in the Year II. In fact, however, these two *Représentants en mission* always behaved above all as agents of the central government; it is a man like Javogues who epitomizes much more accurately the failure of the 'anarchical' Terror to provide a co-ordinated system of government.

In equal contrast with Javogues's behaviour was Le Bon's unquestioning submission to the dictates of the Committee of Public Safety, especially in the speed with which he obeyed his recall. Javogues, however, steadfastly ignored instructions from Paris and major pieces of legislation. Clearly, therefore, his activities could not contribute towards the co-ordination and coercion of the nation behind the leadership of the government. Again, it was not until frimaire that the divergence between the government's views and those of Javogues became apparent. On the one hand, his activities were unexceptionable until he started to implement his democratic programme in the Saône-et-Loire and the Loire; on the other, the policies of the Committee of Public Safety were in the main somewhat fluid until the decisions of late brumaire, which prepared the great change of course in frimaire. Thus, precisely at the moment when the Committee was moving in one direction, Javogues was moving in the other. It was at this point that the Committee lost control over him. Writing to it from the Saône-et-Loire on 18 frimaire/8 December, Javogues launched into the typical complaints of the overworked *Représentant* and demanded his recall.[1] Before receipt of this letter, the Committee had already complied by including him among several proconsuls recalled on 21 frimaire/11 December.[2] Javogues, however, changed his mind and moved on to the Loire in defiance of this order. He was recalled a second time, when he was not included among those *Représentants* appointed on 9 nivôse/29 December for the organization of the *gouvernement révolutionnaire*.[3] The powers of all *Représentants en mission* excluded from the list were terminated at this point. Javogues ignored the whole question. On 10 pluviôse/29 January, the Committee wrote

[1] A.N., AF II 186, d. 1539, p. 13, letter received 26 frim.
[2] A.N., AF II 36, d. 295, pp. 76–7.
[3] A.N., AF II 37, d. 296, pp. 6, 15.

him a letter which, considering the increasingly bitter criticisms levelled against him, was surprisingly mild. It pointed out that the Loire was now under the supervision of the *Représentants* at Commune-affranchie, thus rendering his mission purposeless, and it expressed its confidence that he would be all the more eager to return, since the Committee had granted more than a month ago his request for a recall because it had found his reasons so convincing.[1] Eventually Javogues's compliance was obtained only by a decree of the Convention on 20 pluviôse/8 February threatening him with arrest unless he returned within eight days.[2]

Thus, Javogues had defied the Committee of Public Safety for two months. It is not altogether clear why the Committee allowed him to get away with it. This situation suggests that, ultimately, it had very little hold over a *Représentant en mission* who simply refused to obey. In the last resort, it could only coerce such men through the wrath of the Convention. Yet it could not afford to use this weapon too often, for that would undermine its authority, which, as with all the institutions of the Terror, resided much more in what it could threaten to do than in what it actually did. It only had recourse to the Convention when it was politic to make an example, as was the case in mid pluviôse. Javogues was not the only proconsul to disobey a recall, though few could match his supreme indifference and usually offered objections and excuses. In nivôse–pluviôse, Chasles remained at Lille for nearly a month on the pretext of his wound, while in ventôse the Committee gave up an attempt to transfer Florent Guiot from the Nord to Brittany.[3] Both these cases date from after the law of 14 frimaire, as does that of Javogues: by itself this law did little to change the insubordination of proconsuls beyond laying down rules for their conduct and giving a pretext for a purge of the less pliable and less orthodox elements among those already out on mission.

The legality of the whole of Javogues's second period in the Loire is therefore debatable. Already his actions in the Ain

[1] Ibid., p. 68, rough draft. This mildness seems to have been standard technique: Carrier was handled in the same way (Martin, op. cit., p. 370).

[2] *Procès-verbal de la Convention nationale*, xxxi. 98.

[3] Pichois and Dautry, op. cit., pp. 65–7; Jacob, op. cit., i. 324–6.

could be questioned in this respect. Admittedly, his original commission had included this department. But the fact that in brumaire the Convention issued him with powers for the Saône-et-Loire, which had also been in his original commission, indicates that the government thought that this had expired with the fall of Lyon. Similarly, the fact that Collot wrote asking for powers for Javogues in the Ain reveals that both of them were uncertain of the situation. Beyond all this, however, it is Javogues's reaction to the law of 14 frimaire that marks most clearly his relationship with the central government and his place in the history of the Terror. Before this law, Javogues certainly behaved impoliticly and did not operate altogether as intended, but he rarely acted illegally; after this law, his most important actions were either illegal or supported by justifications so tenuous as to amount to pure chicanery.

The text of the law was officially received by the Department of the Loire on 3 nivôse/23 December and immediately circulated.[1] However, even in the Loire it was already known before that date,[2] while at Commune-affranchie it was read out to the *Commission Temporaire* on 20 frimaire/10 December, although, significantly enough, it was not applied by that body until 25 frimaire/15 December.[3] Therefore the text was being studied and discussed in the circle of the proconsuls there precisely at the time Javogues passed through on his way to the Loire. Unfortunately one can reach no firm conclusion as to whether Javogues's subsequent behaviour reflects the first reactions of Fouché, Collot d'Herbois, and Laporte. If so, this would suggest that Collot, member of the Committee of Public Safety, was not consulted during the drafting of this legislation, which united a substantial consensus of opinion in the Committee.[4]

Javogues's disobedience to the law of 14 frimaire went far beyond his failure to report to the Committee of Public Safety every ten days. He denied that the law could be

[1] A.D.L., L 79, fol. 32.

[2] Cf. A.D.L., L 81, Dist. of Armeville to Depart., 2 niv.

[3] A.D.R., 31 L 50, 25 frim. It was registered by the Depart. of the Rhône on 1 niv. (A.D.R., 1 L 87).

[4] Cf. Richard Cobb, *Les Armées révolutionnaires*, ii. 748–53.

applied to the department of the Loire and he therefore proceeded to ignore it. He based this argument upon article 20 of section III:

> Aucune force armée, aucune taxe, aucun emprunt forcé ou volontaire ne pourront être levés qu'en vertu d'un décret. Les taxes révolutionnaires des représentants du peuple n'auront d'exécution qu'après avoir été approuvées par la Convention, à moins que ce ne soit en pays ennemi ou rebelle.

Javogues claimed that the Loire was a 'pays rebelle'. On this premise he could legitimately impose a *taxe révolutionnaire* in spite of the law. However, his *arrêté* which prescribed a tax throughout the department had to admit that, in these terms, it was a case of prevention, that it was only by forcing the rich to help the poor that one could avoid an insurrection.[1] But even on this premise, the text of article 20 only applied to *taxes révolutionnaires*. It did not justify him, as he said that it did, in maintaining the *armée révolutionnaire*.[2] Thus Claude Javogues, without any proper authority even to be on mission, kept the government in ignorance of his activities and maintained institutions and practices specifically abolished in the interests of national homogeneity and political expediency. Indeed, only in one instance did he ever refer publicly in an *arrêté* to the law of 14 frimaire.[3] In all this Javogues was far less cautious than his colleagues at Ville-affranchie. They felt that they could go no further than state that the law of 14 frimaire was not retroactive and that *taxes révolutionnaires* imposed previously would be collected.[4]

Javogues's policy of dechristianization also revealed his contempt for legislation that did not please him. In this case again, he was more frankly hostile to the government than the proconsuls at Ville-affranchie. There, the excesses against religion took place well before the law of 16 frimaire/6 December, which forbade 'toutes violences et mesures contraires à la liberté des cultes'.[5] The *arrêté* of Fouché, Albitte, and Laporte of 17 nivôse/6 January was a masterly demonstration of just how far one could dechristianize within the

[1] A.N., AF II 114 (861) 14, *arrêté* of 6 niv.
[2] Ibid., other *arrêté* of 6 niv. [3] Ibid.
[4] A.N., AF II 137 (1062), d. 6, p. 7, *arrêté* of 26 frim.
[5] E. Herriot, *Lyon n'est plus*, iii. 90–4, 122–8.

terms of the law of 16 frimaire.[1] In the Loire, however, the dechristianization campaign was at its most intense in nivôse and pluviôse. In this context, it must be emphasized that Javogues had probably learnt of the decree of 16 frimaire during his visit to Commune-affranchie, and that, in any case, he made no effort to rescind his own *arrêté* of 1 nivôse/21 December and stop dechristianization in the light of it.

When Javogues alleged that the department of the Loire was a 'pays rebelle', he was not consciously guilty of sophistry. He did not merely feel that the laws of 14 and 16 frimaire undermined the capacity of the People to defend itself against its enemies and destroyed tools for the construction of the Democratic Republic. For Javogues, these laws were enacted at precisely the moment when the threat to the People from its enemies was very real indeed, so real that he felt that the Loire was on the verge of civil war again. It was his diagnosis of the social and economic crisis of the mid winter of Year II that led him to this conclusion. The manifestations of this crisis appeared to him as symptoms of imminent rebellion. This was the gist of the preambles to his *arrêtés* of 6 nivôse/26 December concerning the *armée révolutionnaire* and the *taxe révolutionnaire*.[2] On the one hand, the *maximum* was being continually violated, food was scarce, and in the mountain areas there were an increasing number of religious riots and attacks on the statues of Liberty as Christmas approached: here, believed Javogues, was the evidence that the plot hatched by the rich landowners, the *négociants*, and the priests was being brought to fruition. On the other hand, the murmurings of the populace revealed that, tired of the sufferings of hunger and the degradation of beggary, the poor were about to rise up and use violence. Such a combination constituted an emergency, and thus Javogues felt himself to be entirely justified by local conditions in ignoring the developments of governmental policy in frimaire–nivôse. But this decision constituted a definitive rupture between Javogues and the Committee of Public Safety. In the first place, as the incidents caused by his activities increased, the Committee could tolerate him less and less. He

[1] A.N., AF II 83 (615) 3.
[2] A.N., AF II 114 (861) 14.

was an element of disruption in a system that the Committee wished to be monolithic: on the one hand, he appeared to justify the dangerous moderate offensive against the *gouvernement révolutionnaire*, on the other he represented the equally dangerous ultra-revolutionaries. In the second place, Javogues's view on the laws of 14 and 16 frimaire inevitably led him to suspect the motives of the Committee of Public Safety. These suspicions deepened into certainties when the Committee attempted to remedy the damage done by his initiatives in the Saône-et-Loire and the Ain and when he came into conflict with Couthon, member of the Committee. From there it was only a step to attributing his difficulties with the moderate offensive to the collusion, if not the instigation, of the Committee. And once so pure a revolutionary as Javogues knew himself to be had accepted this as fact, then the conclusion was inescapable. The *liberté des cultes* was synonymous with the rule of religion, he told Collot d'Herbois in mid pluviôse, and the system of *agents nationaux* merely established so many little dictators. Indeed, this latter was, he thought, remarkably like a plan that Dumouriez had had, and all this legislation presented so much material for intrigues and conspiracies that it was quite obvious that there were men working solely for personal gain and still hoping to enslave the People anew:

> Oui, il existe un plan de Contre-Révolution dans le Comité de Salut public; j'en ai vu les faits se développer partout où j'ai passé. On a cherché à faire rétrograder la Révolution en envoyant des hommes qui paralysaient des arrêtés vigoureux. Les patriotes tremblent; je ne sais quel sera le terme où on cessera de les vexer.[1]

From the beginning, the succession of incidents that led ultimately to the decree against Javogues conformed to a fairly consistent pattern. They were usually of Javogues's making, in that his violent character and his political manichaeism provoked him into ill-considered outbursts. Most of the incidents were distorted and indeed sometimes caused by his fierce involvement in local feuds, which, whether ancient or contemporary, were expressed in the political terms of the day. Often his temper was inflamed by the resistance that

[1] A.N., AF II 114 (861) 15, Javogues to Collot, 16 pluv.

moderate and orthodox opposed to his comprehensively energetic programme. His policies of intensive repression suited an area that had been in rebellion. Yet most of the region in which he pursued his mission lay either on the edge of or outside the area of the rebellion and had been implicated in it either indirectly or not at all. The proximity of former centres of rebellion made their uncontaminated neighbours intensely anxious to dissociate themselves from them and from all the acute discomforts attached to their position. Significantly enough, hostility to Javogues in the districts of Armeville and Boën was not usually expressed directly and publicly. He encountered overt resistance above all because his actions tended to assimilate non-rebellious areas to rebellious, because policies of intensive repression appeared to be in themselves proof of guilt. This was a real threat: the District of Marcigny, for example, was remarkably ready to brand neighbouring Roanne as an accomplice of Lyon, while, when Javogues had publicly mentioned (Saint-Symphorien-de-) Lay as a centre of conspiracy, the club at Régny promptly refused affiliation to the club there because of the rumour that the town had been declared to be in rebellion, 'que même il en est en quelque façon parlé par l'arrêté du Représentant du peuple'.[1] Hence almost all Javogues's opponents recounted at great length their patriotic deeds during 1793, all protested against any identification of themselves with Lyon.[2] Moreover, resistance to Javogues was always waged in much the same pattern. In order to guard against the dangers inherent in opposing a *Représentant du peuple* and in order to make their case more convincing against his established patriotism, his enemies always expressed themselves through clubs, revolutionary committees, and recently purged administrations, which provided an ostensible guarantee of their terrorist devotion. Against the might of one *Représentant en mission* they appealed both to other proconsuls (particularly those at Commune-affranchie) and to the central government. In Paris the goodwill of local

[1] A.D. S.-et-L., 1 L 7/43, no. 299, Dist. of Marcigny to Dept. of Saône-et-Loire, 16 niv.; A.D.L., L 416, fol. 6.

[2] e.g. *La Société populaire de Villefranche-sur-Saône à la Convention nationale*, p. 1: 'L'on semble vouloir les faire passer pour des contre-révolutionnaires semblables aux rebelles lyonnais.'

members of the Convention was enlisted as patronage for their lobbying and as testimony to their republican virtue. Thus was formed a consensus of apparently and often genuinely terrorist reprobation against Javogues.

Well before news of Javogues's extravagances in the Loire started to reach Paris, the authorities in the capital had begun to form an unfavourable impression of the proconsul. His quarrelling in the Saône-et-Loire and the Ain had brought a steady stream of reports and petitions against him during the second half of frimaire and early nivôse. In the Saône-et-Loire, the perennial rivalry between the major urban centres had resolved itself by the Year II into an alliance between Mâcon and Autun against Châlon-sur-Saône. Heeding the insinuations of the terrorists of the former towns, Javogues, in a flurry of abuse and accusation about Châlon's counter-revolutionary character, stripped it of the criminal tribunal in favour of Autun.[1] At the same time he abolished the district of Bellevue-les-Bains/Bourbon-Lancy on similar grounds of incorrigible addiction to counter-revolution and incorporated much of the area into the district of Autun, whose authorities had been yearning for just this since 1790.[2] The authorities of both Bellevue and Châlon launched campaigns of self-justification against the allegations of Javogues, sending *commissaires* with petitions and testimonials to the Committee of Public Safety and circulating polemical addresses round the Republic.[3] The campaign by Châlon was particularly effective since, unlike Bellevue-les-Bains, the regular and extra-ordinary authorities here had relatively clean records and could demonstrate without difficulty the inaccuracies and absurdities of the sweeping accusations which Javogues had so typically made. By 25 frimaire/15 December their *commissaires* had persuaded the Committee of Public Safety to annul Javogues's decision on the criminal tribunal. Robespierre, at least, must have been convinced by the disturbing portrait drawn of Javogues, for, after noting that the *Représentant* had already been recalled (on 21 frimaire/11 December), he crossed out in his draft of

[1] A.N., AF II 138 (1077), p. 15, 13 frim. [2] Ibid., p. 16, 13 frim.

[3] e.g. A.N., AF II 59, d. 431, p. 14; *Extrait des registres . . . de la Société populaire de Châlon-sur-Saône*; A.D. S.-et-L., 2 L 94, fol. 3.

this *arrêté* the usual 'témoignage authentique à la vertu républicaine de ce représentant'.[1]

When Javogues moved into the Ain on 20 frimaire/10 December, he ran straight into further trouble. Believing, on the advice of a group of militants from Bourg, that this town was on the verge of open rebellion, he immediately appointed a revolutionary tribunal and set about providing work for it.[2] Within two days this programme had produced a near-riot, which was only averted by the arrival of the *Représentant* Gouly on mission for the implementation of the law of 14 frimaire. Javogues left for Commune-affranchie after a bitter quarrel with Gouly, who hastened to inform the Committee of Public Safety of the situation that he had found at Bourg.[3] The Committee responded swiftly by ordering Gouly to examine all Javogues's *arrêtés* in the Ain and the Saône-et-Loire and to suspend any that he considered useless or harmful.[4] Gouly, a moderate, proceeded to annul all the stringent measures of Terror that Javogues had put into effect. When Javogues heard of this public indictment of his work, he published a long denunciation of 'la perfidie et les complots ténébreux de l'infâme Gouly' and concluded by ordering the arrest of this 'tyran d'azie'.[5] But since, by this time, Javogues was in the Loire and Gouly's mission had come to an end, in practice this amounted to little more than rhetoric.

By mid nivôse all the evidence about Javogues in the possession of the central government pointed one way: that he was a factor of disruption, capable of the most extreme acts of anarchical behaviour. Clearly, the Committee of Public Safety had condemned him. But, having recalled him on 21 frimaire/11 December, the Committee dismissed Javogues from its mind as neutralized. Subsequent complaints from the Saône-et-Loire and the Ain, therefore, simply needed rectifying but did not involve any action against the proconsul. But, on 20 nivôse/9 January, the Convention was presented with the petition of an inhabitant of the Loire who complained

1 A.N., AF II 59, d. 431, p. 13, draft in Robespierre's hand and signed by him.

2 *Vie révolutionnaire de Blanq Desisles*, pp. 22–3; B. Gouly, *Compte rendu à la Convention nationale*.

3 A.N., AF II 186, d. 1540, p. 23.

4 A.N., AF II 84 (621), 14 niv.

5 Ibid., p. 22.

that Javogues had arrested him on false information; a routine incident, which the Convention appropriately handled by forwarding the petition to Javogues—but some must have wondered why Javogues was in the Loire at all.[1] At about the same time, that vindictive moderate Guffroy was receiving Lepoully's detailed denunciation of Javogues's performance at Commune d'Armes; on 17 nivôse/6 January, the Committee of Public Safety received the letter from Javogues and Girard which announced that the *armée révolutionnaire* would be maintained; on 26 nivôse/15 January, it listened to Bardet, president of the revolutionary tribunal at Feurs, who presented a report on the activities of the tribunal together with Javogues's irate letter suspending it—obviously he must have been questioned about the state of affairs in the Loire.[2] Thus, not only was the issue of Javogues not dead, but the Committee of Public Safety possessed a considerable amount of information about him despite his silence, and this was to be augmented rapidly in early pluviôse.

It was not until the end of nivôse that Javogues's behaviour in the Loire began to cause sufficient disturbance to be noticed in Paris. He quarrelled with terrorists and moderates alike and rapidly created a situation in which the protests of the former lent authenticity to the accusations behind which the latter concealed their political manœuvres. His quarrel with the proconsul Girard de l'Aude at Armeville was particularly important in this respect, for although it was not accompanied by the flamboyant publicity that marked so many of his fracas, it provided terrorist evidence of the persistence of Javogues's previous unruly conduct. In part, this was a clash between totally opposed personalities. Javogues could have little in common with a proconsul who wrote to one of the terrorists of the *Commission des Sept* at Commune-affranchie in such terms as 'je me procure une jouissance délicieuse en communiquant avec un vertueux citoyen', 'si tu peux, incorruptible républicain, sans altérer la délicatesse de tes sentiments', etc.[3] In part also it may have

[1] *Arch. parlementaires*, 83, p. 142.

[2] A.N., D III 349, d. Javogues, covering note dated 6 niv.; A.N., AF II 186, d. 1543, p. 3; A.N., D III 349, d. Javogues, Bardet to C.P.S., n.d. (flor. ?).

[3] A.D.R., 42 L 187, d. Ravel, letter dated 4 vent.

been resentment at the way in which the militants of Armeville transferred their allegiance to the more approachable and humane Girard. Certainly, Javogues was convinced that Girard patronized disreputable elements.[1] This belief was aggravated by Girard's friendship with Dorfeuille, for whose arrest Javogues issued a warrant in late nivôse,[2] and also by a denunciation from one of the revolutionary committees at Ville-affranchie against Girard's secretary, to which Javogues responded with an arrest warrant.[3] The dispute between the proconsuls broke out over the 2,000,000 *livres* that Javogues had requested the government to allocate to the district of Armeville for the arms industry and for the conversion of the silk workers.[4] Eventually the government authorized Girard, now in charge of the arms industry, to take the sum from the treasury of the Department. However, the Department viewed Girard and Armeville with as much suspicion as did Javogues, and when *commissaires* came to collect the sum on 27 nivôse/16 January, it warned Javogues, who was then at Montbrisé.[5] The roads were watched and the convoy intercepted.[6] Javogues kept the consignment and sent the *commissaires* back to Armeville 'en leur tenant des discours incendiaires'. Girard sent them back with a letter to Javogues, who told them that they did not have a proper escort for such an important consignment and that he would see to its dispatch. When Girard wrote to the Committee of Public Safety to complain about the whole incident on 6 pluviôse/25 January, the money still had not appeared. Girard's letter could not fail to incriminate his colleague. He recounted the difficulty he had had in restraining the citizens from setting off armed for Montbrisé, for a great many poor were depending upon the arrival of the money, as were all those, especially the armourers, to whom the District owed

[1] A.N., AF II 114 (861) 15, letter dated 22 pluv.: 'Le pauvre Girard qui a des vues droites mais qui s'est laissé mal entourer . . .'

[2] A.D.R., 42 L 170, d. Pignon, Pignon to Javogues, 11 pluv.; Bibl. Lyon, Coste MS. 681, no. 6, Girard to *Repr.* at Cne-aff., 28 niv.

[3] A.D.R., 42 L 171, d. Perier, accused of being an ex-priest and an ex-federalist, 6 pluv.

[4] A.N., AF II 411, d. 3306, p. 56, Girard and Javogues to C.P.S., 2 niv.

[5] A.D.L., L 18, fol. 142.

[6] For the rest of the paragraph, A.N., AF II 411, d. 3306, p. 58, Girard to C.P.S., 6 niv. (= pluv.).

money;[1] he emphasized that, since he had been acting according to the Committee's orders, its power had been openly defied, and concluded that only his restraint had avoided a scandalous scene between two members of the Convention. On 7 pluviôse/26 January the club at Armeville underwrote Girard's reliability in a eulogy to the Convention, although it refrained from mentioning Javogues; on 12 pluviôse/31 January, the Committee of Public Safety received more direct support for Girard from the revolutionary committee, which complained about Javogues's behaviour.[2]

But Javogues's most virulent and effective enemies in the Loire were to be found at Roanne. The persistent moderatism of both the regular and the extra-ordinary administrations in that town inevitably destined it to become a centre for the moderate offensive. Throughout the period the inhabitants of Roanne devoted themselves to avoiding the Terror and especially repression as far as possible. The equivocal behaviour of the oligarchy during the federalist crisis had left it, its property, and its control over the town vulnerable. Since it dominated all the institutions in the town, even after the renewal of the regular authorities in brumaire, it was safe provided that it was left alone. Therefore the whole of its energy was directed towards discrediting and removing all external agents of repression. The basic issue was clear: was Roanne to be classed as an accomplice of Lyon and hence to be subjected to intensive repression in the same way as Montbrisé and Armeville? In order to prevent any affirmative answer to this question, the authorities of Roanne exploited to the full the fact that, however ambiguous the conduct of the administrations, this was the only major town of the Loire not to have welcomed the *muscadins*, and that its National Guard had finally marched against Lyon with apparent willingness. These were the arguments with which the District dispatched *commissaires* to the Convention on 5 frimaire/25 November seeking an end to Lapalus's

[1] When some supply had been received from Cne-aff. in late niv., the Dist. treasurer had paid out 400,000 *livres* in two days, so behind was he; the failure to receive the two millions had meant the suspension of all payments for arms at the end of niv. (A.D.L., L 156, fol. 99).

[2] *Adresse de la Société populaire de Commune d'Armes* . . .; A.N., AF II 37, d. 297, p. 68, C.P.S. to *Repr.* at Cne-aff., 12 pluv.

repressive activities in the area.[1] For Javogues's clash with Roanne developed out of its earlier struggle with this *commissaire* of the Committee of General Security, who represented the most immediate threat in the early period.[2] The club and the revolutionary committee had quickly become centres of resistance to Lapalus in mid October. Tension reached the point where he was threatening to have the club walled up, while the regular and extra-ordinary authorities obstructed his work in the town.

The *commissaires* whom the District had sent to Paris on 5 frimaire/25 November had intended to obtain the arrest of Lapalus and hoped to use Noailly, the deputy from Roanne, as their patron in the matter.[3] However, when they appeared at the Convention on 18 frimaire/8 December, their eloquence was rewarded only by a decree suspending all proceedings against officials in the district of Roanne pending investigations by the *Représentants en mission* at Commune-affranchie. Accordingly, the *Commission Temporaire* sent out *commissaires* to investigate Lapalus's activities in the districts of Villefranche and Roanne, where his dechristianization campaign was provoking increasing unrest in early nivôse. The *commissaires* visited Roanne during the second *décade* of nivôse and entirely accepted the moderates' case against Lapalus. Over thirty suspects were immediately released, while on 14 or 15 nivôse/3 or 4 January the *Commission Temporaire* had already issued a warrant for the arrest of Lapalus. Meanwhile the revolutionary committee was proceeding to arrest a certain number of his supporters in the area.[4] Lapalus, however, escaped from his escort and placed himself under the protection of Javogues. As Javogues's right-hand man during the latter part of nivôse and pluviôse, he naturally became his expert on the affairs of Roanne. There could be no doubt in the mind of an inhabitant of that town as to the nature of his influence upon the proconsul. When he was made a judge on the revolutionary tribunal on 13 pluviôse/1 February, he possessed in a very concrete sense the

1 A.D.L., L 176, fol. 52.

2 For the rest of this paragraph and the next, Colin Lucas, 'La brève carrière du terroriste Jean-Marie Lapalus', *A.H.R.F.* 1968, pp. 522–33.

3 Bibl. Roanne, 3 L (1) 20, Game to Lapalus, n.d. (21 frim.).

4 Ibid. and A.D.R., 42 L 180, d. Game, Game to Javogues, 19 pluv.

means of revenge. Thus Roanne had every reason to fear an association between Javogues and Lapalus.

But it also had every reason to fear Javogues in his own right. Lapalus was not the only hostile voice in the ear of the *Représentant*. His confidants in the Department viewed the administrations of the town with deep suspicion, while his *commissaires* reported on their unpatriotic attitudes and on the campaign against Lapalus.[1] By mid pluviôse, Javogues's hatred of Roanne was such that he was preparing a collection of damning documentary evidence against it for publication.[2] It rapidly became apparent that the victory over Lapalus had achieved nothing for Roanne, since all the evidence indicated that Javogues was preparing to continue the same repressive action. The pattern of his movement through the districts of Armeville and Boën would lead him inexorably on to the district of Roanne. On 19 nivôse/8 January he revealed the attitude that he would adopt on his arrival by ordering the rearrest of two prominent local lawyers recently acquitted by the revolutionary tribunal at Feurs.[3] On 1 pluviôse/20 January, he requested the names of all those under arrest at Roanne, which seemed to point to a massive transfer of prisoners to Feurs similar to that from Armeville and Montbrisé.[4] On 12 pluviôse/31 January, he issued arrest warrants against thirty influential citizens, mostly leading figures in the club and the committee.[5] There were rumours that he intended to remove the District to Le Coteau, to change the personnel of all the institutions, and to set up the guillotine at Roanne.[6] One local militant was taking it for granted on 19 pluviôse/7 February that the *Représentant* was about to operate a 'bouleversement' at Roanne.[7] On 21 pluviôse/9 February, two of Javogues's intimates wrote from Feurs that they would shortly be arriving and would remain at Roanne for at least a month.[8] For the leading citizens of

[1] Bibl. Lyon, Coste MS. 1245, no. 6, Depart. to *Repr.* at Cne-aff., 27 frim. A.D.R., 42 L 168, d. Chartre, Chartre and Guyot to Javogues, 4 pluv.

[2] A.N., AF II 114 (861) 15, letter of 22 pluv.

[3] A.C. Roanne, 1 D 1 (2), fol. 246 (acquitted on 7 niv.).

[4] A.C. Roanne, 1 D 1 (2), fol. 255, Lapalus to Raveaud (1 pluv.).

[5] A.D.R., 42 L 156.

[6] A.D.L., L 413, 16 flor.

[7] A.D.R., 42 L 180, d. Game, Game to Javogues, 19 pluv. Cf. *Papiers inédits omis ou supprimés par Courtois*, ii. 310–11, letter of 20 pluv.

[8] Bibl. Roanne, 3 L (1) 18, Civeton and Costalin to Civeton's wife (?).

Roanne, so concerned to keep the Terror at arm's length, it was therefore a question of mounting urgency in pluviôse to put a stop to Javogues's activities.

Javogues was much more dangerous to Roanne than Lapalus because he commanded a wider range of terrorist weapons. The law of 14 frimaire must have appeared to Roanne as a major guarantee against the more brutal aspects of the Terror. The alacrity with which the administrators dismissed the *armée révolutionnaire* is clear evidence of this. Javogues's infringement of this law meant that he was retaining the weapons which Roanne feared, especially the *armée révolutionnaire* and the *taxe révolutionnaire*. Moreover, his attitude to the law of 14 frimaire suggested to Roanne that even a specific decree of the Convention, such as the suspension of proceedings against its officials, did not in fact afford it any protection. In this they were correct: Javogues told Collot d'Herbois that the Convention was dishonouring itself by absolving such a guilty commune and that he himself would not hesitate to ignore a decree so harmful to liberty.[1] Roanne did not have a sufficiently clean record to permit it to denounce a *Représentant du peuple* with impunity. It adopted indirect tactics. Javogues's judgement on the town was unequivocal: 'si un pays a été constamment en rébellion depuis le commencement de la Révolution, c'est Roanne.'[2] Therefore the authorities continued to pester the government for a statement that this was not the case. This would remove the last vestige of legality from any extension of his revolutionary measures to the district of Roanne, since Javogues's infringement of the law of 14 frimaire was justified by his assertion that the Loire was a 'pays rebelle'. But, since the practical effect of such a statement on the proconsul was doubtful, they also sought to discredit him indirectly and provoke his recall. In the first place, merely by questioning whether his measures were applicable to Roanne and by citing the laws with which these measures conflicted, they were in effect drawing the attention of the government to the irregularities of his conduct. In the second place, they refrained from criticizing Javogues other than by implication and continued to present Lapalus as the chief criminal.

[1] A.N., AF II 114 (861) 15, letter of 16 pluv. [2] Ibid.

Measures such as the reincarceration of men acquitted by the tribunal at Feurs were ascribed to the vengeance of Lapalus who had betrayed Javogues's confidence.[1] On the one hand, Javogues was thus portrayed as dangerous because a plaything of intriguers. On the other, Lapalus was a man whose crimes were, ostensibly at least, already established; the arrest warrant of the *Commission Temporaire* vouchsafed the allegations against him in an unimpeachably terrorist manner. By emphasizing the association between Lapalus and Javogues, Roanne implicated the latter in the former's disrepute.

The manœuvres against Javogues started as early as 8 nivôse/28 December when the District sent a copy of the *arrêté* of 6 nivôse/26 December, maintaining the *armée révolutionnaire*, to the Committee of Public Safety.[2] The administration requested guidance on how to reconcile this with the law of 14 frimaire. During the rest of the month, its energies were mostly devoted to disabling Lapalus. But on 28 nivôse/17 January, the revolutionary committee at Le Coteau drew the attention of the District back to the basic problem.[3] It asked whether it should execute the various *arrêtés* of the proconsuls concerning *taxes révolutionnaires*, since it did not consider that the district of Roanne was a 'pays rebelle'. But the incident that really set the offensive in motion was an *arrêté* issued by Javogues on 2 pluviôse/21 January.[4] He denounced a counter-revolutionary plot against Lapalus in the districts of Roanne and Villefranche and the participation of treacherous administrators in it. He declared all the communes of that area responsible for Lapalus's safety and made the sinister promise that any insult or attack on his person would be avenged in the name of the People. This was not merely a public proclamation of Javogues's adoption of Lapalus; it also gave the proconsul a ready justification for repressive action against Roanne. The District reacted at once by declaring that this *arrêté* was the result of Lapalus's misrepresentations.[5] On 8 pluviôse/27 January, District and

[1] A.N., D III 124, d. Roanne, Barbier to Convention, n.d.

[2] A.N., AF II 186, d. 1543, p. 10. Annotated: 'sous les yeux du Comité' and 'Répondre'.

[3] A.D.L., L 417, fol. 87.

[4] A.N., AF II 114 (861) 15.

[5] A.D.L., L 176, fol. 99.

Municipality sent petitions to the Convention recounting both their patriotic record and Javogues's illegalities, while the revolutionary committee begged the *Représentants* at Ville-affranchie to mediate between Roanne and Javogues.[1] Already on 4 pluviôse/23 January the Convention had received petitions describing the illegal arrest of judges of the district tribunal after acquittal by the revolutionary tribunal.[2] During the second *décade* of pluviôse, pressure built up both at Commune-affranchie and in Paris. Two of the men against whom Javogues had issued arrest warrants fled to Ville-affranchie, saying that they were the victims of a few intriguers who had misled Javogues; the proconsuls there could not but favour them, since they were the president of the club and a member of the committee.[3] In Paris, *commissaires* lobbied the Convention and the Committee of Public Safety, demanding that it be accepted that the district had never been in revolt and that the law of 14 frimaire be applied there without reservation.[4]

It was on 18 pluviôse/6 February that the *commissaires* from Roanne were admitted to the Convention.[5] Faithful to their tactics, they denounced Lapalus; Javogues was indicted only to the extent that he was Lapalus's dupe and that Roanne demanded a proconsul who was not a native of the department. However, Reverchon undertook to emphasize the irregularities in Javogues's conduct, especially his failure to obey his recall. The Convention referred the question of Lapalus to the Committee of General Security and that of Javogues to the Committee of Public Safety. On the next day, the delegation from Roanne renewed the attack. A petition in favour of a suspect arrested by Lapalus was made the excuse for a list of Lapalus's crimes, while the anomaly of a situation in which he was both denunciator and judge was stressed. Again, Reverchon intervened, and it was in response to him that the Convention ordered the arrest of Lapalus. The case of the judges of the district tribunal of Roanne was

[1] Ibid., fol. 103; A.C. Roanne, 1 D 1 (2), fol. 259; A.D.R., 1 L 190.

[2] A.N., D III 124, d. Roanne.

[3] A.C. Roanne, 1 D 1 (2), fol. 270.

[4] A.D.L., L 188, Dist. of Roanne to Convention and C.P.S., 17 pluv.; A.N., F1c III Rhône 8, d. 4, Louvrier to C.P.S., 21 pluv.

[5] For this paragraph, *Arch. parlementaires*, 84, 18 pluv., no. 70, 19 pluv., nos. 9 and 12.

also discussed and their rearrest implicitly condemned as illegal.

Reverchon's role in the debates of 18 and 19 pluviôse/6 and 7 February can be partly explained by the fact that at the end of the siege of Lyon he had accorded a testimonial of good behaviour to Roanne.[1] He was therefore naturally anxious to combat any indirect damage to his own reputation that might result from a general acceptance of the view held by Javogues and Lapalus. Above all, however, his hostility had been kindled by Villefranche-sur-Saône. Most of Lapalus's excesses had in fact taken place in this district, but it was only in mid nivôse, after he had rearrested a number of people released by the *Commission Temporaire*, that the administration joined in the campaign against him. Javogues's *arrêté* of 2 pluviôse/21 January in defence of Lapalus classed Villefranche with Roanne as a centre of the alleged conspiracy, and therefore had much the same effect there as at Roanne. The District protested to the Department of the Rhône, to the proconsuls at Ville-affranchie, and to Reverchon, while the club forwarded a detailed memorandum to Commune-affranchie. Villefranche saw Reverchon as its patron because, as proconsul responsible for the area during the siege of Lyon, he had praised the town. Indeed, the record of Villefranche was infinitely more respectable than that of Roanne. Its loyalty to the Convention during the summer of 1793 had undoubtedly been instrumental in preventing the expansion of Lyon federalism northwards, just as the loyalty of Vienne had prevented the union of the Lyon and Marseille rebellions. Therefore, Javogues had merely succeeded in providing the rather disreputable Roanne with yet another unimpeachable surety, which could not but add credence to its allegations.

However, although Roanne had seriously damaged Javogues's reputation on 18 and 19 pluviôse/6 and 7 February by obtaining the arrest of his confidant and by demonstrating his continued violation of the law of 14 frimaire, it was not Roanne who provoked the decree of 20 pluviôse/8 February against him. This was the direct consequence of his quarrel with Couthon, Maignet, and the Puy-de-Dôme.

[1] For this paragraph, Lucas, art. cit.

Javogues's hatred of Maignet and Couthon developed out of the quarrels between the *Représentants en mission* directing the siege of Lyon.[1] Javogues was one of the proconsuls who organized the siege from the beginning and who, under the inspiration of Dubois-Crancé and Kellerman, adopted a tactic of blockade and regular siege works in order to avoid wasting lives. Couthon, Maignet, and Châteauneuf-Randon, on the other hand, who had been appointed later to hasten the victory with the *levée en masse*, were determined to implement a tactic of frontal assault in order to gain quick success through the sheer numbers of untrained and ill-equipped men at their disposal. The clash between the two groups of proconsuls was bitter. The quarrel between Couthon and Dubois-Crancé dragged on into the Year II and culminated in the latter's expulsion from the Jacobins. Javogues must have shared in the general anger of his team, when the late arrivals took the glory for a victory gained by frontal assault but clearly made possible by the work of their predecessors. Moreover, Javogues had his own particular dispute with one of their rivals, Châteauneuf-Randon, who had accused him of, at best, ineptitude during the campaign in the Forez—Javogues had not properly combined his advance from the south with that of the *levée en masse* from the west. Couthon lost the last shreds of his reputation, as far as Javogues was concerned, by the restraint of his repressive policies in Commune-affranchie immediately after the siege. Javogues, who had courteously forwarded a sequestrated wheel chair to Couthon before the latter's arrival at the siege, was hoping in late brumaire that Collot d'Herbois would be able to repair the damage done at Commune-affranchie by Couthon and the others, who had failed to take any of the steps necessary for the salvation of the Republic.[2] His hatred for Couthon was further intensified by the efforts of the Committee of Public Safety to remedy his irregularities and particularly by the Gouly affair. Javogues attributed his difficulties increasingly to the counter-revolutionary bent of most of the

[1] For this paragraph, Colin Lucas, 'Auvergnats et Foréziens pendant la mission du conventionnel Javogues', *Gilbert Romme et son temps*, pp. 145–6; Dubois-Crancé, ... *aux Jacobins, en rentrant dans la société* and *Réponse* ... *aux inculpations de ses collègues* ..., 2 vols.; A.N., AF II 185, d. 1526, p. 30, Couthon to C.P.S., 6 Oct.

[2] A.N., AF II 58, d. 430, p. 2, letter to Collot d'Herbois, 28 brum.

members, who, he believed, had sworn to destroy him, and was convinced that Couthon was the dominant influence against him in that quarter.[1] In pluviôse the club at Ambert reported him as saying frequently that either Couthon, Maignet, and Châteauneuf-Randon must lose their heads or he must.[2]

The affair of the Puy-de-Dôme was born of the marriage between this tenacious resentment against the two leading Auvergnats in the Convention and the local feud between the inhabitants of the Forez and those of the Auvergne, into which Javogues plunged with his habitual passion.[3] We have seen how the inhabitants of Montbrisé turned against the Auvergnats in an attempt to put an end to repression. The Auvergnats had administered the town in the chaotic closing stages of the siege of Lyon, and the considerable drainage of food and goods towards the army was ascribed by their dispossessed owners to the proverbial dishonesty of the Auvergnats. During the winter the militant terrorists of Montbrisé accepted this charge as they struggled to contain an ill-disciplined garrison of Auvergnats, which they resented as a strain on food and as evidence of Montbrisé's allegedly unreliable political character. Although Javogues had viewed the Auvergnat Committee of Public Safety at Montbrison with benevolence in October, in late nivôse he had clearly adopted the position of his compatriots. Having suspended the revolutionary tribunal for counter-revolutionary attitudes, he arrested the Auvergnat member Meyrand, with whom he had already quarrelled during the siege of Lyon.[4] This incident set off a flurry of protest among the clubs in the Puy-de-Dôme, who wrote to the Convention and in some cases directly to Couthon. *Commissaires* sent to Javogues succeeded in obtaining the release of Meyrand on 13 pluviôse/1 February. But the issue went much deeper than that, as the club at Ambert understood. According to it, Javogues was fulminating in early pluviôse against the Puy-de-Dôme and

[1] A.N., AF II 114 (861) 15, letter to Collot d'Herbois, 16 pluv. Cf. AF II 137 (1069), d. 30, p. 22, proclamation of 13 pluv.: 'Ah! Couthon [. . . connaissant] ton intimité avec *les Gouly* . . .'

[2] A.N., D III, d. Javogues, *soc. pop.* at Ambert to Convention, 5 pluv.

[3] For this paragraph, Lucas, art. cit., and H. Soanen, 'Les sociétés populaires du Puy-de-Dôme et le rappel du conventionnel Javogues', *A.H.R.F.* 1931, pp. 431–7.

[4] A.D. P.-de-D., L 2784, Meyrand *et al.* to C.P.S. of Montbrison, 19 Sept.

against the local Committee of Public Safety of the autumn, demanding denunciations against the Auvergnats and the three *conventionnels* who had directed the *levée en masse*, and was announcing his intention to invade the Puy-de-Dôme to punish it for its crimes.[1] Ambert was considerably alarmed by this information, since it was Montbrisé's nearest neighbour in the Puy-de-Dôme and since the Committee of Public Safety had been composed of its citizens. Therefore, whereas the protests of the other clubs were circumspect, this club addressed a detailed and virulent denunciation against Javogues to the Convention on 5 pluviôse/24 January.[2] This was the most devastating direct attack yet made on the proconsul. Almost Thermidorian in tone, it accused him of a whole gamut of crimes ranging from ultra-revolutionary sentiments, public slander against Robespierre and Couthon, and incitement to civil war to 'lèze-révolution', 'lèze-humanité', persecution of patriots, and propagation of sun-worship. Meanwhile, echoes of Javogues's pronouncements seem to have been reaching Couthon from his friends at Clermont-Ferrand at least by 13 pluviôse/1 February.[3]

It was on 13 pluviôse/1 February that Javogues committed his final blunder. He published two *arrêtés* and a long proclamation which denounced the excesses and criminal depredations wrought by the Auvergnat *levée en masse* and Committee of Public Safety in the Forez.[4] These publications were little more than a torrent of abuse mingling the accusations of the inhabitants of Montbrisé with his own acrimony. But the real targets were Maignet and Couthon, who were accused of having authorized and connived at these crimes. Couthon especially, whose villainy was further revealed by the fact that a mere thirty rebels had been executed during the six weeks of his rule at Commune-affranchie, was attacked with extravagant violence:

Ah Couthon! jusqu'à présent tu n'as été qu'un habile empirique; avec un air apparent de philanthropie, tu n'as jamais cherché le bonheur du peuple; avec le mot de justice sur les lèvres, tu n'avais que

[1] A.N., loc. cit. [2] Ibid.

[3] F. Mège, *Correspondance inédite de Couthon*, p. 289, Couthon to Clermont-Ferrand, 13 pluv.

[4] A.N., AF II 137 (1069), d. 30, pp. 12, 17, 22.

l'injustice dans le cœur; je lis dans le souterrain de tes plus secrètes pensées; tu as voulu allier ce qui de sa nature était inaliable, la richesse avec l'amour de la République . . . Avec le sourire de la bienfaisance, tu es le monstre le plus cruel et l'ennemi le plus implacable des patriotes . . . Sous le vernis de vertus, tu n'as que l'ascendant du crime.

Therefore Javogues ordered an investigation into the Committee of Public Safety of Montbrison and established a *Commission ambulante* to gather denunciations.

Naturally, these publications inflamed the clubs of the Puy-de-Dôme. But their chorus of denunciation did not reach the Convention until after the recall of Javogues. Similarly, the protests of Châteauneuf-Randon and Maignet, who were both still on mission, had no influence on the debate of 20 pluviôse/8 February.[1] The patriots of Clermont-Ferrand, however, sent a copy of Javogues's proclamation directly to Couthon by express.[2] The public accusations contained in this document were so serious that it was inevitable that Couthon should defend himself publicly. On 20 pluviôse/8 February, he denounced Javogues to the Convention.[3] After pointing out that Javogues had remained on mission quite illegally and was exercising, with a cruelty worthy of Nero, powers that had been withdrawn, he emphasized that when a patriot was slandered, the whole Republic was maligned, for there was between the Republic and the patriot a perfect identity that had to be defended for the salvation of both. He linked Javogues's libel to the existence of a systematic plan to denigrate the purest and most ardent friends of the People with the intention of causing the People to lose confidence in them. He described how Javogues was inciting the department of the Loire against the Puy-de-Dôme and attempting to provoke an incident so as to have a pretext for invading the Puy-de-Dôme with his 'armée prétendue révolutionnaire'. Finally, he suggested that Javogues had wilfully failed to quell federalism in the Forez before the *levée en masse* and questioned whether he had not wanted the federalists to reach the Vendée without hindrance. Couthon then

[1] A.N., AF II 187, d. 1547, p. 12, Châteauneuf-Randon to C.P.S., 3 vent.; Bibl. Clermont-Ferrand, MS. 357bis, fol. 80, Maignet to Convention, 29 pluv.

[2] Mège, op. cit., p. 295, Couthon to Clermont-Ferrand, 22 pluv.

[3] For the rest of the paragraph, *Arch. parlementaires*, 84, 20 pluv., no. 13, and Couthon's commentary in Mège, op. et loc. cit.

proceeded to read out Javogues's proclamation, and 'toute l'assemblée se lève d'indignation'. The subsequent debate consisted largely of a general homage to Couthon's patriotism and this was in itself an automatic condemnation of Javogues. Reverchon stated that throughout his mission Javogues had always been surrounded by brigands and scoundrels, and that it was time that the Convention put an end to his vexatious conduct: 'Je demande que vous preniez à son égard une mesure ferme.' Although Merlin de Thionville remarked that Javogues was more irascible than ill-intentioned, and suggested that perhaps he had gone mad, opinion supported Reverchon and agreed that Javogues and his creatures should be brought before the Convention. Ambert's denunciation, which was then read out, only served to generalize the demand for the arrest of Javogues. Couthon, however, requested the Convention to limit itself to ordering Javogues to return forthwith, and the assembly could hardly go against the wishes of the principal party in the matter. It ordered Javogues to return within eight days, after which time 'il y sera traduit à la diligence des Représentants du peuple dans le département'; the dossier of the affair was formally transmitted to the Committee of Public Safety, and a warrant for the arrest of Duret was added to that for Lapalus issued on the previous day. On the orders of the proconsuls at Commune-affranchie, two members of the *Commission Temporaire* notified Javogues of the decree shortly before midnight on 24 pluviôse/12 February; they arrested Lapalus and Duret, wound up the revolutionary tribunal, transferred the prisoners to Commune-affranchie, and disbanded the *armée révolutionnaire*.[1]

The recall of Javogues in pluviôse is perfectly comprehensible as part of the general pattern by which the Committee of Public Safety progressively imposed the centralized hierarchy of Terror elaborated in the law of 14 frimaire. The Committee seems to have become more preoccupied with the functioning of the *Représentants en mission* in pluviôse—it was on 4 pluviôse/30 January that it sent a circular outlining general principles and reminding proconsuls that 'les développements partiels produiraient des déchirements mortels

[1] A.N., T 781, d. Marino, report by Marino and Delan to *Repr.*, n.d.

à la chose publique. Que tout vive, sente et marche à la fois'.[1] It was on 10 pluviôse/30 January that the Committee sought to bring order more particularly to the area round Commune-affranchie by circularizing the proconsuls in the region to act in concert with those in the town.[2] In these circumstances, Javogues obviously had to be eliminated, for he was quite incapable of living in harmony with other proconsuls, let alone co-ordinating his activity with theirs, while his policies evidently produced nothing but dangerous disaffection. The public debate on his behaviour and the decree against him may indeed be taken as a warning consciously issued by the Committee to other *Représentants en mission* of similar inclinations. It is significant that Taillefer, who had been a notable ultra-revolutionary in his mission, spoke harshly of calling the *suppléant* of those who did not obey recall notices; similarly Dubouchet, whose *commissaires* in the Seine-et-Marne had provoked much protest by their use of the wide powers delegated to them, was one of those who demanded the arrest of Lapalus.[3]

Nevertheless, such considerations do not altogether satisfactorily explain why particularly Javogues, who was only one, though perhaps the worst, of many ill-behaved proconsuls, should have been chosen as an example. Nor do they explain the strange mixture of harshness against his confidants and circumspection with regard to the proconsul which characterized the recall. Moreover, Couthon had received a copy of Javogues's proclamation against him by 18 pluviôse/6 February.[4] Yet it was not until 20 pluviôse that he made use of it. On 19 pluviôse he intervened in the debate on Lapalus, not in order to mention Javogues, but to suggest that Lapalus was perhaps not as guilty as he appeared.[5] On the next day, he said that information had just reached the Committee of Public Safety which proved Lapalus to be 'un méchant homme'.[6] This tends to suggest that Couthon's speech to the Convention was the reflection of a decision in the Committee of Public Safety which had not

[1] A.N., D XLII 7, d. 1, p. 56. [2] A.N., AF II 37, d. 297, p. 59.

[3] *Arch. parlementaires*, 84, 18 pluv., no. 70, and 19 pluv., no. 9.

[4] Mège, op. cit., pp. 292–5, Couthon to Clermont-Ferrand, 22 pluv.

[5] *Arch. parlementaires*, 84, 19 pluv., no. 9.

[6] Ibid., 20 pluv., no. 14.

been taken on the previous day. Therefore the debates of 18–20 pluviôse/6–8 February only achieve their full significance when they are placed in the political context of those days.

In the *ultra* counter-offensive against the gains made by the *citras* since late frimaire, the liberation of Ronsin and Vincent on 14 pluviôse/2 February constituted both a major victory and a substantial encouragement.[1] The Cordeliers immediately organized a violent campaign during the subsequent days for a purge of the *nouveau modéré* elements in the Convention. On 17 pluviôse/5 February, they also inaugurated an assault on the revolutionary committees, which the government had made the basis for the extension of its control over sectional politics. Thus, the Cordeliers were attacking the structure of authority which the Committee of Public Safety was attempting to impose, and also jeopardizing that neutrality above the factions that it had managed to reassert under Robespierre's influence. Certainly, the *ultra* offensive did not reach its climax until early ventôse. By that time, the equilibrium between the factions had been broken, and the Committee abandoned neutrality to strike, first against the *ultras* of the *complot militaire* on 23–24 ventôse/13–14 March, and then against the *Indulgents* on 9–10 germinal/29–30 March. The remainder of both factions was disposed of on 24 germinal/13 April after the trial of the *Conspiration des prisons*. Nevertheless, Robespierre had already acted firmly in mid pluviôse in an attempt to contain the *ultras* and to preserve the balance between the factions. On 17 pluviôse/5 February he delivered an important speech in the Convention which condemned both *citras* and *ultras* as being but two heads of the same body, both aiming to make tyranny triumphant by the disorganization of popular government and the ruin of the Convention. On 19 pluviôse/7 February in the Jacobins, he intervened to have the *ultra* Brichet expelled despite the popularity of his proposals.

The debates on Lapalus and Javogues, therefore, correspond exactly with the first attempts of the Committee of Public Safety to repulse the *ultras*. When Couthon spoke of

[1] For this paragraph, A. Soboul, *Les Sans-culottes parisiens en l'an II*, pp. 350–8, 371–4.

a systematic plan to denigrate the purest and most ardent friends of the People, he was referring to the attacks of the *ultras* and the *citras* on the orthodox, governmental Montagnards. The decree against Javogues and his two confidants appears thus very much as a measure of intimidation against the *ultra* faction. The portrait of Lapalus and Javogues that emerged from the denunciations read out to the Convention provided almost the perfect illustration of the counter-revolutionary ultra-revolutionary recently described in general terms by Robespierre. The disturbance caused by Javogues's energy and his attitude to the law of 14 frimaire fitted Robespierre's denunciation of those who were 'toujours prêt[s] à adopter les mesures hardies, pourvu qu'elles aient beaucoup d'inconvénients; calomniant celles qui ne présentent que des avantages'. His personal extravagance made him 'plein de feu pour les grandes résolutions qui ne signifient rien . . . très attaché . . . aux pratiques extérieures'. As for his dechristianization, 'la guerre déclarée à la divinité n'est qu'une diversion en faveur de la royauté'. Javogues could appear 'sévère pour l'innocence, mais indulgent pour le crime', since he protected Lapalus but arrested Meyrand, Sadet, and Dorfeuille.[1] His attacks on Robespierre, Couthon, and Maignet, his accusations that the Committee of Public Safety was counter-revolutionary, identified him as one of those who cultivated 'le mépris du peuple pour les autorités qu'il a lui-même établies'.[2] Indeed it was above all this attack on the Committee of Public Safety and on its leading members, coupled with his talk of an invasion of the Puy-de-Dôme, which brought Javogues's disgrace. He identified himself publicly as an ultra-revolutionary.[3] It could therefore be argued convincingly that his activities were symptoms of an *ultra* conspiracy aimed at overthrowing the authority of the central government and precipitating civil war. Couthon's speech clearly hinted at the counter-revolutionary nature of Javogues's intentions; writing to his friends at Clermont-Ferrand shortly afterwards, he made this accusation specific,

[1] Both Committee and Convention knew of this because it was reported in the denunciation from Ambert (A.N., D III 349, d. Javogues).

[2] Ibid., although the clearest expression of these views was contained in his letter to Collot of 16 pluv., which did not reach the Committee until after the decree.

[3] Reported by Ambert.

saying that he had intended to plant the seeds of a new federalism.[1] Therefore, the recall of Javogues and the arrest of his confidants must be seen, first, as an attempt to produce evidence in support of Robespierre's explanation of the true character of *ultracisme*; and second, as a warning to the *ultras* in the same category as the speech of 17 pluviôse/5 February and the expulsion of Brichet from the Jacobins. It would have been impossible to issue such a warning by attacking an *ultra* leader in Paris, immediately after the release of Vincent and Ronsin, which had only been conceded under popular pressure. Thirdly, it is possible that one should consider these debates as a warning also to the members of the Convention to refrain from becoming as involved in the *ultra* faction as some of them had in the *citra* faction.

The logic of this argument, however, should have led to the arrest of Javogues as well as that of his confidants. The government's restraint towards him, typified by Couthon's opposition to an arrest warrant, was also a product of the political situation. The crucial issue in the conflicts of the second *décade* of pluviôse was the utility of the repressive weapons. The question of Javogues's recall, which revolved to a large extent around his use of those weapons, was therefore directly relevant to the debate. Moreover, the release of Vincent and Ronsin had by no means silenced the *citras*. They gained considerable encouragement from Robespierre's stand of 17 pluviôse/5 February, despite his care to condemn the *nouveaux modérés* as well, and from the incident in the Jacobins on 19 pluviôse/7 February. Prominent among those who attacked Javogues in the debate of 20 pluviôse/8 February were such men as the Dantonist Thuriot, Bourdon de l'Oise, so bitterly denounced with Camille Desmoulins in nivôse, and Legendre, attacked by Hébert in early pluviôse for his attitude to Lyon. The arrest of Javogues was, therefore, politically inadvisable from two points of view. In the first place, it might have given too much encouragement to the *nouveaux modérés* and further enraged the *ultras* by appearing as a governmental decision on the question of repressive weapons. In the second place, it was dangerous to arrest a member of the Convention, especially an *ultra*, at a time

[1] Mège, op. cit. ,p. 295, Couthon to Clermont-Ferrand, 23 pluv.

when the government was resisting the *ultra* clamour for a purge of the assembly. The arrest of Lapalus and Duret and the public discussion of Javogues's conduct must have been deemed sufficient for the various warnings involved. The arrest of the shadowy Duret, whose name had hardly been mentioned in the Convention, was intended to emphasize that the decree was aimed at the employer of these two men, whereas the arrest of Lapalus alone could well have been taken to refer solely to his earlier misdeeds as a *commissaire* of the Committee of General Security, which had formed the subject of the denunciations by Roanne.

Quite apart from all this, however, the recall of Javogues has another significance in terms of the government's reaction to the *ultra* offensive.[1] With its complaisant proconsuls and large Cordelier colony, Commune-affranchie/Lyon had become the capital of *ultracisme* by this time. Its most dangerous feature was that it was a military *ultracisme* possessing the whole range of extra-ordinary repressive weapons. The *ultra* campaign in Paris revolved around the military figures of Ronsin and Vincent and, significantly enough, it was a *complot militaire* which provided the government with the pretext for the liquidation of the *ultras* in ventôse. Inevitably, therefore, the government kept an anxious eye on their military stronghold in the south. The increasing influence that was now being gained at Paris by the Lyon lobby against the *étrangers* was both a reflection of this preoccupation and an added stimulus to it. Moreover, it was on 7 pluviôse/26 January that the rupture between the indigenous patriots and the imported agents of the Terror was consummated in the club at Ville-affranchie. The gravity of the situation at Ville-affranchie resided to a large extent in the confusion in the surrounding area, which allowed the *ultras* to intervene. Pluviôse saw an increasing flow of protests against them—the exactions of Vauquoy in the district of La Tour-du-Pin, the elucubrations of the amorous Dobigny at Villefranche-sur-Saône, the struggle between the *ultras* and the moderates in the Ain under Albitte, etc. The recall of Javogues was a major step towards reducing this situation to order and with

[1] For this paragraph, Richard Cobb, *Les Armées révolutionnaires*, ii. 788–94; É. Herriot, *Lyon n'est plus*, iii. 344–401.

it the size of the threat from Commune-affranchie. It was just one of a series of such measures starting with the Committee's instruction of 10 pluviôse/30 January to the *Représentants en mission* in the area,[1] proceeding to the decree of 28 pluviôse/16 February limiting the jurisdiction of the *Commission des Sept* to Commune-affranchie, and culminating in the dispersion of the *ultras* of the city and the dismantling of their institutions in germinal.

It is probable that the recall of Javogues, and especially the arrest of Lapalus and Duret, were intended as a warning of the power of the central government to the *ultras* of Commune-affranchie, who held positions in the favour of the *Représentants* similar to those of the arrested men. Certainly, the members of the *Commission Temporaire* sent to implement the decree at Feurs hastened to exclaim: 'Ah! malheureux Javogues, quoique montagnard et avec des intentions pures . . . tu faisais la contre-révolution.'[2] The debate of 20 pluviôse/8 February was fully reported by the *Journal républicain*, probably edited by Duvicquet of the *Commission Temporaire*; by 6 ventôse/24 February, the local *Père Duchesne* was echoing Robespierre's denunciations against both *ultras* and *citras*.[3] But it is doubtful whether Fouché and his colleagues, who were swift to protest at the attacks on the *Commission des Sept*,[4] saw the recall of Javogues in this light. He was proving an increasing source of embarrassment to them. Clear divisions of policy had appeared over matters as diverse as dechristianization and the Gouly affair.[5] They were particularly in evidence over the preservation of the *armée révolutionnaire*, for it is inconceivable that the proconsuls at Ville-affranchie had not at least hearsay knowledge of the *arrêté* of 6 nivôse/26 December when they issued theirs of 20 nivôse/9 January calling the battalion to Commune-affranchie.[6] Javogues became more outrageous as his neighbours, probably under the influence of Méaulle, became

[1] Note that Javogues's third recall coincided with this.

[2] A.N., T 781, d. Marino, report by Marino and Delan, n.d.

[3] *Journal républicain des deux départements de Rhône et de Loire*, no. 19 (28 pluv.), cf. Herriot, op. cit. iii. 344; *Je suis le véritable Père Duchesne, Foutre*, no. 25 (6 vent.).

[4] Herriot, op. cit. iii. 390–1.

[5] They also had denounced Gouly, but Javogues went much further than they were willing to go when he issued a warrant for Gouly's arrest.

[6] Above, p. 173.

more circumspect.[1] His patronage of Lapalus and his arrest warrants against Maccabéo of the Department of the Rhône, Sadet of the *Commission Temporaire*, and, especially, Dorfeuille served to harden their disapproval of him.[2] Their anxiety about his activities had reached such a pitch by mid pluviôse that they ordered refugees from Lapalus returning home to Roanne to let them know of the whereabouts of the proconsul and whether the revolutionary tribunal was functioning.[3] Their informants responded by forwarding the latest set of arrest warrants, which Méaulle annotated: 'une liste de proscription qui ne frappe évidemment que de francs Républicains'.[4] The very fact that they took such care to stipulate what would happen to anyone who ignored their abolition of the tribunal at Feurs reveals the sort of image that they had of the developments in the Loire under Javogues.[5] Thus, the proconsuls had come to accept the arguments of the moderates from Roanne. Indeed, Javogues was entirely without friends in mid pluviôse. Even the powerful Collot d'Herbois, member of the Committee of Public Safety, sometime patron of the *ultras* of Commune-affranchie, and alone among Javogues's colleagues to retain his esteem, was far too preoccupied with attempting to reconcile the warring factions to defend a cause so obviously lost as that of Javogues. Collot was concerned to disengage himself from his previous commitment to intensive repression at Commune-affranchie: it was he who drafted the instruction of 10 pluviôse/29 January to the *Représentants* in the region.[6] Thus, when Javogues requested him to communicate his fulminations against the Committee of Public Safety to the interested party, it is evident that Collot scrupulously obeyed.[7]

[1] Cf. L. Madelin, *Fouché*, i. 143, though one cannot accept his view that Méaulle was frightened by the Terror at Cne-aff. Méaulle was sent as replacement for Albitte to implement the law of 14 frim., and his main activity at Cne-aff. related to that task.

[2] Note the tone of the letters exchanged by Fouché, Laporte, and Méaulle with Albitte, 1 and 4 pluv. (Bibl. Lyon, Coste MS. 681, no. 7, and 1102, no. 2).

[3] A.D.R., 1 L 190, Gay and Pascalis to *Repr.*, 25 pluv.

[4] Ibid.

[5] A.N., T 781, d. Marino, *arrêté* of 23 pluv.

[6] A.N., AF II 37, d. 297, p. 59, in Collot's hand, signed by Collot and Billaud. Note that Collot hardly wrote to Fouché between his return to Paris and, at the earliest, 19 pluv. (Bibl. Lyon, Coste MS. 113, no. 7, Collot to Fouché, 19 pluv.—an insignificant letter relating to colonies and slavery).

[7] A.N., AF II 114 (861) 15, letter of 16 pluv.

If the campaign against Javogues had come to a head a month later, there is little doubt that he would have returned under arrest and possibly have perished with the Hébertists. The connection through him between the *ultras* in Paris and in Commune-affranchie was far too tempting to be ignored. On 30 ventôse/20 March, Couthon, at least, was prepared to exploit it, pointing out to his friends that at the very time Javogues had been fulminating against him in the area round Commune-affranchie, in Paris Ronsin had also been portraying Robespierre and himself as the arch-traitors to be liquidated.[1] Eventually, hounded by Reverchon,[2] Lapalus and Duret were sacrificed in the trial of the *Conspiration des prisons* (21–24 germinal/10–13 April) to the need to emphasize the provincial ramifications of the *ultra–citra* Janus. But the threat still hung over Javogues as a warning to ill-disciplined proconsuls: 'Parmi les derniers scélérats', noted Couthon on 23 germinal/12 April, 'se trouvent les nommés *Lapalus* et *Duret*, amis et confidants du fameux Javogues, il pourrait bien se faire que ce *Monsieur* acquit quelque jour la même célébrité'.[3] He finally extricated himself from this delicate situation by a public apology to Couthon and Maignet in the Convention on 1 floréal/20 April, attributing his proclamation to villains who had gained his confidence under false pretences and had taken advantage of his republican exaltation. Couthon absolved him after a brief homily; they embraced amid the plaudits of the Assembly.[4] Maignet wrote a complacently sententious letter.[5] Dorfeuille forgave him magnanimously.[6]

[1] Mège, op. cit., p. 310, Couthon to Clermont-Ferrand, 30 vent.

[2] Colin Lucas, 'La brève carrière du terroriste Jean-Marie Lapalus', *A.H.R.F.* 1968, pp. 531–2; Herriot, op. cit. iii. 384, 396.

[3] Mège, op. cit., p. 323, Couthon to Clermont-Ferrand, 23 germ.

[4] Ibid., pp. 328–9, Couthon to Clermont-Ferrand, 3 flor. Possibly Javogues helped himself back into Couthon's good graces by turning on Dubois-Crancé: A.N., F7 4683, d. 1 (Dubois-Crancé), *femme* Beauchaton-Rameau to Dubois-Crancé, 14 therm. an II, denouncing attacks on him by Fillion, Émery, Gravier: 'je ne vous parle pas de Javogues, votre opinion doit être formée sur son compte . . .' There is no evidence that he had any hand in the attack on the *Comm. Temp.*, vent.–germ.

[5] Bibl. Clermont-Ferrand, MS. 360, no. 875, Maignet to Javogues, 11 flor.

[6] A.N., D III 216, d. Lyon (2), Jean-Marie Corret to Convention, n.d. (16 therm. an II): 'Il m'a chargé d'aller dire au citoyen Javogues qu'il ne lui voulait point de mal relativement aux dénonciations qu'il avait faites contre lui . . .'

Javogues slipped into the background again, but he maintained his interest in the area of his mission. He cultivated Robespierre's protégé from Commune-affranchie, Gravier, who had furnished evidence against Lapalus, and lent a hand in obtaining supplies of food for Commune-affranchie.[1] He corresponded with the Department of the Loire, relaying the news of Admiral's assassination attempt together with an orthodox platitude on it.[2] He promised patronage in Paris and delivered certificates of good character to men of the Forez.[3] In messidor, he apprehended a refugee suspect from the Saône-et-Loire and brought him to the Committee of General Security.[4] He had developed caution at last: in prairial he had no apparent difficulty with the *scrutin épuratoire* of the Jacobins.[5] But his political views remained unchanged. In early thermidor, he was helping to obtain the release of minor *patriotes prononcés* from the Gravilliers section; in the Jacobins he denounced the way in which the accusation of Hébertism had been used as a pretext for the arrest of 20,000 patriots in the provinces, and alleged that in the Gravilliers the best *sans-culottes* were regarded as partisans of Jacques Roux.[6] With his beliefs unchanged and his resentments unallayed, it was natural that Javogues should take an active part against the Robespierrists during the 9 thermidor crisis. His consistent admiration for Collot d'Herbois, now their arch-enemy, propelled him in the same direction. In the Jacobins he was vociferously one of a very small group round Collot and Billaud-Varenne, who tried on 8 thermidor to oppose Robespierre in the teeth of a frenzied mass of his supporters. He interrupted Robespierre's speech to deny the charge that he and his friends were factious individuals or conspirators, crying that their aim was simply to prevent the domination of one man. Robespierre paused to thank Javogues balefully for revealing his position in such a pronounced manner, thus helping to identify more clearly the enemies of the Republic.[7] It

[1] Bibl. Lyon, Coste MS. 663, no. 5, Gravier to ?, 13 prair.
[2] A.D.L., L 80, fol. 74, Depart. to Javogues, 25 prair.
[3] Bibl. Lyon, Fonds Général, MS. 1610, 13 prair.
[4] A.N., F^7 4659, d. Saône-et-Loire, 16 mess.
[5] F.-A. Aulard, *La Société des Jacobins*, vi. 171.
[6] Ibid. vi. 241, 6 therm.
[7] *Correspondance politique de Paris et des départements*, no. 90, reprinted in *A.H.R.F.* 1924, pp. 498–501.

was hardly surprising, therefore, that his name was among the fourteen members of the Convention designated by the Commune on the night of 9 thermidor as leaders of the conspiracy.[1] 9 thermidor did something to restore Javogues's reputation, for, as one of his colleagues remarked, it did appear as a complete vindication of his denunciation of Couthon.[2] On 19 fructidor/5 September, the Jacobins elected him to their *Comité de Présentation*.[3]

The Thermidorian Reaction naturally undermined his position. The militants of the Loire, with whom he maintained contact throughout the winter of the Year III,[4] were ousted from the administrations and persecuted by the *égorgeurs* during floréal, prairial, and messidor. Javogues was the focus for a great deal of the hatred: to the elderly Decelle of Moingt, who pleaded to be finished off, the *assommeurs* replied: 'ce serait une mort trop douce pour toi, mais en attendant porte ça à Javogues.'[5] A torrent of vituperative denunciation against the former proconsul reached Paris in germinal and floréal.[6] By this time he was clearly among the *Crétois* and was one of the fifty-two who voted for the *appel nominal* over Barère, Billaud-Varenne, Collot d'Herbois, and Vadier on 12 germinal an III/1 April 1795.[7] Inevitably, therefore, Javogues was arrested by the Convention on 13 prairial/1 June at the same time as other former ultra-revolutionary proconsuls—Mallarmé, Dartigoëyte, and Marc-Antoine Baudot.[8] After his release, there was little likelihood that Javogues would leave Paris. In brumaire an IV, his father sent him 9,000 *livres* and warned him that he would never be able to settle in the Loire, 'notre nom

[1] A.N., F7 4432, pl. 1, p. 36.

[2] Bibl. Lyon, Fonds général, MS. 1610, Patrin to Dupuy, 11 therm.

[3] Aulard, op. cit. vi. 418.

[4] e.g. Bibl. Roanne, 3 L (1) 20, 23 niv. an III, Phalippon buying wine for Dupuy, Javogues, and Dubouchet; A.D.L., L 47, fols. 6, 13, Dist. of Montbrison to Javogues and others, brum. and frim. an III; A.D.L., L 60, fols. 98, 116, Depart. to Javogues, therm. and fruct. an II.

[5] A.N., BB18 690, evidence of the woman Cantal.

[6] A.N., D III 349, d. Javogues, D III 343–4, D III 354, d. Méaulle, D III 225, d. Châlon-sur-Saône; D III 343, 'État général des différentes dénonciations . . .', 8 brum. an IV, places Javogues in twelfth position out of 214 deputies mentioned with thirty-seven denunciations.

[7] K. D. Tönnesson, *La Défaite des sans-culottes*, p. 205 n. 63.

[8] A.N., BB3 29, no. 885.

y étant entièrement proscrit'.[1] In any case, he seems to have been amply informed of conditions at home by acquaintances from the area who visited him.[2] His possessions had been ransacked during his detention and he was unable to pay the high rent now being demanded by his landlord in the rue Helvétius.[3] He moved first to his brother's lodgings in the Guillaume Tell section and then into semi-hiding in the rue de Clery with a *carte de sûreté* belonging to an immigrant German, which he later claimed to have picked up in the street.[4] A subscriber to Babeuf's *Tribun du Peuple*, though not to Lebois's *Ami du Peuple*,[5] Javogues soon gravitated towards the other proscribed Montagnards. By nivôse an IV, he could be seen in the Café Chrétien, which was a meeting-place for former Jacobins coming up from the provinces, in the company of his former enemy Maignet, Vadier of the terrorist Committee of General Security, the Jacobin general Rossignol, and Dufresse, a former general of the *armée révolutionnaire*.[6] Javogues was typical of this shattered remnant of the *Crête*, devoted to the memory of the Year II. He preserved the sash and plume of the *conventionnel* 'comme un fanatique porterait une relique', declaring that they were all that he had left and that he would carry them on him until he died; he acquired the habit of carrying a dagger so that, in the image of the Prairial Martyrs, he might turn it against himself if ever the enemies of the Republic should triumph.[7] Indeed, Javogues seems to have become one of the leaders of this group. According to Buonarotti, he was one of those who took the initiative in setting up a Committee of Montagnards in germinal an IV with the aim of taking advantage of a popular insurrection, which they deemed imminent, in order to re-establish the Convention and the Constitution of 1793.[8] He took part in the negotiations of mid floréal between this

1 A.N., W 554, d. 10, letter dated brum. an IV.
2 Ibid., letters of an IV from father and mother.
3 Ibid., Biram to Javogues, 14 brum. an IV.
4 Ibid., interrogation by *juge de paix* of Châtillon, 24 fruct. an IV.
5 A.N., F^7 4278, F^7 4771, d. 3 (Lebois).
6 A. Schmidt, *Tableaux de la Révolution française*, iii. 27.
7 A.N., W 554, d. 10, interrogation, 24 fruct. an IV and declaration by the woman Debrunière, 14 vend. an V.
8 P. Buonarotti, *La Conspiration pour l'Égalité dite de Babeuf* (Éditions sociales, 1957), i. 118. With Ricord, Laignelot, Choudieu, Amar, and later Robert Lindet.

group and the Babouvists, which produced agreement on an insurrection and on the national assembly that was to follow it.[1] When the Babouvists were arrested, the Montagnards attempted to implement themselves the agreed plan of bringing out the troops at the Camp de Grenelle. Thus, in the night of 23–24 fructidor an IV/9–10 September 1796, the former *conventionnels* Javogues, Cusset, and Huguet led a small group of militants, including at least one former terrorist from the Loire,[2] into the ambush prepared by the government.[3] Javogues managed to escape, but was arrested the next morning at an inn at Montrouge. Condemned to death by the *Conseil militaire* on 28 vendémiaire an V/19 October 1796, he was shot on the following day in the company of Huguet, Cusset, Bertrand, the former mayor of Commune-affranchie, etc. 'Tous sont morts en lâches. Javogues, seul, chantait sur la route'—the *Marseillaise*.[4]

[1] P. Buonarotti, op. cit. i. 139.

[2] Dubessey, administrator of the dept. Jean-François Rousset, *marchand chapelier tenant manufacture*, claimed to have arrived from Feurs on 24 vend. an III (A.N., W 554, d. 19); in germ. an III he claimed to have fled from the *égorgeurs* (A.N., F[11] 1181); but he has no identifiable terrorist past. Jean-Marie Lafond, born at Montbrison, had been living in Paris for eleven years (A.N., W 554, d. 8), but had been a member of the rev. com. of his section (A.N., F[7] 6327, d. 1).

[3] For the rest of the paragraph, four articles by G. Javogues: 'L'affaire du Camp de Grenelle', *A.H.R.F.* 1925, pp. 23–32; 'L'arrestation de Claude Javogues', ibid. 1926, pp. 374–83; 'Le procès de Claude Javogues', ibid. 1926, pp. 555–64; 'L'exécution de Claude Javogues', ibid. 1928, pp. 34–45. However, his basic argument that his ancestor was innocent appears both unsubstantiated and improbable.

[4] *La Gazette française*, 30 vend. an V; *Le Journal de Lyon et du département du Rhône*, 5 brum. an V.

CONCLUSION

THE history of the mission of Claude Javogues and of the department of the Loire during this period reveals the variety and the complexities of the Terror. The Terror was never implemented in a uniform fashion in the departments. Not merely did the will of the *Représentant en mission* often conflict with that of the central government, but the directives of both these authorities were consistently modified and distorted in the course of their application at a local level. Simple geographical facts prevented adjacent areas from responding similarly to the same impulses; antagonisms between town and country and between neighbouring urban centres dictated opposing reactions to the same political situation; contrasts in individual temperament and conviction and different types of problem in various towns and villages produced great variations in the activity of similar institutions. Although the Terror was a national phenomenon, it was expressed, at least during the 'anarchical' period, above all in local terms and its development was shaped by local issues.

Nevertheless, it would be incorrect to describe this state of affairs as confusion at a local level. It is evident that, in the Loire, a coherent structure of institutions administering the Terror emerged during the 'anarchical' period. Each of these institutions had a definite sphere of competence and there was surprisingly little conflict and encroachment between them. Even the 'anarchical' Terror appears, therefore, predominantly as a period of order when compared with the years preceding and succeeding it.

It is within this structure of terrorism that the *Représentant en mission* assumes his true dimension. Javogues could hardly be called all-powerful. On the one hand, he was one element in a structure of authorities and institutions which he both organized and used and without which he could not have had any effect on the department. On the other hand, he was never able to impose his views more than superficially on the area and he finally failed to convince the terrorists to accept the character that he wished to give to the Terror. The Terror was only possible in so far as its local agents were either prepared or could be made to administer it; inevitably, therefore, it was they, and not the proconsul, who decided the character of the Terror at this level. The role of the *Représentant en mission* was above all that of an organizer and a stimulant. More generally, however, his importance sprang from his relations with the central government and the other proconsuls. As far as the Loire is concerned, the 'anarchy' of the period resided in the fact that the *Représentant en mission* effectively prevented the department from participating in a co-ordinated, national system. In other words, the *Représentant en mission* was relatively more important in national terms than he was in local terms.

It is in this context that the law of 14 frimaire can be placed in a proper perspective. For the most part it contributed little to the structure of terrorism within the department. The practices which it aimed to destroy were, in any case, those of the proconsul. The career of Javogues illustrates the fact that the greatest enemies of the concept of a centralized Terror were the insubordinate *Représentants en mission* and not small groups of local extremists increasingly disavowed by their terrorist colleagues at a local level. By itself, therefore, the law of 14 frimaire did little to remedy the 'anarchical' Terror. It cannot be dissociated from the purge of the *Représentants en mission*, the elimination of the factions, and the destruction of the Parisian *armée révolutionnaire*. Moreover, it is certainly incorrect to say, at least as far as the Loire is concerned, that the law of 14 frimaire brought order to France overnight or indeed over several nights.

As with all case studies, it is dangerous to generalize from the particular. The Loire is not necessarily typical in all respects of other areas of intensive repression. For example, the decline in the number of arrests after pluviôse was certainly not paralleled either in the Nord or at Nancy or in the Basses-Pyrénées, where there was a recrudescence of repression in ventôse and germinal. The Loire differed from the frontier regions in the sense that repression was essentially retrospective and that, after a time, the arguments for its continuation appeared largely specious to all but a minority of the terrorists themselves. The Loire is also particular in that it was subjected to the influence of only one *Représentant en mission*. The essential orderliness of the period in this region may perhaps be ascribed to this fact and, therefore, the Loire may be untypical of other areas. The emergence of an 'anarchical' situation at a local level was often the fruit of political divergence between proconsuls operating in the same area and of their consequent patronage of separate groups of people with different political attitudes. For instance, the vicissitudes of the struggle between moderates and *ultras* at Nancy during the Year II can be directly related to successive reforms by the moderate Faure, the *ultras* Lacoste and Baudot, the moderate Pflieger, and finally the more terrorist Michaud. Furthermore, the Loire was never troubled by the initiatives of insubordinate *commissaires* which were a characteristic of many areas of intensive repression.

On the other hand, however, the geographical distribution of the revolutionary committees and the structure of terrorism at the lowest level in the Loire suggest that we might be well advised to take a closer look at other areas of intensive repression. It is evident that in those areas of the Loire that were subjected to the most intensive repression, the revolutionary committees were less widespread than in those areas untouched by the rebellion. This is true not only of the district of Roanne as a whole but also of the south-east corner of the department, which had been insulated from the revolt by geographical features. It is also clear that the clubs and the committees were more regimented in the Loire than they were in many other areas of France, but that they were more regimented in the districts of Boën and Armeville than they were in the district of Roanne. It is possible that in areas of intensive repression the threat of counter-revolution was felt to be more immediate, because its effects had been experienced, and that this emphasized the need for an organized riposte. Elsewhere, however, the creation of a committee, for example, had a more preventive than punitive character; it was directed against a threat known to exist but not experienced, and the need to organize was correspondingly less urgent. Indeed, an official programme for the establishment of committees, such as existed in the district of Boën and Armeville, would tend to deter communes from forming them spontaneously. On the one hand, they would feel that this might transgress the rules, and on the other, the move would have less significance as an act of political insurance. In the district of Roanne, however, the communes were left to make their own decisions about the utility of committees and about the political expediency of having them. The pattern in the Loire, therefore, tends to suggest that the 'anarchical' proliferation of extra-ordinary institutions is a phenomenon to be associated less with an area of intensive repression than with the fringe areas that abutted on it.

In general terms, however, it seems to us that both the social basis of the terrorists and the structure and activity of the institutions of the Terror in the Loire are typical of the greater part of France. Moreover, the problems facing the terrorists here were the same as those elsewhere, while the juxtaposition of mountain and plain has allowed us to illustrate the pattern of the Terror in both types of country. Finally, Javogues provides an excellent subject for a case study of the ultra-revolutionaries.

BIBLIOGRAPHY

PRIMARY SOURCES

I. MANUSCRIPT

By far the greater part of the documentation used in this study was gathered from manuscript sources. But it would be unnecessarily fastidious to enumerate the references to all the dossiers exploited and, rather than provide a bald checklist, this bibliography will only characterize the broad areas explored in an effort to supplement the standard *instruments de travail* and to give some general assistance by analogy to others wishing to engage in local studies of the Terror.

* * *

Any historian working on the provincial history of this period must necessarily devote considerable time to research in the **Archives nationales.** But, contrary to a commonly held belief, this repository is frequently disappointing for the Terror in the departments. In contrast to the Directorial period, whose local struggles are often more richly illuminated by the papers in the Archives nationales than by those in the departments, a great deal of the local history of the Terror is hardly reflected here. Part of the explanation of this is inherent in the arguments in this book. Naturally, a historian who wishes to survey a much wider geographical area than that scrutinized in this book, or to pursue a theme in its application to the whole of France, must use the Archives nationales for the sake of convenience. But his work will remain incomplete without some supporting research in local archives. The papers of the provincial Terror in the Archives nationales may be broadly categorized in three ways. Firstly, they illuminate the preoccupations of the central government and the nature of its relationship with the provinces; secondly, they concern or arise out of political police work; thirdly, they reflect the miscellany of issues presented in petitions sent in from the provinces. Of course, the preoccupations of the central government in this period were manifold and the definitions of political crime both various and ambiguous, while the great power and disposition to intervene of the terrorist government attracted petitioning on a whole host of matters of personal and local interest. Thus, one encounters here a great many documents crucial to the understanding of the Terror in the departments, while the range of subject matter is quite unpredictable. None the less, the whole routine of local affairs, whether in the domain of ordinary administration or else in repression and all the activities of the local Terror, tends to be absent from the Archives nationales. For the most part the central government did not inquire too closely into the business of local institutions as long as they could accomplish their tasks adequately and in conformity with political norms. Only when the Terror and its agents were contested, only when the local authorities were unable to solve problems or to satisfy personal or communal grievances, did matters begin to come to the attention of higher authorities. Clearly, this was frequently the case. Some problems, such as food supply or rebellion, were beyond the power of local men to solve, while some areas, especially those fairly close to Paris, and some groups, especially suspects and rival factions, were prone to solicit the interest of the government. But this situation does mean that the greater part of the documents in the Archives nationales on local affairs refers essentially to exceptional cases. However interesting the exceptional may be and however necessary for the comprehension of this *régime d'exception*, the reality of the Terror at this level lay not so much in the exceptional as in the ordinary, the quotidian.

The essential source for a regional study of the kind in this book is provided by the papers of the Committee of Public Safety in the Series AF II. Here is to be found the correspondence exchanged between the Committee and the *Représentants en mission* and institutions in the departments, together with the decisions of the Committee relating to the proconsuls, correspondence with other committees about local affairs, copies of many of the proconsuls' *arrêtés*, and miscellaneous documents sent in from the departments. F.-A. Aulard published many of the elements of this Series in his *Recueil des Actes du Comité de Salut public* (Paris, 1889–1933), but he omitted not only the papers annexed to the correspondence received by the Committee, but also many of the letters themselves. The Series D XLII also contains miscellaneous papers of the Committee of Public Safety, a few of which related to the problems studied in this book. But the Series D § I, which ostensibly is concerned with the *Représentants en mission*, is generally disappointing and contains nothing on the area round Lyon.

The various departmental Sub-series provide the second major source in this repository. They usually consist largely of petitions with their accompanying documents and correspondence. As far as this study was concerned, the departmental section of the Series D III proved to be the most directly relevant, together with the personal dossiers in the same Series of *Représentants en mission* denounced in the Year III. The Series F^2 and F^3, relating to local administration, contained no documents which could be useful within the scope of this book, while, among the Sub-series in the Series F^1 F^{1a}, and F^{1d} appeared largely without interest. However, the departmental cartons in F^{1b} and F^{1c} present a considerable amount of documentation relevant to the Terror, even though the bulk of the material dates from the period of the Directory. Similarly, the departmental cartons in BB^{16} and BB^{18}, containing papers relating to civil and criminal proceedings respectively, are a source which no regional historian of the Terror can afford to neglect since so many terrorists were involved in confrontations of this sort after the Year II. Finally, local issues during the Terror can be illuminated by documents from the Series D IV bis concerning the establishment of the new administrative boundaries of the Revolution and the ensuing quarrels.

The Series F^7 is justly renowned and any study of the provincial Terror must include research in it, especially in the dossiers of the Committee of General Security. The instruments of coercion were the hub of the Terror and thus one is likely to encounter here material relating indirectly to a wide range of subjects; but more directly the papers concern the system of repression, its victims, and also local terrorists in the vicissitudes of their political existence during and after the Terror. However, although a study of a broadly based aspect of provincial history will derive great benefit from its eclectic nature, the historian confining himself to one geographical area may well find the Series arduous and return on time invested fairly low. It can be of uneven value and is difficult to use, especially the departmental Sub-series entitled 'Statistique personnelle et morale'. Similar considerations apply to the Series W. Some interesting discoveries can be made among the petitions, letters, and evidence contained in Fouquier-Tinville's papers and those of the revolutionary tribunal (and also, in the case of this book, among the papers relating to the Camp de Grenelle), but one must expect frustrations if one is locating material for a single area. The sequestrated papers in the Series T present much the same characteristics, although the inventory is more helpful than in the case of several of the other series.

Finally, one should not ignore such series as F^{10}, F^{11}, F^{12}, and F^{20} (all of which provided material for this book) even when one is not primarily concerned with the subjects to which these Series are devoted, for they all contain large numbers of documents whose relationship to the title of the Series is purely incidental.

* * *

The manuscript material in the provinces used for this book was located in three sorts of repository: departmental archives, communal archives, and municipal libraries.

The Series L in the **Archives départementales de la Loire** provided the central core of documentation. The Archives possess a hand-written catalogue which gives a fair general indication of the contents of each dossier, although a few have disappeared since it was drawn up towards the beginning of this century. There is also a useful printed inventory of each item in the *registres des délibérations* of the central administration of the department up to the Year VI. This Series originated as the archives of the successive central administrations of the department before the Consulate. They comprised, on the one hand, the registers and papers relating to the administrations' own business, and, on the other, the archives of various other institutions handed in at the time of their abolition, that is to say essentially the district and the cantonal administrations. The archives of the district administrations in turn contained those of the clubs and the revolutionary committees surrendered in the Year III. The Series has remained largely in its original form with each of these elements forming a Sub-series, although the papers of the local extraordinary institutions of the Terror have been separated from those of the Districts.

As far as the papers of the regular administrations are concerned, they can be divided into three main categories. Firstly, the *registres des délibérations*. In some cases there are separate registers for the *directoire* and *conseil général*, while some of the administrations also kept separate registers for important recurrent topics like food supply and repression. These latter, however, prove to be often incomplete and should be treated with caution. Although the *registres des délibérations* tend to become formalized and narrowly administrative under the Directory, those of the Terror period in the Loire contain not merely the texts of local government decisions, but also an amount of revealing ancillary information in the form of justification for these decisions together with a record of some debates among administrators and transcriptions of more formal speeches. Secondly, the correspondence registers. There was considerable disparity of practice between administrations here. Usually, the correspondence of the *agent national* and his predecessor was recorded in separate registers from that of the administration as a whole; in the best case (the District of Roanne, typically enough), separate registers were also used for incoming and outgoing letters, for correspondence with superior and inferior authorities, and for some major topics. But during the Terror period, when many of the trained *commis* became suspects and patriotism was as much a requisite for such employment as talent, great confusion developed. This was also later the case of the central administration under the Directory when successive teams of administrators tended to purge the employees of their predecessors. It is most unwise to rely on the title of a register (and thus the description in the catalogue) as rendering accurately its contents. Letters are transcribed in the wrong register; some registers are incomplete, others abandoned, yet others used for two or three different purposes either simultaneously or at different periods. None the less, these registers constitute a vital source, since not only do they reflect the whole activity of the administrations and their relations with other institutions, but they also contain a vast amount of information not recorded elsewhere. Thirdly, the dossiers of miscellaneous papers. The most coherent element among these are the papers relating to the administrations' accounts. Although the accounts themselves were of no benefit to the kind of study undertaken in this book, many of the supporting documents were of use since, ultimately, most of the aspects of the Terror found expression in terms of expenditure that had to be accounted for. In general, the other papers in these dossiers are composed of petitions, reports, and letters of every sort. Their contents are quite unpredictable and there is no uniformity in the topics represented in each of the various component archives. While some attempt seems to have been made to group documents according to subject, this is only a significant asset to research when there are enough to make up a whole dossier. Usually, the dossiers have been compiled by amalgamating a number of topics related only in time. Although petitions were listed in registers on their arrival at the administrations, as far as the Loire is concerned this involved only the briefest characterization of content. This very rich and varied source can only be fully tapped by working through nearly all the dossiers.

The Archives of the Loire also contain a body of documents belonging to local authorities during the Terror. Several *registres des délibérations* of Municipalities have found their way here, either because they were subsequently used by a cantonal administration, or else because of some accident: all the registers from Saint-Bonnet-le-Château since 1789 are here, for example, because they were being scrutinized by Lapalus at the time of his arrest. More interesting, and fundamental to this study, are the papers of the local extraordinary terrorist authorities. Although the registers of only three clubs have survived (Charlieu, Régny, and Saint-Chamond), and although the papers of neither the club nor the committee at Roanne and Saint-Étienne are extant, the Archives possess a remarkably extensive collection of material from the revolutionary committees, which, as far as the centre of France is concerned, is rivalled only by the holdings of the Puy-de-Dôme.

At the time that the research for this book was undertaken, there also existed an important supplement to the Series. L. This contained largely miscellaneous material from every category represented in the Series L, but which had reached the Archives subsequent to the establishment of this Series. It also contained elements which were not represented there, especially the papers of the *armée révolutionnaire*, those of the departmental engineer, population statistics, prison records, and the registers of the civil and criminal tribunals, together with those of several justices of the peace. Clearly, these judicial records are a magnificent source for the social history of the period and can also be used to complement the BB Series in the Archives nationales. But their exploitation is rendered extremely laborious by the appallingly crabbed handwriting common to all of them. This supplement has recently been incorporated into the Series L and can be consulted by means of the old inventory on cards which now carry the new reference.

This study also benefited from two other Series in this repository. The Series Q should not be neglected by historians of this period for it contains material on arrested and convicted suspects and also on the operation of the Terror and on the terrorists themselves. For instance, the *procès-verbaux* relating to the desecration of the churches during the Year II are often found here, while the sale of the *biens nationaux* can provide information about the fortune of individual terrorists, as much by their bids as by their purchases. Unfortunately, the summary inventory of this Series in the Loire is more than sybilline and time restricted our investigation to a number of *sondages*. As for the Series C, material from the late Ancien Régime tax records contributed to chapters I and XI. Finally, a private collection acquired by the Archives and entitled the Fonds Chaleyer (inventory on cards) contains a few documents relating to the Terror, notably the registers of the Municipalities of Firminy and Fontanès.

* * *

Research on the area round Lyon necessarily includes work in the **Archives départementales du Rhône**. In general terms, the populous city of Lyon was the centre of gravity of this region and the events of the federalist crisis and the siege had repercussions in every direction. Furthermore, throughout the Terror the *Représentants en mission* in the city had supervisory powers over the whole region and actively intervened at one time or another in every part of it; moreover, many appeals were made to them in an effort to circumvent local authorities. Finally, since the Loire was formed out of the division of the department of the Rhône-et-Loire, much that concerns the Loire in particular is to be found in the Rhône archives. This is especially true of the early years of the Revolution, but even after 1793 an amount of miscellaneous material still found its way there.

As far as this study is concerned, three elements of the Series L (of which there is a printed summary inventory) were found useful. Firstly, the papers of the *Représentants en mission* (in the Sub-series 1 L). Although these are less voluminous for the Terror in the Loire than for the Thermidorian Reaction, for reasons explained in this book, they contain a number of important *arrêtés* together with correspondence and investigations, which illuminate the circumstances leading up to Javogues's recall. Secondly, the papers of the *Commission Temporaire* (Sub-series 31 L). The activities of this institution, which still awaits systematic examination, affected the Loire possibly less than other areas in the region. Above all, it is the papers of the revolutionary tribunals (Sub-series 42 L) which are of capital importance. The tribunals at Lyon dealt not only with inhabitants of the city and with strangers accused of participating in the rebellion, but also with suspects sent in from the whole region and accused of all the crimes in the Law of Suspects. Furthermore, it is here that the papers of the revolutionary tribunals at Feurs are deposited, for they were dispatched to Lyon when the remaining prisoners were forwarded for trial there in pluviôse an II. The papers of each tribunal are grouped separately and comprise correspondence, interrogations, evidence, copies of judgements, and personal dossiers. These last are especially abundant, often containing the suspect's own private papers in addition to information provided by the authorities about him. Also among the papers of these tribunals are the registers of the sections of Saint-Étienne during the summer of 1793, of the federalist *comité central* of the district of Saint-Étienne, and the registers of the Municipality of Gumières (42 L 40–43).

* * *

Finally, the **Archives départementales du Puy-de-Dôme** contributed the important papers of the Committee of Public Safety of Montbrison (L 2781–5), taken back there by its Auvergnat members, while some of Couthon's papers (L 322) also related to the early period of the Terror in the Loire. The **Archives départementales de la Saône-et-Loire** provided some supplementary details concerning the supply of food to the Loire as well as Javogues's first quarrels.

* * *

Departmental archives contain essentially a different kind of document from that discovered in the Archives nationales, despite an amount of duplication. Similarly, **communal archives** preserve in the minutes of the Municipalities material rarely encountered elsewhere in more than fragmentary form and thus they complement the sources consulted at the departmental and national levels. Here is a qualitatively different vision of local affairs, which in its immediacy, in its naïvety indeed, provides the historian with his closest contact with the grass-roots. A list of items held in the communal archives is kept at the Archives départementales. The larger towns usually have a separate archival service, as is the case at Saint-Étienne, Roanne, and Saint-Chamond in the Loire; but in the smaller towns and villages these papers are kept in a cupboard or an attic and it is advisable to write in advance of a visit in order to give the staff of the *mairie* time to remember where they are. One should also check opening hours, since the smaller *mairies* are not always open every day. This study made use of the *registres des délibérations* of the Municipalities of Chazelles-sur-Lyon, Feurs, Moingt, Montbrison, Noailly, Roanne (Sub-series 1 D 1), Saint-Chamond, Saint-Étienne (Sub-series 1 D 10), and

Saint-Rambert; the correspondence register (Sub-series 2 D 2) and tax documents (Sub-series 1 G 1) from Roanne, and the collection of proclamations (Sub-series 2 D 12) and tax documents (Sub-series 2 G 66) from Saint-Étienne were also used.

* * *

In the **Bibliotheque municipale de Lyon,** the Fonds Coste contains a large number of manuscripts relating to the whole region as well as to the city. Built up in the early nineteenth century, in part at least with documents from the papers of local administrations, this magnificent collection was partially acquired by the Municipality of Lyon in the middle of that century. Unfortunately concerned only to document the 'glorious' period of the city's history, the Municipality acquired primarily the documents relating to the federalist crisis and the siege of Lyon. Many of these are duplicates of those found elsewhere. The documents relating to the Terror were in a number of cases scorned, resulting in the loss to a public depot of vital documents on Lyon and the surrounding departments. A useful catalogue of the collection was published before the sale: A. Vingtrinier, *Catalogue de la bibliothèque de Monsieur Coste* (Lyon, Paris, 1853). Most documents are clearly identified and a number are summarized. The classification has not been retained by the municipal library, but a copy of the catalogue with the new reference numbers marked in it may be obtained from the counter in the reading-room.

* * *

The **Bibliothèque municipale de Roanne** contains a small and jealously guarded collection of disparate documents, of which the most useful for this study were the miscellaneous papers relating to the local extra-ordinary institutions (Sub-series 3 L (1)). The library also possesses the minutes of the *juge de paix* and the district tribunal from the Year III to the Year VI. The municipal library at **Saint-Étienne** contributed Claude Pupil's notes on his recollections of the Revolution (MS. 310), while a few references were used from Maignet's papers in the municipal library at **Clermont-Ferrand** (MSS. 357 *bis* and 360).

2. PRINTED

The printed versions of the *arrêtés* of the *Représentants en mission* are not included. Unless otherwise stated, all these documents are to be found in the *Bibliothèque nationale*.

MODERN EDITIONS AND COLLECTIONS

Archives parlementaires (*Les*), vols. 81, 83, 84

Aulard, F.-A., *Recueil des Actes du Comité de Salut public* (Paris, 1889–1933)

—— *La Société des Jacobins* (Paris, 1889–97)

Béraud, Marcellin, *Compte rendu à ses commettants*, ed. J.-M. Devet (Saint-Étienne, 1884)

Buonarotti, Ph., *La Conspiration pour l'Égalité dite de Babeuf* (Paris, 1957)

Correspondance politique de Paris et des départements, no. 90, *A.H.R.F.* 1924, pp. 498–501

(Couthon), *Correspondance inédite de Couthon*, ed. F. Mège (Paris, 1872)
Donot, P., and Neufbourg, L. de, *Le Forez pendant la Révolution* (Lyon, 1888)
Procès-verbaux des séances du conseil général du département de Rhône-et-Loire, 1790–3, 2 vols., ed. G. Guigue (Trévoux, 1895)
Procès-verbaux des séances de la Commission populaire républicaine et de Salut public de Rhône-et-Loire, ed. G. Guigue (Trévoux, 1899)
Puy, C.-J., *Expédition des Lyonnais dans le Forez*, ed. L. Chaleyer *et al.* (Lyon, 1889: Bibl. Lyon, 318. 510)
'Registre de la thaille, subsidiaire et vingtième de Montbrison, année 1789', *Bulletin de la Diana*, 1941, pp. 227–443
Registre des délibérations de la commune de Savigneux . . ., ed. J. Cerisier (Montbrison, 1945: Bibl. Lyon, 149. 130)
Registre des procès-verbaux de la société républicaine de Saint-Chamond, ed. G. Lefebvre (Lyon, 1890)
Schmidt, A., *Tableaux de la Révolution française*, vol. iii (Leipzig, 1869)
Sée, A., *Le Procès Pache* (Paris, 1911)

GENERAL

Almanach national, 1793 and an II
Billaud-Varenne, *Rapport fait . . . sur un mode de gouvernement provisoire et révolutionnaire* (an II)
Châteauneuf-Randon, *Rapport des missions* (messidor an III)
Courtois, E.-B., *Rapport fait au nom de la commission chargée de l'examen des papiers trouvés chez Robespierre* (nivôse an III)
—— *Papiers inédits . . . supprimés ou omis par Courtois*, 3 vols. (Paris, 1828)
Cusset, *Adresse aux vertueux électeurs de Rhône-et-Loire* (August 1792) (Bibl. Lyon, 350. 873)
Dorfeuille, *Discours prononcé . . . après la lecture du décret sur les hommes de couleur* (ventôse an II)
—— *Aux habitants du district de Roanne* (Roanne, 1793) (Bibl. Roanne, 1 L 8)
Dubois-Crancé, *Aux Jacobins, en rentrant dans la société* (thermidor an II) (A.N., F7 4683, d. 1)
Dubouchet, *Compte moral* (an V) (A.N., AD XVI 45)
Expilly, *Dictionnaire géographique, historique et politique des Gaules et de la France*, 6 vols. (Amsterdam, 1764)
Javogues *et al.*, *Mémoire à consulter pour Sieur Jacques Marie Simon* (March 1788) (Bibl. Saint-Étienne, C XIII, p. 8)
—— *Compte rendu de ce qu'il a dépensé dans les missions dont il a été chargé* (an III)
—— *Discours prononcé à la société des sans-culottes républicains de Bourg* (frimaire an II) (A.N., AF II 84 (623))
Procès-verbal de la Convention nationale, vols. 16, 17, 24, 31

NEWSPAPERS

Gazette française (*La*)
Moniteur (*L'Ancien*)

Je suis le cousin du Père Duchesne, foutre! (Commune-affranchie, an II)
Je suis le véritable Père Duchesne, foutre! (ibid.)
Journal de Commune-affranchie et des départements de Rhône et Loire
Journal de Lyon ou Moniteur du département de Rhône-et-Loire
Journal de Lyon et du département du Rhône
Journal républicain des deux départements de Rhône et de Loire
Soirées de la campagne ou le voyageur révolutionnaire (*Les*) (Commune-affranchie, état-major de l'armée révolutionnaire, nivôse an II: Bibl. Lyon, 350. 614)

LOIRE

Adresse aux Foréziens (n.d.) (A.N., AD XVI 45).
Compte rendu de la gestion du directoire du district de Montbrison (germinal an III) (A.D.L., 273)
Liste des cent plus fort imposables de la commune de Montbrison (1812) (A.N., F1b II Loire 10, d. Montbrison)
Liste des cent plus fort imposables de la commune de Saint-Chamond (1812) (F1b II Loire 14, d. Saint-Chamond)
Liste des électeurs du département de Rhône-et-Loire (1791) (Bibl. Lyon, 350. 863)
Liste des notables du département de la Loire (an X) (A.N., AD XVI 45)
Mémoire présenté à M. Necker . . . par les citoyens de Mont-Brison et de son département (January 1789) (A.N., D IVbis 16, d. 271)
Tableau des conspirateurs et des personnes suspectes du ci-devant district de Montbrisé (n.d.) (A.N., BB16 646, d. 1793)
Tableau des conspirateurs et des personnes suspectes du district d'Armeville, ci-devant Saint-Étienne (n.d.) (ibid.)
Tableau général des émigrés, condamnés, déportés, fugitifs et reclus du district de Roanne (thermidor an II) (A.D.L., L suppl. 274)
Alléon-Dulac, *Mémoires pour servir à l'histoire naturelle des provinces de Lyonnais, Forez et Beaujolais* (Lyon, 1765)
Barges *et al.*, *A leurs commettants* (Feurs, an II) (A.D.R., 42 L 148)
Bourgeois, *Réponse aux discours du citoyen Pignon* (Saint-Étienne, 1793) (Bibl. Saint-Étienne, 2501, p. 2)
Dubien, *Aux citoyens d'Armeville . . ., Montbrisé, Feurs, Roanne, Boën etc.* (n.d.) (ibid. CX, p. 29)
Forest *et al.*, *Sur les élections du département de la Loire* (an VI) (A.N., AD XVI 45)
Lafaye, *Discours à la société populaire de Feurs* (n.d.) (Bibl. Roanne, 10 L 6)
Laforest, *Nécessité des mœurs républicaines* (Saint-Étienne, 1793) (Bibl. Saint-Étienne, C. XIII, p. 7)
Lenoble, *Mission patriotique* (n.d.) (A.N., F1c III Rhône 8, d. 4)
Méaudre *et al.*, *Mémoire sur le département de la Loire* (thermidor an V) (A.N., F1b II Loire 10, d. Objets généraux)
Pignon, *Discours en l'honneur de Simonneau* (n.d.) (Bibl. Saint-Étienne, 2634, p. 20)
—— *Discours lors de la réintégration des sociétés populaires* (Saint-Étienne, 1793) (ibid. 2501, p. 2)

Pointe, *Compte rendu à la Convention nationale* (n.d.)
Pressavin and Reverchon, *Rapport des commissaires-députés, envoyés dans les départements de Rhône-et-Loire et Saône-et-Loire* (April 1793) (Bibl. Lyon, 350. 565)
(Rive-de-Gier), *A l'Assemblée nationale* (Lyon, 1789) (A.N., AD XVI 45)
Roanne, *Société populaire, règlements* (May 1793) (A.D.L., L 419)
—— *A la Convention nationale* (Roanne, 1793) (A.N., loc. cit.)
—— *Mémoire adressé au Comité de Sûreté générale* (nivôse an II) (Bibl. Roanne, 3 L (1) 18)
Roland, *Lettres écrites de Suisse, d'Italie, et de Sicile, et de Malthe en 1776, 1777, et 1778*, vol. vi (Amsterdam, 1780)
(Saint-Chamond, *Société populaire*), *Citoyens Représentants* (Feurs, an II)
(Commune d'Armes/Saint-Étienne, *Société populaire*), *Adresse à la Convention nationale* (Commune d'Armes, pluviôse an II) (A.N., loc. cit.)
Siauve, *Discours prononcé dans une assemblée de la société populaire* (Saint-Étienne, 1792)
Thiolière *et al.*, *Compte rendu à ses commettants* (August 1793) (A.D.R., 42 L 157)
Voytier, *Discours à ses concitoyens* (Saint-Étienne, 1793) (Bibl. Saint-Étienne, 2501, p. 2)

COMMUNE-AFFRANCHIE/LYON

Almanach astronomique et historique de la ville de Lyon et des provinces de Lyonnais, Forez et Beaujolais, 1759 and 1789
Histoire du siège de Lyon (Lausanne, 1795)
Lettre écrite à l'auteur d'un journal très connu (n.d.) (Bibl. Lyon, 350. 550)
Liste générale des dénonciateurs et des dénoncés tant de la ville de Lyon que des communes voisines (Lausanne, 1795)
(Commission Temporaire), *Instruction adressée aux autorités constituées . . .* (brumaire an II)
Couthon, *Première partie du rapport sur le siège de Commune-affranchie* (n.d.)
Dubois-Crancé, *Première, seconde et troisième partie de la réponse aux inculpations de ses collègues* (n.d.)
Guillon, A., *Histoire du siège de Lyon*, 2 vols. (Paris, 1797)
Tallien, *Rapport à la Convention sur les troubles à Lyon* (February 1793)
(Villefranche-sur-Saône, *Société populaire*), *A la Convention nationale* (an II) (A.N., AD XVI 63)
Vingtrinier, A., *Catalogue de la bibliothèque lyonnaise de M. Coste* (Lyon, 1853)

SAÔNE-ET-LOIRE

(Bellevue-les-Bains, *Société populaire*, etc.), *Au département de Saône-et-Loire* (brumaire an II) (A.N., D IVbis 89, d. Saône-et-Loire)
(Châlon-sur-Saône, *Société populaire*), *Extrait des registres des délibérations* (frimaire an II) (A.N., AD XVI 65)
—— *Justification contre les inculpations* (frimaire an II) (ibid.)
Paillet, J., *L'Expédition lyonnaise* (n.d.)

AIN

Coup d'œil sur les manœuvres des intriguants de la commune de Bourg (an III)
Grand Voyage du cousin du Père Duchesne dans le district de Trévoux (Le) (an II)
Sans-culottes de Bourg . . . députés par la commune entière (Les) (n.d.)
(Bourg), *Dénonciation contre Amar, Javogues, Albitte et Méaulle* (an III)
Gouly, B., *Compte rendu à la Convention nationale* (ventôse an II)
—— *Supplément au compte rendu* (n.d.)

SECONDARY WORKS

The following have been used for reference or for comparison:

Billacois, F., 'La batellerie de la Loire au XVIIe siècle', *Revue d'histoire moderne et contemporaine*, 1964, pp. 163–90
Calvet, H., 'Les rapports du comité de surveillance et les autorités constituées du département de Loir-et-Cher', *A.H.R.F.* 1928, pp. 430–41
Cobb, R. C., *Les Armées révolutionnaires*, 2 vols. (Paris, 1961–3)
Gershoy, L., *Bertrand Barère* (Princeton, 1962)
Godechot, J., *Les Institutions de la France sous la Révolution et l'Empire* (Paris, 1951)
—— 'Le comité de surveillance révolutionnaire de Nancy', *R.f.* 1927, pp. 249–62, 295–311
Imberdis, F., *Le Réseau routier de l'Auvergne au XVIIIe siècle* (Paris, 1966)
Jacob, L., *Joseph Le Bon*, 2 vols. (Paris, 1934)
Labrousse, C.-E., *Esquisse du mouvement des prix et des revenus en France au XVIIIe siècle* (Paris, 1933)
Madelin, L., *Fouché*, 2 vols. (Paris, 1901)
Martin, G., *Carrier et sa mission à Nantes* (Paris, 1922)
Mautouchet, P., *Le Gouvernement révolutionnaire* (Paris, 1912)
Meunier, L., 'Albitte, conventionnel en missions', *A.H.R.F.* 1946, pp. 49–66, 238–77
Pichois, C., and Dautry, J., *Le Conventionnel Chasles et ses idées démocratiques* (Aix-en-Provence, 1958)
Richard, A., 'Le comité de surveillance et les suspects de Dax', *A.H.R.F.* 1930, pp. 24–40
Rouff, M., *Les Mines de charbon en France au XVIIIe siècle* (Paris, 1922)
Sangnier, G., *La Terreur dans le district de Saint-Pol*, 2 vols. (Paris, 1938)
Sirich, J. B., *The Revolutionary Committees in the Departments of France, 1793–4* (Cambridge, Mass., 1943)
Soboul, A., *Les Sans-culottes parisiens en l'an II* (Paris, 1962)
Tönnesson, K. D., *La Défaite des sans-culottes* (Paris, 1959)
Vaillandet, P., 'La Mission de Maignet en Vaucluse', *A.H.R.F.* 1926, pp. 168–78, 240–63

On Claude Javogues:

Birembaut, A., 'Javogues vu par C.-A. Alexandre', *A.H.R.F.* 1967, pp. 402–3
*Gonon, F., *Un Forézien célèbre, Claude Javogues* (Saint-Étienne, 1938)

* I was able to consult this extremely rare book thanks to the kindness of the Father Abbot and the community of the Abbaye de Saint-Benoît at Fleury-sur-Loire.

Javogues, G., 'Une défense de Claude Javogues', *Ann. rév.* 1922, pp. 417–19
—— 'Lamartine et Claude Javogues', ibid. 1923, pp. 288–95
—— 'L'affaire du Camp de Grenelle', *A.H.R.F.* 1925, pp. 23–32
—— 'L'arrestation de Claude Javogues', ibid. pp. 374–83
—— 'Le procès de Claude Javogues', ibid. 1926, pp. 555–64
—— 'L'exécution de Claude Javogues', ibid. 1928, pp. 34–45
—— 'Un conventionnel forézien: Claude Javogues', *Amis du Vieux Saint-Étienne*, 1932
Marion, M., 'La guerre aux riches en 1793 et le conventionnel Javogues', *Revue universelle*, 15 April 1925, pp. 125–46
Soanen, H., 'Les sociétés populaires du Puy-de-Dôme et le rappel du conventionnel Javogues', *A.H.R.F.* 1931, pp. 431–7
Tézenas du Montcel, P., *Deux régicides: Claude Javogues et Noël Pointe* (Saint-Étienne, 1952)
—— 'Notes sur la famille de Claude Javogues', *Revue du Sud-Est illustrée*, July 1905

Some fine local studies exist on the Loire and the neighbouring region. Galley's work on the Revolution is particularly remarkable for the density and accuracy of information, but unfortunately the absence of an index makes it difficult to use. The same criticism applies to Herriot. Riffaterre remains one of the best books on the federalist crisis anywhere in France.

Dubois, E., *Histoire de la Révolution dans l'Ain*, 6 vols. (Bourg, 1931–5)
Galley, J. B., *L'Élection de Saint-Étienne à la fin de l'Ancien Régime* (Saint-Étienne, 1903)
—— *Saint-Étienne et son district pendant la Révolution*, 3 vols. (Saint-Étienne, 1904–6)
Herriot, E., *Lyon n'est plus*, 4 vols. (Paris, 1937–40)
Mège, F., *Le Puy-de-Dôme en 1793 et le proconsulat de Couthon* (Paris, 1877)
Pothier, F., *Roanne pendant la Révolution, 1789–1796* (Roanne, 1868)
Riffaterre, C., *Le Mouvement antijacobin et antiparisien à Lyon et dans le Rhône-et-Loire en 1793*, 2 vols. (Lyon, 1912–28)

Much more disappointing, however, are:

Bauzon, L. *et al.*, *Recherches historiques sur la persécution religieuse dans le département de Saône-et-Loire pendant la Révolution*, 4 vols. (Châlon-sur-Saône, 1889–1903)
Brossard, E., *Histoire du département de la Loire pendant la Révolution française, 1789–1799* (Paris, 1904–7)

This latter needs to be used with particular caution after the Year II.

Material can also be found in the following works:

Balleydier, A., *Histoire politique et militaire du peuple de Lyon*, 3 vols. (Paris, 1845–6)
Broutin, A., *Histoire de la ville de Feurs* (Saint-Étienne, 1867)
—— *Histoire des couvents de Montbrison avant 1793*, 2 vols. (Saint-Étienne, 1874–6)
Buenner, (Dom), *Madame de Bavoz, abbesse de Pradines de l'ordre de Saint Benoît, 1768–1838* (Lyon, 1961)

Cobb, R. C., 'Un comité révolutionnaire du Forez. Le comité de surveillance de Bonnet-la-Montagne (Loire)', *A.H.R.F.* 1957, pp. 296–315
—— *L'Armée révolutionnaire parisienne à Lyon* (Lyon, n.d.)
Cohas, J., *Saint-Germain-Laval pendant la Révolution, 1789–1795* (Charlieu, 1906)
Devet, J. M., *Dénonciation des Stéphanois contre le Représentant Javogues* (Saint-Étienne, 1884)
—— *Une Taxe révolutionnaire en faveur de l'humanité souffrante* (ibid.)
—— *La Contribution patriotique de 1789* (Saint-Étienne, 1885)
—— *Une Prison en 1793 et 1794. Registre d'écrou* (Saint-Étienne, 1890)
—— *Montbrison sous la Terreur. Les premières arrestations* (Saint-Étienne, 1897)
Dumoulin, M., *Charlieu au XVIIIe siècle* (Roanne, 1898)
Estier, R., 'La crise de la papeterie auvergnate au XVIIIe siècle', *Cahiers d'histoire*, 1966, pp. 181–205.
Gardette, P., 'Carte linguistique du Forez', *Bulletin de la Diana*, 1943, pp. 259–81.
Gonon, F., *Histoire de la chanson stéphanoise et forézienne* (Saint-Étienne, 1906)
Gras, L.-J., *Histoire du commerce locale . . . dans la région stéphanoise* (Saint-Étienne, 1910)
—— *Les Routes du Forez et du Jarez* (Saint-Étienne, n.d.)
Guyonnet, M.-C., 'Jacques de Flesselles, Intendant de Lyon, 1768–1784', *Albums du crocodile*, 1956
Huguet, A., *Le Cloître de Notre-Dame de Montbrison en 1791* (Montbrison, 1894)
Labouré, M., *Roanne et le Roannais: études historiques* (Lyon, 1957)
La Chapelle, S. de, *Histoire des tribunaux révolutionnaires de Lyon et de Feurs* (Lyon, 1879)
Lefebvre, G., *Souvenirs de cent ans. Saint-Chamond et Rive-de-Gier* (Paris, 1889)
Lucas, C., 'La guillotine à Feurs (Loire) en l'an II', *A.H.R.F.* 1965, pp. 216–17
—— 'Le désarmement du comte de Saint-Polgues', ibid. 1965, pp. 367–8
—— 'Auvergnats et Foréziens pendant la mission du conventionnel Javogues', *Gilbert Romme et son temps* (Paris, 1966), pp. 129–47
—— 'La brève carrière du terroriste Jean-Marie Lapalus', *A.H.R.F.* 1968, pp. 489–533
Palluat de Bessat, 'La résistance à la constitution civile du clergé dans le district de Montbrison, 1791–1792', *Amitiés foréziennes et vellaves*, 1926, pp. 305–10, 398–410, 492–503
Perrin, E., *Le Tombeau des muscadins* (Montbrison, 1918)
Portallier, A., *Tableau général des victimes et martyrs de la Révolution en Lyonnais, Forez et Beaujolais* (Saint-Étienne, 1911)
Pothier, F., *Le Pont de Roanne et les inondations de la Loire* (Roanne, 1868)
Ricau, O., 'La Révolution vue de Grézolles', *Actes du 88e Congrès national des Sociétés savantes*, 1963, pp. 233–42
Straka, G., *Poèmes du XVIIIe siècle en dialecte de Saint-Étienne*, 2 vols. (Paris, 1964)
Tomas, F., 'Géographie sociale du Forez en 1788', *Bulletin de la Diana*, 1965, pp. 80–117

INDEX

For abbreviations see p. xiii.
For revolutionary place names see p. xiv.